# MCTS 70-642 Cert Guide: Windows Server® 2008 Network Infrastructure, Configuring

Don Poulton

800 East 96th Street
Indianapolis, Indiana 46240 USA

# MCTS 70-642 Cert Guide: Windows Server® 2008 Network Infrastructure, Configuring

Printed in the United States of America

First Printing: February 2012

ISBN-978-0-7897-4830-0

ISBN-0-7897-4830-4

Library of Congress Cataloging-in-Publication data is on file.

## Trademarks

All terms mentioned in this book that are known to be trademarks or service marks have been appropriately capitalized. Pearson cannot attest to the accuracy of this information. Use of a term in this book should not be regarded as affecting the validity of any trademark or service mark.

## Warning and Disclaimer

Every effort has been made to make this book as complete and as accurate as possible, but no warranty or fitness is implied. The information provided is on an "as is" basis. The author and the publisher shall have neither liability nor responsibility to any person or entity with respect to any loss or damages arising from the information contained in this book or from the use of the CD or programs accompanying it.

## Bulk Sales

Que Publishing offers excellent discounts on this book when ordered in quantity for bulk purchases or special sales. For more information, please contact

**U.S. Corporate and Government Sales**

1-800-382-3419

corpsales@pearsontechgroup.com

For sales outside of the U.S., please contact

**International Sales**

international@pearsoned.com

**Associate Publisher**
Dave Dusthimer

**Acquisitions Editor**
Betsy Brown

**Development Editor**
Box Twelve
Communications, Inc.

**Managing Editor**
Sandra Schroeder

**Project Editor**
Mandie Frank

**Copy Editor**
Sheri Cain

**Indexer**
Tim Wright

**Proofreader**
Leslie Joseph

**Technical Editors**
Chris Crayton
Darril Gibson

**Publishing Coordinator**
Vanessa Evans

**Multimedia Developer**
Timothy Warner

**Interior Designer**
Gary Adair

**Page Layout**
Mark Shirar

# Contents at a Glance

# Table of Contents

# About the Author

**Don Poulton** (A+, Network+, Security+, MCSA, MCSE) is an independent consultant who has been involved with computers since the days of 80-column punch cards. After a career of more than 20 years in environmental science, Don switched careers and trained as a Windows NT 4.0 MCSE. He has been involved in consulting with a couple of small training providers as a technical writer, during which time he wrote training and exam-prep materials for Windows NT 4.0, Windows 2000, and Windows XP. Don has written or contributed to several titles, including *Security+ Lab Manual* (Que, 2004), *MCSA/MCSE 70-299 Exam Cram 2: Implementing and Administering Security in a Windows 2003 Network (Exam Cram 2)* (Que, 2004), *MCSE 70-294 Exam Prep: Planning, Implementing, and Maintaining a Microsoft Windows Server 2003 Active Directory Infrastructure* (Que, 2006), *MCTS 70-620 Exam Prep: Microsoft Windows Vista, Configuring* (Que, 2008), *MCTS 70-680 Exam Prep: Microsoft Windows 7, Configuring* (Que, 2011), and *MCTS 70-640 Exam Prep: Microsoft Windows Server 2008 Active Directory, Configuring* (Que, 2011).

In addition, Don has worked on programming projects, both in his days as an environmental scientist and, more recently, with Visual Basic to update an older statistical package used for multivariate analysis of sediment contaminants.

When not working on computers, Don is an avid amateur photographer who has had his photos displayed in international competitions and published in magazines such as *Michigan Natural Resources Magazine* and *National Geographic Traveler*. Don also enjoys traveling and keeping fit.

Don lives in Burlington, Ontario, with his wife, Terry.

# Dedication

*I would like to dedicate this book to my wife, Terry, who has stood by my side and supported me throughout the days spent writing this book. This project would not have been possible without her love and support.*

# Acknowledgments

I would like to thank the staff at Pearson and, in particular, Betsy Brown for making this project possible. My sincere thanks goes out to Chris Crayton and Darril Gibson for their helpful technical suggestions, as well as Jeff Riley, development editor, and Sheri Cain, copy editor, for their improvements to the manuscript.

—Don Poulton

# About the Technical Reviewers

**Christopher A. Crayton** is an author, technical editor, technical consultant, security consultant, trainer, and SkillsUSA state-level technology competition judge. Formerly, he worked as a computer and networking instructor at Keiser College (2001 Teacher of the Year); as network administrator for Protocol, a global electronic customer relationship management (eCRM) company; and at Eastman Kodak Headquarters as a computer and network specialist. Chris has authored several print and online books, including *The A+ Exams Guide*, Second Edition (Cengage Learning, 2008), *Microsoft Windows Vista 70-620 Exam Guide Short Cut* (O'Reilly, 2007), *CompTIA A+ Essentials 220-601 Exam Guide Short Cut* (O'Reilly, 2007), *The A+ Exams Guide*, *The A+ Certification and PC Repair Handbook* (Charles River Media, 2005), and *The Security+ Exam Guide* (Charles River Media, 2003) and *A+ Adaptive Exams* (Charles River Media, 2002). He is also co-author of the *How to Cheat at Securing Your Network* (Syngress, 2007). As an experienced technical editor, Chris has provided many technical edits/reviews for several major publishing companies, including Pearson, McGraw-Hill, Cengage Learning, Wiley, O'Reilly, Syngress, and Apress. He holds MCSE, A+, and Network+ certifications.

**Darril Gibson** has authored or coauthored more than a dozen books and contributed as a technical editor to many more. He holds several IT certifications, including CompTIA A+, Network+, Security+, CASP, (ISC)2 SSCP, CISSP, MCSA, MCSA Messaging (2000, 2003), MCSE (NT 4.0, 2000, 2003), MCDBA (SQL 7.0, 2000), MCITP (Vista, Windows 7, Server 2008, SQL 2005, SQL 2008), MCTS (Server 2008, SQL Server 2008), MCSD (6.0, .NET), and ITIL Foundations v 3.0. He is the CEO of Security Consulting and Training, LLC, and actively teaches, writes, and consults on a variety of IT topics. He regularly blogs at blogs.getcertifiedgetahead.com.

## We Want to Hear from You!

As the reader of this book, *you* are our most important critic and commentator. We value your opinion and want to know what we're doing right, what we could do better, what areas you'd like to see us publish in, and any other words of wisdom you're willing to pass our way.

As an associate publisher for Pearson, I welcome your comments. You can e-mail or write me directly to let me know what you did or didn't like about this book—as well as what we can do to make our books better.

*Please note that I cannot help you with technical problems related to the topic of this book. We do have a User Services group, however, where I will forward specific technical questions related to the book.*

When you write, please be sure to include this book's title and author, as well as your name, e-mail address, and phone number. I will carefully review your comments and share them with the author and editors who worked on the book.

E-mail: feedback@pearsonitcertification.com

Mail: Dave Dusthimer
Associate Publisher
Pearson Education
800 East 96th Street
Indianapolis, IN 46240 USA

## Reader Services

Visit our website and register this book at www.quepublishing.com/register for convenient access to any updates, downloads, or errata that might be available for this book.

# Introduction

*MCTS Windows Server 2008 Network Infrastructure Configuring Cert Guide (Exam 70-642)* is designed for network administrators, network engineers, and consultants who are pursuing the Microsoft Certified Technology Specialist (MCTS) or Microsoft Certified IT Professional (MCITP) certifications for Windows Server 2008. This book covers the TS: Windows Server 2008 Network Infrastructure, Configuring exam (70-642), which earns you the Microsoft Certified Technology Specialist: Windows Server 2008 Network Infrastructure, Configuration certification. The exam measures your skill and ability to implement, administer, and troubleshoot network infrastructure services running on Windows Server 2008. Microsoft not only tests you on your knowledge of network infrastructure, but it has purposefully developed questions on the exam to force you to problem-solve in the same way that you would when presented with a real-life error. Passing this exam demonstrates your competency in administration.

This book covers all the objectives that Microsoft has established for exam 70-642. It doesn't offer end-to-end coverage of networking in Windows Server 2008; instead, it helps you develop the specific core competencies that you need to master as a network services administrator. You should be able to pass the exam by learning the material in this book, without taking a class.

## Goals and Methods

This book's #1 goal is simple: to help you get ready to take—and pass—Microsoft Certification Exam 70-642, "TS: Windows Server 2008 Network Infrastructure, Configuring." You will find information within this book that helps ensure your success as you pursue this Microsoft exam and the Technology Specialist or IT Professional certification.

Because Microsoft certification exams stress problem-solving abilities and reasoning more than memorization of terms and facts, this book helps you master and understand the required objectives for the 70-642 exam.

To aid you in mastering and understanding the MCTS certification objectives, this book uses the following:

- **Opening topics list:** Defines the topics covered in each chapter; it also lists the corresponding 70-642 exam objectives.

- **Do I Know This Already quizzes:** At the beginning of each chapter is a quiz. The quizzes, and answers/explanations (found in Appendix A), gauge your knowledge of the subjects. If the answers to the questions don't come readily to you, be sure to read the entire chapter.

- **Foundation topics:** The heart of the chapter. Explains the topics from a hands-on and a theory-based standpoint. This includes in-depth descriptions, tables, and figures that are geared to build your knowledge so that you can pass the exam. The chapters are broken down into several topics.

- **Key topics:** Indicate important figures, tables, and lists of information that you should know for the exam. They are interspersed throughout each chapter and are listed in table format at the end of each chapter.

- **Memory tables:** Can be found on the CD within Appendix B, "Memory Tables." Use them to help memorize important information.

- **Key terms:** Key terms without their definitions are listed at the end of each chapter. Write down the definition of each term and check your work against the complete key terms in the Glossary, which can also be found on the CD.

## Study and Exam Preparation Tips

It's a rush of adrenaline during the final day before an exam. If you've scheduled the exam on a workday, or following a workday, you will find yourself cursing the tasks you normally cheerfully perform because the back of your mind is telling you to read just a bit more, study another scenario, practice another skill so that you will be able to get this exam out of the way successfully.

The way that Microsoft has designed its tests lately does not help. I remember taking Microsoft exams many years ago and thoroughly understanding the term "paper certified." Nowadays, you can't get through a Microsoft exam without knowing the material so well that, when confronted with a problem, whether a scenario or real-life situation, you can handle the challenge. Instead of trying to show the world how many MCSEs are out there, Microsoft is trying to prove how difficult it is to achieve a certification, including the newly created MCTS and MCITP, as well as the MCSE and MCSA, thereby making those who are certified more valuable to their organizations.

# Learning Styles

To best understand the nature of preparation for the test, it is important to understand learning as a process. You are probably aware of how you best learn new material. You might find that outlining works best for you, or, as a visual learner, you might need to "see" things. Or, as a person who studies kinesthetically, the hands-on approach serves you best. Whether you might need models or examples, or maybe you just like exploring the interface, or whatever your learning style, solid test preparation works best when it takes place over time. Obviously, you shouldn't start studying for a certification exam the night before you take it; it is important to understand that learning is a developmental process. Understanding learning as a process helps you focus on what you know and what you have yet to learn.

People study in a combination of different ways—by doing, seeing, and hearing and writing. This book's design fulfills all three of these study methods. For the kinesthetic, key topics are scattered throughout each chapter. You will also discover step-by-step procedural instructions that walk you through the skills you need to master networking in Windows Server 2008. The visual learner can find plenty of screen shots that explain the concepts described in the text. The auditory learner can reinforce skills by reading out loud and copying down key concepts and exam tips scattered throughout this book. You can also practice writing down the meaning of the key terms defined in each chapter, and in completing the memory tables for most chapters found on the accompanying CD. While reading this book, you will realize that it stands the test of time. You will be able to turn to it over and over again.

Thinking about how you learn helps you recognize that learning takes place when you are able to match new information to old. You have some previous experience with computers and networking. Now, you are preparing for this certification exam. Using this book, software, and supplementary materials will not just add incrementally to what you know; as you study, the organization of your knowledge actually restructures as you integrate new information into your existing knowledge base. This leads you to a more comprehensive understanding of the tasks and concepts outlined in the objectives and of computing in general. Again, this happens as a result of a repetitive process rather than a singular event. If you keep this model of learning in mind as you prepare for the exam, you will make better decisions concerning what to study and how much more studying you need to do.

# Study Tips

There are many ways to approach studying, just as there are many different types of material to study. However, the following tips will work well for the type of material covered on Microsoft certification exams.

## Study Strategies

Although individuals vary in the ways they learn information, some basic principles of learning apply to everyone. You should adopt some study strategies that take advantage of these principles. One of these principles is that learning can be broken into various depths. Recognition (of terms, for example) exemplifies a rather surface level of learning in which you rely on a prompt of some sort to elicit recall. Comprehension or understanding (of the concepts behind the terms, for example) represents a deeper level of learning than recognition. The ability to analyze a concept and apply your understanding of it in a new way represents further depth of learning.

Your learning strategy should enable you to know the material at a level or two deeper than mere recognition. This will help you perform well on the exams. You will know the material so thoroughly that you can go beyond the recognition-level types of questions commonly used in fact-based multiple-choice testing. You will be able to apply your knowledge to solve new problems.

### Macro and Micro Study Strategies

One strategy that can lead to deep learning includes preparing an outline that covers all the objectives and subobjectives for the particular exam that you are planning to take. You need to delve a bit further into the material and include a level or two of detail beyond the stated objectives and subobjectives for the exam. Then, you should expand the outline by coming up with a statement of definition or a summary for each point in the outline.

An outline provides two approaches to studying. First, you can study the outline by focusing on the organization of the material. You can work your way through the points and subpoints of your outline, with the goal of learning how they relate to one another. For example, be sure you understand how each of the main objective areas for exam 70-642 is similar to and different from another. Then, you should do the same thing with the subobjectives; you should be sure you know which subobjectives pertain to each objective area and how they relate to one another.

Next, you can work through the outline, focusing on learning the details. You should memorize and understand terms and their definitions, facts, rules and tactics, advantages and disadvantages, and so on. In this pass through the outline, you should attempt to learn detail rather than the big picture (the organizational information that you worked on in the first pass through the outline).

Research has shown that attempting to assimilate both types of information at the same time interferes with the overall learning process. If you separate your studying into these two approaches, you will perform better on the exam.

### Active Study Strategies

The process of writing down and defining objectives, subobjectives, terms, facts, and definitions promotes a more active learning strategy than merely reading the material does. In human information-processing terms, writing forces you to engage in more active encoding of the information. Simply reading over the information leads to more passive processing. Using this study strategy, you should focus on writing down the items that are highlighted in this book—bulleted or numbered lists, key topics, notes, cautions, and review sections, for example.

You need to determine whether you can apply the information you have learned by attempting to create examples and scenarios on your own. Think about how or where you could apply the concepts that you are learning. Again, write down this information to process the facts and concepts in an active fashion.

### Common-Sense Strategies

You need to follow common-sense practices when studying: Study when you are alert, reduce or eliminate distractions, and take breaks when you become fatigued.

## Pretesting Yourself

Pretesting allows you to assess how well you are learning. One of the most important aspects of learning is what has been called *meta-learning*. Meta-learning has to do with realizing when you know something well or when you need to study some more. In other words, you recognize how well or how poorly you have learned the material you are studying.

For most people, this can be difficult to assess. Memory tables, practice questions, and practice tests are useful in that they objectively reveal what you have learned and what you have not learned. Use this information to guide your review and further studying. Developmental learning takes place as you cycle through studying, assessing how well you have learned, reviewing, and assessing again until you feel you are ready to take the exam.

You might have noticed the practice exam included in this book. You should use it as part of the learning process. The ExamGear test-simulation software included on this book's CD-ROM also provides you with an excellent opportunity to assess your knowledge.

You should set a goal for your pretesting. A reasonable goal is to score consistently in the 90 percent range.

# Pearson Cert Practice Test Engine and Questions on the CD

The CD in the back of this book includes the *Pearson IT Certification Practice Test* engine, which is software that displays and grades a set of exam-realistic multiple-choice questions. Using the Pearson IT Certification Practice Test engine, you can either study by going through the questions in Study Mode or take a simulated 70-642 exam that mimics real exam conditions.

Installation of the test engine is a two-step process. The CD in the back of this book has a copy of the Pearson IT Certification Practice Test engine. However, the practice exam (that is, the database of 70-642 exam questions) is not on the CD.

**NOTE**   The cardboard CD case in the back of this book includes the CD and a piece of paper. The paper lists the *activation code* for the practice exam associated with this book. Keep the activation code. Also, on the opposite side of the paper from the activation code is a unique, one-time use coupon code for the purchase of the *70-642 Cert Guide, Premium Edition eBook and Practice Test* product.

## Install the Software from the CD

The Pearson IT Certification Practice Test is a Windows-only desktop application. You can run it on a Mac using a Windows virtual machine, but it was built specifically for a Windows platform. The minimum system requirements are

- Windows XP (SP3), Windows Vista (SP2), or Windows 7
- Microsoft .NET Framework 4.0 Client
- Microsoft SQL Server Compact 4.0
- Pentium class 1GHz processor (or equivalent)
- 512 MB RAM
- 650 MB disc space plus 50 MB for each downloaded practice exam

The software installation process is similar to other wizard-based installation processes. If you have already installed the Pearson IT Certification Practice Test software from another Pearson product, there is no need for you to reinstall the software. Simply launch the software on your desktop and proceed to activate the practice exam from this book, using the activation code included in the CD sleeve. The following steps outline the installation process:

1. Insert the CD into your PC.

2. The software that automatically runs is the Pearson IT Certification software to access and use all CD-based features, including the exam engine, video training, and any CD-only appendices. From the main menu, click the option *Install the Exam Engine.*

3. Respond to the wizard-based prompts.

The installation process gives you the option to activate your exam with the activation code supplied on the paper in the CD sleeve. This process requires that you establish a Pearson website login. You need this login to activate the exam; so register when prompted. If you already have a Pearson website login, there is no need to register again. Just use your existing login.

## Activate and Download the Practice Exam

After the exam engine is installed, you can activate the exam associated with this book (if you did not do so during the installation process) as follows:

1. Start the *Pearson IT Certification Practice Test* (PCPT) software from the Windows *Start* menu or from your desktop shortcut icon.

2. To activate and download the exam associated with this book, from the *My Products* or *Tools* tab, select the **Activate** button.

3. At the next screen, enter the *Activation Key* from the paper inside the cardboard CD sleeve in the back of this book. Once entered, click the **Activate** button.

4. The activation process will download the practice exam. Click **Next**, and then click **Finish**.

Once the activation process is completed, the *My Products* tab should list your new exam. If you do not see the exam, make sure you selected the *My Products* tab on the menu. At this point, the software and practice exam are ready to use. Simply select the exam and click the **Open Exam** button.

To update an exam you have already activated and downloaded, simply select the *Tools* tab and select the **Update Products** button. Updating your exams ensures that you have the latest changes and updates to the exam data.

If you want to check for updates to the Pearson Cert Practice Test exam engine software, simply select the *Tools* tab and select the **Update Application** button. This ensures that you are running the latest version of the exam engine.

### Activating Other Exams

The exam software-installation process, and the registration process, only occurs once. Then, for each new exam, only a few steps are required. For instance, if you buy another new Pearson IT Certification Cert Guide, extract the activation code from the CD sleeve in the back of that book (you don't even need the CD at this point). From there, all you have to do is start the exam engine (if not still up and running), and perform Steps 2 through 4 from the previous list.

### Premium Edition

In addition to the free practice exam provided on the enclosed CD, you can purchase additional exams with expanded functionality directly from Pearson IT Certification. The Premium Edition eBook and Practice Test for this title contains an additional two full practice exams as well as an eBook (in both PDF and ePub format). Also, the Premium Edition title also has remediation for each question to the specific part of the eBook that relates to that question.

Because you purchased the print version of this title, you can purchase the Premium Edition at a deep discount. There is a coupon code in the CD sleeve that contains a one-time use code and instructions for where you can purchase the Premium Edition.

To view the Premium Edition product page, go to http://www.pearsonitcertification. com/store/product.aspx?isbn=0132939576.

## Exam Prep Tips

After you master the subject matter, the final preparatory step is to understand how the exam will be presented. Make no mistake: An MCTS exam challenges both your knowledge and your test-taking skills. Preparing for the 70-642 exam is a bit different than preparing for those old Microsoft exams. The following is a list of things that you should consider doing:

■ **Combine your skill sets into solutions:** In the past, exams would test whether you knew to select the right letter of a multiple choice answer. Today, you need to know how to resolve a problem that may involve different aspects of the material covered. For example, on exam 70-642, you could be presented with a problem that informs you that users at some client computers are unable to access a given server (although other users can access this server), and to troubleshoot this network access problem. The skills themselves are simple. Being able to zero in on what caused the problem and then to resolve it for a specific situation is what you need to demonstrate. In fact, you should not only be able to select one answer, but also multiple parts of a total solution.

- **Delve into excruciating details:** The exam questions incorporate a great deal of information in the scenarios. Some of the information is ancillary—it will help you rule out possible issues, but not necessarily resolve the answer. Some of the information simply provides you with a greater picture, like you would have in real life. Some information is key to your solution. For example, you may be presented with a question that lists the components of a Windows-based network such as the number of server and client computers, the IP addressing and subnet configuration, and so on. When you delve further into the question, you realize that the subnetting configuration is the problem. Other times, you will find that the subnetting configuration simply eliminates one or more of the answers that you could select. If you don't pay attention to what you can eliminate, the answer can elude you completely. And other times, the hardware configuration simply lets you know that the hardware is adequate.

- **Microsoft likes to quiz exam takers on the latest modifications of its technology:** From time to time, Microsoft feeds new questions into its exam database and beta tests these questions on exam takers. During the beta period for each question, its answer is not taken into account in computing the final score. However, when Microsoft is satisfied with the question's performance, it becomes live and is scored appropriately. You can expect to see questions that test your knowledge of the latest changes in server networking technology, including the enhancements introduced in 2009 with Windows Server 2008 R2.

- **It's a GUI test:** Microsoft has expanded its testing criteria into interface recognition. You should be able to recognize each dialog box, properties sheet, options, and defaults. You will be tested on how to perform typical configuration actions in server networking. In fact, Microsoft has begun to include performance-based questions on its exams that instruct you to perform a given task and presents you with a live version of some network configuration tool. You must complete the required actions and no others; otherwise, your response will be scored as incorrect.

- **Practice with a time limit:** The tests have always been time restricted, but it takes more time to read and understand the scenarios now and time is a whole lot tighter. To get used to the time limits, test yourself with a timer. Know how long it takes you to read scenarios and select answers.

# Self-Assessment

Before you attempt to take the exam covered by this book, it is imperative that you know considerable information about Windows Server 2008 R2 itself. There is so much breadth to this exam that I felt it necessary to include a Self-Assessment within this book to help you evaluate your exam readiness. Within this portion of the book, let us look at what is needed to pass the exam and achieve further Microsoft certifications. When you go through the actual Self-Assessment contained within this section, you will have a good idea how far along you are toward taking the exam.

## MCTSs and MCITPs in the Real World

To complete the MCITP certification as a Windows Server 2008 administrator, you will have to be a well-rounded server-aware individual. The new generation of Microsoft Certifications is much more meaningful and map more closely to the everyday work environment found in the real world. With that said, you will also likely find this particular exam challenging to complete successfully.

The exam requires you to have at least a base level of knowledge about the entire Windows Server 2008 product, including the latest enhancements introduced in Windows Server 2008 R2. You need to know how Windows Server 2008 networks with other computers running previous editions of Windows Server and with client computers running Windows XP/Vista/Windows 7. You must be aware of general server management, including user accounts, groups, access controls, Active Directory, and so on. The exam is broad in nature and tests you across the full realm of the Windows Server 2008 R2 networking software.

Increasing numbers of people are attaining Microsoft certifications, so the goal is within reach. You can get all the real-world motivation you need from knowing that many others have gone before, so you can follow in their footsteps. If you're willing to tackle the process seriously and do what it takes to obtain the necessary experience and knowledge, you can take—and pass—all the certification tests involved in obtaining an MCITP certification. If you're willing to tackle the preparation process seriously and do what it takes to gain the necessary experience and knowledge, you can take and pass the exam. In fact, the *Cert Guides* and the companion *Exam Crams* are designed to make it as easy as possible for you to prepare for these exams, but prepare you must!

## The Ideal MCITP Candidate

Just to give you some idea of what an ideal candidate is like, here is some relevant information about the background and experience such an individual should have.

Don't worry if you don't meet these qualifications or don't even come that close—this is a far-from-ideal world, and where you fall short is simply where you'll have more work to do:

- Academic or professional training in network theory, concepts, and operations. This includes everything from networking media and transmission techniques through network operating systems, services, and applications.

- Three-plus years of professional networking experience, including experience with various types of networking media, including Ethernet and wireless. This must include installation, configuration, upgrading, and troubleshooting experience.

- Two-plus years in a networked environment that includes hands-on experience with Windows Server 2000/2003/2008/R2, Windows 2000 Professional, Windows XP Professional, Windows Vista Business/Enterprise/Ultimate, and Windows 7 Professional/ Enterprise/Ultimate. A solid understanding of each system's architecture, installation, configuration, maintenance, and troubleshooting is also essential.

- Knowledge of the various methods for installing Windows Server 2008 R2, including manual and automated installations and server virtualization.

- Familiarity with key Windows Server 2008-based, Active Directory Domain Services (AD DS) and its enhancements, including Active Directory Lightweight Directory Services (AD LDS), Active Directory Certificate Services (AD CS), and Active Directory Federation Services (AD FS), plus familiarity with one or more of the following: Internet Information Services (IIS), Index Server, and Internet Security and Acceleration Server.

- An understanding of how to implement security for key network data in a Windows Server 2008 environment.

- A good working understanding of Windows Server networking concepts. Obviously, this book prepares you for the Windows Server 2008 R2 network configuration exam, but it is helpful if you have real-world exposure to a server-based networking environment. Familiarity with network theoretical models, such as the Open Systems Interconnect (OSI) layered model, and how it relates to the four-layer TCP/IP protocol stack structure is strongly desirable. We recommend that you find out as much as you can about networking in Windows Server environments and acquire as much experience using this technology as possible. In addition, knowledge of how Windows-based computers network with non-Windows computers, such as Macintosh, UNIX, and Linux, is also helpful. The time you take learning about server-based networking will be time well spent!

Although a bachelor's degree in computer science can be helpful, a strong willingness to learn new techniques and technologies together with as many of these qualifications as possible, is key to your success. We believe that well under half of all certification candidates possess such experience, and that, in fact, most meet less than half of these requirements—at least when they begin the certification process. But, because all the people who already have been certified have survived this ordeal, you can survive it, too, especially if you heed what our Self-Assessment can tell you about what you already know and what you need to learn.

### Put Yourself to the Test

The following series of questions and observations are designed to help you figure out how much work you'll face in pursuing Microsoft certification and what kinds of resources you can consult on your quest. Be absolutely honest in your answers, or you'll end up wasting money on an exam you're not ready to take. There are no right or wrong answers only steps along the path to certification. Only you can decide where you are ready.

Two things should be clear from the outset, however:

- Even a modest background in computer science will be helpful.

- Hands-on experience with Microsoft products and technologies is an essential ingredient for success.

### Educational Background

1. Have you ever taken any computer-related classes? (Yes or No.)

   If Yes, proceed to question 2; if No, proceed to question 4.

2. Have you taken any classes on computer operating systems? (Yes or No.)

   If Yes, you will probably be able to handle Microsoft's architecture and system component discussions. If you're rusty, brush up on basic operating system concepts, especially virtual memory, multitasking regimes, user mode versus kernel mode operation, and general computer security topics.

   If No, consider some basic reading in this area. We strongly recommend a good general operating systems book, such as *Operating System Concepts*, Eighth Edition, by Abraham Silberschatz, Peter B. Galvin, and Greg Gagne (John Wiley & Sons, 2008). If this title doesn't appeal to you, check out reviews for other similar titles at your favorite online bookstore.

3. Have you taken any networking concepts or technologies classes? (Yes or No.)

If Yes, you will probably be able to handle Microsoft's networking terminology, concepts, and technologies (brace yourself for frequent departures from normal usage). If you have passed an entry-level exam, such as the CompTIA Network+ exam, you should be readily capable of understanding the concepts behind the material covered in this book. If you're rusty, brush up on basic networking concepts and terminology, especially networking media, transmission type, the OSI reference model, and networking technologies, such as Ethernet, WAN links, and wireless networking concepts and protocols.

If No, you might want to read one or two books in this topic area. The two best books that we know of are *Computer Networks*, Fifth Edition, by Andrew S. Tanenbaum (Prentice-Hall, 2010) and *Computer Networks and Internets*, Fifth Edition, by Douglas E. Comer (Prentice-Hall, 2008).

Skip to the next section, "Hands-On Experience."

4. Have you done any reading on operating systems or networks? (Yes or No.)

If Yes, review the requirements stated in the first paragraphs after questions 2 and 3. If you meet those requirements, move on to the next section.

If No, consult the recommended reading for both topics. A strong background will help you prepare for the Microsoft exams better than just about anything else.

## Hands-On Experience

Perhaps the most important key to success on any certification exam is hands-on experience, especially with Windows Server 2008 and Windows 7, plus the many add-on services and BackOffice components around which so many of the Microsoft certification exams revolve. If we leave you with only one realization after taking this Self-Assessment, it should be that there's no substitute for time spent installing, configuring, and using the various Microsoft products on which you'll be tested repeatedly and in depth.

Have you installed, configured, and worked with:

- Windows 2000 Server, Windows Server 2003, or Windows Server 2008/R2? (Yes or No.)

  If Yes, make sure you understand basic concepts as covered in Exam 70-640 and/or Exam 70-646.

You can download objectives, practice exams, and other data about Microsoft exams from the Microsoft Learning page at www.microsoft.com/learning/default.mspx. Use the Certification link to obtain specific exam information.

If you haven't worked with Windows Server 2008 R2, you must obtain one or two machines and a copy of the operating system. Then, learn the operating system and any other software components on which you'll also be tested. Search the Microsoft website for low-cost options to obtain evaluation copies of the software that you need.

In fact, we recommend that you obtain two computers, each with a network interface, and set up a two-node network on which to practice. You can also download Microsoft Virtual PC 2007 for free at www.microsoft.com/windows/virtual-pc/default.aspx. Use the links on this page to learn more about how you can run multiple operating systems from a single computer using this product.

- Windows 7 Professional or Windows 7 Ultimate? (Yes or No.)

If Yes, make sure you understand the concepts covered in exam 70-680.

If No, you will want to obtain a copy of Windows 7 Professional or Ultimate and learn how to install, configure, and maintain it. You can use *MCTS 70-680 Cert Guide: Microsoft Windows 7, Configuring* by Don Poulton (Que Certification, 2011) to guide your activities and studies, or you can work straight from Microsoft's test objectives if you prefer.

For any and all of these Microsoft exams, the Resource Kits for the topics involved are a good study resource. You can purchase soft cover Resource Kits from Microsoft Press (search for them at www.microsoft.com/mspress), but most of the information in the Resource Kits is also available from the TechNet website (http://technet.microsoft.com/en-us/default.aspx). Along with the Cert Guide and Exam Cram series, we believe that Resource Kits are among the best tools you can use to prepare for Microsoft exams.

**TIP**  If you have the funds or your employer will pay your way, consider taking a class led by a professional instructor. In particular for those just starting out or with limited knowledge or access to state-of-the-art computer systems. Microsoft has designed very good courses available to be taken in most communities. In addition, the course includes trial versions of the software that is the focus of your course, along with the operating system that it requires.

Testing Your Exam Readiness

Whether you attend a formal class on a specific topic to get ready for an exam or use written materials to study on your own, some preparation for the certification exams is essential. You pay for your exam attempts—pass or fail—so you want to do everything you can to pass on your first try. Not only can failed attempts be expensive to your pocketbook, but they can also be very discouraging.

This book includes a comprehensive 120-question practice exam, so if you don't score well on the questions related to a particular chapter or chapters, you can study more and then tackle the questions at the end of this book or on the CD again.

For any given subject, consider taking a class if you've tackled self-study materials, taken the practice test, and failed anyway. If you can afford the privilege, the opportunity to interact with an instructor and fellow students can make all the difference in the world. For information about systems auditing classes, visit the Find Training page at http://learning.microsoft.com/Manager/Catalog.aspx.

If you can't afford to take a class, visit the Microsoft Learning page anyway, because it also includes pointers to free practice exams and to Microsoft Certified Professional Approved Study Guides and other self-study tools. And even if you can't afford to spend much at all, you should still invest in some low-cost practice exams from commercial vendors.

1. Have you taken a practice exam on your chosen test subject? (Yes or No.)

   If Yes and you scored 90 percent or better, you're probably ready to tackle the real thing. If your score isn't above that crucial threshold, keep at it until you break that barrier. If you answered No, go back and study the book some more, and repeat the practice tests. Keep at it until you can comfortably break the passing threshold.

**TIP**   There is no better way to assess your test readiness than to take a good-quality practice exam and pass with a score of 90 percent or better. When I'm preparing, I shoot for 95+ percent, just to leave room for the "weirdness factor" that sometimes shows up on Microsoft exams.

One last note: I hope it makes sense to stress the importance of hands-on experience in the context of the exams. As you review the material for the exams, you'll realize that hands-on experience with server configuration and best practices is invaluable.

### Well, Let's Get to It

After you assess your readiness, undertaken the right background studies, obtained the hands-on experience that will help you understand the products and technologies at work, and reviewed the many sources of information to help you prepare for a test, you'll be ready to take a round of practice tests. When your scores come back positive enough to get you through the exam, you're ready to go after the real thing. If you follow our assessment regimen, you'll not only know what you need to study, but you'll also know when you're ready to take the exam. Good luck!

## Microsoft 70-642 Exam Topics

Table I-1 lists the exam topics for the Microsoft 70-642 exam. It also lists where each exam topic is covered in this book.

**Table I-1**   Microsoft 70-642 Exam Topics

| Chapter | Topics | 70-640 Exam Objectives Covered |
|---|---|---|
| 1 | Concepts of TCP/IP | Configuring Addressing and Services |
|  | IPv4 Addressing | ■ Configure IPv4 and IPv6 addressing |
|  | IPv6 Addressing |  |
|  | Resolving IPv4 and IPv6 Network Connectivity Issues |  |
| 2 | How DHCP Works | Configuring Addressing and Services |
|  | Installing and Configuring a DHCP Server | ■ Configure Dynamic Host Configuration Protocol (DHCP) |
|  | DHCP Scopes and Options |  |
|  | Managing and Troubleshooting a DHCP Server |  |
| 3 | The Need for Routing and Routing Tables | Configuring Addressing and Services |
|  | Routing and Remote Access Service (RRAS) in Windows Server 2008 R2 | ■ Configure routing |
|  | Managing and Maintaining Routing Servers |  |
| 4 | Configuring Windows Firewall | Configuring Addressing and Services |
|  | Using the Windows Firewall with Advanced Security Snap-in | ■ Configure Windows Firewall with Advanced Security |
|  | Using IPSec to Secure Network Communications |  |

| Chapter | Topics | 70-640 Exam Objectives Covered |
| --- | --- | --- |
| 5 | Introduction to DNS<br><br>Installing DNS in Windows Server 2008 R2<br><br>Configuring DNS Server Properties | Configuring Names Resolution<br>■ Configure a Domain Name System (DNS) server |
| 6 | Zone Types and their Uses<br><br>Configuring DNS Zones<br><br>Configuring DNS Zone Transfers and Replication<br><br>Troubleshooting DNS Zones and Replication | Configuring Names Resolution<br>■ Configure DNS zones<br>■ Configure DNS replication |
| 7 | Resource Record Types and Their Uses<br><br>Configuring Resource Record Properties | Configuring Names Resolution<br>■ Configure DNS records |
| 8 | Configuring DNS Client Computer Settings<br><br>Other Types of Name Resolution | Configuring Names Resolution<br>■ Configure name resolution for client computers |
| 9 | Shared Folders in Windows Server 2008 R2<br><br>NTFS Permissions<br><br>Data Encryption<br><br>Additional File Server Management Resources | Configuring File and Print Services<br>■ Configure a file server |
| 10 | DFS Concepts<br><br>Managing DFS Namespaces<br><br>Managing DFS Replication | Configuring File and Print Services<br>■ Configure Distributed File System (DFS) |
| 11 | Protecting Data with Windows Backup<br><br>Volume Shadow Copies<br><br>Restoring Data from Backup | Configuring File and Print Services<br>■ Configure backup and restore |
| 12 | File Server Resource Manager (FSRM)<br><br>Configuring Disk and Volume Quotas<br><br>Storage Manager for SANs | Configuring File and Print Services<br>■ Manage file server resources |
| 13 | Printing Terminology in Windows Server 2008 R2<br><br>Installing, Sharing, and Publishing Printers<br><br>Managing and Troubleshooting Printers | Configuring File and Print Services<br>■ Configure and monitor print services |

| Chapter | Topics | 70-640 Exam Objectives Covered |
|---|---|---|
| 14 | Remote Access Protocols<br><br>Configuring Dial-Up Connections<br><br>Network Address Translation<br><br>Virtual Private Networking<br><br>Connection Manager | Configuring Network Access<br><br>■ Configure remote access |
| 15 | Wireless Networking Protocols and Standards<br><br>RADIUS in Windows Server 2008 R2 | Configuring Network Access<br><br>■ Configure Network Policy Server (NPS) |
| 16 | Concepts of NAP<br><br>NAP Enforcement<br><br>System Health Validation | Configuring Network Access<br><br>■ Configure Network Access Protection (NAP) |
| 17 | Concepts of DirectAccess<br><br>Configuring the DirectAccess Server<br><br>Group Policy and DirectAccess | Configuring Network Access<br><br>■ Configure DirectAccess |
| 18 | Concept of WSUS<br><br>Installing and Configuring a WSUS Server<br><br>Configuring Client Computers for WSUS | Monitoring and Managing a Network Infrastructure<br><br>■ Configure Windows Server Update Services (WSUS) server settings |
| 19 | Performance Monitor<br><br>Data Collector Sets<br><br>Reliability Monitor | Monitoring and Managing a Network Infrastructure<br><br>■ Configure performance monitoring |
| 20 | Event Viewer<br><br>Customizing Event Logs<br><br>Configuring Event Log Subscriptions<br><br>Configuring Tasks from Events | Monitoring and Managing a Network Infrastructure<br><br>■ Configure event logs |
| 21 | Simple Network Management Protocol (SNMP)<br><br>Network Monitor<br><br>Connection Security Rules Monitoring | Monitoring and Managing a Network Infrastructure<br><br>■ Gather network data |

# How This Book Is Organized

Although this book could be read cover-to-cover, it is designed to be flexible and allow you to easily move between chapters and sections of chapters to cover just the material that you need more work with. Each chapter is designed to meet the requirements of one specific objective within the published Microsoft exam description. If you do intend to read all the chapters, the order in the book is an excellent sequence to use.

The core chapters, Chapters 1 through 21, cover the following topics:

- **Chapter 1, "Configuring IPv4 and IPv6 Addressing"**—TCP/IP is the core networking protocol used by all modern computer networks. With version 4 of this protocol running out of addresses, more and more companies are switching to the newer IPv6 protocol, which offers virtually unlimited addresses. This chapter focuses on the various types of IPv4 and IPv6 addresses and methods used to troubleshoot network addressing and subnetting problems.

- **Chapter 2, "Configuring Dynamic Host Configuration Protocol (DHCP)"**—DHCP is used to automatically assign IPv4 or IPv6 addresses to computers on the network. This chapter shows you how to set up, configure, and troubleshoot DHCP servers on the network.

- **Chapter 3, "Configuring Routing"**—As networks become more involved, you can divide them into multiple segments connected by routers. This chapter shows you how to configure a Windows Server 2008 computer to route traffic between multiple segments in order to optimize network traffic and reduce bottlenecks.

- **Chapter 4, "Configuring Windows Firewall with Advanced Security"**—This chapter discusses the use of Group Policy with rules that determine the types of network traffic allowed into and out of computers on your network. You can specify custom rules and profiles according to the location of computers, their domain membership, authorized users and computers, and other options. You also learn how to configure rules used by IP Security (IPSec) to encrypt and secure network data.

- **Chapter 5, "Installing and Configuring Domain Name System (DNS)"**—DNS is the name resolution system used on all modern Windows networks and is used by Active Directory to locate computers, printers, and other network resources. This chapter introduces the concepts behind the DNS protocol and shows you how to set up DNS servers and forwarders.

- **Chapter 6, "Configuring DNS Zones and Replication"**—DNS servers store information about the network namespace in portions known as zones; each zone is looked after by a specific authoritative DNS server. In this chapter, you learn the various types of DNS zones, how and when to create them, how to integrate DNS zone information with Active Directory, and how to ensure that zone data is properly replicated among each other. DNS in Windows Server 2008 R2 includes options that enable you to configure secure replication and troubleshoot problems when they occur.

- **Chapter 7, "Configuring DNS Records"**—This chapter discusses the various types of DNS records used to store data about the various computers located within a DNS zone and shows you how to configure and troubleshoot DNS record information.

- **Chapter 8, "Configuring Client Computer Name Resolution"**—This chapter shows you how to ensure that client computers on your network are able to access servers locally and remotely. Included are alternate name resolution technologies such as HOSTS files and Windows Internet Name System (WINS) that can be useful when DNS servers are not available.

- **Chapter 9, "Configuring File Servers"**—This chapter shows you how to configure a Windows Server 2008 R2 computer to share files and folders and how to secure shared resources so that only allowed users and groups can access them. You also learn methods for encrypting and decrypting these resources.

- **Chapter 10, "Configuring Distributed File System (DFS)"**—DFS enables you to set up a root share that includes shared folders on multiple file servers, thereby facilitating access by users. In this chapter you learn how to set up and manage a DFS root and ensure its security, reliability, and availability.

- **Chapter 11, "Configuring Backup and Restore"**—Data on a disk volume or file server can easily be lost if a backup is not available, and days or weeks of work could be wiped out. This chapter discusses how you can back up data so that the risk of loss is minimized. It also covers methods you can use to recover data when server failure, corruption, or other damage has occurred.

- **Chapter 12, "Managing File Server Resources"**—This chapter discusses other items you need to know of when managing file servers such as File Server Resource Manager (FSRM), disk and volume quotas, and Storage Manager for SANs.

- **Chapter 13, "Configuring and Monitoring Print Services"**—Printing is an important component of file server functionality and you must ensure that users are able to print their documents in a timely and proper fashion. Windows Server 2008 R2 enables you to share and publish printers as well as configure and troubleshoot problems that keep users from printing.

- **Chapter 14, "Configuring Remote Access"**—This chapter shows you how to configure a server that enables a user to connect to the network from a remote location using various connection protocols. You learn the type of protocols that are required under certain conditions and how to authenticate users attempting to access your network.

- **Chapter 15, "Configuring Network Policy Server (NPS)"**—A NPS server is Microsoft's implementation of Remote Authentication Dial-In User Service (RADIUS) and is used to authenticate users connecting remotely to your network. This chapter shows you how to configure policies for wired and wireless connections and connection requests.

- **Chapter 16, "Configuring Network Access Protection (NAP)"**—Computers connecting from remote locations can be an entry point for viruses and other types of malware to your network. NAP enables you to verify that computers attempting to connect remotely to your network are free of malware and up-to-date with regard to security updates and antimalware definitions.

- **Chapter 17, "Configuring DirectAccess"**—DirectAccess enables users to directly connect to your network from any Internet connection without the need to establish a virtual private network (VPN) connection first. This chapter discusses the requirements for a DirectAccess connection and then shows you how to configure, secure, and troubleshoot this type of network connection.

- **Chapter 18, "Windows Server Update Services (WSUS) Server Settings"**—You can use a WSUS server to distribute updates from Microsoft and other sources in a reliable and timely fashion without the need for each individual computer to access the Internet for these updates. This chapter shows you how to configure and troubleshoot policies that govern user access to the WSUS server.

- **Chapter 19, "Configuring Performance Monitoring"**—This chapter focuses on computer performance and looks at factors that might cause degraded performance and steps you might take to restore performance to an acceptable level.

- **Chapter 20, "Configuring Event Logs"**—Windows Server 2008 R2 includes a series of logs that capture a considerable range of events that occur on the computer, including errors and warnings that can pinpoint causes of trouble. This chapter shows you how to configure Event Viewer to display appropriate types of logs and specify actions that the server can automatically take when a certain type of event is logged.

- **Chapter 21, "Collecting Network Data"**—This chapter shows you how to monitor the various types of network traffic passing to and from your servers. The data so obtained can be useful in detecting and reporting unauthorized network access by intruders. You also learn how to monitor IPSec connection security rules set up in Windows Firewall with Advanced Security.

In addition to the 21 main chapters, this book includes tools to help you verify that you are prepared to take the exam. The CD includes the Glossary, practice test, and memory tables that you can work through to verify your knowledge of the subject matter.

This chapter covers the following subjects:

- **Concepts of TCP/IP:** TCP/IP is a complex stack of related networking protocols. This section introduces the various protocols involved and explains their relationship with one another.

- **IPv4 Addressing:** Version 4 of the IP protocol has been used for many years and is still common today. This section describes the 32-bit IPv4 address classes and shows you how to configure your computer for IPv4 addressing.

- **IPv6 Addressing:** With the increasing large number of computers and other devices that connect to the Internet, IPv4 is running out of addresses. The 128-bit IP version 6 was developed to alleviate this problem. In this section, you are introduced to the various types of IPv6 addresses that are available. You then learn how to configure your computer with IPv6 and connect to other computers using either IPv4 or IPv6.

- **Resolving IPv4 and IPv6 Network Connectivity Issues:** Many factors can result in an inability to access other computers on the network or can result in intermittent connectivity. This section introduces common troubleshooting techniques you should be aware of when your computer cannot connect to others.

# CHAPTER 1

# Configuring IPv4 and IPv6 Addressing

At its heart and soul, computer networking is all about getting computers to talk to one another and exchange information. For computers to talk to one another, they must know how to contact each other. When I want to talk to another person across the city, the country, or the world, I pick up the phone and call his number. In the same fashion, a computer wanting to talk to another one must call its number. That number is the computer's IP address. In my first career as an environmental scientist, one day in the 1980s, a fellow scientist in another agency told me that I could send some data from my computer to his if I entered a series of numbers that he dictated to me. That series of numbers was an IP address, and that was my first exposure to TCP/IP. Upon transitioning to a computer networking career with Windows NT, I quickly discovered that you need to use and be proficient with TCP/IP to operate large networks and the Internet. While considered by Microsoft as an elective, the exam offered by Microsoft in TCP/IP networking in Windows NT was really mandatory for anyone who wanted to become proficient in server and network management.

Beginning with Windows 2000 and becoming much more so with successive versions of Windows Server, TCP/IP came into its forefront as the primary networking protocol, relegating other networking protocols such as NetBEUI to the museum. In fact, Microsoft made TCP/IP the required networking protocol for Active Directory (AD). This is largely because of Active Directory's dependence on the Domain Name System (DNS) to provide the computer name and address resolution for all resources in Active Directory. In reading this book to prepare for the 70-642 exam, you will learn about all the latest Windows Server 2008 R2 networking technologies used by businesses to keep users connected with each other and their data, regardless of where they are accessing the network from and the tasks that they are expected to perform.

For many years, version 4 of the IP protocol with its 32-bit addressing scheme provided an abundant supply of IP addresses for all the computers wanting to access the Internet. However, the Internet Engineering Task Force (IETF) foresaw the day that IPv4 would run out of address space and began the introduction of version 6 of this protocol, featuring a 128-bit address space in the late 1990s. Simply known as IPv6, this protocol provides for 128-bit addressing, which allows for a practically infinite number of possible addresses. Because IPv4 is still in common use, Microsoft expects you to know how to configure both IPv4 and IPv6 for the 70-642 exam, and this chapter presents a comprehensive introduction to both versions of the TCP/IP networking protocol.

## "Do I Know This Already?" Quiz

The "Do I Know This Already?" quiz allows you to assess whether you should read this entire chapter or simply jump to the "Exam Preparation Tasks" section for review. If you are in doubt, read the entire chapter. Table 1-1 outlines the major headings in this chapter and the corresponding "Do I Know This Already?" quiz questions. You can find the answers in Appendix A, "Answers to the 'Do I Know This Already?' Quizzes."

**Table 1-1**    "Do I Know This Already?" Foundation Topics Section-to-Question Mapping

| Foundations Topics Section | Questions Covered in This Section |
| --- | --- |
| Concepts of TCP/IP | 1–2 |
| IPv4 Addressing | 3–6 |
| IPv6 Addressing | 7–10 |
| Resolving IPv4 and IPv6 Network Connectivity Issues | 11–14 |

1. Which layer of the OSI model is responsible for establishing, maintaining, synchronizing, and managing communication dialog between entities on a network?

    **a.** Network

    **b.** Transport

    **c.** Session

    **d.** Presentation

2. At which layer of the TCP/IP reference model does the TCP protocol operate?

    **a.** Application

    **b.** Presentation

    **c.** Internet

    **d.** Transport

    **e.** Network interface

3. You need to ensure that your IPv4-enabled computer can access other subnets on your company's network, as well as the Internet. Which addressing component should you ensure is specified properly?

   a. IP address

   b. Subnet mask

   c. Default gateway

   d. DNS server address

   e. WINS address

4. Your computer is configured with the IP address 131.107.24.5. To which class does this IP address belong?

   a. A

   b. B

   c. C

   d. D

   e. E

5. Your network is configured to use DHCP for assignment of IP addresses and other TCP/IP configuration information such as DNS server addresses. Which of the following options should you ensure are selected in the Internet Protocol Version 4 (TCP/IPv4) Properties dialog box? (Choose two.)

   a. **Obtain an IP address automatically**

   b. **Use the following IP address**

   c. **Obtain DNS Server address automatically**

   d. **Use the following DNS Server addresses**

6. Your computer is configured to use the IPv4 address 169.254.183.32. What system is being used by your computer?

   a. Automatic Private Internet Protocol Addressing (APIPA)

   b. Dynamic Host Configuration Protocol (DHCP)

   c. Alternate IP configuration

   d. Private IPv4 network addressing

7. Your company has transitioned to using the IPv6 protocol and you are responsible for configuring Internet servers that need direct access to the Internet. Which of the following types of IPv6 addresses should you use for this purpose?

   a. Global unicast

   b. Link-local unicast

   c. Site-local unicast

   d. Multicast

   e. Anycast

8. Your computer is using an IPv6 address on the fe80::/64 network. What type of IPv6 address is this?

   a. Global unicast

   b. Site-local unicast

   c. Link-local unicast

   d. Teredo

9. You are responsible for adding IPv6 to your company's network. Two computers that are separated by an IPv4-only network infrastructure are configured with the IPv6 addresses of fe80::5efe:172.16.21.3 and fe80::5efe:192.168.12.51, respectively. Which of the following address types is being used to ensure IPv6-IPv4 connectivity in this example?

   a. ISATAP

   b. Teredo

   c. 6to4

   d. IPv4-mapping

10. You have configured a Windows Server 2008 R2 computer with the Internet Configuration Sharing (ICS) feature to enable IPv6 forwarding on both the 6to4 tunneling and private interfaces. Which of the following networking components is configured on this machine?

    a. 6to4 host

    b. 6to4 router

    c. 6to4 host/router

    d. 6to4 relay

11. Your computer is configured to use DHCP on the IPv4 network 192.168.4.0, but is unable to connect to other computers. You run **ipconfig /all** and notice that the computer is using the address 169.254.231.98. You must try again immediately to connect to other network computers. Which parameter of the ipconfig command should you use?

    a. /release

    b. /renew

    c. /flushdns

    d. /displaydns

12. You are troubleshooting the inability of your computer to connect to others on the network, so you are planning to run several TCP/IP utilities. Arrange the following in the sequence in which you should perform them.

    a. Ping the computer's own IP address.

    b. Ping a host that is on another subnet.

    c. Ping 127.0.0.1 or ::1.

    d. Run ipconfig /all.

    e. Ping the default gateway.

13. Computers on your network are configured to use static IP addresses. Your computer has been able to connect to the network most mornings when you start up, but one morning when you do not arrive until 9:30 a.m., your computer is unable to connect. Which of the following is the most likely reason for this problem?

    a. Your computer is configured with an IP address that is a duplicate of another one that has started up first.

    b. Your computer is using APIPA.

    c. Your computer is configured with an incorrect subnet mask.

    d. Your computer is configured with an alternate IP address and is using the alternate.

**14.** You are using the `ping` command to verify connectivity on your IPv6 network. You want to verify connectivity with a machine whose IPv6 address is fe80::9f:00ff:3a87:e364. Which of the following should you do? (Each answer represents part of the solution. Choose three.)

   **a.** Run the `ipconfig /displaydns` command.

   **b.** Run the `netsh interface ipv6 show interface` command.

   **c.** Run the `netsh interface ipv6 show neighbors` command.

   **d.** Run the `netsh interface ipv6 delete neighbors` command.

   **e.** Type `ping fe80::9f:00ff:3a87:e364 %<ID>`, where <ID> is the zone ID for the sending interface.

## Foundation Topics

# Concepts of TCP/IP

You might think of TCP/IP as a single networking protocol. However, this is not true—TCP/IP is actually a suite, or stack, of networking protocols that have been developed over the past several decades to provide a robust, scalable mechanism for networking computers both on a local and long-distance scale. Before introducing the components of the TCP/IP protocol stack, let's quickly look at how this protocol stack came to be.

## TCP/IP History in Brief

In the late 1960s, the Advanced Research Projects Agency of the US Department of Defense (ARPA, which was later renamed DARPA, The Defense Advanced Research Projects Agency) began sponsoring research into connecting geographically remote computers. TCP/IP began its development as part of ARPANET, a U.S. Department of Defense (DOD) packet-switched, wide-area network. ARPANET's initial reason for existence was to connect four mainframe computers located at the University of California at Los Angeles, Stanford Research Institute, University of California at Santa Barbara, and the University of Utah. The network was gradually extended, and by 1981, was comprised of 200 mostly academic and research-oriented-sites.

In the 1980s, mini- and microcomputers were also evolving and growing in power and complexity. Many of these machines ran on Berkeley Software Distribution (BSD) UNIX. It was actually at the U.S. government's urging that the TCP/IP protocol was incorporated into the BSD version of UNIX. The sharing of knowledge could be made easier if everyone involved (and their computers) used a common set of communication protocols. Whatever the government's motives may have been, the Internet is in part a result of this coming together and this standardization.

Several of the more important milestones of the early development of TCP/IP include the following:

- In 1970, ARPANET began to use the Network Control Protocol (NCP).

- In 1973, Request for Comment (RFC) 454 described the File Transfer Protocol (FTP).

- In 1974, detailed specifications for TCP were defined.

- In 1981, RFC 1791 described the IP protocol standard.

- In 1982, the Defense Communications Agency (DCA) and ARPA established TCP and IP as the TCP/IP protocol suite.

- In 1983, ARPANET began to use TCP/IP instead of NCP.

- In 1984, the Domain Name System (DNS) was introduced to provide a common name resolution standard for computers on the Internet.

> **NOTE**   RFCs are officially registered documents that describe the internal workings of the Internet, including all standards and enhancements pertaining to TCP/IP versions 4 and 6. They propose revisions and enhancements to its present standards and methods. IETF working groups oversee the development, revision, and acceptance of each RFC. The beginnings of IPv4 were described in RFC 791; many additional RFCs have been published that describe additional components of and improvements to IPv4 throughout the years. IPv6 was first described in RFC 1884, and was updated in RFCs 2373 and 3513.

## TCP/IP Protocol Stack

You can generally describe network protocols as being implemented in layers. The bottom layer typically deals with the physical aspects of networking. As one ascends through the layers, functions and descriptions become increasingly less physical and more abstract. A model that is commonly used to describe networking functionality is the Open Systems Interconnection (OSI) reference model, which is briefly introduced here.

### OSI Reference Model

During the time that most common networking protocols were being developed, the OSI reference model was created and published. The model serves to describe the work of protocols in a standardized fashion. This standardization allows differing system to communicate and provides protocol developers a list of common protocol tasks and a blueprint for designing protocol suites. The OSI model can be used to describe network communication in two ways: across boundary layers from a higher layer to a lower layer or as virtual, peer-to-peer, communication between corresponding layers on two different machines.

The OSI model as outlined in Table 1-2 is the ISO standard for connecting both similar and dissimilar network systems. This model describes network communications by referencing seven layers—each layer is associated with a specifically defined function or job.

**Table 1-2**  OSI Model Layers

| OSI Layer | Description |
| --- | --- |
| Application layer | Handles program-to-program transfer of information. This typically includes file transfers, database access, print services, and e-mail in a networked environment. The application layer can be described as the window into the network at large. |
| Presentation layer | Translates data into a format that can be understood by the different applications and the computers they run on. Compression, decompression, encryption, and decryption are also functions of this layer. |
| Session layer | Establishes, maintains, synchronizes, and manages communication dialog between entities on a network. These dialogs are called sessions. This also allows higher OSI layers to identify and connect with various network services. |
| Transport layer | Provides flow control and error handling, and aids in solving problems related to the transmission and reception of segments of data over a network. It is usually connection oriented, and makes up for less reliable connection services at the lower layers. It also acknowledges receipt of information. |
| Network layer | Translates logical network names and addresses into physical addresses. This means that networks and hosts on the network must have unique network addresses. Data routing, packet switching and network congestion are handled at the network layer. Routers operate at the network layer. |
| Data link layer | Organizes bits from the physical layer into groups called packets or frames. On the sending end, the data link layer sends data frames from the network layer to the physical layer as bits. This layer also controls data flow, detects and corrects errors, and identifies devices on the network. This layer adds segmentation and frame type information to the data being sent. Bridges, intelligent hubs, and network adapter cards are associated with the data link layer. |
| Physical layer | Converts bits into signals for outgoing messages and signals into bits for incoming messages. Network hardware is defined at this layer. Repeaters and amplifiers function at this layer. |

### Four-Layer TCP/IP Model

TCP/IP protocols correspond to a four-layer reference model, similar to the seven-layer OSI model, as shown in Figure 1-1. Here also, the four layers represent related standards. These standards serve to define the architecture of a TCP/IP network. They also define how TCP/IP communicates. The four layers that comprise the TCP/IP protocol suite are application, transport, Internet, and network interface.

Each layer corresponds to one or more layers of the seven-layer OSI model, as shown in the figure. If you remember your networking essentials, you are aware that logical communication takes place between the corresponding layers of a reference model as found on two machines on a network. That is, the application layer on one machine has important things to say to the application layer on another machine.

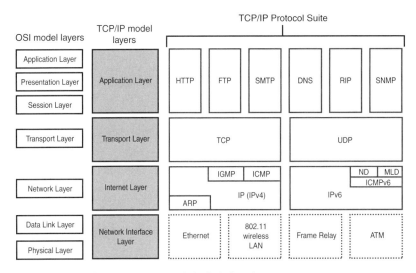

**Figure 1-1**   TCP/IP architecture is built in four layers.

Physical communication takes place between adjacent layers within the reference model on one machine. That is, the transport layer passes information to and receives information from the Internet layer as found on one machine, for example. A basic familiarity with the layers helps understand how TCP/IP operates.

### Application Layer

Like the OSI model's application layer, this layer is the access point that applications use to begin communicating with the network. Most applications conform to a client/server architecture. This layer defines numerous protocols (HTTP, FTP, SMTP, DNS, RIP, and SNMP) used by applications to communicate across the network; more applications that use this layer are always in development.

### Transport Layer

*Transmission Control Protocol (TCP)* and *User Datagram Protocol (UDP)* are the two protocols that operate at the transport layer. They are principally responsible for enabling delivery of packets transmitted by the network layer.

TCP is the protocol used for connection-oriented, reliable communication between two hosts—typically involving large amounts of data. Note that a *host* includes any device on the network (such as a computer, switch, or router) that is configured for TCP/IP. UDP is used for non-connection-oriented communications with no guarantee of delivery—typically small short bursts of data. Applications that are using UDP data are responsible for checking their data's integrity.

### Internet Layer

The Internet layer is primarily concerned with the routing and delivery of packets. This layer corresponds closely to the OSI network layer. Both versions 4 and 6 of the IP operate at this layer.

Routing is accomplished mainly by means of IP. Other protocols that function at the Internet layer are the Internet Control Messaging Protocol (ICMP), Internet Group Management Protocol (IGMP), Address Resolution Protocol (ARP), Neighbor Discovery (ND) protocol, and the Multicast Listener Discovery (MLD) protocol.

### Network Interface Layer

The network interface layer provides an interface for the layer above it to the network media. This layer controls the way frames are ultimately built and sent out on to the network media (Ethernet cables, network adapter cards, wireless cards, and so on) or received from the network media and sent to the upper layers. It is also responsible for controlling how frames are received from the network media and transmitted to the upper layers. The network interface layer needs to furnish an interface allowing the Internet layer to communicate with it from above. The Internet layer, in turn, is responsible for communicating directly with the network interface layer below.

**TIP** You will not be tested on either the history of TCP/IP or the OSI model stack on the 70-642 exam. These sections are included to provide a foundational background that helps form a better understanding of the concepts behind Windows Server 2008 networking.

### TCP/IP Component Protocols

As already described and shown in Figure 1-1, the TCP/IP protocol suite consists of a large number of component protocols. This section introduces these protocols.

### Transmission Control Protocol

The *Transmission Control Protocol (TCP)* provides connection-oriented, reliable communication between two hosts, typically involving large amounts of data. This kind of communication also involves acknowledgments that data has been correctly received. TCP works by establishing a connection, or session, between two hosts before transmitting data. Once established, this connection is maintained for the duration of a session. The connection is closed at the end of session.

TCP is described as a reliable protocol because it makes every effort to deliver data to its destination. TCP accepts messages from upper-layer protocols and provides an acknowledged connection-oriented delivery service to the transport layer at a remote host. Operating at the transport layer, TCP provides a reliable and guaranteed delivery mechanism to a destination host. TCP can guarantee delivery of packets by tracking the transmission and error-free receipt of individual packets during communication. TCP reliability is the result of TCP assigning a sequence number to each data segment transmitted. TCP also informs upper network layers of errors if it cannot transmit data successfully. In addition, TCP is responsible for ensuring that data is sent in the proper sequence. TCP uses a checksum feature to validate both the packet header and its data for correctness. If a packet is lost or corrupted during transmission, TCP is responsible for initiating a retransmission of that packet. All of the above characteristics of TCP add overhead in terms of transmission speed and processing.

### User Datagram Protocol

The *User Datagram Protocol (UDP)* is used for fast, non-connection-oriented communications with no guarantee of delivery—typically small short bursts of data. It guarantees neither delivery nor correct sequencing of packets. Applications using UDP data transmission are responsible for checking their data's integrity. UDP operates with less overhead than TCP. It is also used sending data from a single source to multiple destinations.

In general, UDP is best for handling transmission of large amounts of data where a dropped packet or two is not a major catastrophe. This can also include streaming and multimedia applications that require fast delivery of large amounts of data. Users of these applications won't notice that a few bits are out of place in a sound or a picture. Digital media are still far more accurate in terms of reproduction than their analog alternatives.

## Internet Protocol

The *Internet Protocol (IP)* handles, addresses, and routes packets between hosts on a network. It performs this service for all other protocols in the TCP/IP protocol suite.

IP is a connectionless protocol. Connectionless protocol transmissions occur without a pre-established path between the source and destination. This means that packets may take different routes between the source and destination. Packets may arrive at their destinations by different paths and in random order. They may also be duplicated or delayed. Although there is no way to guarantee delivery, IP will always make a "best effort" to deliver packets using the limited means at its disposal.

This best effort does not include acknowledgment for data that is received. Nor is the sender or receiver informed by IP when a packet goes missing or is sent out of sequence. Instead, the higher layer protocols, particularly TCP, take on the job of making sure packets reach their destination without error and of making acknowledgments in general.

By default, IP always first checks to see whether the destination IP address involved is for a local or a remote host. If the destination address is identified as a local one, IP sends the packet directly to the host. Should the destination address be a remote one, IP looks first to the local routing table for a route to the destination host or network. If IP cannot find a path in the routing table, it sends the packet to the source host's default gateway (assuming one is configured).

## Address Resolution Protocol

Within the TCP/IP protocol suite, other protocols are used by IP for special tasks. For two systems to communicate across a TCP/IP network, the system sending the packet must map the address of the destination computer to the physical or MAC address, which is a unique 12-digit hexadecimal number that is burned into ROM on every network adapter card. The *Address Resolution Protocol (ARP)* detects and updates a table that matches up physical addresses with IP addresses. This table is cached or stored in RAM for a limited time.

## Internet Control Message Protocol

The *Internet Control Message Protocol (ICMP)* delivers messages to hosts on a TCP/IP network. ICMP is specifically responsible for reporting errors and messages regarding the delivery of IP datagrams. It is not responsible for error correction. Higher layer protocols use information provided by ICMP to recover from transmission problems. Network administrators may also be able to use ICMP to detect network problems. ICMP is required in every IPv4 network implementation; IPv6 networks use a newer implementation of this protocol: ICMPv6.

### Internet Group Management Protocol

The *Internet Group Management Protocol (IGMP)* is used at the host level to report host group memberships to local multicast routers. IGMP provides membership in a multicast group to individual TCP/IP hosts. Multicasting is a limited form of broadcasting because broadcasts are directed to members of the multicast group only. These machines are also assigned special network addresses by TCP/IP. When using IGMP, a computer or other device sends a single copy of a message to a multicast service provider as a single operation. The service provider delivers that message to members of a group specified in the transmission. Note that IGMP is used in IPv4 only; on IPv6 networks, IGMP has been replaced by MLD, which serves to manage multicast groups on IPv6 networks.

### Application Layer Protocols

The following protocols, located within the application layer of the four-layer TCP/IP model, provide ancillary application-related services to their host computers:

- **Hypertext Transfer Protocol (HTTP):** Provides a file transfer capability for web-based pages as requested by a browser.

- **File Transfer Protocol (FTP):** Provides bidirectional file transfers between a Windows-based computer and any TCP/IP host running FTP server software.

- **Simple Mail Transport Protocol (SMTP):** Provides a simple service for transferring e-mail messages and their attachments.

- **Domain Name System (DNS):** Resolves host names on the Internet and local networks to IP addresses. DNS is such an important technology on Windows networks that we spend four chapters on this topic.

- **Routing Internet Protocol (RIP):** Used by routers to exchange routing information across IP subnetworks. Windows Server 2008 supports the updated version of this protocol: RIP v2.

- **Simple Network Management Protocol (SNMP):** Gathers network-management information from network devices, such as routers, bridges, and servers, and provides this information to network management consoles.

You study most of these protocols in detail in later chapters of this *Cert Guide*.

**NOTE**   For additional information on the component protocols in the TCP/IP protocol suite and their functions, refer to "Chapter 2—Architectural Overview of the TCP/IP Protocol Suite" at http://technet.microsoft.com/en-us/library/ bb726993.aspx. Also, refer to "IPv4 Protocols" for information on packet headers at http://technet.microsoft.com/en-us/library/dd392264(WS.10).aspx.

## IPv4 Addressing

IPv4 is installed as the default TCP/IP networking protocol in both the original and R2 versions of Windows Server 2008. Much of IPv4 is transparent to users when you've configured it properly. The administrator may need to configure the address information applied to the network interface. Table 1-3 describes this address information.

**Table 1-3**   IPv4 Addressing Components

| Addressing Component | Description |
|---|---|
| IP address | The unique, logical 32-bit address, which identifies the computer (called a host or node) and the subnet on which it is located. The IP address is displayed in dotted-decimal notation (each decimal represents an octet of binary ones and zeroes). For example, the binary notation of an address may be 10000000.00000 001.00000001.00000011, which in dotted-decimal notation is 128.1.1.3. |
| Subnet mask | The subnet mask is applied to an IP address to determine the subnetwork address and the host address on that subnet. All hosts on the same subnet must have the same subnet mask for them to be correctly identified. If a mask is incorrect, both the subnet and the host address will be wrong. (For example, if you have an IP address of 128.1.1.3, and an incorrect mask of 255.255.128.0, the subnet address would be 128.1.0 and the host address would be 1.3. If the correct subnet mask is 255.255.255.0, the subnet address would be 128.1.1 and the host address would be 3.) |
| Default gateway | The address listed as the default gateway is the location on the local subnet to which the local computer sends all data meant for other subnets. In other words, this is the IP address for the local network side of the router that is capable of transmitting the data to other networks. |

**Table 1-3**   IPv4 Addressing Components (*Continued*)

| Addressing Component | Description |
| --- | --- |
| DNS server address | The IP address to which names of IP hosts are sent so that the DNS server will respond with an IP address. This process is called *name resolution*. DNS is a distributed database of records that maps names to IP addresses, and vice versa. |
| Windows Internet Naming Service (WINS) address | The WINS server address is the location where network computers send requests to resolve NetBIOS names to IP addresses. WINS is used on Microsoft Windows networks where older Windows computers or applications require NetBIOS name resolution. When a user types in a NetBIOS name, such as JACKSPC, the computer sends the name to the WINS server. Because WINS is a flat-file database, it returns an IP address or a `Name not found` message. WINS server addresses, like DNS server addresses, are optional. |

**NOTE**   In this discussion and elsewhere in this book, the term "Windows Server 2008" includes both the original and R2 versions unless otherwise noted. The term "Windows Server 2008 R2" is used when referring to new features added with this version of the server software.

## Static IPv4 Addressing

IP addresses indicate the same type of location information as a street address within a city. A building on a street has a number, and when you add it to the street name, you can find it fairly easily because the number and the street will be unique within that city. This type of address scheme—an individual address plus a location address—allows every computer on a corporate network or the Internet to be uniquely identified.

A static IP address is one that is manually assigned to a computer on the network. Certain computers require static IP addresses because of their functions, such as routers or servers. Client computers are more often assigned dynamic addresses because they are more likely to be moved around the network or retired and replaced. DSL and cable modem users are usually given a static IP address, whereas dial-up users are provided with dynamic addresses.

IP addresses consist of two parts: one that specifies the network and one part that specifies the computer. These addresses are further categorized with classes, as described in Table 1-4.

**Table 1-4**  IPv4 Address Classes

| Class | Dotted-Decimal Hosts per Range | Default Subnet Mask | First Octet Binary | Usage | Number of Networks | Number of Hosts per Network |
|---|---|---|---|---|---|---|
| A | 1.0.0.0– 126.255.255.255 | 255.0.0.0 | 0xxxxxxx | Large networks/ISPs | 128 | 16.777.214 |
| B | 128.0.0.0– 191.255.255.255 | 255.255.0.0 | 10xxxxxx | Large or mid-size ISPs | 16,384 | 65,534 |
| C | 192.0.0.0– 223.255.255.255 | 255.255.255.0 | 110xxxxx | Small networks | 2,097,152 | 254 |
| D | 224.0.0.0– 239.255.255.255 | N/A | 1110xxxx | Multicasting | N/A | N/A |
| E | 240.0.0.0– 254.255.255.255 | N/A | 1111xxxx | Reserved for future use | N/A | N/A |

**NOTE**   The concept of loopback testing is the usage of a predefined IP address that a computer can dial itself up to see whether the TCP/IP stack is properly set up. If TCP/IP is configured, you should be able to run the `ping 127.0.0.1` command when troubleshooting a connectivity problem. More about this command is provided later in this chapter.

The portion of the address that decides on which network the host resides varies based on the class, and, as you will see further on, the subnet mask. In the following list, the uppercase *N*s represent the part of the IP address that specifies the network, and the lowercase *C*s represent the part of the address that specifies the computer. This explains why there are differing numbers of networks per class, and different numbers of hosts per network, as listed in Table 1-4.

- Class A: NNNNNNNN.cccccccc.cccccccc.cccccccc

- Class B: NNNNNNNN.NNNNNNNN.cccccccc.cccccccc

- Class C: NNNNNNNN.NNNNNNNN.NNNNNNNN.cccccccc

These address portions coincide with the default subnet masks for each address class. A Class A subnet mask is 255.0.0.0, a Class B subnet mask is 255.255.0.0, and a Class C subnet mask is 255.255.255.0.

Take, for example, the IP address 192.168.5.137 on a default Class C network. In binary notation, this address is as follows:

11000000 10101000 00000101 10001001

The network portion of the address is the first three octets: 11000000 10101000 00000101 and the host portion is represented by the final octet: 10001001. This division follows directly from the information provided in Table 1-4.

In recent years, it has become popular to use *classless inter-domain routing (CIDR)*, also known as the *slash notation* or *CIDR notation*, to refer to the number of bits represented by the network portion of the IP address. This provides a simple means of defining a network address and subnet mask together; simply suffix the network address with a "/" followed immediately by the number of bits in the network portion of the address. Table 1-5 compares the different notations of the default subnet masks for Class A, B, and C networks.

**Table 1-5**   Default Subnet Masks in Different Notations

| Class | Binary Subnet Mask Notation | Decimal Subnet Mask Notation | CIDR Notation |
|-------|------------------------------|-------------------------------|----------------|
| A | 11111111 00000000 00000000 00000000 | 255.0.0.0 | /8 |
| B | 11111111 11111111 00000000 00000000 | 255.255.0.0 | /16 |
| C | 11111111 11111111 11111111 00000000 | 255.255.255.0 | /24 |

## Subnetting and Supernetting in IPv4

IPv4 does not restrict you to the default subnet masks already introduced for Classes A, B, and C networks. If it did, the use of IP address space would be extremely inefficient and IPv4 addresses would have been exhausted decades ago. By employing subnetting, you can divide the address space of your network into subnets of an efficient size that relates to the number of hosts that each subnet must support.

### Using Subnetting to Divide a Network

The process of *subnetting* enables you to reconfigure which portion of the subnet mask constitutes the network portion and which portion constitutes the host portion. When you apply the subnet mask to the IP address by using a "bitwise logical AND" operation, as discussed in the previous section, the result is a network number. A bitwise logical AND operation adds the bit, whether 1 or 0, to the corresponding bit in the subnet mask. If the subnet mask bit is a 1, the corresponding IP address bit is passed through as a result. If the subnet mask bit is a 0, a zero bit is passed through. For example, if the IP address is 141.25.240.201 with the default Class B subnet mask of 255.255.0.0 or /16, you will have the following:

- IP address: 10001101.00011001.11110000.11001001
- Subnet mask: 11111111.11111111.00000000.00000000
- Result from bitwise logical AND
- Network: 10001101.00011001.00000000.00000000

This shows the network address as 141.25.0.0 and the host address to 0.0.240.201. If you add bits to the mask, you will be able to have additional subnetworks when you perform a bitwise logical AND, and each subnetwork will have fewer hosts because fewer bits are available for the host portion of the address. If you use the same address and five bits to the subnet mask, you would receive the following:

- IP address: 10001101.00011001.11110000.11001001
- Subnet mask: 11111111.11111111.11111000.00000000
- Result from bitwise logical AND
- Network: 10001101.00011001.11110000.00000000

In this case, the subnet mask changes the network address to 141.25.240.0 or /21. The host address changes to 0.0.0.201. Other IP addresses that are under the default Class B subnet mask that would otherwise be part of the same network, such as 140.25.192.15 and 140.25.63.12, are now on different subnets.

For an organization with a large number of physical networks where each requires a different subnet address, you can use the subnet mask to segment a single address to fit the network. You can easily calculate how many subnets and hosts you will receive when you subnet a network. To calculate the number of subnets, use the formula $2^s$, where $s$ is the number of bits in the subnet portion of the address. $2^s$ is the number 2 raised to the power of the number of subnet bits. To calculate the number of hosts available on each subnet, use the formula $2^b - 2$, where $n$ is the number of bits in the host portion of the address. $2^b$ is the number 2 raised to the power of the number of host bits, and that result minus 2 (the addresses represented by all 1s and all 0s) equals the available hosts. Therefore, if you have a subnet of 5 bits as previously shown, you are able to achieve $2^5 = 32$ subnets. Because there are 11 bits left for host addresses, each subnet will have $2^{11} - 2 = 2048 - 2 = 2,046$ hosts.

Table 1-6 compares the number of networks and hosts provided by subnetting a Class B network. You should be easily able to compute similar numbers for other network classes.

**Table 1-6**   Subnetting a Class B Network

| Dotted-Decimal Subnet Mask | CIDR Notation | Number of Subnets | Number of Hosts per Subnet |
|---|---|---|---|
| 255.255.128.0 | /17 | 2 | 32,766 |
| 255.255.192.0 | /18 | 4 | 16,382 |
| 255.255.224.0 | /19 | 8 | 8190 |
| 255.255.240.0 | /20 | 16 | 4094 |
| 255.255.248.0 | /21 | 32 | 2046 |
| 255.255.252.0 | /22 | 64 | 1022 |
| 255.255.254.0 | /23 | 128 | 510 |
| 255.255.255.0 | /24 | 256 | 254 |

**NOTE**   For more information on subnetting Class A, B, and C IPv4 networks, refer to "Host and Subnet Quantities" at www.cisco.com/en/US/tech/tk365/technologies_tech_note09186a0080093f33.shtml.

**TIP**   Be sure that you understand the various notations of IPv4 subnet masks thoroughly, both for the 70-642 exam and for the real world. You are most likely to encounter questions on the exam that ask you to determine the subnet mask that will accommodate a given number of hosts.

**NOTE**   For more information on subnetting, refer to "Subnetting" at http://technet.microsoft.com/en-us/library/cc958834.aspx. For more information on all aspects of IP addressing, refer to "Chapter 3—IP Addressing" at http://technet.microsoft.com/en-us/library/bb726995.aspx.

## Using Supernetting to Provide for Additional Hosts on a Network

The process of subnetting, as outlined in the preceding section, enables you to sub-divide a network according to the number of hosts on each segment. But, you might encounter the opposite problem—you might require a larger number of hosts than what a given network can accommodate. Suppose that you are responsible for an organization that requires IPv4 addressing for as many as 2000 hosts. Recall from Table 1-4 that a Class C network can accommodate up to 254 hosts, so your company would require eight separate Class C networks or a single Class B network. However, the latter, which can accommodate 65,534 hosts, would waste IPv4 addresses. So, InterNIC assigns your company a contiguous block of eight Class C network addresses that you combine to form a single network. This practice is known as *supernetting*. In doing so, a company can "supernet" two (or more) Class C addresses to put more than 254 hosts on a single physical network. Supernetting is the process of subtracting bits from the default subnet mask. This adds bits to the host portion, increasing the number of hosts available. CIDR is used in conjunction with super-netting so that only a single routing table entry is required for the eight Class C networks assigned in this example. A possible CIDR notation for the network in this example could be 192.168.1.0/21. Table 1-7 shows how you can supernet several Class C networks together.

**Table 1-7**   Supernetting a Class C Network

| Dotted-Decimal Subnet Mask | CIDR Notation | Number of Network Addresses Combined | Number of Hosts Accommodated |
|---|---|---|---|
| 255.255.192.0 | /18 | 64 | 16,382 |
| 255.255.224.0 | /19 | 32 | 8190 |
| 255.255.240.0 | /20 | 16 | 4094 |
| 255.255.248.0 | /21 | 8 | 2046 |
| 255.255.252.0 | /22 | 4 | 1022 |
| 255.255.254.0 | /23 | 2 | 510 |

**NOTE**   For more information on supernetting, refer to "Planning Supernetting and Classless Interdomain Routing" at http://technet.microsoft.com/en-us/library/cc783978(WS.10).aspx.

### Understanding Private IPv4 Networks

IPv4 specifications define sets of networks that are specified as *private IPv4 networks*. The private IP address classes are used on private networks that do not need to be accessed directly from the public Internet. Internet routers are preconfigured to not forward data that contains these IP addresses. Table 1-8 describes these networks.

**Table 1-8**   Private IPv4 Network Addresses

| Class | Dotted-Decimal Hosts per Range | First Octet Binary | Number of Networks | Number of Hosts per Network |
|-------|-------------------------------|--------------------|--------------------|-----------------------------|
| A | 10.0.0.0–10.255.255.255 | 00001010 | 1 | 16,777,214 |
| B | 172.16.0.0–172.16.255.255 | 10101100 | 16 | 65,534 |
| C | 192.168.0.0–192.168.255.255 | 11000000 | 256 | 254 |

### Dynamic IP Addressing

Dynamic IP addresses are provided to a computer when it needs to be connected to the network. The provider is the Dynamic Host Configuration Protocol (DHCP) server. Such an IP address is leased for a specified period of time (the administrator specifies this time period when configuring the DHCP server), and when the lease is up, the IP address is placed back in an IP address pool and can be delivered to another computer. You learn more about DHCP and dynamic IP addressing in Chapter 2, "Configuring Dynamic Host Configuration Protocol (DHCP)."

### Configuring IPv4 Address Options

You can configure TCP/IP version 4 on a Windows Server 2008 computer either manually or dynamically. The default method is to dynamically configure TCP/IP. If the infrastructure includes DHCP services that deliver IP addresses to network computers, a Windows Server 2008 computer can connect upon log on with the default configuration of the network adapter. However, if you need to apply a static IPv4 address and other parameters (which is required for servers that provide infrastructure services, such as DHCP or DNS servers or domain controllers), your only option is to manually configure the network adapter. Use the following procedure to configure your server with a static IPv4 address:

1. Click **Start**, right-click **Network**, and choose **Properties**.

2. From the left side of the Network and Sharing Center, click **Change adapter settings**. On a server running the original version of Windows Server 2008, click **Manage Network Connections**. This opens the Network Connections page, as shown in Figure 1-2.

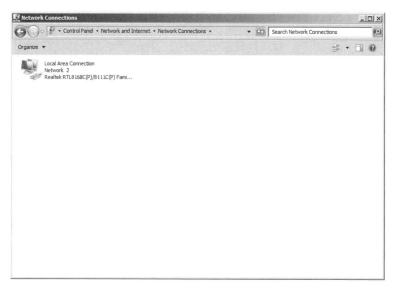

**Figure 1-2**    The Network Connections page displays the network connections configured for your computer.

3. Right-click the connection that represents the adapter you are going to configure and select **Properties**. The Local Area Connection Properties dialog box opens, as shown in Figure 1-3.

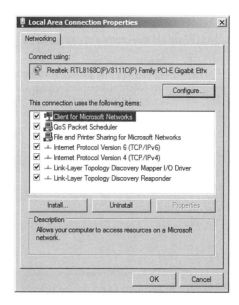

**Figure 1-3**    The Local Area Network Connection Properties dialog box enables you to configure TCP/IP addressing options.

4. Click to select **Internet Protocol Version 4 (TCP/IPv4)**. (You might need to scroll through other services to reach this item.) Click **Properties**. The Internet Protocol Version 4 (TCP/IPv4) Properties dialog opens, as shown in Figure 1-4.

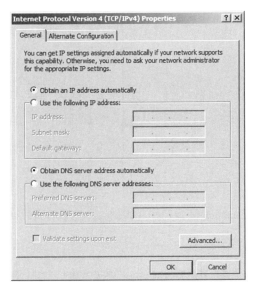

**Figure 1-4** The Internet Protocol Version 4 (TCP/IPv4) Properties dialog box lets you define manual or dynamic IPv4 address information.

5. To use DHCP services, make sure that **Obtain an IP address automatically** is selected, and if the DHCP server provides extended information—including the DNS server information—you would also select **Obtain DNS server address automatically**. To manually configure the IP address, click **Use the following IP address**.

6. In the **IP address** box, type the address that will function on the current network segment. For example, if the network segment uses a Class C address 192.168.1.0 with a subnet mask of 255.255.255.0, and you've already used 192.168.1.1 and 192.168.1.2, you could select any node address from 3 through 254 (255 is used for broadcasts), in which case, you would type `192.168.1.3`.

7. In the **Subnet mask** box, type the subnet mask. In this case, it is `255.255.255.0`.

8. In the **Default gateway** box, type the IP address that is assigned to the router interface on your current segment that leads to the main network or the public network. For example, suppose that the IP address of the router on your

segment is 192.168.1.1 and the IP address of the router's other interface is 12.88.54.179. In the Default gateway box, you would type `192.168.1.1`.

9. To configure an alternate IP address on a computer configured to use DHCP, click the **Alternate Configuration** tab. Then, enter the required IP address, subnet mask, default gateway, and DNS and WINS server information.

10. Click the **Advanced** button. The Advanced TCP/IP Settings dialog box opens, as shown in Figure 1-5.

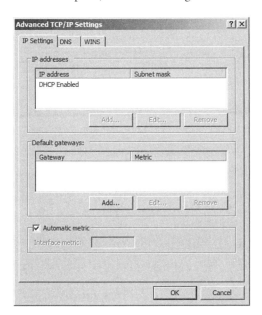

**Figure 1-5**   The Advanced TCP/IP Settings dialog box allows you to control granular IP addressing options.

11. If you require more than one IP address for a computer, such as for hosting two different websites, you can configure the additional IP addresses in this dialog box by clicking the **Add** button. You cannot configure any additional IP addresses if you are using DHCP.

12. If your network segment is connected to more than one router leading to the main or outside networks, you can configure these gateway addresses in the Default Gateways section by clicking the **Add** button.

13. When finished, click **OK** twice and then click **Close** to return to the Network Connections dialog box.

**NOTE** If you configured your server to receive an IP address from DHCP and the observed IPv4 address is in the range of 169.254.0.1 to 169.254.255.254, your server has been unable to access the DHCP server and has used APIPA to assign itself an IP address. While possibly useful on a small LAN, this is usually a symptom of network connectivity problems. See the section, "Resolving IPv4 and IPv6 Network Connectivity Issues," for troubleshooting information.

**TIP** An alternate configuration as described in Step 9 of the preceding procedure is useful with a portable computer that might move to a network without a DHCP server. If such a computer is unable to locate a DHCP server, it defaults to the alternate IP configuration rather than assigning itself an APIPA address.

### Using the Command Line to Configure IPv4 Addressing Options

Windows Server 2008 provides the `netsh` command that enables you to configure TCP/IP networking and addressing options from the command line. `netsh` also enables you to configure and display the status of various networking server roles and components. This command is useful for scripting network configuration for a series of computers, and it is the only means of configuring TCP/IP options at a machine running the Server Core option of Windows Server 2008.

**NOTE** In the Server Core option of Windows Server 2008 R2, you can also use `sconfig.cmd` to configure TCP/IP settings. For information on using this command, refer to "Configuring a Server Core installation of Windows Server 2008 R2 with `Sconfig.cmd`" at http://technet.microsoft.com/en-us/library/ee441254(WS.10). aspx.

`Netsh` uses the following general command syntax:

```
Netsh [-a AliasFile] [-c Context] [-r RemoteComputer] [-u
[DomainName\UserName] [-p Password | *} [{NetshCommand
| -f ScriptFile}]
```

Table 1-9 describes the parameters of this command. All parameters are optional unless otherwise specified.

**Table 1-9** `Netsh` Command Parameters

| Parameter | Description |
|---|---|
| `-a` | Specifies that you are returned to the `netsh` prompt after running *AliasFile*. |
| `AliasFile` | Specifies the name of a text file containing one or more `netsh` subcommands. |
| `-c` | Specifies that `netsh` enters the specified `netsh` context. |
| `Context` | Specifies the `netsh` context that you want to enter. For more information, refer to "Enter a `Netsh` Context" at http://technet. microsoft.com/en-us/library/cc754580(WS.10).aspx. |
| `-r` | Specifies that you want to run the `netsh` command on a remote computer. |
| `RemoteComputer` | Specifies the remote computer to be configured. |
| `-u` | Specifies an alternate user account under which the `netsh` command is to be run. |
| `DomainName\` | Specifies the domain name where this user account is located. If absent, the local domain is used. |
| `UserName` | Specifies the user account name to be used. |
| `-p Password` | Specifies the password to be used with this user account. |
| `NetshCommand` | Specifies the `netsh` command to be executed. |
| `-f` | Specifies that you want to run a script file. |
| `ScriptFile` | Specifies the script file to be run. |

In addition to these parameters, you can use the `netsh` command in this format:

```
Netsh subcommand
```

Here, `subcommand` refers to the networking component you are configuring. You learn about numerous subcommands used with `netsh` in various chapters of this *Cert Guide*. With respect to configuring IPv4, the command syntax used is as follows:

```
Netsh interface ip [parameters]
```

`parameters` represents the string of parameters required to accomplish a given task. For example, to configure the computer's local area connection with the static IP address 192.168.0.2, subnet mask 255.255.255.0, and default gateway 192.168.0.1, use the following command:

```
Netsh interface ip set address "Local Area Connection"
static 192.168.0.2 255.255.255.0 192.168.0.1
```

To add the IP address 192.168.0.3 as a preferred DNS server address, use the following command:

```
Netsh interface ip add dnsserver name="Local Area Connection"
addr=192.168.0.3 index=[DNSIndex]
```

*DNSIndex* specifies the position of the added DNS server in the list of DNS servers. This parameter has the value of 1 for the preferred DNS server and 2 or higher for an alternate DNS server.

> **NOTE**   For additional information on commands used to configure IPv4 and IPv6 interfaces using the `netsh` command, refer to "`Netsh` Commands for Interface (IPv4 and IPv6)" at http://technet.microsoft.com/en-us/library/cc770948(WS.10).aspx. For more information on `netsh` commands in general, refer to "The `Netsh` Command-Line Utility" at http://technet.microsoft.com/en-us/library/cc785383(WS.10). aspx, "`Netsh` Technical Reference" at http://technet.microsoft.com/en-us/library/ cc725935(WS.10).aspx, and "`Netsh` Overview" at http://technet.microsoft.com/ en-us/library/cc732279(WS.10).aspx.

## IPv6 Addressing

The 128-bit addressing scheme used by IPv6 enables an unimaginably high number of $3.4 \times 10^{38}$ addresses, which equates to a total of $6.5 \times 10^{23}$ addresses for every square meter of the Earth's surface. Consequently, this is a complicated addressing scheme, as described in the following sections.

By default, versions of Windows prior to Windows Server 2008 have used version 4 of the IP protocol, simply known as IPv4. With its 32-bit address space, this version has performed admirably well in the over 25 years since its initial introduction. However, with the rapid growth of the Internet, its address space has approached exhaustion and security concerns have increased. In fact, a news story in February 2011 reported that the last five blocks of IPv4 addresses have recently been allocated to the five Regional Internet Registries (RIR), which will distribute these addresses to Internet service providers (ISP). Consequently, the IETF introduced version 6 of the IP protocol with RFC 1883 in 1995 and added RFCs 2460, 3513, and 4193 in more recent years.

The introduction by the IETF of 128-bit IPv6 addressing provides for a practically infinite number of possible addresses, as well as the following benefits:

- **Efficient hierarchical addressing scheme:** IPv6 addresses are designed to enable an efficient, hierarchical, and summarizable routing scheme, making way for multiple levels of ISPs.

- **Simpler routing tables:** Backbone routers on the Internet are more easily configured for routing packets to their destinations. Routing is discussed in Chapter 3, "Configuring Routing."

- **Stateful and stateless address configuration:** IPv6 simplifies host configuration with the use of stateful address configuration (configuring IP addresses in the presence of a DHCP server) or the use of stateless address configuration (configuring IP addresses in the absence of a DHCP server). Stateless address configuration enables the automatic configuration of hosts on a subnetwork according to the addresses displayed by available routers.

- **Improved security:** IPv6 includes standards-based support for IP Security (IPSec). In fact, IPv6 requires IPSec support. You can configure IPSec connection security rules for IPv6 in the same fashion as with IPv4. IPSec is discussed in Chapter 4, "Configuring Windows Firewall with Advanced Security."

- **Support for Link-Local Multicast Name Resolution (LLMNR):** This enables IPv6 clients on a single subnet to resolve each other's names without the need for a DNS server or using NetBIOS over TCP/IP.

- **Improved support for Quality of Service (QoS):** IPv6 header fields improve the identification and handling of network traffic from its source to destination, even when IPSec encryption is in use.

- **Extensibility:** You can add extension headers after the IPv6 packet header, which enable the inclusion of new features as they are developed in years to come.

By using a TCP/IP implementation known as the Next Generation TCP/IP stack (first included with Windows Vista), both the original and R2 versions of Windows Server 2008 as well as Windows 7 enable a dual IP layer architecture enabling the operation of both IPv4 and IPv6 at the same time. Unlike with Windows XP and older Windows versions, Windows Server 2008 does not require you to install a separate IPv6 component; IPv6 is installed and enabled by default.

**NOTE**   For more introductory information on IPv6, refer to "Microsoft's Objectives for IP Version 6" at http://technet.microsoft.com/en-us/library/bb726949.aspx.

### IPv6 Address Syntax

Whereas IPv4 addresses use dotted-decimal format, as already explained earlier in this chapter, IPv6 addresses are subdivided into eight 16-bit blocks. Each 16-bit block is portrayed as a 4-digit hexadecimal number and is separated from other blocks by colons. This addressing scheme is referred to as *colon-hexadecimal*.

For example, a 128-bit IPv6 address written in binary could appear as follows:

0011111111111110 1111111111111111 0010000111000101
0000000000000000 0000001010101010 0000000011111111
1111111000100001 0011101000111110

The same address written in colon-hexadecimal becomes 3ffe:ffff:21a5:0000:00ff: fe21:5a3e. You can remove any single set of contiguous leading zeros, converting this address to 3ffe:ffff:21a5::ff:fe21:5a3e. This process is known as *Zero compression*. In this notation, note that the block that contained all zeros appears as ::, which is called *double-colon*. You can always figure out how many blocks of zeros are contained within a double-colon because all IPv6 addresses consist of eight 16-bit blocks.

### IPv6 Prefixes

Corresponding to the network portion of an IPv4 address is the prefix, which is the part of the address containing the bits of the subnet prefix. IPv6 addresses do not employ subnet masks, but use the same CIDR notation used with IPv4. For example, an IPv6 address prefix could be 3ffe:ffff:21a5::/64, where 64 is the number of bits employed by the address prefix.

### Types of IPv6 Addresses

IPv6 uses the following three types of addresses:

- **Unicast:** Represents a single interface within the typical scope of unicast addresses. In other words, packets addressed to this type of address are to be delivered to a single network interface. Unicast IPv6 addresses include global unicast, link-local, and unique local addresses. Two special addresses are also included: unspecified addresses (all zeros or ::, equivalent to the IPv4 address of 0.0.0.0) and the loopback address, which is 0:0:0:0:0:0:0:1 or ::1, which is equivalent to the IPv4 address of 127.0.0.1. By default, all unicast addresses are divided into a 64-bit network component and a 64-bit host component.

- **Multicast:** Represents multiple interfaces to which packets are delivered to all network interfaces identified by the address. Multicast addresses have the first eight bits set to ones, so begin with ff.

- **Anycast:** Represents multiple interfaces. Anycast packets are delivered to a single network interface that represents the nearest (in terms of routing hops) interface identified by the address.

Table 1-10 provides additional details on the IPv6 classes and subclasses.

**Table 1-10**   IPv6 Address Classes and Subclasses

| Class | Address Prefix | Additional Features | First Binary Bits | Usage |
|---|---|---|---|---|
| Global unicast | 2000::/3 | Use a global routing prefix of 45 bits (beyond the initial 001 bits), which identifies a specific organization's network; a 16-bit subnet ID, which identifies up to 65,536 subnets within an organization's network; and a 64-bit interface ID, which indicates a specific network interface within the subnet. | 001 | Globally routable Internet addresses that are equivalent to the public IPv4 addresses. |
| Link-local unicast | fe80::/64 | Equivalent to APIPA-configured IPv4 addresses in the 169.254.0.0/16 network prefix. | 111111101000 | Nonroutable addresses used for communication between neighboring nodes on the same subnet. These addresses are assigned automatically when you configure automatic addressing in the absence of a DHCP server. |

**Table 1-10**    IPv6 Address Classes and Subclasses (*Continued*)

| Class | Address Prefix | Additional Features | First Binary Bits | Usage |
|---|---|---|---|---|
| Unique local IPv6 unicast | fc00::/7 | Prefix followed by a local (L) flag, a 40-bit global ID, a 16-bit subnet ID, and a 64-bit interface ID. | 11111100 | Provide addresses that are private to an organization but unique across all the organization's sites. |
| Multicast | Ff | Use the next 4 bits for flags (Transient [T], Prefix [P], and Rendezvous Point Address [R]), the following 4 bits for scope (determines where multicast traffic is forwarded), and the remaining 112 bits for a group ID. | 11111111 | Multiple interfaces to which packets are delivered to all network interfaces identified by the address. |
| Anycast | (From unicast addresses) | Assigned from the unicast address space with the same scope as the type of unicast address within which the anycast address is assigned. | (Varies) | Only utilized as destination addresses assigned to routers. |

Consider the following sample IPv6 addresses:

- **2003:414:ab86:731f::230:1:45ab:** This is a global unicast address in which 2003:414:ab86 represents the global routing prefix specifying the organizations site, 731f is a subnet identifier, and 0:230:1:45ab represents the host ID. Note that the presence of multiple zeros is implied by the presence of the double-colon.

- **fe80::cc33:456a:3719:1234%8:** This is a link local address in which the host ID is cc33:456a:3719:1234; included at the end of each link local address (but not part of the actual address itself) is a zone ID specified in the form %ID (%8 in this example). This ID appears when you run the `ipconfig` command and specifies the network interface and is typically equal to the interface index of the interface connected to the link on which the destination is located. It distinguishes the networks to which a computer with multiple network adapters is connected. Windows Server 2008 assigns a zone ID according to a parameter called the interface index for each network interfaces. To view a list of interface indexes on a computer, open a command prompt and type `netsh interface ipv6 show interface`.

- **fd12:cde6:1208:9::f92b:** This is a unique local address in which the first 7 bits are all ones; the eighth bit is also one, which is the local (L) flag. The next 40 bits are 02:cde6:1208 and represent a global network ID, which is a randomly generated site-specific value. The 16-bit subnet ID has a value of 0009; its use is for further subnetting the internal network in an analogous manner to the IPv4 subnetting discussed previously. Finally, the last 64 bits are 0:0:0:f92b, which specifies the unique host interface ID. Again, the zeroes are represented by the double-colon.

**NOTE**  You might also find mention of the site-local IPv6 address class. This address class was equivalent to the private IPv4 addresses mentioned in Table 1-8; however, site-local addresses have been deprecated as of 2004. Refer to "Deprecating Site Local Addresses" at http://tools.ietf.org/html/rfc3879 for more information.

### Connecting to a TCP/IP Version 6 Network

You can let IPv6 configure itself automatically with a link-local address described previously in Table 1-10. You can also configure IPv6 to use an existing DHCP server, or manually configure an IPv6 address as required. The configuration of IPv6 addresses is similar to the procedure used with configuration of IPv4 addresses, as the following procedure shows:

1. Click **Start**, right-click **Network**, and choose **Properties**.

2. From the left side of the Network and Sharing Center, click **Change adapter settings**. On a server running the original version of Windows Server 2008, click **Manage Network Connections**. This opens the Network Connections page, as previously shown in Figure 1-2.

3. Right-click the connection that represents the adapter you are going to configure and select **Properties**.

4. Click to select **Internet Protocol Version 6 (TCP/IPv6)**. (You might need to scroll through other services to reach this item.) Click **Properties**. The Internet Protocol Version 6 (TCP/IPv6) Properties dialog opens, as shown in Figure 1-6.

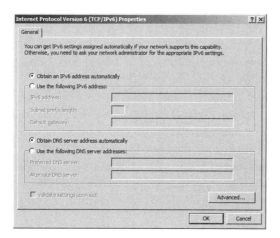

**Figure 1-6**   The Internet Protocol Version 6 (TCP/IPv6) Properties dialog box lets you define manual or dynamic IPv6 address information.

5. To use DHCP, ensure that the **Obtain an IPv6 address automatically** radio button is selected. If the DHCP server provides DNS server information, ensure that the **Obtain DNS server address automatically** radio button is also selected. You can also select these options to configure IPv6 automatically with a link-local address using the address prefix fe80::/64, previously described in Table 1-10.

6. To manually configure an IPv6 address, select **Use the following IPv6 address**. Then, type the **IPv6 address**, **Subnet prefix length**, and **Default gateway** in the text boxes provided. For unicast IPv6 addresses, set the prefix length to its default value of 64.

7. To manually configure DNS server addresses, select **Use the following DNS server addresses**. Then, type the IPv6 addresses of the preferred and alternate DNS server in the text boxes provided.

8. Click **Advanced** to display the Advanced TCP/IP Settings dialog box shown in Figure 1-7.

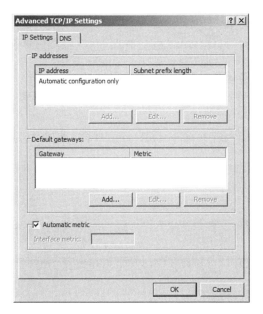

**Figure 1-7** The Advanced TCP/IP Settings dialog allows you to control granular IPv6 addressing options.

9. As with IPv4, you can configure additional IP addresses if you are not using DHCP. Click **Add** and type the required IP address in the dialog box that appears.

10. As with IPv4, if your network segment is connected to more than one router, configure additional gateway addresses in the Default Gateways section by clicking the **Add** button.

11. When finished, click **OK** until you return to the Network Connections dialog box.

---

**TIP** You can also use the `netsh` tool with the `interface IPv6` subcommand to configure IPv6 from the command line. For example, the `netsh interface IPv6 set address "local area connection 2" fec0:0:0:ffee::3` sets the IPv6 address of the second local-area connection to the specified address. For more information, and other IPv6-related `netsh` subcommands, refer to "IPv6 Configuration Information with the `Netsh.exe` Tool" at http://technet.microsoft.com/en-us/library/bb726952. aspx#EBAA.

### Interoperability Between IPv4 and IPv6 Addresses

Many organizations are considering moving to IPv6, but currently have large numbers of servers and client computers using IPv4 addressing technology. Indeed, nodes using IPv4 will be with us for years to come. In designing IPv6, this fact was recognized early in the process and the designers adopted several transition criteria into the recommendations outlined in RFC 1752:

- You can upgrade existing IPv4 hosts at any time and independently of other devices on the network.

- You can add new IPv6-only hosts at any time without dependencies on other hosts or devices.

- After IPv6 is set up, existing IPv4 hosts can continue to use their IPv4 addresses without the need for new IPv6 addresses.

- It should be easy to upgrade existing IPv4 hosts to IPv6 or deploy new IPv6 hosts without much additional preparation.

To assist in upgrading networks to IPv6, the following node types were defined in RFC 2893:

- **IPv4 node:** Uses IPv4, but can also be an IPv6/IPv4 node.

- **IPv6 node:** Uses IPv6, but can also be an IPv6/IPv4 node.

- **IPv4-only node:** Uses IPv4 and cannot support IPv6.

- **IPv6-only node:** Uses IPv6 and cannot support IPv4.

- **IPv6/IPv4 node:** Uses both IPv4 and IPv6.

To assist in the migration from IPv4 to IPv6 and their coexistence, the following address types were defined:

- Compatibility addresses

- Intra-Site Automatic Tunnel Addressing Protocol (ISATAP) addresses

- 6to4 addresses

- Teredo addresses

The following sections introduce these address types.

### Compatibility Addresses

The following two types of compatibility addresses are defined for nodes that communicate on IPv4 and IPv6 networks:

- **IPv4-compatible addresses:** Nodes communicating between IPv4 and IPv6 networks can use an address represented by 0:0:0:0:0:0:*w.x.y.z*, where *w.x.y.z* is the IPv4 address in dotted decimal.

- **IPv4-mapped address:** An IPv4-only node is represented as ::ffff:.w.x.y.z to an IPv6 node. This address type is used only for internal representation and is never specified as a source or destination address of an IPv6 packet.

### ISATAP Addresses

As defined in RFC 4214, ISATAP is a tunneling technology that enables unicast IPv6 connectivity between IPv6/IPv4 hosts over an IPv4 intranet. You do not need to perform any manual configuration actions on an ISATAP host; ISATAP addresses are created using standard autoconfiguration mechanisms.

An ISATAP address utilizes the locally administrative interface identifier ::0:5efe:*w.x.y.z*, where *w.x.y.z* is any private unicast IPv4 address, or ::200:5efe:*w.x.y.z*, where *w.x.y.z* is a public IPv4 unicast address. You can combine either of these ISATAP identifiers with any 64-bit unicast IPv6 prefixes, including link-local, unique local, and global prefixes already described in Table 1-10.

For example, suppose you have two ISATAP hosts, Computer1 and Computer2, that are separated by an IPv4-only network infrastructure, as shown in Figure 1-8. These machines have been configured with the IPv4 addresses 172.16.21.3 and 192.168.12.51, as shown. When the IPv6 protocol is added to the network, these computers are automatically configured with the ISATAP addresses of fe80::5efe:172.16.21.3 and fe80::5efe:192.168.12.51, respectively. When Computer1 sends an IPv6 message to Computer2 using Computer2's link local ISATAP address, the source and destination addresses for the IPv4 and IPv6 packet headers are as shown in Figure 1-8.

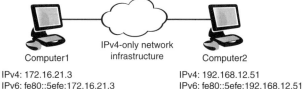

**Figure 1-8**  Sample ISATAP configuration.

### 6to4 Addresses

Two nodes running both IPv4 and IPv6 across an IPv4 routing infrastructure use this address type when communicating with each other. You can form the 6-to-4 address by combining the prefix 2002::/16 with the 32-bit public IPv4 address to form a 48-bit prefix of the form 2002:*wwxx:yyzz*::/48 in the case of a public IPv4 address *w.x.y.z*. The 6to4 address is completed with a 16-bit subnet ID and a 64-bit interface ID. This tunneling technique is described in RFC 3056.

By using 6to4, you can assign global IPv6 addresses to your corporate computers, which can reach IPv6 locations on the Internet without the need to obtain a connection to the IPv6 Internet or use an IPv6 global address prefix supplied by an ISP.

Within the 6to4 addressing framework, you can have the following components:

- **6to4 host:** Includes any host configured with at least one 6to4 address with the 2002::/16 address prefix. These hosts do not require any manual configuration; the 6to4 address is created automatically using autoconfiguration.

- **6to4 router:** Includes any IPv6/IPv4 router that uses a 6to4 tunneling interface to forward 6to4 addressed traffic between 6to4 hosts and routers, host/routers, or relays on the IPv4 Internet. These routers might need additional manual configuration.

- **6to4 host/router:** Includes IPv6/IPv4 hosts that use 6to4 tunneling to exchange 6to4-addressed traffic with other 6to4 routers, host/routers, or relays on the IPv4 Internet. Unlike 6to4 routers, these host/routers do not forward traffic for other 6to4 hosts. An example could be a Windows Server 2008 R2 computer that is directly connected to the Internet and assigned a public IPv4 address. When a public IPv4 interface is assigned to the host's external interface, IPv6 automatically configures a 6to4 address with a 2002::/16 route that forwards all 6to4 traffic to IPv6 destinations encapsulated with an IPv4 header. A DNS query is also performed to obtain the IPv4 address of a 6to4 relay on the IPv4 Internet.

- **6to4 relay:** Includes IPv6/IPv4 routers that forward 6to4 addressed traffic between 6to4 routers and 6to4 host/routers on the IPv4 Internet and hosts on the IPv6 Internet. Such computers utilize the Internet Configuration Sharing (ICS) feature to enable IPv6 forwarding on both the 6to4 tunneling and private interfaces. A 64-bit IPv6 subnet prefix of the form 2002:*wwxx:yyzz:Interf aceIndex*://64 is also determined, where *InterfaceIndex* is the interface index of the private interface.

**NOTE**   For information on `netsh` commands used for manual configuration of 6to4 routers and ISATAP routers, refer to "Manual Configuration for IPv6" at http://technet.microsoft.com/en-ca/library/bb878102.aspx.

### Teredo Addresses

Teredo is a tunneling communication protocol that enables IPv6 connectivity between IPv6/IPv4 nodes across network address translation (NAT) interfaces, thereby improving connectivity for newer IPv6-enabled applications on IPv4 networks. Teredo is described in RFC 4380. Teredo makes use of a special IPv6 address that includes the following components in the sequence given:

- A 32-bit Teredo prefix, which is 2001::/32 in Windows Vista/7 and Windows Server 2008/R2

- The 32-bit IPv4 address of the Teredo server involved in creating this address

- A 16-bit Teredo flag field and an obscured 16-bit UDP port interface definition

- An obscured external IPv4 address corresponding to all Teredo traffic across the Teredo client interface

A computer running Windows 7 or Windows Server 2008 R2 includes a Teredo client that is enabled but inactive by default. To activate Teredo, you must install an application that recognizes Teredo on the computer or configure Windows Firewall to allow Teredo on a per-application basis. After activation, the Teredo client obtains information such as the type of NAT device in use, thereby setting up and maintaining a communication tunnel for the Teredo client through its NAT device.

**NOTE**   More information on compatibility addresses and technologies used for transition to IPv6 is available in "Internet Protocol Version 6, Teredo, and Related Technologies in Windows 7 and Windows Server 2008 R2" at http://technet. microsoft.com/en-us/library/ee126159(WS.10).aspx. A comprehensive description of the technologies discussed in this section is found in "IPv6 Transition Technologies" at http://technet.microsoft.com/en-us/library/bb726951.aspx.

### Using Group Policy to Configure IPv6 Transition Technologies

On a Windows 7 or Windows Server 2008 R2 computer, you can use Group Policy to configure settings for ISATAP, 6to4, and Teredo settings. In an Active Directory Domain Services (AD DS) environment, this enables you to configure settings applicable to all computers in the domain, site, or organizational unit (OU). Note that these settings are not available in the original version of Windows Server 2008.

To do this, access the Group Policy Management Editor focused on the appropriate Group Policy object (or the Local Group Policy Editor in a non-domain environment) and navigate to the **Computer Configuration\Policies\Administrative Templates\Network\TCP/IP Settings\IPv6 Transition Technologies** node. You receive the settings shown in Figure 1-9. To enable any policy, right-click the desired policy and choose **Edit**, as shown for the 6to4 Relay Name policy in Figure 1-10. Select **Enabled** and specify any options pertaining to the policy being configured. You can also enable IP-HTTPS, which is a tunneling technology that uses IP-Hypertext Transfer Protocol Secure (HTTPS) to enable IP connectivity to a remote network. For more information on all the IPv6 transition technology policies, consult the help information provided with each policy's dialog box as shown for the 6to4 Relay Name policy in Figure 1-10.

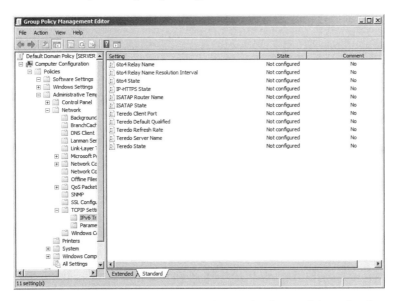

**Figure 1-9**   You can configure IP transition technology policies using Group Policy in Windows Server 2008 R2.

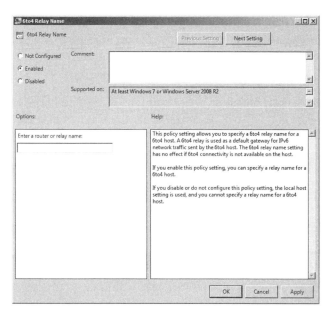

**Figure 1-10**   Configuring the 6to4 Relay Name policy in Windows Server 2008 R2.

**NOTE**   For more information on IP-HTTPS and Teredo and the IP Transition Technology Group Policy settings, refer to "Support for IPv6 in Windows Server 2008 R2 and Windows 7" at http://technet.microsoft.com/en-us/magazine/2009.07.cableguy.aspx. Also, note that computers running the original version of Windows Server 2008 do not have any IPv6 transition technology settings in Group Policy. For these computers, you must configure these settings individually using `netsh interface` commands. The reference quoted here provides information on these commands. For details, refer to "`Netsh` commands for Interface 6to4" at http://technet.microsoft.com/en-us/library/cc730854(WS.10).aspx, "`Netsh` commands for Interface ISATAP" at http://technet.microsoft.com/en-us/library/cc732516(WS.10).aspx, and "`Netsh` commands for Interface Teredo" at http://technet.microsoft.com/en-us/library/cc732065(WS.10).aspx.

## Resolving IPv4 and IPv6 Network Connectivity Issues

With any type of computer network, connectivity problems can and do occur whether you have configured your network to use IPv4, IPv6, or both. You need to be aware of the types of problems that you might encounter, and the steps to use to determine the source of the problem and the means to correct it.

### Windows Server 2008 Network Diagnostics Tools

Windows Server 2008 provides several tools that are often useful in troubleshooting network and Internet connectivity failures. These tools provide wizards that ask questions as to what problems might exist and suggest solutions or open additional troubleshooters.

The Network and Sharing Center provides a comprehensive networking problem troubleshooter. Click **Troubleshoot problems** from the **Change your networking settings** list to obtain the Troubleshoot problems–Network and Internet dialog box shown in Figure 1-11. Clicking any of the options on this dialog box takes you to a wizard that attempts to detect a problem associated with the selected option. If the wizard is unable to identify a problem, it suggests additional options that you might explore.

**Figure 1-11**    You can click any option to open a wizard that attempts to troubleshoot problems with any of these network and printing categories.

You can also check the status of a LAN connection from the Network Connections page previously shown in Figure 1-2. Right-click your connection icon and choose **Status** to display the Local Area Connection Status dialog box, which is shown in Figure 1-12. This dialog box provides information on your LAN connectivity. To obtain details on your LAN connection, click **Details**. The Network Connection Details dialog box shown in Figure 1-13 provides a subset of the information also provided by the ipconfig command discussed in the next section. To view or configure the properties of the connection, click the **Properties** button shown in Figure 1-12. This takes you to the same Local Area Connection Properties dialog box, which was discussed earlier and was shown in Figure 1-3.

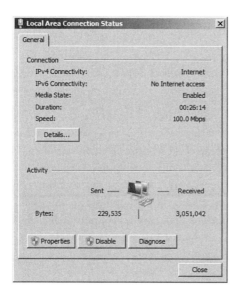

**Figure 1-12**   The Local Area Connection Status dialog box provides information on the connectivity of your LAN connection.

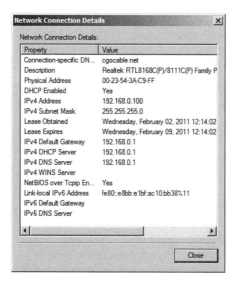

**Figure 1-13**   The Network Connection Details dialog box provides IPv4 and IPv6 configuration information.

If you suspect a problem, click the **Diagnose** button shown in Figure 1-12 to open a troubleshooter. You are informed of any problem that exists, such as a disconnected network cable or malfunctioning network adapter card.

## Using TCP/IP Utilities to Troubleshoot TCP/IP

The TCP/IP protocol suite includes a number of tools that can help you isolate the source of connectivity problems. Both versions of Windows Server 2008 incorporates these tools as command-line executables. Each tool is different in what information it provides and when you might want to use it.

When you are troubleshooting a connectivity problem, remember that sometimes the problem is the hardware—a failed network adapter, a failed port on the hub, a failed switch, and so on. If the communication is between two different physical segments, it could be a problem with the router between them. And if you were able to communicate in the past, and now cannot, the most likely suspect is a configuration change on one of the computers and the second most likely is that a piece of equipment has failed. To check whether there is an adapter failure, look at the Device Manager.

### ARP

After data reaches the segment on which the IP address resides, it needs to discover the MAC address of the machine. As introduced earlier, ARP is the protocol in the TCP/IP suite that resolves IP addresses to MAC addresses by creating an address resolution table in each host that transmits data on the network segment.

The `arp` command is useful for viewing the ARP cache. If two hosts on the same subnet cannot even ping each other successfully, try running the `arp -a` command on each computer to see if they have the correct MAC addresses listed for each other. You can determine a host's MAC address by using `ipconfig /all`. If another host with a duplicate IP address exists on the network, the ARP cache may have had the MAC address for the other computer placed in it. In addition, if you cannot contact a host or connect to an unexpected host, the results of this command will help in determining the source of the connectivity problems. `arp -d` can be used to delete an entry that may be incorrect. Entries can be added using `arp -s`.

### FTP

File Transfer Protocol (FTP) is not normally considered to be a troubleshooting tool. Sometimes, you need to make sure that a protocol can move data from one network segment to another, and this utility can help because it verifies TCP specifically, as well as all the protocols down to the Physical layer of the stack.

If you want to verify whether TCP is functioning across a router, you can use FTP to download a file from an FTP server on another subnet.

`ipconfig`

Windows Server 2008 uses the `ipconfig` utility without any additional parameters to display summary information about the IP address configuration of its network adapters. When you experience a problem with connectivity, this is the first thing you need to check (besides the link lights on the network adapter). If you are using DHCP, you can see whether the adapter was able to obtain an IP address lease. If you are using a static IP address, you can verify and validate whether it has been configured correctly. You can use `ipconfig` with the following switches:

- **`ipconfig /all`**: Displays a comprehensive set of IPv4 and IPv6 address data for all network adapters including IPv6 Teredo interfaces, as shown in Figure 1-14. Any configured serial ports (RAS) are also displayed. Use this command to see whether an adapter has been misconfigured or the adapter did not receive a DHCP lease. You can also determine whether the IP address the computer is using has been provided by APIPA; check the `Autoconfiguration Enabled` line of this output. If this line states Yes and the IP address is 169.254.0.1 through 169.254.255.254, you are using an APIPA address. This is also true if you observe an IPv6 address on the fe80::/64 network. Output may be redirected to a file and pasted into other documents by using standard Windows commands (for example, `ipconfig /all > ipstatus.txt`).

Key Topic

Figure 1-14   The `ipconfig /all` command provides a comprehensive set of TCP/IP configuration information.

- **ipconfig /release:** Releases the current DHCP lease. Use this command to remove an IP address that is misconfigured or when you have moved from one network to another and the wrong IP address is still leased to the adapter.

- **ipconfig /release6:** Same as the /release switch for IPv6.

- **ipconfig /renew:** Renews (or tries to renew) the current DHCP lease. Use this command to see whether the computer can contact the DHCP server.

- **ipconfig /renew6:** Same as the /renew switch for IPv6.

- **ipconfig /displaydns:** Displays the contents of the DNS cache. Use this command when the computer connects to the wrong network.

- **ipconfig /flushdns:** Flushes the contents of the DNS cache. Use this command when the computer connects to the wrong network, and you see incorrect entries after using the ipconfig /displaydns command.

- **ipconfig /registerdns:** Refreshes all adapters' DHCP leases and reregisters the DNS configuration. Use this command when the computer has temporarily disconnected from the network and you have not rebooted it.

- **ipconfig /showclassid *adapter*:** Shows the DHCP class ID. If you use the asterisk (*) in place of *adapter*, you see the DHCP class ID for all adapters.

- **ipconfig /setclassid *adapter*:** Changes the DHCP class ID for an adapter. If you use the asterisk (*) in the place of *adapter*, you set the DHCP class ID of all adapters.

### Nbtstat

The Nbtstat utility is used on networks that run NetBIOS over TCP/IP. This utility checks to see the status of NetBIOS name resolution to IP addresses. You can check current NetBIOS sessions, add entries to the NetBIOS name cache, and check the NetBIOS name and scope assigned to the computer.

### Netstat

The Netstat command-line tool enables you to check the current status of the computer's IP connections. If you do not use switches, the results are port and protocol statistics and current TCP/IP connections. Netstat -a displays all connections and listening ports, even those not presently involved in a connection. This allows you to check whether a connection to a remote host that does not appear to be responding is hung. Netstat -r displays the route table, plus active connections. The -n switch tells netstat not to convert addresses and port numbers to names. The `-e` switch displays Ethernet statistics, and may be combined with the `-s` switch, which shows protocol statistics.

You should use `Netstat` to look for the services that are listening for incoming connections, if you have already checked the IP configuration and, although it is correct, the computer still displays a connectivity problem.

### Nslookup

Name Server Lookup, or `Nslookup`, is a command-line utility that communicates with a DNS server. There are two modes to `Nslookup`: interactive and non-interactive. The interactive mode opens a session with a DNS server and views various records. The non-interactive mode asks for one piece of information and receives it. If more information is needed, a new query must be made. More information on this utility is provided in Chapter 8, "Configuring Client Computer Name Resolution."

### ping

`ping` is a valuable tool for determining whether there is a problem with connectivity. The `ping` command uses an ICMP echo packet at the network layer—the default is to send a series of four echoes in a row—transmitting the packets to the IP address specified. The echo returns an acknowledgment if the IP address is found. The results are displayed in the command window. If an IP address is not found, you see only the response `Request timed out`. You see similar results to those shown in Figure 1-15, where the first address that was pinged was found and the second address was not found. The `ping` command indicates how long each packet took for the response. You can use the `ping` command to determine whether a host is reachable, and to determine whether you are losing packets when sending/receiving data to a particular host.

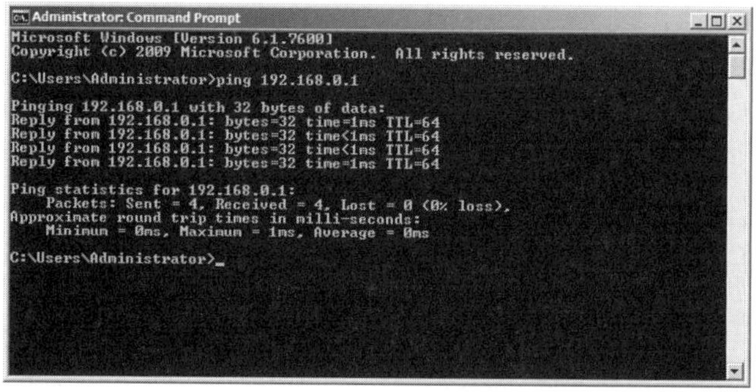

**Figure 1-15**    The `ping` command displays its results in a command window.

`ping` also has several command-line options. Type **`ping -?`** to see the available options. For example, `ping` allows you to specify the size of packets to use, how many to send, whether to record the route used, what TTL value to use, and whether to set the "don't fragment" flag.

You can use the `ping` command to determine whether the internal TCP/IP protocol stack is functioning properly by pinging the loopback testing address. The command for IPv4 is

```
ping 127.0.0.1
```

For IPv6, the command is

```
ping ::1
```

**NOTE**    Firewall settings can prevent you from receiving responses from pinged hosts. In Windows Server 2008 R2, by default you cannot ping other computers on your network. We take a look at configuring firewall settings and policies in Chapter 4, "Configuring Windows Firewall with Advanced Security."

`tracert`

When you have a problem communicating with a particular host, yet you have determined that your computer is functioning well, you can use `tracert` (trace route) to tell you how the data is moving across the network between your computer and the one that you are having difficulty reaching. `tracert` uses the IP Time-to-Live (TTL) field and ICMP error messages to determine the route from one host to another through the network. The `tracert` command offers a somewhat higher level of information than `Ping`. Rather than simply tell you that the data was transmitted and returned effectively, as `ping` does, `tracert` logs each hop through which the data was transmitted. Figure 1-16 shows the results of a `tracert` command. Keep in mind that some network routers strip out or refuse to reply to `tracert` requests. When this happens, you see `Request timed out` messages.

```
Administrator: Command Prompt                                           _ □ x
Microsoft Windows [Version 6.1.7600]
Copyright (c) 2009 Microsoft Corporation. All rights reserved.

C:\Users\Administrator>tracert que.com

Tracing route to que.com [213.171.197.55]
over a maximum of 30 hops:

  1     1 ms    <1 ms    <1 ms  192.168.0.1
  2     *        *        *     Request timed out.
  3    10 ms    10 ms     8 ms  d226-9-169.home.cgocable.net [24.226.9.169]
  4     9 ms    13 ms     9 ms  64.34.137.61
  5    33 ms    27 ms    27 ms  10ge.xe-0-3-0.nyc-telx-dis-1.peer1.net [216.187.
114.194]
  6    33 ms    33 ms    25 ms  10ge.xe-0-0-0.nyc-telx-dis-2.peer1.net [216.187.
115.182]
  7   119 ms   131 ms   119 ms  oc48-so2-2-0.ldn-teleh-dis-1.peer1.net [216.187.
115.34]
  8   107 ms   105 ms   105 ms  195.66.224.98
  9   110 ms   111 ms   123 ms  88.208.255.61
 10   121 ms   113 ms   117 ms  88.208.255.102
 11   113 ms   113 ms   114 ms  server213-171-197-55.live-servers.net [213.171.1
97.55]

Trace complete.

C:\Users\Administrator>_
```

**Figure 1-16**  The `tracert` command provides detailed information about the path that data travels between two IP hosts.

### pathping

The `pathping` command combines the actions of the `ping` and `tracert` utilities into a single command that tests connectivity to a remote host and maps the route taken by packets transmitted from your computer to the remote host. It also provides data on packet loss across multiple hops, thereby providing an estimate of the reliability of the communication links being used.

## Troubleshooting IPv4 and IPv6 Problems

Many problems can result in your inability to reach other hosts on your local subnet, other subnets on your local network, or the Internet. The 70-642 exam will present you with scenarios in which you must figure out the cause of and solution to problems with IPv4 and IPv6 connectivity failures. This section covers the use of the TCP/IP troubleshooting tools already presented to test connectivity, and follows this up with additional suggestions you can use for troubleshooting connectivity problems, both on the 70-642 exam and in the real world.

### Suggested Response to a Connectivity Problem

Microsoft recommends a troubleshooting procedure for TCP/IP connectivity problems similar to the following:

1. Verify the hardware is functioning.

2. Run `Ipconfig /all` to validate the IP address, subnet mask, default gateway, and DNS server, and whether you are receiving a DHCP leased address.

3. Ping 127.0.0.1 or ::1, the loopback address, to validate that TCP/IP is functioning.

4. Ping the computer's own IP address to eliminate a duplicate IP address as the problem.

5. Ping the default gateway address, which tells you whether data can travel on the current network segment.

6. Ping a host that is not on your network segment, which shows whether the router will be able to route your data. By pinging the host name, you can verify that DNS is resolving the name, and by pinging the IP address, you can verify network connectivity.

Additional possible troubleshooting steps you can use include the following:

- FTP a file from an FTP server not on your network, which tells you whether higher-level protocols are functioning. TFTP a file from a TFTP server on a different network to determine whether UDP packets are able to cross the router.

- Check the configuration of routers on a network with multiple subnets. You can use the `tracert` and `pathping` commands to verify connectivity across routers to remote subnets. Also, use the `route print` command to check the configuration of routing tables in use. This command is covered in Chapter 3.

- Clear the ARP cache by opening a command prompt and typing `netsh interface ip delete arpcache`.

- Check the computer's DNS configuration. You can also clear the DNS client resolver cache by using the `ipconfig /flushdns` command.

Many LAN connection problems can be traced to improper TCP/IP configuration. Before looking at the use of TCP/IP utilities for troubleshooting these problems, this section reviews briefly some of the problems you might encounter.

### Network Discovery

Network Discovery is a tool that is enabled by default on Windows 7 and Windows Server 2008 R2 computers. For computers to connect to one another, ensure that Network Discovery has not been turned off at either the source or destination computer. To check this setting, access the Network and Sharing Center and click **Change advanced sharing settings**, which is found in the list on the left side. As shown in Figure 1-17, you can configure a series of sharing options for different network profiles. Ensure that the **Turn on network discovery** option is selected and then click **Save changes**.

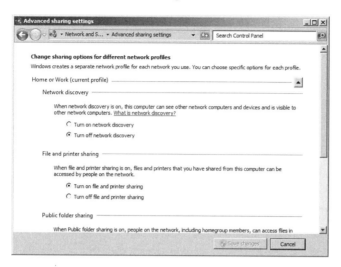

**Figure 1-17**   Checking the Network Discovery setting.

### Incorrect IPv4 Address or Subnet Mask

Recall from earlier in this chapter that the subnet mask determines the number of bits assigned to the network portion of the IP address and the number of bits assigned to the host portion. Be aware of the fact that the network portion of the IP address must match properly on all computers within a network segment and that the subnet mask must be configured appropriately to ensure that the computer is able to determine whether the computer to which it is attempting to connect is on the same or different subnet. An incorrect subnet mask may result in intermittent connections. Sometimes, the connection works; sometimes, it doesn't. Problems occur when the IP address of the destination host results in the packet being routed when it shouldn't be, or when it is not routed when it should be.

For example, suppose you are at a computer configured with an IP address of 192.168.1.2 and a subnet mask of 255.255.255.0. If you want to reach a computer with the IP address of 192.168.2.1, the subnet mask indicates that this computer is located on a different subnet. Connection will take place across a router. If the computer you are at is configured with the same IP address but a subnet mask of 255.255.248.0 indicates that the destination computer with the IP address of 192.168.2.1 is on the same subnet. If, in fact, this computer is located across a router on another subnet, you will fail to connect to it. Router problems could also cause a failure to access a computer on another subnet. This topic is discussed in Chapter 3.

### Incorrect Default Gateway

The default gateway is the IP address of the near side of the router used to communicate with external networks. It is used only for outgoing communication. If specified incorrectly, the host can communicate with other hosts on the local network, but is unable to communicate with external hosts. External hosts can send messages to the incorrectly configured host, but any return message will not reach the external host. In addition, when using DHCP, if the default gateway of the DHCP server is incorrectly specified, clients will be unable to contact the DHCP server to obtain IP address leases. This results in the clients being unable to contact anyone, as they will be configured with an inappropriate IPv4 address using APIPA or a link-local IPv6 address.

### Unable to Connect to a DHCP Server

If you configure your computer to automatically receive an IPv4 address and the DHCP server is down, the computer will assign itself an APIPA address as already described. If you notice this when using `ipconfig /all`, check the connectivity to the DHCP server or contact an administrator responsible for this server.

### Duplicate IP Address

If your computer is using an IP address that duplicates another computer on the network, you will be unable to connect to any computer on the network. When this happens, the first computer on the network performs properly but receives a message when the second computer joins the network. Ping your computer's IP address to check for this problem. This problem cannot occur if you are using DHCP to obtain an IP address automatically or if your computer is configured for an IP address using APIPA.

### Unable to Configure an Alternate TCP/IPv4 Configuration

The Alternate Configuration tab of the TCP/IPv4 Properties dialog box (refer to Figure 1-4) enables you to configure an alternate IPv4 address, which is useful in situations where you need to connect to a second network (for example, when you are using a portable computer and traveling to a branch office of your company). However, to use the alternate configuration, your primary connection must be set to obtain an IP address automatically. If this is not the case, this tab does not appear.

## Using Event Viewer to Check Network Problems

One of Windows Server 2008's standard troubleshooting tools is Event Viewer, which is incorporated into the Server Manager console. You can rely on this utility to be able to see errors and system messages. The ones that would be of most concern for a network problem are in the System Event log. You learn about Event Viewer in more detail in Chapter 20, "Configuring Event Logs."

## Additional Troubleshooting Hints When Using IPv6

When verifying IPv6 network connectivity, you may need to specify a zone ID for the sending interface with the `ping` command. The zone ID is a locally defined parameter that you can obtain from the `ipconfig /all` command or the `netsh interface ipv6 show interface` command. Using this zone ID, to verify connectivity with a machine whose IPv6 address is fe80::b3:00ff:4765:6db7, you would type **`ping fe80::b3:00ff:4765:6db7%12`** at a command prompt if the zone ID is 12.

Before using `ping` to check IPv6 network connectivity, clear the neighbor cache on your computer. This cache contains recently resolved link-layer IPv6 addresses. To view this cache, open an administrative command prompt and type **`netsh interface ipv6 show neighbors`**; to clear it, type **`netsh interface ipv6 delete neighbors`**.

**NOTE**   For further suggestions with regard to troubleshooting IPv6 network connectivity, refer to "The Cable Guy—March 2005" at http://technet.microsoft.com/en-us/library/bb878005.aspx.

## Exam Preparation Tasks

## Review All the Key Topics

Review the most important topics in this chapter, noted with the key topics icon in the outer margin of the page. Table 1-11 lists a reference of these key topics and the page numbers on which each is found.

**Table 1-11**  Key Topics for Chapter 1

| Key Topic Element | Description | Page Number |
|---|---|---|
| Paragraphs | Introduce the various TCP/IP component protocols. | 38 |
| Table 1-3 | Describes important addressing components of TCP/IP version 4. | 41 |
| Table 1-4 | Describes the various IPv4 address classes. | 43 |
| Table 1-5 | Default subnet masks in different notations. | 44 |
| Paragraph | Explains how to use subnet masks to separate the network and machine portions of an IPv4 address. | 44 |
| Table 1-6 | Describes subnetting. | 46 |
| Table 1-7 | Describes supernetting. | 47 |
| Table 1-8 | Describes private IPv4 networks. | 48 |
| List | Explains how to configure a network adapter with a static IPv4 address. | 48 |
| Figure 1-5 | Shows the advanced TCP/IP settings that you can configure. | 51 |
| Paragraph | Introduces the netsh command-line tool and its purposes. | 52 |
| List | Describes the major benefits achieved by using IPv6. | 55 |
| Table 1-10 | Explains IPv6 address classes and subclasses. | 57 |
| List | Explains how to configure your computer to connect to an IPv6 network. | 59 |
| Paragraph | Describes ISATAP addressing. | 63 |
| Paragraph | Describes 6to4 addressing. | 64 |
| Paragraph | Describes Teredo addressing. | 65 |
| Figure 1-12 | Using the Local Area Connection Status dialog box to check LAN connection status. | 69 |
| Figure 1-14 | Use of the ipconfig /all command. | 71 |
| List | Describes a procedure that tests your computer's IP connectivity. | 75 |

## Complete the Tables and Lists from Memory

Print a copy of Appendix B, "Memory Tables," (found on the CD), or at least the section for this chapter, and complete the tables and lists from memory. Appendix C, "Memory Tables Answer Key," also on the CD, includes the completed tables and lists to check your work.

## Definition of Key Terms

Define the following key terms from this chapter, and check your answers in the Glossary.

6to4, Address Resolution Protocol (ARP), Anycast IPv6 address, Automatic Private IP Addressing (APIPA), classless inter-domain routing (CIDR), default gateway, dynamic IP address, global unicast IPv6 address, host, Internet layer, Internet Protocol (IP), Internet Control Message Protocol (ICMP), Internet Group Management Protocol (IGMP), Intra-Site Automatic Tunnel Addressing Protocol (ISATAP), IP version 4 (IPv4), IP version 6 (IPv6), IP address, IPv4-compatible address, IPv4-mapped address, Ipconfig, link local IPv6 address, multicast IPv6 address, netsh, network interface layer, Open Systems Interconnection (OSI) reference model, private IPv4 network, static IP address, subnet mask, subnetting, Teredo, Transmission Control Protocol (TCP), User Datagram Protocol (UDP)

This chapter covers the following subjects:

- **How DHCP Works:** This section introduces the concept of DHCP and describes how the four-stage DHCP process works with IPv4. It follows this up by describing important new features of DHCPv6.

- **Installing and Configuring a DHCP Server:** DHCP in Windows Server 2008 is installed as a server role. This section takes you through the process of installing a DHCP server, both from the Server Manager tool and from the command line.

- **DHCP Scopes and Options:** All DHCP servers have one or more scopes, which define the range of IP addresses available to clients. In this section, you learn how to create scopes and configure the various options available at various levels.

- **Managing and Troubleshooting a DHCP Server:** This section discusses several additional tasks that you should be familiar with, and introduces you to several techniques that you can use in monitoring and troubleshooting your DHCP server.

# CHAPTER 2

# Configuring Dynamic Host Configuration Protocol (DHCP)

Chapter 1, "Configuring IPv4 and IPv6 Addressing," introduced you to the various types of IP addresses used in modern computer networks. You learned that every computer on the network must have its own unique IP address, together with additional configuration options, such as the subnet mask or IPv6 subnet prefix length, the default gateway, and other parameters. On a small network, you could manually specify these options for each computer on the network, but what happens if you're responsible for networking hundreds, or even thousands, of computers together? Attempting to maintain manual TCP/IP configuration for more than a handful of computers becomes an extreme headache. This is where DHCP comes to the rescue.

DHCP automatically assigns these networking parameters and more to every computer on your network. It maintains a database of all configured options and prevents problems from occurring, such as duplicate IP addresses and more. DHCP eliminates most of the problems associated with manual configuration, because it can furnish all essential TCP/IP information to all DHCP-enabled clients on a TCP/IP network. When problems do arise, they are generally easier to trace on a DHCP-controlled network than on a manually configured one.

## "Do I Know This Already?" Quiz

The "Do I Know This Already?" quiz allows you to assess whether you should read this entire chapter or simply jump to the "Exam Preparation Tasks" section for review. If you are in doubt, read the entire chapter. Table 2-1 outlines the major headings in this chapter and the corresponding "Do I Know This Already?" quiz questions. You can find the answers in Appendix A, "Answers to the 'Do I Know This Already?' Quizzes."

**Table 2-1**   "Do I Know This Already?" Foundation Topics Section-to-Question Mapping

| Foundations Topics Section | Questions Covered in This Section |
| --- | --- |
| How DHCP Works | 1–4 |
| Installing and Configuring a DHCP Server | 5–7 |
| DHCP Scopes and Options | 8–10 |
| Managing and Troubleshooting a DHCP Server | 11–13 |

1. Your client computer running Windows 7 Ultimate is requesting an IPv4 address from the local network's DHCP server. Which of the following messages are exchanged between the two computers? (Choose all that apply; arrange your answers in the proper sequence in which the messages are exchanged.)

   a. DHCPREQUEST

   b. DHCPOFFER

   c. DHCPINFORM

   d. DHCPACK

   e. DHCPADVERTISE

   f. DHCPDISCOVER

2. By default, at what percentage of the lease time will a DHCP client first attempt to renew its lease?

   a. 50

   b. 80

   c. 87.5

   d. 95

3. An IPv6 client computer can automatically configure itself with a unique address by using router discovery without the use of a DHCPv6 server. What is this process called?

   a. Stateful address configuration

   b. Stateless address configuration

   c. Managed address configuration

   d. Automatic Private IP Addressing

4. Which of the following messages are exchanged between an IPv6 client computer and DHCPv6 server when requesting configuration information? (Choose all that apply; arrange your answers in the proper sequence in which the messages are exchanged.)

   **a.** Discover

   **b.** Offer

   **c.** Advertise

   **d.** Request

   **e.** Solicit

   **f.** Confirm

   **g.** Reply

5. Which of the following situations might result in a failure of DHCP to install properly on a Windows Server 2008 R2 computer? (Choose two.)

   **a.** The computer is configured with IPv6 only.

   **b.** The computer is configured to obtain an IP address automatically.

   **c.** The computer is not configured as a domain controller.

   **d.** You are logged onto the computer as a nonadministrative user.

6. Under which of the following conditions is it most likely that you would want to specify the IP address of a WINS server when installing DHCP?

   **a.** The network contains two or more segments separated by routers, and you want all network segments serviced from the same DHCP server.

   **b.** Users will be frequently logging onto the network from remote locations and require the capability of locating resources on the local network.

   **c.** The network still contains Windows XP and Windows Server 2003 computers, despite these operating systems being almost a decade old.

   **d.** The network still contains Windows NT 4.0 or Windows 98 computers, despite these operating systems being more than a decade old.

7. You are installing DHCP on a server that runs the Server Core version of Windows Server 2008 R2. Which of the following commands should you run to install DHCP on this server?

   a. `Start /w ocsetup DHCPServerCore`

   b. `Dism /online /enable-feature /featurename:DHCPServerCore`

   c. `servermanagercmd -install DHCPServerCore`

   d. Use Server Manager from a remote computer by connecting to the Server Core computer and remotely install DHCP.

   e. None of these. Server Core does not support DHCP installations.

8. You are configuring options on your DHCP server that need to be applied to various subsets of the computers on your network. You realize that there are four levels at which these options can be applied. Which of the following represents the sequence in which these options are applied?

   a. Server, client, class, scope

   b. Server, scope, class, client

   c. Scope, class, client, server

   d. Client, server, scope, class

9. You want all desktop computers to retain their IP leases for 14 days to reduce the network overhead on the DHCP server. At the same time, you want the laptop computers connecting from external locations to give up their leases within 12 hours. What should you do?

   a. Specify a user class option that sets the lease interval to 12 hours for all laptop computers.

   b. Specify a vendor class option that sets the lease interval to 12 hours for all laptop computers.

   c. For each laptop computer, specify a client option that sets the lease interval to 12 hours.

   d. Create a separate scope for all laptop computers and specify a scope option that sets the lease interval to 12 hours.

**10.** You installed DHCP on a Windows Server 2008 R2 computer and are now creating a scope that will deploy IP addresses to computers on the 192.168.3.0/24 network. The network contains three file servers that must always have the IP addresses 192.168.3.101, 192.168.3.102, and 192.168.3.103. These servers should receive other IP configuration information from the DHCP server. What should you do? (Each answer represents part of the solution. Choose two.)

   **a.** Create an exclusion range on the scope that prevents these addresses from being assigned to client computers.

   **b.** Create two scopes: one that assigns the IP addresses 192.168.3.1 to 192.168.3.99 and the other that assigns the IP addresses 192.168.3.104 to 192.168.3.254.

   **c.** Create three reservations in DHCP, one for each of the three file servers.

   **d.** Create a superscope that includes the IP addresses 192.168.3.101 to 192.168.3.103.

   **e.** Configure each of the three file servers with static IP addresses.

**11.** You installed DHCP on a Windows Server 2008 R2 computer that is a member server on your company's AD DS network and created a scope that is to assign IP addresses on the 192.168.4.0 network. The next day, you notice that the DHCP server has not started and client computers on your network are autoconfiguring themselves with IP addresses on the 169.254.0.0 network. What do you need to do?

   **a.** Deactivate and reactivate the scope.

   **b.** Create a scope option that disables the use of APIPA.

   **c.** Promote the DHCP server to domain controller.

   **d.** Authorize the DHCP server in Active Directory.

12. You are responsible for managing a DHCP server on your company's network, which consists of two subnets separated by a legacy router. You created two scopes, one for each subnet. The DHCP server is located on subnet A. Client computers on this subnet are receiving proper IP addressing information, but those on subnet B are autoconfiguring themselves with IP addresses on the 169.254.0.0 network. They cannot communicate with computers on the first subnet. What should you do?

   a. Install a DHCP relay agent on a server located on subnet A.

   b. Install a DHCP relay agent on a server located on subnet B.

   c. Specify a scope option for client computers on subnet B that specifies the IP address of the DHCP server.

   d. Specify the IP address of the DHCP server manually in the TCP/IP properties of each computer on subnet B.

13. You are responsible for ensuring that file and web servers on your company's network always are configured with the same IP address, so you are creating IP address reservations on your DHCP server. When you attempt to reserve an IP address for a server named WEB1, you receive a message stating `The specified DHCP client is not a reserved client`. What should you do to provide the proper IP address while ensuring that this server receives all other required options?

   a. Modify the DHCP scope to include the IP address to be reserved for WEB1.

   b. Configure a scope option that specifies the IP address to be reserved for WEB1.

   c. Locate the machine that is already using this IP address and type `ipconfig /release` at this machine so that the required IP address becomes available.

   d. Configure a static IP address for WEB1 instead.

## Foundation Topics

# How DHCP Works

Dynamic Host Configuration Protocol (DHCP) works by providing IP addressing information from a pool of addresses called a *scope*, which is defined in the DHCP server's database. If a client accepts the address, it can use the address for a pre-defined period called a *lease*. If a client cannot obtain a lease of an IP address from a DHCP server, it cannot initialize TCP/IP normally.

DHCP used in Windows Server 2008 is based on standards defined by the Internet Engineering Task Force (IETF), which set out specifications in Request for Comment (RFC) 2131: Dynamic Host Configuration Protocol and RFC 2132: DHCP Options and BOOTP Vendor Extensions. With the advent of IPv6, IETF provided the specifications for using DHCP on IPv6-based networks in RFC 3315: Dynamic Host Configuration Protocol for IPv6 (DHCPv6). This section introduces you to the processes used by DHCP in configuring IPv4 and IPv6 clients; although they are conceptually similar, some important differences are presented in the way that IPv6 clients are configured.

**NOTE**   For more information on DHCPv6, its specific advantages, and its message details, refer to "The Cable Guy: The DHCPv6 Protocol" at http://technet. microsoft .com/en-us/magazine/2007.03.cableguy.aspx.

### Four-Phase DHCP IPv4 Leasing Process

The DHCP server and the DHCP client both need to go through a four-phase process before DHCP configures the client with a working set of TCP/IP parameters. Note that many of the communications are in the form of broadcasts. The broadcast nature of these communications can present a major problem, if routers on an internetwork are not capable of forwarding these DHCP messages.

Figure 2-1 is a schematic view of the DHCP leasing process.

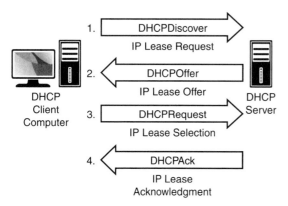

**Figure 2-1**  Four-step DHCP process.

The following sections describe the four DHCP communication phases. Note that the actual process, described at the packet level, uses slightly different terminology and can take a few more twists and turns than those briefly described here.

The client must use the IP lease process when it is in any of the following states:

- A client configured to use DHCP is initializing TCP/IP for the first time.

- A client requests a specific IP address but the server has denied that IP address, as could occur if a DHCP server dropped a lease.

- The client had previously leased an IP address, but has since released that IP address and now requires a new lease. This can occur when the user has typed the `ipconfig /release` and `ipconfig /renew` commands.

### IP Lease Request (DHCPDISCOVER)

When an IPv4 client computer starts up and discovers that it requires an IP address, it initializes a limited version of TCP/IP and then broadcasts a request for the location of a DHCP server. This broadcast indicates to the listening server that the client needs IP addressing information. The broadcast packet sent by the DHCP client at this stage contains the lease request, as well as the source address for the client, 0.0.0.0 and the destination address, which is the broadcast address, 255.255.255.255. The packet also includes the client's hardware (MAC) address and computer name; recall that network communication often boils down to a hardware address of one kind or another. The inclusion of the hardware address reveals the origin of the request to DHCP servers.

The actual packet that the client issues to request an IP address from a DHCP server is called a DHCPDISCOVER packet. The DHCPDISCOVER packet, and all that it contains, represent the client's IP lease request.

### IP Lease Offer (DHCPOFFER)

Any DHCP server with valid IP addressing information responds to a needy DHCP client with an offer of IP addressing information. It responds with one of the unassigned IP addresses from a scope of addresses, which are valid for that specific host. To be able to respond to a DHCPDISCOVER packet, a DHCP server must have valid IP configuration information for the client. Any DHCP server with valid IP information can respond to the client with a DHCPOFFER packet, containing the following information:

- The client's hardware address (allows the unique identification of the DHCP client)

- An offered IP address

- An appropriate subnet mask

- A duration for the lease

- A server ID, which would be the IP address of the DHCP server

The server sends a DHCPOFFER packet to the client's hardware (MAC) address, because the client does not yet have an IP address. Similar to other DHCP messages, this packet is sent as a broadcast message, which is converted to the MAC address on the network. The DHCP server is also smart enough to reserve the IP address it has just offered. This ensures that it will not offer it to another DHCP client, thus avoiding duplicate IP addresses. It's worth remembering that the world does not stand still during this process; a DHCP server may be handling DHCP traffic from multiple clients at any given time. Therefore, it needs to keep track of the IP addresses it is offering and dishing out.

### IP Lease Selection (DHCPREQUEST)

The DHCP client selects the IP addressing information it requires from the first DHCPOFFER packet it receives; that is, the offer from the server quickest off the mark to supply the information. At this time, it broadcasts this information out onto the network. In this broadcast, the client requests the IP address that the server has proposed for it. The explanation for including the IP address request in the broadcast is that the client could have received more than one offer, if there are other DHCP servers on the network. By broadcasting its request, the client announces to any other DHCP servers that this client will not be accepting their offers. To further ensure that there is no confusion over which server's offer the client is accepting, the client includes the following additional information in the request packet:

- The IP address of the server whose offer it accepted

- The client's hardware address

- The IP address that the client is accepting

The name of the actual packet sent is a DHCPREQUEST packet. In addition to requesting a specific IP address from a DHCP server, this packet asks other DHCP servers on the network to withdraw their offers of an IP address, if they have made any.

### IP Lease Acknowledgment (DHCPACK)

The DHCP server responds to the client that made the selection by assigning IP addressing information to the client. After it does so, it also acknowledges that it has assigned IP addressing information to that client through a special acknowledgment packet called a DHCPACK, which it sends to the client. This message contains a valid lease for an IP address and other configuration information, which a network administrator may have specified in a DHCP scope.

Occasionally, a DHCP lease request can be unsuccessful after the client accepts a lease offered by the server. This can happen in situations such as the following:

- The IP address is not valid because the client has been moved to another subnet.

- The client is attempting to lease its previous IP address, and the IP address is no longer available.

In either of these situations, the server would broadcast an unsuccessful (negative) acknowledgment packet or DHCPNACK. A client that receives a DHCPNACK must start the entire DHCP initialization process over from scratch. That is, it must broadcast another DHCPDISCOVER packet looking for a fresh IP address from any available DHCP server.

### Renewing an IPv4 Lease

A DHCP server leases an IP address to the DHCP client for only a specified term. The default term is eight days. To continue using its leased IP address, a DHCP client attempts to renew its lease before it expires. This occurs at default intervals during the life of the lease. It automatically sends the renewal request, if TCP/IP is still initialized on the client. The client receives a response if it is still on the same network or subnet and is able to communicate with the DHCP server.

When 50 percent of the lease time has expired, a client attempts to renew its lease with the DHCP server that provided its lease and configuration information. It makes the renewal attempt by sending a DHCPREQUEST packet directly to that DHCP server. If the DHCP server and the IP address are both available, the server renews the client's IP addressing information by sending a DHCPACK to the client with the renewed lease duration and any updated configuration information. Upon receipt of the DHCPACK, the client updates its configuration.

If the client is unable to renew its lease with the original DHCP server at this time, it continues to use its currently leased IP address and any other configuration data it received from its DHCP server with the original lease. The client can still use the address because only 50 percent of the lease duration has expired.

If a client still does not have a renewed lease after 87.5 percent of the active lease period has gone by, it attempts to communicate with any DHCP server on the network to secure IP addressing and configuration information by broadcasting a DHCPREQUEST packet. The listening DHCP servers can make two possible responses:

- Any DHCP server can respond with a DHCPACK message to renew the lease. However, the renewal is most likely to come from the DHCP server that originally leased the IP address, although the location of an IP address or an IP address scope is not tied to one DHCP server forever. For the record, it is possible for a DHCP client to renew the same IP address lease from a different DHCP server.

- Any DHCP server can respond with a DHCPNACK message. DHCPNACK messages force a client to reinitialize and to obtain a lease for a different IP address.

If the client cannot make contact with a DHCP server and consequently fails to maintain its lease, the client must discontinue use of the IP address and begin the entire process again by issuing a DHCPDISCOVER packet. If this is also not possible, it resorts to Automatic Private IP Addressing (APIPA) to give itself an IP address when the lease expires.

## How DHCPv6 Works

IPv6 clients can use address autoconfiguration to automatically configure themselves without the use of DHCPv6 using a link-local address and router discovery. This enables the host to determine the addresses of routers, servers, and other configuration parameters. The following types of address configuration can be used:

- **Stateless address autoconfiguration:** Uses Router Advertisement messages to configure link-local addresses and additional addresses by exchanging Router Solicitation and Router Advertisement messages with neighboring routers.

- **Stateful address autoconfiguration:** Uses a stateful address configuration protocol, such as DHCPv6, to obtain non-link-local addresses and other IPv6 configuration parameters.

- **Both types of addresses:** Uses Router Advertisement messages that include address prefixes and stateful address configuration protocols.

Two address autoconfiguration flags are used to determine the use of stateful and stateless address autoconfiguration on an IPv6 network:

- **Managed Address Configuration (M) flag:** Determines when DHCPv6 is used to obtain IPv6 stateful addresses. When set to 0, DHCPv6 is not used and stateless addresses are obtained. When set to 1, DHCPv6 is used to assign stateful addresses to IPv6 clients.

- **Other Stateful Configuration (O) flag:** Determines how additional IPv6 configuration parameters are obtained. This includes such settings as the IPv6 addresses of Domain Name System (DNS) servers. When set to 1, DHCPv6 is used to obtain these types of information. If the M flag is set to 0 and the O flag is set to 1, a combination known as DHCPv6 stateless is being used, where DHCPv6 assigns additional stateless configuration settings but not stateful addresses to IPv6 clients.

An IPv6 client attempts DHCPv6 configuration according to the values of the M and O flags in router advertisement messages. If the M flag is set to 1, the client requesting addressing information participates in a four-step process similar to that used with IPv4, as follows:

1. The client sends a Solicit message from its link-local address to the All_DHCP_Relay_Agents_and_Servers address of FF02::1:2. This message corresponds to the DHCPDISCOVER message used with IPv4.

2. A DHCP server receiving this message sends an Advertise message (which corresponds to the DHCPOFFER message) to the client. This message informs the client that the server can provide address and configuration settings.

3. The client sends a Request message to the server to request address and configuration settings (corresponding to the DHCPREQUEST message). If the

client does not receive an Advertise message, it uses a stateless address configuration protocol to obtain IPv6 configuration information.

4. The DHCP server sends a Reply message (which corresponds to the DHCPACK message) to the client to confirm acceptance of the Request message and assignment of the IPv6 address and configuration settings.

**NOTE**   To extend an expiring IPv6 address lease, the DHCPv6 server will send a Renew message. Several other types of DHCPv6 messages are possible; for information on other DHCPv6 messages, refer to "DHCP Protocols" at http://technet. microsoft.com/en-us/library/dd145321(WS.10).aspx. This reference also provides information on the structure of various DHCPv6 messages.

**TIP**   To view the settings of the M and O flags, first obtain the index of the desired interface by using the `netsh interface ipv6 show interface` command. Then, view the settings of the interface by using the `netsh interface ipv6 show interface <number>` command, where `<number>` is the interface index (Idx) number. The results of the latter command include a large number of connection parameters for the specified interface. To configure a Windows Server 2008 R2 router to set the M flag to 1 in router advertisements, use the `netsh interface ipv6 set interface InterfaceName managedaddress=enabled` command. To set the O flag to 1, use the `netsh interface ipv6 set interface InterfaceName otherstateful=enabled` command.

## Installing and Configuring a DHCP Server

In Windows Server 2008, DHCP is installed and configured as a server role. Before installing DHCP, ensure that the server is configured with a static IP address that is compatible with the scope that you will be configuring for lease purposes. You can do this from the Properties dialog box for your network adapter, which is accessible from the Network and Sharing Center:

1. From the left panel, select **Change adapter settings**. On a server running the original version of Windows Server 2008, click **Manage Network Connections**.

2. Right-click your network connection and choose **Properties**.

   3. From the Local Area Connection Properties dialog box that appears, select either **Internet Protocol Version 4 (TCP/IPv4)** or **Internet Protocol Version 6 (TCP/IPv6)** as required and click **Properties**.

   4. In the dialog box that appears, select the **Use the following IP address** option and then type the IP address, subnet mask or subnet prefix length, and the default gateway.

Use the following procedure to install DHCP on a Windows Server 2008 R2 computer:

   1. Open Server Manager and expand the Roles node.

   2. Click **Add Roles** to start the Add Roles Wizard.

   3. If you receive the Before You Begin page, click **Next**. Note that you can disable the appearance of this page by selecting the check box labeled **Skip this page by default**.

   4. The Select Server Roles page enables you to select the roles you want to install on your server. Select **DHCP Server** (as shown in Figure 2-2) and click **Next**.

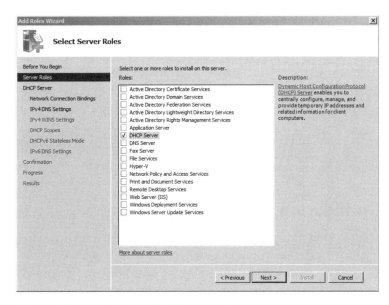

**Figure 2-2**   Selecting the DHCP server role.

5. You receive the Introduction to DHCP Server page shown in Figure 2-3. To learn more about DHCP, click the links provided. When you're ready to proceed, click **Next**.

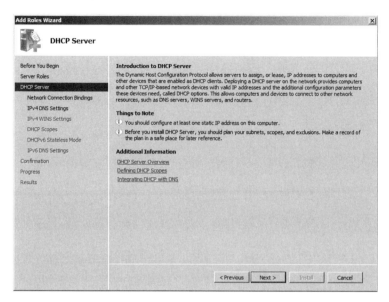

**Figure 2-3**   The Introduction to DHCP Server page enables you to obtain more information on DHCP.

6. The Select Network Connection Bindings page displays all the available network connections that are configured with a static IP address. You can use different network connections to serve DHCP clients on separate subnets, if desired. Select the network connections to be used by DHCP and click **Next**.

7. The Specify IPv4 DNS Server Settings page enables you to specify the IP addresses of DNS servers and the name of an DNS domain to be used by client computers for name resolution. Type the name of the domain and the IP address of the preferred DNS server (as shown in Figure 2-4) and optionally the alternate DNS server. Then, click **Next**.

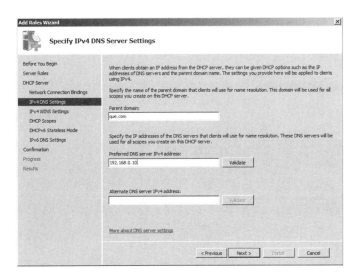

**Figure 2-4**   Specifying IPv4 DNS server settings.

**8.** The Specify IPv4 WINS Server Settings enables you to specify the IP address of a WINS server if one is in use. Unless this is true, leave the default of **WINS is not required for applications on this network** selected, and then click **Next**.

**9.** The Add or Edit DHCP Scopes page shown in Figure 2-5 enables you to add, edit, or delete DHCP scopes. We discuss scopes in the next section. Click **Add** to specify a new scope, **Edit** to modify an existing one, or **Delete** to remove one. When finished, click **Next**.

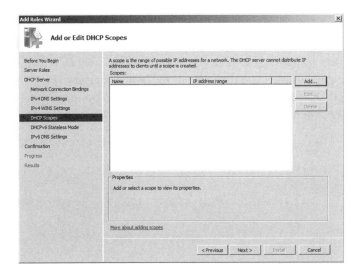

**Figure 2-5**   You can add or edit DHCP scopes while installing your DHCP server.

10. On the Configure DHCPv6 Stateless Mode page shown in Figure 2-6, select whether to enable DHCPv6 stateless mode as discussed in the previous section. Then, click **Next**.

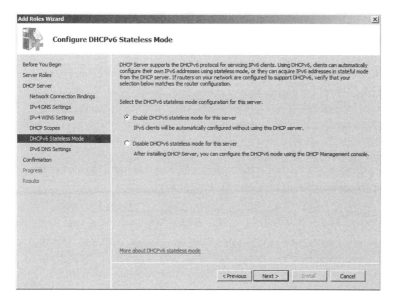

**Figure 2-6** You can choose whether to enable DHCPv6 stateless mode on your DHCP server.

11. If you enable DHCPv6 stateless mode, the Specify IPv6 DNS Server Settings page enables you to specify similar options to those previously shown in Figure 2-4 for DNS server settings. Specify these settings as required and then click **Next**.

12. If your server is a domain controller or domain member server, you receive the Authorize DHCP Server page, which informs you that Active Directory Domain Services (AD DS) stores a list of DHCP servers that are authorized to service clients on the network. If the credentials you are using to install DHCP are adequate, leave the default of **Use current credentials** selected. Otherwise, select **Use alternate credentials** and click **Specify** to enter the username and password of a user entitled to authorize the DHCP server. Then, click **Next**. Note that if you are installing DHCP on a standalone server, you will not receive this page.

13. You receive the Confirm Installation Selections page that summarizes the options you specified. Verify that these selections are complete and then click **Install**.

14. The Installation Progress page tracks the progress of installing DHCP. When informed that the installation is complete, click **Close**.

After you finish installing DHCP, the DHCP Microsoft Management Console (MMC) snap-in is added to the set of administrative tools accessed from the Administrative Tools folder. The remainder of this chapter discusses configuration of the options available from this console.

### Using the Command Line to Install DHCP

Windows Server 2008 R2 uses the Deployment Image Servicing and Management (DISM.exe) tool to install and configure server roles, such as DHCP. This is unlike the original version of Windows Server 2008, which used the servermanagercmd.exe tool to install server roles.

Use the following command to install DHCP on a computer that runs the Server Core version of Windows Server 2008 R2. (Note that this command is case-sensitive and DHCPServerCore must be typed exactly as indicated.)

```
Dism /online /enable-feature /featurename:DHCPServerCore
```

On a computer running the original version of Windows Server 2008, use the following command to install DHCP:

```
start /w ocsetup DHCPServerCore
```

After installing DHCP, you need to configure the DHCP server service to start automatically and then start it manually for the first time. To configure automatic start, type the following:

```
sc config dhcpserver start= auto
```

To start the DHCP service, type

```
Net start dhcpserver
```

After you install and start the DHCP server service on a Server Core computer, use the netsh dhcp command line context to configure the server. The more common uses of this command are covered in later sections of this chapter.

**NOTE**  For more information on installing server roles and role services from the command line in Windows Server 2008 R2, refer to "Installing a server role on a server running a Server Core installation of Windows Server 2008 R2: Overview" at http://technet.microsoft.com/en-us/library/ee441260(WS.10).aspx. For more information on DISM commands, refer to "DISM Command-Line Options" at http://technet.microsoft.com/en-us/library/dd772580(WS.10).aspx.

# DHCP Scopes and Options

After you install and start the DHCP server service, you need to configure a scope of configuration information. Every DHCP server requires at least one scope with a pool of IP addresses available for leasing to clients. You can create a scope for each physical subnet on your network and use this scope to define networking parameters, such as the range of IP addresses and their subnet mask, lease duration values, scope options, and client reservation options. You can create multiple scopes to act as a backup method for other DHCP servers and for assigning IP addresses specific to a subnet, such as default gateway addresses. You can create, edit, or remove scopes during installation of the server as already discussed, or at any time afterwards from the DHCP console.

### Creating DHCP Scopes

Windows Server 2008 provides the Create Scope Wizard to facilitate the creation of new scopes. Use the following procedure to create a new DHCP scope:

1. Click **Start > Administrative Tools > DHCP** to open the DHCP console.

2. In the console tree, expand the node for your server to reveal subnodes for IPv4 and IPv6.

3. Right-click either **IPv4** or **IPv6** as required and choose **New Scope**.

4. The New Scope Wizard starts with a Welcome page. Click **Next**.

5. On the Scope Name page, type a name (required) and optional description for the scope, and then click **Next**.

6. On the IP Address Range page, specify the start and end points of the address range (as shown in Figure 2-7) to be provided by the scope. Change the subnet mask length and value if required, and then click **Next**.

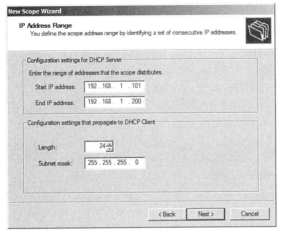

**Figure 2-7**    Specifying the range of IP addresses to be provided by the scope.

   **7.** The Add Exclusions and Delay page shown in Figure 2-8 enables you to specify a range of addresses to be excluded from distribution to clients. This is useful to exclude IP addresses configured for servers or other devices with static
IP addresses from being distributed. Specify the start and end IP addresses (as
shown in Figure 2-8), click **Add**, and then click **Next**.

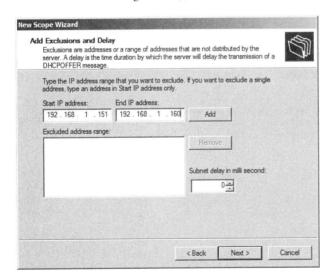

**Figure 2-8**    Specifying a range of IP addresses to be excluded from your scope.

   **8.** The Lease Duration page enables you to choose how long a client is entitled
to use an IP address from the scope. By default, this period is 8 days. If you

wish, choose the number of days, hours, and minutes desired for the lease duration period. Then, click **Next**.

9. You receive the Configure DHCP Options page shown in Figure 2-9. Leave the default of **Yes, I want to configure these options now** selected to specify options for domain name, lease duration, and router location. Click **No, I will configure these options later** to complete the wizard and specify these options later. These options are discussed later in this section.

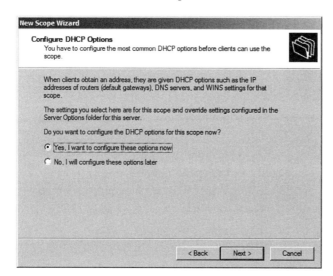

**Figure 2-9**   The wizard enables you to choose whether to specify several common options now.

10. When you finish configuring these options, you are asked whether you want to activate the scope now. To provide IP addressing information to clients, you must activate the scope. Click **Yes, I want to activate this scope now**, and then click **Next**. Note that you do not receive this page if you choose the **No, I will configure these options later** option in Step 9; you will have to activate the scope after completing the wizard.

11. Click **Finish** to create your scope.

Creating an IPv6 scope is similar. After you specify the name of the scope, the wizard asks for a scope prefix (refer to Table 1-10 in Chapter 1). It then asks if you want to add exclusions (similar to Figure 2-8 for IPv4) and the lease duration.

**CAUTION** DHCP servers don't share scope information, so it's important that each scope contains unique IP addresses. Otherwise, more than one DHCP server could lease the same address to different DHCP clients, causing duplicate IP address problems. Microsoft recommends that you use the 80/20 rule for allocating scope addresses between two DHCP servers. Simply put, this means that you configure one DHCP server to allocate 80 percent of the addresses in any scope and a second server to allocate the remaining 20 percent. For a second scope, simply reverse these percentages between the DHCP servers. This provides for fault tolerance in the event that a DHCP server becomes unavailable. For additional suggestions regarding scope creation, refer to "More about adding scopes" at http://technet.microsoft.com/en-us/library/cc754471.aspx.

## Using the Command Line to Create Scopes

Windows Server 2008 provides the `netsh dhcp` command-line context that enables you to perform DHCP management tasks from the command line. This is useful for scripting tasks to be run from multiple servers or for working at a Server Core machine. Use the following command to create a scope:

```
netsh dhcp server add scope ScopeAddress SubnetMask ScopeName
[ScopeComment]
```

In this command, `ScopeAddress` specifies the scope to be added by IP network number, `SubnetMask` specifies the subnet mask, `ScopeName` specifies the scope's name, and `ScopeComment` specifies an optional comment. For example, the following command adds a scope with scope address 10.2.2.0, subnet mask 255.255.255.0, a scope name of MyScope, and a scope comment of MyComment:

```
add scope 10.2.2.0 255.255.255.0 MyScope MyComment
```

**NOTE** For more information on using the `netsh` command-line tool for configuring and scripting DHCP, refer to "`Netsh` commands for DHCP" at http://technet.microsoft.com/en-us/library/cc787375(WS.10).aspx.

## Superscopes

Superscopes are useful in situations where you are running out of IP addresses in a regular scope. Using a superscope, you can combine two or more scopes into a single logical scope, and the DHCP server can hand out IP addresses to a client from either scope. To ensure proper communication, you have to configure important servers that use static IP addresses with an address from each scope contained within the superscope. Superscopes are useful in situations such as the following:

- Supporting DHCP clients on a single physical network segment that includes multiple logical IP networks (referred to as multinets). In such a situation, you might need to enable routing to allow clients on different logical IP networks to communicate with each other.

- Supporting DHCP clients located in a multinet on the other side of Bootstrap Protocol (BOOTP) relay agents.

- Migration of clients to a new scope.

To define a superscope, first define at least one of the scopes to be included using the New Scope Wizard, as already described. Having done this, right-click the IPv4 subnode in the DHCP console and choose **New Superscope**, and then follow the instructions provided by the New Superscope Wizard. This wizard asks you for a name for your superscope and then lets you choose the scope or scopes to be included.

**NOTE** For more information on superscopes, including sample configurations of various superscope scenarios, refer to "Managing DHCP Superscopes" at http://technet.microsoft.com/en-us/library/dd183662(WS.10).aspx.

## Multicast Scopes

Multicast scopes hand out IP addresses to multicast-enabled applications on the network. A multicast message is one that is sent once but received by more than one destination computer configured with a Class D IP address. DHCP in Windows Server 2008 includes Multicast Address Dynamic Client Allocation Protocol (MADCAP), which facilitates the configuration of multicast groups on the network.

Analogous to the use of DHCP for assigning unicast IP addresses, MADCAP allocates IP multicast network addresses to its clients. MADCAP actually operates independently of DHCP, although both services are supported by DHCP servers. Clients of one do not depend on the configuration of the other.

To create a multicast scope, right-click the IPv4 node in the DHCP console and choose **New Multicast Scope**. Then, follow the instructions provided by the New Multicast Scope Wizard, which are similar to those in the New Scope Wizard discussed earlier in this section.

**NOTE**   For more information on multicast scopes, refer to "Managing DHCP Multicast Scopes" at http://technet.microsoft.com/en-us/library/dd183599(WS.10).aspx.

### Split Scopes

It is usual on all but the smallest networks to operate two or more DHCP servers to provide for fault tolerance and load balancing. Windows Server 2008 R2 provides a new Split-Scope Configuration Wizard that improves on the more error-prone manual split-scope configuration method previously used. This wizard enables you to minimize the possibility of depletion of address pools. Use the following procedure to configure a split scope:

1. In the DHCP snap-in, expand either **IPv4** or **IPv6** to locate the scope to be split.

2. Right-click this scope and choose **Advanced > Split-Scope**.

3. The DHCP Split-Scope Configuration Wizard starts with an introduction page. Click **Next**.

4. On the Additional DHCP Server page, type the name or IP address of the server to be added or select it by clicking the **Add Server** button. Then, click **Next**.

5. Specify the IP addresses to be used by each DHCP server. Microsoft suggests that you use the 80/20 rule when splitting a scope—in other words, assign 80 percent of the IP addresses in the scope to the primary DHCP server and the remaining 20 percent of the IP addresses to the secondary DHCP server.

6. On the Delay in DHCP Offer page, configure the primary DHCP server with the default value of 0 and the secondary (Added DHCP Server) with a non-zero value, such as 1000 milliseconds, and then click **Next**. This enables the secondary server to send DHCPOFFER messages only after the stated delay value, thereby preventing the exhaustion of IPv4 addresses from the scope at the secondary server.

7. On the completion page, click **Finish**.

**NOTE**   For more information on configuring split scopes in Windows Server 2008 R2, refer to "DHCP Step-by-Step Guide: Demonstrate DHCP Split Scope with Delay on a Secondary Server in a Test Lab" at http://technet.microsoft.com/en-us/library/ee405264(WS.10).aspx.

## Exclusions

An *exclusion* is a range of IP addresses within a scope that you do not want to have used by DHCP in leasing addresses to clients. Typically, these are IP addresses of computers such as servers that are configured with static IP addresses.

You can create an exclusion when first creating a scope with the New Scope Wizard, as already described. Use the following procedure:

1. In the console tree of the DHCP console, double-click the required scope under the IPv4 node to expand it.

2. Select **Address Pool**, right-click it, and select **New Exclusion Range**.

3. In the Add Exclusion dialog box, type the starting and ending IP addresses of the desired exclusion range in the Start IP Address and End IP Address fields, and then click **Add**.

4. Repeat as needed to define additional exclusion ranges. When finished, click **Close**.

You can also use the `netsh dhcp` command to create an exclusion from the command line. Type the following:

```
netsh dhcp server scope add excluderange StartIP EndIP
```

In this command, `StartIP` and `EndIP` specify the IP addresses of the start and end points of the exclusion range. For example, to exclude the range 192.168.1.101 to 192.168.1.199, use the following command:

```
netsh dhcp server scope add excluderange 192.168.1.101 192.168.1.199
```

**NOTE**   For more information on managing scopes in general, refer to "Managing DHCP Server Scopes" at http://technet.microsoft.com/en-us/library/dd183624(WS.10).aspx.

## Configuring DHCP Scope Properties

Each scope you create on your DHCP server has a set of properties associated with it. Right-click the scope and choose **Properties** to display the dialog box shown in Figure 2-10. The four tabs enable you to configure the following properties:

- **General tab:** Enables you to adjust the IP address range and lease duration, as shown in Figure 2-10.

- **DNS tab:** Enables you to automatically update the host (A) and pointer (PTR) records on the authoritative DNS servers. More information on this process is provided in Chapter 7, "Configuring DNS Records."

- **Network Access Protection tab:** Enables you to set up Network Access Protection (NAP) settings for the scope. More information is provided in Chapter 16, "Configuring Network Access Protection (NAP)."

- **Advanced tab:** Enables you to select whether the scope provides IP addressing information to DHCP clients, BOOTP clients, or both. You can adjust the lease duration for BOOTP clients, which is 30 days by default.

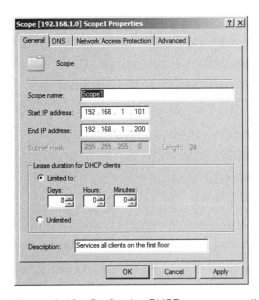

**Figure 2-10**   Configuring DHCP scope properties.

## Configuring DHCP Options

As already noted, the Create Scope Wizard enables you to specify several options related to the scope. DHCP in Windows Server 2008 provides a considerable range of options that you can use to specify additional TCP/IP-related parameters to client computers on your network. You can specify these options at any of the following four levels:

- Server (specific for either IPv4 or IPv6; serves as defaults for all scopes configured on the server).

- Scope (applies only to the scope for which it is specified).

- Option class (applies to all computers belonging to the defined option class). Option classes are discussed later in this chapter.

- Client (applies only to the specified client computer).

Any option applied at a later stage in this sequence always overwrites a conflicting option that was applied earlier in this sequence. For example, server options are overwritten by any conflicting option applied at any of the other levels and client options always overwrite other options applied at any level.

Table 2-2 summarizes the more important DHCP server options.

**Table 2-2**  Common DHCP Options

| DHCP Option | Description |
|---|---|
| 003 Router | Specifies the IP address of the default gateway. |
| 006 DNS Servers | Specifies the IP addresses of the network's DNS name servers. |
| 015 DNS Domain Name | Specifies the DNS domain name used for client reservations. |
| 044 WINS/NBNS Servers | Specifies the IP addresses of the network's NetBIOS name servers. |
| 046 WINS/NBT Node Type | Specifies the type of NetBIOS over TCP/IP name resolution to be used by the client:<br><br>1 = B-node (broadcast)<br><br>2 = P-node (peer)<br><br>4 = M-node (mixed)<br><br>8 = H-node (hybrid) |
| 047 NetBIOS Scope ID | Specifies the local NetBIOS scope ID. Hosts can communicate only with other hosts configured with the same scope ID. |
| 060 Vendor class Identifier | Specifies the vendor type and configuration of the DHCP client. |
| 066 Boot Server Host Name | Specifies the host name of the TFTP server used in servicing PXE boot clients. |
| 067 Boot File Name | Specifies the name of a boot image file on the TFTP server used in servicing PXE boot clients. |

**NOTE**    For a complete list of available DHCP options and their associated parameters, refer to "DHCP Tools and Options" at http://technet.microsoft.com/en-us/library/dd145324(WS.10).aspx and "RFC 2132–DHCP Options and BOOTP Vendor Extensions" at www.faqs.org/rfcs/rfc2132.html.

### Server Options

As already noted, you can configure DHCP options at any of four levels. Use the following procedure to configure DHCP options at the server level:

1. In the console tree of the DHCP console, right-click **Server Options** under either **IPv4** or **IPv6** as required and choose **Configure Options**.

2. From the General tab of the Server Options dialog box, select the option to be configured. The lower part of this dialog box expands to reveal parameters specific to the option selected, as shown in Figure 2-11 for the 003 Router option.

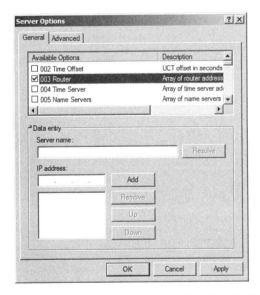

**Figure 2-11**    Configuring the 003 Router DHCP server option.

3. Click **Apply** to apply your changes and then select another option as required. When finished configuring options, click **OK**.

Note that if you specified any of these options while installing the DHCP server role, they will appear in the Server Options dialog box. You can modify any of these options simply by selecting the required option and making any needed changes.

To add a server option from the command line, use the following command:

```
netsh dhcp server add optiondef OptCode OptName {BYTE | WORD | DWORD
| STRING | IPADDRESS} [[IsArray=]{0 | 1}] [vendor=VendorClass]
[comment=OptComment] [DefValue}
```

In this command, OptCode is the option type and OptName is the name of the option type (for example, the code and name in each line of Table 2-2), and {BYTE | WORD | DWORD | STRING | IPADDRESS} indicates the data type of the option. All these parameters are required. The remaining optional parameters are as follows: [IsArray=]{0 | 1} indicates whether the data type is arrayed or non-arrayed: 0 = non-arrayed (default), 1 = arrayed. vendor=VendorClass specifies the vendor class for the option. If unspecified, the default vendor class, the DHCP standard options class, is used. comment=OptComment specifies a comment to be added. DefValue specifies a default value to be used with this option type.

For example, to add a new option type named ExtensionsPath with code 18, a STRING data type, and join it to the DHCP standard options class, and assign it a default value of c:\Temp, use the following command:

```
netsh dhcp server add optiondef 18 ExtensionsPath STRING 0 c:\Temp
```

## Scope Options

To configure options at the scope level, expand the desired scope to reveal the Scope Options subnode, as shown in Figure 2-12. As shown, any options specified at the server level appear in the details pane of the DHCP console. Right-click this node, choose **Configure Options**, and then proceed as described previously for server options.

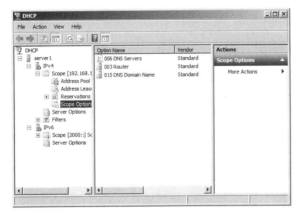

**Figure 2-12**   Specifying DHCP options at the scope level.

To set an option value for the current scope from the command line, use the following command:

```
netsh dhcp scope set optionvalue OptCode {BYTE | WORD | DWORD |
STRING | IPADDRESS} OptionValue
```

In this command, *OptionValue* specifies the assigned value for the option type that is specified in *OptCode*. Other parameters are as defined previously for adding server options. For example, to set the default gateway for the scope at 192.168.0.0 to 192.168.0.1, use the following command:

```
netsh dhcp server scope 192.168.0.0 set optionvalue 003 IPADDRESS
192.168.0.1
```

## Option Classes

DHCP in Windows Server 2008 provides *option classes*, which facilitate the introduction of custom applications on enterprise networks. By specifying option classes, you can differentiate groups of DHCP clients and specify customized options that apply only to the specified group of clients. The following two types of option classes are available in Windows Server 2008:

- **Vendor classes:** Identify a client's vendor type and configuration when obtaining a DHCP lease. You can use the vendor class ID option (code 60) to specify vendor classes. This option includes an identifier with a string of character data readable by the DHCP servers. Often used with vendor classes are standard reserved hardware and operating system codes defined in RFC 1700.

- **User classes:** Differentiate clients according to their type, such as desktop, laptop, or server computer. For example, you can group mobile computers into a specific class and apply options, such as shorter lease times, to only these computers by supplying them with the relevant class ID. You can also define class identifiers that specify information, such as a client's software configuration, physical location within a building, operating system in use, and so on.

**TIP**   DHCP in Windows Server 2008 provides for a default user class, to which all DHCP clients belong by default. Any options you define for this class automatically apply to all DHCP clients. Options assigned to this class can be overridden by options assigned to other user classes.

Use the following procedure to define a custom user class:

1. In the console tree of the DHCP console, right-click the **IPv4** or **IPv6** node as required under the DHCP server and choose **Define User Classes**.

2. When defining a user class, the DHCP User Classes dialog box appears. As shown in Figure 2-13, three default user classes are provided. To define a new user class, click **Add**.

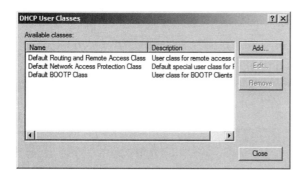

**Figure 2-13**   DHCP provides three user classes by default.

3. In the New Class dialog box that appears (see Figure 2-14), type the required information and click **Add**.

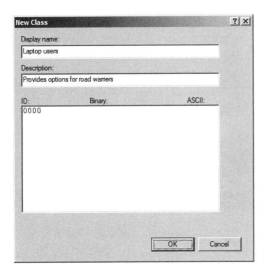

**Figure 2-14**   Specifying user class information.

You can define a custom vendor class by using a similar procedure. Right-click **IPv4** or **IPv6** and select **Define Vendor Classes**. Default vendor classes are provided for Microsoft Windows 2000 Options, Microsoft Windows 98 Options, and Microsoft Options.

To specify DHCP options for user or vendor classes, select the **Advanced** tab of either the Server Options or Scope Options dialog box. (Refer to Figure 2-11 for the Server Options dialog box.) Specify the class ID to be assigned and then configure the required options as previously described.

**NOTE**   For more information on option classes, refer to "DHCP Architecture" at http://technet.microsoft.com/en-us/library/dd183602(WS.10).aspx.

### Client Reservations and Options

You can configure DHCP so that a DHCP server always assigns the same IP address to a client computer. This feature is known as a *client reservation*. It maps the IP address to a specific MAC address, which is useful for configuring servers that must always be reached at the same IP address with a specified set of options. You can include client-specific options that override conflicting server and scope-based options. Proceed as follows:

1. In the console tree of the DHCP console, expand the required scope to reveal the **Reservations** node.

2. Right-click this node and select **New Reservation**.

3. In the dialog box that appears (see Figure 2-15), type the correct IP address (for example, `192.168.1.173`) and MAC address (`ab-17-3f-42-69-7c`) for the reservation and click **Add**.

**Figure 2-15** Specifying a client reservation.

4. Repeat to add additional client reservations as needed. When finished, click **Close**.

5. To specify client-based options similar to those already mentioned for server and scope options, right-click the client reservation and select **Configure Options**.

To add a client reservation from the command line, use the following command:

```
netsh dhcp server add reserevedip ReservedIP MACAddress [ClientName]
[ClientComment] [{DHCP | BOOTP | BOTH}]
```

In this command, *ReservedIP* specifies the IP address to be reserved, *MACAddress* specifies the MAC address of the adapter to be associated with the reserved IP address, and *ClientName* and *ClientComment* are an optional client name and client comment to be associated with the reserved client entry. {**DHCP** | **BOOTP** | **BOTH**} specifies the type of clients to be associated with this entry; DHCP is the default.

For example, to reserve the IP address 192.168.1.173 for a server named MailServer1 and using the MAC address ab-17-3f-42-69-7c, use the following command:

```
netsh dhcp server add reserevedip 192.168.1.173 ab173f42697c
MailServer1
```

> **TIP**   Remember that DHCP options are applied in the sequence server, scope, user class, and client reservation. Options applied at a later stage of this sequence always override those applied earlier.

## Managing and Troubleshooting a DHCP Server

Exam 70-642 tests your ability to perform several additional managerial tasks on your DHCP server, including the following:

- Authorizing the server in Active Directory
- Configuring DHCP relay agents
- Configuring PXE boot
- Monitoring and troubleshooting your DHCP server

### Authorizing a DHCP Server in Active Directory

In an Active Directory Domain Services (AD DS) domain, you must authorize the DHCP server in Active Directory before it can lease IP addresses. This prevents rogue DHCP servers from leasing improper IP addresses that would result in communication problems. When a domain controller or member server running DHCP starts up, it queries AD DS for the list of authorized servers as identified by their IP addresses. If its IP address is not present on this list, the DHCP server service does not complete its startup sequence.

To authorize your DHCP server, you must be a member of the Enterprise Admins group. Use the following procedure:

1. At the top of the console tree of the DHCP console, right-click **DHCP** and choose **Manage authorized servers**.

2. On the Manage Authorized Servers dialog box that appears, click **Authorize**.

**3.** On the Authorize DHCP Server dialog box, type the name or IP address of the server to be authorized, as shown in Figure 2-16, and click **OK**.

**Figure 2-16** Authorizing a DHCP server in Active Directory.

**4.** Click **OK** to confirm the authorization.

To authorize your DHCP server from the command line, use the following:

```
netsh dhcp add server ServerDNS ServerIP
```

In this command, *ServerDNS* is the DNS domain name of the DHCP server to be authorized, and *ServerIP* is the IP address of this server. Both parameters are required.

### Configuring DHCP Relay Agents

Recall from earlier in this chapter that when a client computer starts up, it broadcasts a DHCPDISCOVER message to locate a DHCP server and obtain TCP/IP configuration information. What happens if there is no DHCP server on the subnet to which the client belongs? Broadcast messages do not cross routers to access servers on another subnet unless the router is compliant with the RFC 1542 standard, "Clarifications and Extensions for the Bootstrap Protocol." Such a router can recognize and pass BOOTP broadcasts to other subnets, a feature known as BOOTP-forwarding. Note that nearly all current routers are RFC 1542 compliant, but you might still encounter legacy routers that are not compliant.

There is another means to forward BOOTP broadcasts to other subnets in search of a DHCP server—this is a *DHCP relay agent*. A DHCP relay agent is a Windows Server 2008 computer that is configured with Routing and Remote Access (RRAS) to pass BOOTP broadcasts, and is thereby compliant with RFC 1542. This server acts as a DHCP proxy by listening for DHCPDISCOVER broadcasts and translating them into DHCPINFORM messages that are directed to the IP addresses of all DHCP servers on adjacent subnets that the DHCP relay agent knows about.

Before configuring a Windows Server 2008 computer as a DHCP relay agent, you must set up RRAS. The installation of RRAS is covered in Chapter 3, "Configuring

Routing." After installing RRAS, use the following procedure to configure a Windows Server 2008 computer as an IPv4 DHCP relay agent:

1. Open the RRAS snap-in by clicking **Start** > **Administrative Tools** > **Routing and Remote Access**.

2. From the console tree of the RRAS snap-in, expand **IPv4**, right-click the **General** subnode, and choose **New Routing Protocol**.

3. From the New Routing Protocol dialog box, select **DHCP Relay Agent** (as shown in Figure 2-17) and click **OK**.

**Figure 2-17**   You must select DHCP Relay Agent from the New Routing Protocol dialog box.

4. DHCP relay agent is added to the console tree of the RRAS snap-in. Right-click it and choose **New Interface**.

5. In the New Interface for DHCP Relay Agent dialog box (shown in Figure 2-18), select the required network interface and click **OK**.

**Figure 2-18**   Configuring the DHCP relay agent.

6. Ensure that **Relay DHCP packets** is selected and click **OK**.

7. Right-click **DHCP Relay Agent** and choose **Properties**.

8. On the General tab of the DHCP Relay Agent Properties dialog box, type the IP addresses of the DHCP servers that will service the RRAS server's clients, click **Add**, and click **OK**.

Configuring a DHCPv6 relay agent is slightly different, as the following procedure shows:

1. Open the RRAS snap-in by clicking **Start** > **Administrative Tools** > **Routing and Remote Access**.

2. From the console tree of the RRAS snap-in, expand **IPv6**, right-click **General**, and click **New Routing Protocol**.

3. In the New Routing Protocol dialog box, select **DHCPv6 Relay Agent** and click **OK**.

4. Right-click **DHCPv6 Relay agent** and choose **New Interface**.

5. Select the required interface and click **OK**.

6. In the DHCPv6 Relay Properties dialog box, select **Relay DHCP packets** and click **OK**.

7. Right-click **DHCPv6 Relay Agent** and choose **Properties**.

8. On the Servers tab of the DHCP Relay Agent Properties dialog box, type the IPv6 addresses of the DHCP servers that will service the RRAS server's clients, click **Add**, and click **OK**.

**NOTE**   For more information on capabilities of the DHCP Relay Agent, refer to "RRAS DHCP Relay Agent (IPBOOTP)" at http://technet.microsoft.com/en-us/library/cc773747(WS.10).aspx and "RRAS DHCPv6 Relay Agent" at http://technet.microsoft.com/en-us/library/cc733646(WS.10).aspx. Also, refer to "DHCP Processes and Interactions" at http://technet.microsoft.com/en-us/library/dd183657(WS.10).aspx.

## PXE Boot

When using Windows Deployment Services (WDS) to install operating systems such as Windows 7 or Windows Server 2008 R2 on new computers, the network interface card (NIC) of the new computer must be compliant with the Preboot Execution Environment (PXE), which enables a computer to access an image across the network for installation purposes. Such a computer connects to a WDS server, which then installs the operating system across the network without the need for a CD or DVD.

When such a computer initializes a PXE boot, the PXE ROM requests an IP address from the DHCP server using the normal four-step process described earlier. The DHCPDISCOVER message indicates to the server that the client computer is PXE-enabled, and after the client receives a valid IP address, it attempts to locate and connect to the WDS server to download a network boot program.

**NOTE**   For more information on WDS and its use in deploying Windows 7 to large numbers of client computers, refer to *MCTS 70-680 Microsoft Windows 7, Configuring Cert Guide* (by Don Poulton, Pearson 2011). For information on installing and configuring the WDS server, refer to "Windows Deployment Services Getting Started Guide" at http://technet.microsoft.com/en-us/library/cc771670(WS.10).aspx.

### Monitoring and Troubleshooting a DHCP Server

As with any other server role, things can—and do—go wrong with a DHCP server. If problems occur with a DHCP server, client computers might not receive proper IP leases and network communication errors might result. Furthermore, it is important that you know whether your DHCP server is encountering performance bottlenecks or other issues.

You can obtain DHCP server monitoring data from any of the following three locations:

- DHCP statistics
- Statistical information provided by Performance Monitor
- Events recorded by Event Viewer

DHCP statistics are provided for each scope configured on the server. To access DHCP statistics, right-click the required scope in the DHCP console and choose **Display Statistics**. The dialog box shown in Figure 2-19 provides statistical information.

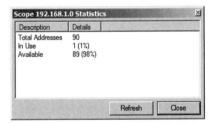

**Figure 2-19**   Displaying DHCP statistical data.

When you install DHCP, a series of statistical counters is added to Performance Monitor. These counters enable you to track server performance and monitor server activity, such as the number and types of messages sent and received by the server, the processing time required by the DHCP server to deal with requests sent to it, and whether message packets are being dropped because of internal server delays. Performance Monitor is discussed in Chapter 19, "Configuring Performance Monitoring."

**NOTE**   For a list of DHCP performance counters and their description, refer to "Monitoring DHCP Server Performance" at http://technet.microsoft.com/en-us/library/dd145323(WS.10).aspx.

Each time the DHCP server receives a lease request, offers a lease, or acknowledges or denies it, a record is written to the DHCP event log, which you can view in Event Viewer. Errors or warning messages encountered during this activity are also recorded, which enables you to locate and track problems related to the DHCP server. Event Viewer is discussed in Chapter 20, "Configuring Event Logs."

If disk space is causing a problem, you can move the database file to another location. By default, the database is stored at `%systemroot%\system32\dhcp`, as shown in Figure 2-20. Use the following procedure to move the database to another location:

1. In the console tree of the DHCP snap-in, right-click the server and choose **Properties**.

2. Click **Browse** opposite the Database path field to move the database file to another location.

3. You are warned that changing the database path might result in loss of data. Click **Yes** to continue, and then on the Browse for Folder dialog box that appears, select the desired location. Click **Make New Folder**, if desired, to create a new folder.

4. Click **OK** twice to complete the operation.

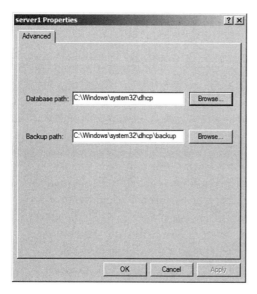

**Figure 2-20**   The Properties dialog box for a DHCP server enables you to change the location of the database and backup files.

**TIP**   You might also be able to save disk space by compacting the DHCP database file. To do so, open a command prompt, change to the `%systemroot%\system32\dhcp` folder, type `jetpack dhcp.mdb temp.mdb`, and press **Enter**. Then, copy the compacted DHCP database back to the original location.

The following are a few problems you might encounter with a DHCP server, together with suggestions for resolution:

- **IP address conflicts:** This can occur if a user manually configures a computer with a static IP address that is within the range of a DHCP scope. Ensure that the user chooses the **Obtain an IP address automatically** option. If there is a reason that the chosen IP address must be retained, configure an exclusion so that the DHCP server does not lease this address. This error might also occur if more than one DHCP server is configured with overlapping scopes.

- **Failure to obtain an IP address reservation:** If you attempt to add a reservation for an IP address outside the range of a configured scope, you receive a message stating `The specified DHCP client is not a reserved client`. You must use an IP address that is contained within an existing scope when configuring an IP address reservation. Use an exclusion range to ensure that another client does not receive the same IP address.

- **Clients are unable to receive an IP address:** This might mean that all available IP addresses within the range of existing scopes have been allocated. You should extend the scope or create a new scope, according to the overall network configuration.

- **After restoring the DHCP server from backup, clients receive IP addresses that are already in use:** After restoring the DHCP server from backup, it might be unaware of which IP addresses it has leased from a given scope. The Conflict detection parameter is provided for this purpose. By default, this parameter is set to 0, which disables conflict detection. When this parameter is set to a nonzero value, the DHCP server uses the `ping` utility to test an IP address before leasing it to a client; the value represents the number of times the server performs this test. The value can range from 0 to 6; higher values perform a more thorough test at the expense of server resources. To specify a value for this parameter, right-click the DHCP server in the console tree of the DHCP snap-in. From the Advanced tab of the Properties dialog box, type a value between 1 and 6 in the **Conflict detection attempts** text box, and click **OK**.

- **Client obtains an inappropriate IP address:** Such an error can cause inability to communicate on the network. This might occur if the client is connected to the wrong network or if the scope has been incorrectly configured. Check the scope configuration and the location of the client computer.

**NOTE**   For additional information on potential DHCP errors and their remediation, refer to "DHCP Server" at http://technet.microsoft.com/en-us/library/cc726909(WS.10).aspx.

## Exam Preparation Tasks

## Review All the Key Topics

Review the most important topics in this chapter, noted with the key topics icon in the outer margin of the page. Table 2-3 lists a reference of these key topics and the page numbers on which each is found.

**Table 2-3**   Key Topics for Chapter 2

| Key Topic Element | Description | Page Number |
|---|---|---|
| Paragraphs | Describe the four-step DHCP lease process. | 90 |
| List | Describes DHCPv6 autoconfiguration options. | 94 |
| List | Describes how to install the DHCP server role. | 96 |
| List | Describes how to create a scope on the DHCP server. | 101 |
| Figure 2-7 | Use the New Scope Wizard to define the range of IP addresses to be offered to clients. | 102 |
| Figure 2-9 | Define options for your scope while creating it. | 103 |
| List | Describes the four levels at which you can create DHCP options. | 108 |
| Table 2-2 | Describes the more common DHCP options. | 109 |
| List | Shows how to create server options. | 110 |
| List | Describes available option classes. | 112 |
| Figure 2-15 | Shows how to configure a client reservation. | 115 |
| Figure 2-16 | Shows how to authorize a DHCP server in Active Directory. | 117 |
| Figure 2-17 | Shows how to create a DHCP relay agent. | 118 |

## Complete the Tables and Lists from Memory

Print a copy of Appendix B, "Memory Tables," (found on the CD), or at least the section for this chapter, and complete the tables and lists from memory. Appendix C, "Memory Tables Answer Key," also on the CD, includes the completed tables and lists to check your work.

## Definition of Key Terms

Define the following key terms from this chapter, and check your answers in the Glossary.

Bootstrap Protocol (BOOTP), broadcast, client reservation, Dynamic Host Configuration Protocol (DHCP), DHCP options, DHCP relay agent, DHCP scope, exclusion, lease, Managed Address Configuration (M) flag, multicast, Multicast Address Dynamic Client Allocation Protocol (MADCAP), Other Stateful Configuration (O) flag, Preboot Execution Environment (PXE), reservation, stateful address configuration, stateless address configuration, superscope. user class, vendor class

This chapter covers the following subjects:

- **The Need for Routing and Routing Tables:** Every Windows computer maintains its own routing table. In this section, you learn what the entries in the routing table mean. You also learn about routing protocols and important routing terminology.

- **Routing and Remote Access Service (RRAS) in Windows Server 2008 R2:** This section introduces you to the RRAS server, shows you how to install it, and shows you how to configure this server as an IP router.

- **Managing and Maintaining Routing Servers:** In this section, you learn about demand-dial routing and IGMP router and proxy settings.

# CHAPTER 3

# Configuring Routing

As you have already seen, computer networks of any significant size consist or a series of subnetworks or subnets, each configured with their own TCP/IP parameters, whether they use version 4 or 6 of the venerable internetworking protocol. You have also seen how these networks are connected by devices known as routers, whose primary purpose is to relay messages from one subnet to the next one. In Chapter 1, "Configuring IPv4 and IPv6 Addressing," you learned that the default gateway parameter is the IP address of a router that sends messages to other networks. Chapter 2, "Configuring Dynamic Host Configuration Protocol (DHCP)," introduced you to the use of a Windows Server 2008 computer running Routing and Remote Access Service (RRAS) as a DHCP relay agent to forward DHCP messages between subnets. This is but one small function that a computer configured with RRAS can perform.

In modern computer networks, dedicated hardware routers handle most of the heavy load of sending packets between subnetworks and forwarding them across the Internet to their destinations, even when these destinations are halfway around the world. Smaller organizations often do not need to use hardware routers to interconnect their subnets; in these cases, the router built into RRAS in Windows Server 2008 can do a fully adequate routing job. This chapter introduces you to the routing side of RRAS. As its name implies, RRAS also functions as a remote access server to connect and authenticate external users accessing your network. This function of RRAS is covered in Chapter 14, "Configuring Remote Access."

## "Do I Know This Already?" Quiz

The "Do I Know This Already?" quiz allows you to assess whether you should read this entire chapter or simply jump to the "Exam Preparation Tasks" section for review. If you are in doubt, read the entire chapter. Table 3-1 outlines the major headings in this chapter and the corresponding "Do I Know This Already?" quiz questions. You can find the answers in Appendix A, "Answers to the 'Do I Know This Already?' Quizzes."

**Table 3-1**   "Do I Know This Already?" Foundation Topics Section-to-Question Mapping

| Foundations Topics Section | Questions Covered in This Section |
| --- | --- |
| The Need for Routing and Routing Tables | 1–3 |
| Routing and Remote Access Service (RRAS) in Windows Server 2008 R2 | 4–8 |
| Managing and Maintaining Routing Servers | 9–10 |

1. A router is determining which path to use to send a message to a server located across the country. With several possible paths available, the router needs to choose the fastest and easiest path for sending the message to its destination. What measuring standard does the router use in making the selection?

   a. Hop

   b. Metric

   c. Protocol

   d. Proxy

2. Which of the following is a distance-vector routing protocol that is used by routers running Windows Server 2008 R2 RRAS and provides a high level of capability, including support for such components as CIDR and variable-length subnet masks?

   a. Open Shortest Path First (OSPF)

   b. Routing Information Protocol version 1 (RIP v1)

   c. Routing Information Protocol version 2 (RIP v2)

   d. Bootstrap Protocol (BOOTP)

3. How would you display your computer's routing table, including all static and dynamic routes that packets sent from your computer might utilize?

   a. From a command prompt, type the `route display` command.

   b. From a command prompt, type the `route print` command.

   c. From the RRAS snap-in, right-click **Static Routes** and choose **Show IP Routing Table**.

   d. From the RRAS snap-in, right-click **General** and choose **Show IP Routing Table**.

4. You just finished installing Windows Server 2008 R2 on a brand new computer and now want to configure this server to act as a router. Which of the following actions should you do? (Each answer represents part of the solution. Choose two.)

   a. From the Add Roles Wizard, select **Network Policy and Access Services** and complete the remaining steps of the wizard.

   b. From the Add Roles Wizard, select **Routing and Remote Access Service (RRAS)** and complete the remaining steps of the wizard.

   c. From the Add Features Wizard, select **Routing and Remote Access Service (RRAS)** and complete the remaining steps of the wizard.

   d. From the RRAS snap-in, right-click your server and choose **Configure and Enable Routing and Remote Access**. In the wizard that appears, select the **Remote access (dial-up or VPN)** option and select **LAN routing**.

   e. From the RRAS snap-in, right-click your server and choose **Configure and Enable Routing and Remote Access**. In the wizard that appears, select the **Custom configuration** option and select **LAN routing**.

5. You want to add protocols to your router to provide complete functionality to client computers on your IPv4-enabled network, so you right-click **General** and choose **New Routing Protocol**. Which of the following protocols are available from the New Routing Protocol dialog box that appears? (Choose all that apply.)

   a. DHCP relay agent

   b. IGMP router and proxy

   c. NAT

   d. RIP version 1 for Internet Protocol

   e. RIP version 2 for Internet Protocol

   f. OSPF

6. You are configuring RIP v2 on your Windows Server 2008 R2 router and want it to ignore announcements originating from routers on the 172.24.10.0 network. How should you proceed?

   a. Use the `route -i add 172.24.10.0` command.

   b. Access the **Neighbors** tab of the RIP Properties dialog box. Select **Ignore announcements from all listed routers** and specify addresses of routers on the 172.24.10.0 network.

   c. Access the **Security** tab of the RRAS server's Properties dialog box. Select **Ignore announcements from all listed routers** and specify addresses of routers on the 172.24.10.0 network.

   d. Access the **Security** tab of the RIP Properties dialog box. Select **Ignore announcements from all listed routers** and specify addresses of routers on the 172.24.10.0 network.

7. You are responsible for configuring static routes on your Windows Server 2008 R2 server, which is configured with RRAS. You want to add a route to the 192.168.3.0 network with a subnet mask of 255.255.255.0. The default gateway should be 192.168.2.1. In addition, you must ensure that this route is not removed from your server when updates are installed and the server must be rebooted. Which of the following commands should you execute?

   a. `route -p add 192.168.3.0 MASK 255.255.255.0 192.168.2.1 metric 2`

   b. `route -p add 192.168.2.1 MASK 255.255.255.0 192.168.3.0 metric 2`

   c. `route -f add 192.168.3.0 MASK 255.255.255.0 192.168.2.1 metric 2`

   d. `route -f add 192.168.2.1 MASK 255.255.255.0 192.168.3.0 metric 2`

8. You are examining the static routing table for your Windows Server 2008 R2 router and are looking for a route that specifies that only an exact match of the destination network number can use the route. Which of the following characteristics informs you of this fact?

   a. The network mask is 0.0.0.0.

   b. The network mask is 255.255.255.0.

   c. The network mask is 255.255.255.255.

   d. The destination and network mask numbers are equal to each other.

9. You want to limit the number of redial attempts on your demand-dial routing server to 3. Further, you want to specify that the server waits 2 minutes between redial attempts. What should you do?

    a. From the Security tab of the demand-dial interface's Properties dialog box, specify the maximum number of redial attempts and the redial interval.

    b. From the Options tab of the demand-dial interface's Properties dialog box, specify the maximum number of redial attempts and the redial interval.

    c. From the Networking tab of the demand-dial interface's Properties dialog box, specify the maximum number of redial attempts and the redial interval.

    d. From the Networking tab of the demand-dial interface's Properties dialog box, click the **Advanced** button. Then, specify the maximum number of redial attempts and the redial interval.

10. You want to configure your RRAS server to forward multicast traffic to groups of computers. In particular, you want to connect a single-router intranet to a multicast-capable intranet or the Internet. What should you do?

    a. Configure the RRAS server's outbound interface for IGMP router mode.

    b. Configure the RRAS server's inbound interface for IGMP router mode.

    c. Configure the RRAS server's outbound interface for IGMP proxy mode.

    d. Configure the server's inbound interface for IGMP proxy mode.

**Foundation Topics**

# The Need for Routing and Routing Tables

Suppose you're at your desk and want to access a website on the far side of the continent. You enter a URL and your browser locates a DNS server that can translate the URL into its corresponding IP address (more about this later in Chapter 5, "Installing and Configuring Domain Name System (DNS)"). But, your network only knows about local IP addresses. However, you've configured your TCP/IP properties with an IP address for the default gateway (or the network DHCP server has supplied this address for you). This address is that of your network router, and it knows that it must send your message onward. But, there's a veritable maze of networks and routers out there. Without some kind of directing authority, your message could bounce around these routers forever. Figure 3-1 gives you an idea of the type of problem each message packet must face in its journey to the destination.

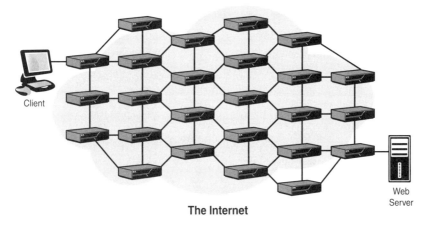

**Figure 3-1**  An Internet message must cross large numbers of routers to reach its destination.

Each of those routers out there needs to know how to get that packet to its far-off destination. And this is where the concept of a *routing table* comes in. Simply put, the routing table is a table of best routes through any network situation from the smallest local network to the worldwide Internet cloud. Each router has its own routing table, which it consults when requested by an incoming packet to determine which router should next be queried to take the packet. And should one router fail to respond to such a request, the routing table provides a route to an alternate router that can continue the message towards its eventual destination. As you can see from Figure 3-1, many such alternate routes can exist. And similar alternate routes can also exist in the LAN or WAN environment associated with most medium-sized or large corporations.

How does the router know where it should send each packet? Complex routing algorithms are built into each router, whether it be a Windows Server 2008 computer running RRAS or a dedicated hardware router made by a company such as Cisco. Such algorithms take many factors into consideration, including the speed, bandwidth, availability, and cost of each link. They look at these factors in real time and note the amount of traffic any given link is carrying at a given time. Routers share this data with other routers so that network traffic can be optimized as conditions change.

When studying how routing functions, be aware of the following terminology:

- **Hop:** This is a step taken by a packet from one router to the next one as it travels across the network. You could compare this to flying from one city to another. A direct flight would be a single hop, but if you need to change planes en route, your flight has two hops, and so on. The total number of hops is often called the hop count.

- **Metric:** A measuring standard, such as a hop count, that is employed by routing algorithms in calculating the best path to the destination.

- **Routing algorithm:** Mappings that the router uses when directing each packet to its destination. You could compare these to mapped highway routes used in a long-distance road trip. On a simple network, administrators can set up static routing algorithms that do not change unless the administrator modifies them. Although these can be used on small LANs, routers on large networks and the Internet make use of dynamic routing algorithms that adjust as conditions change to optimize the routes taken by messages to destinations across the city, country, or the world.

**NOTE**   You can find a comprehensive glossary of definitions for network standards and protocols at http://msdn.microsoft.com/library/ff358762.aspx.

## Routing Protocols

Windows Server 2008 uses Routing Information Protocol (RIP, also sometimes known as Routing Internet Protocol) in exchanging information among routers in an internetwork. The purpose of a routing protocol is to facilitate the capability of routers to automatically adjust network paths according to network conditions such as overuse or failure of a given network connection.

> **NOTE**   Support for the Open Shortest Path First (OSPF) routing protocol, previously used in older versions of Windows Server, has been removed in Windows Server 2008. This link-state protocol built a map of the entire network, which it then loaded into memory and sent to other routers in the form of link-state advertisements. However, OSPF requires additional server resources, such as RAM, to function adequately.

RIP is a distance-vector routing protocol that is simple to configure and deploy on networks of various sizes. In a distance-vector routing protocol, every router communicates the routes it knows about to all neighboring routers to which it is directly connected. These neighboring routers then broadcast the changes to their neighbors, and so on.

Originally defined in 1988 with RFC 1058, RIP version 1 used IP broadcast packets for router announcements. RFCs 1723 and 2453 updated this protocol to version 2 (RIP v2), which is still the version commonly used on Windows Server 2008-based routers. RIP v2 can use either broadcast or multicast packets for its announcements; these packets are sent over UDP port 520. Some of the capabilities of RIP v2 include the following:

- Support for simple password authentication. Defined in RFC 1723, simple password authentication works by using a key that authenticates routing information to the router. This helps prevent unauthorized or misconfigured RIP routers from being introduced to the network. However, the simple password is not secure because it is sent in clear text format that can be read with a protocol analyzer, such as Microsoft Network Monitor. RIP v2 can also use newer authentication methods, such as message digest 5 (MD5).

- Support for multicast announcements and increased flexibility in subnetted networks and those using Classless Interdomain Routing (CIDR). RIP version 1 routers cannot interpret the subnet mask field in the route and can misinterpret variable length subnet masks (subnetting or supernetting as introduced in Chapter 1). Multicast RIP v2 packets use the IP multicast address 224.0.0.9.

- The capability to automatically add and remove routes as peer routers are added and removed from the network. To enable this capability, you must ensure that all routers have RIP v2 enabled to receive all RIP-based route announcements.

- The capability for peer routers to announce and update changes to the routing table whenever the RIP protocol is initialized.

- The use of socket operations to receive RIP packets from neighboring routers.

- Use of a Routing Table Manager (RTM) as a central repository for routing information for all RRAS-based routers. RTM maintains a user-mode routing table that includes all routes from all possible route sources. Information about the IP address of each router is included, helping to prevent packets from being forwarded through excessive routers.

**NOTE**    In this chapter, when RIP is mentioned without qualification, it refers to either RIP v1 or RIP v2.

**CAUTION**    You can use a mixture of RIP v1 and RIP v2 routers on your network. However, if you use a mixture of the two versions, you should not employ multicasting. Remember that RIP v1 routers cannot communicate with RIP v2 routers when the latter are using multicasting for communication of updated routes.

RIP determines the best route for packets based on the shortest number of hops to their destination. This can be disadvantageous if this route includes a slow link; in such a case, sometimes a route with a higher hop count can be faster. It is possible to assign a higher hop count to a slow link so that routers ignore this link and utilize it only in cases where the faster link is unavailable for any reason. If more than one route has the same hop count, RIP performs a round-robin load balance that distributes traffic among the links.

RIP can handle hop counts up to a maximum of 15 hops; if a network is more than 15 hops away, RIP considers it to be unreachable. This can be an advantage or a disadvantage. By limiting the number of hop counts, the possibility of routing loops in which packets circle endlessly between a series of routers is reduced. But, the scaling of RIP to large internetworks is difficult to impossible because of this maximum hop count.

## Routing Table

The routing table is a complete description of all the routes available from any computer, not just a server configured for routing. You can view the routing table by executing the `route print` command from a command prompt. Figure 3-2 shows a typical routing table.

**Figure 3-2**   Typical routing table as displayed by the `route print` command.

Windows Server 2008 and Windows 7 computers display routing tables for both IPv4 and IPv6 routes, assuming that neither of these protocols has been disabled. Table 3-2 describes the more important components of the routing table.

**Table 3-2**   Routing Table Components

| Component | Description |
|---|---|
| Interface list | Contains entries for each network adapter card installed on the computer plus interfaces representing IPv6 to IPv4 transition technologies. The digits displayed for network adapter cards represent each adapter's MAC address. |
| Network destination | Used with the netmask to determine the location to which matching IP packets should be sent. Consider the following:<br><br>■ A destination of 0.0.0.0 represents a default route.<br><br>■ A destination of 127.0.0.0 or 127.0.0.1 represents the loopback interface. You can ignore these lines.<br><br>■ A destination of 224.0.0.0 represents a multicast address.<br><br>■ A destination of 255.255.255.255 represents a broadcast address for all hosts on the same network segment. |

| Component | Description |
|---|---|
| Netmask | The subnet mask that is applied to the destination IP address when matching it to the value in the network destination. Use the following criteria when interpreting this value:<br><br>■ When sent to 0.0.0.0, this specifies the default gateway.<br><br>■ When set to 255.255.255.0, this specifies an interface. You can ignore lines with this value. |
| Gateway | When paired with a netmask of 0.0.0.0, represents the default gateway for this interface as configured in the TCP/IP properties or supplied by DHCP. In general, this represents the IP address of the next hop. "On-link" represent routes that are directly reachable. |
| Interface | The IP address configured on the computer for the local network adapter in use when an IP packet is forwarded on the network. For a multihomed computer, you will see lines with the IP address of each network adapter on the computer. |
| Metric | An indication of the cost of using a route, typically the number of hops to the IP destination. |
| Persistent routes | Represents static routes that have been added to the routing table. More about persistent routes later in this chapter. |

**NOTE**  For more information on the routing table and routing in general, refer to "Chapter 5—IP Routing" at http://technet.microsoft.com/en-us/library/bb727001.aspx. For more information on the IPv6 component of the routing table, refer to "Understanding the IPv6 Routing Table" at http://technet.microsoft.com/en-ca/library/bb878115.aspx and "Using Windows Tools to Obtain IPv6 Configuration Information" at http://technet.microsoft.com/en-us/library/bb726952.aspx.

## Routing and Remote Access Service (RRAS) in Windows Server 2008 R2

As already mentioned, configuring Windows Server 2008 to act as a router uses RRAS, which is configured as a server role. Use the following procedure to install RRAS on a Windows Server 2008 R2 computer:

1. Open Server Manager and expand the Roles node.

2. Click **Add Roles** to start the Add Roles Wizard.

3. From the Select Server Roles page shown in Figure 3-3, select **Network Policy and Access Services** and click **Next**.

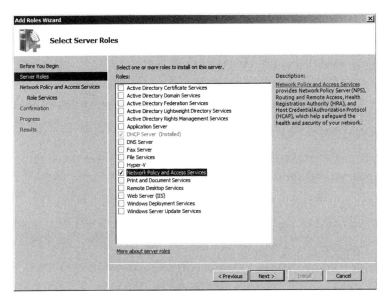

**Figure 3-3**   You must select **Network Policy and Access Services** to install RRAS.

4. You receive the Introduction to Network Policy and Access Services page shown in Figure 3-4. To learn more about Network Access Protection (NAP) and policy services, click the links provided. When you're ready to proceed, click **Next**.

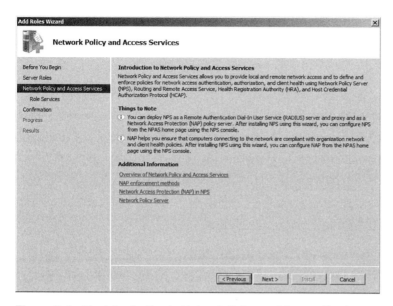

**Figure 3-4**  The Introduction to Network Policy and Access Services page enables you to obtain more information on these services.

5.  On the Select Role Services page, select **Routing and Remote Access Services** (as shown in Figure 3-5) and click **Next**.

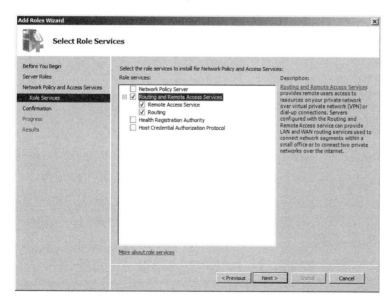

**Figure 3-5**  Selecting the RRAS role service.

6. On the Confirm Installation Selections page, click **Install**.

7. The Installation Progress page tracks the progress of installing RRAS. When informed that the installation is complete, click **Close**.

### Configuring RRAS as a Router

After installing RRAS, the Routing and Remote Access service, which is a Windows service automatically included on all Windows Vista/7/Server 2008 computers, becomes enabled and is configured for automatic start. However, the server is not yet enabled to act as a router. Use the following procedure:

1. Open the RRAS snap-in by clicking **Start** > **Administrative Tools** > **Routing and Remote Access**.

2. Right-click your server and choose **Configure and Enable Routing and Remote Access**. The Routing and Remote Access Server Setup Wizard starts.

3. Click **Next** to bypass the welcome page.

4. By default, the Configuration page indicates that remote access by dial-up or VPN will be configured. To set up routing, click **Custom Configuration** (as shown in Figure 3-6) and click **Next**.

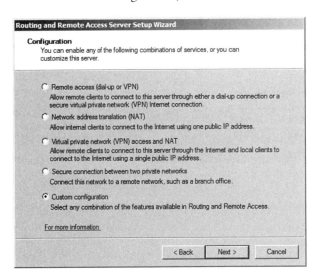

**Figure 3-6**   The Routing and Remote Access Server Setup Wizard provides five options for enabling specific services.

5. The Custom Configuration page provides several options for enabling services. To set up a router, select **LAN routing**, as shown in Figure 3-7. To enable demand-dial routing as described later in this chapter, also select **Demand-dial connections**. Then, click **Next**.

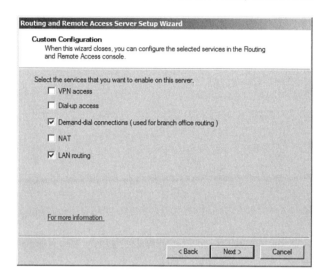

**Figure 3-7**   Configuring your server for LAN routing and demand-dial routing.

6. Click **Finish** to complete setting up your RRAS server.

7. If you receive a message box asking you to start the RRAS service, click **Start Service** and wait while the RRAS service is initialized.

8. The configured services are displayed in the console tree of the RRAS snap-in.

You can modify the routing services configured on your server at any time afterwards. To do so, right-click your server in the console tree of the RRAS snap-in and choose **Properties**. Make the desired changes from the General tab of the server's Properties dialog box as shown in Figure 3-8, and then click **OK**.

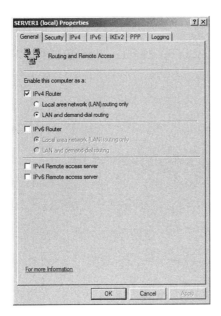

**Figure 3-8**   The General tab of the RRAS server's Properties dialog box enables you to specify which services are enabled on your router.

### Configuring RIP

By enabling RIP, your server can advertise routes to neighboring routers and automatically detect neighboring routers and remote networks. Use the following procedure to enable RIP:

1. In the console tree of the RRAS snap-in, expand either **IPv4** or **IPv6** as required. You see two subnodes: General and Static Routes.

2. Right-click **General** and choose **New Routing Protocol**.

3. In the New Routing Protocol dialog box, select **RIP Version 2 for Internet Protocol** (as shown in Figure 3-9), and click **OK**.

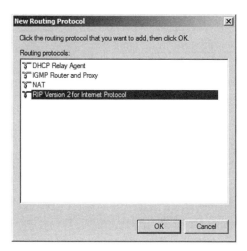

**Figure 3-9**  The New Routing Protocol dialog box enables you to add any of four protocols to your router.

4.  RIP is added as a subnode in the console tree of the RRAS snap-in. Right-click it and choose **New Interface**.

5.  On the New Interface for RIP Version 2 for Internet Protocol dialog box, select the desired interface and then click **OK**.

6.  In the RIP Properties dialog box that appears, configure settings to match those of other routers on the network. In many cases, the default settings will work. This dialog box has the four tabs shown in Figure 3-10 and described in Table 3-3.

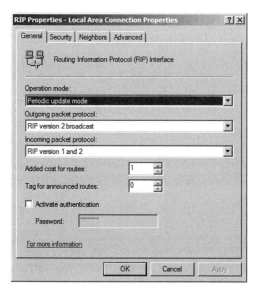

**Figure 3-10**  The RIP Properties dialog box enables you to configure properties related to RIP on your router.

**Table 3-3**   Functions of the RIP Properties Dialog Box

| Tab | Functions |
| --- | --- |
| General | Enables you to provide an added route cost (as explained earlier, this can increase the apparent number of hops used on a slow route) and insert password-based authentication. You can also configure the following:<br><br>■ **Operation mode:** By default, this is periodic update mode. You can also select autostatic update mode, which sends out RIP announcements only when updates are requested by other routers. Note that autostatic update mode is the default for demand-dial interfaces.<br><br>■ **Outgoing packet protocol:** Select the protocol used by packets sent from this router. By default, this is RIP version 2 broadcast. You can also select **RIP version 1 broadcast**, **RIP version 2 multicast**, or **silent RIP**.<br><br>■ **Incoming packet protocol:** Select protocols on incoming packets that this router will send along. By default, the router will process both versions 1 and 2 packets. You can also select either version alone, or choose to ignore incoming packets. |
| Security | Enables you to specify the ranges of IP addresses of incoming routes from which packets will be accepted, as well as the ranges of IP addresses of outgoing routes that will be announced. By default, all incoming packets are accepted and all outgoing routes are announced |
| Neighbors | Enables you to specify how the router interacts with neighboring routers. By default, this is broadcast or multicast only. You can choose to use neighbors in addition to or instead of broadcast or multicast and specify which IP addresses will use neighbors. |
| Advanced | Enables you to configure several additional RIP parameters including the periodic announcement interval (30 seconds by default), the time before routes expire (180 seconds by default), and the time before the route is removed (120 seconds by default). For explanations of these parameters and the other settings available from this tab, click the For more information link at the bottom of this dialog box. |

7. Configure settings for your interface from the options in this dialog box as required. When finished, click **OK**. The new interface is displayed under RIP in the details pane of the RRAS snap-in.

After you add and configure your interface, it is displayed in the details pane of the RIP snap-in. You can modify the settings you configured for the interface by right-clicking it and choosing **Properties**. This displays the same dialog box previously shown in Figure 3-10.

## Configuring Static Routing

In some cases, you might want to add a static route to your Windows Server 2008 router. Doing so ensures that the router knows about a specific network, including the address of the gateway serving as the next hop, and the interface to which it should forward packets being sent to this network. You can use either the RRAS snap-in or the `route` command to create a static route.

### Using the RRAS Snap-In to Create a Static Route

Use the following procedure to create an IPv4 static route:

1. In the console tree of the RRAS snap-in, expand either **IPv4** or **IPv6** as required. You see two subnodes: General and Static Routes.

2. Right-click **Static Routes** and choose **New Static Route**. This displays the IPv4 Static Route dialog box shown in Figure 3-11.

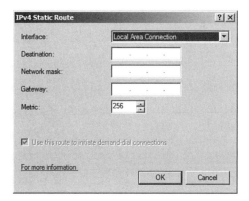

**Figure 3-11**    The IPv4 Static Route dialog box enables you to create a new static route.

3. From the Interface drop-down list, choose the interface to be used in sending packets to the network for which you are creating the route.

4. Specify the IPv4 network address, subnet mask, and default gateway for this network. The gateway is the IPv4 address of the router used for the next hop with forwarded packets; it must be directly accessible from the network being configured.

5. Specify a cost value for this route in the Metric spin list. This value is typically the number of routers between your server and the destination network; however, you can specify a higher metric to reflect factors such as bandwidth and availability.

6. Click **OK**. The new route is displayed in the details pane of the RRAS snap-in.

Configuring a new IPv6 static route is similar. Right-click **Static Routes** under IPv6 and choose **New Static Route**. The required parameters are the same except that a prefix length is specified instead of a subnet mask. Typically, the prefix length is 64; however it can be a lower value when creating a summarized route.

If you need to modify a configured static route, right-click it in the details pane and choose **Properties**. This re-displays the dialog box previously shown in Figure 3-11. Make the required changes and then click **OK**. To delete a static route, right-click it and choose **Delete** (or press the **Delete** key).

### Using the `route` Command to Create a Static Route

You have already learned how to use the `route` command to view the routing table on your computer. You can also use this command to create a static route. Use the following command:

```
route [-p] [-f] add [destination] [MASK netmask] [gateway]
[METRIC metric]
```

The parameters of this command are as described in Table 3-4.

**Table 3-4**   `route` add Parameters

| Parameter | Purpose |
|---|---|
| `-p` | Makes the route persistent. If omitted, the route is nonpersistent and remains in the routing table only until the server is restarted or the interface is deactivated. |
| `-f` | Clears the routing table of all gateway entries. |
| `Add` | Required subcommand that instructs the server to add the specified route. |
| `Destination` | The IP address of the network being specified in the route. |
| `MASK netmask` | Specifies the subnet mask used with the destination address. |
| `Gateway` | Specifies the default gateway or next hop router. |
| `METRIC metric` | Specifies a cost value to be assigned to the route, as described previously. |

For example, to add a persistent route to the 10.0.0.0 network that uses a subnet mask of 255.0.0.0, a gateway of 192.168.11.1, and a cost metric of 3, use the following command:

```
route -p add 10.0.0.0 MASK 255.0.0.0 192.168.11.1 METRIC 3
```

You can also use this command to modify or delete a static route by using the `route change` or `route delete` command.

### Choosing a Default Gateway

You have seen how you can use the `route add` parameter or the IPv4 Static Route dialog box to add an entry to the routing table. It is important to remember that when a network is connected to other networks by means of two or more routers, you can use the path to only one of these routers as the default gateway. Choose a default gateway that routes packets via the fastest, most reliable connection. Remember that this default gateway must be the IP address of the network adapter facing the network on which you are configuring it. If computers are unable to connect to remote subnets, use the `route print` command to check the value of the default gateway, and then add or change this parameter as required.

### Displaying the Static Routing Table

You can display the static routing table from the RRAS snap-in. This differs from the routing table displayed with the `route print` command, in that it does not include dynamic routes added by RIP. Right-click **Static Routes** and choose **Show IP Routing Table** to display this routing table for your server, as shown in Figure 3-12.

| Destination | Network mask | Gateway | Interface | Metric | Protocol |
|---|---|---|---|---|---|
| 0.0.0.0 | 0.0.0.0 | 192.168.0.1 | Local Area Connection | 276 | Network management |
| 127.0.0.0 | 255.0.0.0 | 127.0.0.1 | Loopback | 51 | Local |
| 127.0.0.1 | 255.255.255.255 | 127.0.0.1 | Loopback | 306 | Local |
| 192.168.0.0 | 255.255.255.0 | 0.0.0.0 | Local Area Connection | 276 | Network management |
| 192.168.0.100 | 255.255.255.255 | 0.0.0.0 | Local Area Connection | 276 | Network management |
| 192.168.0.255 | 255.255.255.255 | 0.0.0.0 | Local Area Connection | 276 | Network management |
| 224.0.0.0 | 240.0.0.0 | 0.0.0.0 | Local Area Connection | 276 | Network management |
| 255.255.255.255 | 255.255.255.255 | 0.0.0.0 | Local Area Connection | 276 | Network management |

**Figure 3-12**   Displaying the static routing table.

In this table, note that a network mask of 0.0.0.0 means that any destination can use this route. A network mask of 255.255.255.255 means that only an exact match of the destination network number can use the route. The destination of 224.0.0.0 and mask of 240.0.0.0 is used for multicast packets.

**NOTE**   For more information on planning and using static routes, refer to "Static Routing" at http://technet.microsoft.com/en-ca/library/dd469762(WS.10).aspx.

# Managing and Maintaining Routing Servers

Additional tasks involved in managing and maintaining routing servers that you should be aware of for the 70-642 exam include configuring demand-dial routing, specifying packet filtering, and configuring an Internet Group Management Protocol (IGMP) proxy.

> **NOTE**   You can configure most of the router options discussed in this chapter from the command line by using the `netsh routing ip` command context. For information on this command and its large list of subcommands, refer to "Netsh Routing IP Context Commands" at http://technet.microsoft.com/en-us/library/cc730801(WS.10).aspx.

### Demand-Dial Routing

RRAS in Windows Server 2008 enables you to create demand-dial interfaces. This is a logical interface representing a point-to-point connection, either a physical connection such as two routers connected with an analog phone line, or a logical connection such as two routers using a VPN connection. It typically requires an authentication process when connection is being established. Two types of demand-dial connections are available:

- **On-demand connection:** A point-to-point connection that is only established when required. This connection is terminated when not in use, thereby providing cost savings.

- **Persistent connection:** Once established, this connection remains in a connected state. This connection remains open when not in use.

### Establishing a Demand-Dial Interface

Use the following procedure to set up a demand-dial interface:

1. In the console tree of the RRAS snap-in, expand your server (if necessary), right-click **Network Interfaces**, and then choose **New Demand-Dial Interface**.

2. This starts the Demand-Dial Interface Wizard with a welcome page. Click **Next**.

3. On the Interface Name page, type a name for the interface and click **Next**.

4. On the Connection Type page, make a choice from the following three connection types:

   - **Connect using a modem, ISDN adapter, or other device** (available only if the appropriate hardware is installed on the server)

   - **Connect using virtual private networking (VPN)**

   - **Connect using PPP over Ethernet (PPPoE)**

5. If you select the **VPN** option, choose the protocol to be used from **Point-to-Point Tunneling Protocol (PPTP)**, **Layer 2 Tunneling Protocol (L2TP)**, or **Automatic protocol selection**. If you select **PPP over Ethernet**, type the name of the service providing the broadband connection. Then, click **Next**.

6. On the Destination Address page, type the host name or IP address of the router to which you're connecting and click **Next**.

7. The Protocols and Security page shown in Figure 3-13 provides four choices of transport and security options. The available choices depend on the connection type. Select appropriate option(s) and click **Next**.

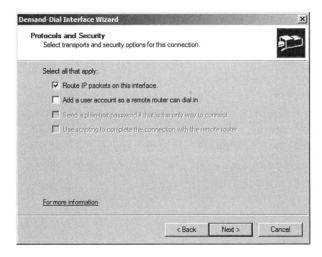

**Figure 3-13**   The Protocols and Security page of the Demand-Dial Interface Wizard provides transport and security options.

8. The Static Routes for Remote Networks page enables you to add persistent routes. Click **Add** to display the Static Route dialog box, as shown in Figure 3-14. Supply the required information for an IPv4 or IPv6 remote network as required, click **OK**, and then click **Next**.

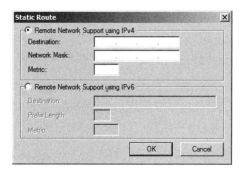

**Figure 3-14**   Supplying remote network information.

9. On the Dial-Out Credentials page, specify the username, password, and do-main name to be used for connecting to the remote router, and then click **Next**. Note that these credentials must match those specified for dial-in at the remote router.

10. Click **Finish**. The demand-dial interface is created and displayed in the details pane of the RRAS snap-in.

> **TIP**   Demand-dial routing connections as described here can be either one-way or two-way. A one-way connection can be initiated from only one end, while a two-way connection can be initiated from either end. To configure a two-way connection, set up a demand-dial interface on each RRAS server using the procedure discussed in this section. The user account used for authenticating the connection must be config-ured on each server, and its username must be identical to the name assigned at the demand-dial interface of the calling router. In addition, a static route must be config-ured at each interface as previously shown in Figure 3-14.

## Configuring Demand-Dial Interface Properties

Right-click the demand-dial interface from the details pane of the RRAS snap-in and choose **Properties** to bring up the Properties dialog box, which enables you to configure the following properties:

- **General tab:** Enables you to modify the host name or IP address of the desti-nation router.

- **Options tab:** Enables you to specify either a demand-dial or persistent con-nection type, as already discussed. If you select the **Demand-Dial** option, you can specify the idle time that must elapse before hanging up as well as a dialing policy that indicates the number of redial attempts and the average redial intervals in case the destination router does not answer.

- **Security tab:** As shown in Figure 3-15, you can specify several security-related parameters, including encryption, authentication, and the protocols used to authenticate the connection. VPN authentication protocols are discussed in Chapter 14.

- **Networking tab:** Enables you to specify the types of networking protocols used with the connection. The available items are similar to those available for local area networking properties and discussed in Chapters 1 and 2.

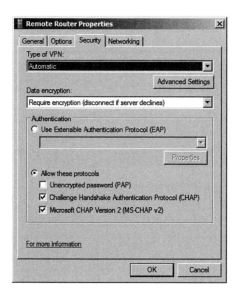

**Figure 3-15**    The Security tab of the demand-dial interface's Properties dialog box enables you to specify parameters such as encryption and authentication for the demand-dial connection.

### Specifying Packet Filtering

IP packet filtering enables you to specify the types of traffic that can use the connections specified on the router. The filter enables you to specify the ports and protocols that are allowed or denied passage across the router. Use the following procedure to add a packet filter:

1. Expand the entries in the console tree of the RRAS snap-in to reveal the interfaces that you've configured under IPv4 or IPv6.

2. Right-click the desired interface and choose **Properties**.

3. On the General tab of the interface's Properties dialog box shown in Figure 3-
   16, click either **Inbound Filters** or **Outbound Filters** as required.

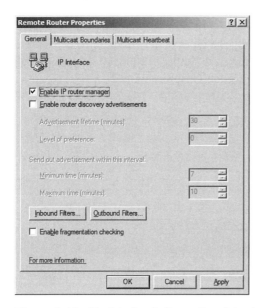

**Figure 3-16**   The interface's Properties dialog box enables you to configure packet filtering and
several other properties.

4. In the Inbound Filters or Outbound Filters dialog box, click **New**.

5. In the Add IP Filter dialog box, specify the source and/or destination networks
   and protocol option (as shown in Figure 3-17), and then click **OK**.

**Figure 3-17**    Configuring packet filter options.

6. Select the appropriate filter action that matches the criteria you added. (You can choose either **Receive all packets except those that meet the criteria below** or **Drop all packets except those that meet the criteria below**.)

7. To add additional filters, click **New** again and repeat Steps 5 and 6 as required. When finished, click **OK**. Repeat Steps 3 to 6 if needed to configure filters for the opposite direction.

**NOTE**    For more information on demand-dial routing, refer to "What is Demand-Dial Routing?" at http://technet.microsoft.com/en-us/library/dd458986(WS.10).aspx and "How Demand-Dial Routing Works" at http://technet.microsoft.com/en-us/library/cc781790(WS.10).aspx. For more information on packet filtering, refer to "Packet Filtering" at http://technet.microsoft.com/en-us/library/cc732746(WS.10).aspx.

### IGMP Proxy

As already mentioned, you can use a RRAS server to forward multicast traffic to groups of computers. In doing so, RRAS uses IGMP as an IP routing protocol component. IP multicasting operates by sending messages to a group that is identified by an IP multicast address in the class D range such as the 224.0.0.9 destination mentioned earlier in this chapter. Destination hosts inform a local router to join the group.

When the network is enabled for IP multicasting, any host can send multicast messages to any group address, and any host in the group can receive messages from any group address regardless of its location. Hosts use IGMP to establish group membership, and routers use multicasting protocols to forward messages.

You can configure router interfaces to use either of two operating modes:

- **IGMP router mode:** Forwards multicast traffic in a single-router intranet. When supporting IPv4 multicast applications or connecting this intranet to the Internet, you would configure the RRAS server's outbound interface for IGMP router mode.

- **IGMP proxy mode:** Connects a single-router intranet to a multicast-capable intranet or the Internet. In cases described here, you would configure the server's inbound interface for IGMP proxy mode.

Use the following procedure to add IGMP to the router and enable IGMP proxy mode:

1. In the console tree of the RRAS snap-in, right-click **General** under either IPv4 or IPv6 as required and choose **New Routing Protocol**.

2. You see the New Routing Protocol dialog box, previously shown in Figure 3-9. Select **IGMP Router and Proxy** and click **OK**.

3. IGMP is added to the list of items under IPv4 or IPv6. Right-click it and choose **New Interface**.

4. From the New Interface for IGMP Router and Proxy dialog box, select the interface on which you want to run this protocol and then click **OK**.

5. You receive the IGMP Properties dialog box. If configuring an IGMP Router, leave the default option selected and choose the desired IGMP protocol version. To configure your router as an IGMP proxy, select the **IGMP proxy** option as shown in Figure 3-18. The Router tab of this dialog box contains additional options applicable only when **IGMP Router** is selected. Click **OK** when finished.

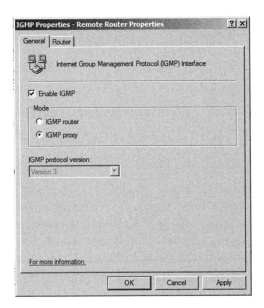

**Figure 3-18**    Specifying IGMP proxy.

**NOTE**    For more information on the use of IGMP in a routing context, refer to "Internet Group Management Protocol" at http://technet.microsoft.com/en-us/library/dd458978(WS.10).aspx and "RRAS IGMP" at http://technet.microsoft.com/en-us/library/cc733679(WS.10).aspx.

## Exam Preparation Tasks

## Review All the Key Topics

Review the most important topics in this chapter, noted with the key topics icon in the outer margin of the page. Table 3-5 lists a reference of these key topics and the page numbers on which each is found.

**Table 3-5**   Key Topics for Chapter 3

| Key Topic Element | Description | Page Number |
|---|---|---|
| List | Describes important terms related to IP routing. | 133 |
| Paragraph | Describes the RIP routing protocol and discusses the advantages of RIP v2. | 134 |
| Table 3-2 | Describes the components of a Windows routing table. | 136 |
| List | Shows you how to install a RRAS server. | 138 |
| Figure 3-7 | Configuring your RRAS server as a router. | 141 |
| Figure 3-9 | Adding routing protocols to your RRAS server. | 143 |
| Figure 3-10 | Configuring RIP routing properties. | 143 |
| Figure 3-11 | Shows how to configure a static route. | 145 |
| List | Shows how to set up a demand-dial interface. | 148 |
| List | Shows how to specify packet filtering. | 152 |

## Complete the Tables and Lists from Memory

Print a copy of Appendix B, "Memory Tables," (found on the CD), or at least the section for this chapter, and complete the tables and lists from memory. Appendix C, "Memory Tables Answer Key," also on the CD, includes the completed tables and lists to check your work.

## Definition of Key Terms

Define the following key terms from this chapter, and check your answers in the Glossary.

demand-dial interface, dynamic route, hop, IGMP proxy, metric, packet filter, persistent route, router, routing algorithm, Routing Information Protocol (RIP), routing table, static route

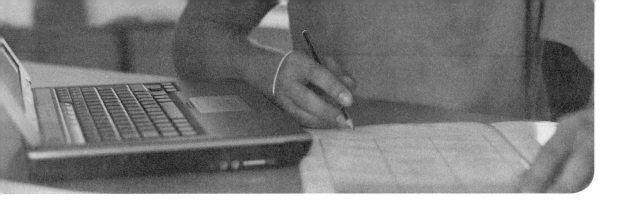

This chapter covers the following subjects:

- **Configuring Windows Firewall:** All Windows computers come with an easily configurable firewall tool that can block undesired communications, including those that attempt to install malicious software. This section shows you how to configure the most important options that come with Windows Firewall.

- **Using the Windows Firewall with Advanced Security Snap-In:** This section builds upon the first section by showing you how to configure the various types of security rules available with the Windows Firewall with Advanced Security snap-in. It then shows you how to use Group Policy so that these rules can apply to all computers to which the policy applies.

- **Using IPSec to Secure Network Communications:** IPSec can create a secure, authenticated, encrypted communications channel that protects network traffic either locally or across the Internet. This section shows you how to configure IPSec to apply locally or across the domain.

# CHAPTER 4

# Configuring Windows Firewall with Advanced Security

The Internet is truly a 21st century version of the Wild West out there. All sorts of villains lurk behind seemingly innocuous web pages, looking to steal your money and identity. They want to install their various malicious software programs, such as adware, spyware, rootkits, Trojan horses, worms, and other nasty bits of malware. Companies have used hardware devices called firewalls for many years that block undesired network communications from accessing their networks and servers. Starting with Windows Server 2003 and Windows XP prior to SP2, Microsoft introduced a software firewall known as the Internet Connection Firewall. This was upgraded and renamed Windows Firewall in Windows XP SP2. Microsoft has further improved and refined Windows Firewall in the original and R2 versions of Windows Server 2008, with parallel improvements being added to Windows Vista and 7. This version of Windows Firewall was the first to block both incoming and outgoing traffic unless specifically configured to pass. Included was the blocking of actions by malicious programs such as Trojan Horses that attempt to send data to an unauthorized location.

Internet Protocol Security (IPSec) was designed by the Internet Engineering Task Force (IETF) as a series of open standards for using cryptographic security features for providing end-to-end protection of IP network communications. Working at the Network layer of the OSI model, IPSec provides application-transparent encryption services for traffic crossing an IP network between servers and clients, as well as remote access traffic on virtual private networks (VPN) using the Layer 2 Transport Protocol (L2TP). Microsoft designed IPSec and Windows Firewall to work together with IPSec providing complex static filtering based on IP addresses and Windows Firewall providing stateful filtering for all addresses across network interfaces.

## "Do I Know This Already?" Quiz

The "Do I Know This Already?" quiz allows you to assess whether you should read this entire chapter or simply jump to the "Exam Preparation Tasks" section for review. If you are in doubt, read the entire chapter. Table 4-1 outlines the major headings in this chapter and the corresponding "Do I Know This

Already?" quiz questions. You can find the answers in Appendix A, "Answers to the 'Do I Know This Already?' Quizzes."

**Table 4-1**    "Do I Know This Already?" Foundation Topics Section-to-Question Mapping

| Foundations Topics Section | Questions Covered in This Section |
| --- | --- |
| Configuring Windows Firewall | 1–2 |
| Using the Windows Firewall with Advanced Security Snap-In | 3–6 |
| Using IPSec to Secure Network Communications | 7–12 |

1.  Your company's web server, which is located on a perimeter network but is a member of the Active Directory Domain Services (AD DS) domain, has been hacked and all pages replaced by messages of an undesirable nature. You want to temporarily prevent outsiders from accessing this server while you restore the proper pages and check the server for malicious software. What should you do?

    a.  In Window Firewall, select the **Turn off Windows Firewall** option under the Home or Work (Private) Network Location Settings section of the Customize Settings dialog box.

    b.  In Window Firewall, select the **Block all incoming connections, including those in the list of allowed programs** option, under the Home or Work (Private) Network Location Settings section of the Customize Settings dialog box.

    c.  In Window Firewall, select the **Turn off Windows Firewall** option under the Public network location settings section of the Customize Settings dialog box.

    d.  In Window Firewall, select the **Block all incoming connections, including those in the list of allowed programs** option, under the Public network location settings section of the Customize Settings dialog box.

2.  Which of the following actions can you perform from the Windows Firewall Control Panel applet on your Windows Server 2008 R2 computer? (Choose three.)

    a.  Specify ports that are allowed to communicate across the Windows Firewall.

    b.  Specify programs that are allowed to communicate across the Windows Firewall.

   **c.** Set the firewall to block all incoming connections, including those in the list of allowed programs.

   **d.** Configure logging settings for programs that are blocked by the firewall.

   **e.** Specify a series of firewall settings according to the type of network to which you are connected.

**3.** You open the Windows Firewall with Advanced Security snap-in and notice that a large number of firewall rules have already been preconfigured. Which of the following rule settings types does *not* include any preconfigured firewall rules?

   **a.** Inbound rules

   **b.** Outbound rules

   **c.** Connection security rules

   **d.** Monitoring rules

**4.** Which of the following profiles are available for configuration from the Windows Firewall with Advanced Security snap-in? (Choose three.)

   **a.** User

   **b.** Computer

   **c.** Private

   **d.** Domain

   **e.** Public

**5.** You are using the New Rule Wizard to create an incoming rule in the Windows Firewall with Advanced Security snap-in. You want to ensure that authentication, integrity, and privacy are all enabled on communications permitted by this rule. What should you do?

   **a.** From the Action page of the wizard, select the **Allow the connection if it is secure** option. Then, select the **Require the connections to be encrypted** option on the Customize Allow if Secure Settings dialog box that appears.

   **b.** From the Action page of the wizard, select the **Allow the connection if it is secure** option. Then, select the **Allow the connection if it is authenticated and integrity-protected** option on the Customize Allow if Secure Settings dialog box that appears.

   **c.** From the Action page of the wizard, select the **Allow the connection** option. Then, select the **Require the connections to be encrypted** option on the Customize Allow if Secure Settings dialog box that appears.

   **d.** From the Rule Type page of the wizard, select the **Authentication exemption** option. Then, select the **Allow the connection if it is authenticated and integrity-protected** option on the Customize Allow if Secure Settings dialog box that appears.

6. You are in charge of configuring Windows Firewall with Advanced Security on a Windows Server 2008 R2 computer on which confidential research files are stored. You are using the New Rule Wizard to create an inbound rule that is designed to allow members of the Research global security group in your company's AD DS domain to access this server. How should you proceed?

   **a.** From the Action page of the wizard, select the **Allow the connection if it is secure** option. Then, from the Users page of the wizard that appears, select **Only allow connections from these users** and add the Research group.

   **b.** From the Action page of the wizard, select the **Allow the connection if it is secure** option. Then, from the Users page of the wizard that appears, select **Skip this rule for connections from these users** and add the Research group.

   **c.** From the Action page of the wizard, select the **Allow the connection** option and complete the rest of the steps in the wizard. Then, in the details pane of the Windows Firewall with Advanced Security snap-in, right-click the new rule and choose **Properties**. Then, from the Users tab of the dialog box that appears, select **Only allow connections from these users** and add the Research group.

   **d.** From the Action page of the wizard, select the **Allow the connection** option and complete the rest of the steps in the wizard. Then, in the details pane of the Windows Firewall with Advanced Security snap-in, right-click the new rule and choose **Properties**. Then, from the Users tab of the dialog box that appears, select **Skip this rule for connections from these users** and add the Research group.

7. You configured a new inbound rule that limits connections by a specific application on your computer to only those connections that have been authenticated using IPSec. The next day, when you start your application, you realize that you should have configured this rule as an outbound rule. What should you do to correct this error with the least amount of effort?

   **a.** Access the Scope tab of the Properties dialog box for your rule and change the scope from Inbound to Outbound.

   **b.** Access the Advanced tab of the Properties dialog box for your rule and change the interface type from Inbound to Outbound.

   **c.** Select the rule from the list of inbound rules in the details pane of Windows Firewall with Advanced Security and drag the rule to the Outbound Rules node in the console tree.

   **d.** You must deactivate or delete the inbound rule you configured and then use the New Outbound Rule Wizard to set up a new rule that is specific to your application.

**8.** You are planning the use of IPSec to secure network traffic on a link that must use the Internet to communicate with your company's branch offices. Which mode of IPSec should you use to ensure the confidentiality and integrity of data?

   **a.** AH tunnel mode

   **b.** AH transport mode

   **c.** ESP tunnel mode

   **d.** ESP transport mode

**9.** You are planning the use of IPSec to secure communications between servers and client computers within your company's AD DS domain. Servers run a mix of Windows Server 2003 R2 and Windows Server 2008 R2, and client computers run a mix of Windows XP Professional and Windows 7 Professional. You must ensure that the highest level of security is provided by the encryption algorithm while enabling all computers on the network to communicate with IPSec. Which of the following encryption algorithms should you use?

   **a.** DES

   **b.** 3DES

   **c.** AES

   **d.** ESP

**10.** You are using Group Policy to create a policy designed to enforce IPSec communications between users and computers throughout your company's AD DS forest, which consists of a forest root domain and three child domains. Which authentication protocol should you select?

   **a.** Kerberos v5

   **b.** Certificates

   **c.** Preshared key

   **d.** IKE

**11.** You are responsible for maintaining your company's network, including security of network transmissions. Computers on the network run Windows 7 or
Windows Server 2008 R2. You have implemented policies requiring IPSec-
secured transmissions. However, while troubleshooting possible network connectivity problems, a junior desktop support technician informs you that when
he attempts to ping computers on the network, he always receives the `Request
timed out` message. Even when he pings between two computers that he
knows are able to communicate, he still receives this message. What should
you do to enable the desktop support technician to use the `ping` tool properly?

    **a.** Use Group Policy to apply the Client (Respond Only) policy setting to
domain computers.

    **b.** Use Group Policy to create a new connection security rule that includes
an authorization exemption.

    **c.** Configure an IPSec tunnel authorization.

    **d.** Configure an IPSec exemption.

**12.** Your network, which is configured as an AD DS domain, has a Windows
Server 2008 R2 member server that you want to ensure accepts only authenticated and secured communications from other domain computers. What
policy setting should you configure?

    **a.** Domain isolation

    **b.** Server isolation

    **c.** IPSec tunnel authorization

    **d.** IPSec exemptions

## Foundation Topics

## Configuring Windows Firewall

Windows Firewall is a stateful host-based firewall that you can configure to allow or block specific network traffic. It includes a packet filter that uses an access control list (ACL) specifying parameters (such as IP address, port number, and protocol) that are allowed to pass through. When a user communicates with an external computer, the stateful firewall remembers this conversation and allows the appropriate reply packets to reach the user. Packets from an outside computer that attempts to communicate with a computer on which a stateful firewall is running are dropped unless the ACL contains rules permitting them. Using Windows Firewall reduces the chance that an attacker will compromise your server, resulting in actions such as crashing your computer, modifying or deleting data, copying unwanted files or information to your computer, creating user accounts with elevated privileges, and using these accounts to access other computers or devices on your network.

The original version of Windows Server 2008 introduced considerable improvements to its original implementation in Windows Server 2003 SP1, including outbound traffic protection, support for IPSec and IP version 6 (IPv6), improved configuration of exceptions, and support for command-line configuration. In Windows Server 2008 R2, Microsoft has improved Windows Firewall even further. The following are some of the important new features in the Windows Server 2008 R2 implementation (which are shared with all editions of Windows 7):

- Support for multiple active profiles. If your computer is connected to more than one network, you can have each network adapter assigned to a different profile (public, private, or domain).

- Additional rules are available from the Windows Firewall with Advanced Security tool, including more specific disabling of its features.

- The ability to selectively disable features that might be in conflict with components of a third-party firewall.

- You can use Windows Firewall with Advanced Security to specify port numbers or protocols in connection security rules, as well as ranges of port numbers. In previous versions of Windows Firewall, you had to use the `netsh` command-line tool to perform this action.

- Creation of IPSec connection security rules has been simplified with the use of dynamic encryption.

■ When securing tunnel-mode connections, you can specify the authorized users and computers that can set up an inbound tunnel to an IPSec gateway server.

■ You can exempt DHCP traffic from IPSec requirements.

■ You can specify that an outbound Allow rule can override block rules when secured with an IPSec connection security rule.

■ Additional options have been added for configuring authentication for an IP-Sec tunnel-mode rule.

■ A new main mode configuration capability includes additional configuration options for specific origin and destination IP addresses or network location protocols. Network connections matching a main mode rule use these settings rather than the global defaults or those specified in connection security rules.

Windows Firewall enables you to specify multiple profiles, each of which is a series of firewall settings customized according to the environment in which the computer is located. The following firewall profiles are available:

■ **Domain Profile:** Specifies firewall settings for use when connected directly to an AD DS domain; more specifically, this profile is applied when a computer is able to access a domain controller in its domain. If the network is protected from unauthorized external access, you can specify additional exceptions that facilitate communication across the LAN to network servers and client computers.

■ **Private Profile:** Specifies firewall settings for use when connected to a private network location, such as a home or small office. You can open up connections to network computers and lock down external communications as required. Settings in this profile should be more restrictive than those in the domain profile.

■ **Public Profile:** Specifies firewall settings for use when connected to an insecure public network, such as a Wi-Fi access point at a hotel, restaurant, airport, or other location where unknown individuals might attempt to connect to your computer. This profile should contain the most restrictive settings of all three profiles. By default, network discovery and file and printer sharing are turned off, inbound connections are blocked, and outbound connections are allowed. Although mentioned for completeness purposes, it is extremely unlikely that you would ever use this profile on a server computer.

You can perform basic configuration of Windows Firewall from a Control Panel applet; you can also perform more advanced configuration of Windows Firewall, including the use of security policies from a Microsoft Management Console (MMC) snap-in. We look at each of these in turn.

## Basic Windows Firewall Configuration

The Windows Firewall Control Panel applet, found in the System and Security category (see Figure 4-1), enables you to set up firewall rules for each of the same network types introduced earlier in this chapter for configuring network settings.

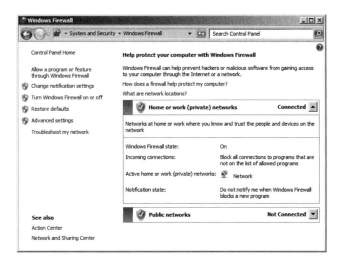

**Figure 4-1**   The Windows Firewall Control Panel applet enables you to configure basic firewall settings for different network locations.

**NOTE**   If your computer is joined to an Active Directory Domain Services (AD DS) domain, an additional location is added in Figure 4-1, called Domain Networks. Settings in this location are configured through domain-based Group Policy and cannot be modified in this location.

You can enable or disable the Windows Firewall separately for each connection. In doing so, you are able to use Windows Firewall to protect a computer connected to the Internet via one adapter, and not use Windows Firewall for the adapter connected to the private network. Use the following instructions to perform basic firewall configuration:

1. Open the Windows Firewall applet by using any of the following methods:

   - Click **Start > Control Panel > System and Security > Windows Firewall**.

   - Click **Start** and type `firewall` in the Search field. From the list of programs displayed under Control Panel, click **Windows Firewall**.

■ Click **Start**, right-click **Network**, and then click **Properties**. Select **Windows Firewall** from the bottom-left corner of the Network and Sharing Center.

2. From the left pane, select **Turn Windows Firewall on or off**. If you receive a User Account Control (UAC) prompt, click **Continue**. This displays the Customize settings for each type of network page shown in Figure 4-2.

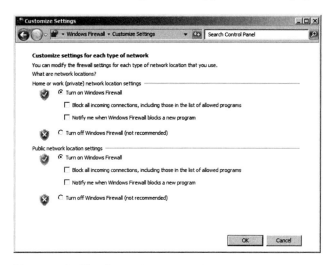

**Figure 4-2**   The Customize settings for each type of network dialog box enables you to turn the firewall on or off and to block incoming connections.

3. If you are connected to a corporate network with a comprehensive hardware firewall, you might need to select **Turn off Windows Firewall (not recommended)** under the Home or Work (Private) Network Location Settings section. This is true because some hardware firewalls might conflict with Windows Firewall or turn it off automatically. However, from a defense-in-depth perspective, it's best to keep both enabled if at all possible.

**NOTE**   If you connect at any time to an insecure network, such as an airport or restaurant Wi-Fi hot spot, select the **Block all incoming connections, including those in the list of allowed programs** option under Public network location settings. This option disables all exceptions you've configured on the Exceptions tab.

**WARNING**   Don't disable the firewall unless absolutely necessary, even on the Home or Work (Private) Network Location Settings section. Never select the **Turn off Windows Firewall** option in Figure 4-2 unless you're absolutely certain that your network is well protected with a good firewall. The only exception should be temporarily to troubleshoot a connectivity problem; after you solve the problem, be sure to immediately re-enable the firewall.

4. To configure program exceptions, return to the Windows Firewall applet and click **Allow a program or feature through Windows Firewall**.

5. From the list shown in Figure 4-3, select the programs or ports you want to have access to your computer on either of the Home or Work (Private) or Public profiles. Table 4-2 describes the more important items in this list. Clear the check boxes next to any programs or ports to be denied access, or select the check boxes next to programs or ports to be granted access.

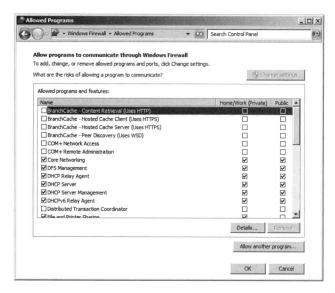

**Figure 4-3**   The Allow programs to communicate through Windows Firewall page enables you to specify which programs are allowed to communicate through the firewall.

**Table 4-2**   Windows Firewall Configurable Exceptions

| Exception | Description | Enabled by Default? |
|---|---|---|
| Core Networking | Enables your computer to connect to other network computers or the Internet | Yes |
| DFS Management | Enables you to manage Distributed File System (DFS) shares on a file server | Yes |
| DHCP Relay Agent, DHCP Server, DHCP Server Management, and DHCPv6 Relay Agent | Enables your computer to act as a DHCP server and relay agent; also enables you to manage your DHCP server remotely | Yes |
| Distributed Transaction Coordinator | Coordinates the update of transaction-protected resources, such as databases, message queues, and file systems | No |
| File and Printer Sharing | Enables your computer to share resources such as files and printers with other computers on your network | Yes (not on public networks) |
| iSCSI Service | Used for connecting to iSCSI target servers and devices | No |
| Key Management Service | Used for machine counting and license compliance in enterprise environments | No |
| Netlogon Service | Maintains a secure channel between domain clients and a domain controller for authenticating users and services | Only on a computer joined to an Active Directory domain |
| Network Discovery | Allows computers to locate other resources on the local network | Yes, for home or work only |
| Performance Logs and Alerts | Allows remote management of the Performance Logs and Alerts service | No |
| Remote Administration | Enables an administrator to connect with and administer a remote server | No |
| Remote Desktop | Enables a user to connect with and work on a remote computer | No |
| Remote (*Item*) Management | Enables an administrator to manage items on a remote computer, including event logs, scheduled tasks, services, and disk volumes | No for all these tasks |

| Exception | Description | Enabled by Default? |
|---|---|---|
| Routing and Remote Access (RRAS) | Enables remote users to connect to a server to access the corporate network (used on RRAS server computers only) | Yes |
| Windows Remote Management | Enables you to manage a remote Windows computer | No |

6. To add a program not shown in the list, click **Allow another program**. From the Add a Program dialog box shown in Figure 4-4, select the program to be added, and then click **Add**. If necessary, click **Browse** to locate the desired program. You can also click **Network location types** to choose which network type is allowed by the selected program.

**Figure 4-4**   The Add a Program dialog box enables you to allow specific programs access through the Windows Firewall.

7. In the Allow programs to communicate through Windows Firewall dialog box (refer to Figure 4-3), to view properties of any program or port on the list, select it and click **Details**.

8. To remove a program from the list, select it and click **Remove**. You can do this only for programs you have added using Step 6.

9. If you need to restore default settings, return to the Windows Firewall applet previously shown in Figure 4-1 and click **Restore defaults**. Then, confirm your intention in the Restore Default Settings dialog box that appears.

10. If you are experiencing networking problems, click **Troubleshoot my network** to access a network troubleshooter window.

11. When you finish, click **OK**.

**TIP** When allowing additional programs to communicate through the Windows Firewall, by default, these programs are allowed to communicate through the Home/Work network profile only. You should retain this default, unless you need a program to communicate through the Internet from a public location, which is sometimes true for a client computer but almost never the case for a server.

## Using the Windows Firewall with Advanced Security Snap-In

Enhanced in Windows Server 2008 R2 over the version introduced in the initial edition of Windows Server 2008, the Windows Firewall with Advanced Security snap-in enables you to perform a comprehensive set of configuration actions. You can configure rules that affect inbound and outbound communication and you can configure connection security rules and the monitoring of firewall actions. Inbound rules help prevent actions such as unknown access or configuration of your computer, installation of undesired software, and so on. Outbound rules help prevent utilities on your computer performing certain actions, such as accessing network resources or software without your knowledge. They can also help prevent other users of your computer from downloading software or inappropriate files without your knowledge.

When you install a server role, role service, or feature that uses incoming or outgoing connections, Windows Server 2008 automatically configures the appropriate firewall rules. For example, Figure 4-3 shows DHCP firewall rules that were automatically added to Windows Firewall when this role was installed, thereby enabling the DHCP server to function properly on the network. However, third-party applications that you install on your server might not necessarily create the firewall rules needed for proper communication on the network. In this case, you need to use the Windows Firewall with Advanced Security snap-in to create the required rules.

To access this snap-in, type `firewall` in the Search field of the Start menu, and then select **Windows Firewall with Advanced Security** from the Programs list. You can also click **Advanced settings** from the task list in the Windows Firewall applet. After accepting the UAC prompt (if you receive one), you receive the snap-in shown in Figure 4-5.

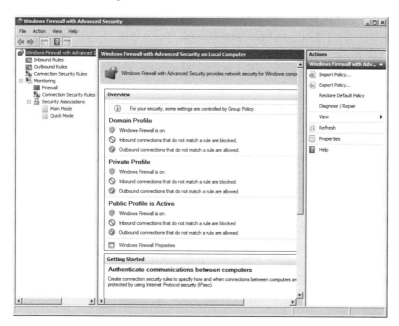

**Figure 4-5**   The Windows Firewall with Advanced Security snap-in enables you to configure firewall settings for each of the domain, private, and public firewall profiles.

When the snap-in first opens, it displays a summary of configured firewall settings. From the left pane, you can configure any of the following types of properties:

- **Inbound Rules:** Displays a series of defined inbound rules. Enabled rules are shown with a green check mark icon. If the icon is dark in appearance, the rule is not enabled. To enable a rule, right-click it and select **Enable Rule**; to disable an enabled rule, right-click it and select **Disable Rule**. You can also create a new rule by right-clicking **Inbound Rules** and selecting **New Rule**. We discuss creation of new rules later in this section.

- **Outbound Rules:** Displays a series of defined outbound rules, also with a green check mark icon for enabled rules. You can enable or disable rules, and create new rules in the same manner as with inbound rules.

- ■ **Connection Security Rules:** By default, this branch does not contain any rules. Right-click it and choose **New Rule** to create rules that are used to determine limits applied to connections with remote computers.

- ■ **Monitoring:** Displays a summary of enabled firewall settings and provides links to active rules and security associations. This includes a domain profile for computers that are members of an AD DS domain. The following three links are available from the bottom of the details pane:

  - ■ **Firewall:** Displays enabled inbound and outbound rules.

  - ■ **Connection Security Rules:** Displays enabled connection security rules that you have created.

  - ■ **Security Associations:** Displays IPSec main mode and quick mode associations.

**NOTE**   For additional information on all aspects of using the Windows Firewall with Advanced Security snap-in, refer to "Windows Firewall with Advanced Security Getting Started Guide" at http://technet.microsoft.com/en-us/library/cc748991(WS.10).aspx and "What's New in Windows Firewall with Advanced Security" at http://technet.microsoft.com/en-us/library/cc755158(WS.10).aspx.

### Configuring Multiple Firewall Profiles

A *profile* is simply a means of grouping firewall rules so that they apply to the affected computers dependent on where the computer is connected. The Windows Firewall with Advanced Security snap-in enables you to define different firewall behavior for each of the domain, private, and public profiles introduced earlier in this chapter.

To configure settings for these profiles from the Windows Firewall with Advanced Security snap-in, right-click **Windows Firewall with Advanced Security** at the top left corner and choose **Properties**. This opens the dialog box shown in Figure 4-6.

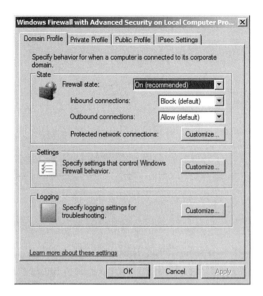

**Figure 4-6**   The Windows Firewall with Advanced Security on Local Computer Properties dialog box enables you to configure several properties that are specific for domain, private, and public profiles.

You can configure the following properties for each of the three profiles individually from this dialog box:

- **State:** Enables you to turn the firewall on or off for the selected profile and block or allow inbound and outbound connections. For inbound connections, you can either block connections with the configured exceptions or block all connections. Click **Customize** to specify which connections you want Windows Firewall to help protect.

- **Settings:** Enables you to customize firewall settings for the selected profile. Click **Customize** to specify whether to display notifications to users when programs are blocked from receiving inbound connections or allow unicast responses. You can also view but not modify how rules created by local administrators are merged with Group Policy-based rules.

- **Logging:** Enables you to configure logging settings. Click **Customize** to specify the location and size of the log file and whether dropped packets or successful connections are logged (see Figure 4-7).

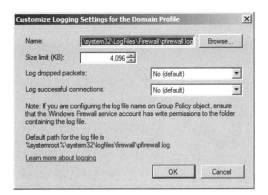

**Figure 4-7**    You can customize logging settings for each of the Windows Firewall profiles.

In addition, you can configure IPSec settings from the IPSec Settings tab (refer to Figure 4-6), including defaults and exemptions. IPSec authentication rules enable you to configure bypass rules for specific computers that enable these computers to bypass other Windows Firewall rules. Doing so enables you to block certain types of traffic while enabling authenticated computers to receive these types of traffic.

### Configuring New Firewall Rules

The Windows Firewall with Advanced Security snap-in enables you to create inbound, outbound, and connection security rules, as described earlier in this section.

### Configuring Inbound Rules or Outbound Rules

By clicking **New Rule** under Inbound Rules or Outbound Rules in the Windows Firewall with Advanced Security snap-in (refer to Figure 4-5), you can create rules that determine programs or ports that are allowed to pass through the firewall. Use the following procedure to create a new rule:

    **1.** Right-click the desired rule type in the Windows Firewall with Advanced Security snap-in and choose **New Rule**. This starts the New (Inbound or Outbound) Rule Wizard, as shown in Figure 4-8. (We chose a new inbound rule, so our example shows the New Inbound Rule Wizard.)

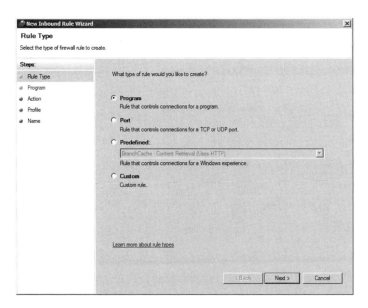

**Figure 4-8**   The New (Inbound or Outbound) Rule Wizard starts with a Rule Type page, which enables you to define the type of rule you want to create.

2. Select the type of rule you want to create:

   ■ **Program:** Enables you to define a rule that includes all programs or a specified program path.

   ■ **Port:** Enables you to define rules for specific remote ports using either the TCP or UDP protocol.

   ■ **Predefined:** Enables you to select from a large quantity of predefined rules covering the same exceptions described previously in Table 4-2 and shown in Figure 4-3. Select the desired exception from the drop-down list.

   ■ **Custom:** Enables you to create rules that apply to combinations of programs and ports. This option combines settings provided by the other rule-type options.

3. After you select your rule type, click **Next**.

4. The content of the next page of the wizard varies according to which option you select. For example, the following steps show you how to define a port rule with port 3389 used on a terminal server with Remote Desktop Protocol (RDP).

**5.** On the Protocol and Ports page shown in Figure 4-9, select **TCP** and the **Specific local ports** option. Type **3389** in the text box provided and click **Next**.

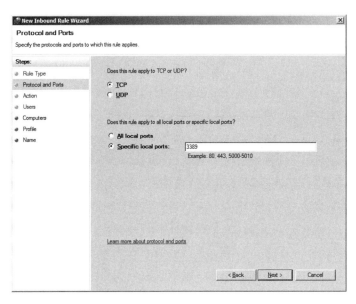

**Figure 4-9**   The Protocol and Ports page enables you to specify whether the rule applies to TCP or UDP, and specify the port or ports to which the rule will apply.

**6.** On the Action page, specify the action to be taken when a connection matches the specified conditions, as shown in Figure 4-10.

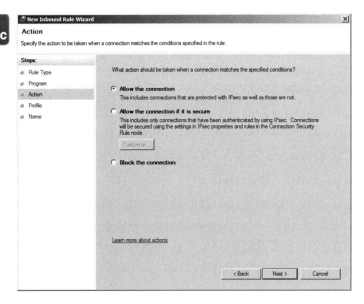

**Figure 4-10**   The Action page enables you to specify the required action type.

7. If you choose the **Allow the Connection if it is secure** option, click **Customize** to display the dialog box shown in Figure 4-11. From this dialog box, select the required option as explained on the dialog box and click **OK**. If you desire that encryption be enforced in addition to authentication and integrity protection, select the **Require the connections to be encrypted** option and select the check box provided if you want to allow unencrypted data to be sent while encryption is being negotiated.

**Figure 4-11**   The Customize Allow if Secure Settings dialog box enables you to select additional actions to be taken for packets that match the rule conditions being configured.

8. Click **Next** to display the Users page. By default, connections from all users are authorized to make a connection specified by the rule. To limit connections to authorized users or groups, select **Only allow connections from these users** and click the **Add** button. In the Select Users, Computers, or Groups dialog box that appears, type the name of the authorized user or group and then click **OK**. Repeat as desired to add additional users or groups. When finished, click **Next**.

9. The Computers page enables you to limit the computers that are allowed to use the rule. By default, connections from all computers are authorized to make a connection. To limit connections to authorized computers, select **Only allow connections from these computers** and click the **Add** button. In the Select Computers or Groups dialog box that appears, type the name of the

authorized computer or group, and then click **OK**. Repeat as desired to add additional computers. When finished, click **Next**.

10. On the Profile page, select the profiles (**Domain**, **Private**, and **Public**) to which the rule is to be applied. Then, click **Next**.

11. On the Name page, specify a name and optional description for your new rule. Click **Finish** to create the rule, which will then appear in the details pane of the Windows Firewall with Advanced Security snap-in.

**NOTE**  In general, you do not need to create rules for filtering outbound traffic. Windows Server 2008 includes outbound filters for basic networking services, such as DHCP or DNS requests, Group Policy communications, and networking protocols, such as IPv6 and Internet Group Management Protocol (IGMP). Blocking outbound communications can prevent many default Windows features such as Windows Update from communicating properly. However, malware such as worms, viruses, and Trojan horses can be blocked from spreading to other computers by using appropriate outbound traffic filters.

**TIP**  If you create outbound filters to help secure your network against malware propagation, be sure to test third-party applications running on your network to ensure that they communicate properly.

**NOTE**  For more information on creating inbound and outbound rules, refer to "Creating New Rules" at http://technet.microsoft.com/en-us/library/cc771477(WS.10).aspx.

## Configuring Connection Security Rules

Creating a new connection security rule is similar to that for inbound or outbound rules, but the options are slightly different. Windows Firewall with Advanced Security provides the following types of connection security rules:

- **Isolation:** Enables you to limit connections according to authentication criteria that you define. For example, you can use this rule to isolate domain-based computers from external computers such as those located across the Internet. Such a rule enables you to implement server or domain isolation strategies, which are discussed later in this chapter. You can request or require authentication and specify the authentication method that must be used.

- **Authentication exemption:** Enables specified computers, such as DHCP and DNS servers, to be exempted from the need for authentication. Computers listed here do not require authentication to communicate with computers in an isolated domain. You can specify computers by IP address ranges or subnets or you can include a predefined set of computers.

- **Server-to-server:** Enables you to protect communications between two specified groups of computers (known as endpoints). Specify the endpoints by IP address range or those that are accessible through a specified connection type such as a wireless connection.

- **Tunnel:** Enables you to secure communications between two computers by means of IPSec tunnel mode. We discuss IPSec modes later in this chapter. This encapsulated network packets that are routed between the tunnel endpoints. You would typically use this rule type to secure connections across the Internet between security gateways. You can choose from several types of tunnels, as shown later in Figure 4-13; you can also exempt IPSec-protected computers from the defined tunnel.

- **Custom:** Enables you to create a rule that requires special settings not covered explicitly in the other options. All wizard pages except those used to create only tunnel rules are available.

Use the following procedure to create a connection security rule:

1. From the Windows Firewall with Advanced Security dialog box previously shown in Figure 4-5, right-click **Connection Security Rules** and choose **New Rule** to display the New Connection Security Rule Wizard, as shown in Figure 4-12. Connection security rules manage authentication of two machines on the network and the encryption of network traffic sent between them using IPSec. Security is also achieved with the use of key exchange and data integrity checks.

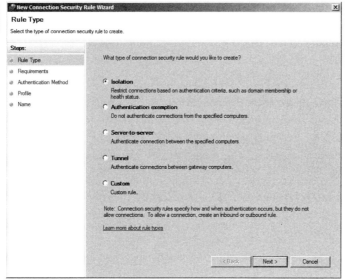

**Figure 4-12**    The New Connection Security Rule Wizard enables you to create five types of connection security rules.

2. Choose from one of the five types of connection security rules already described, and then click **Next**. The Tunnel Type page appears (see Figure 4-13).

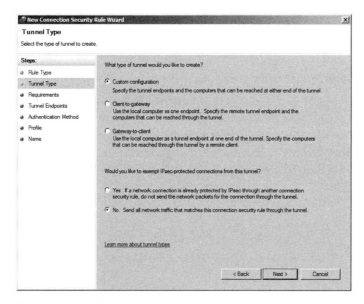

**Figure 4-13**    Configuring an IPSec tunnel mode connection security rule.

3. The remaining pages of the wizard depend on the type of rule you are configuring. The following steps take you through creating a server-to-server rule. Select **Server-to-Server** and click **Next**.

4. On the Endpoints page, select the range of IP addresses to be included in endpoints 1 and 2. By default, computers from any IP addresses are included. To limit the rule's application, select **These IP addresses under either endpoint** and click **Add**. In the IP Address dialog box that appears, choose an option for an IP address or subnet, a range of IP addresses, or a predefined set of computers as required. When finished, click **OK**, and then repeat for the other endpoint if needed. Then, click **Next**.

5. On the Requirements page, select one of the authentication options shown in Figure 4-14, and then click **Next**.

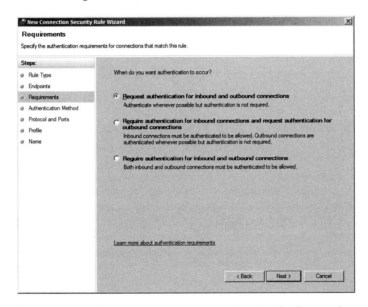

**Figure 4-14**  You can choose from several authentication requirements when configuring a connection security rule.

6. On the Authentication Method page, select one of the authentication methods shown in Figure 4-15. If you select the **Computer Certificate** option, choose a signing algorithm and certificate store type (the figures show the defaults). Click **Browse** to locate a suitable certification authority. If you select the Advanced option, click Customize and provide information for the first and second authentication settings in the dialog box that appears. When finished, click **Next**.

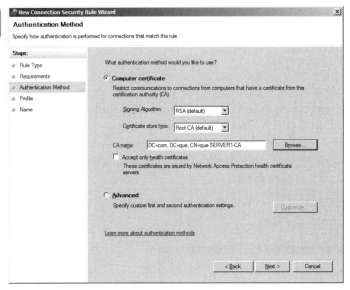

**Figure 4-15**   You can choose from several authentication methods when configuring a connection security rule.

7. All rule types enable you to select any or all of the domain, private, or public profiles described earlier in this chapter. Make the appropriate choice and click **Next**.

8. Specify a name and optional description for the rule on the last page of the wizard, and then click **Finish**. The rule appears in the details pane of the Windows Firewall with Advanced Security snap-in.

**NOTE**   For more information on creating connection security rules, refer to "Creating Connection Security Rules" at http://technet.microsoft.com/en-us/library/cc725940(WS.10).aspx.

### Configuring Rule Properties

All firewall rules in Windows Firewall with Advanced Security come with a Properties dialog box that enables you to modify an extensive set of rule properties. Right-click the desired rule and choose **Properties** to display its Properties dialog box. We discuss the more important of these properties that you need to be aware of here. Note that, for default rules, many of the options contained in this dialog box are fixed and cannot be modified; however, these options are available for any new rules that you might have created using the New Rule Wizard.

### Authorizing Users and Computers

Windows Firewall enables you to require that remote users or computers be authorized before they can connect to your server. This can be useful in some situations; for example, if your company has a customized billing application that uses a specific TCP port, any user that connects to the server across this port can access data that should only be available to authorized users or computers. Windows Firewall enables you to limit inbound connections to users who are members of a specific group for which access has been permitted. This enables you to add access control to custom applications without the need to add specific access-control code to the application. If users or computers are not on the authorized lists you've specified, attempted connections will be dropped immediately.

Use the following procedure to authorize users and computers in Windows Firewall:

1. On the General tab of the rule's Properties dialog box, select **Allow the connection if it is secure**, as shown in Figure 4-16. Then, click **Apply**. This enables you to designate authorized or excepted users or computers.

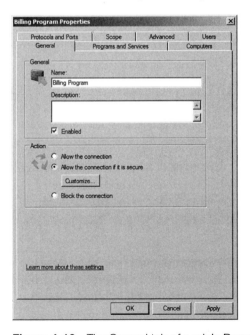

**Figure 4-16**   The General tab of a rule's Properties dialog box enables you to modify the action taken by the rule.

**2.** To limit the users that are enabled to connect using the rule, select the **Users** tab. Select the check box labeled **Only allow connections from these users** and click **Add**.

**3.** Type the name of the user or group allowed to use this connection in the Select Users or Groups dialog box and click **OK**. The user or group is added to the Authorized users group, as shown in Figure 4-17.

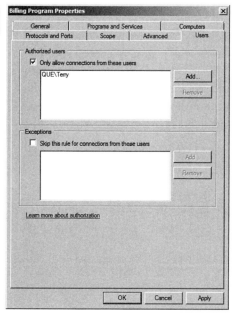

**Figure 4-17**   The Users tab of a rule's Properties dialog box enables you to limit the users authorized to use the connection covered by the rule.

**4.** To designate users or groups whose traffic is to be blocked by Windows Firewall despite being included in the Allowed list, select the check box labeled **Skip this rule for connections from these users** and click **Add**. Type the required user or group name in the Select Users or Group dialog box and click **OK**.

**5.** To limit the computers that are allowed to access the server through this connection, first add the names of the computers to an appropriate security group. From the **Computers** tab, select the check box labeled **Only allow connections from these computers**. Click **Add**, add the group name in the Select Groups dialog box that appears, and then click **OK**.

**6.** You can also designate computers whose traffic is to be blocked by Windows Firewall despite being included in the Allowed list in a similar manner. Select the check box labeled **Skip this rule for connections from these computers**, click **Add**, and add the group name in the Select Groups dialog box. Then, click **OK**.

**NOTE**   The Users tab is provided for inbound rules only; it is not available for outbound rules.

**TIP**   The purpose of the **Skip this rule for connections from these (users or computers)** option is to block traffic from users or computers that would otherwise be allowed by virtue of their group membership. For example, if user1 is a member of a group that has been authorized on the Users tab but you want to block this user's communications, include user1 in the Skip this rule section. Note that the original version of Windows Server 2008 did not include this feature; it included just the Allow function, which was combined in a single tab for both users and computers.

### Modifying Rule Scope

The Scope tab of a rule's Properties dialog box enables you to limit the scope of connections from your internal network and block connections from undesired network segments, internal or external. This helps you to limit access to a specific server to users or computers that have the need to access resources on this server, blocking those with no need to access the server. This can include web servers such as those configured for intranet websites only.

Use the following procedure to modify the scope of a rule:

1. On the Scope tab of the rule's Properties dialog box, select the option labeled **These IP addresses** under **Remote IP address**.

2. Click **Add**. As shown in Figure 4-18, specify the IP address or subnet either as a single IPv4 or IPv6 address or network number, or an IPv4 or IPv6 address range limited by the addresses you specify in the From and To fields. Then, click **OK**.

**Figure 4-18**   The Scope tab of a rule's Properties dialog box enables you to limit the IP addresses that are allowed to access your server.

3. The IP address or range you specify is displayed on the Scope tab. Click **Add** again to add another IP address range or **OK** to finish configuring IP addresses.

### Additional Rule Properties

The other tabs of a rule's Properties dialog box enable you to configure the following additional functions related to each firewall rule:

- **Programs and Services tab:** Enables you to specify the program or service that is permitted to communicate using this rule. By default, all programs that meet conditions specified elsewhere in the rule's properties are allowed to communicate. To limit the programs being used, select the **This program** option and either type the complete path to the program's executable file or click **Browse** to locate the required program. To limit the services that can communicate using the rule, click the **Settings** command button and select the appropriate services in the Customize Service Settings dialog box.

- **Protocols and Ports tab:** Enables you to specify the protocol type and the local and remote ports covered by the rule. A comprehensive list of available protocols and ports is included in the drop-down lists on this tab. You can add a custom protocol by selecting the **Custom** option and typing any protocol number designated by the Internet Assigned Numbers Authority (IANA). (For a list of the most often-used protocols and their numbers, refer to http://technet.microsoft.com/en-us/library/dd421720(WS.10).aspx.) Note that the local port is the port on the computer on which you are configuring the rule and the remote port is the port on any computer that is sending or receiving communications from the local port.

- **Advanced tab:** Enables you to specify the profiles (domain, private, or public) to which the rule applies. You can also specify the interface types (local-area network, remote access, and/or wireless) and whether edge traversal (traffic routed through a Network Address Translation [NAT] device) is allowed or blocked for incoming rules. The following edge traversal options are available:

  - **Block edge traversal:** Blocks the reception of unsolicited Internet traffic through a NAT device

  - **Allow edge traversal:** Enables applications to receive unsolicited Internet traffic through a NAT device

  - **Defer to user:** Enables the user to decide whether traffic from the Internet will be allowed through a NAT device when requested by an application

  - **Defer to application:** Enables each application to determine whether Internet traffic will be allowed through a NAT device

**NOTE**    For additional information on the various tabs of the firewall rule's Properties dialog box, refer to the references cited at "Firewall Rule Properties Page" at http://technet.microsoft.com/en-us/library/dd421727(WS.10).aspx.

### Configuring Notifications

You can configure Windows Firewall with Advanced Security to display notifications when a program is blocked from receiving inbound connections according to the default behavior of Windows Firewall. When you select this option and no existing block or allow rule applies to this program, a user is notified when a program is blocked from receiving inbound connections.

To configure this option, right-click **Windows Firewall with Advanced Security** at the top of the left pane in the Windows Firewall with Advanced Security snap-in and then choose **Properties**. This opens the dialog box previously shown in Figure 4-6. Select the tab that corresponds to the profile you want to configure, and then click the **Customize** command button in the Settings section. From the Customize Settings for the (selected) Profile dialog box, select **Yes** under Display a Notification (as shown in Figure 4-19), and then click **OK** twice.

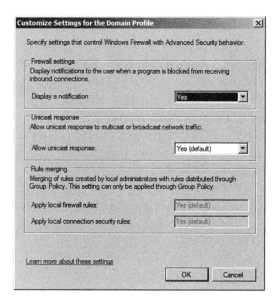

**Figure 4-19**   Configuring Windows Firewall to display notifications.

### Importing and Exporting Policies

All the Windows Firewall with Advanced Security settings that have been discussed in this section, including the domain, private, and public profiles, are included in a policy file with the .wfw extension. You can export a configured policy and import it to a new location.

These actions are helpful if you decide to restore Windows Firewall with Advanced Security defaults, which you might want to do should problems arise with firewall settings. Doing so deletes all firewall settings, firewall rules, and IPSec-connection security rules that have been configured on the computer. Exporting the firewall policy enables you to restore your settings later if desired. To export your policy, right-click **Windows Firewall with Advanced Security** and choose **Export Policy**. Provide a name and path for the export file, and then click **Save**.

To import a saved policy configuration, right-click **Windows Firewall with Advanced Security** and choose **Import Policy**. You receive the warning shown in Figure 4-20, which says that importing a policy overwrites all the current settings. Click **Yes**, specify the name of the policy file to be imported, and then click **Open**.

**Figure 4-20**   You are warned that importing a policy will overwrite all current firewall policy settings.

**NOTE**   You can configure most of the Windows Firewall with Advanced Security options discussed in this section from the command line using the `netsh advfirewall` command-line tool. For more information on this tool, refer to "Netsh Commands for Windows Firewall with Advanced Security" at http://technet.microsoft.com/en-us/library/cc771920(WS.10).aspx.

# Using IPSec to Secure Network Communications

IPSec is a set of protocols that defines standards for securing communication across IP networks using cryptographic methods to protect data while in transit. The Internet Engineering Task Force (IETF) has developed standards for data integrity, authentication, encryption, and anti-replay as defined in RFCs 2401–2409. Note that these standards not only apply to Windows networks, but to networks involving all computer operating systems currently in use. All Windows operating systems from Windows 2000 onward support IPSec. You can use the Windows Firewall with Advanced Security snap-in as well as Group Policy to configure the use of IPSec on Windows Server 2008-based networks.

### IPSec Modes

Because IPSec can be used for securing data transmitted across a single network or between different networks, the following two modes exist:

- **Transport mode:** Enables you to secure transmissions within a single network, such as server-to-server or client-to-server, as shown in Figure 4-21.

- **Tunnel mode:** Enables you to secure transmissions between two networks, as shown in Figure 4-22. This mode creates a tunneled path between subnets or across the Internet, through which secured data passes. When using this mode, tunnel endpoints, which are normally router interfaces, are defined, and you can specify the types of authentication and encryption protocols used to secure traffic passing through the tunnel.

### IPSec Transport Mode

**Figure 4-21**   IPSec transport mode provides secure communication from endpoint to endpoint within a network.

### IPSec Tunnel Mode

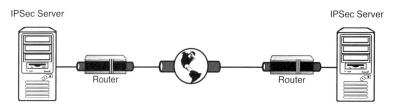

**Figure 4-22**   IPSec tunnel mode provides for secure communications between two networks.

Within either IPSec mode, the following two IPSec protocols are available:

- **Encapsulating Security Payload (ESP):** Specified as IP Protocol 50 and defined in RFC 2406, ESP provides data confidentially, authentication, integrity, and anti-replay for the payload contained within each packet, but not the entire packet. Header information is allowed to change in transit.

- **Authentication Header (AH):** Specified as IP Protocol 51 and defined in RFC 2402, AH provides data authentication, integrity, and anti-replay for the entire packet (including both the IP header and the data contained within the packet). Although it protects data from modification, AH does not provide data confidentiality (in other words, it does not encrypt the payload). Some information within the header is allowed to change in transit because of a need for modification as they are transmitted between routers.

**NOTE**   You can use ESP alone or in combination with AH to provide total protection for the entire packet as it passes across networks in IPSec tunnel mode.

## IPSec Encryption

As already noted, IPSec using ESP provides encryption to ensure data privacy. The following encryption algorithms are used:

- **Data Encryption Standard (DES):** Uses a block cipher encryption protocol with a 56-bit encryption key. This type of protocol is an encryption algorithm that operates on a fixed size data block, in this case, a 64-bit block. You should generally avoid using DES unless you need to communicate with an older computer that cannot use higher levels of encryption.

- **Triple DES (3DES):** By using a three-step encryption process in which the data is passed through a 56-bit key three times, 3DES provides for a higher level of security. This is the most secure option on networks with Windows XP or Windows Server 2008 computers.

- **Advanced Encryption Standard (AES):** Uses a symmetric block cipher that encrypts data in 128-bit blocks using a 128-bit, 192-bit, or 256-bit encryption key. This provides even greater security but with the need for greater processor utilization. Cipher block chaining is used to hide patterns of identical data blocks within each packet. AES is supported only on computers running Windows Server 2008/R2 and Windows Vista/7.

**NOTE**   For more information on key exchange protocols, integrity and encryption algorithms, and authentication methods supported by various Windows versions, refer to "IPSec Algorithms and Methods Supported in Windows" at http://technet.microsoft.com/en-us/library/dd125380(WS.10).aspx and "Descriptions of the IPSec Algorithms and Methods" at http://technet.microsoft.com/en-us/library/dd125356(WS.10).aspx.

### Using Group Policy to Create IPSec Policies

Group Policy provides an IPSec node that enables you to create policies that apply to a single computer or an AD DS domain. Use the following procedure:

1. In an AD DS domain, open the Group Policy Management Editor focused on a Group Policy object (GPO) linked to the appropriate site, domain, or organizational unit (OU). In a non-domain environment or for a local computer, open the Local Group Policy Editor.

> **TIP**  Don't forget the rule for GPO precedence. GPOs are applied in the sequence local, site, domain, OU unless configured otherwise with the No Override or Block Inheritance settings; conflicting policies in GPOs applied at a later stage overwrite those applied at an earlier stage.

2. Navigate to **Computer Configuration\Policies\Windows Settings\ Security Settings\IP Security Policies on (Active Directory** or **Local Computer)**, depending on whether you're configuring AD DS or local policy.

3. Right-click this node and choose **Create IP Security Policy**.

4. The IP Security Policy Wizard starts with a Welcome page. Click **Next**.

5. Provide a name for your security policy on the IP Security Policy Name page, and then click **Next**.

6. The Requests for Secure Communication page enables you to choose whether to activate the default response rule. Note that this option applies only to computers running Windows Server 2003 or Windows XP. Select this option only if you are not configuring IPSec for computers running Windows Vista/7/ Server 2008/R2. Then, click **Next**.

7. The wizard displays a completion page with a default option to edit the policy properties. Leave this option selected and click **Finish**. The Properties dialog box for your IP security policy appears, as shown in Figure 4-23.

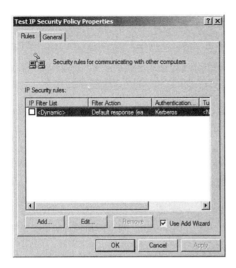

**Figure 4-23**    Configuring the properties of your IP security policy.

8.  You can leave the Use Add Wizard check box selected to run the Create IP
    Security Rule Wizard to create your security rule. If so, leave this check box
    selected and click **Add**. Otherwise, clear the check box and click **Add** to use
    the dialog box to add a rule.

9.  If you cleared the check box, you receive the New Rule Properties dialog box
    shown in Figure 4-24. Specify the properties for your security rule, as de-
    scribed in Table 4-3.

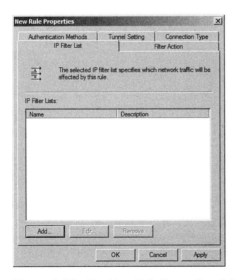

**Figure 4-24**    The New Rule Properties dialog box enables you to define a range of properties
for your IP security rule.

**Table 4-3**   Options Provided by the New Rule Properties Dialog Box

| Tab | Options Available |
|---|---|
| IP Filter List | Click **Add** to specify one or more IP filter lists. A wizard is provided that enables you to specify IP traffic source and destination according to several criteria, as shown in Figure 4-25. You can also choose a specific IP protocol or any protocol. Note that you must select the radio button next to your desired IP filter list. |
| Filter Action | Click **Add** to specify a filter action that determines whether this rule will permit or block traffic, or negotiate security. Several additional filter action properties are available, as shown in Figure 4-26.<br><br>■ **Permit** or **Block**: Permits or blocks all traffic.<br><br>■ **Negotiate Security**: Enables you to choose a security method from **Integrity and encryption**, **Integrity only**, or **Custom**. By default, 3DES is selected; if you want to use a different encryption algorithm, select the **Custom** option and choose the desired integrity and encryption algorithms from the Custom Security Method Settings dialog box that appears. You can also select any or all of the following options:<br><br>  ■ **Accept unsecured communication, but always respond using IPSec**: IPSec negotiates security associations and the sending or receiving of IPSec-protected traffic. Unsecured traffic will be permitted if the destination host cannot use IPSec.<br><br>  ■ **Allow fallback to unsecured communication if a secure connection cannot be established**: IPSec falls back to unsecured communication if required.<br><br>  ■ **Use session key perfect forward security (PFS)**: Requires the generation of new session master keys before each new session is initiated.<br><br>Note that you must select the radio button next to the desired filter action. |
| Authentication Methods | Choose from one of the following three authentication methods:<br><br>■ **Kerberos v5**: This is the default protocol and is the default protocol used by AD DS for authentication in domains. It is the most secure method for authentication across all domains in an AD DS forest.<br><br>■ **Certificate**: In a non-domain situation, you can use a certificate from a specified certification authority (CA).<br><br>■ **Preshared key**: This is a previously agreed-upon string value that you might use for authenticating standalone computers; it can be used for authentication protection only and cannot be used for data integrity or encryption. It is the least secure method, because you have no way of telling whether it might have been compromised by an intruder. |
| Tunnel Setting | If configuring a transport mode IPSec rule, leave the default of **This rule does not specify an IPSec tunnel** selected. For tunnel mode, select the option labeled **Tunnel endpoints are specified by these IP addresses** and specify an IPv4 or IPv6 tunnel endpoint. |

| Tab | Options Available |
| --- | --- |
| Connection Type | Select the range of network connections to which the rule should apply from **All network connections** (the default), **Local area network** (LAN), or **Remote Access**, as required. |

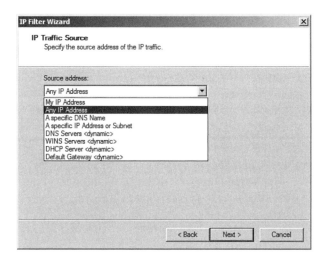

**Figure 4-25** You have several options for specifying the source address of the IP traffic. The same options are available on a later wizard page for the IP traffic destination.

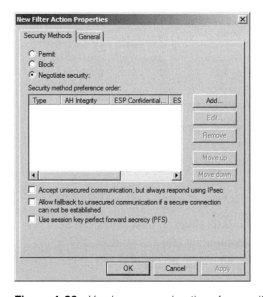

**Figure 4-26** You have several options for specifying the desired filter action.

**10.** When you finish configuring your rule properties, click **Close**. You are returned to the Properties dialog box for your IP security policy.

**11.** If you want to add additional security rules, repeat the previous steps. When finished, select one or more filter lists to be applied, and then click **OK**. The Group Policy Management Editor snap-in displays the IP security policy you configured in the details pane.

**NOTE**  Windows Server 2008 provides two snap-ins that can be used for configuring and monitoring IPSec on computers running Windows XP or Windows Server 2003. However, these snap-ins are provided for backward-compatibility purposes only; computers running Windows Vista, Windows 7, or Windows Server 2008 do not recognize any settings that you may have configured with these snap-ins. In a non-domain environment, Windows Server 2008 R2 no longer contains the Client (Respond Only), Server (Request Security), and Secure Server (Require Security) policy settings in the IP Security Policies on (Active Directory or Local Computer) node that were present in the original version of Windows Server 2008 or in Windows Server 2003. However, these policy settings are available when configuring Group Policy on a domain controller.

**NOTE**  For more information on creating IPSec policies, refer to "Creating and Using IPSec Policies" at http://technet.microsoft.com/en-us/library/cc730656(WS.10).aspx.

### Using Group Policy to Configure Windows Firewall Policies

Group Policy enables you to define IPSec policies that apply to all computers in your AD DS domain, site, or OU. As with other Group Policy settings, you can define these policies in a GPO linked to a site, domain, or OU as required.

#### Creating Windows Firewall with Advanced Security Policies

Group Policy enables you to configure Windows Firewall with Advanced Security so that the configured options apply to all computers affected by the GPO in the AD DS object to which it is linked. Use the following procedure:

1. From the Group Policy Management Editor focused on the appropriate GPO, navigate to **Computer Configuration\Policies\Windows Settings\ Security Settings\Windows Firewall with Advanced Security\Windows Firewall with Advanced Security**.

2. Expand this node. You will notice subnodes for Inbound Rules, Outbound Rules, and Connection Security Rules, as shown in Figure 4-27.

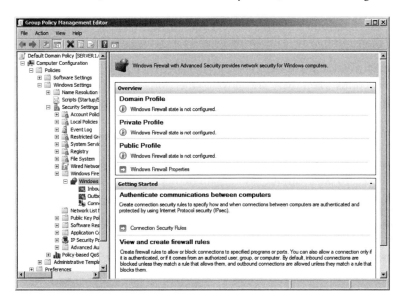

**Figure 4-27**   Using Group Policy to configure Windows Firewall with Advanced Security options.

3. To configure a Group Policy-based IPSec policy, right-click **Connection Security Rules** and choose **New Rule**.

4. The New Rule Wizard starts with the Rule Type page, which provides you with the same five rule types previously shown in Figure 4-12. Select the desired rule type and click **Next**.

5. Complete the New Rule Wizard as described earlier in this chapter; you receive the same pages previously shown in Figures 4-13 to 4-15. After clicking Finish, your rule appears in the details pane of the Group Policy Management Editor snap-in.

If you need to modify any policy rules, right-click the required rule in the details pane and choose **Properties**. You can modify all the same options that the New Rule Wizard initially configures. You can also disable a policy rule if required by right-clicking the rule and choosing **Disable Rule**. This option then changes to **Enable Rule** so that you can re-enable it later.

### Windows Firewall Group Policy Property Settings

Group Policy also enables you to define several properties that apply to all policies configured in a given GPO. In the Group Policy Management Editor, right-click the second **Windows Firewall with Advanced Security** node and choose **Properties**. For each of the domain, private, and public profiles you can specify the behavior of the firewall state (on, off, or not configured), plus several settings that control Windows Firewall behavior and logging options. Available settings are similar to those previously shown in Figure 4-6 for local computer firewall properties. The IPSec Settings tab, shown in Figure 4-28, provides the following options:

- **IPSec defaults:** Click **Customize** to specify settings used by IPSec to establish secured connections when there are active connection security rules. The Customize IPSec Settings dialog box that appears enables you to specify settings for key exchange, data protection, and authentication method.

- **IPSec exemptions:** You can choose whether or not to exempt ICMP from IPSec requirements. Choosing the **Yes** option enables ICMP packets, such as `ping` or `tracert`, to pass without being examined by IPSec rules. This can assist in troubleshooting network connectivity problems.

- **IPSec tunnel authorization:** By clicking **Advanced**, you can customize the computers and/or users that are authorized to use the IPSec tunnel or deny connections. This dialog box works in a similar fashion to that shown previously in Figure 4-17.

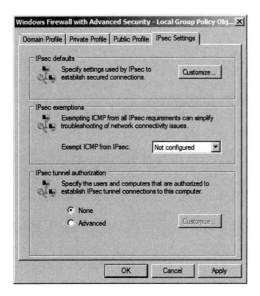

**Figure 4-28**   You can choose from three authentication methods when configuring a connection security rule.

## Isolation Policies

As you have seen, Windows Firewall with Advanced Security enables you to create connection security rules that specify the use of IPSec for securing network traffic. You can also use IPSec authentication to require each computer that is an AD DS domain member to positively identify the other computer to which it connects; this feature is known as *domain isolation*, because it effectively isolates these computers from any computers that do not belong to the domain.

In a similar fashion, you can isolate specific domain member servers to accept only authenticated and secured communication from other computers within the domain. This feature is known as *server isolation*, because it isolates the specified servers and domain member client computers from other excluded machines. Furthermore, you can extend the server isolation policy to limit communications to domain member computers that are members of specified security groups configured within AD DS.

To configure domain isolation, configure settings in a GPO linked to the domain that require all incoming communication requests be authenticated using Active Directory. You can optionally require encrypted communications among domain members. Furthermore, you can configure exemptions to enable specific trusted non-domain member computers to initiate unprotected communications with computers in the isolated domain. To configure server isolation, configure a connection security rule in Windows Firewall with Advanced Security or in a local GPO that requires similar authentication as members of an authorized group for incoming communications.

**NOTE**   For more information on domain and server isolation policies, refer to "Introduction to Server and Domain Isolation" at http://technet.microsoft.com/en-us/library/cc725770(WS.10).aspx, "Deploying a Basic Domain Isolation Policy" at http://technet.microsoft.com/en-us/library/cc730709(WS.10).aspx, and "Server Isolation with Microsoft Windows Explained" at http://technet.microsoft.com/en-us/library/cc770626(WS.10).aspx. Also, refer to additional documents referenced in each of these sources.

**NOTE**   For a comprehensive guide to deploying Windows Firewall with Advanced Security, including practice scenarios involving the use of Group Policy and IPSec, refer to "Windows Firewall and IPSec Policy Deployment Step-by-Step Guide" at http://technet.microsoft.com/en-us/library/deploy-ipsec-firewall-policies-step-by-step(WS.10).aspx.

## Exam Preparation Tasks

## Review All the Key Topics

Review the most important topics in this chapter, noted with the key topics icon in the outer margin of the page. Table 4-4 lists a reference of these key topics and the page numbers on which each is found.

**Table 4-4**   Key Topics for Chapter 4

| Key Topic Element | Description | Page Number |
|---|---|---|
| List | Describes the available Windows Firewall profiles. | 166 |
| List | Shows you how to use the Windows Firewall Control Panel applet. | 167 |
| Figure 4-3 | You can choose to allow individual programs through the Windows Firewall Control Panel applet for either the Home/Work or Public profiles. | 169 |
| Figure 4-5 | Windows Firewall with Advanced Security enables you to configure settings for each of the domain, private, and public profiles. | 173 |
| List | Describes the available properties of each of the three firewall profiles and when you would use them. | 175 |
| Figure 4-8 | Shows the types of rules you can create using the New Rule Wizard. | 177 |
| Figure 4-10 | You can choose from three actions when a connection matches rule criteria. | 178 |
| Figure 4-12 | Shows the custom rule types you can create using the New Connection Security Rule Wizard. | 182 |
| Figure 4-14 | Choosing an authentication requirement for a connection security rule. | 183 |
| Figure 4-15 | Choosing an authentication method for a connection security rule. | 184 |
| List | Describes how to authorize users and computers in Windows Firewall. | 185 |
| Figure 4-17 | Modifying a rule's scope to define which computers are affected by the rule. | 186 |
| List | Defines modes available with IPSec. | 191 |
| List | Defines IPSec transport and tunnel protocols. | 192 |
| List | Shows you how to use Group Policy to create an IPSec policy. | 194 |
| Table 4-3 | Describes options you can select when creating a filter rule for your IPSec policy. | 196 |
| Figure 4-27 | Using Group Policy to create a Windows Firewall with Advanced Security rule. | 199 |

## Definition of Key Terms

Define the following key terms from this chapter, and check your answers in the Glossary.

authentication, authentication header (AH), connection security rule, domain isolation policy, Encapsulating Security Payload (ESP), filter action, firewall, firewall profile, firewall rule, IP Security (IPSec), server isolation policy, stateful firewall, transport mode, tunnel mode, Windows Firewall, Windows Firewall with Advanced Security

This chapter covers the following subjects:

- **Introduction to DNS:** This section provides you with background knowledge by introducing you to the fundamentals under which DNS is built. It then shows you how DNS works to resolve computer names to IP addresses under various situations that might be encountered.

- **Installing DNS in Windows Server 2008 R2:** This section shows you how to install the DNS server role on a Windows Server 2008 R2 computer, both by using the Add Roles Wizard and from the command line.

- **Configuring DNS Server Properties:** Each DNS server has a Properties dialog box associated with it from which you can configure a large number of server-specific properties. This section shows you how to configure the functions of the tabs in the DNS Server Properties dialog box.

# CHAPTER 5

# Installing and Configuring Domain Name System (DNS)

When you go onto the Internet and type in an address, like www.microsoft. com, into your browser, the browser has to locate this name by finding the correct IP address associated with it. This requires a system of name resolution. Back in the early days of the Internet, when there were only a few hundred computers (or hosts) connected together in what was then a defense-oriented network that was also used by a few university researchers, a text-based file called HOSTS was developed that mapped host names directly to IP addresses. Whenever a new computer, either a server or a local workstation, was added to the Internet, a mapping was added to the HOSTS file, which was then posted for everyone to download. This worked well in the small and slowly changing environment of those days. But, as more computers joined the network and the rate of change increased, all these changes had to be manually entered into the HOSTS file and this file replicated to that increasing number of computers out there. Clearly, a better means of resolving computer names was needed. This is where Domain Name System (DNS) comes in.

DNS has its beginnings in the Berkeley Internet Name Domain (BIND), developed at the University of California in Berkeley and originally defined in Request for Comments (RFC) 1034 and 1035. As you will see, DNS was conceived as a hierarchical naming system, thereby allowing for an almost infinite possibility of expansion as more computers are added, limited only by the limitations of the IP addressing system itself. With the increasing use of IPv6, DNS has truly become an infinite system. In fact, ever since the inception of Active Directory in Windows 2000, a Microsoft domain running Active Directory Domain Services (AD DS) cannot function without DNS; if the DNS service becomes unavailable, users cannot log on or access any resources, such as servers or printers, until DNS is restored. Consequently, DNS is an extremely important component of any Microsoft domain and is therefore a well-tested topic on several Microsoft certification exams.

## "Do I Know This Already?" Quiz

The "Do I Know This Already?" quiz allows you to assess whether you should read this entire chapter or simply jump to the "Exam Preparation Tasks" section for review. If you are in doubt, read the entire chapter. Table 5-1 outlines the major headings in this chapter and the corresponding "Do I Know This Already?" quiz questions. You can find the answers in Appendix A, "Answers to the 'Do I Know This Already?' Quizzes."

**Table 5-1**  "Do I Know This Already?" Foundation Topics Section-to-Question Mapping

| Foundations Topics Section | Questions Covered in This Section |
|---|---|
| Introduction to DNS | 1–3 |
| Installing DNS in Windows Server 2008 R2 | 4–5 |
| Configuring DNS Server Properties | 6–10 |

1. Which of the following are components of the DNS namespace? (Choose all that apply.)

   a. Root domains

   b. Top-level domains

   c. Second-level domains

   d. Host names

   e. NetBIOS names

2. Which of the following are valid fully qualified domain names (FQDN)? (Choose all that apply.)

   a. SERVER1

   b. http://www

   c. www.certguide.com

   d. mailserver.acme.co.uk

   e. webserver.anydomain.

   f. fileserver1.mycompany.biz

**3.** Which of the following best describes the procedure followed during an iterative query for resolving a FQDN?

    **a.** A client sends a query to its local DNS server, which forwards the query to a DNS server hosted by the company's ISP. The latter server returns the appropriate IP address directly to the client.

    **b.** A client sends a query to its local DNS name server, which forwards the query to a DNS server that is authoritative for the host name specified in the query. This DNS server forwards this information to a DNS server that is authoritative for the second-level domain, which in turn forwards the information to a DNS server that is authoritative for the top-level domain. Finally, this last DNS server returns the result to the local DNS name server, which returns the result to the client.

    **c.** A client sends a query to its local DNS name server, which forwards the query to a root name server. The root name server returns the IP address of a DNS server that is authoritative for the specified top level domain. This server replies with the IP address of a DNS server that is authoritative for the specified second-level domain, which resolves the query and returns the result to the local DNS name server, which returns the result to the client.

    **d.** A client sends a query to a root name server, which forwards the query to a DNS server that is authoritative for the specified top level domain. This server then forwards the query to a DNS server that is authoritative for the specified second-level domain. This next server forwards the query to a DNS server that is authoritative for the host name, which resolves the query and returns the result to the client.

**4.** Which of the following tools can you use to install DNS on a Windows Server 2008 R2 computer? (Each correct answer represents a complete solution. Choose three).

    **a.** Add Roles Wizard

    **b.** Add Features Wizard

    **c.** Control Panel Add or Remove Programs

    **d.** `Start /w ocsetup` command

    **e.** `dcpromo` command

    **f.** `dnscmd` command

    **g.** DNS Manager

5. Which of the following is most likely to cause a problem when installing a DNS server?

   a. The server is not configured as a domain controller.

   b. The server is not configured with a static IP address.

   c. The server has only a single network adapter.

   d. The server is not configured with the Application Server role.

6. After users on your company's network report that they are unable to reach the company's intranet website, you check the DNS server and realize that the DNS service has not started. In Event Viewer, you notice that an error with ID 408 has been logged. What is the most likely cause of this problem?

   a. The DNS server is located on a separate subnet from that of the users and messages from the users are unable to cross the router to the DNS server.

   b. The network adapter on the DNS server has failed and needs to be re-placed.

   c. You have not specified the IP address of the intranet server on the For-warders tab of the DNS server's properties.

   d. You configured the Interfaces tab of the DNS server's properties to re-spond only to a specified IP address, but the IP address you entered is incorrect.

7. Your company has entered into a partnership arrangement with another com-pany, and you want to configure your company's DNS server to send queries for resources in the partner company to their DNS server. You need to ensure that requests for Internet resources do not go to the partner company DNS server. What should you do?

   a. Right-click the Conditional Forwarders node of the DNS snap-in and choose **New Conditional Forwarder**. Then, specify the DNS domain of the partner company and the IP address of their DNS server.

   b. On the Forwarders tab of your DNS server's Properties dialog box, specify the IP address and FQDN of the partner company's DNS server.

   c. Ask the administrator of the partner company's DNS server to specify the IP address and FQDN of your DNS server on the Forwarders tab of their DNS server's Properties dialog box.

   d. On the Root Hints tab of your DNS server's Properties dialog box, specify the IP address and FQDN of the partner company's DNS server.

8. You are responsible for configuring the DNS server on your network. Users at your company report that they are unable to access external websites. You check network connectivity and find that you can access external websites by IP address but not by name. Which of the following should you check at the DNS server?

   a. Conditional forwarders

   b. Root hints

   c. Trust anchors

   d. Round robin

9. You want to create a record of packets sent to and from your DNS server and store this information in a text file for later analysis. What feature should you enable?

   a. DNS monitoring

   b. Event logging

   c. DNS Notify

   d. Debug logging

10. Users in your company report that queries to Internet websites often end up retrieving inappropriate sites. You direct users to flush their cache using the `ipconfig /flushdns` command, but they still receive inappropriate sites. Which of the following should you check on your DNS server, which runs Windows Server 2008 R2?

    a. Root hints

    b. Cache locking

    c. Conditional forwarders

    d. Trust anchors

**Foundation Topics**

# Introduction to DNS

Back in the early 1980s, computers on the Internet still used HOSTS files, as described in the introduction, to locate each other. However, around this time, growth on the Internet really took off, and it was quickly evident that this system could not be continued. So, the Internet community came up with a solution of distributing the process of name resolution among a series of servers. And so the DNS system was born in 1984. At the same time, a central clearinghouse for Internet names was established, called the Internet Network Information Center (InterNIC). Today, a large series of name registrars have been accredited with the Internet Corporation for Assigned Names and Numbers (ICANN) (www.icann.org) for registering Internet names. InterNIC still keeps track of names registered by any name registrar and requires that all Internet domains have at least two DNS servers running and containing a database of the domain's machines.

So, when you want to go to a website, for example, www.microsoft.com, you enter this name into your browser and a DNS query is sent to your local server. This query works its way up the hierarchy of DNS servers as you will see shortly, and returns an IP address of 65.55.21.250 and makes the connection. Actually, to complete this connection, it must then use the Address Resolution Protocol (ARP) to locate the hardware, or MAC address, of the server that will respond to the query. But, this is another matter. Likewise, when you need to access some resource, such as a folder or printer located on another computer in your network, you use a program such as the Network and Sharing Center or type a UNC path, such as \\server1\ documents, and a DNS query is used to resolve the computer name to its IP address. Furthermore, when you first log onto your computer on an AD DS network, the Netlogon service must access a domain controller to verify your credentials. The DNS naming scheme is used to create the structure of the AD DS namespace, permitting interoperability with Internet technologies; therefore, the concept of namespaces is central to Active Directory. By integrating this concept with the system's directory services, Active Directory facilitates the management of multiple namespaces that are often found in the heterogeneous software and hardware environments of corporate networks. Your client computer uses DNS to determine the location of resources such as shared folders, printers, and so on, on the network. Again, DNS is used for this purpose.

### Hierarchical Nature of DNS

Nowadays, there are most likely over one billion machines hosting websites on the Internet! Imagine that number of machines referenced in a flat database: a HOSTS file containing references to all these machines would be at least tens of *gigabytes* in length! Imagine trying to search this file, let alone update it when a new machine is added to the Internet or replicate it to other servers.

So, DNS was developed as a hierarchical name resolution system that is distributed among servers located around the world. It includes the following properties:

- **Companies registered with the InterNIC operate their own DNS servers, which describe their own machines to others on the Internet**. So, when you point your browser to a location, such as www.microsoft.com, a machine owned by Microsoft and not one owned by the InterNIC responds to your request with the correct IP address. Only Microsoft has responsibility for these machines, and the only thing that InterNIC knows about them is the correct IP addresses of all DNS servers operated by Microsoft.

- **InterNIC functions as a central group to keep track of Internet domain names and their DNS servers**. They keep a large database that contains the names of registered domains and the DNS servers that serve these domains. Because InterNIC has the final say on registering Internet domain names, they will not register a name without knowing the IP addresses of at least two DNS servers that will be responsible for a new domain. So, InterNIC can tell you the IP addresses of several DNS servers operated by Microsoft that can provide the IP address of www.microsoft.com, or any other domain name, such as search. Microsoft.com that Microsoft operates.

- **DNS server software is capable of referring queries to other DNS servers as required**. As you will see shortly, local DNS servers can refer queries to external locations to other DNS servers that can respond with an IP address. They actually do two jobs: resolving local or external queries for machines on your network, and referring queries to external networks to the appropriate location.

- **DNS servers can remember recently resolved names**. As individuals tend to go frequently to the same Internet sites as opposed to going everywhere on the Internet at random, it is important that DNS servers can cache the results of recent name resolutions. Otherwise, think of the name resolution traffic that could result.

Let's look more closely at the hierarchical nature of DNS.

The hierarchical database of DNS, as represented schematically (and extremely simplified!) in Figure 5-1, is called the domain namespace. Within this namespace, every computer is identified by its fully qualified domain name (FQDN). Name servers themselves are grouped into different levels of domains and subdomains. Domains define the different levels of authority in the hierarchical structure of DNS.

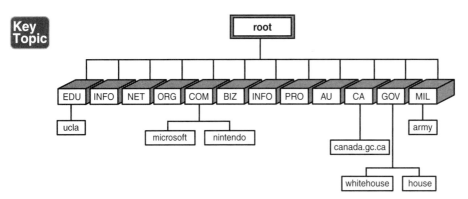

**Figure 5-1**   Hierarchical structure of DNS.

### Root-Level Domains

The top of the hierarchy is called the root domain. The root node uses a null label and is specified by . (a period or dot). Connecting the top-level domains, it is not included in domain names.

### Top-Level Domains

Starting in the 1980s, ICANN set up a system of top-level domain names, including those described in Table 5-2. In more recent years, ICANN has expanded the series of top-level domain names, with currently about two dozen top-level domain names assigned. In addition, two-letter ISO standard country name abbreviations are used as top-level domains (for example, .ca for Canada and .au for Australia). A few countries sell space in their top-level domains (for example, .tv for Tuvalu sometimes is often linked to television broadcasts or programs).

**Table 5-2**  Original Top-Level Domain Names

| DNS Name | Type of Organization |
|---|---|
| .arpa | Used by Advanced Research Project Agency for reverse mapping of IP addresses to DNS domain names (for example, in-addr.arpa) |
| .com | Commercial (for example, microsoft.com for Microsoft Corporation) |
| .edu | Educational (for example, mit.edu for Massachusetts Institute of Technology) |
| .gov | Government (for example, whitehouse.gov for the White House in Washington, D.C.) |
| .int | International organizations (for example, nato.int for NATO) |
| .mil | U.S. Military operations (for example, army.mil for the Army) |
| .net | Networking organizations (for example, nsf.net for NSFNET) |
| .org | Noncommercial organizations, such as churches and charities (for example, unitedway.org) |

Beginning in 2000, ICANN introduced new top-level domains, so that now approximately 20 top-level domain names are in use across the Internet today. Table 5-3 describes the more notable additional top-level domain names. Some of these are sponsored; i.e., an organization is delegated some defining policy-formulation authority regarding the use of such a domain that ensures its appropriate usage (for example, ensuring that .edu domain names are limited to educational organizations). Others are unsponsored and operate under policies established by the global Internet community by means of processes sponsored by ICANN.

**Table 5-3**  Additional Top-Level Domain Names

| DNS Name | Type of Organization |
|---|---|
| .aero | Aviation-related organizations (for example, www.desktop.aero for Desktop Aeronautics, an aerospace consulting firm) |
| .biz | Businesses (introduced to take some load off the .com top-level domain; for example, cindyking.biz for Cindy King Social Media & Cross-Cultural Communication for International Businesses) |
| .coop | Cooperatives, wholly owned subsidiaries, and other organizations that support cooperatives (for example, Ica.coop for the International Co-operative Alliance) |
| .info | Informative Internet resource-related organizations (for example, mta.info for the New York Metropolitan Transit Authority) |

**Table 5-3** Additional Top-Level Domain Names (*Continued*)

| DNS Name | Type of Organization |
| --- | --- |
| .museum | Museums, museum associations, and individual members of the museum profession (for example, www.penn.museum for the University of Pennsylvania Museum of Archaeology and Anthropology) |
| .name | Individuals for representation of personal names, nicknames, pseudonyms, and so on. Operated by VeriSign as of 2009 (for example, www.iranians.name for Persian Iranian Farsi Names for Boys and Girls) |
| .pro | Government-certified professionals, such as lawyers, accountants, physicians, and engineers (for example, www.registry.pro for registration of businesses, professionals, and other entities around the world) |

**NOTE**   For more information on the use and history of top-level domains, refer to "Top-level Domains (gTLDs)" at www.icann.org/en/tlds/ and "Top-Level domains: Domain Name System (DNS)" at http://technet.microsoft.com/en-us/library/cc784663(WS.10).aspx.

### Second-Level Domain Names

Under the top-level domains are additional groupings referred to as second-level domains. For example, que.com would be a second-level domain and is actually a subdomain of the .com top-level domain. Second-level domains can be divided into their own subdomains (for example, accounting.que.com). In turn, these subdomains can be further subdivided, up to a limit of 127 levels. The responsibility of designing, naming, and maintaining these lower-level domains or subdomains rests with the administrator of the DNS server at the second-level domain. Authority for these subdomains can be delegated to organizations so that they can manage their own namespace. This is true at all levels of the DNS hierarchy.

### Host Names

Individual computers exist within a domain. Each computer in the domain must have its own name, referred to as the host name. The combination of a host name, an organization's domain name, and the Internet top-level domain name creates what is called a *fully qualified domain name* (FQDN) that is unique across the Internet. Host names used inside domains are added at the beginning of the domain name and are also referred to by their FQDN. For example, a computer-called search in the Microsoft domain has a FQDN of search.Microsoft.com. The "www" is actually the name (or one of the names) used by a particular computer. Note that the maximum length of a FQDN is 255 characters.

In NetBIOS networking, as used by older versions of Microsoft operating systems, no two computers can share the same NetBIOS name. The same is true regarding host names, but only in so far as every domain or subdomain is concerned. This is possible because of the hierarchical nature of DNS names. Because the FQDN contains both the host name and domain name, two hosts from different domains can share the same host name (for example, search.Microsoft.com and search.zdnet.com). Also, note that NetBIOS names are derived from the first 15 characters of the host name, so many organizations limit the host name to 15 characters to prevent duplication of NetBIOS names. More about NetBIOS names is found in Chapter 8, "Configuring Client Computer Name Resolution."

## DNS Name Resolution Process

A client can make three common types of queries to a DNS server:

- Recursive queries
- Iterative queries
- Reverse lookup queries

While discussing name resolution, keep in mind that a DNS server can be a client to another DNS server. They often are.

Both recursive and iterative queries try to do the same task in different ways. These are both types of forward lookup queries, and are used to resolve a FQDN located somewhere on the Internet to its IP address. They are analogous to locating a phone number for a person whose name you know. A reverse lookup query is the opposite: given an IP address, it attempts to locate the FQDN of the host using this address. An analogy would be the locating of an individual or company that is using a known telephone number.

### Recursive Queries

When you type a FQDN into the address field of your browser and press **Enter**, you are sending out a query to the server configured as a preferred DNS server for the IP address of this FQDN. The name server receiving this query must respond with either the IP address for a name or with an error stating that data of the requested type doesn't exist or that the domain name specified doesn't exist. The name server cannot simply refer the DNS client to another name server. This type of query is known as a *recursive query*.

A DNS client (often called a *resolver*) typically makes this type of query to a DNS server. Also, if a DNS server is configured to use a *forwarder* (this is another DNS server set up to handle requests forwarded to it), the request from this DNS server to its forwarder will be a recursive query. In other words, name servers that receive recursive requests need to do some digging on behalf of their clients. In networking terms if all forward queries were recursive there would be a lot more traffic on the network, a lot more activity. However, another option exists. The query can be referred onwards to another DNS server. This option is known as an *iterative query*, and is detailed in the next section.

### Iterative Queries

In an *iterative query*, the queried name server provides the best answer it currently has back to the resolver. A DNS server typically performs this type of query to other DNS servers after it has received a recursive query from a resolver. As a rule clients don't make iterative queries. Upon receipt of an iterative query that it does not have a best answer for a DNS server it can respond by saying, in effect, "I can't help you, why don't you try someone else like..." This "someone else" is, of course another DNS server.

Figure 5-2 shows an example of recursive and iterative queries. The numbered steps refer to the following procedure.

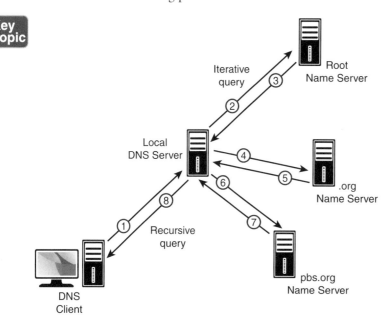

**Figure 5-2**   An iterative query can be described as a "call for help."

1. The resolver sends a recursive DNS query to its local DNS server asking the DNS server to resolve the name www.pbs.org to an IP address. The client expects an answer from the local name server. It cannot be referred to another name server.

2. The local name server can't find the requested information in its zone files or in its cache. It sends an iterative query for www.pbs.org to a root name server located up the DNS tree. Iterative queries are always directed elsewhere.

3. The root name server has authority for the root domain and it sends back the IP address of a name server for the org top-level domain.

4. The local name server sends an iterative query for www.pbs.org to the server that handles the .org top-level domain. (It is able to do this because it has been given the IP address of the .org server by the root name server.)

5. The .org name server responds to the local name server with IP address of the name server that looks after the pbs.org domain.

6. The local name server sends an iterative query for the IP address of www.pbs. org to the pbs.org name server.

7. The pbs.org name server can resolve www an IP address within its domain. It replies to local name server with IP address for www.pbs.org.

8. The local name server now has the exact information it needs to respond to the resolver. It sends the IP address of www.pbs.org to the resolver that needed the name resolved in the first place.

Note that a *zone* as mentioned in Step 2 of this procedure is a discrete portion of the Internet namespace for which a particular DNS server is primarily responsible. You learn more about DNS zones and their configuration in Chapter 6, "Configuring DNS Zones and Replication."

## Reverse Lookup Queries

You have seen how a forward lookup query works. In summary, the client sends the name to the DNS server and the DNS server replies with the IP address. But, what if a resolver has the IP address and needed to know the host name for a particular machine? In this instance, a resolver furnishes an IP address to the name server and requests that it be resolved to a host name. This is the purpose of a *reverse lookup query*. In reverse lookup, the client sends the IP address to the DNS server and the DNS server replies with the name. Normally, a name server would need to perform an exhaustive search of all DNS domains to make sure it found the name that corresponded to an IP address. In our analogy, that would be like having a phone number and having to scan the phone book from A to Z looking for that phone number in order to find out the name of the individual associated with it. To do this, there needs to be a root server that maps IP addresses to names. In fact, there is such a server.

To address this problem, a special domain "in-addr.arpa" in the DNS namespace was created. Domain names, as we have learned, become more specific when moving from right to left. On the other hand, IP addresses become more specific when read from left to right. The most specific part of the IP address 172.48.4.23 is the 23. So, if our name server and all the other name servers in DNS need to answer a question about a particular IP address, they should start in their own neighborhood at the most specific. They would only need to trouble another name server if their investigations didn't yield a result. This means that the record for the IP address 172.48.4.23 should read "backwards" as 23.4.48.172. That is, in fact, the kind of record in-addr.arpa contains. Such would also be true in resolving a phone number. The most specific part of the number 123-456-7890 is the 7890; you could resolve this by looking for the city or town in area code 123 whose numbers begin with the 456 prefix. Resolving the IP address works exactly the same way. The in-addr.arpa domain suffix is discussed in detail in RFC 2317. We look at the mechanics of reverse lookup zones in detail in Chapter 6.

## Installing DNS in Windows Server 2008 R2

In Windows Server 2008 R2, DNS is present as a server role. You can install DNS on any server by using the Add Roles Wizard. DNS now provides complete support for IP version 6 (IPv6). After you install DNS, the DNS Manager MMC snap-in is available in the Administrative Tools folder, from which you can perform all configuration activities associated with DNS.

Before installing DNS on your server, ensure that your server is configured to use a static IP address. You can do this from the Properties dialog box for your network adapter, accessible from the Network and Sharing Center:

1. From the left panel, select **Change adapter settings**.

2. Right-click your network connection and choose **Properties**.

3. From the Local Area Connection Properties dialog box that appears, select either **Internet Protocol Version 4 (TCP/IPv4)** or **Internet Protocol Version 6 (TCP/IPv6)** as required and click **Properties**.

4. In the dialog box that appears, select the **Use the following IP address** option and then type the IP address, subnet mask or subnet prefix length, and default gateway.

Use the following procedure to install DNS on a Windows Server 2008 R2 computer:

1. Open Server Manager and expand the Roles node.

2. Click **Add Roles** to start the Add Roles Wizard.

3. If you receive the Before You Begin page, click **Next**. Note that you can disable the appearance of this page by selecting the check box labeled **Skip this page by default**.

4. The Select Server Roles page enables you to select the roles you want to install on your server. Select **DNS Server** (as shown in Figure 5-3) and click **Next**.

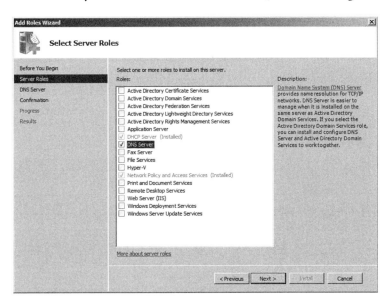

**Figure 5-3**  Selecting the DNS server role.

5. You receive the Introduction to DNS Server page shown in Figure 5-4. To learn more about DNS, click the links provided. When you're ready to proceed, click **Next**.

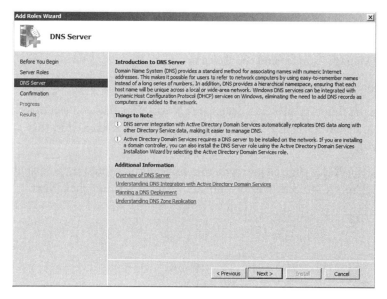

**Figure 5-4**    The Introduction to DNS Server page enables you to obtain more information on DNS.

6. The Confirm Installation Selections page informs you that DNS Server and Domain Name Server will be installed. To proceed, click **Install**.

7. The Installation Progress page tracks the progress of installing DNS. When informed that the installation is complete, click **Close**.

> **NOTE**    For additional information on installing DNS and pre-installation considerations, refer to "Install a DNS Server" at http://technet.microsoft.com/en-us/library/cc725925.aspx.

> **NOTE**    If you use the `dcpromo.exe` utility to install AD DS on your server, the Active Directory Installation Wizard automatically installs DNS on your server if it cannot find another DNS server on the network.

## Using the Command Line to Install DNS

You can also install DNS on a Windows Server 2008 R2 computer from the command line. This is the only method available when installing DNS on a Server Core machine. Similar to the procedure introduced in Chapter 2 for DHCP, you can use DISM.exe to install and configure the DNS server role. Use the following command:

```
Dism /online /enable-feature /featurename:DNS-Server-Core-Role
```

To remove DNS from a Windows Server 2008 R2 computer, use the following command:

```
Dism /online /disable-feature /featurename:DNS-Server-Core-Role
```

On a computer running the original version of Windows Server 2008, use the following command to install DNS:

```
start /w ocsetup DNS-Server-Core-Role
```

Note that in both instances, the keyword DNS-Server-Core-Role is case sensitive and must be entered exactly as shown here.

If you need to remove the DNS server role, use the same command by adding the /uninstall keyword at the end of the command. You can also install DNS on a Server Core machine when using dcpromo.exe to promote the server to a domain controller. This involves use of an answer file, which you can create when promoting a server running a regular installation of Windows Server 2008 to a domain controller.

After installing DNS on a Server Core machine, you can manage DNS by using the dnscmd command at the Server Core machine, or you can connect to this computer from another server by right-clicking **DNS** at the top of the DNS Manager snap-in and choosing **Connect to another computer**. More information on the dnscmd command is provided in the next section.

**NOTE**  For more information on installing DNS and other server roles on a Server Core computer, refer to "Installing and Uninstalling Roles and Features Using Ocsetup" at http://technet.microsoft.com/en-us/magazine/dd673656.aspx.

## Using the Command-Line for DNS Server Administration

You can perform most of the DNS administrative tasks outlined in this and later chapters from the command line by using the *Dnscmd.exe* utility provided with Windows Server 2008 DNS. This is especially useful for scripting repetitive tasks and is the only method available for configuring DNS locally on a Server Core computer (you can also connect to a Server Core computer from a remote computer running the DNS Manager snap-in). Using this command, you can display and modify the properties of DNS servers, zones, and resource records. You can also force replication between DNS server physical memory and DNS databases or data files.

To use this utility, open a command prompt and type the following:

**dnscmd** *server_name command* {*parameters*}

In this command, *server_name* is the name or IP address of the DNS server against which the command is to be executed (if omitted, the local server is used), *command* represents the **dnscmd** subcommand to be executed, and *parameters* represents additional parameters required by the subcommand being executed. Table 5-4 summarizes many of the more useful **dnscmd** subcommands.

**Table 5-4**   Useful dnscmd Subcommands

| Subcommand | Description |
| --- | --- |
| Clearcache | Clears resource records from the DNS cache memory. |
| Config | Enables the user to modify a range of configuration values stored in the registry and individual zones. |
| Enumzones | Displays a complete list of zones configured for the server. |
| Info | Displays DNS server configuration information as stored in the server's registry. You can specify which setting for which information will be returned. |
| Statistics | Displays or clears statistical data for the specified server. You can specify which statistics are to be displayed according to ID numbers. |
| zoneadd *zone_name* | Adds a zone to the DNS server. |
| zonedelete *zone_name* | Deletes the specified zone from the DNS server. |
| zoneexport *zone_name* | Exports all resource records in the specified DNS zone to a text file. |
| zoneinfo *zone_name* | Displays registry-based configuration information for the specified DNS zone. |

For example, use the following command to clear the cache at a server named Server1:

```
dnscmd server1 /clearcache
```

To add a primary forward lookup zone named TestZone whose data is stored in a file named testzone.dns, use the following command at a server named Server1:

```
dnscmd server1 /zoneadd TestZone /primary testzone.dns
```

**NOTE** For a complete list and description of available **dnscmd** commands, including parameters used with the **dnscmd config** command, refer to "Dnscmd" at http://technet.microsoft.com/en-us/library/cc772069(WS.10).aspx. For more information on dnscmd, refer to "Dnscmd Overview" at http://technet.microsoft.com/en-us/library/cc778513(WS.10).aspx.

## Configuring DNS Server Properties

Every DNS server has a Properties dialog box that enables you to configure server properties that are applied to all zones hosted by the server. In the DNS Manager console, select the DNS server, right-click it, and choose **Properties** to display this dialog box. The following sections describe the functions of the eight available tabs.

### Interfaces Tab

On a multihomed DNS server, you can specify the IPv4 and IPv6 addresses of the network interfaces used by DNS to listen for queries from client computers. Doing so ensures that only servers and clients configured to use the specified IP addresses can query the DNS server. This is useful in the case of DNS servers that are also connected to the Internet; in such cases, you can ensure that only clients on the internal network can query your server for DNS name resolution. By default, the DNS server service listens on all IP interfaces on the server, including the following:

- Any additional IP addresses specified for a single network interface
- Individual IP addresses specified for separate interfaces when more than one interface is present on the server

To limit the interfaces to which the DNS server listens for queries, select the **Only the following IP addresses** option on the Interfaces tab, as shown in Figure 5-5.

Type the required IP address to be enabled on the server and then click **Add**. Repeat for any additional interfaces on which the DNS server is to listen for queries.

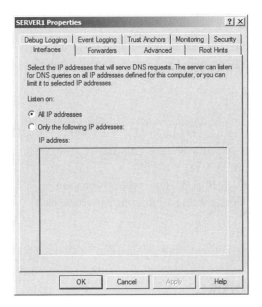

**Figure 5-5**   The Interfaces tab of the DNS server's Properties dialog box enables you to limit the interfaces on which the DNS server listens for queries.

**CAUTION**   Ensure that all IP addresses you enter on the Interfaces tab are valid for the DNS server. If you specify an invalid network interface, the DNS server logs an error with event ID 408, and the DNS server service might not start. Refer to "Event ID 408—DNS Server Configuration" at http://technet.microsoft.com/en-us/library/dd349681(WS.10).aspx for more information.

### Forwarders Tab

As already introduced, the act of forwarding refers to the relaying of a DNS request from one server to another one, when the first server is unable to process the request. This is especially useful in resolving Internet names to their associated IP addresses. By using an external forwarder, the internal DNS server passes off the act of locating an external resource, thereby reducing its processing load and network bandwidth. The use of forwarding is also helpful for protecting internal DNS servers from access by unauthorized Internet users. It works in the following manner:

1. A client issues a request for a FQDN on a zone for which its preferred DNS server is not authoritative (for example, an Internet domain such as www. google.com).

2. The local DNS server receives this request but has zone information only for the internal local domain and checks its list of forwarders.

3. Finding the IP address of an external DNS server (such as one hosted by the company's ISP), it forwards the request to the external server (forwarder).

4. The forwarder attempts to resolve the required FQDN. Should it not be able to resolve this FQDN, it forwards the request to another forwarder or uses an iterative query process to resolve the FQDN.

5. When the forwarder is able to resolve the FQDN, it returns the result to the internal DNS server by way of any intermediate forwarders, which then returns the result to the requesting client.

You can specify external forwarders from the Forwarders tab of the DNS server's Properties dialog box, as shown in Figure 5-6. Click **Edit** to open the Edit Forwarders dialog box, as shown in Figure 5-7. In the space provided, specify the IP address of a forwarder and click **OK** or press **Enter**. The server resolves this IP address to its FQDN and displays these in the Forwarders tab. You can also modify the sequence in which the forwarding servers are contacted by using the **Up** and **Down** command buttons, or you can remove a forwarding server by selecting it and clicking **Delete**.

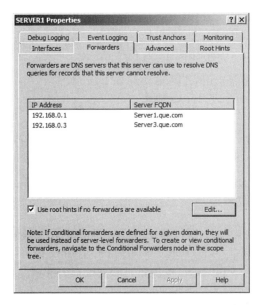

**Figure 5-6**   The Forwarders tab of the DNS server's Properties dialog box enables you to specify forwarders used by the current DNS server.

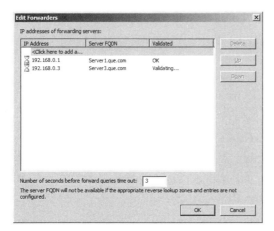

**Figure 5-7**   The Edit Forwarders dialog box enables you to add or remove forwarding servers, or modify the sequence in which they are contacted.

You can also specify forwarders from the command line by using the `dnscmd` command. Open an administrative command prompt and use the following command syntax:

**dnscmd** *ServerName* **/ResetForwarders** *MasterIPaddress* ...
[/TimeOut *Time*] [/Slave]

The parameters of this command are as follows:

- *ServerName* specifies the DNS host name of the DNS server. You must include this parameter; use a period to specify the local computer.

- **/ResetForwarders** indicates that you are configuring a forwarder.

- *MasterIPaddress* ... specifies a space-separated list of one or more IP addresses of DNS servers to which queries are forwarded.

- /TimeOut specifies a timeout (*Time*) setting in seconds, which is the number of seconds that the DNS server waits for a response from the forwarder. Default is 5 seconds.

- /Slave determines whether the DNS server uses recursion when querying for the domain name specified by *ZoneName*.

For example, the following command resets forwarders at the server1.que.com DNS server and specifies that this server forwards queries that it is unable to resolve to the DNS server located at 192.168.0.1 with a timeout value of 7 seconds. In addition, the DNS server does not perform its own iterative queries:

```
Dnscmd server1.que.com /resetforwarders 192.168.0.1 /timeout 7
/slave
```

### Conditional Forwarders

You can configure a DNS server as a conditional forwarder. This DNS server handles name resolution for specified domains only. In other words, the local DNS server forwards all the queries that it receives for names ending with a specific domain name to the conditional forwarder. This is especially useful in situations where users in your company need access to resources in another company with a separate AD DS forest and DNS zones, such as a partner company. In such a case, specify a conditional forwarder that directs such queries to the DNS server in the partner company while other queries are forwarded to the Internet. Doing so reduces the need for adding secondary zones for partner companies on your DNS servers.

The DNS snap-in provides a Conditional Forwarders node where you can specify forwarding information. Use the following procedure to specify conditional forwarders:

1. Right-click the Conditional Forwarders node and choose **New Conditional Forwarder** to display the dialog box shown in Figure 5-8.

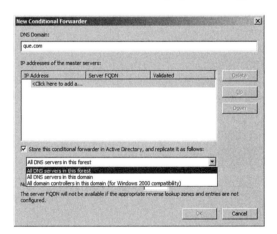

**Figure 5-8**   Creating a new conditional forwarder.

2. Type the DNS domain (for example, que.com) that the conditional forwarder will resolve and the IP address of the server that will handle queries for the specified domain.

3. If you want to store the conditional forwarder information in AD DS, select the check box provided (this check box is enabled when you configure an Active Directory–integrated zone, which is a zone that is configured to store its data in AD DS rather than in a zone.dns file) and choose an option in the drop-down list, as shown in Figure 5-8, that specifies the DNS servers in

your domain or forest that will receive the conditional forwarder information. Then, click **OK**.

Information for the conditional forwarder you have configured is added beneath the Conditional Forwarders node in the DNS Manager snap-in. Name queries for the specified DNS domain will now be forwarded directly to this server.

> **NOTE**   For more information on forwarders and conditional forwarders, refer to "Understanding Forwarders" at http://technet.microsoft.com/en-us/library/cc730756.aspx.

### Advanced Tab

The Advanced tab of the DNS server's Properties dialog box shown in Figure 5-9 contains a series of options that you should be familiar with.

**Figure 5-9**   The Advanced tab of the DNS server's Properties dialog box enables you to configure several additional server options.

## Server Options

The Server Options section of this dialog box contains the following six options, the last three of which are selected by default:

- **Disable recursion:** Prevents the DNS server from forwarding queries to other DNS servers, as described later in this section. Select this check box on a DNS server that only provides resolution services to other DNS servers, because unauthorized users can use recursion to overload a DNS server's resources and thereby deny the DNS Server service to legitimate users.

- **BIND secondaries:** During zone transfer, DNS servers normally utilize a fast transfer method that involves compression. If UNIX servers running a version of Berkeley Internet Name Domain (BIND) prior to 4.9.4 are present, zone transfers will not work. These servers use a slower uncompressed data transfer method. To enable zone transfer to these servers, select this check box. Zone transfers are discussed in Chapter 6. This option is only relevant if the network contains UNIX servers running BIND. For a pure Microsoft DNS setup, this option can remain cleared.

- **Fail on load if bad zone data:** When selected, DNS servers will not load zone data that contains certain types of errors. The DNS service checks name data using the method selected in the Name Checking drop-down list on this tab.

- **Enable round robin:** Enables round robin, as described in Chapter 7, "Configuring DNS Records."

- **Enable netmask ordering:** Prioritizes local subnets so that when a client queries for a host name mapped to multiple IP addresses, the DNS server preferentially returns an IP address located on the same subnet as the requesting client. This topic is discussed further in Chapter 7.

- **Secure cache against pollution:** Cache pollution takes place when DNS query responses contain malicious items received from nonauthoritative servers. This option prevents attackers from adding such resource records to the DNS cache. The DNS servers ignore resource records for domain names outside the domain to which the query was originally directed. For example, if you sent a query for `que.com` and a referral provided a name such as `quepublishing.com`, the latter name would not be cached when this option is enabled.

## Disable Recursion

As discussed earlier, the act of recursion refers to the name-resolution technique where a DNS server queries other DNS servers on behalf of the requesting client to obtain the required FQDN, which it returns to the client. Unauthorized individuals can use recursion to overload a DNS server's resources, thereby causing a denial of service (DoS) attack on the DNS server and preventing its servicing of legitimate name resolution requests.

To reduce the possibility of a DoS attack on an internal network DNS server that does not need to process recursive queries, you should disable recursion on the DNS server. To do so, select the check box labeled **Disable recursion (also disables forwarders)** from the Advanced tab of the server's Properties dialog box previously shown in Figure 5-9.

You can also disable recursion from the command line. Open an administrative command prompt and type the following command:

```
dnscmd <ServerName> /Config /NoRecursion {1|0}
```

In this command, the /Config parameter specifies that the server indicated by *ServerName* is being configured, and the /NoRecursion parameter together with the numeral 1 disables recursion. To re-enable recursion, re-issue the same command with the numeral 0.

**NOTE**   For more information on disabling recursion, refer to "Disable Recursion on the DNS Server" at http://technet.microsoft.com/en-us/library/cc771738.aspx.

### Name Checking

The Name checking setting (refer to Figure 5-9) enables you to configure the DNS server to permit names that contain characters that are not allowed by normal DNS standards outlined in RFC 1123. You can select the following options:

- **Strict RFC (ANSI):** Uses strict name checking according to RFC 1123 host naming specifications. Non-compliant DNS names generate error messages.

- **Non RFC (ANSI):** Permits nonstandard names that do not conform to RFC 1123 host naming specifications. ASCII characters that are not compliant to RFC 1123 specifications are accepted.

- **Multibyte (UTFB):** Enables the transformation and recoding of multibyte non-ASCII characters according to Unicode Transformation Format (UTF-8) specifications. This is the default setting.

- **All names:** Permits names containing any types of characters.

If you receive an error with ID 4006, indicating that the DNS server was unable to load the records in the specified name found in the Active Directory–integrated zone, this means that the DNS name contains unsupported characters. You can resolve this problem by selecting the **All names** option and restarting the DNS service. This enables the DNS names to be loaded. If the names are improper, you can delete them and then reset the Name Checking setting.

### Loading Zone Data

When a DNS server containing an Active Directory-integrated zone starts up, it normally uses information stored in this zone and in the Registry to initialize the service and load its zone data. The Load zone data on startup option (refer to Figure 5-9) enables you to specify that the DNS server starts from the Registry only, or from a file named `Boot` and located in the `%systemroot%\System32\Dns` folder. This optional file is similar in format to that used by BIND servers.

> **TIP**   If you have improperly configured options on this tab and want to return to the default options, click the **Reset to Default** command button at the bottom of this tab and then click **Apply** to apply this change without closing the dialog box (or **OK** to apply the changes and close the dialog box).

### Root Hints Tab

As already discussed, a DNS server that is unable to resolve a name directly from its own database or with the aid of a forwarder sends the query to a server that is authoritative for the DNS root zone. The server must have the names and addresses of these servers stored in its database in order to perform such a query. These names and addresses are known as *root hints*, and they are stored in the `cache.dns` file, which is found at `%systemroot%\system32\dns`. This is a text file that contains resource records for every available root server. Resource records are discussed in Chapter 7.

When you first install DNS on a server that is connected to the Internet, it should download the latest set of root hints automatically. You can verify that this has occurred by checking the Root Hints tab of the server's Properties dialog box. You should see a series of FQDNs with their corresponding IP addresses, as shown in Figure 5-10.

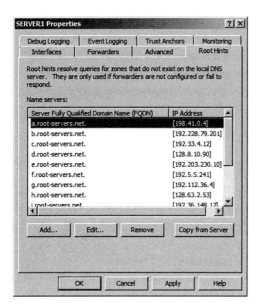

**Figure 5-10**   The Root Hints tab of the DNS server's Properties dialog box displays the names and IP addresses of the Internet root zones.

If your internal DNS server does not provide access to Internet name resolution, you can improve network security by configuring the root hints of the internal DNS servers to point to the DNS servers that host your root domain and not to Internet root domain DNS servers. To modify the configuration on this tab, perform one or more of the following actions:

- Click **Add** to display the New Name Server Record dialog box, from which you can manually type the FQDN and IP addresses of one or more authoritative name servers.

- Select an entry and click **Edit** to display the Edit Name Server Record dialog box, which enables you to modify it or add an additional IP address to an existing record.

- Select an entry and click **Remove** to remove a record.

- Click **Copy from Server** to copy a list of root hints from another DNS server. Type the DNS name or IP address in the dialog box that appears. This action is useful if your server was not connected to the Internet at the time DNS was installed.

> **TIP**  You can also use the Configure a DNS Server Wizard to configure root hints for your server. Right-click your server in the console tree of the DNS Manager snap-in and choose **Configure a DNS Server**. Click **Next** and then select the **Configure root hints only (recommended for advanced users only)** option from the Select Configuration Action page of the wizard.

### Debug Logging Tab

The Debug Logging tab enables you to configure packet-level logging for debugging purposes. Packets sent to and from the DNS server are logged to a text file named `dns.log`. This file is stored in the `%systemroot%\system32\dns` folder.

To enable debug logging, select the **Log packets for debugging** check box on the Debug Logging tab, which makes all other check boxes available, as shown in Figure 5-11. Table 5-5 describes the available logging options.

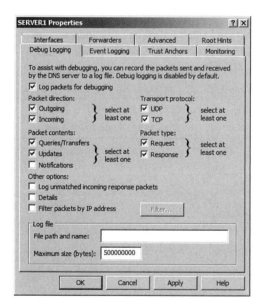

**Figure 5-11**  Configuring debug logging.

**Table 5-5** DNS Debug Logging Options

| Option | Description |
|--------|-------------|
| Packet direction | Determines the direction of packets logged, incoming or outgoing or both. |
| Transport protocol | Select **UDP** to log the number of DNS requests received over a UDP port and select **TCP** to log the number of DNS requests received over a TCP port. |
| Packet contents | Select at least one of the available options to determine the types of packets logged by the server:<br><br>■ **Queries/Transfers:** Logs packets containing standard queries, according to RFC 1034.<br><br>■ **Updates:** Logs packets containing dynamic updates, according to RFC 2136.<br><br>■ **Notifications:** Logs packets containing notifications, according to RFC 1996. |
| Packet type | Determines whether the request or response (or both) packets are logged. |
| Other options | Select **Details** to enable logging of detailed information.<br><br>Select **Filter** to limit the packets that are logged according to IP address. This logs packets sent from specific IP addresses to the DNS server or from the DNS server to these specific IP addresses (according to the incoming or outgoing choice). |
| Log file | Enables you to change the default file path, name, and maximum size. If the maximum size is exceeded, the DNS server overwrites the oldest logged data. |

**CAUTION** Configure debug logging only when absolutely necessary, only on required DNS servers, and only on a temporary basis. Its use is highly resource intensive. It is for this reason that debug logging is disabled by default.

To view the DNS log, first stop the DNS service by right-clicking the DNS server in DNS Manager and choosing **All Tasks > Stop**. Then, open the log in either Notepad or WordPad. When you are finished, restart the DNS service by right-clicking the DNS server and choosing **All Tasks > Start**.

### Event Logging Tab

The Event Logging tab of the DNS server's Properties dialog box, shown in Figure 5-12, enables you to control how much information is logged to the DNS log, which appears in Event Viewer. You can choose from one of the following options:

- **No events:** Suppresses all event logging (not recommended).

- **Errors only:** Logs error events only.

- **Errors and warnings:** Logs errors and warnings only.

- **All events:** Logs informational events, errors, and warnings. This is the default.

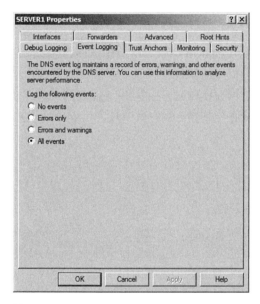

**Figure 5-12**   The Event Logging tab enables you to control the quantity of information that is logged to the DNS log in Event Viewer.

Choosing either the **Errors only** or **Errors and warnings** option might be useful to reduce the amount of information recorded to the DNS event log.

### Trust Anchors Tab

You should configure a trust anchor for signed zones on every DNS server that will attempt to validate DNS data from that zone. A trust anchor is a preconfigured public key associated with a specific zone in DNS. Such a trust anchor is used to support the DNSKEY resource record on a Windows Server 2008 R2 DNS server; it provides additional security against certain types of intrusions such as spoofing, man-in-the-middle, and cache-poisoning attacks.

Because of vulnerabilities in DNS to these types of intrusions, DNS security extensions (DNSSEC) were developed to add additional security to the DNS protocol. Outlined in RFCs 4033, 4034, and 4035, DNSSEC is a suite of DNS extensions that adds security to the DNS protocol by providing origin authority, data integrity, and authenticated denial of existence. Although an older form of DNSSEC was used in Windows Server 2003 and the first iteration of Windows Server 2008, DNSSEC has been updated completely according to the specifications in the above-mentioned RFCs. The newest form of DNSSEC is available for Windows Server 2008 R2 and Windows 7 only.

DNSSEC enables DNS servers to use digital signatures to validate responses from other servers and resolvers. Signatures are stored in a new type of resource record called DNSKEY within the DNS zone. Upon resolving a name query, the DNS server includes the appropriate digital signature with the response, and the signature is validated by means of a preconfigured *trust anchor*. This is a preconfigured public key associated with a specific zone. The validating server is configured with one or more trust anchors. Besides DNSKEY, DNSSEC adds RRSIG, NSEC, and DS resource records to DNS.

The Trust Anchors tab of the DNS server's Properties dialog box enables you to view zones that are signed with DNSSEC, as shown in Figure 5-13.

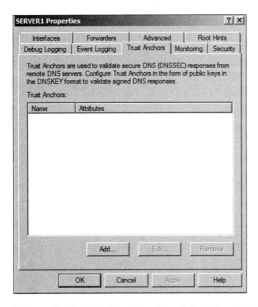

**Figure 5-13**   The Trust Anchors tab of the DNS server's Properties dialog box enables you to view and specify trust anchors configured on your DNS server.

To specify a trust anchor, click **Add**. Provide the information requested in the New Trust Anchor dialog box, including its name and public key value, and then click **OK**. The public key value must be formatted as a Base64 encoding value. It needs to come from the other server because it's matched to that server's private key; for more information on the public key, refer to www.rfc-archive.org/getrfc.

php?rfc=4034. Doing so adds the trust anchor to the Trust Anchors tab and enables its use for signing DNS query responses.

> **NOTE**  For more information on how DNSSEC works, refer to "DNSSEC Security Extensions (DNSSEC)" at http://technet.microsoft.com/en-us/library/ee683904(WS.10).aspx, "Introduction to DNSSEC" at http://technet.microsoft.com/en-us/library/ee649205(WS.10).aspx, and "Understanding DNSSEC in Windows" at http://technet.microsoft.com/en-us/library/ee649277(WS.10).aspx.

### Monitoring Tab

The Monitoring tab enables you to perform test queries that verify the proper installation and operation of the DNS server. Shown in Figure 5-14, this tab enables you to perform two types of test queries:

- **Simple query:** The DNS client software performs a local query to a zone stored in the DNS server (including Active Directory-integrated zones).

- **Recursive query:** A recursive query is forwarded to another DNS server for resolution.

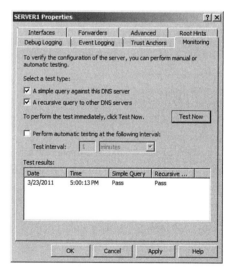

**Figure 5-14**  The Monitoring tab enables you to perform simple and recursive test queries against the DNS server.

To perform these queries, select the appropriate check boxes, as illustrated in Figure 5-14, and click the **Test Now** command button. The result is displayed in the Test results field directly below. You can also schedule the test to occur automatically at preconfigured intervals by selecting the check box labeled **Perform automatic testing at the following interval** and then selecting a test interval in minutes or hours from the drop-down list.

A `Pass` result for the simple test confirms that DNS has been correctly installed on this server. If the recursive test fails, check the connectivity to the remote server as well as the presence and correctness of the root hints file (`cache.dns`). Note that it is best to use the automatic testing option and obtain a series of test results. As seen in Figure 5-12, each test includes a date and time stamp. Although a single failure might occur because of a temporary outage, multiple failures generally indicate a name resolution problem. Failure of all recursive query tests might indicate that the Disable Recursion option on the Advanced tab has been selected.

**NOTE**   Refer to "Monitor your DNS Servers on Windows Server 2008 R2" at http://technet.microsoft.com/en-us/magazine/ff521760.aspx for more information on using the Monitoring tab.

DNS also adds a log to the Event Viewer and several objects and counters to the Performance Monitor. We discuss these tools in Chapter 19, "Configuring Performance Monitoring," and Chapter 20, "Configuring Event Logs."

## DNS Socket Pooling

New to Windows Server 2008 R2 is the concept of *DNS socket pooling*, also known as *source port randomization*. This enables the server to select random source ports from a pool of available sockets when answering queries from DNS clients. In doing so, the server is protected against DNS cache poisoning attacks. In the original version of Windows Server 2008 or older servers, DNS used a predictable source port when answering queries, which enabled an intruder to access a known port used in the DNS query and thereby execute a successful cache poisoning attack.

By default, the size of the socket pool is 2500. You can specify a value between 0 and 10,000; larger values provide greater protection against DNS spoofing attacks. To configure the size of the socket pool, open a command prompt, type the following command, and then restart the DNS server service:

```
dnscmd /Config /SocketPoolSize <value>
```

The `<value>` keyword specifies the desired size of the socket pool. To view the current size of the socket pool, use this command with the `/Info` keyword. Figure 5-15 shows an example of determining the current socket pool size and then setting this size to 5000.

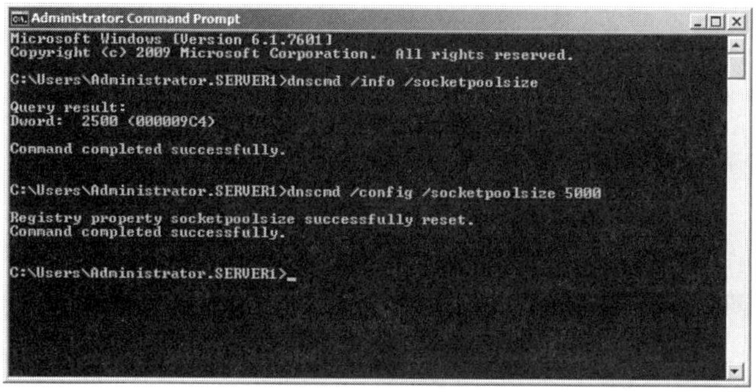

**Figure 5-15**   Configuring the socket pool size.

You can also exclude port ranges from the socket pool by using the following command:

```
dnscmd /Config /SocketPoolExcludedPortRanges <excluded port ranges>
```

Specify the range of ports to be excluded with the `<excluded port ranges>` keyword.

**NOTE**   These commands modify values of registry keys associated with the socket pool. For more information on the registry keys and configuration of the socket pool size, refer to "Configure the Socket Pool" at http://technet.microsoft.com/en-us/library/ee649174(WS.10).aspx.

## DNS Cache Locking

New to DNS in Windows Server 2008 R2 is the concept of cache locking, which is a security feature that enables you to control the overwriting of information stored in the DNS cache. As already mentioned, a DNS server stores the results of recent queries in its cache, so that it can rapidly resolve repeated queries for the same FQDN without the need to forward these queries. This cached information is stored for a period known as the Time to Live (TTL). However, information in the cache can be updated before expiry of the TTL should the DNS server receive updated information about a query. An intruder that successfully overwrites information in the cache might be able to redirect network traffic to a malicious site.

On a Windows Server 2008 R2 computer, you can configure a percent value for cache locking. This refers to the percent of the TTL within which the DNS server will not overwrite a cached entry. For example, if this value is set to 50, the DNS server does not overwrite the cached entry for 50 percent of the TTL. By default, the cache locking value is 100 percent.

To modify the cache locking value, type the following command from an elevated command prompt, and then restart the DNS server service:

```
dnscmd /Config /CacheLockingPercent <percent>
```

Specify the desired cache locking percent in the `<percent>` keyword as a value between 0 and 100 in decimal format. If omitted, cache locking value is set to 0. To view the current value of the cache locking percent value, use this command with the `/Info` keyword.

Figure 5-16 shows an example of determining the current cache locking value and then resetting this value to 75 percent.

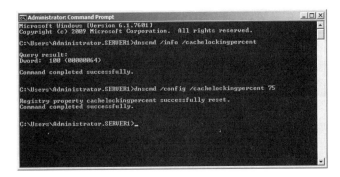

**Figure 5-16**   Configuring the cache locking value.

**NOTE**   This command modifies the value of a registry key associated with the cache locking percent value. For more information, refer to "Configure Cache Locking" at http://technet.microsoft.com/en-us/library/ee649148(WS.10).aspx.

## Exam Preparation Tasks

## Review All the Key Topics

Review the most important topics in this chapter, noted with the key topics icon in the outer margin of the page. Table 5-6 lists a reference of these key topics and the page numbers on which each is found.

**Table 5-6**  Key Topics for Chapter 5

| Key Topic Element | Description | Page Number |
| --- | --- | --- |
| Figure 5-1 | Shows you how the Internet namespace is set up. | 212 |
| Paragraph | Introduces the types of DNS queries. | 215 |
| Figure 5-2 | Shows you how recursive and iterative queries for domain names work. | 216 |
| List | Describes the procedure for installing the DNS server role. | 219 |
| Figure 5-6 | Shows how to specify DNS forwarders. | 225 |
| List | Shows how to create a conditional forwarder. | 227 |
| Figure 5-9 | Displays advanced DNS server configuration options. | 228 |
| Table 5-5 | Describes debug logging options. | 234 |
| Figure 5-14 | Shows you how to perform test queries against a DNS server. | 237 |

## Definition of Key Terms

Define the following key terms from this chapter, and check your answers in the Glossary.

conditional forwarding, dnscmd, DNS Manager, DNSSEC (Domain Name System Security Extensions), Domain Name System (DNS), forward lookup query, forwarding, fully qualified domain name (FQDN), host name, iterative query, recursion, reverse lookup query, root hints, trust anchor

This chapter covers the following subjects:

- **Zone Types and Their Uses:** This section introduces you to primary, secondary, and stub zones. It also shows you when you should use each zone type and discusses integration of these zones with Active Directory.

- **Configuring DNS Zones:** After you install DNS, you need to create and configure the zones to be hosted by your server. After showing you how to create new zones, this section looks at the various properties available for DNS zones; it also shows you how to create subdomains and delegated zones.

- **Configuring DNS Zone Transfers and Replication:** It is important that you understand how information in DNS zones is replicated among DNS servers. Two types of zone transfers are used in Windows Server 2008; in addition, Active Directory–integrated zones are replicated by means of Active Directory replication.

- **Troubleshooting DNS Zones and Replication:** Problems can occur with DNS and the replication of zones among servers. These can manifest themselves with failures of clients to resolve Internet names or improper resolution of names. This section discusses several troubleshooting tools provided with DNS.

# CHAPTER 6

# Configuring DNS Zones and Replication

In Chapter 5, "Installing and Configuring Domain Name System (DNS)," you learned what DNS is all about and how to set up a DNS server and configure its general properties. You were briefly introduced to the concept of DNS *zones* as subdivisions of the overall DNS namespace. Management of DNS would be a daunting, overwhelming task without some methodology of subdividing the namespace, and this is where the concept of zones fits in. Simply put, a zone is a discrete portion of the namespace that is managed as a unit and stored on a server as a specific database file. Such a file can be managed on its own or it can be integrated into the hierarchical database of Active Directory Domain Services (AD DS).

To ensure that DNS zone data is always available to client computers requesting name resolution services, copies of zones must be made available to more than one server. It is for this purpose that DNS uses a system of *zone transfer*, also known as *zone replication*. To ensure that up-to-date copies of zone data are always available, you must be able to configure and troubleshoot zone transfers. This chapter introduces you to all the facts you need to know to manage DNS zones on your network.

## "Do I Know This Already?" Quiz

The "Do I Know This Already?" quiz allows you to assess whether you should read this entire chapter or simply jump to the "Exam Preparation Tasks" section for review. If you are in doubt, read the entire chapter. Table 6-1 outlines the major headings in this chapter and the corresponding "Do I Know This Already?" quiz questions. You can find the answers in Appendix A, "Answers to the 'Do I Know This Already?' Quizzes."

**Table 6-1**  "Do I Know This Already?" Foundation Topics Section-to-Question Mapping

| Foundations Topics Section | Questions Covered in This Section |
| --- | --- |
| Zone Types and Their Uses | 1–4 |
| Configuring DNS Zones | 5–8 |
| Configuring DNS Zone Transfers and Replication | 9–10 |
| Troubleshooting DNS Zones and Replication | 11–12 |

1. What DNS zone type contains source information about authoritative name servers for its zone only?

   a. Primary zone

   b. Secondary zone

   c. Forwarding zone

   d. Stub zone

   e. Active Directory–integrated zone

2. You set up two Windows Server 2008 R2 servers as domain controllers and configured them with Active Directory–integrated DNS zones. You configured another Windows Server 2008 R2 computer as a DNS server. You do not intend to promote this server to domain controller, but you want it to include a backup copy of the DNS zone data for your domain. What DNS zone type should you configure?

   a. Primary zone

   b. Secondary zone

   c. Forwarding zone

   d. Stub zone

   e. Active Directory–integrated zone

3. Your network has several older servers that have static records with single-label names. Historically, you have used WINS for name resolution with these servers, but the WINS server is being removed as your network is being converted to IPv6. What zone type should you configure to support these servers?

   a. Primary zone

   b. Secondary zone

   c. GlobalNames zone

   d. Stub zone

4. Which of the following is *not* a benefit of hosting a secondary DNS name server on your network?

   a. Load balancing.

   b. Fault tolerance.

   c. Faster name resolution across a slow link.

   d. It is not involved with zone transfers, so network traffic across slow links is reduced.

5. You are configuring a reverse lookup zone for your network, which uses the Class C network address range of 192.168.8.0/24. Which of the following addresses should you use for the reverse lookup zone?

   **a.** `8.168.192.in-addr.arpa`

   **b.** `0.8.168.192.in-addr.arpa`

   **c.** `192.168.8.in-addr.arpa`

   **d.** `192.168.8.0.in-addr.arpa`

6. You are responsible for a DNS server that is configured as a secondary name server for its zone. The processor on the corresponding primary name server has failed and it will take a week or two to repair this server and get it back online, so you want to reconfigure this zone as a primary zone. What should you do?

   **a.** Right-click your server in the DNS Manager snap-in and choose **Properties**. From the General tab of the server's Properties dialog box, choose the **Primary name server** option.

   **b.** Right-click the zone in the DNS Manager snap-in and choose **Properties**. From the Name Servers tab of the zone's Properties dialog box, specify the FQDN of the current secondary server as a primary name server.

   **c.** Right-click the zone in the DNS Manager snap-in and choose **Properties**. From the General tab of the zone's Properties dialog box, click **Change** and specify the **Primary** zone type.

   **d.** Back up the zone information and delete the zone. Then, use the New Zone Wizard to create a new primary zone and finally restore the zone information to this zone.

7. Desktop support technicians have been busy replacing older Windows XP computers in your company with new Windows 7 machines, and you noticed that the performance of your DNS servers has been declining. Checking the zone data, you notice that many stale resource records are present in the DNS zone file database. What should you do to delete these resource records as soon as possible?

   **a.** Right-click your server in the console tree of DNS Manager and choose **Scavenge Stale Resource Records**. Then, click **Yes** in the message box that appears.

   **b.** Right-click your server in the console tree of DNS Manager and choose **Properties**. On the Advanced tab of the server's Properties dialog box,

select the **Enable automatic scavenging of stale records** option and
specify a short time frame as the scavenging period.

**c.** Right-click your server in the console tree of DNS Manager and choose
**Set Aging/Scavenging for All Zones**. Then, select the **Scavenge stale
resource records** check box and specify short values for the no-refresh
and refresh intervals.

**d.** Right-click the zone in the console tree of DNS Manager and choose
Properties. From the General tab, click **Aging** and on the Zone Aging/
Scavenging Properties dialog box, select the **Enable automatic scavenging of stale records** option and specify a short time frame as the
scavenging period.

**8.** Administrators in the Engineering department of your company want the ability to manage their own DNS server and its namespace while existing within
the overall company DNS namespace. How should you configure DNS to enable this?

**a.** In DNS Manager, right-click **Forward Lookup Zone** and choose **New
Zone**. In the New Zone Wizard, select **Primary Zone**. Type Engineering on the Zone Name page and complete the remaining steps of the
wizard. Then, right-click **Reverse Lookup Zone**, choose **New Zone**,
and repeat the same options as for the forward lookup zone.

**b.** In DNS Manager, right-click **Forward Lookup Zone** and choose **New
Zone**. In the New Zone Wizard, select **Secondary Zone**. Type Engineering on the Zone Name page and complete the remaining steps
of the wizard. Then, right-click **Reverse Lookup Zone**, choose **New
Zone**, and repeat the same options as for the forward lookup zone.

**c.** In DNS Manager, right-click your company's forward lookup zone and
choose **New Domain**. Then, type `Engineering` in the New DNS Domain dialog box that appears and click **OK**. Then, repeat this action with
your company's reverse lookup zone.

**d.** In DNS Manager, right-click your company's forward lookup zone and
choose **New Delegation**. On the Delegated Domain Name page of the
New Delegation Wizard that appears, type `Engineering`, and then complete the remaining steps of this wizard.

9. You are responsible for maintaining the DNS servers on your company's AD DS forest, which contains three domains and 10 DNS servers. One of these servers is still running Windows 2000 and it is also hosting an application that still has not been updated for use with newer Windows versions. You have installed a new DNS server and need to ensure that it can replicate its zone data to all servers including the Windows 2000 server. Which replication scope option should you choose?

   a. **To all DNS servers running on domain controllers in this forest**

   b. **To all DNS servers running on domain controllers in this domain**

   c. **To all domain controllers in this domain**

   d. **To all domain controllers in the scope of this directory partition**

10. You are responsible for managing DNS in your company's AD DS domain, which includes five DNS servers. You want to ensure that zone transfers within the domain are secured using IPSec. What should you do?

    a. Open the Group Policy Management Editor focused on a domain-based GPO and navigate to the **Computer Configuration\Policies\ Windows Settings\Security Settings\Windows Firewall with Advanced Security\Windows Firewall with Advanced Security\Connection Security Rules** node. Create a new connection security rule that requires authentication for inbound and outbound connections using the Kerberos V5 protocol.

    b. Open the Group Policy Management Editor focused on a domain-based GPO and navigate to the **Computer Configuration\Policies\ Windows Settings\Security Settings\Windows Firewall with Advanced Security\Windows Firewall with Advanced Security\Inbound Rules** node. Create a new inbound rule that requires authentication for inbound and outbound connections using the Kerberos V5 protocol. Then, repeat these steps to create a similar outbound rule.

    c. On each DNS server, right-click the forward lookup zone in DNS Manager and choose **Properties**. From the Zone Transfers tab, select the **Only to servers listed on the Name Servers tab** option and specify the IP addresses of the other DNS servers on this tab.

    d. On each DNS server, right-click the forward lookup zone in DNS Manager and choose **Properties**. From the Zone Transfers tab, select the **Only to the following servers** option, click **Edit**, and specify the IP addresses of the other DNS servers.

    e. On each DNS server, right-click the DNS server in DNS Manager and choose **Properties**. From the Advanced tab, select the **Enable zone transfers using** IPSec option.

**11.** A user in your company reports that he is unable to access shares on a file server. At his computer, you attempt to ping the file server by name but are unsuccessful; however, you are successful when you ping the file server by IP address. Which of the following might be useful in troubleshooting this problem? (Choose all that apply.)

   **a.** Use the `nslookup` command to query the DNS server.

   **b.** Perform simple and recursive test queries at the DNS server.

   **c.** Use the `ipconfig /release` and `ipconfig /renew` commands at the user's computer.

   **d.** Use the `ipconfig /flushdns` command at the user's computer.

   **e.** Check the event logs on the DNS server for errors.

**12.** Which of the following commands would provide you with the host name of a computer whose IP address is `10.0.5.25`?

   **a.** `ping 10.0.5.25`

   **b.** `nslookup 10.0.5.25`

   **c.** `ipconfig /all`

   **d.** `ipconfig 10.0.5.25`

## Foundation Topics

# Zone Types and Their Uses

As introduced in Chapter 5, each DNS server stores information about a portion of the Internet namespace. Such a portion is known as a *zone*, and the DNS server that is primarily responsible for each zone is considered to be authoritative for that zone. In other words, the DNS server is the main source of information regarding the Internet addresses contained within the zone. A zone can be considered a part of the big database that is DNS, and can contain information on one or more domains. Zones are defined by who looks after maintaining the records that they contain.

## DNS Zone Types

Windows Server 2008 R2 enables you to configure the four different types of DNS zones introduced in Table 6-2.

**Table 6-2**   DNS Zone Types

| Zone Type | Description |
|---|---|
| Primary zone | A master writable copy of zone data stored in a text file and administered from the server on which it is created |
| Secondary zone | A copy of an existing zone that has been replicated from another DNS server and is stored as a read-only text file |
| Active Directory–integrated zone | A master writable copy of zone data that is stored and replicated from within AD DS |
| Stub zone | A secondary copy of an existing zone that contains only the resource records needed to identify the authoritative DNS servers for the corresponding primary zone |

### Primary Zones

Each primary contains the read/write database for its zone and is stored on a DNS name server known as the *primary name server*. This DNS server is the primary source for information concerning this zone, and is referred to as being authoritative for its zone. By default, this primary zone is called `zone_name.dns` and is stored in the `%systemroot%\system32\dns` folder on the server. Note that any client computer can update its records within the primary zone.

### Secondary Zones

Other DNS servers can host secondary zones that are replicas of the primary zone located on another name server across the network that is authoritative for that zone. The process of obtaining this zone information (that is, the database file) across the network is referred to as a *zone transfer*. The file itself is read-only. Changes to zone information cannot be made to a zone file stored on a secondary name server. Such a zone is stored as a text file in the `%systemroot%\system32\dns` folder on its server, and cannot be integrated with AD DS. Zone transfers are discussed in detail later in this chapter.

### Active Directory–Integrated Zones

When you host your primary zones on a domain controller, the option to integrate these zones with AD DS becomes available. These zones are stored as directory objects in the AD DS database file and replicated to other domain controllers as a component of AD DS replication. Using Active Directory–integrated zones provides the following benefits:

- **Zone security is enhanced:** You can configure zone updates to be secured so that intruders cannot modify zone data to redirect clients to rogue servers on the Internet. You can also use access control list (ACL) editing to secure DNS zone objects within the directory tree.

- **Zone data are automatically replicated and synchronized to all domain controllers:** Each domain controller always stores a copy of directory-integrated zones, thereby providing redundancy and fault tolerance. When you add a new domain controller to the network, it automatically receives an up-to-date copy of the DNS zone database.

- **Administration of zone file replication across your network is facilitated:** You can use only a single replication topology for replicating both the directory database and zone data, thereby simplifying administrative requirements.

- **Faster and more efficient replication is possible:** AD DS replication propagates only relevant changes to each zone database, requiring the synchronizing of smaller quantities of data.

> **NOTE**   For more information on Active Directory–integrated zones, refer to "Understanding Active Directory Domain Services Integration" at http://technet.microsoft.com/en-us/library/cc726034.aspx.

## Stub Zones

A stub zone is similar to a secondary zone, but includes only information about the zone's authoritative name servers. As with a secondary zone, information is replicated from the authoritative server hosting the corresponding primary zone.

A stub zone is useful for the following purposes:

- **Maintain current delegated zone information:** By updating each stub zone on a regular basis, the DNS server hosting both the parent zone and the stub zone maintains a current list of authoritative DNS servers for the zone.

- **Improve name resolution:** By using a stub zone, DNS servers can perform recursion using the list of name servers contained in the stub zone without having to query the Internet or an internal root server for the DNS namespace.

- **Simplify DNS administration:** By utilizing stub zones within your DNS infrastructure, you can distribute lists of the authoritative DNS servers without the need for secondary zones. Note that stub zones are not an alternative for enhancing redundancy and load balancing.

The following two lists of DNS servers are involved in the loading and maintenance of a stub zone:

- The list of master servers involved in the maintenance of the stub zone. These servers might be a primary or secondary server for the zone. The server hosting the stub zone will have a complete list of the DNS servers for the zone.

- The list of authoritative DNS servers for the zone, as maintained in the stub zone using name server (NS) resource records. We study resource records in detail in Chapter 7, "Configuring DNS Records."

Note that a stub zone can be integrated with Active Directory.

## Forward and Reverse Lookup Zones

All the zone types discussed in this section can occur as either forward or reverse lookup zones. The forward lookup zones are the commonly used ones that resolve fully qualified domain names (FQDN) to IP addresses. As introduced in Chapter 5, DNS can also take an IP address and resolve it to its corresponding FQDN. This process is known as a reverse lookup query, and each DNS server hosts a reverse lookup zone file that makes this process possible.

The reverse lookup files maps IP addresses to host names, by using a special domain name that ends in "in-addr.arpa" and contains the octets of the network portion of the IP address in reverse sequence as described earlier in this chapter. On an IPv6 network, a domain name ending in "ip6.arpa" is used, as described in Request for Comment (RFC) 3596. The use of a reverse lookup file allows a resolver to provide an IP address and request a matching host name. Pointer (PTR) records, which you learn about in Chapter 7, are used to provide a static mapping of IP addresses to host names within a reverse-lookup zone. They can be created either manually or automatically when A records are added to the forward lookup zone file.

You can have reverse lookup zones in any of the primary, secondary, or Active Directory–integrated zone types.

**NOTE**   For more information on reverse lookup zones, refer to "Understanding Reverse Lookup" at http://technet.microsoft.com/en-us/library/cc730980.aspx. Also, refer to "DNS Extensions to Support IP Version 6" at http://tools.ietf.org/html/rfc3596.

### GlobalNames Zones

A *GlobalNames* zone is a special type of Active Directory–integrated zone that enables you to resolve static, global records with single-label names without the need for a Windows Internet Name Service (WINS) server. You can use this zone to manage older servers that are assigned static IP addresses and have been managed using WINS. However, the GlobalNames zone is not designed to completely replace WINS. You should not use this zone type to support the name resolution of records that are dynamically registered in WINS.

The following are several situations in which it is useful to deploy a GlobalNames zone:

- You are retiring WINS or planning to convert your network to using only IPv6 (WINS will not work in an IPv6 network.)

- You require single-label name resolution only for important servers or websites that can be statically registered in DNS. Note that the GlobalNames zone cannot register host names using dynamic updates.

- You are unable to rely on the suffix search lists on client computers for providing single-label name resolution, perhaps because there is a large number of target domains where the possibility of duplicated host names exists.

- All the DNS servers that are authoritative for your zones run Windows Server 2008. This is needed so that names registered in the GlobalNames zone can be properly resolved.

A GlobalNames zone is not a unique zone type in the sense of the other zone types mentioned in this section; it is simply an Active Directory–integrated zone that is called GlobalNames.

You need to use dnscmd when enabling support for a GlobalNames zone on your network. At every authoritative DNS server in the forest, run the following command:

```
dnscmd ServerName /config /enableglobalnamessupport 1
```

In this command, `ServerName` is the name of the DNS server hosting the Global-Names zone.

### DNS Name Server Roles

DNS servers can store and maintain the database of names in several different ways and are referred to as name servers. The servers need to be specifically configured to perform these roles. Keep in mind that name servers can store the data for one or more zones. This depends, of course, on the way they are configured. The name server roles are described in the following sections.

### Primary Name Servers

A name server provides names to its clients. Where does it get this information? Each primary zone is maintained on a name server known as the primary name server. This server provides zone data to fulfill queries from the original zone file that it is storing. As well, the primary name server handles all changes made to the zone file for a zone, such as adding domains or hosts. For this reason, a primary name server is described as authoritative for its zone. It has the last word on host name to IP address resolution within its zone, and therefore does not have to issue an iterative query to another server in order to resolve a host name for a machine located in its zone. There can only be one primary name server for any given zone.

Additional characteristics of primary name servers that are shared with all DNS servers include the following:

- **They can boot from either the registry or a boot file:** By default, the Windows Server 2008 DNS server obtains operational data from the registry. Information is located in the following key:

    ```
    HKEY_LOCAL_MACHINE\SYSTEM\CurrentControlSet\Services\
    DNS\parameters\BootMethod
    ```

However, Windows Server 2008 DNS also provides a file that is named BOOT, which is stored (like other DNS database files) at the `%systemroot%\system32\dns` folder. You can use the BOOT file by modifying the server properties in the DNS snap-in, as discussed in Chapter 5.

- **They cache all previously resolved queries:** As already described, clients often request the same FQDNs. Upon receipt of a successful resolution of an iterative query with another DNS server, the server places the query results in its cache. This information is stored in memory, and retained for the time specified as the TTL, or until the server is rebooted. As cache information is lost whenever a DNS server is rebooted, it is best to avoid rebooting the DNS server unless absolutely necessary.

- **All DNS servers have available the IP addresses of the Internet root name servers:** The DNS servers store this information in a file called `cache.dns` that is located in the same folder as the DNS zone data files just mentioned. It uses this information to locate a root server that can handle an iterative name query.

### Secondary Name Servers

A secondary name server hosts the secondary zone file referred to in the previous section. Secondary name servers are provided for several reasons:

- **Redundancy:** The secondary server provides a measure of fault tolerance as it can resolve host names in the event that the primary server fails.

- **Remote location:** If clients are located across a slow link, one can provide a secondary server for faster name resolution. This means that most DNS clients will not communicate across the slow link to obtain their information from the primary name server. The secondary name server does this for them, typically using a zone transfer on a periodic basis. The zone transfer can be configured to take place at a time of light traffic such as at night.

- **Load balancing:** Even if clients and servers are not separated by a slow link, having a secondary name server available helps to distribute some of the load normally placed on the primary server to the secondary server. Certain clients can be configured to connect a particular server first to make this happen. Even in the absence of a slow link, a single DNS server could be overwhelmed under conditions of heavy query traffic, and the secondary DNS server takes part of this load.

Because information for each zone is stored in separate files, a server computer can have a number of different zone files stored on it—for a number of different zones.

This allows a particular computer to act as both a primary name server for one or more zones and as secondary name server for one or more other zones. This can occur as the primary or secondary designation is always defined at the zone level.

### Caching-Only Servers

DNS servers don't rely solely on the information in their zone files. All DNS name servers cache queries that they have resolved. By contrast, caching-only servers are DNS name servers whose only job is to perform queries, cache the answers, and return the results. A caching-only server can only provide information based on the results of queries that it has already performed; it does not provide any type of zone file. It is not authoritative for any zone.

Some of the useful properties of caching-only servers are as follows:

- **They reduce the query load on primary and secondary DNS servers:** By caching already resolved names, caching-only servers are able to resolve subsequent queries from clients for previously requested FQDNs. The cache takes the place of the zone database file on a primary or secondary name server and takes on some of the load of responding to clients. A primary or secondary name server would otherwise need to shoulder this load.

- **They are not involved with zone transfers:** Because caching-only servers do not have the need to store zone data, they are not involved in the zone transfer process and the network traffic that it generates.

- **They are useful at the far end of a WAN link:** By situating a caching-only server at the far-end of a WAN link such as at a small branch office, clients in the office can reach remote hosts more rapidly on the second or subsequent times that they connect to the same host.

- **They can be used as forwarders:** Because unauthorized clients cannot obtain zone information from a caching-only server, these servers are excellent candidates for a forwarder role, discussed in the next section.

### Forwarders

A forwarder is a special DNS server that accepts requests for name resolution from another DNS server. It is especially useful for protecting internal DNS servers from access by Internet users. It works in the following manner:

1. A client issues a request for an FQDN on a zone for which its preferred DNS server is not authoritative.

2. This DNS server forwards the request to another server, which is the forwarder. In other words, the client's preferred DNS server is acting as a forwarding server in relaying the request to the forwarder.

3. The forwarder attempts to resolve the required FQDN and returns the result to the client's preferred (forwarding) server, which then returns the result to the requesting client. If the forwarder cannot resolve the FQDN, the forwarding server issues an iterative query to resolve the name.

The major factor here is that the client's preferred DNS server first uses the forwarder to resolve the query, and only issues an iterative request if the forwarder cannot complete the resolution. As already mentioned, caching-only servers make ideal candidates for forwarders.

## Slave Servers

A server that is paired with a forwarder and operates exclusively with this server is known as a *slave server*. Upon receiving a query from a client, this server attempts to resolve it against its own zone files and cache. If this fails, it sends the client's request to the forwarder, and then relays the forwarder's response back to the client. If the forwarder cannot resolve the name, the client receives an error. A caching-only slave works in a similar fashion, except that it does not have any zone files; if it cannot resolve a query from its cache, it sends the query on to the forwarder.

The combination of a slave server with a forwarder is useful in maintaining the security of a company's zone data, in combination with a firewall. It prevents users that are external to the firewall from being able to access information on a company's internal DNS servers. Suppose that you have a DNS server in your company that is used only to resolve DNS requests inside the corporate network. Requests from internal users do not present a security risk, but there is a potential security risk when internal users request an externally located FQDN.

Why is this so? When the client makes this request, the internal DNS server sends out an iterative query that is resolved by DNS servers out there somewhere. The response has to be sent back across the firewall to the internal DNS server, exposing it and its zone data to external users on the Internet. How do you avoid this? One way is to configure a caching-only server as a forwarder and locate it on the outside of the company's firewall. At the same time, configure an internal DNS server as a slave server. When a request for an external FQDN is issued, the slave server passes the request to the forwarder, which attempts to resolve the FQDN to its IP address. If this request is successful, the IP address is sent though the forwarder back to the slave server and hence to the host. If it is not successful, the forwarder reports the fact to the slave server, which does not attempt to resolve the FQDN itself. No responses from DNS servers on the Internet are ever sent directly to this internal

DNS server when this mechanism is used. Thus, the internal DNS records are not exposed to the Internet.

## Configuring DNS Zones

If you promote your Windows Server 2008 computer to domain controller, DNS zones relevant to the domain being hosted on the domain controller are automatically created when DNS is installed. When you install DNS on a member server or a standalone server, no DNS zones are created by default. Consequently, one of the first activities you perform when configuring a new DNS server is to specify forward and reverse lookup zones.

The following two types of DNS lookup zones exist:

- **Forward lookup:** This is the usual action in which a client requires the IP address of a remote computer as found in the DNS server's A or AAAA (host) resource record.

- **Reverse lookup:** This occurs when a client computer knows the IP address of another computer and requires its host name, which can be found in the DNS server's PTR (pointer) resource record.

By creating primary forward and reverse lookup zones, you can create a primary name server that is authoritative for the zone that you have created. Alternately, you can create a secondary name server for any zone that you have already created on another DNS server. Note that you can create any number of zones on a single DNS server and that one DNS server can contain any combination of primary and secondary zones.

### Creating New DNS Zones

Windows Server 2008 provides the New Zone Wizard to facilitate the creation of all types of zones. It is simple to create a new forward lookup zone, as the following procedure shows:

1. Open the DNS snap-in by clicking **Start > All Programs > Administrative Tools > DNS**. Alternatively, you can click **Start**, right-click **Computer** and choose **Manage** to open Server Manager. Within the Roles node, scroll to the DNS node and select **Go to DNS Server**.

2. Expand the node containing the name of your server. You see nodes for Forward Lookup Zones and Reverse Lookup Zones.

3. Right-click **Forward Lookup Zone** and choose **New Zone**. The New Zone Wizard starts with a Welcome page. Click **Next**.

   4. On the Zone Type page as shown in Figure 6-1, select **Primary zone** and
      click **Next**.

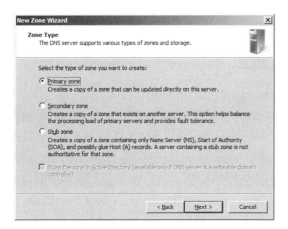

**Figure 6-1**  Selecting the type of zone to be created.

   5. On the Zone Name page, type the name of the zone to be created and click
      **Next**.

   6. On the Zone File page shown in Figure 6-2, the default is to create a new zone
      file with a name consisting of the zone name you just supplied suffixed with
      a `.dns` extension. You can modify this if you need to or choose the option of
      using an existing file that has been saved to the `%systemroot%\system32\dns`
      folder. Make your choice and click **Next**.

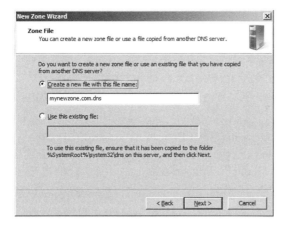

**Figure 6-2**  Choosing a zone filename.

**7.** On the Dynamic Update page shown in Figure 6-3, select an option for allowing dynamic updates, and then click **Next**.

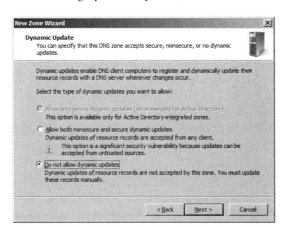

**Figure 6-3**    The Dynamic Update page enables you to choose whether to allow dynamic updates.

**8.** Review the information provided on the Completing the New Zone Wizard page and click **Finish**. If you need to make any modifications, click **Back**.

The zone you just created is displayed in the console tree of the DNS snap-in under the Forward Lookup Zones container.

**NOTE**   For more information on using and creating forward lookup zones including the use of dnscmd from the command line, refer to "Add a Forward Lookup Zone" at http://technet.microsoft.com/en-us/library/cc771566.aspx.

### Creating a Reverse Lookup Zone

As has already been mentioned, a reverse lookup zone enables you to obtain the FQDN for any computer whose IP address you already know. Recall that the reverse lookup zone name is derived in IPv4 from the forward lookup zone name by reversing the order of the octets of the network portion of the IP address and suffixing the name "in-addr.arpa" (for example, 0.168.192.in-addr.arpa for the Class C network address range of 192.168.0.0/24). A similar procedure is used in IPv6 to create a reverse lookup zone suffixed by "ip6.arpa." To create the reverse lookup zone for the primary lookup zone you just created, proceed as follows:

1. In the DNS snap-in, right-click **Reverse Lookup Zone** and choose **New Zone**. This again starts the New Zone Wizard.

2. Click **Next**, and choose the appropriate zone type from the Zone Type page, as previously shown in Figure 6-1, and click **Next** again.

3. On the Reverse Lookup Zone Name page shown in Figure 6-4, choose whether to create an IPv4 or IPv6 reverse lookup zone.

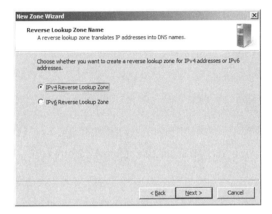

**Figure 6-4**   You are provided with a choice between IPv4 and IPv6 reverse lookup zones.

4. On the Reverse Lookup Zone page shown in Figure 6-5, type the first one, two, or three octets of your network's IP address (according to whether it is Class A, B, or C) in normal sequence in the Network ID text box (for example, 192.168.0, as shown in the figure). If creating an IPv6 reverse lookup file, enter the IPv6 address prefix including the prefix length. In either case, the filename is automatically filled in according to the naming rule already discussed for the reverse lookup zone name. Then, click **Next**.

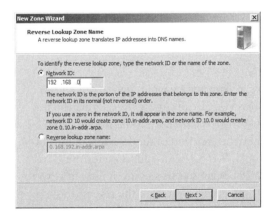

**Figure 6-5**   The Reverse Lookup Zone Name page assists you in creating the proper name for your reverse lookup zone file.

5. The Zone File page gives you a choice of creating a new zone file with the name you just created or using an existing file. In most cases, you will create the file with the name specified. If you have another zone file, ensure that it is copied to the location specified and then select the **Use this existing file** option. Then, click **Next**.

6. You receive the same options previously shown for forward lookup zones in Figure 6-3 for allowing dynamic updates. Make your choice and click **Next**.

7. Review the information provided on the Completing the New Zone Wizard page, and then click **Finish**. If you need to make any modifications, click **Back**.

The zone you just created is displayed in the console tree of the DNS snap-in under the Reverse Lookup Zones container.

After you create either type of DNS zone, you can specify additional zone properties. The various zone properties are discussed in the following sections and in Chapter 7.

**NOTE**   For more information on using and creating reverse lookup zones including the use of dnscmd from the command line, refer to "Add a Reverse Lookup Zone" at http://technet.microsoft.com/en-us/library/cc753997.aspx.

**TIP**   You can create a pair of forward and reverse lookup zones at the same time from the Configure a DNS Server Wizard. To access this wizard, right-click your server at the top of the DNS Manager console tree and choose **Configure a DNS Server** and then select the **Create forward and reverse lookup zones (recommended for large networks)** option.

### Creating Secondary Zones

Recall that secondary DNS servers are created for reasons of redundancy, load balancing, and facilitation of connections across slow links. To create a secondary forward lookup zone, proceed in a similar manner to that already described, selecting **Secondary zone** from the Zone Type page, previously shown in Figure 6-1. At this point, you receive the Master DNS Servers page shown in Figure 6-6. Specify the master DNS server by IP address or FQDN by clicking where indicated and typing the master server's FQDN or IP address. Then, click **Next** and complete the remaining steps in the wizard.

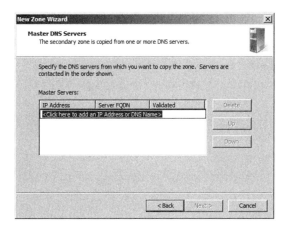

**Figure 6-6**   Use the Master DNS Servers page to specify the servers from which zone information is copied to create the secondary zone.

Creating a secondary reverse lookup zone is similar to creating a primary reverse lookup zone, with the exception of receiving the Master DNS Servers page as described here.

### Creating Stub Zones

Creating a stub zone is also similar to creating other forward or reverse lookup zones. Simply select the **Stub zone** option from the Zone Type page of the New Zone Wizard, as previously shown in Figure 6-1, and then complete the remaining steps of the wizard as described earlier in this section, including the Master DNS Servers page shown in Figure 6-6.

**NOTE**   For more information on using and creating stub zones including the use of dnscmd from the command line, refer to "Add a Stub Zone" at http://technet. microsoft.com/en-us/library/cc754190.aspx.

### Creating a GlobalNames Zone

As already introduced, a GlobalNames zone is simply a special Active Directory–integrated zone that is called GlobalNames. Use the following procedure to create a GlobalNames zone:

1. On a domain controller running DNS, start the New Zone Wizard, as already described for creating a forward lookup zone.

2. On the Zone Type page previously shown in Figure 6-1, select **Primary zone** and ensure that the **Store the zone in Active Directory** option is selected. (This option is available only on domain controllers.)

3. On the Zone Name page, type `GlobalNames` as the name of the new zone.

4. Complete the remaining steps of the New Zone Wizard as previously described.

5. Enable the new zone for GlobalNames support by issuing the following command on every authoritative DNS server in the forest:

   ```
   dnscmd <ServerName> /config /enableglobalnamessupport 1
   ```

   In this command, `ServerName` is the DNS name or IP address of the server on which you created the GlobalNames zone.

6. Replicate the GlobalNames zone to other DNS servers in the forest. Replication of DNS zones is discussed later in this chapter.

7. Populate the GlobalNames zone by adding an alias (CNAME) record to the GlobalNames zone. CNAME and other resource records are discussed in Chapter 7.

**NOTE**   For more information on GlobalNames zones and their creation and use, refer to "Deploying a GlobalNames Zone" at http://technet.microsoft.com/en-us/library/cc731744.aspx.

### Configuring DNS Zone Properties

The Properties dialog box for each DNS zone enables you to configure a large number of zone-related properties, including the following:

- Zone types
- Authoritative secondary servers
- Dynamic and secure dynamic updating
- Scavenging and time to live
- Integration with WINS

Right-click the zone in the console tree of DNS Manager and choose **Properties** to display the dialog box shown in Figure 6-7. The following sections outline the configuration of the more important properties that you should be aware of.

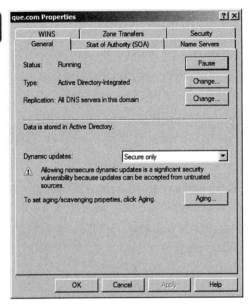

**Figure 6-7**   The General tab of a zone's Properties dialog box provides several important details on the zone and enables you to configure zone types, replication, dynamic updates, and scavenging properties.

### Configuring Zone Types

The Properties dialog box for a DNS zone enables you to change the zone type and determine whether the zone files are stored in Active Directory. In DNS Manager, right-click the zone and choose **Properties**. On the General tab of the zone's Properties dialog box shown in Figure 6-7, click the **Change** button opposite the Type entry. This brings up the Change Zone Type dialog box shown in Figure 6-8, which displays the current zone type and enables you to select the zone type and determine whether the zone data is stored in Active Directory. Click **OK** when finished.

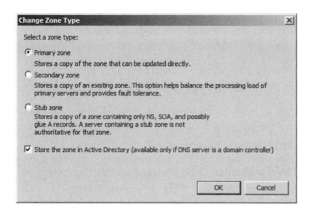

**Figure 6-8**    The Change Zone Type dialog box enables you to configure zone types.

## Adding Authoritative DNS Servers to a Zone

When you use secondary DNS servers, you need to add these servers to the NS records to specify them as authoritative for the zone. To do this, proceed as follows:

1. Access the Name Servers tab of the zone's Properties dialog box.

2. Click **Add** to display the New Name Server Record dialog box shown in Figure 6-9.

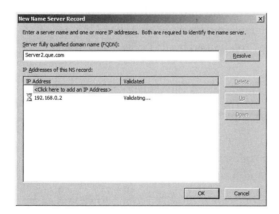

**Figure 6-9**    The New Name Server Record dialog box enables you to add authoritative DNS servers to your zone.

3. Specify the FQDN and IP address of a DNS server that is to be authoritative for the zone. Alternately, you can specify the name and click **Resolve** to resolve the name entered to its corresponding IP address.

4. If necessary, you can add additional server names in the same manner. When finished, click **OK**.

Repeat this procedure as required to add additional authoritative DNS servers. If you need to remove a DNS server, select it on the Name Servers tab and click **Remove**.

### Dynamic DNS, Non-Dynamic DNS, and Secure Dynamic DNS

Dynamic DNS (DDNS) enables DNS zone files to be updated on the fly, so to speak, whenever DNS client computers update their TCP/IP configuration information. In other words, DNS clients can dynamically update their A and PTR records in the master zone file on startup or whenever their configuration changes. First introduced in Windows 2000, client computers automatically report their TCP/IP information to the DNS server. If your network is using Dynamic Host Configuration Protocol (DHCP), the DHCP server can update the DDNS server with each client computer's current IP address whenever it renews client IP address leases.

Non-dynamic DNS (NDDNS) was the default prior to Windows 2000. At that time, the administrator was required to enter A records manually to keep the DNS database up-to-date, although it was possible to integrate DNS with WINS to provide a "pseudo" dynamic version of DNS.

Secure dynamic DNS (SDDNS) is an enhancement that enables you to permit dynamic updates only from authorized client computers in an Active Directory–integrated zone. Secure dynamic updates are defined by RFC 2137 and offer the following benefits:

- Only computers with existing domain accounts can update DNS records.

- Only computers that create (and therefore own) a DNS record can update the record.

- Only authorized users can modify zones and resource records, thereby protecting them from unauthorized modification.

- You can specify which users and groups are authorized to modify zones and resource records.

You can configure the type of update being used from the General tab of the zone's Properties dialog box, previously shown in Figure 6-7. From the Dynamic updates drop-down list, select **None** for NDDNS, **Nonsecure and secure** for DDNS, or **Secure only** for SDDNS. The default for Active Directory–integrated zones is Secure only.

**CAUTION**   You cannot have secure dynamic updates on a zone that is not integrated with Active Directory. Microsoft recommends that you not allow dynamic updates when creating such a zone, because dynamic updates can be accepted from untrusted sources. The New Zone Wizard cautions you to this fact when creating such a zone.

**TIP**   Know the purpose of the various dynamic update options available here. An exam question might present a scenario in which your DNS server's primary zone contains entries for unknown computers. You must select the **Secure only** option to prevent this problem from occurring. Also, remember that the zone must be Active Directory–integrated to enable this option.

**NOTE**   For more information on dynamic updates and their use, refer to "Understanding Dynamic Update" at http://technet.microsoft.com/en-us/library/cc771255.aspx.

### Zone Scavenging

Strange situations can occur in which resource records are not automatically removed from the DNS database. This can happen if a client such as a remote access client disconnects improperly from the network. In this case, the A resource record that is left behind is known as a *stale* resource record. These records take up space on a DNS server and might be used in attempts to resolve queries, resulting in errors and reduced DNS server performance. If computers are frequently added to or removed from the network (for example, when many portable computers are in use), many stale resource records can accumulate. These records can degrade the DNS server's performance.

For locating and removing these stale resource records, a process known as *scavenging* is employed. In this process, the DNS server searches for and deletes aged resource records. You can control the scavenging process by specifying which servers can scavenge the records, which zones are to be checked, and which records are to be scavenged if they become stale. Scavenging is disabled by default. You should enable scavenging if computers are frequently added to or removed from the network to ensure continued optimum performance of DNS servers.

Use the following procedure to enable scavenging:

1.  Access the **General** tab of the zone's Properties dialog box and click the **Aging** command button. Alternately, you can right-click your server in the console tree of DNS Manager and choose **Set Aging/Scavenging for All Zones**. Either of these actions brings up the Zone Aging/Scavenging Properties dialog box shown in Figure 6-10.

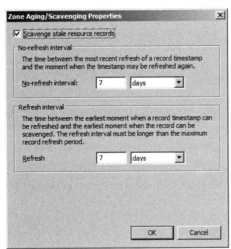

**Figure 6-10**    You can configure scavenging properties from the Zone Aging/Scavenging Properties dialog box.

2.  To enable scavenging, select the **Scavenge stale resource records** check box and then specify values for the No-refresh interval and Refresh interval, as shown in Figure 6-10.

**TIP**    You can also perform an immediate scavenging of all stale resource records on a DNS server without first configuring scavenging properties. To do so, right-click the DNS server in the console tree of DNS Manager and choose **Scavenge Stale Resource Records**. Then, click **Yes** in the message box that appears.

By selecting the **Enable automatic scavenging of stale records** check box found on the Advanced tab of the DNS server's Properties dialog box, the DNS server checks the age of each dynamically assigned record and removes records that are older than the scavenging period that you specify in this option (7 days by default). Note that Windows computers send a request to the DNS server to update their records every 24 hours; consequently, DNS records from active computers never become stale even if their TCP/IP configuration does not change.

**NOTE**   You can also set server scavenging properties by right-clicking the server in the console tree of DNS Manager and choosing **Set Aging/Scavenging for All Zones**. The Server Aging/Scavenging Properties dialog box that displays offers the same options previously shown in Figure 6-10 for zone scavenging; however, these settings are applied to all zones hosted by this server.

## Integrating DNS with WINS

If your network is still using WINS servers to resolve computer names not found within the DNS namespace, you can enable WINS lookup integration on your DNS server. This uses two special resource records called WINS and WINS-R. If the DNS server is unable to resolve a name resolution query, it forwards the query to the WINS servers that are configured in these resource records. The WINS resource resolves forward lookup queries, while the WINS-R resource record handles reverse lookup queries.

Use the following procedure to enable WINS integration:

1. Access the WINS tab of the zone's Properties dialog box.

2. Select the **Use WINS forward lookup** check box.

3. Type the IP address of the WINS server to be used for name resolution and click **Add**, as shown in Figure 6-11.

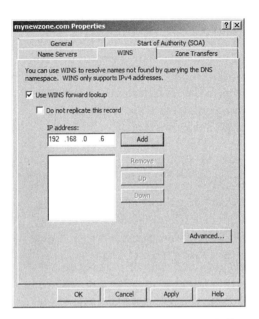

**Figure 6-11**   The WINS tab of the zone's Properties dialog box enables you to specify a WINS server.

4. To modify default timeout values, click **Advanced**. The Advanced dialog box that appears enables you to modify the cache timeout (15 minutes by default) and lookup timeout (2 seconds by default) values.

The procedure for enabling WINS integration on a reverse lookup zone is similar, except that the tab is labeled WINS-R. In this case, select the **Use WINS-R lookup** check box, and then type the required domain name on the **Domain to append to returned name** field.

## Subdomains and Zone Delegation

Parallel to the Active Directory tree structure of parent and child domains is the concept of subdomains, which exist beneath a parent domain in the hierarchical DNS namespace. Also similar to the reasons for creating Active Directory child domains, you could create subdomains for purposes of dividing administrative or geographical branches of your company. For example, you could have a subdomain named marketing.certguide.com directly beneath the certguide.com parent domain.

As shown in Figure 6-12, you can create the following two types of subdomains in Windows Server 2008 DNS:

- **Delegated subdomain:** This type of subdomain exists in its own DNS zone and has one or more DNS servers specifically delegated to it as containing the authoritative zone files. There exists a parallel between this concept and that of any second level domain in the Internet namespace, because you wouldn't want all computers within a large domain such as the com top-level domain to be managed from one location—this would get away from the idea of distributed management. So therefore, domains like Microsoft.com manage their own namespaces.

- **Non-delegated subdomain:** A non-delegated subdomain is a separate entity beneath the parent domain but is part of its zone.

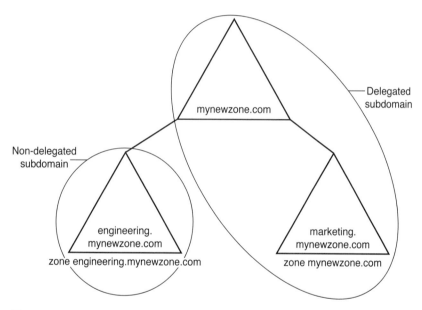

**Figure 6-12**   Example of zones and subdomains.

To create a non-delegated subdomain, right-click the forward or reverse lookup zone in which it is to be created and choose **New Domain**. In the New DNS Domain dialog box, as shown in Figure 6-13, type the new domain name (only the newest hierarchical portion, not the entire FQDN) (for example, `marketing`). It appears in the DNS snap-in as a folder located beneath the zone in which it was created.

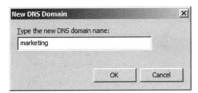

**Figure 6-13**   The New DNS Domain dialog box enables you to create a non-delegated subdomain.

To create a delegated subdomain, right-click the zone. Proceed as follows:

1. Right-click the zone in which you want to create a delegated subdomain and choose **New Delegation**. This starts the New Delegation Wizard with a Welcome page. Click **Next**.

2. On the Delegated Domain page, type the name of the subdomain to be created (for example, `engineering`), as shown in Figure 6-14. Then, click **Next**.

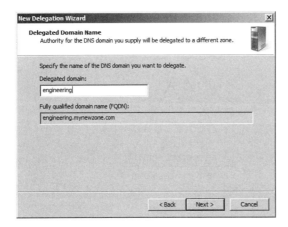

**Figure 6-14**   Specifying the name of a delegated domain.

3. On the Name Servers page, click **Add** to specify the name and IP address of a DNS server that will be authoritative for the new zone, as shown in Figure 6-15.

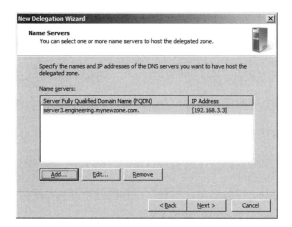

**Figure 6-15**   Specifying the server that will be authoritative for the new zone.

4.  In the dialog box that displays, you can either specify the host name and IP address of the server, or specify the FQDN and click **Resolve**. This should re-solve the FQDN to its IP address and display it in the appropriate field. Then, click **OK**.

5.  You can specify additional DNS servers if you want. Then, click **Next**.

6.  Review the information and click **Finish**.

The subdomains created by this procedure appear under the Forward Lookup Zone containers in the DNS snap-in, as shown in Figure 6-16.

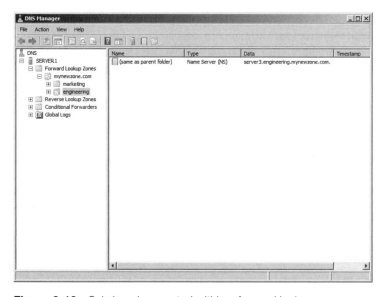

**Figure 6-16**   Subdomains created within a forward lookup zone.

> **TIP** The servers that you listed do not automatically receive a copy of the zone. For replication to occur, you must configure the listed servers as secondary servers for the zone or configure an Active Directory–integrated zone.

## Configuring DNS Zone Transfers and Replication

When changes are made to zone data on the master DNS server, these must be replicated to all DNS servers that are authoritative for the zone. This is essential so that the data is available for answering queries. Otherwise, if only a single DNS server is available and if it fails to respond for any reason, the query would fail.

The following two methods of DNS replication are available in Windows Server 2008 DNS:

- Active Directory replication, which is used for replicating Active Directory–integrated zones.

- Zone transfer, which can be used by all types of DNS zones. Active Directory–integrated zones also use zone transfer to replicate data to a standard secondary zone located on another DNS server operated for purposes of fault tolerance, load balancing, and reduction of DNS network traffic.

### Active Directory DNS Replication

As already discussed, in an AD DS domain you can integrate your DNS zones with Active Directory so that zone data is automatically replicated to other domain controllers as part of Active Directory replication. Within Active Directory, each DNS zone becomes an Active Directory container object (DnsZone). Information for each zone is stored on an application directory partition that is replicated throughout the forest or domain in which it is located.

### Application Directory Partitions

First introduced in Windows Server 2003, an *application directory partition* (also simply called an *application partition*) is a data structure in AD DS that contains application-specific data that needs to be replicated only to specific domain controllers in one or more domains of the Active Directory forest. DNS stores its Active Directory–integrated zone data in the following application directory partitions, which are automatically created when you install DNS during creation of your domain:

- **ForestDnsZones:** Contains forestwide DNS zone data, one partition per forest. By default, this partition is replicated among all DNS servers in its forest.

- **DomainDnsZones:** Contains domainwide DNS zone data, one partition for each domain in the forest. By default, this partition is replicated among all domain controllers in its domain that are configured as DNS servers.

By using application directory partitions, Active Directory replicates its DNS data to other domain controllers as stated here. A benefit of application directory partitions is that their data can be replicated to only specific domain controllers, as opposed to domain partitions, which are replicated to all domain controllers in the domain. Consequently, replication traffic is reduced. For example, DNS application directory partitions are replicated only to those domain controllers that are running DNS. The same application directory partition can replicate to domain controllers in more than one domain in the forest.

**NOTE** Windows 2000 stored its DNS data in the domain directory partition, which was replicated to all domain controllers in its domain regardless of whether they were configured as DNS servers or not. This increased replication traffic. If your domain is configured with the Windows 2000 native domain functional level, this type of DNS replication is used. Consequently, you should upgrade your domain and forest functional levels if no Windows 2000 domain controllers remain on the network. For more information on functional levels, refer to *MCTS 70-640 Cert Guide, Windows Server 2008 Active Directory, Configuring* (by Don Poulton) or "What Are Active Directory Functional Levels?" at http://technet.microsoft.com/en-us/library/cc787290(WS.10).aspx.

## Replication Scope

The replication scope of an Active Directory–integrated DNS zone refers to the subset of DNS servers or domain controllers that actively participate in replication of the specific zone. DNS in Windows Server 2008 makes available the replication scopes described in Table 6-3.

**Table 6-3**  Available DNS Replication Scopes

| Replication Scope | Description |
|---|---|
| All DNS servers in the forest hosted on domain controllers running Windows Server 2003 or 2008 | Replicates zone data to all Windows Server 2003 or 2008 domain controllers running DNS in the AD DS forest. By replicating zone data to the ForestDNSZones application directory partition, it provides the broadest replication scope. |
| All DNS servers in the domain hosted on domain controllers running Windows Server 2003 or 2008 | Replicates zone data to all Windows Server 2003 or 2008 domain controllers running DNS in the AD DS domain, by replicating zone data to the DomainDNSZones application directory partition. This is the default replication scope. |
| All domain controllers in the AD DS domain | Replicates zone data to all domain controllers in the AD DS domain. This scope is required if you want Windows 2000 DNS servers to be included in the scope of an Active Directory–integrated zone. When this scope is used, zone data is stored in the domain directory partition. |
| All domain controllers hosting a specified application directory partition | Replicates zone data according to the replication scope of the specified application directory scope. Enables the replication of zone data to domain controllers in multiple domains without replicating the data to the entire AD DS forest. |

You can change the replication scope of an Active Directory–integrated primary or stub forward lookup zone, but not that of a secondary forward lookup zone. To change the replication scope of a zone, right-click the zone in DNS Manager and choose **Properties**. On the General tab of the zone's Properties dialog box, click **Change** next to **Replication**. From the dialog box shown in Figure 6-17, select the desired option and then click **OK**.

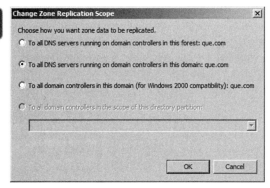

**Figure 6-17**  The Change Zone Replication Scope dialog box offers options for configuring a zone's replication scope.

Note that replication scope is not available for DNS zones that are not integrated with Active Directory. These zones use the zone transfer method only for replication.

You can also specify an application directory partition within which a zone will be stored from the command line. Open an administrative command prompt and type the following command:

```
dnscmd ServerName /ZoneChangeDirectoryPartition ZoneName
 NewPartitionName
```

In this command, the **/ZoneChangeDirectoryPartition** parameter directs that the zone specified by *ZoneName* will be stored in the application directory partition whose FQDN is specified as *NewPartitionName*.

**TIP**   If you have any Windows 2000 DNS servers, you must select the **To all domain controllers in this domain** option in Figure 6-17. If you upgrade all Windows 2000 DNS servers to Windows Server 2003 or 2008, you can change the replication scope to any of the other available options.

**NOTE**   For more information on replication scope within Active Directory–integrated zones, refer to "Understanding DNS Zone Replication in Active Directory Domain Services" at http://technet.microsoft.com/en-us/library/cc772101.aspx and "Change the Zone Replication Scope" at http://technet.microsoft.com/en-us/library/cc754916.aspx.

### Types of Zone Transfers

Every version of DNS since Windows 2000 has supported two types of zone transfer: *full zone transfer (AXFR)* and *incremental zone transfer (IXFR)*.

### Full Zone Transfer

The original specifications for DNS supported only the full zone transfer process, in which the master server transmits the entire zone database to that zone's secondary servers. When a new secondary DNS server is added to the network, it uses AXFR to obtain a full copy of the zone's resource records. AXFR was the only zone transfer process supported by Windows NT 4.0 DNS. Furthermore, a Windows Server

2008 server, when replicating with non-Windows DNS servers, such as UNIX BIND servers, must use AXFR.

### Incremental Zone Transfer

The process of incremental zone transfer, as specified in RFC 1995, replicates only the modified portion of each zone file. It is therefore more efficient and uses less bandwidth than the full zone transfer process.

The DNS servers involved in the IXFR process use the following sequential procedure:

1. The secondary DNS server sends an IXFR request to the primary server. This request contains a serial number for the secondary server's current zone database, which is found in its SOA resource record. This serial number is incremented each time the zone information changes. The SOA record also contains a number called the refresh interval, which is 15 minutes by default and determines how often the server sends the IXFR request.

2. The master server checks the secondary server's serial number against the current one.

3. If the two serial numbers are equal, the master server determines that no zone transfer is needed at the current time and the process ends.

4. If the primary server's serial number is higher, it determines that a zone transfer is required.

5. This server checks its history file that indicates which portions of the zone have been modified at what time. It uses this file to determine the updates that must be sent in response to the IXFR request.

6. When the secondary server receives the incremental zone transfer, it creates a new version of the zone file and replaces the updated records with the new ones, beginning with the oldest one.

7. When the secondary server has updated all the records, it replaces the old version of the zone with the newest version of the zone.

A full zone transfer may still take place rather than an incremental zone transfer under the following conditions:

- If the master DNS server does not support incremental zone transfers.

- If the bandwidth required for sending an incremental zone transfer is greater than that required for sending a full zone transfer.

- If the master DNS server does not possess all the data required for the incremental zone transfer, such as an accurate history file.

DNS servers that load zone data from Active Directory use a similar process, in which they poll the directory at an interval determined by the refresh interval in the SOA record for updating and refreshing their zone.

**NOTE**   For more information on incremental zone transfers, refer to "Incremental Zone Transfer in DNS" at www.ietf.org/rfc/rfc1995.txt.

### Configuring Zone Transfers

The Zone Transfers tab of a zone's Properties dialog box enables you to configure the scope of zone transfers. Use the following procedure:

1. Right-click the zone in DNS Manager, choose **Properties**, and select the **Zone Transfers** tab.

2. Select one of the following options displayed in Figure 6-18 to specify the scope of zone transfers.

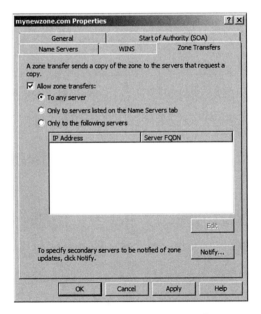

**Figure 6-18**   Specifying the scope of zone transfers.

- **To any server:** Enables zone transfers to all DNS servers.

- **Only to servers listed on the Name Servers tab:** Enables zone transfers to all DNS servers for which NS records are specified in the zone data. The Name Servers tab and its configuration are discussed in Chapter 7.

- **Only to the following servers:** Enables you to specify DNS servers that are to receive zone transfers according to IP address or FQDN. Click **Edit** and specify the IP address(es) of the required server(s).

3. If you selected the **Only to the following servers** option, specify the IP address and FQDN of the required servers in the fields provided.

4. Click **OK** or **Apply** to apply your choices.

You can specify the scope of a zone transfer from the command line. Open an administrative command prompt and type the following:

```
dnscmd ServerName /ZoneResetSecondaries ZoneName {/NoXfr | /NonSecure |
    /SecureNs | /SecureList [SecondaryIPAddress...]}
```

The parameters of this command are as follows:

- *ServerName*: Specifies the DNS host name of the DNS server. You must include this parameter; use a period to specify the local computer.

- `/ZoneResetSecondaries`: Required, indicates that you are modifying the scope of the zone transfer.

- *ZoneName*: Required, specifies the FQDN of the zone being configured.

- `/NoXfr`: Disables zone transfers for the specified zone.

- `/NonSecure`: Permits zone transfers to any DNS server.

- `/SecureNs`: Permits zone transfers to only those DNS servers specified by the `/SecureList` parameter.

- `/SecureList`: Permits zone transfers to only those DNS servers that are specified by `SecondaryIPAddress`.

- *SecondaryIPAddress*: Required if `/SecureList` is used, specifies the IP addresses of DNS servers to which zone transfers are permitted.

Additional parameters are available for this command. For more information, open a command prompt and type **dnscmd /ZoneResetSecondaries /?**.

---

**NOTE**  If you are using Active Directory–integrated zones, zone data is automatically replicated to all other domain controllers in the domain. Consequently, you cannot limit zone transfers for Active Directory–integrated zones.For more information on configuring zone transfer settings, refer to "Modify Zone Transfer Settings" at http://technet.microsoft.com/en-us/library/cc816693(WS.10).aspx.

## Configuring DNS Notify

*DNS Notify* is a process in which the master DNS server for a zone notifies secondary servers of changes to the zone, so that the secondary servers can check to determine whether they need to initiate a zone transfer. You can configure the DNS server for DNS notify by specifying the list of IP addresses to which notifications are to be sent. Configuring the notify list also helps you to prevent attempts by unknown DNS servers to request zone updates from your server.

To configure the notify list, proceed as follows:

1. Access the Zone Transfers tab of the zone's Properties dialog box, previously shown in Figure 6-18, and click the **Notify** command button.

2. In the Notify dialog box shown in Figure 6-19, ensure that **Automatically notify** is selected.

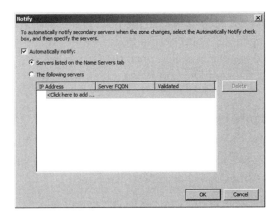

**Figure 6-19**   Specifying a DNS notify list.

3. Select **Servers listed on the Name Servers tab** to use the list of DNS servers for which NS records are configured or **The following servers** to specify the desired servers by IP address.

4. When finished, click **OK** to close the Notify dialog box and click **OK** again to close the zone's Properties dialog box.

**NOTE**   The notify list is required only for servers that operate as secondary DNS servers for zones that are not integrated with AD DS. You do not need to configure DNS notify for Active Directory–integrated zones. For more information on configuring DNS Notify, refer to "Create and Manage a Notify List for a Zone" at http://technet. microsoft.com/en-us/library/cc816637(WS.10).aspx.

### Secure Zone Transfers

If you are using DNS servers running BIND 9 or higher, you can specify that zone transfers be digitally signed. This feature enables secondary DNS servers to verify that zone transfers are being received from a trusted source.

As already discussed, you cannot limit the scope of zone transfer when using Active Directory–integrated zones. If you are concerned about zone data passing through an unsecured network segment, you can use a security mechanism such as IP Security (IPSec) to specify rules that secure the zone transfer process. We introduced IPSec in Chapter 4, "Configuring Windows Firewall with Advanced Security." When used, only zone transfers between servers whose IP addresses are specified on the Zone Transfers tab and that meet the conditions specified in the IPSec rule, are permitted.

To specify an IPSec secure zone transfer policy, use the following procedure:

1. At the DNS server, click **Start** and type `gpedit.msc` in the Start menu Search field. Then, select **gpedit.msc** to open the Local Group Policy Editor. If the DNS server is configured as a domain controller, open the Group Policy Management Editor focused on the Default Domain Policy GPO or another suitable GPO.

2. Navigate to the **Computer Configuration\Policies\Windows Settings\ Security Settings\Windows Firewall with Advanced Security\Windows Firewall with Advanced Security\Connection Security Rules** node.

3. Right-click **Connection Security Rules** and choose **New Rule**.

4. On the Rule type page of the New Connection Security Rule Wizard, select **Custom**, and click **Next**.

5. On the Endpoints page, specify the IP address ranges of the computers between which secure zone transfers are to be permitted. To do so, select **These IP addresses** under the appropriate endpoint and click **Add**. As shown in Figure 6-20, you can specify IP address ranges as single addresses, subnets, ranges of addresses, or predefined sets of computers (which includes a DNS Servers option). Perform this task for both endpoints and click **Next**.

**Figure 6-20**    The New Connection Security Rule Wizard provides several means of identifying the range of computers to which the rule applies.

6. You receive the Requirements page previously shown in Figure 4-13 in Chapter 4. Select the **Require authentication for inbound and outbound connections** option and then click **Next**.

7. On the Authentication Method page, select **Computer (Kerberos V5)** and click **Next**.

8. On the Protocol and Ports page, ensure that **Any** is selected next to Protocol Type and click **Next**.

9. On the Profile page, ensure that all three check boxes are selected and click **Next**.

10. On the Name page, type a name and optional description for the rule and click **Finish**. You have now enabled an IPSec policy rule for secured zone transfers.

**NOTE**    For more information on configuring secured zone transfers, refer to "Secure Zone Transfers with IPSec" at http://technet.microsoft.com/en-us/library/ee649192(WS.10).aspx.

### Auditing of DNS Replication

When you have configured your DNS zones to be Active Directory–integrated, auditing of zone transfers and replication becomes possible. The new Advanced Audit

Policies subnode in the Group Policy Management Editor in Windows Server 2008 R2 enables you to configure granular auditing policies for ten categories, including four subcategories of DS (Directory Service) Access. In previous versions of Windows Server, a single DS Access category controlled the auditing of all directory service events. The available DS Access subcategories include the following:

- **Directory Service Access:** Tracks all attempts at accessing AD DS objects whose system access control lists (SACL) have been configured for auditing. This includes deletion of objects.

- **Directory Service Changes:** Tracks modifications to AD DS objects whose SACLs have been configured for auditing. The following actions are included:

  - When an attribute of an object has been modified, the old and new values of the attribute are recorded in the Security log.

  - When a new object is created, values of their attributes, including new attribute values, are recorded in the Security log. This includes objects moved from another domain.

  - When objects are moved from one container to another, the distinguished names of the old and new locations are recorded in the Security log.

  - When objects are undeleted, the location in which they are placed is recorded in the Security log. Any added, modified, or deleted attributes are also recorded.

- **Directory Service Replication:** Tracks the beginning and end of the synchronization of a replica of an Active Directory naming context. This includes replication of the DomainDnsZones and ForestDnsZones application directory partitions.

- **Detailed Directory Service Replication:** Tracks additional AD DS replication events, including the establishment, removal, or modification of an Active Directory replica source naming context, replication of attributes for an AD DS object, or removal of a lingering object from a replica. Again, these event types on the DomainDnsZones and ForestDnsZones application directory partitions are included.

Use the following procedure to enable auditing of the DNS-related application directory partitions:

1. Open the Group Policy Management Editor focused on the Default Domain Policy Group Policy object (GPO) or any other suitable GPO.

2. Navigate to the **Computer Configuration\Policies\Windows Settings\ Security Settings\Advanced Audit Policy Configuration\Audit Policies\ DS Access** node.

3. Click this node to display the four available policies in the details pane, as shown in Figure 6-21.

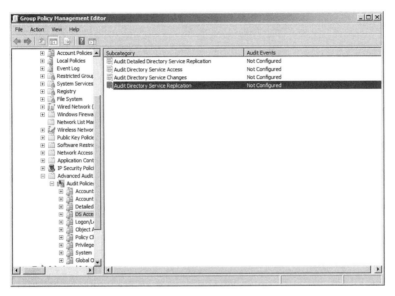

**Figure 6-21**   Windows Server 2008 R2 makes four directory service access auditing policies available.

4. Right-click **Audit Directory Service Replication** or **Audit Detailed Directory Service Replication** as required and choose **Properties**.

5. In the Properties dialog box for the policy, select **Configure the following audit events** and then choose **Success**, **Failure**, or both, as desired (see Figure 6-22). Then, click **OK**. New to Windows Server 2008, the Explain tab of each policy's Properties dialog box provides more information on what the setting does.

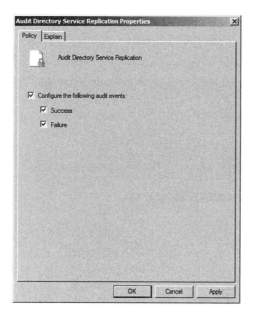

**Figure 6-22**   Enabling auditing of directory service replication.

**NOTE**   For additional information on configuring audit policies, including a comprehensive guide for setting up a series of policies on a test network, refer to "Advanced Security Audit Policy Step-by-Step Guide" at http://technet.microsoft.com/en-us/library/dd408940(WS.10).aspx. For more information on the available advanced policy settings, refer to "Advanced Security Audit Policy Settings" and references cited therein at http://technet.microsoft.com/en-us/library/dd772712(WS.10).aspx.

**TIP**   You need to ensure that advanced audit policy settings are not overwritten by basic audit policy settings. To do so, navigate to the **Computer Configuration\Policies\Windows Settings\Security Settings\Local Policies\Security Options** node and enable the **Audit: Force audit policy subcategory settings (Windows Vista or later) to override audit policy category settings** policy setting.

After you configure directory services auditing, attempts to access audited objects appear in the Security Log, which you can view from Event Viewer either in Server Manager, as shown in Figure 6-23, or in its own snap-in from the Administrative

Tools folder. For more information on any audited event, right-click the event and choose **Event Properties**. Event Viewer is discussed in Chapter 20, "Configuring Event Logs."

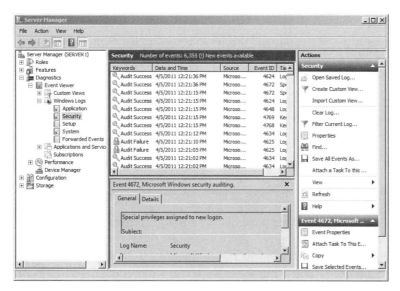

**Figure 6-23**  Event Viewer displays failed attempts at audited events with a lock icon.

# Troubleshooting DNS Zones and Replication

Failure of DNS queries on the network may lead to significant problems, particularly in the case of AD DS-enabled networks. If a user is unable to access a domain controller due to DNS failure, she cannot log on except with the aid of cached credentials. Resources on the network may become inaccessible. Furthermore, users may become unable to access intranet or Internet websites. DNS in Windows Server 2008 includes several utilities that can assist you in locating and troubleshooting DNS problems.

Chapter 5 introduced you to the Debug Logging, Event Logging, and Monitoring tabs of the DNS Server Properties dialog box. If users are unable to resolve FQDNs or reach improper locations, perform the simple and recursive test queries on your DNS server, as previously shown in Figure 5-12. Select the **Perform automatic testing at the following interval option** on this dialog box and view the test results later in this dialog box to determine whether sporadic failures are occurring.

### Using the `ipconfig`, `ping`, and `nslookup` Commands

You can use the `ipconfig`, `ping`, and `nslookup` commands to test connectivity and name resolution on a DNS-enabled network. We introduced these commands in Chapter 1, "Configuring IPv4 and IPv6 Addressing."

Recall that the `ipconfig /all` command displays a complete list of the computer's TCP/IP configuration parameters. The following commands are especially useful when encountering name resolution problems:

- **`ipconfig /displaydns`:** Displays the contents of the local DNS resolver cache, which includes both entries preloaded from the HOSTS file and any recently obtained DNS query results.

- **`ipconfig /flushdns`:** Flushes the client cache, which contains the results of recently resolved FQDNs. Execute this command on any client computer that resolves FQDNs incorrectly because of DNS server cache errors.

- **`ipconfig /registerdns`:** Performs a manual dynamic registration for DNS names and IP addresses configured on the computer. This command is useful for troubleshooting failed DNS name registration or resolving a dynamic update problem between a client and the DNS server without the need to reboot the client computer.

If users are unable to ping a computer on the network by name but can ping the computer by IP address, some type of name resolution problem is evident. Perform simple and recursive test queries on the DNS servers on the network; also, check the DNS event log for errors and use the `nslookup` command to query the DNS server, as described here.

The `nslookup` command enables you to check the connectivity to DNS servers and display information from these servers from a command prompt. You can use this command in either of two modes:

- **Interactive mode:** If you need to look up more than one piece of data, use interactive mode. Type **nslookup** with no subcommands. The command prompt enters interactive mode where you can type subcommands directly. Use the `exit` subcommand to end interactive mode.

- **Noninteractive mode:** Type **nslookup** with the appropriate subcommand to obtain a single item of data. The syntax is as follows:

  ```
  Nslookup [-option ... ] [computer | - [server]]
  ```

  In this command,

- `[-option ... ]` specifies one or more nslookup commands as a command-line option. Each option consists of a hyphen (-) followed immediately by the command name and, in some cases, an equal sign (=) and then a value. For example, to change the default query type to host information and the initial timeout to 10 seconds, you would type:

```
nslookup -querytype=hinfo -timeout=10
```

- `[computer]` specifies the name or IP address of a computer to be found. If you specify the name, nslookup returns the IP address, and if you specify the IP address, nslookup returns the FQDN. The current DNS domain name is automatically appended to the host name specified here unless it is appended with a period. To look up a computer outside of the current DNS domain, append a period to the name. If you type a hyphen (-) instead of a computer name, the command prompt changes to `nslookup` interactive mode.

- `[server]` specifies the DNS server to be used. If omitted, the current default DNS server is used.

For example, you can obtain the host name of a computer knowing its IP address (for example 192.168.4.7) as follows:

```
nslookup 192.168.4.7
```

To obtain the IP address of a server when you know its FQDN (for example, `server3.certguide.com`), type the following:

```
nslookup server3.certguide.com
```

If you are unsure that a particular DNS server is responding, type the following:

```
nslookup <server_IP_address> 127.0.0.1
```

Where `<server_IP_address>` is the IP address of the DNS server you are testing. If the server responds, the name `localhost` is returned. If not, test the network connectivity to the DNS server and verify the proper operation of the server.

A failure to resolve a FQDN when using `nslookup` can indicate the need to clear the DNS server cache or restart the DNS server service. Incorrect name resolution can indicate improper entries in the DNS server or client cache; type **ipconfig / flushdns** to clear the DNS client cache. More information about the DNS client cache and client name resolution is included in Chapter 8.

**NOTE**   For a comprehensive list of `nslookup` subcommands and their uses, refer to "Nslookup" at http://technet.microsoft.com/en-us/library/cc725991(WS.10). aspx. You can also type **help** at an interactive `nslookup` prompt to obtain a list of subcommands.

### Use of the DNSLint Tool

Microsoft provides the DNSLint tool that assists you in diagnosing several DNS name resolution properties. Among other tasks, it enables you to verify the consistency of specific sets of DNS records and verify that DNS records used specifically for AD DS replication are correct.

DNSLint is available as a free download from Microsoft; navigate to http://support. microsoft.com/kb/321045 and select the link provided to download this tool. Three important functions available with this tool are as follows:

- **dnslint /d** requests domain name tests; this parameter is useful for troubleshooting issues related to lame delegation.

- **dnslint /ql** enables you to perform DNS query tests from a list included in a text input file. Queries on A, PTR, CNAME, SRV, and MX resource records are supported. Information on these records is provided in Chapter 7.

- **dnslint /ad** performs Active Directory tests, including the verification of DNS records used specifically for AD DS replication. This option uses the local computer's Lightweight Directory Access Protocol (LDAP) service; optionally, you can specify a remote server's LDAP service by IP address.

When you download this tool, unzip it to a convenient folder, from which you can run it from a command prompt. It takes a minute or two to run and then provides an HTML-based report that opens automatically in Internet Explorer or your preferred browser.

**NOTE**   For additional information and a comprehensive list of available DNSLint switches and parameters, refer to "Description of the DNSLint Utility" at http:// support.microsoft.com/kb/321045.

## Exam Preparation Tasks

## Review All the Key Topics

Review the most important topics in this chapter, noted with the key topics icon in the outer margin of the page. Table 6-4 lists a reference of these key topics and the page numbers on which each is found.

**Table 6-4** Key Topics for Chapter 6

| Key Topic Element | Description | Page Number |
|---|---|---|
| Table 6-2 | Describes available DNS zone types. | 249 |
| List | Describes the benefits of integrating DNS zones with Active Directory. | 250 |
| List | Describes the purposes of stub zones. | 251 |
| List | Describes the benefits of secondary zone servers. | 254 |
| List | Shows you how to create a new DNS zone. | 257 |
| Figure 6-3 | Shows options for allowing dynamic DNS zone updates. | 259 |
| Figure 6-7 | Setting properties of a DNS zone. | 264 |
| Figure 6-10 | Configuring zone scavenging properties. | 268 |
| List | Describes types of DNS subdomains. | 271 |
| Paragraph | Describes replication of DNS zones in Active Directory. | 274 |
| Table 6-3 | Describes available DNS replication scopes. | 276 |
| Figure 6-17 | Shows how to configure zone replication scopes. | 276 |
| Paragraph | Describes types of DNS zone transfers. | 277 |
| Figure 6-18 | Shows how to specify the scope of zone transfers. | 279 |
| List | Shows how to configure an IPSec-secured zone transfer policy. | 282 |
| List | Shows how to enable auditing of DNS zone partitions. | 284 |
| Paragraph | Describes several DNS troubleshooting tools. | 288 |

## Complete the Tables and Lists from Memory

Print a copy of Appendix B, "Memory Tables," (found on the CD), or at least the section for this chapter, and complete the tables and lists from memory. Appendix C, "Memory Tables Answer Key," also on the CD, includes the completed tables and lists to check your work.

## Definition of Key Terms

Define the following key terms from this chapter, and check your answers in the Glossary.

Active Directory-integrated zone, application directory partition, caching-only server, DNS Notify, dynamic DNS (DDNS), full zone transfer (AXFR), GlobalNames zone, incremental zone transfer (IXFR), non-dynamic DNS, nslookup, primary zone, replication scope, secondary zone, secure dynamic DNS (SDDNS), secure zone transfer, stub zone, zone, zone delegation, zone file, zone transfers

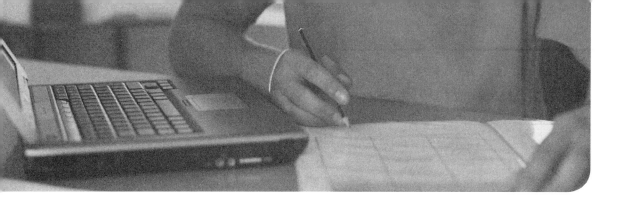

This chapter covers the following subjects:

- **Resource Record Types and Their Uses:** Resource records in DNS contain all the information required for DNS servers to resolve client queries. This section introduces the most common record types and shows you how to create them.

- **Configuring Resource Record Properties:** This section introduces you to the various configurable properties of the different resource record types, in particular the SOA and NS records. It also discusses additional tasks you need to be familiar with concerning resource records, such as configuring the Time-to-Live parameter, registering records, netmask ordering, DNS record security, and so on.

# CHAPTER 7

# Configuring DNS Records

Reviewing what you know about the Domain Name System (DNS) so far, you learned in Chapter 5, "Installing and Configuring Domain Name System (DNS)," how DNS resolves domain names to their corresponding IP addresses. You also learned how to install DNS on a Windows Server 2008 computer and configure server properties. Chapter 6, "Configuring DNS Zones and Replication," turned your attention to how the zone files in DNS work and the importance of replicating this data to all available DNS servers. Now, it is time to take a look at the contents of these zones. Each DNS zone contains a series of entries known as *resource records*, which contain information about a particular component of the DNS namespace. When a DNS server receives a query from a client, it depends on the resource records in its database to be able to answer the query with the appropriate information.

## "Do I Know This Already?" Quiz

The "Do I Know This Already?" quiz allows you to assess whether you should read this entire chapter or simply jump to the "Exam Preparation Tasks" section for review. If you are in doubt, read the entire chapter. Table 7-1 outlines the major headings in this chapter and the corresponding "Do I Know This Already?" quiz questions. You can find the answers in Appendix A, "Answers to the 'Do I Know This Already?' Quizzes."

**Table 7-1**  "Do I Know This Already?" Foundation Topics Section-to-Question Mapping

| Foundations Topics Section | Questions Covered in This Section |
| --- | --- |
| Resource Record Types and Their Uses | 1–3 |
| Configuring Resource Record Properties | 4–8 |

1. Which type of resource record would you use to specify a host name to IPv6 address mapping for a computer in your domain?

   a. A

   b. AAAA

   c. NS

   d. PTR

2. Your AD DS network contains a Windows Server 2008 R2 machine that hosts both a web server and an FTP server, which are configured with two different FQDNs. You want to ensure that clients are directed properly to this machine. What type of resource record should you specify?

   a. A

   b. NS

   c. CNAME

   d. SRV

   e. MX

3. Your AD DS network is configured with DNS servers that host an Active Directory–integrated zone. Which type of resource record is used to specify the location of domain controllers?

   a. A

   b. NS

   c. CNAME

   d. PTR

   e. SRV

4. Your network is experiencing heavy traffic to and from the DNS server because of large numbers of client requests. On examining DNS server logs and talking to users on the network, you discover that many users are repeatedly accessing the same FQDNs. What should you do to reduce the DNS network traffic in this situation?

   a. Increase the refresh interval.

   b. Reduce the refresh interval.

   c. Increase the minimum default TTL value.

   d. Reduce the minimum default TTL value.

5. You are configuring the properties of a secondary DNS server on your network. You want to ensure that the secondary DNS server is kept up-to-date with respect to changes in resource records at the primary DNS server, so you access the Start of Authority (SOA) tab of your server's Properties dialog box. What should you do?

   a. Increase the retry interval.

   b. Reduce the retry interval.

   c. Increase the refresh interval.

   d. Reduce the refresh interval.

6. You are responsible for a secondary name server named DNS2 that has two network adapters with IP addresses 192.168.1.21 and 192.168.2.21. You want to ensure that users on both subnets can use this server for name resolution. The server is currently configured with an NS record that points to the address 192.168.1.21. What should you do?

   a. From the Name Servers tab of the zone's Properties dialog box, select the entry for DNS2 and click **Edit**. In the Edit Name Server Record dialog box, add the IP address `192.168.2.21`.

   b. From the Name Servers tab of the zone's Properties dialog box, click **Add**. In the New Resource Record dialog box, type `DNS2` for the name and `192.168.2.21` for the IP address.

   c. From the Name Servers tab of the zone's Properties dialog box, select the entry for DNS2 and click **Remove**. Then, click **Add** and in the New Resource Record dialog box, type `DNS2` for the name and `192.168.1.21` and `192.168.2.21` for the IP addresses.

   d. Right-click the zone in DNS Manager and choose **New Name Server (NS)**. In the New Name Server (NS) Resource Record dialog box, type `DNS2` and `192.168.2.21` for the name and IP address of the server.

   e. Right-click the zone in DNS Manager and choose **Other New Records**. In the Resource Record Type dialog box, select **Name Server (NS)**, and in the New Name Server (NS) Resource Record dialog box, type `DNS2` and `192.168.2.21` for the name and IP address of the server.

7. Your network's Active Directory–integrated zone is configured for secure dynamic updates. A DHCP server named Server05 requires hardware updates and has been removed from the network. A second DHCP server named Server06 is continuing to provide services on the network. Several users report that they are unable to access resources on the network by server name. What should you do?

    **a.** Add all DNS servers on the network to the DnsUpdateProxy group.

    **b.** Add all DHCP servers on the network to the DnsUpdateProxy group.

    **c.** At the users' computers, type `ipconfig /registerdns`.

    **d.** From the zone's Properties dialog box in DNS Manager, select the option to allow both nonsecure and secure dynamic updates.

**8.** You want to ensure that requests for a host name that is mapped to multiple IP addresses on different subnets always returns an IP address located on the same subnet as the requesting client. What should you do?

    **a.** In the SRV resource record properties for each DNS server, increase the **Priority** value corresponding to the IP address of its subnet.

    **b.** In the NS resource record properties for each DNS server, increase the **Priority** value corresponding to the IP address of its subnet.

    **c.** In the Advanced tab of each DNS server's Properties dialog box, ensure that the **Enable round robin** option is selected.

    **d.** In the Advanced tab of each DNS server's Properties dialog box, ensure that the **Enable netmask ordering** option is selected.

## Foundation Topics

# Resource Record Types and Their Uses

Each zone file contains a series of entries known as *resource records* for a DNS domain. If your zone is `certguide.com`, your zone database file is called `certguide.com.dns`. A copy of this database is stored at `%systemroot%\System32\dns\backup`. Windows Server 2008 supplies a sample database file called `place.dns`, located in the `%systemroot%\System32\dns\Samples` folder, as a template. This file is duplicated and renamed whenever you create a new zone using the New Zone Wizard. In doing so, the minimum resource records that are required for a new zone to function are automatically placed in the zone file.

Table 7-2 contains descriptions of the most common resource records found in the zone file.

**Table 7-2**   Common DNS Resource Records

| Resource Record | Description |
|---|---|
| SOA (Start of Authority) | The first record in any zone file, it identifies the primary name server within the domain. It also includes other properties, such as an administrator e-mail address and caching properties for the zone. |
| A and AAAA (host) | Contains the computer name to IPv4 (A) or IPv6 (AAAA) address mappings for all hosts found in the domain, thereby identifying these host names. |
| NS (name server) | Contains the DNS servers that are authoritative in the domain. This includes both the primary DNS servers and any secondary DNS servers. |
| SRV (service location) | Stores information about where computers that provide a specific service are located on the network. Information in these records includes the name of the service and the DNS name of the host that is providing the service. A computer stills need to access the A or AAAA record for a service provider to resolve the name to an IP address. Examples include web services associated with a web server or logon services associated with a domain controller on an Active Directory Domain Services (AD DS) domain. |
| CNAME (alias) | Provides aliases (canonical names), which are additional names that point to a single host. Machines will respond to either the original name or the alias. This facilitates doing such things as hosting both an FTP server and a web server on the same machine, or for server migrations. |

**Table 7-2**   Common DNS Resource Records (*Continued*)

| Resource Record | Description |
| --- | --- |
| PTR (pointer) | Allows for reverse lookups by containing IP address-to-name mappings. |
| MX (mail exchanger) | Identifies preferred mail servers on the network. When there is more than one mail server, they are listed in order of precedence. |

### Creating New Resource Records

While dynamic DNS allows the creation of many of the resource records automatically with the assistance of the DHCP server, you need to configure some of these yourself, in particular resource records for downlevel clients. In addition, if you have not yet configured your server to accept dynamic updates, you need to configure all the resource records yourself.

You can create new DNS resource records if required. Right-click your DNS zone and choose the appropriate option from those shown in Figure 7-1. Provide the requested information in the dialog box that appears and then click **OK**. The Other New Records option enables you to select from a complete list of available resource record types and provides a description of each of the available record types.

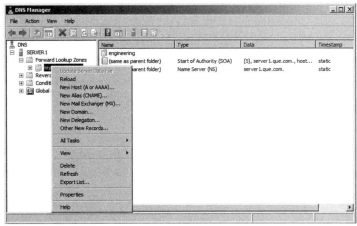

**Figure 7-1**   You can create new resource records in DNS by right-clicking your zone name and choosing the appropriate option.

Also visible in Figure 7-1 are the two resource records automatically created whenever you use the New Zone Wizard as described in Chapter 6 to create a new zone—the SOA and NS resource records. You never need to create a new SOA resource record because each zone file contains only one of these records. You might need to create additional NS resource records; the procedure for creating these records is slightly different, as will be discussed later. We look at the properties of these resource records later in this chapter.

### New Host (A or AAAA) Records

A host resource record maps the FQDN of any computer (host) in the domain to its IP address. Normally, the appropriate host record is dynamically added or updated when the host obtains its IP configuration from DHCP. An A resource record is used on an IPv4 network and an AAAA resource record is used on an IPv6 network; if your network is configured to use both IPv4 and IPv6, each host will have both A and AAAA resource records. However, if your network doesn't include a DHCP server, you will need to create your own host records. Furthermore, a non-Windows computer such as a UNIX server cannot perform dynamic updates; you will need to create a host record for such a computer so that clients can locate it by name.

Right-click the zone and choose **New Host (A or AAAA)** to bring up the New Host dialog box shown in Figure 7-2. You need only enter the host name (for example, `server2`) and IP address for the new host (for example, `192.168.0.102`); the FQDN is generated from the host name you specified plus the zone you right-clicked. Additionally, select either or both of the following options as required:

- **Create associated pointer (PTR) record:** Automatically creates a PTR resource record, which enables reverse lookup queries to function. Recall that a reverse lookup query enables an IP address to be resolved to its associated FQDN.

- **Allow any authenticated user to update DNS records with the same owner name:** Enables an administrator to create a secure resource record for a new host that is not yet online and enables this resource record to be updated dynamically when the host comes online and uses DHCP to obtain its TCP/IP configuration. Normally, the host that requests an update receives permission to modify the resource record, but other administrative permissions are not enabled in the resource record's access control list (ACL).

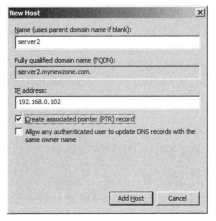

**Figure 7-2**   The New Host dialog box enables you to create either A or AAAA resource records.

## New Alias (CNAME) Records

Also known as a canonical name, an alias enables you to associate more than one name with a single computer. This is frequently used with Internet-facing machines, such as web and FTP servers. In addition, you can use CNAME records in a situation such as a web server farm, where a generic name such as www needs to be resolved to a series of individual machines each with its own A or AAAA record; doing so facilitates the distribution of incoming queries among all servers in the group.

Right-click the zone and choose **New Alias (CNAME)** to bring up the New Resource Record—Alias (CNAME) dialog box, as shown in Figure 7-3. Specify the alias to be used (for example, www) and the host's FQDN (for example, server3.mynewzone.com); the FQDN is generated from the target host FQDN and the alias name you typed. You can also browse for the appropriate host. Select the check box provided if you want to permit the resource record to be updated dynamically. Using this option, you can create a secure resource record for a host that is not yet online, similar to the option previously shown in Figure 7-2 for A or AAAA resource records.

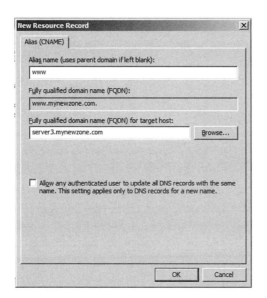

**Figure 7-3**   The New Alias (CNAME) Resource Record dialog box enables you to associate more than one name with a single host, such as a web server.

### New Mail Exchanger (MX) Records

Right-click the zone and choose **New Mail Exchanger (MX)** to bring up the New Resource Record—Mail Exchanger (MX) dialog box, as shown in Figure 7-4. This allows you to specify a mail exchange server for your DNS domain name, which allows the outside world to locate your SMTP/POP3 e-mail server and send messages to it. To define the MX record, specify the following values in the fields provided:

- **Host or child domain:** Provide the single-part name for a mail exchanger in the zone being configured. If left blank, mail is delivered to the parent domain.

- **Fully qualified domain name (FQDN):** Provide the FQDN of the server that is to act as a mail server for the domain specified in the Host or child domain field (for example, `mailserver.mynewzone.com`). You can also click **Browse** to locate the appropriate mail server.

- **Mail server priority:** Provide a preference value in the range of 0 to 65,535 (by default, this value is `10`) that specifies which mail server will be contacted first when more than one mail server has been configured; the lower the number, the higher the priority.

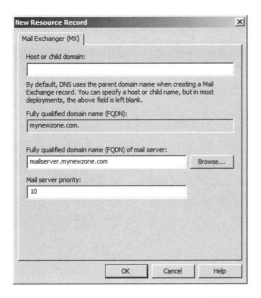

**Figure 7-4**   The New Mail Exchanger (MX) Resource Record dialog box enables you to specify an SMTP/POP3 e-mail server for your domain.

### Additional New Resource Records

DNS in Windows Server 2008 R2 provides a large number of additional resource records. To create any type of resource record, right-click your zone and choose **Other New Records**. This displays the Resource Record Type dialog box shown in Figure 7-5.

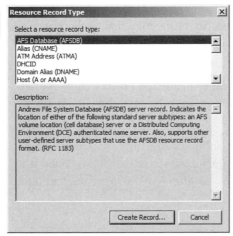

**Figure 7-5**   The Resource Record Type dialog box enables you to create any of the possible types of resource records in Windows Server 2008 R2 DNS.

Select the desired type of resource record and click **Create Record** to bring up a dialog box that enables you to properly define the selected record type. Some of the available record types are as follows:

- **Pointer (PTR):** Pointer records are created automatically if you specified this option in the New Host dialog box, or if the appropriate option has been configured at the DHCP server for dynamic DNS. If not, choose this option and specify the required octet(s) of the host's IP address, and specify or browse to the host name that corresponds to this IP address (see Figure 7-6).

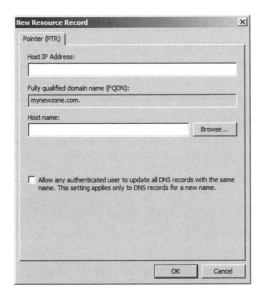

**Figure 7-6** Creating a new PTR resource record.

- **ATM Address (ATMA):** Specify a host name and FQDN of an asynchronous transfer mode (ATM) host in this zone. Also specify the ATM address (ATMA) of the ATM host and the format being used (either E164, which represents the E.164 address format, or NSAP, which specifies an address that conforms to the Network Service Access Protocol [NSAP] address model).

- **Service Location (SRV):** Used to specify the location of specific services in the zone being configured, so that SRV-aware client applications can locate application servers (see Figure 7-7). For example, the Netlogon service searches for SRV records that specify the Lightweight Directory Access Protocol (LDAP) service to locate AD DS domain controllers.

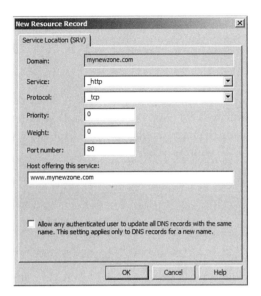

**Figure 7-7**   Creating a new SRV resource record.

To complete the description of this record, specify the following information (as shown in Figure 7-7):

- **Service:** Specifies the universal symbolic name of the TCP/IP service being located with this SRV record.

- **Protocol:** Specifies the transport protocol used by the service (generally either TCP or UDP).

- **Priority:** Specifies a priority number that functions similarly to that in the MX resource record, determining which server will be contacted first when more than one server has been configured for the service in use; the lower the number, the higher the priority.

- **Weight:** Specifies a value used by the clients to determine which server to contact, in cases where multiple records with the same priority exist. This number functions as a load-balancing mechanism. This number can have a value between 0 and 65,535; servers with higher weights are contacted first.

- **Port number:** Specifies the port number used by the service. This is generally (but not always) a well-known port number as defined in RFC 1700.

- **Host offering this service:** Displays the FQDN of the server associated with this record.

- **Allow any authenticated user to update all DNS records with the same name:** Select this option to permit the resource record to be updated dynamically. This grants the host requesting the update permission to modify the resource record, but removes all other nonadministrative permissions from the ACL associated with the record.

> **TIP**   The SRV resource records for a domain controller are important in enabling clients to locate the domain controller. The Netlogon service on domain controllers registers this resource record whenever a domain controller is restarted. You can also re-register a domain controller's SRV resource records by restarting this service from the Services branch of Server Manager or by typing `net start netlogon`. An exam question might ask you how to troubleshoot the non-registration of SRV resource records.

> **NOTE**   For more information on the SRV resource record, refer to "Service Location (SRV) Resource Record Dialog box" at http://technet.microsoft.com/en-us/library/cc742513.aspx. For more information on the more common DNS resource records, including samples of their structure in the DNS database, refer to "DNS Physical Structure" at http://technet.microsoft.com/en-us/library/dd197495(WS.10).aspx.

### Using the Command Line to Create Resource Records

You can use the `dnscmd` command to create resource records from the command line. Use the following command syntax:

```
dnscmd [<ServerName>] /recordadd <ZoneName> <NodeName> <RRType>
<RRData>
```

The parameters of this command are as follows:

- `<ServerName>`: Specifies the local or remote DNS server being managed by IP address, host name, or FQDN. If omitted, the local server is used.
- `/recordadd`: Required, adds a resource record.
- `<ZoneName>`: Specifies the zone in which the record is located.
- `<NodeName>`: Specifies a specific node in the zone.
- `<RRType>`: Specifies the type of resource record being added.
- `<RRData>`: Specifies the type of data that is expected.

## Configuring Resource Record Properties

When you have created the resource records for your DNS zone, you can view information about the existing resource records by selecting the zone in the console tree of the DNS snap-in. As shown in Figure 7-8, summary information about all available records appears in the details pane.

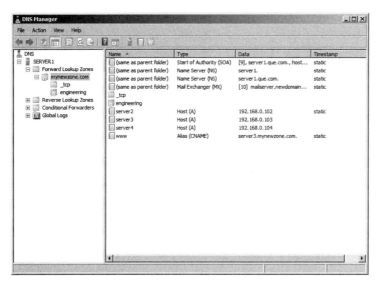

**Figure 7-8**   The details pane of the DNS snap-in displays all existing resource records for each zone.

For any zone that is not integrated with Active Directory, the DNS zone file is stored as an ASCII file at `%systemroot%\system32\dns\`*zone_name*.dns, where *zone_name* is the name of the zone. As shown in Figure 7-9, you can view (and even edit) this file in Notepad; however, it is best to use the DNS snap-in and the various Properties dialog boxes to edit the zone file and avoid any possible syntax errors.

**Figure 7-9**   DNS resource records in a zone file are viewable and editable in Notepad.

## Configuring SOA Resource Record Properties

As already mentioned, the SOA resource record is always the first record in each DNS zone file. Right-click this record and choose **Properties** to bring up the dialog box shown in Figure 7-10. You can also right-click the zone in the console tree of DNS Manager, choose **Properties**, and then select the **Start of Authority (SOA)** tab to display this dialog box.

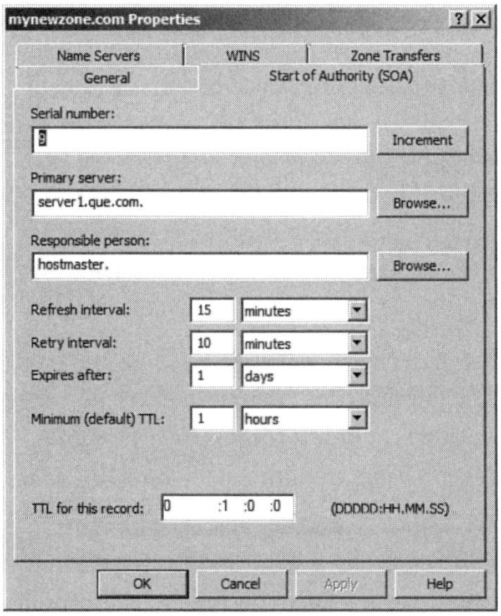

**Figure 7-10**   The Start of Authority tab enables you to configure several zone properties including the TTL for caching externally resolved queries.

The Start of Authority tab contains the additional settings described in Table 7-3 that you should be aware of; all of these are related to the information contained in the server's SOA resource record.

**Table 7-3**   SOA Tab Settings

| Setting | Description |
| --- | --- |
| Serial Number | Starts at one and is incremented every time that a change to some property of the zone occurs. You normally do not change this number. A secondary server that is querying the primary server for updates uses this number to determine if changes to the zone file have occurred. If so, the data is replicated to the secondary server using the zone transfer process. |
| Primary Server | Designates the primary server for the domain by its FQDN. If you need to change the primary server for any reason, you can either browse to locate a suitable server, or type its name here. If zone transfers are failing, check this name for accuracy, because if it is incorrect, zone transfers cannot take place. |
| Responsible Person | Names the designated administrator by his/her Simple Mail Transfer Protocol (SMTP) e-mail address. Even though e-mail addresses generally use the @ symbol to separate the name from the domain, you need to use a period in this address. If zone transfers are not working properly, a message can be sent to this e-mail address. |
| Refresh Interval | Specifies the interval at which the secondary server queries the master server to see if the zone data has changed. By default, this value is 15 minutes. A low value enables the secondary DNS server to be more up to date, but at the expense of increased network traffic. |
| Retry Interval | Specifies how much time will elapse before the secondary server tries again to contact the master server, in the event that the master server does not respond to the initial refresh attempt. By default, this value is 10 minutes. |
| Expires After | Specifies the length of time that a secondary server will resolve queries using the current information when it has been unable to contact the master server for an update. When this interval has been reached, the secondary server will stop resolving queries until it is again able to contact the master server. By default, this value is 1 day. |
| Minimum (default) TTL | Specifies the default Time to Live (TTL) of the zone, which determines the time interval used by other servers before cached information becomes expired and is discarded. By default, this value is 3600 seconds (1 hour). Most resource records created by the DNS server service inherit this value from the SOA record. |
| TTL for This Record | Specifies the TTL used by this specific resource record. Any value specified here overrides the value specified for the minimum (default) TTL. Modifying this value affects it only for the resource record where it is modified; other resource records in the zone still default to the value specified under Minimum (default) TTL. |

**CAUTION**   Try not to confuse the refresh and retry intervals. The refresh interval determines how often other DNS servers hosting the zone will attempt to renew the zone data. It is 15 minutes by default. The retry interval determines how often other DNS servers retry a request for updating the zone every time the refresh interval occurs. It is 10 minutes by default.

**NOTE**   For more information on configuring the SOA resource record, including the use of dnscmd from the command line, refer to "Modify the Start of Authority (SOA) Resource Record for a Zone" at http://technet.microsoft.com/en-us/library/cc816941(WS.10).aspx.

Time to Live

Client computers often request the same FQDNs. Upon receipt of a successful resolution of an iterative query with another DNS server, the server places the query results in its cache. This information is stored in memory, and is available to the client (or any other client on the network requesting the same FQDN) without the need for sending an external query. It is retained for the time known as the *Time to Live* (TTL), which is a configurable retention time interval that specifies the length of time that the server will retain cached information for a zone. This value and the next one are both specified as days:hours:minutes:seconds. Increase this value if zone information does not change frequently. A longer TTL reduces the amount of network traffic but consumes more memory utilization on the DNS server.

You can configure a DNS zone's TTL property from the Start of Authority (SOA) tab of the zone's Properties dialog box, as previously shown in Figure 7-10. In the list box labeled Minimum (default) TTL, type a number and select a unit (days, hours, minutes, or seconds). By default, this TTL is one hour. Note that the **TTL for this Record** entry immediately beneath specifies the TTL for the SOA record.

**Configuring Name Server Resource Record Properties**

The Name Server (NS) resource records are used to define the servers that are authoritative for the zone in which they are found. From this tab, you can configure secondary name servers that are authoritative for the zone, which are DNS servers that receive zone updates for zones that are not integrated with AD DS. When you designate additional servers as authoritative, NS records for these servers are automatically added. Properties of these servers are found in the Name Servers tab of the zone's Properties dialog box. Right-click the required zone in the console tree of the DNS Manager snap-in and choose **Properties**. On selecting the **Name Servers** tab you receive the dialog box shown in Figure 7-11. You can also reach this dialog box by right-clicking a NS resource record in the details pane and choosing **Properties**. This tab enables you to specify the names and IP addresses of the name servers that are authoritative for this zone. These servers are specified in Name NS resource records.

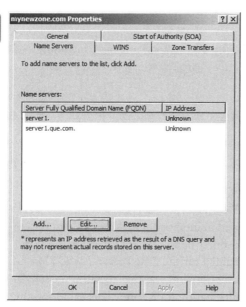

**Figure 7-11**   The Name Servers tab lists the FQDN and IP address of all servers authoritative for its zone.

To add a new name server to the list, click the **Add** button and specify the name and IP address of the server in the New Name Server Record dialog box, as shown in Figure 7-12. Alternately, you can enter the name of the server and click the **Resolve** button (on the New Resource Record dialog box) to resolve the server's name to its IP address.

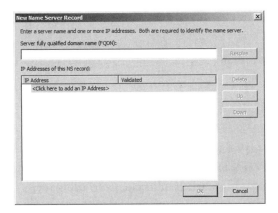

**Figure 7-12**   The New Name Server Record dialog box enables you to designate additional authoritative name servers.

To edit an entry in the Name Servers tab, select it and click **Edit**. The Edit Name Server Record dialog box, which is similar to the New Name Server Record dialog box, enables you to add additional IP addresses or modify the name of the server. You can prioritize the IP addresses on the IP address list by using the **Up** button or **Down** button or by deleting an IP address by selecting it and clicking **Delete**. You can also delete an entry from the Name Servers tab by selecting it and clicking **Remove**.

You can also specify name servers from the command line by using the dnscmd tool. Open an administrative command prompt and type the following:

```
dnscmd ServerName /RecordAdd ZoneName NodeName [/Aging] [/OpenAcl]
    [Ttl] NS {HostName | DomainName}
```

The parameters of this command are as follows:

- *ServerName*: Specifies the DNS host name of the DNS server. You must include this parameter; use a period to specify the local computer.

- /RecordAdd: Required; adds a resource record.

- *ZoneName*: Required; specifies the FQDN of the zone being configured.

- *NodeName*: Required; specifies the FQDN of the node in the DNS namespace for which you are adding a SOA record.

- /Aging: Enables aging and scavenging of the resource record. If not used, the resource record stays in the DNS database until manually deleted or updated.

- /OpenAcl: Specifies that any user is permitted to modify the new records. If not used, only administrators have permission to modify the new record.

- *Ttl*: Specifies the TTL setting for the resource record. If not used, the default TTL in the SOA resource record is used.

- NS: Required; specifies that you are adding a name server (NS) resource record to the specified zone.

### Registering Resource Records

The act of creating A (or AAAA) and PTR resource records is sometimes referred to as the *registering* of resource records. On a DHCP-enabled network, the DHCP server can automatically update these records on behalf of its clients by using the information contained within the DHCP option 81 (Client FQDN), which provides instructions to the DHCP server used by the DNS server to process DNS dynamic updates on behalf of the client. When this option is specified, the DHCP client sends its FQDN to the DHCP server in the DHCPREQUEST packet. The DHCP server then replies with the DHCPACK message including the FQDN option.

As with other DHCP options, you can configure option 81 at the server, scope, option class, or client level. Refer to Chapter 2, "Configuring Dynamic Host Configuration Protocol (DHCP)," for instructions on configuring options at each of these levels.

You can also manually force a refresh of a client's name registration in DNS. Open a command prompt at the client and type **ipconfig /registerdns**. This command forces the registration of the client's A (or AAAA) and PTR records. This is the procedure you need to use when dealing with a client that uses static TCP/IP configuration.

> **NOTE**   For more information on DHCP option 81 and its use in registering DNS records, refer to "Integrating DHCP with DNS" at http://technet.microsoft.com/en-us/library/cc771732.aspx and "Configuring Secure Dynamic Update" at http://technet.microsoft.com/en-us/library/dd145315(WS.10).aspx. The latter reference also contains additional information regarding the DnsUpdateProxy group discussed in the next section.

### Using the DnsUpdateProxy Group

You saw in Chapter 2 how a DHCP server can be configured to dynamically register A and PTR records for client computers. It is possible that a default configuration of DNS secure update can cause stale records. For example, if a DHCP server performs a secure dynamic update on a client computer name, this server becomes the owner of that name and only this server can update the name. It can cause a problem in case the original DHCP server becomes unavailable for any reason and a second DHCP server were to update the client's TCP/IP configuration. Because the second DHCP server did not own the client's name, it would be unable to update these records.

This problem is solved by adding all available DHCP servers to a security group known as the *DnsUpdateProxy group*. Any DHCP server that is a member of this group automatically updates a client's A (or AAAA) and PTR records whenever it updates the client's TCP/IP configuration. This is a built-in global security group in AD DS. Use the following procedure:

1. Open Active Directory Users and Computers and expand the **Users** node.

2. Right-click **DnsUpdateProxy** and choose **Properties**.

3. On the Members tab of the DnsUpdateProxy Properties dialog box, click **Add**.

4. On the Select Users, Contacts, Computers, Service Accounts, or Groups dialog box, as shown in Figure 7-13, type the name of the DHCP server (for example, `server4`) and click **OK**. The added server appears in the Members tab of the DnsUpdateProxy Properties dialog box.

5. Repeat Steps 3 and 4 as required to add additional DHCP servers to this group.

6. Click **OK** to return to the Active Directory Users and Computers snap-in.

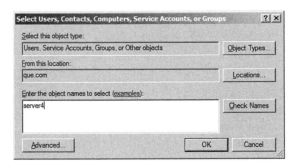

**Figure 7-13**  Adding the DHCP server to the DnsUpdateProxy group.

**TIP**  In Windows Server 2008 R2, you can also use the Active Directory Administrative Center snap-in to add a server to the DnsUpdateProxy group. Right-click this group, choose **Properties**, scroll down to the Members section, and click **Add** to display the Select Users Contacts, Computers, Service Accounts, or Groups dialog box, as previously shown.

### Configuring Round Robin

*Round robin* is a load-balancing mechanism used by DNS servers to distribute name resolution activity among all available DNS servers. If multiple A or AAAA resource records are found in a DNS query (for example, on a multihomed computer), round robin sequences these resource records randomly in repeated queries for the same computer. An example of a situation in which round robin is useful is a situation where you have multiple terminal servers in a server farm that users access for running applications. DNS uses round robin to randomize the sequence in which terminal service users access given servers.

**TIP**   Remember that you should always ensure that round robin is selected when you have configured multiple DNS servers to perform name resolution for client computers in a medium to large corporate environment.

**NOTE**   For more information on using round robin in a terminal server environment, refer to "TS Session Broker Load Balancing Step-by-Step Guide" at http://technet.microsoft.com/en-us/library/cc772418(WS.10).aspx.

By default, round robin is enabled on Windows Server 2008 R2 DNS servers. Use the following procedure to verify or modify this setting:

1. Right-click the DNS server in the console tree of DNS Manager and choose **Properties**.

2. Select the **Advanced** tab.

3. Select or clear the check box labeled **Enable round robin** as required, as shown in Figure 7-14. Then, click **OK**.

**Figure 7-14**   Configuring round robin in Windows Server 2008 R2 DNS.

### Enabling Netmask Ordering

Netmask ordering is a mechanism used by DNS servers for prioritizing local subnets so that when a client queries for a host name mapped to multiple IP addresses, the DNS server preferentially returns an IP address located on the same subnet as the requesting client.

Netmask ordering is enabled by default in Windows Server 2008 R2. To verify or modify this setting, access the Advanced tab of the DNS server's Properties dialog box as already shown in Figure 7-14 and select or clear the check box labeled **Enable netmask ordering**.

### Configuring DNS Record Security and Auditing

The Security tab of the zone Properties dialog box allows you to modify permissions for secure dynamic updates to resource records in an Active Directory-integrated zone. This tab is not present for other types of DNS zones. As shown in Figure 7-15, this tab is configured with a default set of permissions.

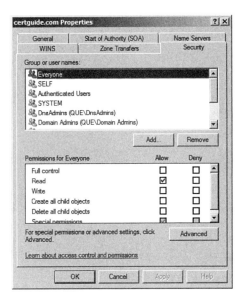

**Figure 7-15**   The Security tab of a zone's Properties dialog box enables you to specify security permissions for the zone.

To add additional groups or users, click the **Add** button to bring up the Select Users, Computers, Service Accounts, or Groups dialog box. Click the **Advanced** button to bring up the Advanced Security Settings dialog box as shown in Figure 7-16. From this dialog box, you can specify granular permissions, auditing properties, or ownership. You can also check the effective permissions applied to a user or group as a result of multiple group memberships. Functions available on this dialog box are similar to those used with NTFS file and folder permissions, and are covered in detail in Chapter 9, "Configuring File Servers."

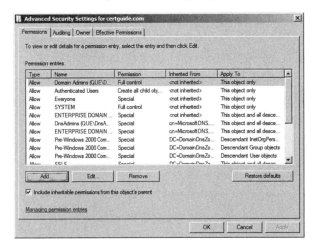

**Figure 7-16**   The Advanced Security Settings for [zone] dialog box enables you to specify granular permissions, auditing, and ownership for the zone.

## Exam Preparation Tasks

## Review All the Key Topics

Review the most important topics in this chapter, noted with the key topics icon in the outer margin of the page. Table 7-4 lists a reference of these key topics and the page numbers on which each is found.

**Table 7-4**  Key Topics for Chapter 7

| Key Topic Element | Description | Page Number |
|---|---|---|
| Table 7-2 | Introduces the most important types of resource records in Windows Server 2008 DNS. | 299 |
| Figure 7-1 | Create new resource records in a zone by right-clicking the zone in DNS manager. | 300 |
| Figure 7-2 | Creating host records. | 302 |
| Figure 7-5 | Use the New Resource Record dialog box to create different types of resource records. | 304 |
| Table 7-3 | Describes the important properties of the Start of Authority (SOA) record that you must be able to configure. | 310 |
| Figure 7-11 | The Name Servers tab contains listings for all servers that are authoritative for its zone. | 312 |
| Paragraph | Describes the importance of the DnsUpdateProxy group. | 314 |

## Complete the Tables and Lists from Memory

Print a copy of Appendix B, "Memory Tables," (found on the CD), or at least the section for this chapter, and complete the tables and lists from memory. Appendix C, "Memory Tables Answer Key," also on the CD, includes the completed tables and lists to check your work.

## Definition of Key Terms

Define the following key terms from this chapter, and check your answers in the Glossary.

Alias (CNAME) record, DnsUpdateProxy group, Host (A or AAAA) record, Name Server (NS) record, netmask ordering, Pointer (PTR) record, Resource record, round robin, service location (SRV) record, Start of Authority (SOA) record, Time to Live (TTL), Weighting records

This chapter covers the following subjects:

- **Configuring DNS Client Computer Settings:** Client computers using DNS for name resolution normally work properly without additional configuration, particularly when supplied with DNS server addresses by means of Active Directory domain membership or DHCP. This section discusses several settings you must be aware of for ensuring that client computers can resolve names properly; it also provides some tips in the event that names are not resolved properly.

- **Other Types of Name Resolution:** This section discusses name resolution methodologies that are useful on networks where DNS servers do not exist. This includes NetBIOS name resolution, use of WINS servers, and Link-Local Multicast Name Resolution (LLMNR).

# CHAPTER 8

# Configuring Client Computer Name Resolution

The previous chapters provided a comprehensive introduction to the use of Domain Name System (DNS) on Windows Server 2008 networks, including the latest enhancements offered by Windows Server 2008 R2 and Windows 7. It is now time to turn your attention to the job of ensuring that client computers on the network are able to resolve computer names successfully. In most cases, client computers receive all the information they need through membership in an Active Directory Domain Services (AD DS) domain or from a server running Dynamic Host Configuration Protocol (DHCP). But, on a small network or an ad-hoc wireless network, client computers may be unable to resolve names without being pointed to the proper resource. In many cases, this is a DNS server. However, in the absence of a DNS server, computers need other means of resolving names. NetBIOS naming has been around for a long time and can still be useful on computers running Windows 7 and Windows Server 2008 R2; however, the latest versions of Windows can also use LLMNR as a simple name resolution technology in the absence of a DNS server. In this chapter, you learn about these and other tips and tricks used for client computer name resolution.

## "Do I Know This Already?" Quiz

The "Do I Know This Already?" quiz allows you to assess whether you should read this entire chapter or simply jump to the "Exam Preparation Tasks" section for review. If you are in doubt, read the entire chapter. Table 8-1 outlines the major headings in this chapter and the corresponding "Do I Know This Already?" quiz questions. You can find the answers in Appendix A, "Answers to the 'Do I Know This Already?' Quizzes."

**Table 8-1**  "Do I Know This Already?" Foundation Topics Section-to-Question Mapping

| Foundations Topics Section | Questions Covered in This Section |
| --- | --- |
| Configuring DNS Client Computer Settings | 1–6 |
| Other Types of Name Resolution | 7–10 |

1. You need to configure a client computer running Windows 7 Professional to respond to three different DNS servers in order to resolve all names on the network. What should you do?

   a. From the General tab of the Internet Properties dialog box, select the **Use the following DNS server addresses** option and type the IP addresses of the three DNS servers in the text boxes provided.

   b. From the General tab of the Internet Properties dialog box, select the **Use the following DNS server addresses** option and type the IP addresses of the two most used DNS servers in the text boxes provided. Then, select the **Alternate Configuration** tab and type the IP address of the third DNS server at this tab.

   c. From the General tab of the Internet Properties dialog box, select the **Use the following DNS server addresses** option and click the **Advanced** button. On the Advanced TCP/IP Settings dialog box that appears, click **Add** and type the three DNS server IP addresses, one at a time. Then, ensure that they are sequenced in the order they will most likely need to be accessed.

   d. You cannot specify more than two DNS servers at the client computer; you must configure the DHCP server to supply the required DNS server IP addresses.

2. Which of the following best describes the act of DNS devolution?

   a. A client computer that has appended a multilevel DNS suffix, such as `certguide.com`, to an unqualified host name, such as `server1`, attempts to resolve the FQDN `server1.certguide.com`; if this query fails, the client attempts to resolve the FQDN `server1.com`.

   b. A client computer that has appended a multilevel DNS suffix, such as `certguide.com`, to an unqualified host name, such as `server1`, attempts to resolve the FQDN `server1.com`; if this query fails, the client attempts to resolve the FQDN `server1.certguide.com`.

   c. A client computer that has appended a multilevel DNS suffix, such as `certguide.com`, to an unqualified host name, such as `server1`, attempts to resolve the FQDN `server1.certguide.com`; if this query fails, the client sends the query to a second DNS server that can resolve the .com top-level domain and then to a third DNS server that can resolve the certguide.com second-level domain.

   d. A client computer appends a series of DNS suffixes in turn to an unqualified host name, such as `server1`, and attempts to resolve each of the resulting FQDNs in turn until it finds one that resolves successfully.

3. You want to enable the use of DNS dynamic updates to register the IP addresses and the connection-specific domain name of this connection, in addition to the primary name of the computer, so you access the DNS tab of the Advanced TCP/IP Settings dialog box. What should you do?

   a. Select the **Append primary and connection specific DNS suffixes** and **Append parent suffixes of the primary DNS suffix** options.

   b. Select the **Append these DNS suffixes (in order)** option and then click **Add** and type all the required DNS suffixes in the dialog box that appears.

   c. Ensure that the **Register this connection's addresses in DNS** option is cleared, and then select the **Use this connection's DNS suffix in DNS registration** option.

   d. Ensure that the **Register this connection's addresses in DNS** option is selected, and then select the **Use this connection's DNS suffix in DNS registration** option.

4. You are responsible for a standalone Windows 7 Ultimate computer that is not to be joined to an AD DS domain. You need to configure a primary DNS suffix for this computer. What should you do?

   a. From the Computer Name tab of the System Properties dialog box, click **Change** to display the Computer Name/Domain Changes dialog box. On the Workgroup field of this dialog box, type the required primary DNS suffix.

   b. From the Computer Name tab of the System Properties dialog box, click **Change** to display the Computer Name/Domain Changes dialog box. Then click **More** to display the DNS Suffix and NetBIOS Computer Name dialog box and type the required primary DNS suffix in the text box provided.

   c. From the General tab of the Internet Protocol Properties dialog box, click **Advanced** to display the Advanced TCP/IP Settings dialog box. Select the **Append these DNS suffixes (in order)** option and type the required primary DNS suffix.

   d. From the General tab of the Internet Protocol Properties dialog box, click **Advanced** to display the Advanced TCP/IP Settings dialog box. Type the required primary DNS suffix in the text box labeled **DNS suffix for this connection**.

5. After hearing from a user named Beth that she is unable to access the company's intranet website, you check the configuration of your DNS server and realize that the web server's A record is incorrect. After correcting this record, you inform Beth that the problem has been corrected. But, she is still unable to access the intranet website. What should you do first?

   a. Ask Beth to open a command prompt on her computer and type `ipconfig /flushdns`.

   b. Ask Beth to open a command prompt on her computer and type `ipconfig /registerdns`.

   c. Ask Beth to log off and log back on her computer.

   d. Check the configuration of the web server and reboot it if necessary.

   e. Check the network configuration for disconnected cables.

6. Your company uses two DNS servers named Server1 and Server2 to resolve host names to IP addresses on the network. After making a change to statically configured A resource records at Server1, users at some client computers report that they receive outdated information when attempting to access resources on the network. What should you do?

   a. At each client computer, open a command prompt and type `ipconfig / flushdns`.

   b. At each client computer, open a command prompt and type `ipconfig / renew`.

   c. At Server1, open a command prompt and type `ipconfig /flushdns`.

   d. At Server2, open a command prompt and type `dnscmd /clearcache`.

7. Your computer is configured for use of NetBIOS name resolution. It is currently configured to try broadcasting to locate NetBIOS names. If this is not successful, it will attempt to locate a NetBIOS name server such as a WINS server. What NetBIOS node type is in use?

   a. b-node

   b. p-node

   c. m-node

   d. h-node

8. Your computer is configured to use a static IPv4 address on a small office network that is configured as a workgroup. You attempt to reach a server named Server1 by using a UNC path, such as \\server1\docs, but are unsuccessful. What should you do?

   a. Access the WINS tab of the Advanced TCP/IP Settings dialog box and select the **Enable NetBIOS over TCP/IP** option.

   b. Access the WINS tab of the Advanced TCP/IP Settings dialog box and select the **Disable NetBIOS over TCP/IP** option.

   c. From the Local Group Policy editor snap-in, disable the **Turn off Multicast Name Resolution** policy.

   d. From a command prompt, type the `ipconfig /registerdns` command.

9. What statically configured file can be used to resolve host names to IP addresses in the absence of a DNS server?

   a. Cache

   b. WINS

   c. HOSTS

   d. LMHOSTS

10. You are using a Windows 7 computer and ping a remote host by using an unqualified host name. You receive a response that includes the IPv6 address of the remote host but no domain name suffix. What technology is being used to resolve this name?

   a. NetBIOS

   b. LLMNR

   c. WINS

   d. Connection-specific DNS suffixes

**Foundation Topics**

# Configuring DNS Client Computer Settings

In the typical business network, client computers obtain settings required for resolving network names through DHCP or by means of membership in an AD DS domain. However, if you have any computers that are configured with static TCP/IP settings or standalone computers that are not members of a domain, it is necessary to configure DNS settings manually through the Advanced TCP/IP Settings dialog box. This section looks at the various settings you must be familiar with, both for the 70-642 exam and the real world.

## Specifying DNS Server Lists

For efficient name resolution purposes, DNS clients require a prioritized list of DNS name servers. This list determines which DNS servers are contacted to resolve name queries—for example, when you type a server name in a Windows Explorer address field or at the **Start > Run** command. Chapter 1, "Configuring IPv4 and IPv6 Addressing," introduced you to the Internet Protocol Version 4 (TCP/IPv4) Properties and Internet Protocol Version 6 (TCP/IPv6) Properties dialog boxes. As shown in Figure 8-1, you generally want to leave the **Obtain DNS server address automatically** option selected; this option enables the computer to obtain DNS server addressing information from DHCP or from AD DS membership. With DHCP servers running Windows Server 2003 or later, you can have a list of up to 25 DNS servers specified by configuring the DHCP option 006, DNS Servers. For more information on this option, refer to Chapter 2, "Configuring Dynamic Host Configuration Protocol (DHCP)."

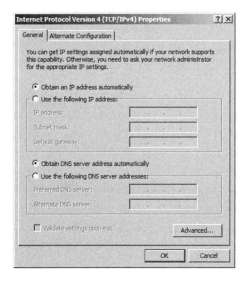

**Figure 8-1**   You can configure preferred and alternate DNS server IP addresses if required.

For standalone clients or clients configured with static IP addresses, you need to select the **Use the following DNS server addresses** option, which allows you to type the IP addresses of preferred and alternate DNS servers in the text boxes provided.

Use the following procedure if you need to specify more than two DNS server addresses:

1. Click the **Advanced** button to display the Advanced TCP/IP Settings dialog box. Select the **DNS** tab to display the options shown in Figure 8-2.

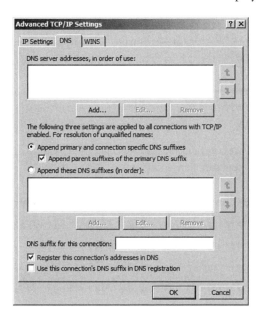

**Figure 8-2**    The DNS tab of the Advanced TCP/IP Settings dialog box enables you to configure several DNS-related options.

2. Click **Add** to display the TCP/IP DNS Server dialog box shown in Figure 8-3.

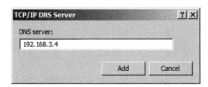

**Figure 8-3**    Adding the IP address of a DNS server.

3. Type the IP address of a required server (for example, `192.168.3.4`) and click **Add** to add the IP address of the server to the DNS server addresses in order of use list box.

4. Repeat Steps 2 and 3 as required to add additional DNS servers.

5. If you need to modify the order of the DNS server addresses as listed, select a server address and use the arrow buttons provided.

> **TIP**   Try to choose a preferred DNS server that is always available and located on a dependable, fast network connection. The client attempts to contact the preferred DNS server first and uses alternates only if the preferred server is not available.

### Configuring DNS Suffix Search Order Lists

By configuring a DNS suffix search order list for a client computer, you can extend or revise the DNS search capability available from that computer. This enables the DNS Client service to append additional DNS name suffixes to the original name, thereby generating alternate fully qualified domain names (FQDN) that can be sent to the DNS server for querying.

By default, client computers use the following DNS suffix search order when the user types an unqualified host name:

1. The client appends its own primary DNS suffix to generate a default FQDN, which is sent to the DNS server for resolution. For example, a computer with the FQDN `computer1.que.com` searching for `server1` will try the FQDN `server1.que.com`.

2. If this query fails, the computer queries for alternate FQDNs by appending additional DNS suffixes that have been configured for network connections. If the alternate suffix is `certguide.com`, the above computer will next try the FQDN `server1.certguide.com`.

3. If this query fails, the computer retries queries based on systematic reduction of the primary suffix; in this case, a search for `server1.com` will be attempted. This type of query is also known as *devolution*.

4. If none of these queries succeed or additional suffixes are not available, the query fails and a `Name not found` message is returned.

**TIP**  Remember that devolution in AD DS environments enables client computers in child domains to access resources in parent domains without the need to specify a complete FQDN of the desired resource.

**NOTE**  For more information on how DNS devolution works on Windows Server 2008 R2 and Windows 7 computers, refer to "DNS Devolution" at http://technet.microsoft.com/en-us/library/ee683928(WS.10).aspx.

You can configure the DNS suffix search list from the DNS tab of the Advanced TCP/IP Settings dialog box previously shown in Figure 8-2. The following settings are available:

- **Append primary and connection specific DNS suffixes:** The default option, this enables the client to resolve unqualified names by appending the primary DNS suffix plus any connection-specific DNS suffixes that have been specified, either manually or from DHCP using the 015 DNS Domain Name option mentioned in Chapter 2. Note that the primary DNS suffix is the suffix that has been assigned to the computer and configured from the Computer Name tab of the System Properties dialog box. The next section describes how to configure this DNS suffix.

- **Append parent suffixes of the primary DNS suffix:** Enables the client to search the parent suffixes of the primary DNS suffix up to the second-level domain, when resolving unqualified host names. Selected by default.

- **Append these DNS suffixes (in order):** Select this option to enable the client to resolve an unqualified name by appending the suffixes from the list specified here. When selected, the client uses the names specified here in sequence and does not use any other domain names. Click **Add** to add a suffix to this list, **Edit** to modify a suffix already on the list, or **Remove** to remove an unwanted suffix from the list. Use the arrows provided to modify the sequence used by the client.

- **DNS suffix for this connection:** Type a DNS suffix in this text box to specify a DNS suffix for this specific connection. You can distinguish different connections on a computer for which more than one network adapter is configured, by specifying a DNS suffix here. When used, the DNS client service ignores any DNS suffix obtained from the DNS Domain Name DHCP option.

- **Register this connection's addresses in DNS:** Enables the use of DNS dynamic update to register the IP addresses of this connection and the primary domain name of this computer, which consists of the host name combined with the primary suffix. Selected by default in Windows Vista, Windows 7, Windows Server 2008, and later.

- **Use this connection's DNS suffix in DNS registration:** Enables the use of DNS dynamic update to register the IP addresses and the connection-specific domain name of this connection, in addition to the primary name of the computer. This option is not selected by default. You must select the **Register this connection's addresses in DNS** option to select this option.

**NOTE**   For more information about specifying DNS suffixes, refer to "Understanding DNS Client Settings" at http://technet.microsoft.com/en-us/library/cc754152. aspx and "IPv4 and IPv6 Advanced DNS tab" at http://technet.microsoft.com/en-us/library/cc754143(WS.10).aspx.

### Configuring a Client Computer's Primary DNS Suffix

You can also use the System Properties dialog box to modify the primary DNS suffix used by a standalone computer that is not a member of an AD DS domain. The following procedure describes how to do this on a Windows 7 computer; the procedure for computers running Windows XP, Vista, Server 2003, or Server 2008 is similar:

1. Click **Start**, right-click **Computer**, and select **Properties**.

2. Select the **Advanced system settings** option to display the System Properties dialog box.

3. From the Computer Name tab, click **Change** to display the Computer Name/ Domain Changes dialog box.

4. On this dialog box, click **More** to display the DNS Suffix and NetBIOS Computer Name dialog box, as shown in Figure 8-4.

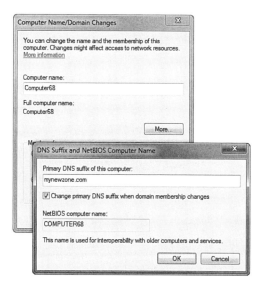

**Figure 8-4**   Specifying a primary DNS suffix on a Windows 7 computer.

5. Type the required primary DNS suffix of the computer (for example,
   **mynewzone.com**) in the text box provided and click **OK**.

6. The primary DNS suffix is added to the computer name to create the full
   name displayed in the Computer Name/Domain Changes dialog box. Click
   **OK**.

### Using Group Policy to Configure DNS Client Settings

Group Policy enables you to configure a series of DNS client settings that are applied to all computers affected by the Group Policy object (GPO) in which you configure them. You can also use Group Policy to specify a primary DNS suffix for all
computers affected by the policy. Use the following procedure:

1. Open the Group Policy Management Editor focused on an appropriate GPO.

2. Navigate to **Computer Configuration\Policies\Administrative Tem-
   plates\Network\DNS Client**. You receive the policy settings shown in
   Figure 8-5. The following list describes the more important settings that you
   should be aware of.

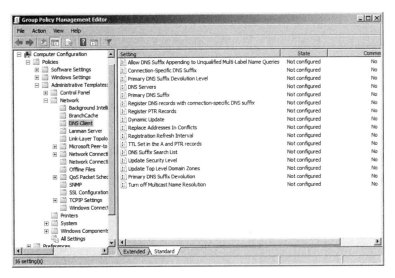

**Figure 8-5**   Group Policy allows you to configure several settings related to DNS client behavior.

- **Allow DNS Suffix Appending to Unqualified Multi-Label Name Queries:** Enables computers to attach DNS suffixes to an unqualified multilabel name when sending additional DNS queries when the original name query fails. Note that unqualified multilabel names are names that contain dots but are not dot-terminated, such as `server1.que` (compared to a FQDN, which ends in a terminating dot, such as `server1.que.com`).

- **Primary DNS Suffix Devolution Level:** Specifies the minimum number of labels that must be retained in a query string when primary DNS suffix devolution takes place.

- **Primary DNS Suffix:** Specifies a primary DNS suffix that applies to all affected computers and overrides any suffixes set in the Advanced TCP/IP Settings dialog box.

- **Register PTR Records:** Enables the registration of PTR resource records. If enabled, you can choose whether or not registration of PTR records is performed or only if registration of A records succeeds.

- **Dynamic Update:** Enable this policy for computers to use dynamic DNS registration on each available network connection. When disabled, computers are not able to use dynamic DNS registration for any network connections, regardless of how individual network connections have been configured.

- **Registration Refresh Interval:** Specifies the interval at which A and PTR resource records are refreshed on computers that use dynamic update.

- **TTL Set in the A and PTR records:** Specifies the Time-to-Live (TTL) value in seconds in the A and PTR records registered by the client computers.

- **DNS Suffix Search List:** Enables you to specify a series of DNS suffixes attached to a query for an unqualified computer name.

- **Update Security Level:** Specifies whether the affected computers can use unsecured or secured dynamic update when registering DNS records.

- **Primary DNS Suffix Devolution:** Determines whether client computers perform primary DNS suffix devolution in the name resolution process.

- **Turn off Multicast Name Resolution:** Enable this policy to disable the use of LLMNR, as described later in this chapter.

3. To apply any policy setting, right-click it and choose **Edit**.

4. On the dialog box that appears (as shown in Figure 8-6 for the Primary DNS Suffix policy), select **Enabled** and enter any required information in the field provided, and then click **OK**. Note that the dialog box for each policy setting provides additional information on the setting's use.

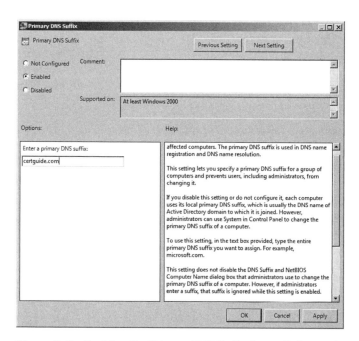

**Figure 8-6**   Enabling the Primary DNS Suffix Group Policy setting.

**TIP**  It is important that you remember—both for the 70-642 exam and the real world—the use of the DNS Client Group Policy settings for configuring DNS suffixes and devolution. Configuring these settings ensures their uniform application throughout an AD DS domain or organizational unit (OU) to which they apply.

## Using the `ipconfig` Command to Update and Register DNS Records

The `ipconfig` command has several parameters that you can use with respect to a client computer's DNS client cache, as follows:

- **`ipconfig /registerdns`:** Forces a registration of all client host records in DNS. An appropriate primary DNS suffix must be present and the DNS server must be hosting properly configured forward and reverse lookup zones.

- **`ipconfig /renew`:** Besides renewing a client's TCP/IP configuration as obtained from a DHCP server, this command enables the update of PTR records by the DHCP server in a non-domain environment. For this to work, both the DNS client and the DNS server must be configured with the address of the DNS server as the preferred DNS server. In addition, the **Register this connection's address in DNS** setting (refer to Figure 8-2) must be enabled and an appropriate DNS suffix must be present.

- **`ipconfig /displaydns`:** Displays the contents of the DNS client cache, including any entries loaded from the client's HOSTS file. This file is discussed later in this chapter. Remember that this cache contains the results of recently resolved FQDNs and is checked before a client queries a DNS server for name resolution.

- **`ipconfig /flushdns`:** Clears the contents of the DNS client cache. This command is useful if incorrect data makes its way into the DNS client cache. This includes negative responses from failed DNS queries that were executed earlier.

## Using the `dnscmd` Command to Update the DNS Server Cache

Besides the client cache referred to in the previous section, the DNS server also maintains a cache, in which it stores the results of recent iterative or recursive queries. Using this cache, the DNS server can immediately resolve additional queries for the same FQDN that it might receive from other client computers, without the need to refer the query to other DNS servers.

Occasionally, it might be necessary to make manual changes to a DNS resource record, as described in Chapter 7, "Configuring DNS Records." If other DNS servers in your organization have cached information from the server on which you have made such changes, the cache is not automatically updated; you need to clear the cache manually to ensure that clients receive the updated information. If you stop the DNS server service or reboot the DNS server, the DNS server cache is cleared automatically. You can clear the DNS server cache without restarting the DNS server service or rebooting the server by opening a command prompt and typing `dnscmd /clearcache`. To clear the DNS server cache on a different server (for example, server2), type `dnscmd server2 /clearcache`.

## Other Types of Name Resolution

Besides DNS, Windows Server 2008 also offers several other types of name resolution: The HOSTS file offers a static means of resolving host names; the LM-HOSTS file offers static resolution of NetBIOS names, the WINS server provides a dynamic means of resolving NetBIOS names, and Link-Local Multicast Name Resolution (LLMNR) offers name resolution for computers running IPv6 without the need for contacting any infrastructure server. This section looks at these name-resolution technologies.

### HOSTS Files

Chapter 5, "Installing and Configuring Domain Name System (DNS)," introduced the HOSTS file as the original means of resolving host names when the Internet was in its infancy in the 1980s. The HOSTS file is a static file (see Figure 8-7) used to map host names to IP addresses. In all recent Windows versions, this file is located in the `%systemroot%\system32\drivers\etc` folder. As it is a static file, someone needs to edit the file to keep its information up to date whenever changes occur. In essence, a HOSTS file is a fairly simple database file. Being an ASCII file, you can edit it in any text editor, such as Notepad. Its data is comprised of as many records as needed, with just two fields: an IP address and a friendly name of some kind that is associated with that IP address. You can also include comments by prefixing them with the # character.

**Figure 8-7**   The HOSTS file is an ASCII text file that is viewable and editable in Notepad.

Microsoft HOSTS files provide compatibility to UNIX-type HOSTS files. Most larger networks, regardless of the operating system, do not employ HOSTS file to any great extent. HOSTS files are troublesome to maintain. You should not use HOSTS files on Windows 7/Server 2008 networks unless they are necessary. Older Windows operating systems may still need to use them. Modern Windows networks would likely use HOSTS files to remain compatible with older network operating systems.

The following are several characteristics of HOSTS files:

- A single entry consists of an IP address corresponding to one or more host names.

- A HOSTS file can contain entries for both IPv4 and IPv6 computers.

- `ping` and other such TCP/IP utilities can reference the HOSTS file to resolve a host name to an IP address on both local and remote networks.

- The HOSTS file is parsed (meaning that its contents are interpreted) whenever a host name is referenced. Names are read in a linear way. For this reason, commonly used names should be placed near the top of the file.

- By default, the host name `localhost` is an entry in the HOSTS file.

- You must place the HOSTS file on every computer on the network. When a change occurs, you must update the HOSTS file on every computer.

With these limitations, the HOSTS file has been relegated to nothing much more than an extreme fallback, only to be used in the event that other name resolution technologies fail.

### NetBIOS Name Resolution

NetBIOS originated in the early 1980s as an application programming interface (API) running at the Session layer of the Open Systems Interconnect (OSI) reference model. We introduced the OSI model in Chapter 1. It provides a frame work for network communication interfaces, session management and data transport functions. Both Transmission Control Protocol (TCP) and User Datagram Protocol (UDP) are supported.

NetBIOS name resolution is used in certain actions performed on Windows computers. For example, when you issue the `net use` command to map a network drive, NetBIOS name resolution is used to obtain the IP address associated with the computer name you specify with this command.

NetBIOS provides for three name resolution methods: broadcasts, the LMHOSTS file, and the WINS server. We briefly look at each of these in turn.

### NetBIOS Broadcasts

By default, computers on the local network running IPv4 have NetBIOS over TCP/IP (NetBT) broadcasting enabled. These computers can use a name query broadcast message sent to the broadcast address (255.255.255.255). In addition, a NetBIOS name cache is included on each computer. A NetBIOS application first checks this cache for a NetBIOS name-to-IPv4 address mapping and then sends out a broadcast message to machines on the local network asking for the holder of the quoted name to reply with its IPv4 address.

NetBIOS name resolution can occur by means of any of four name resolution methods, known as NetBIOS node types and described in Table 8-2. Note that, for any of these node types, the computer first looks in its NetBIOS name cache, which stores resolved names for 10 minutes.

**Table 8-2**  NetBIOS Node Types

| Node Type | Description |
|---|---|
| b-node (broadcast) | Uses broadcasts to resolve NetBIOS names to IP addresses. Limited to resolving names on the local subnet because routers do not typically forward NetBIOS broadcasts. |

**Table 8-2**   NetBIOS Node Types (*Continued*)

| Node Type | Description |
|---|---|
| p-node (point-to-point) | Uses a point-to-point communication with a NetBIOS name server (WINS server) for name resolution. No broadcasts are used; however, if the name server is not available, there is no means to resolve NetBIOS names. |
| m-node (mixed) | First tries a broadcast (b-node) to resolve NetBIOS names; if this is not successful, it attempts to communicate with a NetBIOS name server (p-node). |
| h-node (hybrid) | First uses a WINS query (p-node); if the name server is unavailable, it then tries a broadcast (b-node) query. If both methods fail, the LMHOSTS file is checked and then the HOSTS file. Finally, it will look for a DNS server if configured. |

TCP/IPv4 in Windows Server 2008 and Windows 7 includes a NetBIOS setting that determines whether NetBIOS is enabled. Access the Internet Protocol Version 4 (TCP/IPv4) Properties dialog box and click **Advanced** to bring up the Advanced TCP/IP Settings dialog box. Click the **WINS** tab to display the dialog box shown in Figure 8-8. Then, select one of the three NetBIOS settings shown in the figure.

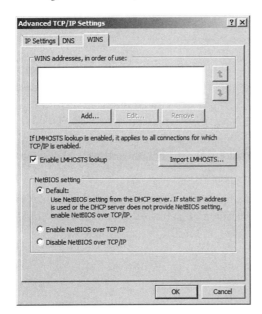

**Figure 8-8**   The WINS tab of the Advanced TCP/IP Settings dialog box provides settings for configuring NetBIOS broadcasts and the location of WINS servers.

You can determine the node type in use (by default, this is h-node). Open a command prompt and type `ipconfig /all`. Near the top of the output, you should see a `Node type` line that tells you which node type is being used (see Figure 8-9).

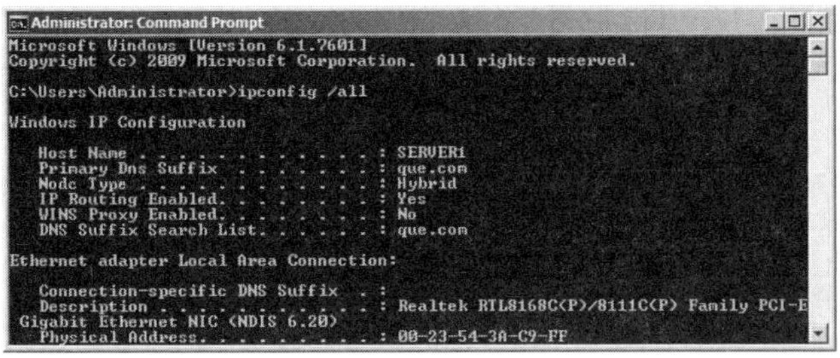

**Figure 8-9**  The output of the `ipconfig /all` command displays the node type in use.

## LMHOSTS Files

LMHOSTS is a static database file of NetBIOS name-to-IPv4 address mappings that is located in the `%systemroot%\system32\drivers\etc` folder on all modern Windows computers. NetBIOS applications can use this file to resolve NetBIOS names for computers running on a local network in the absence of a WINS server. It includes entries consisting of an IPv4 address and its corresponding NetBIOS name. Also included in this file are predefined keywords that start with the # character, including the following:

- **#PRE:** Defines preloaded name resolution entries, which are permanently loaded into the NetBIOS name cache, therefore reducing the number of broadcasts required.

- **#DOM:*DomainName*:** Defines computers for domain-based activities such as logon validation, account synchronization, and computer browsing.

- **#NOFNR:** Avoids the use of NetBIOS name queries for older computers running LAN Manager for UNIX.

- **#INCLUDE *path\filename*:** Loads and searches entries in the *path\filename* file, which is a centrally located and shared LMHOSTS file that is typically specified by use of a Universal Naming Convention (UNC) path, such as `\\`
`servername\sharename`.

- **#BEGIN_ALTERNATE and #END_ALTERNATE:** Defines a list of alternate LM-HOSTS file locations.

- **#MH:** Defines multiple entries used by a multihomed computer.

To enable the use of an LMHOSTS file, access the WINS tab of the Advanced TCP/IP Settings dialog box, as previously shown in Figure 8-8, and ensure that the **Enable LMHOSTS lookup** check box is selected. Note that this check box is selected by default. If you need to import an LMHOSTS file from a remote computer, click the **Import LMHOSTS** command button and browse to the location of the required file.

> **NOTE**  For more information on NetBIOS broadcasts and LMHOSTS files, refer to Chapter 11, "NetBIOS over TCP/IP" at http://technet.microsoft.com/en-us/library/bb727013.aspx.

### WINS Servers

Back in the days of Windows NT and Windows 9x, computers were initially using broadcasts and LMHOSTS files as already described to resolve NetBIOS names to their corresponding IP addresses. But, as already described, LMHOSTS files are static files—each time you added a new computer to the network or updated the TCP/IP configuration on an existing computer, you had to modify this file. Otherwise, broadcasts would become really numerous and errors resulting from the inaccessibility of computers on remote subnets would increase.

To overcome these problems, Microsoft introduced the concept of *Windows Internet Name Service (WINS)*. WINS runs as a server feature in both the original and R2 versions of Windows Server 2008 and maintains a dynamic database of NetBIOS name-to-IPv4 address mappings. Although its function has been largely superseded by DNS on modern Windows networks, older NetBIOS-based applications still can use WINS to locate required resources on the network.

To install WINS, open Server Manager, click **Add Features**, and select **WINS Server** from the list of available server features, as shown in Figure 8-10. Then, follow the instructions in the Add Features Wizard. When completed, you can configure WINS from the WINS snap-in, as shown in Figure 8-11. The WINS snap-in gives you detailed information about your WINS servers, allows you to view the IP address-to-NetBIOS name mappings database, and configure a static mapping.

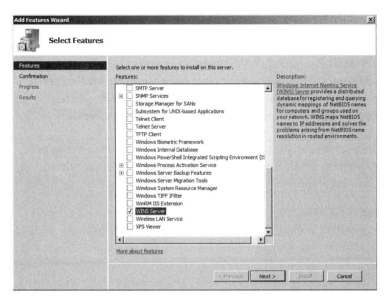

**Figure 8-10**    WINS is installed as a server feature in Windows Server 2008.

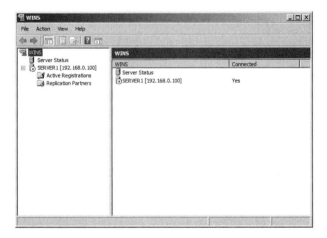

**Figure 8-11**    From the WINS snap-in, you can perform all administrative tasks related to WINS.

The two subnodes in the console tree of the WINS snap-in enable you to perform the following tasks:

- **Active Registrations:** Enables you to view and filter the computer and group records contained within the WINS database. Right-click this node and choose **Display Records**. You can also add static name-to address mappings to the WINS database by right-clicking the node and choosing **New Static**

**Mapping**. In the dialog box that appears, enter the computer name, IP address, and an optional NetBIOS scope.

- **Replication Partners:** Enables replication among different WINS servers on the network. Right-click this node and choose **New Replication Partner** to add a replication partner, which you can specify by name or IP address. To force a replication, right-click this node and choose **Replicate Now**.

Right-click the WINS server entry in the console tree and choose **Properties** to display the server's Properties dialog box, as shown in Figure 8-12. From this dialog box, you can configure the properties described in the following list.

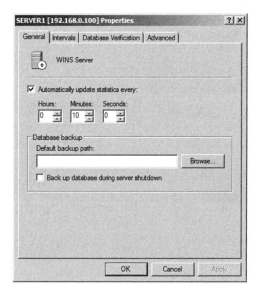

**Figure 8-12**   The WINS Server Properties dialog box enables you to configure several server-based options.

- **General tab:** Enables you to configure the time interval at which statistics are updated and define a database backup path. Select the check box provided to back up the WINS database during shutdown.

- **Intervals tab:** Enables you to define the following time intervals:

  - **Renew interval:** Specifies the interval before a WINS client must refresh its NetBIOS name. Also known as the TTL, this interval is six days by default.

  - **Extinction interval:** Also known as the tombstone interval, specifies the amount of time before a record marked as released is marked as extinct. The maximum allowed value is six days.

- **Extinction timeout:** Also known as the tombstone timeout, specifies the amount of time before a record marked as extinct is deleted from the WINS database. The default is six days.

- **Verification interval:** Specifies the amount of time before a WINS server is required to verify any old names that it does not own. The default is 24 days.

- **Database Verification tab:** Select the check box provided on this tab to verify the consistency of the WINS database, and choose an interval (24 hours by default) and a time at which verification will begin (0200 hours by default).

- **Advanced tab:** Enables you to define the following additional WINS server options: for logging events to the Windows event log, enabling burst handling, and database path location.

  - **Log detailed events to Windows event log:** Enables detailed event logging; the resulting logs are viewable in Event Viewer system log.

  - **Enable burst handling:** The burst handling feature defines the capability of the server to handle large numbers of client requests at one time (such as when many clients start up simultaneously) before these clients are processed and the information physically entered to the WINS database.

  - **Database path:** Enables you to modify the path to the database (`%systemroot%\system32\wins` by default).

  - **Starting version ID:** Specifies an incremental hexadecimal number that tracks changes in the local WINS database.

WINS-enabled clients automatically register themselves at startup, and you do not need to configure the WINS server for them. You do need to configure the clients to use WINS, as explained next. These dynamic mappings reflect any changes in IP address leases as supplied by the DHCP server.

You can configure DHCP to enable WINS clients by specifying scope options as described in Chapter 2. You can also configure static name-to-address mappings from the WINS snap-in. These are non-dynamic entries in the WINS database, and they ensure that WINS clients can resolve the NetBIOS names of the non-WINS enabled computers. DHCP provides the following two options:

- **044 WINS/NBNS Servers:** Instructs the DHCP server to provide the DHCP client with the address of the appropriate WINS server.

- **046 WINS/NBT Node Type:** Instructs the DHCP server to configure the client's node type for use in name resolution.

If you have not configured DHCP to enable WINS name resolution on client computers, you can configure a WINS client manually from the WINS tab of the Advanced TCP/IP Settings dialog box, shown previously in Figure 8-8. From this dialog box, click **Add** to add the IP addresses of the WINS servers to the WINS addresses field, in order of use. Click **Edit** to modify any entry or **Remove** to delete it; use the arrow buttons if you need to modify the sequence in which the WINS servers will be accessed.

**NOTE**  For more information on using a WINS server, refer to "Chapter 12—Windows Internet Name Service Overview" at http://technet.microsoft.com/en-us/library/bb727015.aspx.

**NOTE**  You might occasionally come across the mention of an older networking protocol called NetBEUI. Meaning NetBIOS Extended User Interface, this protocol was used for fast name resolution on NetBIOS-based networks in the days of Windows NT and Windows 9x. It completely depended on the flat namespace used by NetBIOS and was not routable. This protocol is no longer in use and is not included in recent Windows client or server versions. You do not need to worry about this protocol on the 70-642 exam.

## Troubleshooting NetBIOS Problems

If you receive an incorrect response or no response when connecting to a remote host when using commands such as `ping` or `net use`, a name resolution problem exists. Users connecting to network resources or websites generally refer to these resources by name rather than IP address. In fact, they generally do not know the IP address of the desired resource. That name, however, must be resolved to an IP address in order to connect successfully.

As with previous versions of Windows, Windows Server 2008 R2 and Windows 7 provides the `Nbtstat` command-line tool, which is useful for troubleshooting NetBIOS name resolution problems. You can use the various parameters of this command to check other aspects of NetBIOS sessions. The following are several of the more useful parameters:

- **-n:** Displays the NetBIOS name table on the local computer. This includes the names that were registered locally on the system by applications, such as the server and redirector services.

- **-c:** Displays the local NetBIOS name cache, which contains name-to-address mappings for other computers.

- **-R:** Purges the name cache and reloads it from the LMHOSTS file. Note that this parameter is case-sensitive, and must be entered as a capital.

- **-RR:** Releases and re-registers the NetBIOS name cache with LMHOSTS name entries that are configured with the #PRE parameter.

- **-a *<name>*:** Performs a NetBIOS adapter status command against the computer specified by *name*. You can also specify the computer using its IPv4 address. The adapter status command returns the local NetBIOS name table for that computer plus the MAC address of the adapter card.

- **-s:** Lists the current NetBIOS sessions and their status, including statistics.

> **NOTE**   When name resolution problems occur, you should check the event logs for errors. Windows defines several event IDs for naming problems; refer to "NBT Naming" at http://technet.microsoft.com/en-us/library/dd392861(WS.10).aspx for more information. Also, see "Chapter 16—Troubleshooting TCP/IP" at http://technet.microsoft.com/en-us/library/bb727023.aspx for general network troubleshooting tips.

### Link Local Multicast Name Resolution

As you saw in the previous section, IPv4 computers can use NetBT to resolve computer names to IP addresses by using broadcast messages, LMHOSTS files, or WINS servers. However, NetBIOS does not work with IPv6 networks and another name resolution method is needed for IPv6 networks that do not have a DNS server configured, such as might be found in home or small office networks or on ad hoc wireless networks.

Microsoft first introduced Link-Local Multicast Name Resolution (LLMNR) in Windows Vista and Windows Server 2008 to deal with this potential problem. LLMNR provides the capability of computers running IPv6 on the local subnet to resolve each other's names without the need for a DNS server. Recall from Table 1-10 in Chapter 1 that a link-local address is configured in the absence of a DHCP server and exists solely on its own network and cannot be referenced across an external network, such as the Internet. Enabled by default in Windows Vista/7/Server 2008/R2, each computer sends multicast DNS name queries to the IPv6 multicast address of FF02::1:3 rather than unicast queries. These computers listen for multicast LLMNR queries, thereby eliminating the need to perform name resolution on the local subnet by means of NetBT in the absence of a DNS server. It is also possible for LLMNR messages to be sent over an IPv4-based network to the multicast address 224.0.0.252.

You will know that your computer has used LLMNR to resolve an unqualified host name when no domain name suffix is appended to the host name and an IPv6 address is returned from the query, such as the `ping` example shown in Figure 8-13.

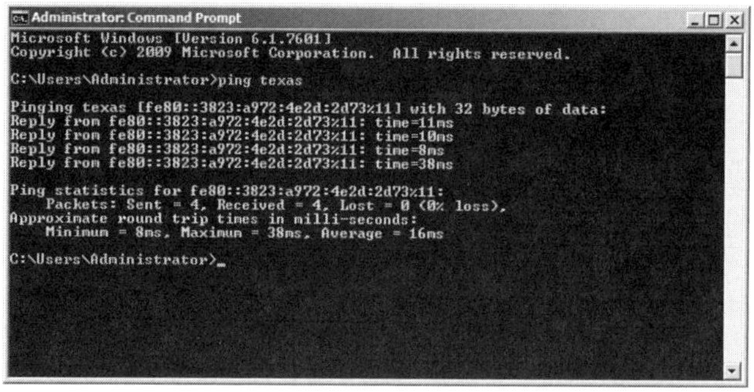

**Figure 8-13** A query using LLMNR for an unqualified host name returns an IPv6 address.

Defined in RFC 4795, LLMNR messages use a similar format as DNS messages but use UDP port 5355 to send name query requests. Responses are stored in an LLMNR resolver cache, which is separate from the DNS resolver cache.

When you enable Network Discovery from the Network and Sharing Center in a computer running Windows Vista/7/Server 2008/R2, this enables the use of LLMNR. In fact, on a computer that has both IPv4 and IPv6 enabled, LLMNR is used before NetBIOS. Consequently, when you use a UNC path such as \\ server1\documents to connect to a remote share, LLMNR is used. When resolving an unqualified host name, a computer on which both IPv4 and IPv6 are enabled will resolve the name as follows:

1. The computer attempts name resolution using DNS by combining the unqualified name with the available DNS suffixes described earlier in this chapter, and then by sending a DNS name query request to the DNS server.

2. If name resolution using DNS is unsuccessful, the computer sends up to two sets of multicast LLMNR name request messages over both IPv4 and IPv6.

3. If LLMNR name resolution is unsuccessful and NetBT is enabled, the computer broadcasts up to three NetBIOS name query request messages.

If the computer is attempting to resolve an unqualified name that is not a single-label name, it does not use either LLMNR or NetBT. When enabled as already described, a computer running Windows Vista or 7 can use LLMNR regardless of whether it has been configured to use a DNS server; this allows the computer to resolve the names of LLMNR-enabled machines that do not have host (A or AAAA) resource records configured on the DNS server.

Be aware that LLMNR has several distinct disadvantages:

- LLMNR is unable to resolve the names of computers running Windows XP, Windows Server 2003, or older Windows versions.

- Network Discovery must be enabled on all computers on the network for LLMNR to function properly.

- LLMNR does not function on an IPv4-only network.

- LLMNR messages do not cross routers, so you cannot resolve the names of computers located on remote subnets.

**NOTE**   You do not normally need to configure any parameters used by LLMNR for proper functionality. However, several configurable variables used by LLMNR, such as the port number and IPv6 multicast address, are found in the registry. For more information on these parameters, refer to "Host Name Resolution for Dual Stack (IPv4/IPv6)" at http://msdn.microsoft.com/en-us/library/ms881910.aspx. For more information on LLMNR in general, refer to "Link-Local Multicast Name Resolution" at http://technet.microsoft.com/en-us/library/bb878128.aspx.

**TIP**   You can use Group Policy to disable the use of LLMNR. From a GPO linked to the appropriate AD DS object, navigate to Computer Configuration\Policies\Administrative Templates\Network\DNS Client. Right-click the **Turn off Multicast Name Resolution** policy, choose **Edit**, and enable this policy. (Refer to Figure 8-5.)

## Exam Preparation Tasks

## Review All the Key Topics

Review the most important topics in this chapter, noted with the key topics icon in the outer margin of the page. Table 8-3 lists a reference of these key topics and the page numbers on which each is found.

**Table 8-3**   Key Topics for Chapter 8

| Key Topic Element | Description | Page Number |
|---|---|---|
| Figure 8-2 | The Advanced TCP/IP Settings dialog box enables you to configure several parameters related to the client computer's use of DNS. | 327 |
| List | Describes the sequence of DNS suffixes used by client computers when attempting to resolve an unqualified host name. | 328 |
| Figure 8-4 | Shows you how to modify the primary DNS suffix used by a client computer that is not joined to an AD DS domain. | 331 |
| List | The `ipconfig` command includes several parameters that are useful in maintaining the proper DNS client cache. | 334 |
| Paragraphs | Describes the use of and importance of NetBIOS name resolution. | 337 |
| Table 8-2 | Describes the available NetBIOS node types. | 337 |
| Paragraphs | Describes the use of WINS servers. | 340 |
| Paragraph | Describes LLMNR. | 345 |

## Complete the Tables and Lists from Memory

Print a copy of Appendix B, "Memory Tables," (found on the CD), or at least the section for this chapter, and complete the tables and lists from memory. Appendix C, "Memory Tables Answer Key," also on the CD, includes completed tables and lists to check your work.

## Definition of Key Terms

Define the following key terms from this chapter, and check your answers in the Glossary.

devolution, HOSTS file, Link Local Multicast Name Resolution (LLMNR), LMHOSTS file, NetBIOS (Network Basic Input/Output System), primary DNS suffix, WINS (Windows Internet Name System), universal naming convention (UNC)

This chapter covers the following subjects:

- **Shared Folders in Windows Server 2008 R2:** This section introduces the concept of file sharing and discusses the available file sharing options and the permissions that you can assign to shared folders on your server.

- **NTFS Permissions:** This section introduces the permissions you can assign to files and folders stored on partitions formatted with the NTFS file system. It then goes on to discuss how permissions assigned at different levels interact with one another, as well as the effective permissions a user receives when accessing a shared resource across the network.

- **Data Encryption:** This section introduces two encryption methods you can use to provide additional security for files and folders on your server. The Encrypting File System (EFS) enables encryption of individual files and folders, and BitLocker enables encryption of entire hard drive volumes.

- **Additional File Server Management Resources:** This section discusses other tools available in Windows Server 2008 R2 for managing file servers and making data available to remote users: Offline Files, BranchCache, and the Share and Storage Management Console.

# CHAPTER 9

# Configuring File Servers

All businesses use data of some kind. This might be inventory databases, product spreadsheets, images, Word documents, or other types of data. But, these are all files of some kind. And these files must be available to everyone who needs them to perform their job. Furthermore, it is just as important that the individuals who really need these files to perform their job are the only ones that should be able to access them. And of those that can access them, only certain individuals should have the capability to modify them. Making sure that files on your network are properly available is one of the big jobs of the network specialist, and Microsoft has created the File Server role in Windows Server 2008 to provide the specialist with a complete set of tools that help him do the job to the best of his abilities. This chapter and the ones to follow provide you with the resources and the know-how to administer and protect files and folders on your Windows Server 2008 network.

## "Do I Know This Already?" Quiz

The "Do I Know This Already?" quiz allows you to assess whether you should read this entire chapter or simply jump to the "Exam Preparation Tasks" section for review. If you are in doubt, read the entire chapter. Table 9-1 outlines the major headings in this chapter and the corresponding "Do I Know This Already?" quiz questions. You can find the answers in Appendix A, "Answers to the 'Do I Know This Already?' Quizzes."

**Table 9-1**  "Do I Know This Already?" Foundation Topics Section-to-Question Mapping

| Foundations Topics Section | Questions Covered in This Section |
|---|---|
| Shared Folders in Windows Server 2008 R2 | 1–2 |
| NTFS Permissions | 3–8 |
| Data Encryption | 9–12 |
| Additional File Server Management Resources | 13–15 |

1. Which of the following are valid permissions you can set for shared folders? (Choose three.)

    a. Full Control

    b. Modify

    c. Change

    d. Read & Execute

    e. Read

2. You are working at a computer running the Server Core version of Windows Server 2008 R2 and want to share a folder. Which command should you use?

    a. Share

    b. Net share

    c. Net user

    d. Netsh

3. You are configuring security permissions for a folder on your Windows Server 2008 R2 computer, and you want other users to be able to view files and run programs in the folder, but you do not want these users to be able to edit or delete files in the folder. What permission should you assign?

    a. Full Control

    b. Modify

    c. Change

    d. Read

    e. Read & Execute

4. You granted a user named Alice the Read NTFS permission on a folder named Documents. Alice is also a member of the Interns group, which has been explicitly denied the Full Control NTFS permission on the Documents folder. What is Alice's effective permission on this folder?

    a. Full Control

    b. Modify

    c. Read

    d. Alice does not have access to the folder.

5. You configured a folder with the basic NTFS permission of Read. Which of the following special access permissions are included in this permission? (Choose all that apply.)

   a. Traverse folder/execute file

   b. List folder/read data

   c. Read attributes

   d. Read extended attributes

   e. Delete

   f. Read permissions

   g. Take ownership

6. You created a shared folder named Documents on your Windows Server 2008 computer, which is a member server in your company's AD DS domain. You assigned the Engineers global group the Full Control NTFS permission to this share. In addition, you assigned the Interns group the Read permission to a subfolder of the Documents folder that is named Specifications. You do not want the members of the Interns group to be able to modify this folder. What should you do?

   a. Access the Advanced Security Settings dialog box for the Specifications folder and clear the check box labeled **Include inheritable permissions from this object's parent**. On the Windows Security dialog box that appears, select the **Remove** option.

   b. Access the Advanced Security Settings dialog box for the Specifications folder and clear the check box labeled **Include inheritable permissions from this object's parent**. On the Windows Security dialog box that appears, select the **Add** option.

   c. Access the Security tab of the Permissions dialog box for the Specifications folder. In this dialog box, select the **Interns** group, and then select the **Full Control** permission under the **Deny** column.

   d. You do not need to do anything because you have not granted any other permission to the Interns group.

7. You granted a user named Peter the Full Control NTFS permission on a shared folder named Documents on your Windows Server 2008 computer, which also has the Read shared folder permission granted to Everyone. Peter will be accessing this folder across the network on his computer. What is Peter's effective permission on this folder?

   a. Full Control

   b. Modify

   c. Read

   d. Peter does not have access to the folder.

8. You granted a user named Fred the Full Control NTFS permission on a shared folder named Documents on your Windows Server 2008 computer, which also has the Read shared folder permission granted to Everyone. Fred will be accessing this folder on your computer. What is Fred's effective permission on this folder?

   a. Full Control

   b. Modify

   c. Read

   d. Fred does not have access to the folder.

9. You want to encrypt the Confidential folder. This folder is located on the D:\ volume, which is formatted with the FAT32 file system. You access the folder's Properties dialog box and click the **Advanced** button. But, the option to encrypt the folder is not available. What do you need to do in order to encrypt this folder? (Each correct answer is a complete solution to the problem; choose two answers.)

   a. Format the D:\volume with the NTFS file system.

   b. Use the `Convert.exe` utility to convert the D:\ volume with the NTFS file system.

   c. Move the Confidential folder to the C:\ volume, which is formatted with the NTFS file system.

   d. Decompress the Confidential folder.

10. You are the default administrator for your company's AD DS domain. You configured Group Policy to permit the use of Encrypting File System (EFS) throughout the domain. Because you're going on vacation for the next three weeks, you want to ensure that your assistant named George can decrypt users' files if they have problems accessing them. George's user account is a member of the Domain Admins group. What should you do?

    **a.** Use Local Group Policy at each user's computer to run the Add Recovery Agent Wizard and designate George's user account as a recovery agent.

    **b.** Use Group Policy on a domain-based GPO to run the Add Recovery Agent Wizard and designate George's user account as a recovery agent.

    **c.** Back up your file encryption certificate and keys, and then give George a USB thumb drive containing a copy of the backed-up certificate and keys.

    **d.** You don't need to do anything; George can decrypt the files himself because he is a member of the Domain Admins group.

11. You want to enable BitLocker on your Windows Server 2008 Standard Edition computer, which is not equipped with a TPM. You go to the System and Security category of Control Panel but are unable to find the BitLocker Drive Encryption applet. What do you need to do before you can use BitLocker? (Each correct answer is part of the solution. Choose two answers.)

    **a.** Use Group Policy to enable the **Require additional authentication at startup** policy and select the **Allow BitLocker without a compatible TPM** option.

    **b.** Configure BitLocker to use a startup key.

    **c.** Upgrade your computer to Windows Server 2008 Enterprise Edition.

    **d.** Use the Add Features Wizard in Server Manager to install BitLocker.

    **e.** Use the Add Roles Wizard in Server Manager to install the File Server role.

356 MCTS 70-642 Cert Guide: Windows Server® 2008 Network Infrastructure, Configuring

12. Your computer is configured to dual boot between Windows Server 2008 R2 and Windows XP Professional. You use BitLocker to encrypt the Windows Server 2008 R2 partition. Upon starting your computer and selecting **Windows Server 2008 R2** from the startup menu, you receive an error message and Windows Server 2008 R2 does not start. What should you do to start Windows Server 2008 R2? (Each correct answer is a complete solution. Choose two answers.)

   a. Boot your computer with the Windows Server 2008 R2 DVD-ROM, select the **Windows Server 2008 R2** installation, and then select the **Startup Repair** option.

   b. Boot your computer with the Windows Server 2008 R2 DVD-ROM, select the **Windows Server 2008 R2** installation, and then select the **System Restore** option.

   c. Press **Enter**, type the recovery password that was automatically created while enabling BitLocker, and press **Enter** again.

   d. Boot your computer to Windows XP, navigate to the partition on which Windows Server 2008 R2 is installed, right-click this partition, and choose **Decrypt Drive**.

   e. Insert the USB drive that contains the recovery password.

13. You configured the Offline Files option on your Windows Server 2008 R2 computer and want to ensure that all available files on a network share are available for caching by users at remote computers running Windows Vista or Windows 7. Which option should you enable?

   a. **Only the files and programs that users specify will be available offline**

   b. **Enable BranchCache**

   c. **All files and programs that users open from the shared folder are automatically available offline**

   d. **Optimize for performance**

14. You are responsible for a Windows Server 2008 R2 file server in the head office of your company, which also operates a small branch office in a nearby city. The branch office has a Windows Server 2008 R2 server that is available to all users in the office. You would like to enable users in the branch office to access files and folders on your file server while minimizing bandwidth requirements. What should you do?

    a. Configure BranchCache using the Distributed Cache mode.

    b. Configure BranchCache using the Hosted Cache mode.

    c. Configure the branch office server with a shared folder and copy the contents of the shared folder on your file server to this folder.

    d. Configure the Offline Files option on your file server and enable the **All files and programs that users open from the shared folder are automatically available offline** option.

15. Which of the following are true about hidden administrative shares? (Choose three.)

    a. These shares are suffixed with the $ symbol and are visible in any Explorer window.

    b. These shares are suffixed with the $ symbol and are only visible in the Share and Storage Management snap-in.

    c. These shares are suffixed with the $ symbol and can be accessed from the Network and Sharing Center.

    d. You can access these shares by entering the UNC path to the share in the Run command.

    e. These shares are created by default when Windows Server 2008 is first installed, and cannot be removed.

## Foundation Topics

# Shared Folders in Windows Server 2008 R2

Sharing is a basic concept of networking in any computer environment. Simply put, sharing means making resources available on a network. Typically, this means a folder on one computer is made accessible to other computers that are connected to the first computer by a network. The purpose of sharing folders is to give users access to network applications, data, and user home folders in one central location. You can use network application folders for configuring and upgrading software. This serves to centralize administration because applications are not maintained on client computers. Data folders allow users to store and access common files, and user home folders provide a place for users to store their own personal information. You can also share other resources such as printers so that users can print to a printer not directly attached to their computer.

### Understanding the File Services Role in Windows Server 2008 R2

Out of the box, a computer running Windows Server 2008 R2 is a capable file server. But, Microsoft has provided a full suite of file-management capabilities and packaged them together in a server role simply called File Services. You learn more about most of the capabilities of the File Services role in this chapter and the chapters to come, but the following briefly summarizes the more important capabilities of the File Server role:

- **File Server Resource Manager:** A set of tools that enables you to manage resources used by files and folders on your server by performing such tasks as limiting the amount of space used by users, restricting the types of files being saved, and monitoring the amount of storage used.

- **Distributed File System (DFS):** Simplifies the logical grouping of shared resources on multiple servers by making them available within a single tree structure. Also included is DFS replication, which optimizes the synchronization of shared resources among multiple locations on your network, thereby providing load balancing and fault tolerance for user access to these resources.

- **Services for Network File System (NFS):** Enables file sharing among servers running Windows and UNIX.

- **Storage Manager for SANs:** A role feature that assists you in creating and managing physical and logical storage solutions pertaining to storage area networks (SANs) that include Fibre Channel and iSCSI disk-drive subsystems.

- **Share and Storage Management:** A role feature that facilitates administration of shared resources. Included is Access-Based Enumeration, which enables the display of only those files and folders that a user is entitled to access according to share and security permissions granted to her account.

- **Windows Search Service:** A role feature that indexes files and folders to facilitate rapid searching by users when connecting to shared folders.

- **Transactional NTFS:** Enables sequential operations on a file volume running NTFS to be performed as a single transaction. This means that all steps in the sequential operation must succeed for the transaction to be completed; if any step fails, the previous steps in the transaction are rolled back.

Use the following procedure to install the File Services role on a Windows Server 2008 R2 computer:

1. Open Server Manager and expand the Roles node.

2. Click **Add Roles** to start the Add Roles Wizard.

3. From the Select Server Roles page, select **File Services** and then click **Next**.

4. The wizard displays the Introduction to File Services page, which enables you to learn more about the File Services role. To do so, click the links provided. When you're ready to proceed, click **Next**.

5. The wizard displays the Select Role Services page shown in Figure 9-1. As shown, you can select from a series of optional role services. Select the required services and then click **Next**.

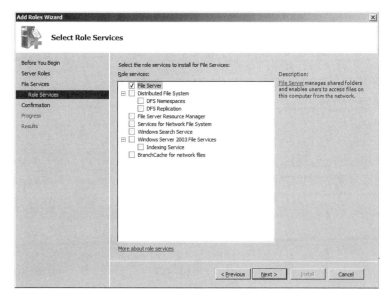

**Figure 9-1**   The Select Role Services page of the Add Roles Wizard enables you to select optional role services for your file server.

6. If any of the role services you select display additional wizard pages, respond as requested and then click **Next**.

7. Review the information provided on the Confirm Installation Selections page, and then click **Install** to proceed.

8. The Installation Progress page tracks the installation of the File Services server role. When informed that installation was successful, click **Close**.

### Using the Network and Sharing Center to Configure File Sharing

First introduced in Windows Vista and Server 2008 and continued in Windows 7 and Windows Server 2008 R2, the Network and Sharing Center, shown in Figure 9-2, brings all networking tasks together in a single convenient location. The diagram at the top indicates your connections to the network and the Internet, and graphically indicates when a connection is unavailable. You can configure connections to other computers and networks, share folders, printers, and media, view devices on your network, set up and manage network connections, and troubleshoot problems from this location.

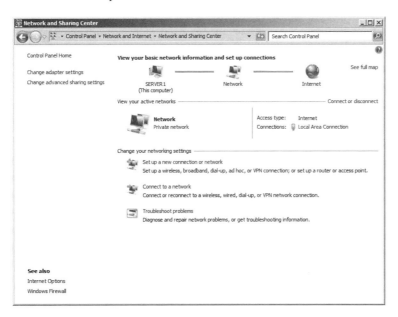

**Figure 9-2** The Network and Sharing Center provides a centralized location for configuring network properties.

You can open the Network and Sharing Center by using any of the following methods:

- Click **Start**, right-click **Network**, and then click **Properties**.

- Click **Start** and click **Network**. At the top of the Network window, click **Network and Sharing Center**.

- Click Start and type `network and sharing` in the Search text box. Then **select Network and Sharing Center** from the Programs list.

- Click **Start** > **Control Panel**. On the Control Panel home page, click **Network and Internet**, and then click **Network and Sharing Center** or **View Network Status and Tasks**.

From the Network and Sharing Center, you can perform actions related to sharing of resources on your computer with others on the network. Click **Change advanced sharing settings** to obtain the Advanced sharing settings dialog box shown in Figure 9-3. Among other networking options, you can specify the following file-sharing options:

- **Network discovery:** Enables the computer to locate other computers and devices on the network and enables these computers to locate your computer. It is expected that you would never turn this option off on a server.

- **File and printer sharing:** Enables the Standard Folder Sharing model, thereby allowing others on the network to access shared files on your computer and print from printers attached to your computer. This is the normal sharing model used by servers that will be discussed in detail later in this section.

- **Public folder sharing:** Enables the Public Folder sharing model, thereby allowing others on the network to access files in your Public folders of each Windows library (Documents, Pictures, Videos, and Music). This is a simplified folder-sharing model that is not normally used on a server-based computer.

- **Password protected sharing:** Increases security by limiting access of shared files and printers to only those who have a user account and password on your computer. You would normally keep this option turned on at a server.

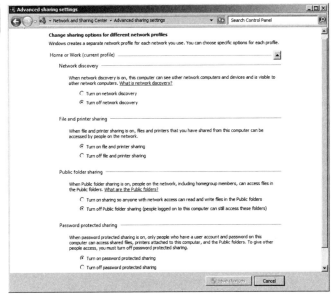

**Figure 9-3**   The Advanced sharing settings dialog box enables you to configure several global file and folder sharing settings.

## Sharing Files, Folders, and Printers

Shared folders are folders on the local hard drive that other users on a network can connect to. For the exam, it is critical that you understand how to manage and troubleshoot connections to shared resources, how to create new shared resources, and how to set permissions on shared resources. The process that Windows Server 2008 uses to share folders is that an administrator selects a folder, regardless of its location in the local folder hierarchy, and shares it through the Sharing tab of the folder's Properties dialog box.

To share files with other users across the network, you must manually do so for each folder containing the files that you want to share. To share a folder with other network users, you can open any Explorer window and use the following procedure:

1. In an Explorer window, navigate to the folder, right-click it, select **Share with**, and then click **Specific people**. The File Sharing dialog box opens, as shown in Figure 9-4.

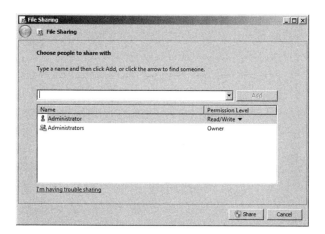

**Figure 9-4**   The File Sharing dialog box enables you to choose those you want to share a file with.

2. Type the name of a user with whom you want to share the folder and click **Add**. The name appears in the Name list with a default permission level of Read.

3. To share with another user, repeat Step 2 as many times as required. When finished, click **Share**.

4. To modify the permission assigned to a user, click that user and select either **Read** or **Read/Write**, as desired. To remove a user from the list, click the user and select **Remove**. When done, click **Share** to apply your changes.

To remove a shared folder, right-click the folder and select **Share with > Nobody**.

### Modifying Shared Folder Properties

When sharing files and folders with other users across a network, your computer becomes vulnerable to both unintentional and intentional attacks. Not only can the data simply be viewed for malicious purposes, such as corporate spying, it can be altered or destroyed on purpose or accidentally. For this reason alone, you should always grant the most restrictive permissions necessary for a network user to conduct work on those files. Granting just enough permission without being too lenient requires careful consideration. If you are too stringent, users can't get their jobs done. If you are too lenient, the data is at risk.

Use the following procedure to modify shared folder properties:

1. In an Explorer window, right-click the shared folder and choose **Properties**.

2. Click the **Sharing** tab (see Figure 9-5).

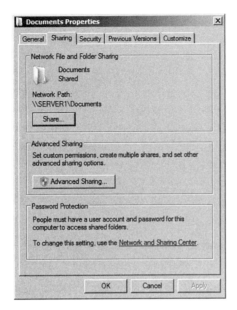

**Figure 9-5**   The Sharing tab of a folder's Properties dialog box enables you to modify shared folder properties.

3. Click **Advanced Sharing.** The Advanced Sharing dialog box shown in Figure 9-6 appears. This dialog box provides the options that are summarized in Table 9-2.

**Table 9-2**   Shared Folder Options in Windows Server 2008 R2

| Option | Description |
|---|---|
| Share this folder | Click to start sharing the folder. |
| Share name | This is the folder name that remote users employ to connect to the share. It appears in a user's Explorer window, or the user can access it by typing **\\computername\sharename** at the Run command or in the address bar of an Explorer window. |
| Comments | This information is optional and identifies the purpose or contents of the shared folder. The comment appears in the Map Network Drive dialog box when remote users are browsing shared folders on a server. |
| User limit | This sets the number of remote users who can connect to a shared resource simultaneously, reducing network traffic. For Windows Server 2008 R2, the limit is 16777216. |

| Option | Description |
|---|---|
| Permissions | Permissions can be assigned to individual users, groups, or both. When a directory (folder) is shared, you can grant each user and each group one of the three types of permissions for the share and all of its subdirectories and files or choose to specifically deny them those permissions. |
| Caching | Enables offline access to a shared folder. Available settings in the Offline Settings dialog box are discussed later in this chapter. |

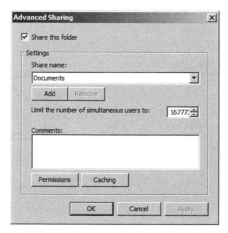

**Figure 9-6**   The Advanced Sharing dialog box enables you to configure several properties of shared folders.

4.  To add an additional share name, click **Add** under the Share name section. (If this command button is dimmed, ensure that the **Share this folder** option is selected and click **Apply**.) An additional share name enables users to access the shared folder under this name. Type the required share name. You can also change the maximum number of simultaneous users accessing with this share name. To do so, type the required number or use the arrows to select a number. In Windows Server 2008, the maximum number of users (displayed by default) is 16,777,216. When finished, click **OK**.

5.  To change shared folder permissions, click **Permissions**. This displays the Permissions for (folder name) dialog box shown in Figure 9-7. By default, the creator of the share receives Full Control permission and other users receive the Read permission. Click **Add** to add an additional user or group and then modify this user's permissions as desired. Click **OK** when finished. Table 9-3 describes the available shared folder permissions.

**Table 9-3**    Shared Folder Permissions

| Permission | Description |
| --- | --- |
| Full Control | Users are allowed to perform any task on the folder or its constituent files, including modifying their individual attributes and permissions used by others accessing them. |
| Change | Users are allowed to view and modify files, but not change the attributes of the shared folder itself. This is equivalent to Read/Write, as described earlier in this section. |
| Read | Users are allowed to view but not modify files. |

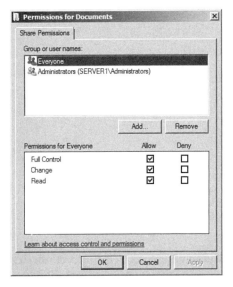

**Figure 9-7**    The Permissions for (folder name) dialog box enables you to configure permissions that apply to users accessing the folder across the network.

**TIP**    If you select permissions from the Deny column, you are explicitly denying access to that user or group. Such an explicit denial overrides any other permissions allowed to this group. Remember this fact if users experience problems accessing any shared resources across the network.

   **6.** To set granular security permissions on the folder, click the **Security** tab (refer to Figure 9-5) and modify the settings in the dialog box shown in Figure

9-8 as required. These permissions apply to everyone accessing the folder either locally or across the network; more restrictive permissions configured here override those configured from the Sharing tab. These settings are discussed in the next section.

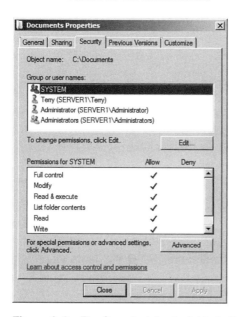

**Figure 9-8**   The Security tab of a folder's Properties dialog box enables you to configure granular permissions for users and groups accessing the folder.

7. When you are finished, click **Close** to close the Properties dialog box. You can also click **Apply** to apply your changes and continue making modifications.

## Mapping a Drive

Mapping a network drive means associating a shared folder on another computer with a drive letter available on your computer. This facilitates access to the shared folder. To map a drive, follow these steps:

1. Click **Start**, right-click **Network**, and select **Map network drive**.

2. In the Map Network Drive Wizard, as shown in Figure 9-9, select the drive letter to be assigned to the network connection for the shared resource from the Drive drop-down box. Drive letters being used by local devices are not displayed in the Drive list. You can assign up to 24 drive letters.

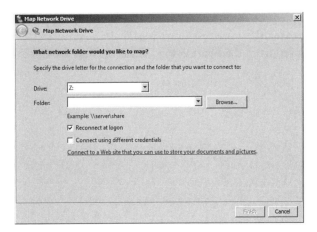

**Figure 9-9**   Mapping a network drive.

3. In the Folder box, enter a UNC path to specify the network path to the computer and the shared folder. For example, to connect to the shared folder Documents on a computer named Server2, type \\Server2\Documents. You can also click **Browse** to find the shared folder and then select the desired path.

4. Select a connection option, as follows:

   ▪ **Reconnect at logon:** This option is enabled by default and creates permanent connections. It reconnects the user to the shared folder each time the user logs on unless the user manually disconnects from the resource.

   ▪ **Connect using different credentials:** This option enables you to connect to a shared folder using a different user account. This option is useful if you are at another user's computer and need to connect to a resource to which the currently logged in user does not have the appropriate access.

5. Click **Finish**.

### Using the `net share` Command to Manage Shared Folders

Windows Server 2008 provides the `net share` command that you can use to manage shared folders. This is useful if you need to use scripts for automating administrative tasks. The syntax is as follows:

```
net share [sharename] [/parameters]
```

In this command, *sharename* is the name of the shared resource, and */parameters* refers to any of a series of parameters that you can use with this command. Table 9-4 describes several of the more common parameters used with this command.

**Table 9-4**   Several Common Parameters Used with the `net share` Command

| Parameter | Description |
|-----------|-------------|
| `/users:number` | Specifies the maximum number of users who can access the shared resource at the same time. Specify unlimited to allow the licensed limit of users. |
| `/cache:option` | Enables offline caching, according to the value of *option*:<br><br>**Documents**: Specifies automatic reintegration of documents<br><br>**Programs**: Specifies automatic reintegration of programs<br><br>**Manual**: Specifies manual reintegration<br><br>**None**: Advises the client that caching is inappropriate |
| `/delete` | Stops sharing the specified resource. |
| `/remark:"text"` | Adds a descriptive comment. Enclose the comment (*text*) in quotation marks. |

Note that you can also use this command without any parameters to display information about all the shared resources on the local computer.

## NTFS Permissions

The previous section introduced you to sharing folders and the permissions you can attach to shared folders. These permissions apply only when you access the folders across the network. Windows Server 2008 provides another means to secure files and folders on the local computer. The New Technology File System (NTFS) that has existed since the early days of Windows NT enables you to secure and manage access to resources on both a network level and on a local level. These NTFS file and folder permissions are also known as *security permissions*; they can apply to both files and folders, and that they apply on your computer to files and folders whether a folder is shared or not shared at all. Keep in mind, however, that although Windows Server 2008 supports FAT and FAT32 partitions, NTFS permissions apply only on partitions that are formatted using NTFS. Because you are already familiar with shared folder permissions, we use that as a jumping-off point to describe NTFS permissions.

### NTFS File and Folder Permissions

Like the shared folder permissions, which you can assign to users and groups, NTFS permissions for a folder control how users access a folder. Folders hold files.

You access a folder to find out what it contains or to create, add, or delete its files. NTFS folder permissions are designed to control this kind of activity. If no explicit permissions are assigned to a folder, a user cannot access that folder at all.

Windows stores an access control list (ACL) with every file and folder on an NTFS partition. The ACL is a list of users and groups that have been granted access for a particular file or folder, as well as the types of access that the users and groups have been granted. Collectively, these kinds of entries in the ACL are called access control entries (ACEs). If you think of the ACL as a list, it isn't hard to conceive that a list contains entries of various kinds. Windows uses the ACL to determine the level of access a user should be granted when he attempts to access a file or folder.

NTFS file permissions control what users can do with files within a folder. More specifically, the permissions control how users can alter or access the data that files contain. Table 9-5 describes the standard NTFS file permissions in detail.

**Table 9-5**   NTFS File and Folder Permissions

| Permission | What a User Can Do on a Folder | What a User Can Do on a File |
|---|---|---|
| Full control | Change permissions, take ownership, and delete subfolders and files. All other actions allowed by the permissions listed in this table are also possible. | Change permissions, take ownership, and perform all other actions allowed by the permissions listed in this table. |
| Modify | Delete the folder as well as grant that user the Read permission and the List Folder Contents permission. | Modify a file's contents and delete the file as well as perform all actions allowed by the Write permission and the Read and Execute permission. |
| Read & execute | Run files and display file attributes, owner, and permissions. | Run application files and display file attributes, owner, and permissions. |
| List folder contents | List a folder's contents, that is, its files and subfolders. | N/A |
| Read | Display file names, subfolder names, owner, permissions, and file attributes (Read Only, Hidden, Archive, and System). | Display data, file attributes, owner, and permissions. |
| Write | Create new folders and files, change a folder's attributes, and display owner and permissions. | Write changes to the file, change its attributes, and display owner and permissions. |

## Applying NTFS Permissions

It is simple to apply NTFS permissions, as the following procedure shows:

1. Right-click a folder or file and choose **Properties**.

2. Select the **Security** tab of the Properties dialog box. Also known as the ACL Editor, the Security tab enables you to edit the NTFS permissions for a folder or file. See Figure 9-10.

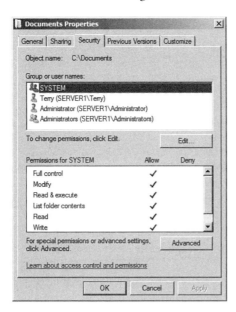

**Figure 9-10**    The Security tab of a file or folder's Properties dialog box displays its security permissions.

3. Click **Edit** to display the dialog box shown in Figure 9-11. You can configure the permissions described in Table 9-6.

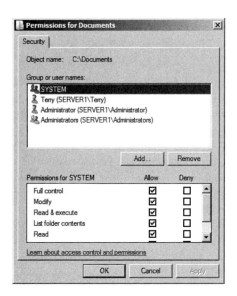

**Figure 9-11**    The Permissions for (file/folder name) dialog box enables you to configure security permissions.

**Table 9-6**    Security Tab Options

| Option | Description |
| --- | --- |
| Group or user names | Start by selecting the user account or group for which you want to change permissions or that you want to remove from the permissions list. |
| Permissions for Authenticated Users | Select the **Allow** check box to allow a permission. Select the **Deny** check box to deny a permission. |
| Add | Click **Add** to open the Select Users or Groups dialog box to select user accounts and groups to add to the Name list. |
| Remove | Click **Remove** to remove the selected user account or group and the associated permissions for the file or folder. |

4. When finished, click **OK** to return to the Security tab shown in Figure 9-10.

5. If you need to configure special permissions or access advanced settings, click **Advanced**. The next section discusses these permissions.

> **NOTE** You can also configure NTFS permissions from the command line by using the `icacls.exe` utility. This utility is useful for scripting permissions configuration or for configuring permissions at a Server Core computer. For more information on this utility, refer to "`Icacls`" at http://technet.microsoft.com/en-us/library/cc753525(WS.10).aspx.

### Specifying Advanced Permissions

For the most part, the standard NTFS permissions are suitable for managing user access to resources. There are occasions where a more specialized application of security and permissions is appropriate. To configure a more specific level of access you can use NTFS special access permissions. It isn't a secret, but it is not obvious in the Windows Server 2008 interface that the NTFS standard permissions are actually combinations of the special access permissions. For example, the standard Read permission is comprised of the List folder/read data, Read attributes, Read extended attributes, and Read permissions special access permissions.

In general, you will only use the standard NTFS permissions already described. In exceptional cases, you might need to fine tune the permissions further, and this is where the special access NTFS permissions come in. To configure special access permissions, use the following steps:

1. From the Security tab of the appropriate file or folder, click **Advanced** to access the Advanced Security Settings dialog box.

2. Click **Change Permissions** to display the Advanced Security Settings dialog box shown in Figure 9-12.

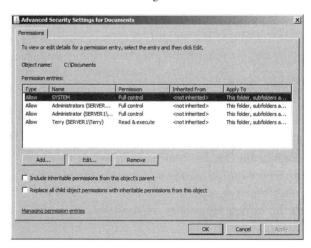

**Figure 9-12** The Advanced Security Settings dialog box displays information about the permissions currently assigned to the file or folder, and enables you to add or edit permissions.

3. Select the user or group account for which you want to apply special access permissions, and then click **Edit** to display the Permission Entry dialog box shown in Figure 9-13.

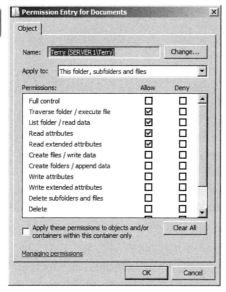

**Figure 9-13**   The Permission Entry dialog box enables you to configure advanced permissions.

4. Configure the following options as required:

- **Name:** The user account or group name appears in this dialog box, but you can select a different one in the scroll box by clicking the **Change** button.

- **Apply to:** You can adjust the level in the folder hierarchy at which the special permissions apply and are inherited. When permissions are not being inherited from a parent folder, you can choose between **This folder, subfolders and files** or any one or two of these components.

- **Permissions:** You can configure any one or more of the special access permissions by selecting their corresponding Allow or Deny check boxes.

- **Apply these permissions to objects and/or containers within this container only:** Here, you can adjust a particular folder's properties so that files and subfolders inherit their permissions from the folder you are working on. Selecting this option propagates the special access permissions to files within and folders below your current location in a folder hierarchy.

- **Clear All:** You can clear all selected permissions.

5. When finished, click **OK**.

Table 9-7 describes the special access file and folder permissions that you can configure from the Permission Entry dialog box:

**Table 9-7** NTFS Special Access Permissions

| Folder Permission | What a User Is Allowed to Do | File Permission | What a User Is Allowed to Do |
|---|---|---|---|
| Full control | Includes all special access permissions. | Full control | Includes all special access permissions. |
| Traverse folder | Navigate through folders that a user normally can't access in order to reach files or folders that the user does have permission to access. | Execute file | Run executable files. |
| List folder | View files or subfolders. | Read data | View data in a particular file. |
| Read attributes | View folder attributes. These attributes are defined by NTFS. | Read attributes | View file attributes. These attributes are defined by NTFS. |
| Read extended attributes | View extended folder attributes. Extended attributes are defined by software and may vary. | Read extended attributes | View extended file attributes. Extended attributes are defined by software and may vary. |
| Create files | Create files within a folder. | Write data | Write changes to or overwrite a file. |
| Create folders | Create subfolders. | Append data | Make changes to the end of a file by appending data. Does not allow changing, deleting, or overwriting existing data. |
| Write attributes | Change the attributes of a folder, such as read-only or hidden. Attributes are defined by NTFS. | Write attributes | Change the attributes of a file, such as read- only or hidden. Attributes are defined by NTFS. |
| Write extended attributes | Change the extended attributes of a folder. Extended attributes are defined by programs and may vary. | Write extended attributes | Change the extended attributes of a file. Extended attributes are defined by programs and may vary. |

**Table 9-7**   NTFS Special Access Permissions (*Continued*)

| Folder Permission | What a User Is Allowed to Do | File Permission | What a User Is Allowed to Do |
|---|---|---|---|
| Delete subfolders and files | Delete subfolders, even if the Delete permission has not been granted on the subfolder. | Delete subfolders and files | Delete files, even if the Delete permission has not been granted on the file. |
| Delete | Delete a folder or subfolder. | Delete | Delete a file. |
| Read permissions | Read permissions for a folder, such as Full Control, Read, and Write. | Read permissions | Read permissions for a file, such as Full Control, Read, and Write. |
| Change permissions | Change permissions for a folder, such as Full Control, Read, and Write. | Change permissions | Change permissions for a file, such as Full Control, Read, and Write. |
| Take ownership | Take ownership of a folder. | Take ownership | Take ownership of a file. |

Taking ownership is a special type of access permission. In Windows Server 2008, each NTFS folder and file has an owner. Whoever creates a file or folder automatically becomes the owner and, by default, has Full Control permissions on that file or folder. If that person is a member of the Administrators group, then the Administrators group becomes the owner. The owner possesses the ability to apply and change permissions on a folder or file that he or she owns, even if the ACL does not explicitly grant them that ability. This does make it possible for the owner of a particular file or folder to deny Administrators access to a resource. But an administrator can exercise the optional right to take ownership of any resource to gain access to it, if this becomes necessary.

In Table 9-5, which described the standard access permissions, you may have noticed that a standard permission like Modify enables a user to do more than one thing to a file or folder. A special-access permission typically enables a user to do one thing only. All special permissions are encompassed within the standard permissions.

### Configuring NTFS Permissions Inheritance

All NTFS permissions are inherited—that is, they pass down through the folder hierarchy from parent to child. Permissions assigned to a parent folder are inherited by all the files in that folder, and by the subfolders contained in the parent folder as well. Unless you specifically stop the process of files and folders inheriting permissions from their parent folder, any existing files and subfolders and any new files and subfolders created within this tree of folders will inherit their permissions from the original parent folder. To use the fancy term, permissions are propagated all the way down the tree.

Windows Server 2008 lets you modify this permissions inheritance sequence if necessary. To check whether permissions are being inherited and to remove permissions inheritance, use the following procedure:

1. From the Advanced Security Settings dialog box previously shown in Figure 9-12, clear the check box labeled **Include inheritable permissions from this object's parent**.

2. You receive the Windows Security dialog box shown in Figure 9-14, which prompts you to specify one of the following permissions inheritance options:

   - **Add:** Click **Add** to add existing inherited permissions assigned for the parent folder to the subfolder or file. This action also prevents subsequent permissions inheritance from the parent folder.

   - **Remove:** Click **Remove** to remove existing inherited permissions assigned for the parent folder to the subfolder or file. Only permissions that you explicitly assign to the file or folder will apply.

   - **Cancel:** Click **Cancel** to abort the operation and restore the Allow inheritable permissions from parent to propagate to this object check box.

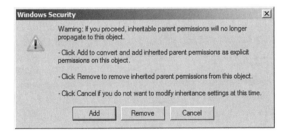

**Figure 9-14**  If you choose to prevent permissions from being inherited, you will need to decide how they are going to be applied.

3. You are returned to the Advanced Security Settings dialog box. Click **OK** or **Apply** to apply your changes.

### Taking Ownership of Files and Folders

In certain cases, you might need to grant the special Take Ownership permission to a user account. This can be valuable if a user is taking over responsibilities and resources from another individual. A user with the Full Control NTFS permission or the Take Ownership special permission can take ownership of a file or folder from the folder's Properties dialog box, as follows:

1. From the Security tab of the folder's Properties dialog box previously shown in Figure 9-10, click **Advanced**, and then click the **Owner** tab to display the dialog box shown in Figure 9-15.

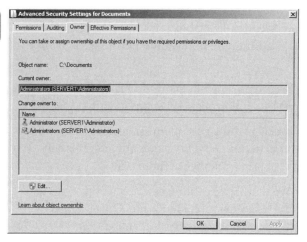

**Figure 9-15**  The Owner tab of the Advanced Security Settings dialog box enables you to take ownership of a file or folder.

2. Click **Edit** to display the Advanced Security Settings dialog box shown in Figure 9-16.

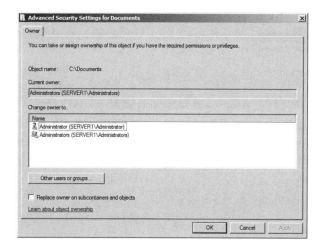

**Figure 9-16**  This dialog box enables you to select a new owner for the desired file or folder.

3. Select the username of the desired owner from the list displayed. If the desired name does not appear, click **Other users or groups** to display the Select User or Group dialog box, from which you can select another user or group.

4. Click **OK**. You are informed that if you have just taken ownership, you will need to close and reopen the object's Properties dialog box to view or change permissions.

5. Click **OK** to accept this message, and then click **OK** again to close the dialog box shown in Figure 9-15.

### Effective Permissions

Users who belong to more than one group may receive different levels of permission. Both shared folder and NTFS permissions are cumulative. Your effective permissions are a combination of all permissions configured for your user account and for the groups of which you are a member. In other words, the effective permission is the least restrictive of all permissions that you have. For example, if you have Read permissions for a given file, but you are also a member of a group that has Modify permissions for the same file, your effective permissions for that file or folder would be Modify.

However, there is one important exception to this rule. If you happen to be a member of yet another group that has been explicitly denied permissions to a resource (the permission has been selected in the Deny column), then your effective permissions will not allow you to access that resource at all. Explicit denial of permission always overrides any allowed permissions.

Putting the two types of permissions together, the rules for determining effective permissions are simple:

- At either the shared folder or NTFS permissions level by itself, if a user receives permissions by virtue of membership in one or more groups, the *least restrictive* permission is the effective permission. For example, if a user has Read permission assigned to his user account and Full Control permission by virtue of membership in a group, he receives Full Control permission on this item.

- If the user is accessing a shared folder over the network and has both shared folder and NTFS permissions applied to it, the *most restrictive* permission is the effective permission. For example, if a user has Full Control NTFS permission on a folder but accesses it across the network where she has Read shared folder permission, her effective permission is Read.

**Key Topic**

- If the user is accessing a shared folder on the computer where it exists, shared folder permissions do not apply. In the previous example, this user would receive Full Control permission when accessing the shared folder locally.

- If the user has an explicit denial of permission at either the shared folder or NTFS level, he is denied access to the object, regardless of any other permissions he might have to this object.

> **TIP** It is important to remember that specifically denying permission to a file within a folder overrides all other file and folder permissions configured for a user or for a group that may contain that user's account. There is no real top-down or bottom-up factor to consider when it comes to denying permissions. If a user is a member of a group that has been denied a permission to a file or folder, or if a user's individual account has been denied a permission to a particular resource, that is what counts. If you are denied access to a folder, it does not matter what permissions are attached to a file inside the folder because you cannot get to it.

### Viewing a User's Effective Permissions

Windows Server 2008 enables you to view a user or group's effective permissions. This is most useful in untangling a complicated web of permissions received by a user who is a member of several groups. Use the following procedure:

1. From the Security tab of the folder's Properties dialog box previously shown in Figure 9-10, click **Advanced**, and then click the **Effective Permissions** tab to display the dialog box shown in Figure 9-17.

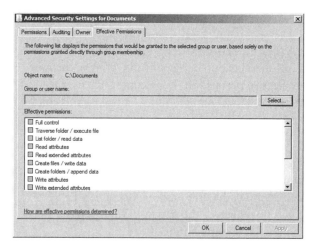

**Figure 9-17** You can view a user or group's effective permissions to a resource from the Effective Permissions tab of the Advanced Security Settings dialog box.

2. Click **Select** to display the Select User or Group dialog box.

3. Select the appropriate user or group and then click **OK**.

4. You are returned to the Effective Permissions tab, which now displays the effective permissions for the user or group.

### Copying and Moving Files and Folders

When you copy or move a file or folder that is configured with NTFS permissions, those NTFS permissions can change. The action that occurs depends on whether you are copying the file or folder or whether you are moving the file or folder.

#### Copying Files and Folders with NTFS Permissions

When you copy a file or folder that is configured with NTFS permissions, those NTFS permissions can change. If you are copying files and folders to a place where the NTFS permissions match exactly, the permissions will stay the same. There are no exceptions to this rule. The potential for change is always there, however, when you copy files and folders with NTFS permissions. To ensure that NTFS permissions are applied effectively on your computer, you will need to keep in mind how copying can change NTFS permissions. There are essentially three possible outcomes, as outlined in Table 9-8.

**Table 9-8**   Effect of Copying Files or Folders on Their NTFS Permissions

| Action | Result |
|---|---|
| Copy a file or folder within the same partition | The copy inherits the NTFS permissions of the destination folder. |
| Copy a file or folder from one NTFS partition to another NTFS partition | The copy inherits the NTFS permissions of the destination folder. |
| Copy a file or folder from an NTFS partition to a FAT or FAT32 partition | The copy of a file or folder loses its NTFS permissions completely. NTFS permissions cannot apply anywhere else but on an NTFS partition. |

To copy files from an NTFS partition you need to have at least the Read permission for the originating folder. To complete the copy operation so that the copied versions are written to disk, you need to have at least the Write permission for the destination folder.

**CAUTION** A close look at Table 9-8 alerts you to the fact that copying a file or folder from an NTFS partition to a FAT or FAT32 partition will strip the file or folder of its NTFS permissions and make it fully available to all users at the local computer.

## Moving Files and Folders with NTFS Permissions

Moving files with NTFS permissions may change those permissions. Depending on the circumstances, especially the destination of the move, the permissions may change or they may stay the same. As outlined in Table 9-9, there are also three possible outcomes.

**Table 9-9** Effect of Moving Files or Folders on Their NTFS Permissions

| Action | Result |
| --- | --- |
| Move a file or folder within the same partition | The file or folder retains its NTFS permissions, regardless of the permissions that exist for the destination folder. |
| Move a file or folder from one NTFS partition to another NTFS partition | The file or folder inherits the NTFS permissions of the destination folder. |
| Move a file or folder from an NTFS partition to a FAT or FAT32 partition | The file or folder loses its NTFS permissions completely. NTFS permissions cannot apply anywhere else but on an NTFS partition. |

To move files within an NTFS partition or between two NTFS partitions, you need to have at least the Modify permission for the originating folder. To complete the move operation so that the moved versions are written to disk, you need to have at least the Write permission for the destination folder. The Modify permission is required at the source so that source files and folders can be deleted after the files or folders are safely relocated to their new home.

**NOTE** Once you have had time to think about how copying and moving files and folders affects NTFS permissions, there is an easy way to remember how all these possible outcomes will work. One simple sentence can serve to summarize what is going on: "Moving within retains." The only sure way to retain existing NTFS permissions during a copy or move operation is to move files within a single NTFS partition. All the other options hold a real potential for altering NTFS permissions.

### Using the Mouse to Copy or Move Objects from One Location to Another

Keep in mind the following facts about dragging objects between locations:

- When you use the mouse to drag an object from one folder to another on the *same* partition, you are *moving* that object.

- If you drag the object to a folder on *another* partition, you are *copying* that object.

- If you hold down the Ctrl key while dragging, you are *copying* the object, whether it is to the same or another partition.

- You can also right-drag the object. In this case, when you release the mouse button, you receive choices of copying the object, moving it, or creating a shortcut to the object in its original location.

## Practical Guidelines on Sharing and Securing Folders

When you share folders, it is important to control how they are used. In order to control the use of shared folders, you need to be aware of how shares are applied in Windows Server 2008. Keep in mind the following facts:

- **Denying permissions overrides all other shared permissions that may be applied to a folder:** If a user is part of a group that is denied permission to access a particular resource, that user will not be able to access that resource, even if you grant her user account access to the share.

- **Multiple permissions accumulate:** You may be a member of multiple groups, each with a different level of permissions for a particular shared resource. Your effective permissions are a combination of all permissions configured for your user account and the groups of which you are a member. As a user, you may have Read permissions for a folder. You may be a member of a group with Change permissions for the same folder. Your effective permissions for that folder would be Change. If you happen to be made a member of yet another group that has been denied permissions to a folder, then your effective permissions will not allow you to access that folder at all. That is the one important exception to this rule.

- **Copying or moving a folder alters the shared permissions associated with that folder:** When you copy a shared folder, the original shared folder is still shared, but the copied folder is not. When you move a shared folder to a new location anywhere, that folder is no longer shared by anyone.

- **When you share a folder that is located on an NTFS volume, you will still need to consider the NTFS permissions that apply to that folder:** There may already be NTFS permissions in place on a folder that you are in the process of sharing. You will need to consider how your NTFS and shared folder permissions combine. (See the next item.) If there aren't any NTFS permissions on that folder, you may need to configure NTFS permissions for your shared folder or it is possible that no one will be able to access it.

■ **When shared folder and NTFS file and folder permissions combine, the most restrictive permissions apply:** When both NTFS and shared folder permissions apply to the same folder, the more restrictive permission is the effective permission for that folder. Do not lose sight of the fact, however, that shared folder permissions have no effect on users that are logged into the computer locally.

■ **When a folder resides on an NTFS volume:** You will need at least the NTFS Read permission to be able to share that folder at all.

## Data Encryption

You often hear news reports that mention thefts of laptop computers containing valuable data. Situations have also occurred in which a server has been stolen and its valuable data used for inappropriate purposes. This could happen in a branch office where a server has been placed in an accessible location such as beneath the receptionist's desk. Presumably such a computer would have been protected with a password but maybe the data was not encrypted. Windows Server 2008 includes the following two systems of data encryption, designed to protect data in any situation where it might be possible that an unauthorized individual might steal the computer or connect to it across an improper network connection:

■ First introduced with Windows 2000 and refined with each successive iteration of Windows, the Encrypting File System (EFS) can be used to encrypt files and folders on any partition that is formatted with the NTFS file system.

■ Introduced with the original version of Windows Server 2008, BitLocker Drive Encryption encrypts a computer's entire system partition.

### Encrypting File System

EFS enables users to encrypt files and folders on any partition that is formatted with the NTFS file system. The encryption attribute on a file or folder can be toggled the same as any other file attribute. When you set the encryption attribute on a folder, all its contents—whether subfolders or files—are also encrypted.

The encryption attribute, when assigned to a folder, affects files the same way that the compression attribute does when a file is moved or copied. Files that are copied into the encrypted folder become encrypted. Files that are moved into the encrypted folder retain their former encryption attribute, whether or not they were encrypted. When you move or copy a file to a file system that does not support EFS, such as FAT or FAT32, the file is automatically decrypted.

**NOTE** For more information on the technology behind EFS, refer to "How EFS Works" at http://technet.microsoft.com/en-us/library/cc962103.aspx.

**TIP** Remember that the file system must be set to NTFS if you want to use EFS, and no file can be both encrypted and compressed at the same time. On the exam, you may be presented with a scenario where a user is unable to use EFS or file compression on a FAT32 volume; the correct answer to such a problem is to convert the file system to NTFS, as described in the section, "Preparing a Disk for EFS."

### Encrypting File System Basics

EFS uses a form of public key cryptography, which utilizes a public and private key pair. The public key or digital certificate is freely available to anyone, while the private key is retained and guarded by the user to which the key pair is issued. The public key is used to encrypt data, while the private key decrypts the data that was encrypted with the corresponding public key. The key pair is created when a user first encrypts a file or folder using EFS. When another user attempts to open the file, she is unable to do so. Therefore, EFS is suitable for data that a user wants to maintain as private, but not for files that are shared.

Windows Server 2008 has the capability to encrypt files directly on any NTFS volume. This ensures that no other user can use the encrypted data. Encryption and decryption of a file or folder is performed in the object's Properties dialog box. Administrators should be aware of the rules to put into practice to manage EFS on a network:

- Only use NTFS as the file system for all workstation and server volumes.

- Keep a copy of each user's certificate and private key on a USB thumb drive or other removable media.

- Remove the user's private key from the computer except when the user is actually using it.

- When users routinely save documents only to their Documents folder, make certain their documents are encrypted by having each user encrypt his own Documents folder.

- Use two recovery agent user accounts that are reserved solely for that purpose for each Active Directory Domain Services (AD DS) organizational unit (OU) if computers participate in a domain. Assign the recovery agent certificates to these accounts.

- Archive all recovery agent user account information, recovery certificates, and private keys, even if obsolete.

- When planning a network installation, keep in mind that EFS does take up additional processing overhead; plan to incorporate additional CPU processing power in your plans.

A unique encryption key is assigned to each encrypted file. You can share an encrypted file with other users in Windows Server 2008, but you are restricted from sharing an entire encrypted folder with multiple users or sharing a single file with a security group. This is related to the way that EFS uses certificates, which are applicable individually to users; and how EFS uses encryption keys, which are applicable individually to files. Windows Server 2008 R2 continues the ability introduced with the original version of Server 2008 to store keys on smart cards. If you are using smart cards for user logon, EFS automatically locates the encryption key without issuing further prompts. EFS also provides wizards that assist users in creating and selecting smart card keys.

You can use different types of certificates with EFS: third-party–issued certificates, certificates issued by certification authorities (CA)—including those on your own network—and self-signed certificates. If you have developed a security system on your network that utilizes mutual authentication based on certificates issued by your own CA, you can extend the system to EFS to further secure encrypted files. For more information on using certificates with EFS, refer to the Windows Server 2008 Help and Support Center.

### Preparing a Disk for EFS

Unlike Windows Server 2003, the system and boot partition in Windows Server 2008 must be formatted with NTFS before you can install Windows Server 2008. However, a data partition can be formatted with the FAT or FAT32 file systems. But you must ensure that such a partition is formatted with NTFS before you can encrypt data using EFS. If it is not, you can convert the hard disk format from FAT to NTFS or format the partition as NTFS. There are two ways to go about this:

- Use the command-line `Convert.exe` utility to change an existing FAT or FAT32 partition that contains data to NTFS without losing the data.

- Use the graphical Disk Management utility to format a new partition, or an empty FAT partition, to NTFS. If the volume contains data, you will lose it. (You can also use the command-line `Format.exe` utility to format a partition as NTFS.)

The `Convert.exe` utility is simple to use and typically problem-free, although you should make certain to back up the data on the partition before you convert it as a precaution. Perform the following steps to use this utility:

1. Log on to the computer as an administrator. Know which drive letter represents the partition that you plan to convert because only the partition that contains the encrypted files needs to be formatted with NTFS. For example, if users store all their data on drive D: and want to encrypt those files, you will convert drive D: to NTFS.

2. Click **Start**, type **cmd** in the Search box, and press **Enter**.

3. The Command Prompt window opens. At the prompt, type **convert d: / fs:ntfs**.

4. The conversion process begins. If you are running the `Convert.exe` utility from the same drive letter prompt as the partition you are converting, or a file is open on the partition, you are prompted with a message that states `Convert cannot gain exclusive access to D:, so it cannot convert it now. Would you like to schedule it to be converted the next time the system restarts (Y/N)?`. Press **Y** at the message.

5. Restart the computer. The disk converts its format to NTFS. This process takes considerable time to complete, but at completion, you can click **Start > Computer**, select the disk you've converted, and note that it is formatted with the NTFS file system.

### Encrypting Files

You can use either the `cipher` command-line utility or the advanced attributes of the file or folder to encrypt a file. To use the cipher utility for encrypting a file named `myfile.txt` located in the `C:\mydir` folder, the full command to use is as follows:

```
cipher /e /s:c:\mydir\myfile.txt
```

Use the following steps to change the Advanced encryption attribute of a file:

1. Click **Start > Computer** and navigate to the file.

2. Right-click the file and select **Properties**.

3. On the General tab, click the **Advanced** button in the Attributes section to open the Advanced Attributes dialog box, as shown in Figure 9-18.

**Figure 9-18**    The Advanced Attributes dialog box enables you to either compress or encrypt a file.

4. Select the **Encrypt contents to secure data** check box (as shown in Figure 9-18) and click **OK**.

5. Click **OK** again to close the file's Properties dialog box.

6. You are given a warning dialog that lets you choose between encrypting just the file that you had selected or both the file and its parent folder. Select one of the options and click **OK**.

**NOTE**    Note that the compression and encryption attributes are mutually exclusive. In the Advanced Attributes dialog box, if you select the **Compress contents to save disk space** check box, the check mark disappears from the Encrypt contents to secure data check box. These two attributes are mutually exclusive—you can select only one.

After a file is encrypted, you can view its encryption attribute details by again right-clicking the file, selecting **Properties**, and then clicking the **Advanced** button on the General tab. In the Advanced Attributes dialog box, click the **Details** button. The User Access to (file) dialog box opens, as shown in Figure 9-19.

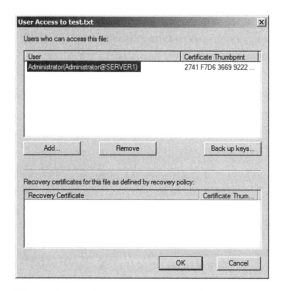

**Figure 9-19**   After a file is encrypted, you can add other users to access the file.

You can see who is able to open the encrypted file and you can add other user accounts to share the encrypted file and view the designated data recovery agent, if any. Click the **Add** button to share the encrypted file. A dialog box listing all the EFS-capable certificates for users opens. If a user has never been issued a certificate, her account does not appear in this dialog box.

**TIP**   If the desired user has not been issued an EFS certificate, she needs only to log on to the computer and encrypt a different file. This automatically creates a certificate that will be visible the next time you attempt to share an encrypted file.

After a file is encrypted, an unauthorized user attempting to open the file is given an error message that says the user does not have access privileges. If an unauthorized user tries to move or copy an encrypted file, he receives an `Access is denied` error message.

### Backing Up EFS Keys

What if a user were to encrypt a file using EFS and then the user's account were to become corrupted or be deleted for any reason? Or what if the user's private key were to become corrupted or lost? You would be unable to decrypt the file and it would be permanently inaccessible. Windows Server 2008 offers the capability for backing up EFS certificates and keys to reduce the likelihood of this occurring. In fact, when you first encrypt a file or folder, Windows Server 2008 prompts you with the dialog box shown in Figure 9-20 to back up your encryption certificates and keys.

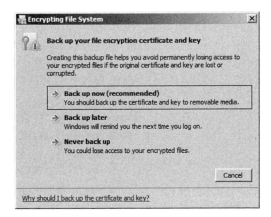

**Figure 9-20**   You are prompted to back up the encryption certificates and keys.

Use the following procedure to back up EFS keys:

1. From the dialog box shown in Figure 9-20, select the **Back up now (recommended)** option. If you don't receive this dialog box, you can access the User Access dialog box previously shown in Figure 9-19 and click the **Back up keys** command button.

2. The Certificate Export Wizard starts. Click **Next**.

3. On the Export File Format page shown in Figure 9-21, the Personal Information Exchange–PKCS #12 (.PFX) format is selected by default. If desired, select the **Include all certificates in the certification path if possible** and **Export all extended properties** options, and then click **Next**.

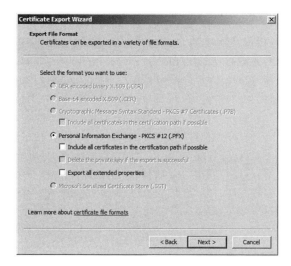

**Figure 9-21**    The Export File Format page of the Certificate Export Wizard enables you to choose a certificate file format.

4. On the Password page, type and confirm a password. This is mandatory, and you should choose a hard-to-guess password that follows the usual complexity guidelines. Then, click **Next**.

5. On the File to Export page, type the name of the file to be exported and click **Next**. By default, this file is created in the user's Documents library with the .pfx extension.

6. Review the information on the completion page, and then click **Finish**.

7. You are informed the export was successful. Click **OK**.

8. You should move this file to a location separate from the computer, such as a floppy disk or USB key that you store securely (such as in a locked cabinet).

## Decrypting Files

The process of decryption is the opposite of encryption. You can either use the cipher command or change the Advanced attribute for encryption on the file.

To use the cipher command to decrypt the file, click **Start**, type **cmd** in the Search box, and then press **Enter**. At the command prompt, type **cipher /d /s:c:\ myfolder\myfile.txt** and press **Enter**. The file will be decrypted.

To use the Advanced Attributes method, open Computer and navigate to the file. Right-click the file and select **Properties**. On the General tab, click the **Advanced** button. In the ensuing Advanced Attributes dialog box, clear the **Encrypt the Contents to Secure Data** check box. Click **OK** and then click **OK** again.

If you are not the person who originally encrypted the file, or if you are not the designated recovery agent, you will receive an error for applying attributes that says the access is denied.

### EFS Recovery Agents

What if the user's keys, even though backed up, were to become lost or corrupted? Without some type of recovery capability, such a file would become permanently inaccessible. EFS in Windows Server 2008 uses the concept of *recovery agents* as a means to recover encrypted data in such a situation.

Designated recovery agents are user accounts authorized to decrypt encrypted files. When a user account is designated as a recovery agent, you essentially are granting it a copy of the key pair. If you lose the key pair, or if they become damaged, and if there is no designated recovery agent, there is no way to decrypt the file and the data is permanently lost. By designating a recovery agent before a user first uses EFS, you can ensure that encrypted files and folders remain accessible by someone responsible for their maintenance.

Windows Server 2008 can include two levels of EFS recovery agents:

- **Local computer:** By default, the local administrator account created when you first install Windows Server 2008 is the recovery agent.

- **Domain:** When you create an AD DS domain, the first domain administrator account is the designated recovery agent. If desired, you can use Group Policy to designate additional recovery agents and you can delegate the responsibility of EFS recovery to other users.

You can use Group Policy to designate additional recovery agents. A user must have an appropriate certificate before he can be designated as a recovery agent. Use the following procedure:

1. Open the Group Policy Management Editor focused on an appropriate Group Policy object (GPO). If operating in a non-domain environment, open the Local Group Policy Editor.

2. Navigate to the **Computer Configuration\Policies\Windows Settings\ Security Settings\Public Key Policies\Encrypting File System** node.

3. Right-click this node and choose **Add Data Recovery Agent**.

4. The Add Recovery Agent Wizard starts with a Welcome page. Click **Next**.

**5.** On the Select Recovery Agents page shown in Figure 9-22, select a user from the Recovery agents list and click **Next**. (If necessary, click **Browse Folders** to locate a certificate for the desired user.)

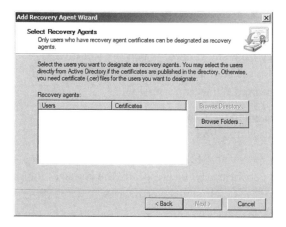

**Figure 9-22**   The Add Recovery Agent Wizard enables you to designate additional users as EFS recovery agents.

**6.** You are informed that you have successfully completed the wizard. Review the information about the designated recovery agents, and then click **Finish**.

## EFS Group Policies

Besides the capability of adding data recovery agents, Group Policy also enables you to control the use of EFS in your network. Right-click the **Computer Configuration\Policies\Windows Settings\Security Settings\Public Key Policies\ Encrypting File System** node and choose **Properties** to open the Encrypting File System Properties dialog box shown in Figure 9-23. This dialog box enables you to configure the following options:

- **File encryption using Encrypting File System (EFS):** To allow the use of EFS and define policies, select **Allow**; to prevent use of EFS on computers affected by this GPO, select **Don't Allow**.

- **Elliptic Curve Cryptography:** Choose to allow, require, or not allow the use of Elliptic Curve Cryptography (ECC) algorithms with EFS. Added in Windows Server 2008 R2 and Windows 7, ECC enables EFS to be compliant with Suite B encryption requirements as defined by the U.S. National Security Agency to meet the requirements of government agencies for protecting classified data.

- **Encrypt the contents of the user's Documents folder:** Automatically encrypts each user's Documents folder. This option is especially useful for protecting documents on portable computers.

- **Require a smart card for EFS:** Users are required to insert a smart card to access files encrypted using EFS.

- **Create caching-capable user key from smart card:** When the **Require a smart card for EFS** option is also selected, users must insert the smart card only when first accessing an encrypted file within a session.

- **Display key backup notifications when user key is created or changed:** When enabled, users are prompted to back up EFS keys when created or changed.

- **Certificates tab:** Enables you to specify an EFS template for automatic certificate requests. For self-signed certificates, you can specify the key sizes for Rivest-Shamir-Adleman (RSA) or ECC self-signed certificates.

- **Cache tab:** Enables you to select the occasions when the encrypted key cache is cleared. You can select a timeout interval (480 minutes by default) or specify that the cache is cleared when the user locks the workstation. Note that smart cards must be removed to ensure that the cache is cleared.

**Figure 9-23**  The Encrypting File Properties dialog box enables you to configure a series of properties related to the use of EFS.

**NOTE**   For more information on using EFS, backing up keys, and designating recovery agents, refer to "Protecting Sensitive Information from Theft on Windows XP Professional in a Workgroup" at http://technet.microsoft.com/en-us/library/cc732774.aspx. Note that, although this article refers to Windows XP, information provided here is generally relevant to Windows Vista, Windows 7, and both versions of Windows Server 2008.

### BitLocker Drive Encryption

First introduced with the original version of Windows Server 2008, BitLocker is a hardware-enabled data encryption feature that serves to protect data on a computer that is exposed to unauthorized physical access. Available on all editions of Windows Server 2008, BitLocker encrypts the entire Windows volume, thereby preventing unauthorized users from circumventing file and system permissions in Windows or attempting to access information on the protected partition from another computer or operating system. BitLocker even protects the data should an unauthorized user physically remove the hard drive from the computer and use other means to attempt access to the data.

BitLocker uses the Trusted Platform Module (TPM) version 1.2 to provide secure protection of encryption keys and checking of key components when Windows is booting. A TPM is a microchip that is built into a computer that is used to store cryptographic information such as encryption keys. Information stored on the TPM is more secure from external software attacks and physical theft. You can store keys and passwords on a USB flash drive that the user must insert to boot his computer. You can also employ an option that requires the user to supply a PIN code, thereby requiring multifactor authentication before the data becomes available for use. If an unauthorized individual has tampered with or modified system files or data in any way, the computer will not boot up.

On a computer that is equipped with a compatible TPM, BitLocker uses this TPM to lock the encryption keys that protect the contents of the protected drive; this includes the operating system and Registry files when you have used BitLocker to protect the system drive. When starting up the computer, TPM must verify the state of the computer before the keys are accessed. Consequently, an attacker cannot access the data by mounting the hard drive in a different computer.

At startup, TPM compares a hash of the operating system configuration with an earlier snapshot, thereby verifying the integrity of the startup process and releasing the keys. If BitLocker detects any security problem (such as a disk error, change to the BIOS, or changes to startup files), it locks the drive and enters Recovery mode.

You can store encryption keys and restoration password on a USB flash drive or a separate file for additional data security and recovery capability. Should a user need to recover data using BitLocker's recovery mode, she merely needs to enter a recovery password to access data and the Windows operating system.

**NOTE**   For more information on how BitLocker works to protect your drives, refer to "BitLocker Drive Encryption Overview" at http://technet.microsoft.com/en-us/library/cc732774.aspx.

Your computer does not need to be equipped with the TPM in order to use BitLocker. If your computer is equipped with TPM, you can use BitLocker in any of the following modes:

- **TPM only:** TPM alone validates the boot files, the operating system files, and encrypted drive volumes during system startup. This mode provides a normal startup and logon experience to the user. However, if the TPM is missing or the integrity of the system has changed, BitLocker enters recovery mode, in which you will be required to provide a recovery key to access the computer.

- **TPM and PIN:** Uses both TPM and a user-supplied PIN for validation. You must enter this PIN correctly or BitLocker enters recovery mode.

- **TPM and startup key:** Uses both TPM and a startup key for validation. The user must provide a USB flash drive containing the startup key. If the user does not have this USB flash drive, BitLocker enters recovery mode.

- **TPM and smart card certificate:** Uses both TPM and a smart card certificate for validation. The user must provide a smart card containing a valid certificate to log on. If the smart card is not available or the certificate is not valid, BitLocker enters recovery mode.

If the computer does not have a TPM, BitLocker uses either a USB flash drive or smart card containing a startup key. In this case, BitLocker provides encryption, but not the added security of locking keys with the TPM.

**NOTE**   Many newer computers are equipped with TPM, but TPM is not always activated. You might need to enter your BIOS setup system to enable TPM. The location of this setting depends on the BIOS in use, but is typically in the Advanced section.

### Preparing Your Computer to Use BitLocker

You can use a computer that does not have a TPM module if you have a USB flash drive to store the encryption keys and password. On such a computer, you need to enable BitLocker without a TPM from Group Policy, as the following procedure describes:

1. Open the Group Policy Management Editor focused on an appropriate GPO to enable TPM in an AD DS environment, or the Local Group Policy Editor in a non-domain environment.

2. Navigate to **Computer Configuration\Policies\Administrative Templates\Windows Components\BitLocker Drive Encryption\Operating System Drives**.

3. Double-click **Require additional authentication at startup**, enable this policy, select the **Allow BitLocker without a compatible TPM** option, and then click **OK**.

4. Close the Group Policy Management Editor or the Local Group Policy Editor.

5. Click **Start**, type `Gpupdate /force` in the Search field, and then press **Enter**. This forces Group Policy to apply immediately.

After you complete this procedure, you are ready to enable BitLocker, which is described next.

### Enabling BitLocker

In Windows Server 2008, BitLocker is present as a server feature. You must first access the Add Features Wizard from Server Manager and then select **BitLocker Drive Encryption** (as shown in Figure 9-24) to install BitLocker. You may be required to restart your computer to complete the installation of BitLocker.

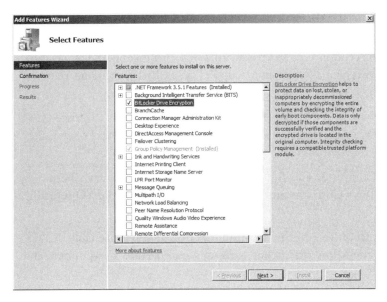

**Figure 9-24**   BitLocker must be installed as a server feature in Windows Server 2008.

If your computer is equipped with a TPM, you can enable BitLocker directly without first accessing Group Policy. Use the following procedure to enable BitLocker on your operating system drive:

1. Click **Start > Control Panel > System and Security > BitLocker Drive Encryption**. You receive the Help protect your files and folders by encrypting your drives dialog box, as shown in Figure 9-25. You can also access this utility by typing `bitlocker` into the Start menu search field and selecting **BitLocker Drive Encryption** from the Programs list.

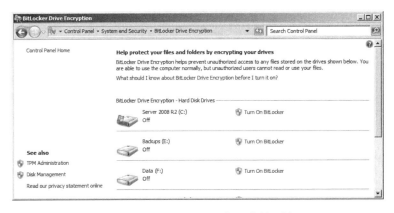

**Figure 9-25**   BitLocker offers to protect all available drives.

**NOTE**   If this dialog box is not available or the BitLocker Drive Encryption link does not appear in the Programs list, it means that the computer does not have a compatible TPM module. You need to perform the procedure given in the previous subsection before you can enable BitLocker.

2. Opposite the drive you want to encrypt, click the **Turn On BitLocker** link. You can also right-click the desired drive in an Explorer window and choose **Turn On BitLocker**.

3. You are asked if you want to start BitLocker setup. Click **Yes** to proceed.

4. You receive a BitLocker Drive Encryption window, and after a few seconds, this window displays the Set BitLocker startup preferences page shown in Figure 9-26. Select from the following options:

   ■ **Use BitLocker without additional keys:** Uses the TPM Only mode for validation, enabling the computer to start up without user interaction. If any hardware component has changed, BitLocker assumes the computer has been tampered with, and will lock up.

   ■ **Require a PIN at every startup:** Enables the TPM and PIN option, requiring the user to enter a PIN at startup.

   ■ **Require a Startup key at every startup:** Creates a startup key and writes it onto a USB flash drive. This is the only option available if your computer is not equipped with a TPM.

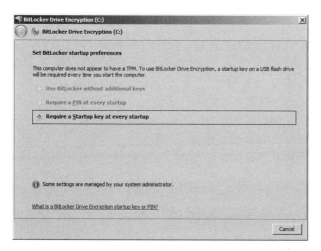

**Figure 9-26**   The BitLocker Drive Encryption applet in Control Panel enables you to encrypt your drive.

5. If you select the **Require a Startup key at every startup** option, insert the USB drive when prompted, and then click **Save** on the Save your Startup Key page. If you select the **Require a PIN at every startup** option, enter and confirm the PIN, and then click **Save**.

6. The How do you want to store your recovery key? page provides the three options shown in Figure 9-27. Use one or more of these options to save the recovery password. If you print it, ensure that you save the printed document in a secure location. If you save it to a USB flash drive, you will see the Save a Recovery Key to a USB Drive dialog box, as shown in Figure 9-28. Click **Save**, and then click **Next**.

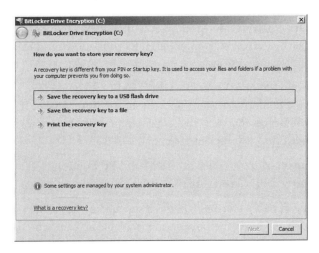

**Figure 9-27**  You are given three options for storing your recovery key.

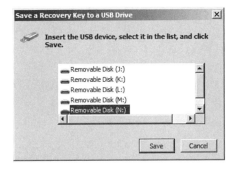

**Figure 9-28**  Select the appropriate USB drive for saving your password.

7. You receive the Are you ready to encrypt this drive? dialog box shown in Figure 9-29. Ensure that the check box labeled **Run BitLocker system check** is selected and then click **Continue** to proceed.

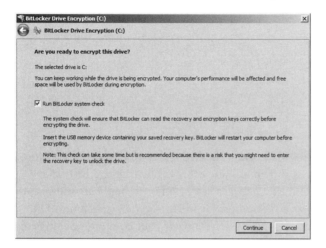

**Figure 9-29**   Select Continue to encrypt your partition.

8. You need to restart your computer to proceed. Click **Restart now**.

9. As the computer restarts, you receive a message informing you that the encryption keys have been saved and that you can remove the USB device. Remove the device, let the computer finish starting up, and log back on as an administrator.

10. Encryption takes place and Windows Server 2008 displays an icon in the notification area. This process can take an hour or longer, but you can use your computer while it is occurring. You can track the progress of encryption by hovering your mouse pointer over this icon. You are informed when encryption is complete. Click **Close**.

After you complete this procedure, you must have the USB drive to start your computer. Alternately, you can use the recovery mode and type the recovery password that was automatically created while enabling BitLocker. BitLocker provides the BitLocker Drive Encryption Recovery Console to enable you to insert the USB drive that contains the recovery password. Or press **Enter**, type the recovery password, and press **Enter** again.

**WARNING**   Ensure that you do not lose the recovery password. If you lose the recovery password, your Windows installation and all data stored on its partition will be permanently lost. You will need to repartition your hard drive and reinstall Windows. Consequently, you should create at least two copies of the password as described in the previous procedure and store these in a secure location. Do not leave the USB flash drive in any location accessible to others; attach it to your key chain or store it elsewhere on your person.

### Managing BitLocker

After you encrypt your drive using BitLocker, the BitLocker applet shows additional options for the protected drive, as shown in Figure 9-30. The Manage BitLocker option enables you to save or print the recovery key again or to duplicate the startup key, thereby enabling you to recover these items while the system is running. You can also back this information up into Active Directory if your computer belongs to an AD DS domain.

**Figure 9-30**   The BitLocker applet displays a distinctive icon for the protected drive and provides several options for its management.

The Suspend Protection option enables you to temporarily disable BitLocker. Select this option and then click **Yes**. After doing so, this option changes to Resume Protection; click it to re-enable BitLocker.

The Turn Off BitLocker option enables you to remove BitLocker protection. To do so, select **Turn Off BitLocker**. On the BitLocker Drive Encryption dialog box that appears, select **Decrypt Drive**. This procedure decrypts your volume and discards all encryption keys; it begins immediately without further prompts. You will be able to monitor the decryption action from an icon in the notification area.

### Configuring BitLocker Group Policies

Besides the policy already mentioned to enable BitLocker on a computer that is not equipped with a TPM, Group Policy has a series of settings that help you to manage BitLocker. You can access these polices from the **Computer Configuration\ Policies\Administrative Templates\Windows Components\BitLocker Drive Encryption** node. This node has three subnodes: Fixed Data Drives, Operating System Drives, and Removable Data Drives, as well as several policies that affect all types of drives. Microsoft provides recommendations for many of these settings at "Best Practices for BitLocker in Windows 7" at http://technet.microsoft.com/en-us/ library/dd875532(WS.10).aspx. Note that these recommendations apply to Windows Server 2008 R2 as well as Windows 7.

### Operating System Drives

As shown in Figure 9-31, you can configure the following policies that govern BitLocker as used on operating system drives:

- **Require additional authentication at startup:** As mentioned earlier, this setting enables you to use BitLocker on a computer without a TPM. By enabling this policy, you can also specify whether BitLocker requires additional authentication including a startup key and/or PIN.

- **Require additional authentication at startup (Windows Server 2008 and Windows Vista):** Enables similar settings for Windows Vista and the original version of Windows Server 2008 computers, except that you cannot use both a startup key and PIN.

- **Allow enhanced PINs for startup:** Enables the use of a PIN that contains additional characters, including uppercase and lowercase letters, symbols, numerals, and spaces.

- **Configure minimum PIN length for startup:** Specifies a minimum length for the startup PIN. You can choose a minimum length of anywhere from 4 to 20 digits.

- **Choose how BitLocker-protected operating system drives can be recovered:** Enables the use of a data recovery agent. We discuss this policy later in this section.

- **Configure TPM platform validation profile:** Enables you to specify how the TPM security hardware secures the BitLocker encryption key. The validation profile includes a set of Platform Configuration Register indices, each of which is associated with components that run at startup. You can select from a series of indices provided in the policy's options.

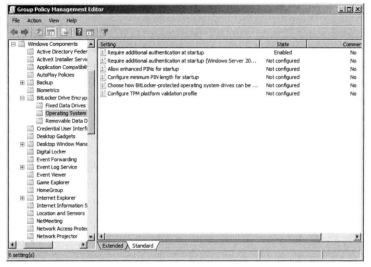

**Figure 9-31**   Group Policy provides these settings for BitLocker used on operating system drives.

## Fixed Data Drive Policies

As shown in Figure 9-32, you can configure the following policies that govern Bit-Locker used on fixed data drives (in other words, internal hard drive partitions containing data but not operating system files):

- **Configure use of smart cards on fixed data drives:** Enables you to specify whether smart cards can be used to authenticate user access to drives protected by BitLocker. You can optionally require the use of smart cards.

- **Deny write access to fixed drives not protected by BitLocker:** Enables you to require BitLocker protection on writable drives. If enabled, any drives not protected by BitLocker are read-only.

- **Allow access to BitLocker-protected fixed data drives from earlier versions of Windows:** Specifies whether or not drives formatted with the FAT or FAT32 file system can be unlocked and viewed on computers running earlier Windows versions (back to Windows XP SP2).

- **Configure use of passwords for fixed data drives:** Enables you to specify whether a password is required for unlocking BitLocker-protected fixed data drives. You can optionally specify that a password is required and you can choose to allow or require password complexity and specify the minimum password length.

- **Choose how BitLocker-protected fixed drives can be recovered:** Similar to the corresponding operating system drives policy.

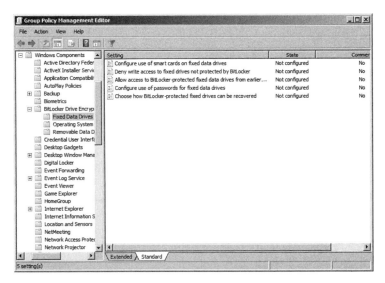

**Figure 9-32**    Group Policy provides these settings for BitLocker used on fixed data drives.

More information on all these policies is available from the Help field in each policy's Properties dialog box. These policies are also available for removable drives (BitLocker To Go) in the Removable Data Drives subnode of Group Policy.

### Using Data Recovery Agents

A data recovery agent (DRA) is a user account that is configured for recovering data encrypted with BitLocker in a manner analogous to the EFS recovery agent described earlier in this chapter. The DRA uses his smart card certificates and public keys to accomplish this action.

To specify a DRA for a BitLocker-protected drive, you must first designate the recovery agent by opening the Local Group Policy Editor and navigating to the **Computer Configuration\Policies\ Windows Settings\Security Settings\ Public Key Policies\BitLocker Drive Encryption** node. Right-click this node and choose **Add Data Recovery Agent**. This starts a wizard that is similar to that used for creating EFS data recovery agents. You can browse for the required certificates or select them from AD DS in a domain environment.

After you specify your data recovery agent, you need to access the **Computer Configuration\Policies\Administrative Templates\Windows Components\ BitLocker Drive Encryption** node of Group Policy and enable the policy labeled

**Provide the unique identifiers for your organizatio**n (see Figure 9-33). In the text boxes provided, specify a unique identifier that will be associated with drives that are enabled with BitLocker. This identifier uniquely associates the drives with your company or department and is required for BitLocker to manage and update data recovery agents. After doing so, this identifier will be automatically associated with any drives on which you enable BitLocker.

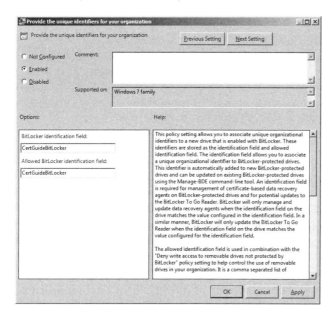

**Figure 9-33**   You need to provide a unique identifier to use a BitLocker DRA.

You can add this identifier to drives previously protected with BitLocker by opening an administrative command prompt and typing the following command:

```
manage-bde -SetIdentifier drive_letter
```

Where *drive_letter* is the drive letter for the BitLocker-protected drive. This utility sets the identifier to the value you specified in Group Policy and displays a message informing you that this identifier has been set.

After you specify a DRA and the unique identifiers, you can configure policies in each subnode of the **Computer Configuration\Policies\Administrative Templates\Windows Components\BitLocker Drive Encryption** node of Group Policy that determine how BitLocker-protected drives can be recovered. Each of the three subnodes contains a similar policy setting that is shown for operating system drives in Figure 9-34. Enable each of these policies as required and select the **Allow data recovery agent** check box. Then, configure the following options as required:

- **48-digit recovery password:** This drop-down list provides choices to allow, require, or do not allow a 48-digit recovery password. Use of a 48-digit recovery password improves DRA security.

- **256-bit recovery key:** This drop-down list provides choices to allow, require, or do not allow a 256-bit recovery key. Use of a 256-bit recovery key improves DRA security.

- **Omit recovery options from the BitLocker setup wizard:** Blocks the appearance of the recovery options previously shown in Figure 9-25; when enabled, these recovery options are determined by policy settings.

- **Save BitLocker recovery information to AD DS for operating system drives:** Enables you to choose the BitLocker recovery information that will be stored in AD DS.

- **Configure storage of BitLocker recovery information to AD DS:** Determines how much recovery information is stored in AD DS when you have selected the preceding option. You can choose to store recovery passwords and key packages or to store recovery passwords only.

- **Do not enable BitLocker until recovery information is stored to AD DS for operating system drives:** When enabled, prevents users from enabling BitLocker unless the computer is attached to the domain and BitLocker recovery information can be backed up to AD DS.

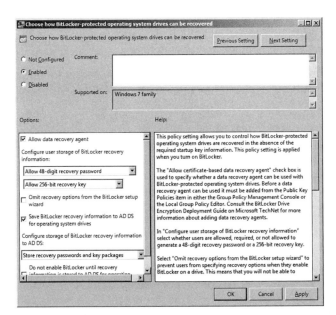

**Figure 9-34**  Group Policy provides these data recovery options for operating system drives.

Similar options are provided for fixed and removable data drives; the wording of the last policy setting changes to reflect the type of drive being configured.

**NOTE**   BitLocker provides several additional DRA management options, including verification of the identification field and listing of configured DRAs. For more information, refer to "Using Data Recovery Agents with BitLocker" at http://technet. microsoft.com/en-us/library/dd875560(WS.10).aspx. For additional information on BitLocker as a whole, refer to "BitLocker Drive Encryption: Frequently Asked Questions" at http://technet.microsoft.com/en-us/library/ee449438(WS.10).aspx. For a comprehensive practice-type scenario outlining the use of BitLocker that is valid for either Windows 7 or Windows Server 2008 R2, refer to "BitLocker Encryption Step-by-Step Guide for Windows 7" at http://technet.microsoft.com/en-us/library/ dd835565(WS.10).aspx.

## Additional File Server Management Resources

Windows Server 2008 provides the following additional file server management resources, which are discussed in this section:

- **Offline Files:** Provides the capability for users to access shared files and folders when not connected to the server at which they are located.

- **BranchCache:** Enables users at branch office to cache shared files and folders from a remote server to a local computer for faster access.

- **Share and Storage Management Console:** Provides a central location for administering shared files and folders, including many tasks discussed earlier in this chapter.

### Using Offline Files

The Offline Files feature in Windows Server 2008 and Windows 7 originated with Windows 2000 and XP. It replaces the My Briefcase feature included with Windows 9x/NT and works only on Microsoft-based networks. The Offline Files feature enables a user to access and work with files and folders stored on a network share when the user is disconnected from that share. For example, such a situation could occur when the user is working from a laptop on the road or at home. This feature ensures that users are always working with the most recent version of their files.

When you enable Offline Files, this feature makes anything you have cached from the network available to you. It also preserves the normal view of network drives, and so on, as well as shared folder and NTFS permissions. When you reconnect to the network, the feature automatically synchronizes any changes with the versions on the network. Also, changes made to your files while online are saved to both the network share and your local cache.

Offline files are stored on the local computer in a special area of the hard drive called a *cache*. More specifically, this is located at `%systemroot%\CSC`, where `CSC` stands for client-side caching. By default, this cache takes up 10 percent of the disk volume space.

You need to configure both the server and the client computer to use the Offline Files feature. Keep in mind that, in this sense, the "server" refers to any computer that holds a shared folder available to users of other computers. Besides a server running Windows 2000 Server, Windows Server 2003, or Windows Server 2008/R2, this may be a computer running Windows 2000 or XP Professional, Vista Business, Enterprise, or Ultimate, Windows 7 Professional, Enterprise, or Ultimate.

**NOTE**   For more information on new features of Offline Files in Windows 7 and Windows Server 2008 R2, refer to "What's New in Offline Files" at http://technet. microsoft.com/en-us/library/ff183315(WS.10).aspx.

### Configuring Servers for Offline Files

To enable the caching of files stored on a shared folder, you need to configure the shared folder on the server and specify the type of caching available. The following procedure shows you how to perform these tasks on a Windows Server 2008 R2 computer:

1. Right-click the shared folder and choose **Properties**.

2. On the Sharing tab of the folder's Properties dialog box, click **Advanced Sharing**.

3. On the Advanced Sharing dialog box, click **Caching** to open the Offline Settings dialog box shown in Figure 9-35.

**Figure 9-35**   The Offline Settings dialog box provides several options for enabling offline caching in Windows Server 2008 R2.

4. Select from the following options and then click **OK**:

- **Only the files and programs that users specify are available offline:**
  Requires that a user connecting to the share specifically indicate the files to be made available for caching. This is the default setting.

- **Enable BranchCache:** Enables computers in a branch office to cache downloaded files and then secure serve these files to other branch office client computers. BranchCache is discussed in the next section.

- **No files or programs from the shared folder are available offline:** Effectively disables the Offline Files feature.

- **All files and programs that users open from the shared folder are automatically available offline:** Makes every file in the share available for caching by a remote user. When a user opens a file from the share, the file is downloaded to the client's cache and replaces any older versions of the file.

- **Optimize for performance:** Enables expanded caching of shared programs so that users can run them locally, thereby improving performance. Note that this option does not provide any enhancement for client computers running Windows Vista or newer.

5. Click **OK** to close the Advanced Sharing dialog box, and then click **Close** to close the Properties dialog box for the shared folder.

**NOTE**   For more information on the available server options for Offline Files, refer to "Configure Offline Availability for a Shared Folder" at http://technet.microsoft.com/en-us/library/cc732663.aspx.

## Configuring Client Computers

By default, the Offline Files feature is enabled on the client computer. A client computer running Windows Vista or Windows 7 provides the Offline Files dialog box, which provides options for managing offline files at the client computer, including the use of the Sync Center for synchronizing offline file content.

To cache all available files from a network share to which you have connected at a computer running Windows Vista, Windows 7, or Windows Server 2008, right-click the shared folder icon and choose **Always available offline**. This automatically caches all available files without your having to open them first. You can also synchronize your cached files manually when you are connected to the network share. To do so, right-click the shared folder icon and choose **Sync > Sync Selected Offline Files**.

**NOTE**   If you want to use a computer running Windows Server 2008 R2 as a client computer to receive offline files, you need to install and enable the Desktop Experience server feature. From Server Manager, start the Add Features Wizard, select this feature from the list provided, and then complete the remaining steps of the wizard. Then, proceed as in the previous paragraph to cache the required files.

**NOTE**   For more information on working with offline files at the client computer, refer to "Configuring New Offline Files Features for Windows 7 Computers Step-by-Step Guide" at http://technet.microsoft.com/en-us/library/ff633429(WS.10).aspx.

## Configuring Offline File Policies

Group Policy makes available a series of policy settings. In Local Group Policy Editor or Group Policy Management Editor, navigate to **Computer Configuration\Policies\Administrative Templates\Network\Offline Files** to display the policy settings shown in Figure 9-36. Note that some of the policy settings available here are applicable to computers running older Windows versions only and are provided for backwards compatibility purposes. Table 9-10 describes the more important policy settings relevant to Windows Server 2008 R2 and Windows 7 computers that you should be aware of.

**Table 9-10**   Offline File Policies

| Policy | Description |
|---|---|
| Administratively assigned offline files | Specifies network files and folders that are always available offline. Type the Universal Naming Convention (UNC) path to the required files. |
| Configure Background Sync | Enables you to control synchronization of files across slow links. You can configure sync interval and variance parameters, as well as blackout periods when sync should not occur. |
| Limit disk space used by offline files | When enabled, limits the amount of disk space in MB used to store offline files. |
| Allow or Disallow use of the Offline Files feature | Determines whether users can enable Offline Files. When enabled, Offline Files is enabled and users cannot disable it; when disabled, Offline Files is disabled and users cannot enable it. |
| Encrypt the Offline Files cache | When enabled, all files in the Offline Files cache are encrypted. |
| Exclude files from being cached | Enables you to exclude file types according to extension from being cached. Specify the extensions to be excluded, separated by semicolons— for example, *.jpg; *.mp3. |
| Enable Transparent Caching | Controls caching of offline files across slow links. You can specify a network latency value above which network files are temporarily cached. More about this policy in the next section. |
| Configure slow-link mode | Controls background synchronization across slow links and determines how network file requests are handled across slow links. |
| Configure slow-link speed | Specifies the threshold link speed value below which Offline Files considers a network connection to be slow. Specify the value in bits per second divided by 100; for example, specify 1280 for a threshold of 128,000 bps. |

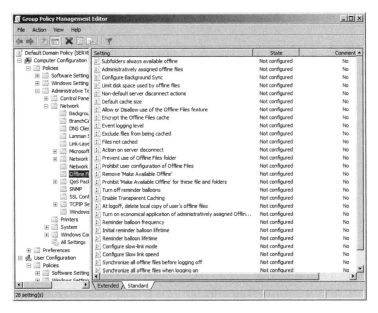

**Figure 9-36**  You can configure a large number of policy settings related to the use of Offline Files.

## Configuring Transparent Caching of Offline Files

New to Windows Server 2008 R2 and Windows 7 is the concept of *transparent file caching*, which enables client computers to temporarily cache files obtained across a slow WAN link more aggressively, thereby reducing the number of times the client might have to retrieve the file across the slow link. Use of transparent caching also serves to reduce bandwidth consumption across the WAN link. Prior to Windows Server 2008 R2 and Windows 7, client computers always retrieved such a file across the slow link.

The first time a user accesses a file across the WAN, Windows retrieves it from the remote computer; this file is then cached to the local computer. Subsequently, the local computer checks with the remote server to ensure that the file has not changed and then accesses it from the local cache if its copy is up-to-date. Note that this type of file caching is temporary; clients cannot access these files when they go offline.

You can configure the Enable Transparent Caching policy so that clients can perform transparent caching. Enable this policy (as shown in Figure 9-37) and set the network latency value, which is the number of milliseconds beyond which the client will temporarily cache files obtained across the WAN.

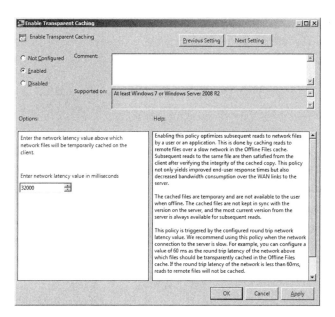

**Figure 9-37**   Enable the Enable Transparent Caching policy setting so that clients can temporarily cache files obtained across a slow WAN link.

### Configuring BranchCache

BranchCache is a new feature of Windows Server 2008 R2 that enables users at client computers running Windows 7 Enterprise and Ultimate to rapidly access data from remotely located file and web servers. For example, users at a small branch office can cache copies of frequently accessed files from head office servers on a local computer. In doing so, users do not need to connect across the low-bandwidth wide area network (WAN) each time they need this content. Not only is access more rapid, bandwidth utilization across the WAN is optimized. When a second client requests the same data, the remote server sends metadata that includes a set of segment and block hashes computed with the use of the Secure Hash Algorithm (SHA)-256 hashing algorithm. The client can compare this hash with that contained in the locally cached version's metadata to check for changes. The client downloads a new version only if there are changes; otherwise, the user receives the content from the local cache. Servers hosting this content in the head office must be running Windows Server 2008 R2.

BranchCache uses the Background Intelligent Transfer Service (BITS) to perform its actions. It can work with web content transferred using Hypertext Transfer Protocol (HTTP), and with data files and documents transferred using Server Message Block (SMB).

BranchCache works in either Distributed Cache mode or Hosted Cache mode:

- **Distributed Cache:** Each user's Windows 7 desktop computer hosts files cached from the remote server. This mode does not require a branch office server, thereby reducing hardware requirements in a small branch office that does not have the need for a server. This mode works on a branch office network containing a single subnet only with no more than 50 client computers. The client computer hosting the cached files must be available for other clients requesting the cached information; otherwise the second client must download the files across the WAN.

- **Hosted Cache:** A server running Windows Server 2008 R2 located in the branch office hosts files cached from the remote server. You need to install the Hosted Cache server feature on this server using Server Manager. When users request these files, they are accessed from this server. Note that you do not require a dedicated server; the server running Hosted Cache can run other applications, such as a file and print server or web server. This enables all clients in the branch office to access a single cache location even if there is more than one subnet; furthermore, it reduces the need for multiple downloads of hosted content because of client computers being offline or in sleep mode.

**NOTE**   For more information on BranchCache, refer to "BranchCache Technical Overview" at www.microsoft.com/downloads/details.aspx?displaylang=en&Family ID=ee07308f-7c53-4c76-9ed9-670bc25a4c9d and "BranchCache Early Adopter's Guide" at http://technet.microsoft.com/en-us/library/dd637762(WS.10).aspx.

You can use either Group Policy or the `netsh` command-line utility to configure BranchCache. With either tool, you need to enable BranchCache, select the required mode, and then configure the client firewall to pass the protocols used by BranchCache.

### Using the `netsh` Command to Configure BranchCache

BranchCache is included as a role service in the Windows Server 2008 R2 File Services role. To enable BranchCache, you need to first install this role service by accessing the File Services role from the Roles node of Server Manager and then clicking **Add role services**. Then, select BranchCache for network files from the Select Role Services page of the Add Role Services Wizard. (This page is similar to the Select Role Services page of the Add Roles Wizard previously shown in Figure 9-1.) Finally, complete the remaining steps of this wizard.

After you install the BranchCache role service, it is simple to enable BranchCache in either mode and then enable the firewall from an administrative command prompt, as follows:

1. Click **Start** and type `cmd` in the Search field. From the program list, right-click `cmd.exe`, choose **Run as Administrator**, and then click **Yes** to accept the UAC prompt that appears.

2. To enable BranchCache in the required mode, type `netsh branchcache set` `options`.

In this command, `options` can have the following values:

- `service mode=DISTRIBUTED:` Enables BranchCache distributed mode.

- `service mode=HOSTEDSERVER:` Enables BranchCache hosted mode and configures a Hosted Cache Server.

- `service mode=HOSTEDCLIENT LOCATION=<fqdn>:` Enables BranchCache hosted mode and configures a Hosted Cache client; `<fqdn>` is the fully qualified domain name (FQDN) of the server hosting the cache.

- `service mode=local:` Enables the client to use local branch caching, where the client stores files retrieved across the WAN in a local cache but does not share its contents with any other branch office client computers. Multiple users on a single computer might find this mode beneficial. You can specify this alternative BranchCache mode only by using the `netsh` command.

- `cachesize size={default | <number>} percent={true | false}:` Specifies the size (`<number>`) of the local cache, either as a percentage of hard disk space (`true`) or as a number of bytes (`false`).

- `localcache directory=<filepath>:` Specifies the location of the local cache when using Hosted Cache mode, where `<filepath>` is the path to the local cache folder.

When you use `netsh` to configure BranchCache, this automatically configures the host computer firewall to pass BranchCache protocol packets.

**NOTE**  The `netsh` commands described here have several additional parameters. For more information, consult "Netsh Commands" at http://technet.microsoft.com/en-us/library/dd637805(WS.10).aspx. This reference provides a comprehensive list of commands used specifically with the BranchCache feature.

## Using Group Policy to Enable BranchCache

You can use Group Policy to enable BranchCache on all client computers located on the remote network. Create a GPO focused on the AD DS site for the remote network or to configure BranchCache for multiple branch offices in a single domain, create a GPO focused on the domain. Then open the Group Policy Management Editor and navigate to the **Computer Configuration\Policies\Administrative Templates\Network\BranchCache** node. As shown in Figure 9-38, this node provides the following five policies:

- **Turn on BranchCache:** Enable this policy to enable BranchCache on all client computers affected by the GPO. You must enable this policy for any of the other policies to be effective.

- **Set BranchCache Distributed Cache mode:** Enable this policy to enable BranchCache Distributed Cache mode.

- **Set BranchCache Hosted Cache mode:** Enable this policy to enable Branch-Cache Hosted Cache mode. As shown in Figure 9-39, type the FQDN of the server hosting the cache in the space provided.

- **Configure BranchCache for network files:** Specify the default round trip network latency value in milliseconds above which network files must be cached. By default, this value is 80 milliseconds.

- **Set percentage of disk space used for client computer cache:** Specify the percent of total client disk space on each client computer available for caching files with BranchCache. By default, this value is five percent of the client computer's total disk space.

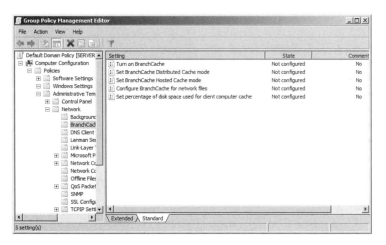

**Figure 9-38**   You can use Group Policy to configure these five BranchCache policies.

**Figure 9-39**   When enabling Hosted Cache mode, you must specify the FQDN of the hosting server.

**TIP**   Although it is convenient to use site-based Group Policy for configuring BranchCache because it applies to all computers in the branch site, remember that domain-based and organizational unit (OU)-based policies override settings in a site-based GPO.

### Specifying BranchCache Firewall Rules

When you use Group Policy to configure BranchCache, you must also configure firewall rules that permit BranchCache messages to pass to the client computers. You can do this by using Windows Firewall with Advanced Security, which we introduced in Chapter 4, "Configuring Windows Firewall with Advanced Security." Proceed as follows:

1. Open the Group Policy Management Editor focused on the same GPO used for enabling BranchCache.

2. Navigate to the **Computer Configuration\Policies\Windows Settings\ Security Settings\Windows Firewall with Advanced Security\Inbound Rules** node.

3. Right-click **Inbound Rules** and choose **New Rule** to start the New Inbound Rule Wizard.

4. As previously shown in Figure 4-8 in Chapter 4, select the **Predefined** option.

5. Ensure that the option reads **BranchCache–Content Retrieval (Uses HTTP)** and follow the remaining steps of the wizard, ensuring that the **Allow the Connection** option is selected. If you are using HTTPS, ensure that the **Branch Cache–Hosted Cache Server (Uses HTTPS)** option is selected instead.

### Understanding BranchCache Network Infrastructure Requirements

Because the client computer at the branch office needs to obtain the requested file only at the time of its first request, network infrastructure requirements are considerably reduced when you enable BranchCache. The BranchCache server in the head office sends a requested file in 64-KB blocks. When it sends the file, it also sends metadata (as mentioned earlier in this section). When another client computer requests the same file, the BranchCache server resends the metadata and the client computer compares the two sets of metadata to determine whether the contents of the requested file have changed. The BranchCache server resends the file only if changes have occurred; even then it might need to send only 64-KB blocks of data that have changed.

Because the metadata can be up to 2,000 times smaller than the file size, the bandwidth requirements are reduced by a factor of up to 2,000 when you enable Branch-Cache. This factor applies only when clients request files multiple times and the files are larger than 64 KB. Security is provided by the use of the Advanced Encryption Standard (AES) with a 128-bit key.

**NOTE**   For more information on network optimization with BranchCache, refer to "End-to-End WAN Optimization with BranchCache" at http://technet.microsoft.com/en-us/magazine/ee914606.aspx.

### Using BranchCache across a Virtual Private Network

You can use BranchCache across remote access virtual private network (VPN) connections that support split tunneling. If DirectAccess is being used for connections from your branch office computers to your head office, you must configure the firewall rules to support such a connection, as follows:

- If using Distributed Cache mode, you must configure IPSec firewall rules to allow the WS-Discovery (UDP multicast on port 3702) and HTTP (TCP port 80) protocols to pass between remote computers.

- If using Hosted Cache mode, you must configure IPSec firewall rules to allow HTTP (TCP port 80) protocols to pass between remote computers and the Hosted Cache server.

**NOTE**   For more information about configuring a VPN, refer to Chapter 14, "Configuring Remote Access."

### Managing Certificates with BranchCache

When using BranchCache with a Hosted Cache server, this server must be trusted by client computers to cache data that might be under access control. The client computers use Transport Layer Security (TLS) to communicate with the Hosted Cache server. Consequently, this server must have a certificate that clients can use to authenticate the server.

You can use Active Directory Certificate Services (AD CS) within an AD DS domain to issue a certificate to the Hosted Cache server that will verify this server's identity to client computers in the branch office accessing documents to be cached. In a non-domain environment, you can also use a server running Certificate Services as a standalone certification authority (CA).

The certificate is imported to the certificate store on the BranchCache server under the local computer account, so that the client computers in the branch office can trust this server. If it is added under the administrator account, clients will be unable to use the certificate to access the Hosted Cache server. To import this certificate, use the Certificates snap-in at the server.

**NOTE**   For further information on configuring a certificate on the BranchCache server, refer to "Hosted Cache Server Setup" at http://technet.microsoft.com/en-us/library/dd637793(WS.10).aspx and "Deploy a hosted cache mode design" at http://technet.microsoft.com/en-us/library/ee649239(WS.10).aspx.

### Using Share and Storage Management Console

The Share and Storage Management Console is a Microsoft Management Console (MMC) snap-in that is installed on your server when you install the File Server role. This console provides a centralized location for managing shared resources including folders, volumes, and other storage resources. It is available from the Administrative Tools folder, and can also be accessed under the Roles node of Server Manager, as shown in Figure 9-40.

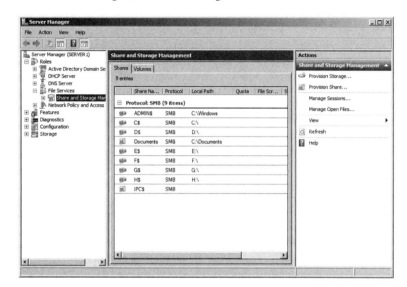

**Figure 9-40** The Share and Storage Management Console provides a convenient location for performing management tasks on folders and disk volumes.

As shown, the details pane displays all shared resources on the computer. Note that each volume is automatically shared with a "$" character suffixed to the drive letter; you can suffix any share with the dollar sign to denote it as a *hidden share*, also known as an *administrative share*. These shares are created automatically when Windows Server 2008 is installed and do not appear in the Computer or Network folders of Windows Explorer. To access such a share from a remote computer, you must use a UNC path from the address bar of an Explorer window or from the Run command.

The Share and Storage Management Console enables you to perform the following tasks:

- Provision shared resources and storage volumes
- Manage existing shared resources, including permissions for shared folders

- Manage existing storage volumes
- Manage shared resources and storage on a remote computer

> **NOTE**   For further information on the basics of the Share and Storage Management tool, refer to "Overview of Share and Storage Management" at http://technet.microsoft.com/en-us/library/cc753175.aspx. Links provided in this reference point to additional information on the various tasks you can perform from this snap-in.

### Using Share and Storage Management to Provision Shared Resources and Volumes

Share and Storage Management enables you to start sharing folders and volumes, configure access permissions, and assign quotas and file screens. Use the following procedure to set up shared resources:

1. Click **Start** > **Administrative Tools** > **Share and Storage Management**. You can also type share in the Start menu Search field, and then select **Share and Storage Management** from the program list.

2. From the console tree of the Share and Storage Management snap-in, right-click **Share and Storage Management** and choose **Provision Share**. This starts the Provision a Shared Folder Wizard, as shown in Figure 9-41.

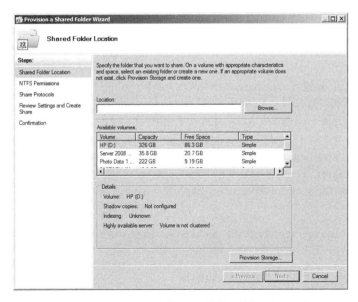

**Figure 9-41**   The Provision a Shared Folder Wizard enables you to create and configure shared folders.

3. Click **Browse** to open the Browse for Folder dialog box, which helps you to locate the folder you want to share. From this dialog box, you can also click **Make New Folder** to create a new folder.

4. Click **Next** to display the NTFS Permissions page. From this page, you can either leave the default of **No, do not change NTFS permissions** selected, or select the **Yes, change NTFS permissions** radio button and click **Edit Permissions** to modify the default permissions. Clicking this button opens the Security tab of the folder's Properties dialog box, similar to that shown previously in Figure 9-10.

5. Click **Next** to display the Share Protocols page, which enables you to select from two protocols over which users can access the share:

   - **SMB:** Uses Server Message Block (SMB), which is the default for Windows users and is generally the only protocol required.

   - **NFS:** Uses Network File System (NFS), which is a UNIX protocol. You need to have the Services for Network File System role service installed to use this protocol.

6. Click **Next** to display the SMB Settings page, which allows you to type a description that users will be able to see when connecting to the share. From this page, you can also click **Advanced** to limit the number of users that can simultaneously access the share. You can also specify caching settings, which are similar to those previously shown in Figure 9-35.

7. Click **Next** to display the SMB Permissions page, which enables you to specify one of the permissions shown in Figure 9-42. If you need to specify customized shared folder permissions, select **Users and groups have custom share permissions** and then click the **Permissions** command button to display a Permissions dialog box similar to that previously shown in Figure 9-7.

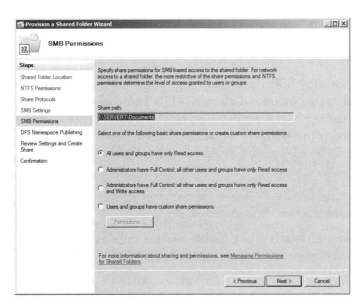

**Figure 9-42**    The SMB Permissions page enables you to configure a default or customized shared folder permission.

8. Click **Next** to display the DFS Namespace Publishing page, which enables you to add the share to a DFS namespace. We discuss DFS namespaces in Chapter 10, "Configuring Distributed File System (DFS)."

9. Click **Next** to display the Review Settings and Create Share page, which displays a summary of the settings you have configured for the shared folder. If you need to change any of the settings, click **Previous** or select the appropriate page from the list on the left. When done, click **Create** to create the shared folder.

10. The Confirmation page informs you that you have successfully created the shared folder. Click **Close** to return to the Share and Storage Management snap-in, which displays the new share among its list of shared resources in the details pane.

You can also use the Provision Storage capabilities to create new volumes from unallocated space on disks in your server or on storage subsystems that support Virtual Disk Service (VDS). Right-click **Share and Storage Management** and choose **Provision Storage** to start a wizard that assists you in performing one of these tasks.

### Using Share and Storage Management to Manage Shared Resources

Share and Storage Management enables you to perform the following management tasks on shared folders and volumes present on your server:

- **View and edit shared folder properties:** Right-click the desired share in the details pane and choose **Properties**. The Properties dialog box that appears enables you to modify the shared folder and NTFS permissions, similar to those discussed earlier in this chapter. You can also click **Advanced** to modify user limits, access-based enumeration, and offline settings.

- **Stop sharing resources:** Right-click the desired share in the details pane and choose **Stop Sharing**. You are warned that users will no longer be able to access files from these shared folders. Click **Yes** to stop sharing or **No** to cancel the operation.

- **Configure offline shared folder availability:** Right-click the desired share in the details pane and choose **Properties**. Then, click **Advanced** and configure the required settings from the Caching tab, which are the same as those already shown in Figure 9-35.

- **Manage sessions:** Each user who connects to one or more shared resources on your server has established a session with the server that you can view and manage. From the console tree, right-click **Share and Storage Management** and choose **Manage Sessions**. The Manage Sessions dialog box that appears displays the users who have sessions active on your server, together with their computer name and statistics on open sessions. If you need to close any sessions, select the desired session and click **Close Selected**; to close all sessions (such as when you need to perform hardware maintenance on the server), click **Close All**. Note that you should notify users that you intend to close their sessions so that they can save their work and avoid data loss.

- **Manage open files:** From the console tree, right-click **Share and Storage Management** and choose **Manage Open Files**. The Manage Open Files dialog box displays all files that users arc connected to, together with the username and statistical options. You can close files or directories from this location in a similar manner to that for sessions; again, you should notify users before closing open files.

> **TIP** You can also use Share and Storage Management to manage shared resources on a remote computer. To do so, right-click **Share and Storage Management** and choose **Connect to another Computer**. Type the name or IP address of the required computer in the dialog box that appears or click **Browse** to locate the required computer. Then, click **OK**.

## Exam Preparation Tasks

## Review All the Key Topics

Review the most important topics in this chapter, noted with the key topics icon in the outer margin of the page. Table 9-11 lists a reference of these key topics and the page numbers on which each is found.

**Table 9-11**   Key Topics for Chapter 9

| Key Topic Element | Description | Page Number |
|---|---|---|
| List | Describes the benefits of the File Server role in Windows Server 2008 R2. | 358 |
| Figure 9-3 | The Advanced sharing settings dialog box enables you to configure several global file-sharing options. | 362 |
| Figure 9-4 | Shows you how to share a folder from Windows Explorer. | 363 |
| Table 9-2 | Describes important file-sharing options available in Windows Server 2008 R2. | 364 |
| Table 9-3 | Describes shared folder permissions. | 366 |
| Table 9-5 | Describes NTFS permissions available on files and folders. | 370 |
| Figure 9-13 | Shows you how to configure advanced NTFS permissions. | 374 |
| Figure 9-14 | You have several options for configuring permissions inheritance. | 377 |
| Figure 9-15 | Shows you how to take ownership of a folder or file. | 378 |
| List | Describes how effective permissions are determined from a combination of share and NTFS permissions configured at different levels. | 379 |
| Figure 9-18 | Use the Advanced Attributes dialog box to either compress or encrypt a file or folder. | 388 |
| List | Shows you how to back up EFS keys. | 390 |
| Paragraph | Describes the use of BitLocker to encrypt a drive volume. | 395 |
| List | Shows you how to enable BitLocker. | 398 |
| Figure 9-30 | The BitLocker applet provides several volume management options. | 402 |
| Figure 9-31 | Using Group Policy to apply BitLocker settings. | 404 |
| Figure 9-34 | You have several options available for recovering BitLocker-protected operating system drives. | 407 |
| Table 9-10 | Describes available offline file policies. | 412 |

| Key Topic Element | Description | Page Number |
|---|---|---|
| List | Describes BranchCache operating modes. | 415 |
| Figure 9-38 | Group Policy provides several policies for configuring BranchCache. | 417 |
| Figure 9-40 | The Share and Storage Management snap-in provides a convenient location for managing folders and volumes. | 421 |
| List | Describes the tasks that Share and Storage Management enables you to perform. | 425 |

## Complete the Tables and Lists from Memory

Print a copy of Appendix B, "Memory Tables" (found on the CD), or at least the section for this chapter, and complete the tables and lists from memory. Appendix C, "Memory Tables Answer Key," also on the CD, includes the completed tables and lists to check your work.

## Definition of Key Terms

Define the following key terms from this chapter, and check your answers in the Glossary.

access control list (ACL), administrative shares, BitLocker Drive Encryption, BranchCache, certificate, decryption, encryption, Encrypting File System (EFS), hidden shares, Network File System (NFS), New Technology File System (NTFS), NTFS permissions, offline files, private key, public key, recovery agent, Share and Storage Management Console, shared folders, shared folder permissions, synchronizing files, Trusted Platform Module (TPM)

This chapter covers the following subjects:

- **DFS Concepts:** This section provides you with an overview of DFS, which places shared folders located on different servers into a single folder tree, from which users can more easily locate and access required resources on the network. It then shows you how to install DFS on a Windows Server 2008 R2 computer.

- **Managing DFS Namespaces:** Namespaces are logical grouping of shared folders that are located on one or more servers on your network. This section shows you how to set up namespaces and perform various configuration tasks.

- **Managing DFS Replication:** DFS replication facilitates replication of data among different servers on the network. This section shows you how to set up, configure, and monitor replication groups and their members.

# CHAPTER 10

# Configuring Distributed File System (DFS)

Chapter 9, "Configuring File Servers," introduced you to the concepts of file sharing and access control in a Windows Server 2008-based network. You learned how to share and manage files and folders so that they are available to users across the network who need access to them to perform their job tasks properly and efficiently. You also learned how to set up a structure of permissions that ensures that only users who require access to given files and folders receive this access, and that users can only modify the appropriate items. Now, we take these file sharing concepts further and look into a Microsoft technology that assists users in locating these resources as their organizations grow in size and add additional file servers—the Distributed File System (DFS). DFS places all the shared resources into a single folder tree that encompasses all these servers and their shares, wherever they might be located on a large, sprawling network.

## "Do I Know This Already?" Quiz

The "Do I Know This Already?" quiz allows you to assess whether you should read this entire chapter or simply jump to the "Exam Preparation Tasks" section for review. If you are in doubt, read the entire chapter. Table 10-1 outlines the major headings in this chapter and the corresponding "Do I Know This Already?" quiz questions. You can find the answers in Appendix A, "Answers to the 'Do I Know This Already?' Quizzes."

**Table 10-1** "Do I Know This Already?" Foundation Topics Section-to-Question Mapping

| Foundations Topics Section | Questions Covered in This Section |
| --- | --- |
| DFS Concepts | 1 |
| Managing DFS Namespaces | 2–4 |
| Managing DFS Replication | 6–8 |

1. Which of the following can you do at the same time you install DFS by using the Add Role Services Wizard? (Choose all that apply.)

   **a.** Create a standalone DFS namespace.

   **b.** Create a DFS namespace that is based in Active Directory.

   **c.** Create a DFS replication group.

   **d.** Specify a DFS replication topology.

2. Which of the following best describes the concept of a folder target in the DFS namespace?

   **a.** The starting point of the namespace and is specified by users when connecting to any object within the namespace.

   **b.** A shared folder that is stored on a namespace server and is directly accessed by a user for purposes of reaching data stored on other servers.

   **c.** Any subfolder on a target server that is specified by users to access data contained within it.

   **d.** A UNC path of a shared folder or another namespace that is associated with a folder in a namespace.

3. You are responsible for configuring a DFS namespace within your company's AD DS network, which consists of a head office and five branch offices. Two of the branch offices are connected to the head office by a high-speed T3 link, one is connected with an ISDN link, and the other two are connected with 28K dial-up lines. All branch office sites are configured with Windows Server 2008 R2 computers as part of a hub and spoke replication topology. You want to ensure that users in the branch offices do not generate excess traffic by requesting data from namespace servers in other offices. What should you do?

   **a.** From the Referrals tab of the namespace's Properties dialog box, select the **Random order** option.

   **b.** From the Referrals tab of the namespace's Properties dialog box, select the **Lowest cost** option.

   **c.** From the Referrals tab of the namespace's Properties dialog box, select the **Exclude targets outside of the client's site** option.

   **d.** From the Referrals tab of the namespace's Properties dialog box, select the **Clients fail back to preferred targets** option.

4. You are responsible for maintaining your company's DFS namespace. You configured all folders within the namespace with shared folder and NTFS permissions that enable users to access data associated with their individual

job tasks, but not other folders. Users are calling and reporting that they frequently receive `Access denied` messages when browsing the DFS namespace. You have verified that all users have access to required files and folders. What should you do to reduce the instance of users receiving these messages?

    **a.** Create additional DFS namespaces that only include folders required for specific groups of users, and provide access to only the required namespaces.

    **b.** Enable access-based enumeration of the DFS namespace.

    **c.** Specify NTFS permissions on the namespace root that limit access to only the required folders for each user.

    **d.** Configure specific denial of NTFS permissions on folder targets that are not required for users performing their job tasks.

5. You are the administrator of an AD DS network that is operating at the Windows 2000 native forest and domain functional levels. You have read about the advantages of DFS Replication and would like to get rid of the older File Replication Service, which has caused many problems in recent years. Which of the following must you do in order to set up a DFS Replication group on your network? (Each correct answer represents part of the solution. Choose three.)

    **a.** Upgrade all servers in the replication group to Windows Server 2003 R2 or higher.

    **b.** Upgrade all servers in the replication group to Windows Server 2008 R2.

    **c.** Convert any FAT32 partitions on replication member servers to the NTFS file system.

    **d.** Ensure that your antivirus software is compatible with DFS replication.

    **e.** Create folder targets that point to all replication member servers.

6. You added three new member servers to your company's DFS replication group. You want to ensure that the new configuration is available for use as soon as possible. What command should you use to force members to poll domain controllers immediately for configuration changes?

    **a.** `Dfsdiag.exe`

    **b.** `Dfsrdiag.exe`

    **c.** `Dfsutil.exe`

    **d.** `Dfsradmin.exe`

7. You configured DFS Replication to make the contents of a folder named Publications available to users in several offices on your network. Managers and journalists should be able to make changes to the contents of this folder from three different servers in the head office. However, you want to ensure that users (including managers and journalists) in two branch offices are unable to make changes to items in this folder. What should you do?

   a. Access the properties of the Publications folder and allow the Managers and Journalists group the Modify NTFS permission. Also, allow the Read shared folder permission to the Everyone group.

   b. Access the properties of the Publications folder and allow the Managers and Journalists group the Modify NTFS permission and the Full Control shared folder permission. Also, allow the Read shared folder permission to groups that include the users in the two branch offices.

   c. In the DFS Management snap-in, access the properties of the replication group. Right-click the replication group and choose **Make read-only**.

   d. In the DFS Management snap-in, access the properties of the replication group. For each branch office server, right-click the **Publications** folder and choose **Make read-only**.

8. You are responsible for configuring and maintaining DFS Replication on your company's network, on which you have configured a single replication group. You want to prepare a report that provides information on replication statistics, error and warning events, backlogged files, and other information for each member of the replication group. What should you do?

   a. Right-click the replication group in the console tree of the DFS Management snap-in and choose **Create Diagnostic Report**. From the wizard that appears, select the **Propagation test** option.

   b. Right-click the replication group in the console tree of the DFS Management snap-in and choose **Create Diagnostic Report**. From the wizard that appears, select the **Propagation report** option.

   c. Right-click the replication group in the console tree of the DFS Management snap-in and choose **Create Diagnostic Report**. From the wizard that appears, select the **Health report** option.

   d. Right-click the replication group in the console tree of the DFS Management snap-in and choose **Create Health Report**.

## Foundation Topics

## DFS Concepts

The typical large organization has many file servers that users require access to as they perform their assigned tasks. Imagine the difficulty that the average user could have in locating the appropriate server from dozens of possibilities when attempting to access that one vital piece of information when putting together that budget forecast for the upcoming fiscal year. And multiply that by the myriads of possibilities when marketing analysts are formulating trends for corporate products and deciding what should be emphasized in both manufacturing and advertising efforts in the months to come. Then, you can see how much simpler such tasks become if the users need to access only a single tree of shared folders that includes all the servers that hold the required files. This is what Distributed File System (DFS) does—a user can type a single universal naming convention (UNC) path, such as \\servername\sharename, or select a single root within the Network folder and obtain access to shares located on multiple servers across the network. Users located in branch offices received optimized access across the wide-area network (WAN) to the most easily accessed file source; further, replication of files and folders can be optimized to facilitate access to everyone regardless of where they might be located within a multisite enterprise network.

First introduced with Windows Server 2003, DFS provides WAN-friendly replication and simplified access to files wherever they are located. DFS includes the two technologies described in Table 10-2.

**Table 10-2**   Components of DFS in Windows Server 2008

| Component | Description |
|-----------|-------------|
| **DFS Namespaces** | Enables you to create logical groupings of shared folders on different servers that facilitate the access to data by users on the network. Such groupings are presented to users as a virtual folder tree or namespace. DFS namespaces is optimized to connect users to data within the same Active Directory Domain Services (AD DS) site wherever possible, thereby minimizing the need for use of WAN links. |
| **DFS Replication** | An efficient multimaster replication component that synchronizes data between servers with limited bandwidth network links. DFS replication replaces the older, problematic File Replication Service (FRS) used in Windows NT/2000 for replicating data across the network. DFS utilizes a new compression algorithm called remote differential compression (RDC), which optimizes file replication by sending only the updated portions of changed files rather than the complete files. On AD DS networks operating at the Windows Server 2008 or higher domain functional level, DFS replication is used for replicating AD DS partitions and the SYSVOL shared folder. |

> **NOTE**   You can use DFS Replication and DFS Namespaces either separately or together; each does not require the presence of the other. You can also use DFS Replication to replicate standalone DFS namespaces.

### Improvements to DFS in Windows Server 2008 R2

Microsoft has improved and updated the technologies included in DFS with Windows Server 2008 R2. The following improvements have been made to DFS Namespaces:

- **Support for access-based enumeration:** Access-based enumeration displays only those files and folders for which a user has been granted access permissions of Read or higher. Other resources are hidden from the user's view. Access-based enumeration is discussed in more detail later in this chapter.

- **New performance counters:** DFS namespaces provides several new performance counters that assist you in the use of Performance Monitor. Performance Monitor is discussed in Chapter 19, "Configuring Performance Monitoring."

- **Performance improvements with large namespaces:** Compared with the original version of Windows Server 2008, startup and connection performance has been improved in Windows Server 2008 R2 with regard to large domain-based namespaces with more than 5000 to 300,000 DFS folders.

- **Support for selectively enabling namespace root referrals:** A root referral is a list of DFS namespace servers that is provided to a client by a Windows Server 2008 R2 domain controller. You can selectively enable or disable referrals to specific namespace servers, enabling you to temporarily take a namespace server offline for maintenance purposes.

- **Improved `Dfsdiag.exe` command prompt help text:** Clearer and more descriptive help and error information has been provided for `Dfsdiag.exe`.

Windows Server 2008 R2 provides the following improvements to DFS Replication:

- **Failover cluster support:** You can add a failover cluster as a member of a replication group. This is discussed later in this chapter.

- **Read-only replicated folders:** You can configure replicated folders as read-only so that users cannot add or modify files. This is convenient for shares such as software installation folders or folders containing published or confidential documents. Prior to Windows Server 2008 R2, you had to manually configure share and security permissions on folders.

- **Read-only SYSVOL folders on read-only domain controllers (RODCs):** Neither users nor administrators can modify the SYSVOL folder on an RODC. Prior to Windows Server 2008 R2, it was possible to modify the SYSVOL folder at an RODC and such changes persisted until the DFS replication service overwrites the change with data from a read-write domain controller.

- **Additional diagnostic functionality within the `Dfsrdiag.exe` command-line utility:** Additional command-line parameters provide DFS replication status diagnostics.

> **NOTE**   For more information on new DFS features in Windows Server 2008 R2, refer to "What's New in Distributed File System" at http://technet.microsoft.com/en-us/library/ee307957(WS.10).aspx.

### Installing DFS on a Windows Server 2008 R2 Computer

DFS is included as an optional role service within the File Server role. You can install either DFS Namespaces, DFS Replication, or both at the time of installing the File Server role, as described in Chapter 9. You can also install either component at a later time by performing the following steps:

1. Open Server Manager and expand the Roles node.

2. In the console tree, expand the Roles node, right-click **File Services**, and then select **Add Role Services.**

3. In the Select Role Services page of the Add Role Services wizard that appears, select **Distributed File System**. This automatically selects the **DFS Namespaces** and **DFS Replication** subnodes. Then, click **Next.**

4. You receive the Create a DFS Namespace page shown in Figure 10-1. To create a namespace now, leave the default of **Create a namespace now, using this wizard**. Type a name for the namespace or use the default of **Namespace1**, and then click **Next.**

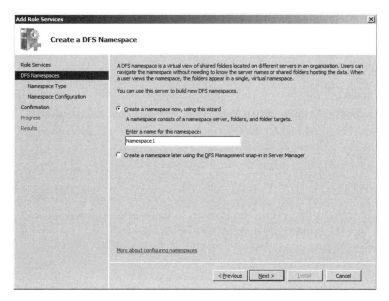

**Figure 10-1**   The Create a DFS Namespace page enables you to create a new DFS namespace.

5. The Select Namespace Type page, as shown in Figure 10-2, offers a choice between domain-based and standalone namespaces (on a standalone server, only the standalone option is available). Note the descriptions provided, make a choice, and then click **Next**.

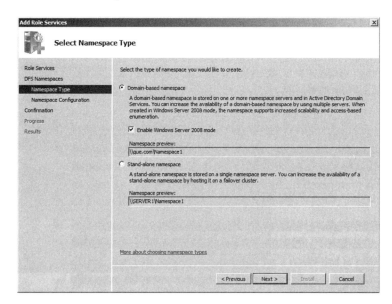

**Figure 10-2**   You can choose between two different types of DFS namespaces.

6. The Configure Namespace page enables you to add shared folders. To add a folder now, click **Add** and browse to the required folder in the Add Folder to Namespace dialog box that appears. After you add your folder (you can also create a new shared folder), click **OK**, and then click **Next**.

7. Confirm your selections on the Confirm Installations page. If you need to modify any selections, click **Previous**. When ready to proceed, click **Install**.

8. Wait while the services are being installed, and then click **Close** when you are informed that installation was successfully completed.

After you install DFS, you can access the DFS Management snap-in from the Administrative Tools folder. As shown in Figure 10-3, this snap-in enables you to perform various tasks related to managing DFS namespaces and DFS replication. These tasks are discussed in later sections.

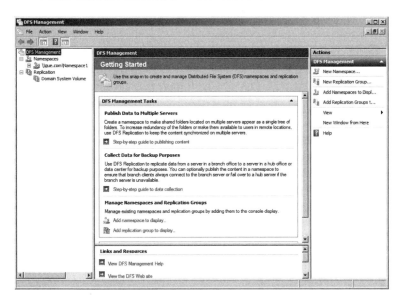

**Figure 10-3**   The DFS Management snap-in enables you to perform management tasks on DFS.

**NOTE**   For more information on configuring DFS Namespaces and DFS Replication, including detailed procedures in a test environment, refer to "DFS Step-by-Step Guide for Windows Server 2008" at http://technet.microsoft.com/en-us/library/cc732863(WS.10).aspx.

# Managing DFS Namespaces

The Namespaces node of the DFS Management snap-in enables you to perform management tasks on namespaces located on your server or AD DS domain. Namespaces are logical groupings of shared folders that are located on one or more servers on your network. Each is defined by a UNC path that is structured similar to the case for ordinary shared folders; for example, `\\namespaceserver\root\folder`, where

- `namespaceserver` refers to the namespace server, which hosts the root of the DFS namespace. This refers to the server on which the namespace was created, and can be on either a domain controller or a member server. For a domain-based namespace, the NetBIOS or DNS name of the AD DS domain is used.

- `root` refers to the namespace root folder as specified when creating the DFS namespace. This root is the starting point of the namespace and is specified by users when connecting to any object within the namespace.

- `folder` refers to any shared folder that you have added to the namespace from the DFS Management tool. Optionally, folders can have folder targets that direct clients to specific server locations. A *folder target* is a UNC path of a shared folder or another namespace that is associated with a folder in a namespace. A folder within a DFS hierarchy can have multiple folder targets that point to shared folders in different geographical locations, thereby enabling a user to access the folder target closest to her location.

## Creating Additional DFS Namespaces

In most cases, you only need the single namespace that you created when installing the DFS role service, as previously noted. However, you can add additional namespaces at any time using the New Namespace Wizard, as follows:

1. In the console tree of DFS Management, right-click the **Namespaces** node and choose **New Namespace**.

2. The New Namespace Wizard starts with the Namespace Server page. Type or browse to the name of the server that will host the namespace and click **Next**.

3. On the Namespace Name and Settings page, type a name for the namespace. The namespace will be created with a default path and share name; to modify these settings or change the default share permission of Read, click **Edit Settings**. When finished, click **Next**.

4. The Namespace Type page provides the same options as previously shown in Figure 10-2. Make a choice and click **Next**.

5. The Review Settings and Create Namespace page provides a summary of the settings you've specified. If necessary, click **Previous** to modify these settings. When ready, click **Create** to create the namespace.

6. The Confirmation page informs you that the namespace has been created successfully. Click **Close**. The namespace is added to the display in the console tree of the DFS Management snap-in.

## Managing Namespaces

When you select a namespace from the console tree of the DFS Management snap-in, the details pane displays four tabs (see Figure 10-4) that provide the following management options:

- **Namespace tab:** Provides entries for all shared folders contained within the namespace.

- **Namespace Servers tab:** Displays all servers hosting shared folders that are included in the DFS namespace. Included for domain-based namespaces is the name of the AD DS site in which each server is located.

- **Delegation tab:** Enables you to delegate management of a portion of the DFS namespace to a user or group. You can grant users who are not members of the Domain Admins group the capability of creating domain-based namespaces. To delegate permissions, right-click the namespace in the console tree and choose **Delegate Management Permissions**. Then, type the name of the required user or group and click **OK**. For more information, refer to "Delegate Management Permissions for DFS Namespaces" at http://technet. microsoft.com/en-us/library/cc754770.aspx.

- **Search tab:** Enables you to locate a shared folder in the DFS namespace. Type the required folder name and click **Search**.

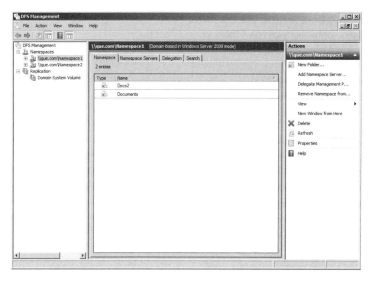

**Figure 10-4**    The DFS Management snap-in provides several namespace management options.

### Adding Folders to DFS Namespaces

For the DFS namespace to be useful to users, you need to add shared folders to it. Doing so enables users to access them from the namespace root. Use the following procedure:

1. In the console tree of DFS Management, expand the Namespaces node, right-click the desired namespace, and choose **New Folder**.

2. You receive the New Folder dialog box shown in Figure 10-5. Type the name of the desired folder in the Name text box.

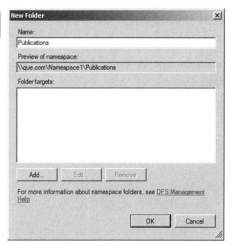

**Figure 10-5**    Adding a folder to a DFS namespace.

3. Click **Add** to add one or more shared folders as folder targets. Users will be able to access these folders as subfolders of the DFS folder you created.

4. Click **Browse** to open the Browse for Shared Folders dialog box, and enter the name of the server that hosts the desired shared folder.

5. Click **New Shared Folder** to specify a shared folder located on the server whose name you entered. Type the name of the folder and enter the local path to the folder on the server. Then, click **OK**. If the folder does not exist, you are prompted to create it.

6. You are returned to the New Folder dialog box, from which you can add additional folder targets if desired. When finished, click **OK** to close this dialog box. The folder is added to the list in the Namespace tab in the details pane.

**TIP**   You can add additional folder targets to a folder at any time. Right-click the folder in the console tree of DFS Management and choose **Add Folder Target**.

### Adding Namespace Servers

You can add additional namespace servers to a domain-based namespace to increase the availability of the namespace and place namespace servers into additional AD DS sites. To do so, right-click the namespace in the console tree of the DFS Management snap-in and choose **Add Namespace Server**. Type the name of the server in the dialog box that appears and click **OK**. The name of the server is added to the list in the Namespace Servers tab.

### Configuring Referrals

A referral is an ordered list of targets that a user receives when she accesses a namespace root or folder from a namespace server or domain controller. A client computer attempts to access the first target in the list to obtain the desired folder; if this target is not available, the client attempts the next target, and so on. You can modify the sequence in which targets are listed, as follows:

1. In the console tree of DFS Management, expand the Namespaces node, right-click the desired namespace or folder, and then choose **Properties**.

2. On the Referrals tab shown in Figure 10-6, select an ordering method from the following:

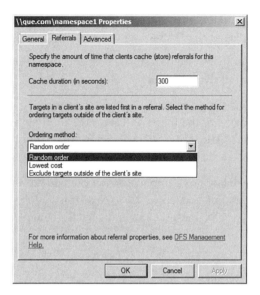

**Figure 10-6**   Selecting an ordering method.

■ **Random order:** Lists the targets in the same AD DS site as the client in random order at the top of the list, and then lists the targets in other sites in random order.

■ **Lowest cost:** Lists the targets in the same AD DS site as the client in random order at the top of the list, and then lists the targets in other sites in sequence of lowest site link cost to highest cost.

■ **Exclude targets outside of the client's site:** Lists only the targets in the same AD DS site as the client, in random order. Targets in other sites are not listed, and if no same-site targets exist, the client is unable to access that portion of the DFS namespace.

3. To modify the length of time that clients cache the referral list before requesting a new one, type the required amount of time in seconds in the Cache duration text box. By default, this duration is 300 seconds (5 minutes).

4. Click **OK**.

**TIP**   You can also configure individual folders in a namespace to exclude targets located outside of the client's site. Right-click the folder, choose **Properties**, and then select either **Exclude targets outside of the client's site** or **Clients fail back to preferred targets** as required.

**NOTE** For more information on configuring referrals, refer to "Set the Ordering Method for Targets in Referrals" at http://technet.microsoft.com/en-us/library/cc732414.aspx.

### Enabling Access-Based Enumeration of a DFS Namespace

Access-based enumeration displays only those files and folders that a user has permission to access. You can enable access-based enumeration of files and folders within a namespace if all namespace servers are running Windows Server 2008 and the namespaces are configured in the Windows Server 2008 mode (the check box labeled **Enable Windows Server 2008 mode**, previously shown in Figure 10-2, must be selected).

To enable access-based enumeration, proceed as follows:

1. In the console tree of DFS Management, expand the Namespaces node, right-click the desired namespace, and then choose **Properties**.

2. From the Advanced tab of the Properties dialog box, as shown in Figure 10-7, select the check box labeled **Enable access-based enumeration for this namespace**.

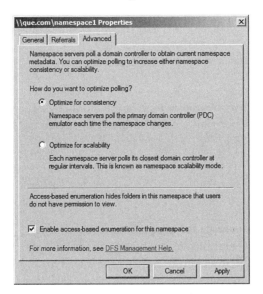

**Figure 10-7** Enabling access-based enumeration of DFS namespaces.

3. By default, access-based enumeration used permissions that are inherited from the local file system of the namespace server. You can also configure explicit view permissions on each folder. To control folder visibility, right-click the desired folder and choose **Properties**. From the Advanced tab of the folder's Properties dialog box, click **Set explicit view permissions on the DFS folder**.

4. Click **Configure view permissions**, and then add or remove users or groups by clicking **Add** or **Remove** as required.

5. For each user or group, click **Allow** to allow them to see the DFS folder or **Deny** to hide the folder from them. Then, click **OK**.

6. Click OK again to close the folder's Properties dialog box and return to the DFS Management snap-in.

**NOTE**   You can also use the `Dfsutil.exe` command-line tool to configure access-based enumeration. For more information on access-based enumeration, refer to "Enable Access-Based Enumeration on a Namespace" at http://technet.microsoft.com/en-us/library/dd919212(WS.10).aspx, "Access-Based Enumeration" at http://technet.microsoft.com/en-us/library/dd772681(WS.10).aspx, and "Using Inherited Permissions with Access-Based Enumeration" at http://technet.microsoft.com/en-us/library/dd834874.aspx.

**TIP**   `Dfsutil.exe` enables you to perform many actions with regard to configuring DFS from a command prompt, and is suitable for working on a Server Core machine or using scripts. For more information, type **dfsutil /?** at a command prompt.

### Configuring Polling of Domain Controllers

In a domain-based DFS namespace, all namespace servers poll the domain's primary domain controller (PDC) emulator operations master hourly for changes in the namespace. This can create increased network traffic and increased load on the PDC emulator if there are more than 16 namespace servers in the domain. To improve scalability in such cases, you can select the **Optimize for scalability** option from the Advanced tab of the namespace properties dialog box already shown in Figure 10-7. (For more information, refer to "Optimize Namespace Polling" at http://technet.microsoft.com/en-us/library/cc732193.aspx.)

## Managing DFS Replication

DFS Replication enables you to synchronize the contents of folders between servers so that users receive the same version of files regardless of which folder target their computer connects to. DFS Replication is an efficient, multimaster replication engine that replaces File Replication Service (FRS) that was used in earlier versions of Windows to synchronize folder content across the network. AD DS uses DFS Replication to synchronize the contents of the SYSVOL shared folder among domain controllers of domains that are operating at the Windows Server 2008 or higher domain functional level.

DFS Replication uses a compression algorithm called remote differential compression (RDC), which detects changes in a file and enables DFS to replicate only the changes rather than the entire file.

To use DFS Replication, you need to create replication groups and add replicated folders. Consider Figure 10-8 as a sample replication group. The group consists of two servers (also known as *members*) configured for DFS Replication, each hosting the replicated folders Budgets and Specifications. These replicated folders remain synchronized across all members of the replication topology. As users make changes to data in each replication folder, DFS replicates these changes across connections between the members of the replication group.

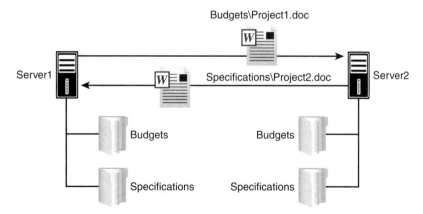

**Figure 10-8**   Sample replication group.

Within a given replication group, all folders are replicated using a common topology, schedule, and bandwidth throttling. You can add additional replicated folders at any time using a wizard launched from the DFS Management snap-in or the `Dfsradmin.exe` command-line tool.

The replication folders located on each member can be hosted by different volumes in each member, and the replicated folders need not be shared folders or part of a namespace. Using the DFS Management snap-in, you can share replicated folders and optionally publish them in an existing namespace.

Also, be aware of the following requirements for DFS Replication:

- All servers in a replication group must be located in the same AD DS forest. You cannot replicate between servers in different forests.

- All members of the replication group must be running Windows Server 2003 R2, Windows Server 2008, or Windows Server 2008 R2.

- All replicated folders must be stored on NTFS volumes.

- Ensure that your antivirus software is compatible with DFS Replication.

- If you are including a failover cluster in a replication group, the failover cluster must be running Windows Server 2008 R2. Failover clusters are discussed later in this section.

**NOTE**   For more information on the concepts of DFS Replication, refer to "Overview of DFS Replication" at http://technet.microsoft.com/en-us/library/cc771058.aspx.

**TIP**   To configure and manage DFS Replication in an AD DS domain environment, you must be a member of the Domain Admins group in the domain where the replication group exists. You can also delegate the ability to manage DFS Replication by right-clicking the **Replication** node or any replication group in the console tree of the DFS Management snap-in and choosing **Delegate Management Permissions**. Click **Add** in the Delegate Management Permissions dialog box that appears and add the desired user or group. For more information, refer to "Delegate the Ability to Manage DFS Replication" at http://technet.microsoft.com/en-us/library/cc771465.aspx.

## Setting Up DFS Replication

To set up DFS Replication for the first time, you need to create a replication group with a primary member. The primary member should contain the most up-to-date files to be replicated to other group members, because the primary member's content is considered "authoritative" during this initial replication; in other words, files replicated from the primary member always replace any conflicting files on other members, regardless of whether these files are older or newer.

Use the following steps to set up a DFS replication group:

1. In the console tree of DFS Management, right-click **Replication** and choose **New Replication Group**.

2. The New Replication Group Wizard starts with a Replication Group Type page. Choose the desired replication group, as described in Figure 10-9, and click **Next**.

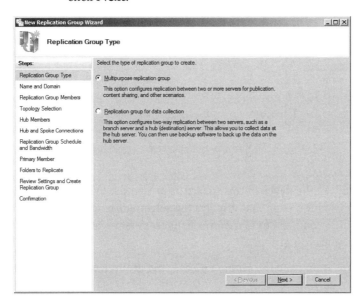

**Figure 10-9**  The Replication Group Type provides a choice between two group types.

3. On the Name and Domain page, type a name and optional description for the replication group. The domain name is automatically filled in; if you are creating a replication group for another domain in your forest, click **Browse** to locate the appropriate domain. Then, click **Next**.

4. The remaining pages of the wizard depend on the replication group type you selected at the first page of this wizard. If you selected the **Multipurpose replication group** type, you need to specify the group members and a topology type (more about this later in this section). If you selected the **Replication**

**group for data collection** type, you need to specify a primary server. Choose the server with the most up-to-date files, as already mentioned. You need to specify the folders to be replicated; on the Replicated Folders page, click **Add** to display the Add Folder to Replicate dialog box, as shown in Figure 10-10, which allows you to designate a folder to be replicated to all members of the replication group. Type or browse to the desired folder and click **OK**. Repeat this process to add all required folders to the group; click **Next** when finished.

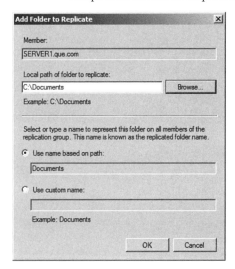

**Figure 10-10**   The Add Folder to Replicate dialog box enables you to designate a folder for replication.

5. Continue to respond to the pages of this wizard as presented. When finished, you receive a Confirmation page that displays the selections you made, and allows you to go back if you need to make any changes. When ready, click **Create** to create the replication group.

6. You receive a notification page informing you that the group has been created. Click **Close**.

**CAUTION**   You need to understand that time is required before replication within the new group begins. Configuration changes must be applied and replicated to all domain controllers, and each group member must poll its nearest domain controller to obtain the changes. The time required depends on AD DS replication latency and the 60-minute polling interval at each member. For more information on setting up a replication group and what happens during the initial phases of DFS replication, refer to "Create a Replication Group" at http://technet.microsoft.com/en-us/library/cc725893.aspx.

### Replication Topologies

The replication topology is simply a framework that describes the available paths across which replication between members of a replication set takes place. All replication topologies are modifications of the following two basic types:

- **Hub and spoke:** This topology requires three or more members. As shown in Figure 10-11, a central hub server replicates to each other server in the replication group. For larger groups, you can designate additional hubs for redundancy purposes. This ensures that a spoke member can still replicate if the original hub member is unavailable.

- **Full mesh:** As shown in Figure 10-12, each member of the group replicates with every other member of the group. This topology works well with groups of 10 or fewer members.

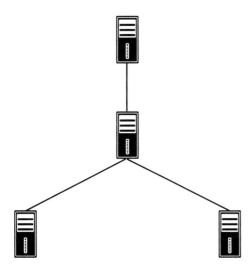

**Figure 10-11**   The hub-and-spoke topology involves a central hub replicating to each other member.

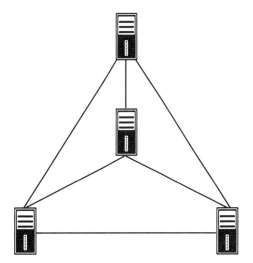

**Figure 10-12**   The full-mesh topology involves replication among all members of the group.

You can create topologies for existing replication groups. From the console tree of the DFS Management snap-in, right-click the replication group and choose **New Topology**. Then, follow the instructions in the New Topology Wizard, which involves the selection of one of these replication topology types.

## Working with Replication Groups

After you create a replication group, the DFS Management snap-in enables you to perform a large number of tasks with replication groups. The paragraphs that follow summarize many of the tasks you can perform from this snap-in.

### Adding New Connections

You can modify the replication topology by creating additional connections at any time. To add a new connection, right-click the required replication group in the console tree of the DFS Management snap-in and choose **New Connection**. In the dialog box that appears, specify the sending and receiving members and choose a schedule to be used for the connection. This creates a one-way replication connection. To create a two-way replication connection, click **Create a second connection in the opposite direction**.

Before the new connection can be used, the new configuration must be replicated to all domain controllers, and each member of the replication group must poll its nearest domain controller to obtain these changes. This takes an interval that depends on AD DS replication latency and the 60-minute polling interval on each member.

You can use the `dfsrdiag.exe` command to force members to poll domain controllers immediately for configuration changes.

**NOTE**   For more information on creating connections and the use of the `dfsrdiag.exe` command, refer to "Create a Connection" at http://technet.microsoft.com/en-us/library/cc771941.aspx.

### Adding Replicated Folders

You can add folders to a replication group at any time. Simply right-click the replication group in the console tree of the DFS Management snap-in and choose **New Replicated Folders**. Then, follow the instructions in the New Replicated Folders Wizard that appears.

### Designating Read-Only Replicated Folders

You can also designate a replicated folder on a particular member of the replication group as being read-only. In such a case, users cannot add or change files at this member of the replication group. This enables you to keep certain folders up-to-date with a central server or servers, such as those that contain published reports or documents. From the DFS Management snap-in, select the appropriate replication group under the Replication node of the console tree. The Memberships tab of the properties that appears in the details pane includes all folders in the group. Right-click the appropriate folder and choose **Make read-only**. You can remove the read-only designation by right-clicking a read-only folder and choosing **Make read-write**.

### Adding Members to Replication Groups

You can add new servers as members of an existing replication group. Right-click the replication group and choose **New Member**. Then, follow the instructions in the New Member Wizard that appears.

### Sharing or Publishing Replicated Folders

You can enable file sharing on a replicated folder and optionally add the folder to a DFS namespace. Use the following steps:

1. In the console tree of DFS Management, expand the Replication node and click the replication group that contains the replicated folder to be shared. The details pane provides information on this group.

2. On the Replicated Folders tab, right-click the desired folder and choose **Share and Publish in Namespace**. This starts the Share and Publish Replicated Folder Wizard.

3. To share the folder, select **Share the replicated folder**. To share and publish the folder in a DFS namespace, select **Share and publish the replicated folder in a namespace**. Then, complete the remaining steps in the wizard.

### Configuring Failover Cluster Support

DFS Replication in Windows Server 2008 R2 enables you to add a failover cluster as a member of a replication group. This provides redundancy and fault tolerance to your replication group. This feature is supported only on servers running Windows Server 2008 R2; the DFS Replication service on older Windows server versions is not designed to coordinate with a failover cluster. To do so, you must first install the Failover Clustering server feature and then install failover cluster support. Use the following procedure to add a failover cluster:

1. Open Server Manager, select the **Features** node, and click **Add Feature** to start the Add Features Wizard.

2. Select the **Failover Clustering** option, as shown in Figure 10-13. Click **Next** and then click **Install**.

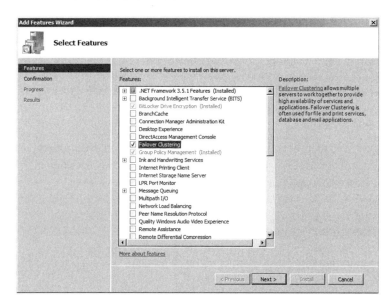

**Figure 10-13**  Adding support for failover clustering.

3. When informed that failover clustering has been installed, click **Close**.

4. Click **Start > Administrative Tools > Failover Cluster Manager**. The Failover Cluster Manager snap-in starts, as shown in Figure 10-14.

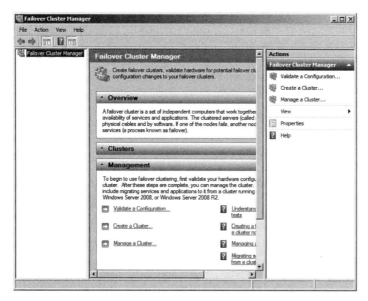

**Figure 10-14**   The Failover Cluster Manager snap-in enables you to perform all tasks associated with failover clusters.

5. In the console tree of this snap-in, right-click **Failover Cluster Manager** and choose **Manage a Cluster**. Then, browse to or type the name of the required cluster and click **OK**. If you need to create a cluster, right-click **Failover Cluster Manager** and choose **Create a Cluster**.

6. Click **Services and Applications** and then, under **Actions** (on the right), click **Configure a Service or Application**.

7. Follow the instructions in the High Availability Wizard that appears. This includes clicking **File Server** from the Select Service or Application page and typing the name of the clustered file server instance on the Client Access Point page.

8. After completing the steps in this wizard, return to the DFS Management snap-in. Use the New Replication Group Wizard or the New Member Wizard as required, and type the name of the clustered file server instance to be added to the replication group. You must store the replicated folder and staging folder on shared storage.

**NOTE**   For more information on using failover clusters, refer to "What's New in Failover Clusters" at http://technet.microsoft.com/en-us/library/dd443539(WS.10). aspx and "Add a Failover Cluster to a Replication Group" at http://technet.microsoft. com/en-us/library/dd759137.aspx.

### Generating Replication Health Reports

You can run diagnostic tests on the health and propagation status of your replication groups from the DFS Management snap-in. This provides the capability of generating the following reports:

- **Propagation test:** Creates a test file in a replicated folder to test replication progress.

- **Propagation report:** Tracks the replication progress for the test file and creates a report on this test. You must run the propagation test first.

- **Health report:** Creates a report that displays the health and efficiency of replication within the replication group. This is an HTML file that provides information on replication statistics, error and warning events, backlogged files, and other information for each member of the replication group.

To generate any of these test reports, right-click the desired replication group in the console tree of the DFS Management snap-in and choose **Create Diagnostic Report**. You receive the Diagnostic Report Wizard, as shown in Figure 10-15. Select the desired test, click **Next**, and then follow the instructions provided. Note that the time required to generate a diagnostic report varies depending on a number of factors, such as the number of replicated folders, available server resources (such as CPU and memory), WAN availability, and the options you selected in the Diagnostic Report Wizard. Microsoft suggests that you do not create diagnostic reports for more than 50 servers at one time.

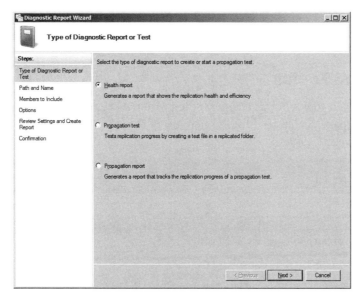

**Figure 10-15**   The Diagnostic Report Wizard enables you to create a health report or propagation test and report.

**NOTE**   You can perform most of the operations associated with DFS replication from the command line using the dfsradmin.exe command-line tool. For more information, refer to "DFS Operations Guide: Using the DFSRAdmin Command-line Tool" at www.microsoft.com/downloads/en/details.aspx?familyid=49caf978-49e9-4eb6-9cc9-72b5dd160505&displaylang=en. You can also type **dfsradmin /?** at a command prompt.

## Exam Preparation Tasks

## Review All the Key Topics

Review the most important topics in this chapter, noted with the key topics icon in the outer margin of the page. Table 10-3 lists a reference of these key topics and the page numbers on which each is found.

**Table 10-3**  Key Topics for Chapter 10

| Key Topic Element | Description | Page Number |
|---|---|---|
| Table 10-2 | Describes the two technologies included within DFS. | 433 |
| List | Shows you how to install the DFS role service. | 435 |
| Figure 10-3 | The DFS Management snap-in enables you to perform all tasks associated with DFS Namespaces and DFS Replication. | 437 |
| Figure 10-5 | Adding a folder to a DFS namespace. | 440 |
| Figure 10-7 | You can optimize polling and configure access-based enumeration from the Advanced tab of a namespace's Properties dialog box. | 443 |
| Figure 10-8 | Describes a DFS replication group. | 445 |
| List | Shows you how to set up a DFS replication group. | 447 |
| List | Describes DFS replication topologies. | 449 |
| Paragraph | Describes failover clustering. | 452 |

## Complete the Tables and Lists from Memory

Print a copy of Appendix B, "Memory Tables," (found on the CD), or at least the section for this chapter, and complete the tables and lists from memory. Appendix C, "Memory Tables Answer Key," also on the CD, includes the completed tables and lists to check your work.

## Definition of Key Terms

Define the following key terms from this chapter, and check your answers in the Glossary.

access-based enumeration, Distributed File System (DFS), DFS folder, DFS folder target, DFS Namespace, DFS Replication, failover cluster, referral, replication group, replication member

This chapter covers the following subjects:

- **Protecting Data with Windows Backup:** When problems arise with your servers, you must have the ability to recover them to a known good point in time. This section describes the various types of backup that you can perform to protect your valuable data.

- **Volume Shadow Copies:** Users occasionally make inappropriate modifications to their documents or these documents might become corrupted for reasons beyond their control. Volume shadow copies enables users to restore documents to a good point in time without the need for performing a complete restore procedure.

- **Restoring Data from Backup:** Windows Server 2008 provides several options for recovering data stored on your file servers, including a complete server or bare metal recovery that enables you to recover your server completely should major problems occur.

# CHAPTER 11

# Configuring Backup and Restore

Backing up and restoring crucial data is an important responsibility for an individual charged with management of file servers. Without some sort of backup strategy in place, loss of critical data could threaten the existence of an organization. At the very least, it can make a computer unusable. A good data backup program can make recovering from a disk crash or restoring a corrupted file a straightforward exercise. Backing up data will never be one of the more enjoyable tasks related to network administration. However, if you do not have backup copies of data stored on a computer, valuable data can be lost forever. Windows Server 2008 R2 provides the Windows Server Backup and Restore server feature that you can use to create backup copies of data on a variety of media including disk, CD-ROM, DVD, and shared network drives.

## "Do I Know This Already?" Quiz

The "Do I Know This Already?" quiz allows you to assess whether you should read this entire chapter or simply jump to the "Exam Preparation Tasks" section for review. If you are in doubt, read the entire chapter. Table 11-1 outlines the major headings in this chapter and the corresponding "Do I Know This Already?" quiz questions. You can find the answers in Appendix A, "Answers to the 'Do I Know This Already?' Quizzes."

**Table 11-1**  "Do I Know This Already?" Foundation Topics Section-to-Question Mapping

| Foundations Topics Section | Questions Covered in This Section |
| --- | --- |
| Protecting Data with Windows Backup | 1–5 |
| Volume Shadow Copies | 6–7 |
| Restoring Data from Backup | 8–10 |

1. You just finished installing Windows Server 2008 R2 on a new computer and have installed the File Server role on this computer. You want to configure Windows Server Backup to perform regular backups of this server, so you open the Administrative Tools folder to select the backup tool. But, you cannot find this tool. What do you need to do?

   a. Click **Start > Run**, type `compmgmt.msc`, and then press **Enter**. Then, select Windows Server Backup from the options in the Computer Management snap-in.

   b. Click **Start > Run**, type `ntbackup`, and then press **Enter**.

   c. Open Server Manager and select Windows Server Backup from the options in the console tree.

   d. Open Server Manager and install Windows Server Backup as a server feature.

2. You want to perform a one-time backup of your file server that will protect you in the event that a catastrophic failure of your server should occur. You should be able to use the Windows Recovery Environment in conjunction with this backup. You start the Back Up Once Wizard and receive the Select Items for Backup page. Which option should you select?

   a. **Bare metal recovery**

   b. **System state**

   c. **System and boot volumes**

   d. **VSS full backup**

3. You have chosen to use a 1-TB portable hard drive to hold scheduled backups of your Windows Server 2008 R2 file server. The hard drive contains two partitions, one of which contains copies of images from your Windows 7 Ultimate desktop computer. You run the Backup Schedule Wizard and select the portable hard drive; the next day after the first backup has been run, you check the portable drive and are unable to locate the partition that contains the images. What is the problem?

   a. You selected the **Back up to a hard disk that is dedicated for backups (recommended)** option, and then selected the portable disk. This option caused the disk to be formatted and dedicated to only store backups; consequently the partition containing the images was erased.

   b. You selected the **Back up to a volume** option, and then selected the partition containing the images. This option caused the images to be erased.

      **c.** You selected the **Back up to a volume** option, and then selected the partition on which you planned to store the backups. However, the partition was not large enough to back up everything that you had selected for backup, so the images were erased.

      **d.** You selected multiple times from the Specify Backup Time page. The multiple backups created by Windows Server Backup caused the images to be erased.

**4.** You want to create a script that will be run on all your company's servers to configure backup. Which of the following tools do you need to use to accomplish this task?

      **a.** `ntbackup`

      **b.** `ntdsutil`

      **c.** `wbadmin`

      **d.** `vssadmin`

**5.** One morning, you receive an alert about a corrupted backup catalog and notice that the overnight scheduled backup did not take place. On checking the event log, you notice an error with event number 514. What do you need to do to ensure that the next overnight backup takes place as scheduled?

      **a.** Replace the disk containing the current backups with a newly formatted, empty disk.

      **b.** Open the Windows Server Backup tool, select **Recover Catalog**, and specify the path to the folder containing the current backups.

      **c.** Open the Windows Server Backup tool and change the location of the stored backups to a remote shared folder.

      **d.** Perform a recovery of system state on your server.

6. You are the network administrator for a company with responsibility for several Windows Server 2008 file servers, on which shared folders are configured for storing user data. You have had several instances of users damaging or corrupting files they are working on. These users have asked you to restore these files and this has taken considerable quantities of time. You want to ensure that users can recover files themselves without calling for assistance and without extra administrative overhead. What should you do?

   a. Install backup and recovery software on each user's computer and hold a seminar to train users to back up their own files.

   b. Add the user accounts of these users to the Backup Operators group.

   c. Install a second hard drive on each user's computer and configure the computer to store duplicates of all files stored to the file server.

   d. Enable shadow copies on all drives containing user files. Then, instruct users to access the Previous Versions tab of a file's Properties dialog box whenever they need to restore a damaged file.

7. You are responsible for file servers in a company where the servers run a mix of the original and R2 versions of Windows Server 2008. Client computers run a mix of Windows XP, Windows Vista, and Windows 7. You have enabled volume shadow copies on file servers used to store user data. A user at a Windows XP computer reports that he accidentally deleted an important file and needs it back. He accessed the properties of the folder containing the file, but was unable to find the Previous Versions tab. What should you do so that he can recover this file with the least amount of administrative effort?

   a. Upgrade his computer to Windows 7.

   b. Download and install client software from Microsoft on his computer.

   c. Add his user account to the Backup Operators group, and then instruct him in the restore procedure.

   d. Restore the file from backup and e-mail the restored file to him.

8. You open the Windows Server Backup application on your file server and select the Recover operation to perform a restore. Which of the following actions can you perform? (Choose all that apply).

   a. Restore individual files and folders.

   b. Restore a volume that does not include the operating system.

   c. Restore the operating system on your server.

   d. Restore the operating system on another server

   e. Create an additional copy of restored files and folders in a new location.

**9.** You need to restore the system state on your file server that is running the
Server Core option of Windows Server 2008 R2. Which of the following commands should you use?

    **a.** `wbadmin start systemstaterecovery –version:`*`MM/DD/YYYY-HH:MM`*
        `-backuptarget:`*`target_drive:`* `-machine:`*`backup_server_name`*
        `-quiet`

    **b.** `wbadmin start sysrecovery –version:`*`MM/DD/YYYY-HH:MM`*
        `-backuptarget:`*`target_drive:`* `-machine:`*`backup_server_name`*
        `-quiet`

    **c.** `ntbackup start systemstaterecovery –version:`*`MM/DD/YYYY-`*
        *`HH:MM`* `-backuptarget:`*`target_drive:`* `-machine:`*`backup_server_name`*
        `-quiet`

    **d.** `ntbackup start sysrecovery –version:`*`MM/DD/YYYY-HH:MM`*
        `- backuptarget:`*`target_drive:`* `-machine:`*`backup_server_name`* `-quiet`

**10.** The system hard disk on a file server running Windows Server 2008 R2 has
failed so you install a new hard disk. Luckily, you performed a bare metal
backup of this server a few days ago. What should you do to restore the server
to operating condition?

    **a.** Press **F8** as the server starts, select **Safe Mode** from the menu that appears, and log on with administrative credentials. Start the Windows
Server Backup program, select **Recover**, select the **A backup stored on
another location** option, and then select the location where the backup
is stored.

    **b.** Start the server from the Windows Server 2008 R2 DVD-ROM, select
**Safe Mode**, select **System Image Recovery**, and then select **Use the
latest available system image (recommended)**.

    **c.** Start the server from the Windows Server 2008 R2 DVD-ROM, select
**Repair your computer**, select **System Image Recovery**, and then select **Use the latest available system image (recommended)**.

    **d.** Use the Windows Server 2008 R2 DVD-ROM to install a new copy of
the operating system. Then, start the Windows Server Backup program,
select **Recover**, select the **A backup stored on another location** option, and then select the location where the backup is stored.

**Foundation Topics**

## Protecting Data with Windows Backup

All computers fail sooner or later. Or perhaps someone (maybe even you) will accidentally delete valuable data. Or a newly released virus could damage your carefully built and configured file folder hierarchy, and the damages could be propagated through normal replication. Perhaps an intruder gets in and does a lot of damage before he's detected; this occasionally happens despite the best security measures being in place. A good backup and recovery strategy is vital to an organization's continued well-being. Without it, your organization's very existence could be threatened. Backup and recovery is critical for your critical production files whether they are stored in a normal folder hierarchy or a Distributed File System (DFS) namespace; the same obviously holds true for your Active Directory Domain Services (AD DS) database.

Windows Server 2008 and Windows Server 2008 R2 include a new backup application called Windows Server Backup. This application enables you to protect against all types of data loss for reasons ranging from hardware or storage media failure to accidental deletion of objects or the entire DFS namespace or AD DS database. It works somewhat differently from the older backup application included with Windows 2000 and Windows Server 2003. The following are some of the more significant differences:

- Windows Server Backup works by backing up critical volumes. These are the volumes that are required for recovering your server, including the system and boot volumes. On a domain controller, they include the SYSVOL volume, as well as the volumes that host the Ntds.dit database file and the AD DS log files.

- Windows Server backup enables you to back up all volumes on your server, selected volumes, folders, or files, or the system state. Windows Server Backup also enables you to create a backup that you can use for bare metal recovery.

- The composition of the *system state data* depends on the server roles installed on the server and the volumes that host the critical operating system and role files. System State consists of at least the following items and can include more depending upon the installed server roles:
  - Registry
  - COM+ Class Registration database
  - System and boot files

- AD DS and Active Directory Certificate Services (AD CS) databases
- SYSVOL folder
- Cluster service information
- Internet Information Services (IIS) metadirectory
- System files that are under Windows Resource Protection

- Windows Server Backup provides several features that enable you to perform backups and recover system and data files, including the following:

  - **Windows Server Backup tools:** Enables you to create backups using the Windows Server Backup MMC snap-in, the Wbadmin command-line tool, or the Windows PowerShell cmdlets for Windows Server backup.

  - **Shadow copies of shared folders:** Enables copies of data in shared folders to be created "on the fly," so to speak. Users can easily recover a file to an earlier point in time to undo intentional or improper changes to the data.

  - **Windows Recovery Environment:** Provides several tools that assist you in recovering a server that will not start up normally.

- You can use Windows Server Backup to perform a manual backup or schedule automated backups to a dedicated backup volume physically located on the server itself.

- In addition to local and network-based hard disk volumes, you can use CDs or DVDs as backup media. Magnetic tape volumes are no longer supported.

- Windows Server Backup does not enable you to back up individual files or folders. You must back up the entire volume that hosts the files or folders to be backed up.

**NOTE** For more information about general concepts and considerations of Windows Server Backup in Windows Server 2008 R2, refer to "Windows Server Backup Overview" at http://technet.microsoft.com/en-us/library/cc772523.aspx and "Backup and Recovery Overview for Windows Server 2008 R2" at http://technet.microsoft.com/en-us/library/dd979562(WS.10).aspx. For more information about new features in Windows Server Backup for Windows Server 2008 R2, refer to "What's New in Windows Server Backup" at http://technet.microsoft.com/en-us/library/ee344835(WS.10).aspx.

### Backup Permissions

Not just anybody has the right to back up and restore data on any files and folders. If this weren't true, anyone could grab data from a computer and make off with it to a competitor's or other unauthorized location. You must have the appropriate permissions and user rights for the data that you want to back up. On a Windows Server 2008 domain controller, this means belonging to the Administrators, Server Operators, or Backup Operators built-in groups by default.

You can modify the default backup rights by using Group Policy. The three groups mentioned here, by default, have the Backup files and directories and Restore files and directories rights assigned to them. It is good practice to separate these rights so that any one individual does not possess both of them. Some companies remove the Restore files and directories right from the Backup Operators group. They then create a Restore Operators group and assign this group the Restore files and directories right.

**NOTE** For more information on using Group Policy to assign user rights, refer to "Assign User Rights to a Group in AD DS" at http://technet.microsoft.com/en-us/library/cc754142.aspx.

**CAUTION** Members of the Backup Operators group can perform manual backups but cannot schedule backups by default. You must possess administrative credentials to schedule backups, and you cannot delegate this privilege.

### Installing Windows Server Backup

Unlike previous versions of Windows, Windows Server Backup is not installed by default; you must install it as a server feature from Server Manager. Use the following procedure to install Windows Server Backup:

1. Open Server Manager and select the **Features** node.

2. In the details pane, click **Add Features**.

3. Scroll the features list to select **Windows Server Backup Features**. If you also want command-line tools for performing backups, expand **Windows Server Backup Features** and select this option, as shown in Figure 11-1.

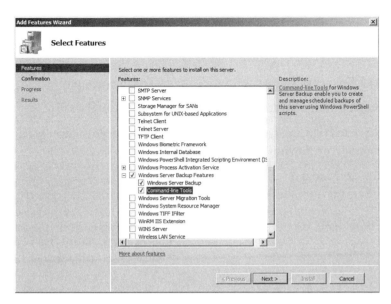

**Figure 11-1**    You need to install Windows Server Backup Features from the Add Features Wizard of Server Manager.

4. If you receive a message asking to install required features, click **Add Required Features**. Then, click **Next**.

5. Review the information provided by the Confirm Installation Selections page and click **Install**.

6. When informed that installation is complete, click **Close**.

7. If you receive a message requesting that you restart your server, click **Yes**.

**TIP**    Be aware of the new backup utilities in Windows Server 2008 and the need to install them before use. Windows Server 2008 no longer supports the `ntbackup.exe` utility or the Automated System Recovery (ASR) tool, as an exam question might attempt to trick you on.

### Backing Up Your File Server

Windows Server Backup enables you to back up your server to different types of media, including fixed or removable hard disk volume installed on the server, a network share, or removable media, such as CDs or DVDs. To perform this type of backup, you must be a member of the Administrators, Server Operators, or Backup Operators group, and an appropriate backup volume must be available. To perform a single backup of critical volumes, proceed as follows:

1. Open Windows Server Backup by using any of the following methods:

    ■ Click **Start > Administrative Tools > Windows Server Backup**.

    ■ Click **Start** and type backup in the Start menu Search field. Then, select **Windows Server Backup** from the list that appears.

    ■ Open **Server Manager**, expand **Storage**, and then select **Windows Server Backup** from this location.

2. From the **Action** menu, select **Backup Once**. A Windows Server Backup message box appears as the program is initialized. After a few seconds, the Backup Once Wizard starts with a Backup Options page, as shown in Figure 11-2.

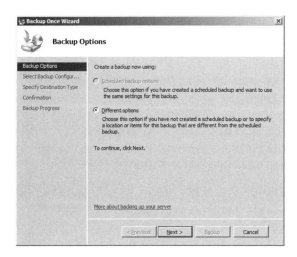

**Figure 11-2**    The Backup Options page provides the choice of using previous options if available and configuring different options.

3. If you have previously scheduled a backup on this server, you can use the **Scheduled backup options** option to perform this backup (in the original version of Windows Server 2008, this option is labeled **The same options that you used in the Backup Schedule Wizard for scheduled backups**). Otherwise, click **Different options** and then click **Next**.

4. The Select Backup Configuration page offers you a choice between a full server backup or custom backup options. To back up the entire server, select the **Full server (recommended)** option. To customize your backup, select **Custom** and click **Next**.

5. If you selected the **Custom** option, you receive the Select Items for Backup page. Click **Add Items**, select the drives that you want to backup, and then click **OK**.

6. You are returned to the Select Items for Backup page, where these items are automatically added, as shown in Figure 11-3.

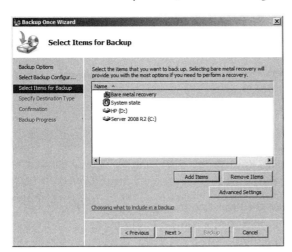

**Figure 11-3**   The Select Items for Backup page displays the items you selected for backup.

7. To choose the type of Volume Shadow Copy Service (VSS) backup to be created, click **Advanced Settings** to display the dialog box shown in Figure 11-4. Select the appropriate option. You can also select types of files that are automatically excluded from backup from the Exclusions tab of this dialog box. When finished, click **OK** to return to the Backup Once Wizard.

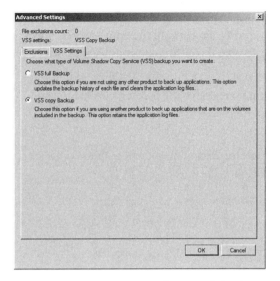

**Figure 11-4**   The Advanced Settings dialog box presents two options for performing a VSS backup.

8. Click **Next** to access the Specify Destination Type page, select either **Local drives** or **Remote shared folder** as required, and click **Next** again.

9. If you choose the **Remote shared folder** option, type the path to the shared folder on the Specify Remote Folder page as shown in Figure 11-5; then, specify logon credentials if requested. If you select the **Local drives** option, select a suitable volume. Then, click **Next**.

**Figure 11-5**   Windows Server Backup enables you to specify a remote location and access control options for your backup.

10. Review the options presented by the Confirmation page and click **Backup** to perform the backup.

11. The Backup Progress page charts the status of the backup operation, as shown in Figure 11-6. When you are informed that the backup is completed, click **Close** (or to allow the backup to continue in the background, click **Close** at any time). Windows Server Backup displays this backup and its results in the main portion of the application window.

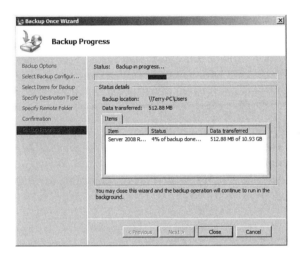

**Figure 11-6**   Windows Server Backup tracks the progress of backing up your files.

**NOTE**   Backups are stored in a folder named WindowsImageBackup located in the location you specified in Step 9 of the previous procedure. Subfolders are automatically created that are named for the computer being backed up; sub-subfolders named for the backup date store the actual backup files.For more information on performing file server backups, refer to "Windows Server Backup Step-by-Step Guide for Windows Server 2008 R2" at http://technet.microsoft.com/en-us/library/ee849849(WS.10).aspx. For additional tips and recommendations with regard to choosing what to backup and where to store your backups, refer to "Backing Up Your Server" at http://technet.microsoft.com/en-us/library/cc753528.aspx.

**TIP**   You can also perform backups to removable media, including recordable CDs, DVDs, or external hard drives. This is especially convenient for creating an additional backup copy for offsite storage purposes, or for preparing to install a new domain controller using the Install from Media option. The procedure is similar to that described in the previous section. Windows Server Backup will ask for additional media as required.

## Performing a Bare Metal Backup

The Windows Server Backup application provides an option to perform a *bare metal* backup. This is essentially a complete backup that enables you to recover your server from the Windows Recovery Environment should a catastrophic failure occur. To do so, use the procedure in the previous section, and at Step 5, when the Add Items dialog box appears, click **Bare metal recovery**. Selecting this option automatically selects the **System state** option, as well as the boot and system volumes. Click **OK** and complete the steps in this procedure. Ensure that you have stored this backup to a network location as previously described in Figure 11-5 or to removable media, such as DVD discs or a portable hard drive.

## Scheduling a Backup

You can schedule a backup to take place when the server utilization is minimized, such as during the night. Scheduling a backup also ensures that it is performed on a regular basis without administrator intervention.

The procedure for scheduling a backup is similar to that described in the previous section, as the following steps show:

1. From the **Action** menu of the Windows Server Backup application, click **Backup Schedule**.

2. The Backup Schedule Wizard starts with a Getting Started page. Click **Next**.

3. The Select Backup Configuration page displays the same options previously described. Make a selection and click **Next**.

4. If you selected the **Custom** option, select the items to be backed up as described in Steps 5 to 8 of the previous procedure and shown in Figure 11-3.

5. From the Specify Backup Time page shown in Figure 11-7, select one or more times a day for the backup to take place and click **Next**.

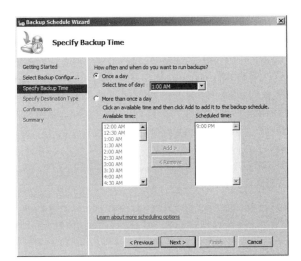

**Figure 11-7**  The Backup Schedule Wizard enables you to specify the time at which you want the backup to occur.

6. Select an appropriate backup volume from the choices given in Figure 11-8 and click **Next**.

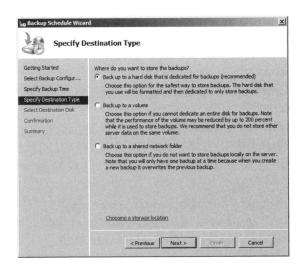

**Figure 11-8**  The Backup Schedule Wizard provides three choices for backup destination.

7. If you choose the default option shown in Figure 11-8, the Select Destination Disk page enables you to select a destination disk. If necessary, click **Show All Available Disks** to locate an available disk. If you choose the **Back up to a volume** option, you receive the Select Destination Volume page. Click **Add**

to select a volume to be added. You receive the warning shown in Figure 11-9 that each scheduled backup will erase the previous one. Click **OK** and then select a destination volume from a wizard page similar to that previously shown in Figure 11-6.

**Figure 11-9**  When performing a scheduled backup to a remote location, each backup erases the previous one.

8. If you choose the default option shown in Figure 11-8, you are warned that the selected disk will be reformatted. Click **Yes** to continue or **No** to select an alternate location. If you click **Yes**, all data on the selected disk (all volumes) will be lost, so ensure that there is no data of value on this disk before you begin this procedure.

9. You receive a Confirmation page listing the options you have configured. Click **Finish** to format the disk or volume and create the backup schedule. After the disk is formatted, note the warning on the Summary page of the wizard and click **Close**. Windows Server Backup provides information on the regularly scheduled backup in its main application window.

After you schedule a backup, the option previously shown in Figure 11-2 becomes available so that you can use the options you specified in running the Backup Schedule Wizard to perform an unscheduled backup at any time.

### Using the wbadmin Command

You can perform backups from the command line with the new wbadmin utility, which is installed with the Add Features Wizard when you select the option described earlier in this chapter to add command-line tools. This tool supports subcommands that enable or disable scheduled backups, run one-time backups, list details of available backups as well as items included in the backups, provide the status of a currently running backup, and perform system state backups and recoveries.

Use the following command syntax to perform a backup:

```
wbadmin start backup -backuptarget:targetdrive: -include:sourcedrive:
```

In this command, *sourcedrive* is the drive whose contents you are backing up and *targetdrive* is the drive on which you are storing the backup. For example, to back up the contents of the C: drive to a portable hard drive in E:, you type

```
wbadmin start backup -backuptarget:e: -include:c:
```

Table 11-2 describes the subcommands supported by wbadmin.

**Table 11-2**   wbadmin Subcommands

| Subcommand | Purpose |
|---|---|
| start backup | Performs a one-time backup |
| stop job | Stops a currently running backup or restore operation |
| get versions | Lists details of available backups at a specified location |
| get items | Lists items currently backed up |
| get status | Displays the status of a currently running backup operation |

All these subcommands use a comprehensive list of parameters. To display available parameters for any subcommand, type **wbadmin *subcommand* /?.**

> **NOTE**   For additional information on the wbadmin utility, including a comprehensive list of the available subcommands, refer to "Wbadmin" at http://technet.microsoft.com/en-us/library/cc754015(WS.10).aspx.

## Restoring the Backup Catalog

Windows Server Backup stores detailed information about backups in a catalog file that is located in the Catalog subfolder of the WindowsImageBackup folder that was previously mentioned. This file includes information such as the volumes that were backed up and where the backups are located and is used to locate specific files and folders during a restore operation. A master catalog is also stored on the computer being backed up at the %systemdrive%\System Volume Information\WindowsImageBackup\Catalog location. If the file becomes corrupted, you are alerted and an error event 514 is logged to the system event log. If this happens, you need to restore the catalog before you perform future backups. In such an event, the Windows Server Backup application provides a Recover Catalog option. (Note that this option appears only if the catalog is corrupted.)

Use the following procedure to restore the backup catalog:

1. From the **Action** menu of the Windows Server Backup application, click **Recover Catalog**.

2. The Catalog Recovery Wizard starts with a Getting Started page. Click **Next**.

3. Perform one of the following actions on the Specify Storage Type page and click **Next**:

   ▪ Click **Local drives**, and if using a locally stored backup, on the Select Backup Location page, select the drive that contains the required backup. If using DVDs or other media, insert the last DVD of the series, and then click **Next**. If using a backup stored on another server, select the server whose backup is to be used.

   ▪ Click **Remote shared folder**, and on the Specify Remote Folder page type the path to the folder containing the required backup.

   ▪ If you don't have a backup that you can use to recover the catalog, click **I do not have any usable backups**. You will be able to delete the corrupted catalog.

4. On the Confirmation page, review the options selected and click **Finish**.

5. When the recovery is complete, you receive a summary page. Click **Close**.

6. Close and re-open Windows Server Backup to refresh the view before proceeding with creation of a new backup.

If no backups are available for recovering the catalog, and you delete the corrupted catalog as mentioned in this procedure, information about previous backups are lost and the backups are inaccessible from Windows Server Backup. In such a case, you should create a new backup after deleting the catalog.

### Managing Backups Remotely

The Server Manager tool or the Windows Server Backup snap-in enable you to perform a backup on a remote server. Right-click **Server Manager** and choose **Connect to Another Computer**. From the Windows Server Backup snap-in, click **Action > Connect to Another Server**. The Connect to Another Server dialog box, as shown in Figure 11-10, enables you to type or browse to the required computer (for example, Server3). Click **OK** and then proceed as described in previous sections.

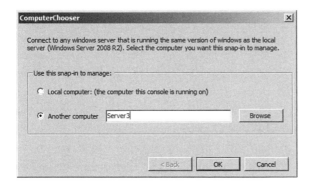

**Figure 11-10** You can connect to another computer to perform a remote backup.

**TIP** Windows Server Backup stores backups in virtual hard disk (VHD) format. You can use Microsoft Virtual PC or Virtual Server to mount a backup image as a disk drive on a virtual machine and browse its contents as if it were a normal disk drive.

## Volume Shadow Copies

Originally introduced in Windows Server 2003, Windows Server 2008 R2 provides the Volume Shadow Copy Service (VSS), which enables you to create point-in-time copies of data that is in use at the time a backup is running. Enabling volume shadow copies enables users to recover files to a previous point in time without the need for performing a complete restore operation. Users can perform actions such as the following without assistance from desktop support staff:

- **Recover accidentally deleted files:** Users can open and copy a previous version of the file.

- **Recover an accidentally overwritten file:** Users can recover overwritten data from a previous version of a file.

- **Compare different versions of a file:** Users can check on changes that have been made to a file (for example, responses to editorial comments) since a previous version was created.

> **TIP**   The Volume Shadow Copy Service is also known as the Volume Snapshot Service. Microsoft appears to use both terms interchangeably, using the acronym VSS for both.

### Using Windows Explorer to Manage Shadow Copies

Shadow copies are not enabled by default. You can enable shadow copies on a per-volume basis for any volume that is formatted with the NTFS file system. To manage shadow copies from Windows Explorer, use the following procedure:

1. Right-click the volume on which you want to configure shadow copies and choose **Configure Shadow Copies**.

2. You receive the Shadow Copies dialog box, which is shown in Figure 11-11.

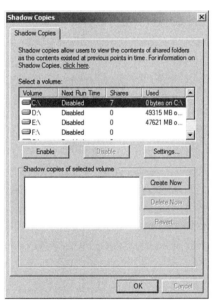

**Figure 11-11**   The Shadow Copies dialog box enables you to specify a volume on which you want to enable shadow copies.

3. Select the volume on which you want to enable shadow copies and click **Enable**.

4. You receive the message box shown in Figure 11-12, informing you that default settings are not appropriate for servers with a high I/O load. Click the

link provided to obtain more information from the Windows Server Help files about shadow copies. Click **Yes** to proceed.

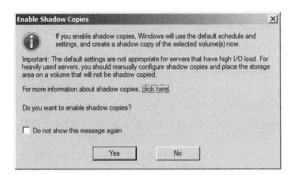

**Figure 11-12**   Enabling shadow copies.

5. You are returned to the Shadow Copies dialog box. A shadow copy is immediately created and the date and time appear in the field provided.

6. To modify the default settings used for creating shadow copies, click the **Settings** command button. The Settings dialog box that appears enables you to configure the following properties (click **OK** when finished):

   - **Storage area:** You can select the volume to be managed if you have enabled shadow copies on more than one volume. You can modify the maximum size used by shadow copies (which is 10 percent of the volume size by default). Specify the desired limit (at least 300 MB) or select the **No limit** option if desired.

   - **Schedule:** Click **Schedule** to modify the schedule at which shadow copies are created. By default, shadow copies are created twice daily on each weekday, at 7:00 a.m. and 12:00 p.m. You can specify additional days, times, or multiple shadow copy schedules.

7. To immediately create a shadow copy, click **Create Now**.

8. To disable shadow copies on any volume, select it and click **Disable**.

9. When finished, click **OK**.

**NOTE**   For more information about using volume shadow copies, refer to "Shadow Copies of Shared Folders" at http://technet.microsoft.com/en-us/library/cc771305.aspx.

### Using the Command Line to Manage Shadow Copies

Windows Server 2008 provides the `vssadmin` command-line utility for managing shadow copies. This command displays currently available shadow copy backups, as well as all installed shadow copy writers and providers. The following are several of the more frequently used commands:

To create shadow copies on the D:\ volume, use the following command:

```
vssadmin create shadow /for=D:
```

To display the shadow copy storage associations, use the following command:

```
vssadmin list shadowstorage
```

To display information about all existing shadow copies on a specified volume, such as the D:\ volume, use the following command:

```
vssadmin list shadows /for=D:
```

To delete shadow copies on an existing volume, such as the D:\ volume, use the following command:

```
vssadmin delete shadows /for=D:\ [/oldest | /all |
/shadow=<ShadowID>] [/quiet]
```

In this command, `/oldest` deletes only the oldest shadow copy, `/all` deletes all shadow copies, and `/shadow=<ShadowID>` deletes the shadow copy specified by *ShadowID*.

> **NOTE**   For more information about the `vssadmin` command and sample command syntaxes, refer to "Vssadmin" at http://technet.microsoft.com/en-us/library/cc754968(WS.10).aspx and select the command you want to view syntax information for.

### Using Volume Shadow Copies to Recover a File or Folder

It is simple to recover a file or folder to a previous version when the Volume Shadow Copies feature is enabled. Right-click a file or folder, choose **Properties**, and then select the **Previous Versions** tab. As shown in Figure 11-13, this tab lists the date and time at which each previous version was created. Select a modification date and time to perform any of the following actions from this tab:

- Click **Open** to open an Explorer window displaying the contents of a folder at the selected date and time. For a file, this action opens the file at the selected date and time using its default application.

- Select **Copy** to open a dialog box that enables you to specify a folder into which you want to copy the folder or file as it existed. This enables you to compare the contents of the current and older versions of the file or folder.

- Select **Restore** to restore the previous version of the file or folder. You receive a message box asking you if you are sure you want to restore the file or folder. Click **Restore** to proceed or **Cancel** to quit. If you click **Restore**, all changes to the file or folder since the selected date will be permanently lost.

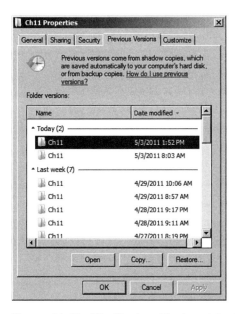

**Figure 11-13**   The Previous Versions tab of a file or folder's Properties dialog box enables you to restore the file or folder to a previous point in time.

**NOTE**   Support for volume shadow copies is included by default for computers running Windows Vista, Windows 7, Windows Server 2008, or later only. You can add support for older computers including Windows XP, Windows Server 2003, and Windows 2000 (Service Pack 3 or later) by downloading and installing client software from http://technet.microsoft.com/en-us/windowsserver/bb405951.aspx.

# Restoring Data from Backup

The whole idea behind planning, organizing, and undertaking a backup job is that data will be easy to recover in the event of a disaster. You should be familiar enough with the Windows Server 2008 restore options to be able to restore a single file or your entire server as required.

## Using Windows Backup to Recover Data

After you perform a backup, Windows Server Backup makes it simple to restore data in the event of a hardware or software failure of some kind. Use the following procedure to restore data.

1. Open Windows Server Backup using any of the methods previously presented.

2. From the **Action** menu, select **Recover**. A Windows Server Backup message box appears as the program is initialized. After a few seconds, the Recovery Wizard starts with a Getting Started page, as shown in Figure 11-14.

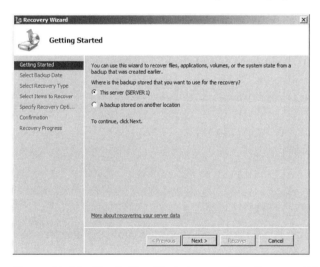

**Figure 11-14**   The Getting Started page of the Recovery Wizard enables you to recover data from either the local computer or a backup stored externally.

3. Select the appropriate location and click **Next**.

4. If you select the **A backup stored on another location** option, you receive the Specify Location Type dialog box, as shown in Figure 11-15.

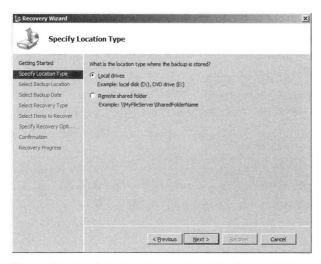

**Figure 11-15**   Selecting the location of the files or folders that you want to restore.

5. Select the location where the backup is stored and click **Next**.

6. Select the local hard drive or type the UNC path to the remote shared folder containing the backup as required, and then click **Next**.

7. On the Select Backup Date page, specify the date and time of the backup to be used and click **Next**.

8. The Select Recovery Type page offers the options shown in Figure 11-16 for specifying the type of items to be recovered. Select the required option and click **Next**.

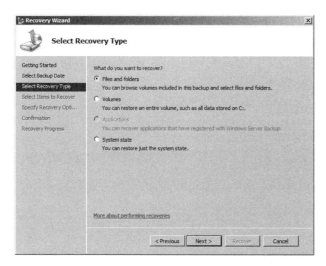

**Figure 11-16**   The Select Recovery Type page offers four options for the items to be recovered.

9. The next page depends on the option chosen in Figure 11-16. If you choose the **Files and folders** option, you receive the Select Items to Recover page, as shown in Figure 11-17. Browse to locate the files or folders to be recovered. When finished, click **Next**.

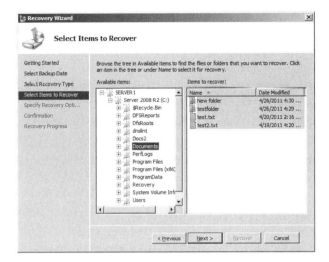

**Figure 11-17**    Selecting the items that will be recovered.

10. You receive the Specify Recovery Options page, as shown in Figure 11-18. Choose an appropriate destination and option for resolving conflicts and click **Next**.

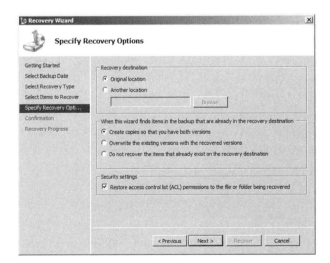

**Figure 11-18**    You have options that determine where the recovered items will be placed and how conflicts with existing items will be resolved.

11. The Confirmation page summarizes the options you selected. If you need to make any changes, click **Previous**. To proceed with recovery, click **Recover**.

12. The Recovery Progress page charts the progress of file restoration. When complete, it informs you. Click **Close**. You return to the Windows Server Backup application, where a message is displayed that informs you of the activity that has taken place.

**CAUTION**    Make a habit of testing your backups and restores. Ensure that you are creating valid backups by performing test restores on a regular basis. Use the **Another location** option, shown in Figure 11-18, to restore data to a different folder and verify that the restored data is present. Otherwise, you may not realize something is wrong with your backups until it is too late.

**NOTE**    The restore tool in the Windows Server Backup utility is not compatible with the .bkf files created using the Windows NT/2000/XP/Server 2003 Ntbackup program. However, Microsoft makes a version of the Windows NT Backup and Restore utility available for download, should you need to restore backups created on an older Windows computer. To obtain details on using this utility and download a version that is appropriate for the edition of Windows that you are running, access "Description of the Windows NT Backup Restore Utility for Windows 7 and for Windows Server 2008 R2" at http://support.microsoft.com/kb/974674.

### Restoring User Profiles

When a user logs on to his computer, the operating system generates a *user profile*. This profile is comprised of desktop settings, files, application data, and the specific environment established by the user. For example, a user named Peter logs on, changes his desktop wallpaper to a picture of his dog, edits the user information in Microsoft Word, configures a dial-up connection to his Internet service provider (ISP), and adjusts the mouse so that it is easier to double-click. When Sharon logs on to the same computer using her own account, she sees the default Windows settings, not Peter's settings. When Peter logs on next, Windows finds Peter's existing profile and loads his settings—the wallpaper, the Word data, the dial-up connection, and the mouse click settings.

For computers that are connected to a Windows network, you can configure a user profile to roam the network with the user. In an AD DS domain environment, you can create a default profile that is supplied to all domain users; you can even make this profile mandatory so that changes made by the user are discarded when she logs off. For a non-domain environment, the profile is stored in a subfolder in the Users folder on the `%systemdrive%` volume. To create a roaming profile, you can configure the profile to be placed on a network drive rather than a local hard disk, thereby making it accessible to the user regardless of which computer she is using. When you back up the Users folder on a Windows 7 or Windows Server 2008 R2 computer, you automatically back up all user profiles that have been configured on the computer.

You can restore a user profile in exactly the same fashion as already described for restoring files and folders. Simply select the **Files and folders** option previously shown in Figure 11-16 and browse to the Users folder. Double-click this folder and then select the username to restore this user's profile. Then, click **Next** and follow the remainder of the procedure already described to complete restoring the user's profile. You can also restore a portion of a user's profile by double-clicking the username to open the profile and then selecting the subfolder or subfolders (such as Contacts, Documents, Downloads, and so on) you need to restore.

### Recovering System State

Recovering system state is similar, but it offers a few different options. If your server is configured as an AD DS domain controller, you need to restart the server in Directory Services Restore Mode (DSRM) by pressing **F8** at startup to access the Advanced Boot Options screen and using the arrow keys to select this option. On a file server not configured as a domain controller, this action is not needed. After doing so, proceed as follows:

1. Perform Steps 1 to 8 of the previous procedure to select the **System state** option from the Select Recovery Type page, shown in Figure 11-16.

2. The Select Location for System State Recovery page shown in Figure 11-19 provides options for recovering your system state backup. New to Windows Server 2008 R2 is the option to perform an authoritative restore of Active Directory files from the Recovery Wizard. Make the appropriate selections and click **Next**.

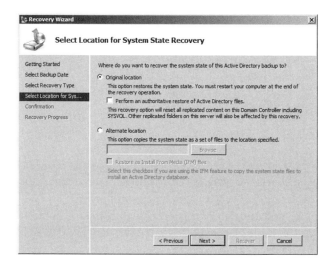

**Figure 11-19**    The Recovery Wizard enables you to recover System State to either the original or another location.

3. You receive the warning shown in Figure 11-20 that all replicated content will be resynchronized after recovery. Click **OK** to proceed.

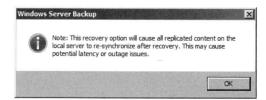

**Figure 11-20**    You are warned that all replicated content will be re-synchronized.

4. Review the information presented on the Confirmation page. If necessary, select **Previous** to make any needed corrections. If you want to reboot the server automatically, select the check box labeled **Automatically reboot the server to complete the recovery process**. Then, click **Recover** to proceed.

5. You receive the message box shown in Figure 11-21 informing you that system state recovery cannot be interrupted or cancelled once started. Click **Yes** to continue.

**Figure 11-21** You cannot interrupt system state recovery while it is in progress.

6. The Recovery Progress page charts the progress of system state recovery. This process takes several minutes; the Recovery Progress page will provide an estimate of the remaining time. You must allow this process to complete before you can click **Close**.

7. Once informed that recovery is complete, the server reboots automatically if you selected this option. Otherwise, you receive a message box informing you must restart the computer to complete recovery. Click **Restart**.

8. Allow the server to reboot into normal mode and log on as the domain administrator (or local administrator on a standalone server).

9. You might receive a message informing you that the restore has completed and asking you to reboot once more. If so, click **Restart now**.

### Performing a Full Server or Bare Metal Recovery of a Windows Server 2008 R2 Computer

If you have a full server backup available, you can also perform a full server recovery of your server. This backup can be located on a separate internal hard drive or on an external hard drive, DVD, or network share. You must also have the Windows Server 2008 R2 installation DVD. The full server recovery procedure restores the operating system, AD DS, and all applications and data from all volumes of the original server.

When performing a full server or bare metal recovery, you need to specify the following:

- The backup that will be used.
- Whether you're performing a full server recovery or just recovering the operating system.

■ Whether you are formatting and repartitioning your disks. If you choose to do so, remember that all existing data will be deleted, including any volumes the server might be currently using but were not included in the backup.

In addition, ensure that a new hard disk is at least as large as the disk that contained the volumes that were backed up, regardless of the size of these volumes. For example, if you backed up a 500-GB hard disk that contained only a 200-GB volume, you must use at least a 500-GB disk when performing the restore operation. Furthermore, when recovering just the operating system, ensure that you have a backup available that contains at least the server's critical volumes. When recovering the full server, ensure that you have a backup available that contains all server volumes. For performing a bare metal recovery, ensure that you have a bare metal or full server backup, as previously mentioned.

Use the following procedure to perform a full server recovery of Windows Server 2008 R2. The steps for the original version of Windows Server 2008 are the same, except that some of the wording on the dialog boxes is different:

1. Insert the Windows Server 2008 R2 DVD-ROM and start your computer.

2. When prompted, press a key to boot the server from the DVD.

3. From the Install Windows screen, click **Next** and then click **Repair your computer**.

4. The System Recovery Options dialog box displays any existing Windows installations on the computer. (If you are recovering to a new disk, the list should be empty.) Select your operating system and click **Next**.

5. On the System Recovery Options dialog box shown in Figure 11-22, select **System Image Recovery**.

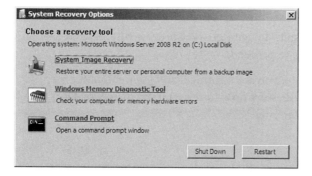

**Figure 11-22**  The System Recovery Options dialog box presents options for recovering a computer that will not start normally.

6. After a few seconds, the Select a system image backup dialog box appears. In most cases, you should leave the default of **Use the latest available system image (recommended)** selected. If you need to select a different image, select **Restore a different backup** to display the **Select the location of the system image** page, and then do one of the following:

- Select the computer that contains the backup to be used, and then click **Next**. Then, on the Select the system image to restore page, select the required backup, and then click **Next**.

- Click **Advanced** to browse for a backup located in a network shared folder and provide the UNC path to the backup. Then, click **Next**.

7. The Choose additional restore options page shown in Figure 11-23 provides additional options. Select any of these that are needed and click **Next**.

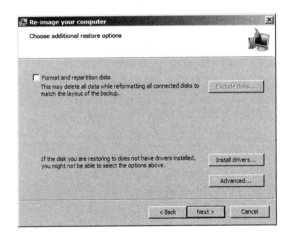

**Figure 11-23**   You can select from these additional restore options.

8. You are warned that the System Image Recovery process will erase all data on the selected disks. Click **Yes** to proceed.

9. When the restore is complete, you are informed, and your computer is restarted automatically. Click **Restart now** to restart immediately or **Don't restart** to restart your computer later.

**NOTE**   For additional information on the options available when performing this procedure and additional cautions you should observe in a domain environment, refer to "Recover the Operating System or Full Server" at http://technet.microsoft.com/en-us/library/cc755163.aspx.

### Using the `wbadmin` Command to Recover Your Server

You learned about the use of the `wbadmin` command-line tool for backing up your server earlier in this chapter. This command also enables you to restore your server. You can use this utility to restore system state from a full server backup, a critical system volumes backup, or a system state backup. Use the following procedure:

1. If necessary, restart your computer into safe mode and log on with an administrative account.

2. Open a command prompt and type the following:

   ```
   wbadmin get versions -backuptarget:target_drive:
      -machine:backup_server_name
   ```

   In this command, `target_drive` is the location of the backup to be restored and `backup_server_name` is the name of the server to be restored. This command returns information on the available backup target that you use for the next command.

3. Type the following command:

   ```
   wbadmin start systemstaterecovery -version:MM/DD/YYYY-HH:MM
      -backuptarget:target_drive: -machine:backup_server_name -quiet
   ```

   In this command, `MM/DD/YYYY-HH:MM` is the version of the backup to be restored, `-quiet` runs the command without user prompts, and the other items are as in the previous command.

4. When you are informed that the restore has completed, restart your computer. If you receive a message that other people are logged on to the computer, click **Yes**.

5. When the computer restarts, log on with an appropriate account, such as a domain account.

**TIP** You can also use the `wbadmin start sysrecovery` command to perform a bare metal recovery of your server. To do so, you need to use the Windows Server 2008 R2 DVD-ROM to access the System Recovery Options dialog box (as described earlier in this section) and choose the **Command Prompt** option, as shown in Figure 11-22. For details of the command syntax involved, refer to "`wbadmin start sysrecovery`" at http://technet.microsoft.com/en-us/library/cc742118(WS.10).aspx.

## Exam Preparation Tasks

## Review All the Key Topics

Review the most important topics in this chapter, noted with the key topics icon in the outer margin of the page. Table 11-3 lists a reference of these key topics and the page numbers on which each is found.

**Table 11-3**   Key Topics for Chapter 11

| Key Topic Element | Description | Page Number |
| --- | --- | --- |
| List | Shows you how to perform a backup of your file server. | 468 |
| Figure 11-3 | Selecting items for backup. | 469 |
| Figure 11-7 | Specifying a time at which the backup should take place. | 473 |
| Table 11-2 | Describes Wbadmin subcommands. | 475 |
| Paragraph | Describes the Windows Server Backup catalog. | 475 |
| Figure 11-11 | Enabling the Shadow Copies feature on Windows Server volumes. | 478 |
| List | Shows how to use Windows Backup to recover data. | 482 |
| Figure 11-16 | You can perform several different types of server recovery. | 483 |
| Figure 11-19 | You have several options when performing a system state recovery. | 487 |
| Figure 11-22 | You have three recovery options when your server is unable to start normally. | 489 |

## Complete the Tables and Lists from Memory

Print a copy of Appendix B, "Memory Tables," (found on the CD), or at least the section for this chapter, and complete the tables and lists from memory. Appendix C, "Memory Tables Answer Key," also on the CD, includes the completed tables and lists to check your work.

## Definition of Key Terms

Define the following key terms from this chapter, and check your answers in the Glossary.

backup catalog file, bare metal backup, bare metal recovery, critical volumes, shadow copies, Startup Repair, System State data, volume shadow copy service (VSS), `vssadmin.exe`, Windows Server Backup, `wbadmin.exe`

This chapter covers the following subjects:

- **File Server Resource Manager (FSRM):** FSRM provides a set of utilities that facilitates the management of files, folders, and volumes on your file server. This section introduces you to the various actions you can perform from the FSRM console.

- **Configuring Disk and Volume Quotas:** Windows Server 2008 provides two means of specifying quotas that limit the amount of disk space used by users storing files on the server. This section compares these two methods and shows you how to use each to configure quotas.

- **Storage Manager for SANs:** This is a server feature that facilitates the management of resources located on a storage-area network (SAN) and enables you to configure volumes on the SAN to appear to users as if they were physically located on the server to which they are connecting.

# CHAPTER 12

# Managing File Server Resources

In recent years, storage space on modern computers has expanded rapidly. Despite this fact, demands on storage space have escalated rapidly and dramatically. Add to that the requirements of various regulatory agencies for maintaining and providing rapid access to critical information that all companies must make available when requested. The File Server role service in Windows Server 2008 provides several tools that facilitate your management of disk space on your server. In this chapter, you learn how to place quotas on users accessing your servers; you also learn about various technologies you can access to create reports on resource usage on the server, as well as a management tool that lets you work with storage area networks that contain disk space accessible to different servers as though they were located on specific servers.

## "Do I Know This Already?" Quiz

The "Do I Know This Already?" quiz allows you to assess whether you should read this entire chapter or simply jump to the "Exam Preparation Tasks" section for review. If you are in doubt, read the entire chapter. Table 12-1 outlines the major headings in this chapter and the corresponding "Do I Know This Already?" quiz questions. You can find the answers in Appendix A, "Answers to the 'Do I Know This Already?' Quizzes."

**Table 12-1**   "Do I Know This Already?" Foundation Topics Section-to-Question Mapping

| Foundations Topics Section | Questions Covered in This Section |
| --- | --- |
| File Server Resource Manager | 1–4 |
| Configuring Disk and Volume Quotas | 5–6 |
| Storage Manager for SANs | 7 |

1. Which of the following tasks can you perform by using the File Server Resource Manager console? (Choose all that apply.)

   a. Configure shared folder and NTFS permissions on files and folders.

   b. Create quotas that limit the amount of disk space users can store within a folder or volume.

   c. Create file screens that restrict the file types users can save.

   d. Define rules that set classification properties on files.

   e. Create scheduled tasks that can be used for applying actions to subsets of files.

2. You want to prevent users from storing audio files with extensions of *.mp* on your file server. However, you have several users who need to store Microsoft Project files with a *.mpp extension on the server. How should you configure the server?

   a. Use FSRM to create a file group and give the group an appropriate name. Specify *.mpp as a set of files to include and *.mp* as a set of files to exclude. Then, create a file screen, specifying the **Active screening** type and the name of the file group that you created.

   b. Use FSRM to create a file group and give the group an appropriate name. Specify *.mpp as a set of files to include and *.mp* as a set of files to exclude. Then, create a file screen, specifying the **Passive screening** type and the name of the file group that you created.

   c. Use FSRM to create a file group and give the group an appropriate name. Specify *.mp* as a set of files to include and *.mpp as a set of files to exclude. Then, create a file screen, specifying the **Active screening** type and the name of the file group that you created.

   d. Use FSRM to create a file group and give the group an appropriate name. Specify *.mp* as a set of files to include and *.mpp as a set of files to exclude. Then, create a file screen, specifying the **Passive screening** type and the name of the file group that you created.

3. You want to generate a report that will inform you which users are storing image files on your file server, so that you can formulate a policy with regards to the types of files users will be allowed to save. For now, you do not want to block storage of these files. What should you do? (Each correct answer represents a complete solution. Choose two.)

   a. Create a file screen that specifies the **Active screening** option and select the **Image Files** file group as a group to block.

    **b.** Create a file screen that specifies the **Passive screening** option and select the **Image Files** file group as a group to block.

    **c.** From the File Server Resource Manager Options dialog box, select the **File Screen Audit** tab and specify the **Files by File Group** option as a group to be reported on.

    **d.** From the File Server Resource Manager Options dialog box, select the **Storage Reports** tab and specify the **Files by File Group** option as a group to be reported on.

**4.** On scanning the contents of several shared folders on your file server, you notice a large number of files that have not been accessed for several years. You want to clean up the contents of these folders by moving these files to another location from which they can be archived and then removed from your server. What should you do?

    **a.** From the Create File Management Tasks dialog box, select the **Action** tab and specify **File Expiration** and specify the folder to which the expired files will be moved. Select the **General** tab and specify the shared folders that will be checked for outdated files. Also, select the **Condition** tab and specify the number of days since the file was last accessed.

    **b.** From Windows Explorer, right-click the shared folder and choose **Properties**. From the folder's Properties dialog box, select the **Action** tab and specify **File Expiration** and specify the folder to which the expired files will be removed. Also, select the **Condition** tab and specify the number of days since the file was last accessed. Repeat for each shared folder as required.

    **c.** From the Storage Reports tab of the File Server Resource Manager Options dialog box, specify the **Least Recently Accessed Files** option and configure the required number of days since the file was last accessed. Then, select the **Automatic Classification** tab of this dialog box and specify the folder to which the expired files will be moved.

    **d.** Create a file screen and specify a file group that includes files older than a specified date. Select the **Command** tab of the File Screen Properties dialog box and include the path to a script that will move files that meet the file screen conditions to another folder from which you can archive them later.

**5.** You are configuring quotas to limit the amount of space users can save files to on your file server. Which of the following is an action that you can accomplish by using the File Server Resource Manager console but cannot be accomplished when using Windows Explorer to configure the quota?

  **a.** You can configure different quotas that apply to individual users.

  **b.** You can configure a quota that applies to a specific shared folder rather than the entire volume.

  **c.** You can deny disk space to users if they exceed their quota limit.

  **d.** You can write events to the Windows system log whenever quota limits are exceeded.

**6.** You are responsible for configuring quotas that will apply to 20 shared folders located on seven file servers in your organization. You want to specify threshold levels that will inform you which users are storing more than 500 MB of data on any one file share. What should you do to accomplish this task with the least amount of administrative effort?

  **a.** Use Windows Explorer to configure a quota template that specifies the 500 MB limit, but do not select the **Deny disk space to users exceeding quota limit** option. Store this template at a shared location accessible to all servers. At each server, use FSRM to create a quota and select the **Auto apply template and create quotas on existing and new subfolders** option and specify the template you've created.

  **b.** Use Windows Explorer to configure a disk quota that specifies the 500 MB limit, but do not select the **Deny disk space to users exceeding quota limit** option. Repeat this action at each file server.

  **c.** Use FSRM to create a custom quota template that includes a soft quota limiting space to 500 MB. Store this template at a shared location accessible to all servers. At each server, use FSRM to create a quota and select the **Auto apply template and create quotas on existing and new subfolders** option and specify the template you've created.

  **d.** Use FSRM to create a custom quota template that includes a hard quota limiting space to 500 MB. Store this template at a shared location accessible to all servers. At each server, use FSRM to create a quota and select the **Auto apply template and create quotas on existing and new subfolders** option and specify the template you've created.

7. You configured seven file servers in your organization as a storage-area network (SAN), and you configured several logical unit numbers (LUN). You want to make data on one of these LUNs inaccessible to users connecting to the SAN, but you do not want to delete this data. What should you do?

   a. Select the **Subsystems** node in Storage Manager for SANs. From the list of subsystems displayed, expand the required subsystem to locate and delete the associated LUN.

   b. Select the **LUN Management** node in Storage Manager for SANs. Then, right-click the required LUN and choose **Rename LUN**.

   c. Select the **LUN Management** node in Storage Manager for SANs. Then, right-click the required LUN and choose **Delete LUN**.

   d. Select the **LUN Management** node in Storage Manager for SANs. Then, right-click the required LUN and choose **Unassign LUN**.

**Foundation Topics**

# File Server Resource Manager

First introduced with Windows Server 2003 R2, File Server Resource Manager (FSRM) is a suite of tools that enables you to perform a series of management tasks on file servers. FSRM helps you to efficiently monitor existing storage resources from a central location, as well as assisting in the planning and implementation of future changes in the file server infrastructure of your network.

FSRM is a Microsoft Management Console (MMC) snap-in that includes five nodes enabling you to perform the following tasks:

- **Quota Management:** Enables you to create quotas for limiting the space users are allowed to store within a volume or folder, and generate notifications that appear automatically when quotas are approached or exceeded. You can also apply these quotas automatically to existing and new subfolders.

- **File Screening Management:** Enables you to create file screens that limit the file types that users can save, and generate notifications when users attempt to save inappropriate files. You can also define templates for quotas and file screens that you can apply to new volumes and folders within your organization.

- **Storage Reports Management:** Enables you to produce scheduled storage reports that help identify trends in disk usage, thereby assisting in the planning of future storage requirements. You can also create on-demand storage reports.

- **Classification Management:** Enables you to define classification property schemas as well as rules that set classification properties on files.

- **File Management Tasks:** Enables you to create scheduled tasks for applying actions to subsets of files.

Windows Server 2008 R2 provides improvements to FSRM that support the classification of files and applying policies based on the information obtained. You can also create file-management tasks that simplify the process of locating subsets of files on a server and applying commands to these files. In addition, you can configure tasks that notify users of any new policies that are to be applied to their files. Management of disk quotas is covered later in this chapter.

### Installing FSRM

FSRM is a role service component of the File Services Role. You can install FSRM when installing the File Services Role as described in Chapter 9, "Configuring File Servers," or you can install it from Server Manager at a later time. To do so, use the following procedure:

1. Open Server Manager to the File Services node.

2. Click **Add Role Services**.

3. The Add Role Services Wizard starts with the Select Role Services page. Select **File Server Resource Manager** and click **Next**.

4. You receive the Configure Storage Usage Monitoring page, which enables you to monitor the amount of space used on each volume on your server and generate storage reports when a specified usage threshold is reached. Storage usage monitoring is discussed later in this section. You can click **Next** without selecting any volumes or select volumes to be monitored first.

5. On the Confirm Installation Services page, click **Install**.

6. The Installation Progress page charts the progress of installing FSRM. When informed that FSRM was installed successfully, click **Close**.

After installing FSRM, you can access it from the File Server node in Server Manager or from the Administrative Tools folder, which opens the FSRM snap-in and displays the five nodes previously mentioned. The following sections introduce you to the available tasks.

### Managing File Screening

File screens enable you to block files belonging to particular file groups from being saved to a volume or folder tree. For example, you can prevent users from storing image files, audio files, or video files on your file server. You have the following two types of file screens:

- **Active screening:** Prevents users from saving disallowed file types on the server, and generates configured notifications if users attempt to save such files.

- **Passive screening:** Sends configured notifications to users who save specific file types but does not prevent users from saving these files.

If disallowed file types have been saved to the configured volume before file screens are set up, these files are not removed. In addition, users and applications are not prevented from accessing these files.

FSRM enables you to create file screen templates for simplified management of file screens. Such a template defines a screening type as already introduced as well as a set of file groups to be blocked and a set of notifications that will be sent when a user attempts to save an unauthorized file. As shown in Figure 12-1, several default screen templates are provided for blocking common file types.

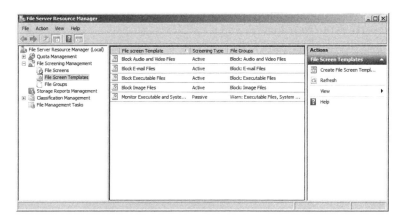

**Figure 12-1**   FSRM provides you with several preconfigured default file screen templates.

## Using File Groups

FSRM uses the concept of a file group for defining files that will be screened or reported on. The file group contains a set of filename patterns that define the types of files that either belong or do not belong in the group. For example, you could define an Audio Files group to include $*.mp*$, which defines the group as including all audio files such as $*.mp2$, $*.mp3$, and so on; you could then specify the $*.mpp$ (Microsoft Project) files are excluded from this group.

FSRM contains several predefined file groups, which you can access from the File Groups subnode of File Screening Management. You can modify these if required or create your own file groups. Use the following steps to create a file group:

1. Right-click **File Groups** and choose **Create File Group**.

2. In the Create File Group Properties dialog box shown in Figure 12-2, provide a name for your file group (for example, Older Word Documents) and type the extensions of file types to be included or excluded in the text boxes provided (for example, $*.doc$ and $*.docx$), clicking **Add** after adding each extension.

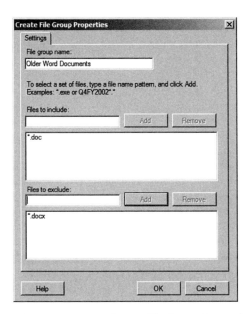

**Figure 12-2**    The Create File Group Properties dialog box enables you to create custom file groups.

3. When finished, click **OK** to add the group to the list in the details pane of FSRM.

You can also modify or delete any of the file groups, either the predefined ones or ones you've added. To do so, right-click a file group and choose **Edit File Group Properties**. Then, make any needed changes in the Edit Group Properties dialog box that appears. To delete a file group, right-click it and choose **Delete** (or select it and press the **Delete** key). Then, click **Yes** in the confirmation message box that appears.

## Creating File Screens and Templates

You can use a file screen to disallow files of specified types from being stored on the file server. FSRM does not provide any file screens by default. Use the following steps to create a file screen:

1. Right-click the **File Screens** subnode and choose **Create File Screen**.

2. In the Create File Screen dialog box shown in Figure 12-3, type or browse to the path of the volume or folder on which you want to disallow storage of given file types.

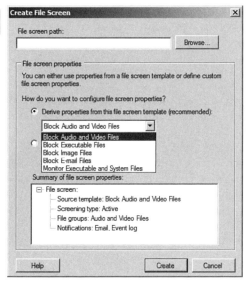

**Figure 12-3**   The Create File Screen dialog box enables you to block storage of files of given types according to settings defined in a template or custom settings.

   **3.** Use a template or custom properties to define the types of files to be blocked. Either select a template from those provided in the drop-down list shown in Figure 12-3 or select the **Custom File Properties** radio button to display the File Screen Properties dialog box shown in Figure 12-4, which provides the following options for customizing your file screen:

     ■ **Settings tab:** Choose the desired screening type (active or passive, as already described) and select the file groups to be blocked. You can choose any of the predefined or customized file groups as defined in the File Groups subnode. You can also create new file groups or edit existing ones by clicking the **Create** or **Edit** command buttons as desired.

     ■ **E-mail Message tab:** Enables you to send e-mail messages to administrators. Specify administrators in the form `account@domain` and use semicolons to separate addresses. You can also send an e-mail message to the user who attempted to save an unauthorized file. Fields are provided for customizing the message to be sent to this user, including variables that are defined according to the user, file type being saved, or other conditions that caused the message to be generated.

     ■ **Event Log tab:** Enables you to create a customized message that will be saved into the event log.

- **Command tab:** Enables you to specify a command or script that will be executed when a user attempts to save a blocked file. Browse to the location of the desired command and specify the arguments required for the command to be executed. You can also specify a command working directory and the service account (Local Service, Network Service, or Local System) under which the account will be run.

- **Report tab:** Enables you to generate any of a series of reports and send reports to administrators or to the user who attempted to save an unauthorized file.

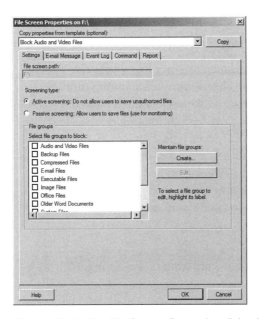

**Figure 12-4**   The File Screen Properties dialog box enables you to select custom properties for your file screen.

4. If you used the File Screen Properties dialog box, click **OK** to return to the Create File Screen dialog box. To finish and create the file screen, click **Create**.

You can also create a file screen template that can be used to create additional file screens at a later time. Right-click **File Screen Templates** and choose **Create File Screen Template**. The Create File Screen Template dialog box provides the same options as previously described and shown in Figure 12-4 for creating your template.

### Creating File Screen Exceptions

At times, you might want to permit exceptions to the rules you've defined in file screening. For example, you might want to block video files from the file server in general; however, you need to permit a group responsible for creating computer-based training videos to save their files. A file screen exception enables you to allow otherwise restricted file types as defined in a file screen. To create a file screen exception, right-click **File Screens** and select **Create File Screen Exception**. In the Create File Screen Exception dialog box that appears, type or browse to the path on which you want to create an exception and select the file groups that will be excluded from screening.

### Monitoring File Screening

In addition to the information provided by e-mail or event log notifications, the details pane of the FSRM snap-in provides general monitoring information. Select the **File Screens** node from the console tree and then select the desired file screen. The panel at the bottom of the details pane provides information on the file screen including the path the file screen was created for, its type (block or exception), the file groups included in the file screen, the template used to create the file screen, and whether the current configuration of the file screen matches the configuration of the template. You can also see the file groups being blocked on the file screen path. Click **Filter** to filter the display according to the file screen type and path.

**NOTE**   For more information on using FSRM to configure file screening, refer to "Screening Files" at http://technet.microsoft.com/en-us/library/dd758760(WS.10). aspx.

## Managing Storage Reports

FSRM enables you to create storage reports that assist you in understanding file usage on your server. The Storage Reports Management node enables you to create report tasks, which you can use to schedule reports to be generated at specified intervals, or you can generate reports on demand. You can also configure reports to be generated automatically when users attempt to perform designated tasks such as exceeding a quota threshold or saving an unauthorized file.

Table 12-2 describes the types of reports that FSRM can generate.

**Table 12-2**  Available Storage Reports in FSRM

| Report | Description |
|---|---|
| Duplicate Files | Lists files with the same name, size, and last-modified time. Helps you to identify and reclaim wasted disk space. |
| File Screening Audit | Lists events generated by file screening that have occurred within a specified number of days. |
| Files by File Group | Lists files that belong to file groups as defined in File Screening. This helps you to identify file group usage patterns and identify often-used file groups, and can facilitate the settings of file screening options. |
| Files by Owner | Lists files according to the users who own them. |
| Files by Property | Lists files by the values of a specified classification property. |
| Large Files | Lists files of a specified size or larger. This helps you to identify files using a large amount of disk space, and assists you in reclaiming disk space. |
| Least Recently Accessed Files | Lists files that have not been accessed for a specified number of days. This helps you decide which files could be archived to save disk space. |
| Most Recently Accessed Files | List files that have been accessed within a specified number of days. This helps you identify information that should always be highly accessible. |
| Quota Usage | Lists quotas for which quota usage is higher than a specified percentage. This helps you modify quotas or take any action that might be appropriate. |

### Specifying Report Parameters

All reports except Duplicate Files have configurable report parameters that vary with the report type. To configure default parameters, use the following procedure:

1. Right-click **File Server Resource Manager** at the top of the console tree in FSRM and choose **Configure Options**.

2. From the Storage Reports tab of the File Server Resource Manager Options dialog box shown in Figure 12-5, select the type of report and click **Edit Parameters**.

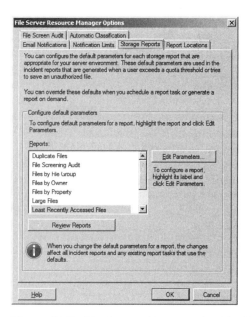

**Figure 12-5**   The Storage Reports tab of the File Server Resource Manager Options dialog box enables you to configure report parameters.

3.  Specify the required options in the dialog box that appears, and then click **OK**.

4.  Repeat these steps for each report type as desired.

5.  To review the default parameters as configured for all reports, click **Review Reports**. Then, click **Close**.

6.  When finished, click **OK**.

### Additional FSRM Options

The File Server Resource Manager Options dialog box introduced in the previous section and shown in Figure 12-5 contains the following additional tabs that enable you to specify additional options that affect the behavior of the FSRM utility:

- **E-mail Notifications tab:** Enables you to specify a Simple Mail Transport Protocol (SMTP) server and default e-mail settings that will be used when sending notifications and storage reports.

- **Notification Limits tab:** Enables you to reduce the number of notifications sent by specifying minimum time intervals between consecutive sending of e-mail notifications, event log notifications, and command notifications. By default, each of these notification intervals is 60 minutes.

- **Report Locations tab:** Enables you to specify the folder in which different types of reports are saved.

- **File Screen Audit tab:** Provides an option to record file screening activity in an auditing database that you can review later by running a File Screen Auditing Report. Select the check box provided to enable this action.

- **Automatic Classification tab:** Enables you to create a schedule at which automatic file classification will take place. You can also select the types of log files and report formats that will be used, as well as specifying an e-mail address in the format `account@domain` to which reports will be sent.

## Scheduling Report Generation

You can configure FSRM to generate a series of reports according to a specified schedule. To do so, create a report task, which specifies which reports will be generated, the parameters to be used, the volumes and folders reported, the frequency of report generation, and the file formats to be saved. Use the following steps:

1. In the console tree of FSRM, right-click **Storage Reports Management** and choose **Schedule a New Report Task**. You receive the Storage Report Task Properties dialog box shown in Figure 12-6.

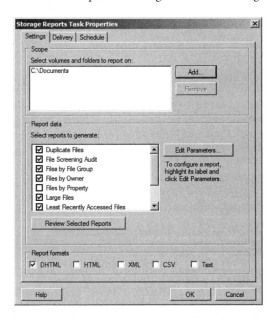

**Figure 12-6**   The Storage Report Task Properties dialog box enables you to configure several report parameters.

2. To select the required volumes or folders, click **Add** under Scope, browse to the required folder, select it, and then click **OK** to add its path to the list. Repeat as required.

3. Specify the reports to be generated by selecting them from the list under Report data.

4. To check the parameters that have been specified, click the **Review Selected Reports** command button. If you need to edit the parameters of a report, select it and click **Edit Parameters**. Make any changes needed in the Report Parameters dialog box that appears, and then click **OK**.

5. Specify report formats by selecting one or more formats under Report Formats.

6. To e-mail reports to administrators, select the **Delivery** tab. Then, select **Send reports to the following administrators**, and enter the names of the administrator accounts in the format **account@domain**.

7. To schedule the reports, select the **Schedule** tab. Click **Create Schedule** to display the Schedule dialog box. Click **New**, and in the Schedule dialog box that appears, modify the default schedule as required, and then click **OK**.

8. Click **OK** to save the report task.

You can also generate reports on demand at any time. To do so, right-click **Storage Reports Management** and choose **Generate Reports Now**. Use Steps 2 to 7 in the previous procedure to define all required report parameters; when finished, click **OK** to open the Generate Storage Reports dialog box shown in Figure 12-7. Select the desired option for generating and viewing the reports.

**Figure 12-7**   The Generate Storage Reports dialog box provides two options for creating and viewing the storage reports.

**NOTE**   For more information on using FSRM to create storage reports, refer to "Generating Storage Reports" at http://technet.microsoft.com/en-us/library/dd758755(WS.10).aspx.

### Managing File Classification

FSRM includes a File Classification infrastructure that assists you in managing your files more effectively by providing insight into the data patterns present in your organization. You can create predefined policies based on the business value of your data that help to automate processes that would otherwise need to be carried out manually. This helps you to accomplish your business needs with regard to factors such as expiration of stale files or protection of important data files. You can use predefined rules for classifying files that help you to more effectively manage data with regard to what should be retained and where it should be stored, and create customized tasks and set up a procedure for automated reporting of data usage. These actions help you to reduce costs of storage and mitigate risks of exposing sensitive data.

The Classification Management node in the console tree of FSRM enables you to create classification properties and rules. Use the following steps:

1. Expand the Classification Management node to reveal Classification Properties and Classification Rules subnodes.

2. To create a classification property, right-click **Classification Properties** and choose **Create Property**. This displays the Create Classification Property Definition dialog box shown in Figure 12-8.

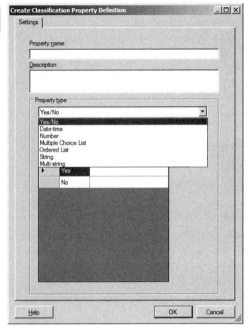

**Figure 12-8** The Create Classification Property Definition dialog box enables you to specify any of seven property types.

3. Specify the property name, optional description, and property type, and then click **OK**. As shown, you have a choice among the following property types:

- **Yes/No:** A Boolean property that can be either Yes or No. When combining multiple values, a No value overwrites a Yes value.

- **Date-time:** A simple date-time property. When combining multiple values, conflicting values prevent reclassification.

- **Number:** A simple number property. When combining multiple values, conflicting values prevent reclassification.

- **Multiple Choice List:** A list of values that can be assigned; you can assign more than one value to a property at a time.

- **Ordered List:** A list of fixed values, only one of which can be assigned at a time.

- **String:** A simple string property. When combining multiple values, conflicting values prevent reclassification.

- **Multi-string:** A list of string values; more than one can be assigned to a property at a time.

Use the following steps to create a classification rule that is used to automatically classify files:

1. In the console tree of FSRM, right-click **Classification Rules** and choose **Create a New Rule**. This displays the Classification Rule Definitions dialog box shown in Figure 12-9.

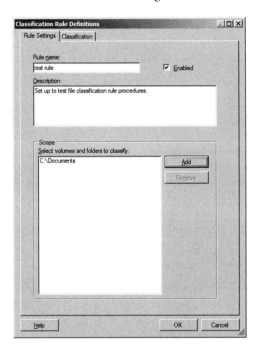

**Figure 12-9**    The Rule Settings tab of the Classification Rule Definitions dialog box enables you to type a name and description for a rule, enable it, and specify a scope for the rule.

2. Specify a rule name and optional description, and then click **Add** to browse to a volume or folder to be classified.

3. Select the **Classification** tab and then specify classification information as shown in Figure 12-10. When finished, click **OK** to enable the classification rule.

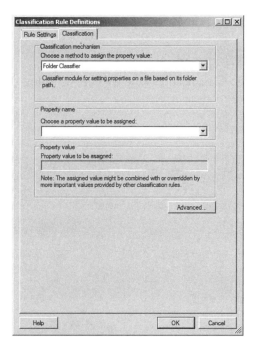

**Figure 12-10** The Classification tab of the Classification Rule Definitions dialog box enables you to specify a classification mechanism, property name, and property value.

**NOTE** For more information on using FSRM to classify files, refer to "Working with File Classification" at http://technet.microsoft.com/en-us/library/dd758765(WS.10).aspx and "FSRM and FCI: Frequently Asked Questions" at http://technet.microsoft.com/en-us/library/ee344836(WS.10).aspx.

### Configuring File-Management Tasks

The File Management Tasks node in FSRM enables you to define file-management tasks that automate the process of locating subsets of files and applying simple commands, such as file expiration to them on a scheduled basis. You can use the following properties to define files that will be processed by the file-management task:

- Location
- Classification properties
- Creation time
- Modification time
- Time last accessed
- Filename

To create a file-management task, right-click **File Management Tasks** and choose **Create File Management Task**. The Create File Management Task dialog box, as shown in Figure 12-11, enables you to define the following items:

- **General tab:** Specify a name, optional description, and scope for the task.

- **Action tab:** Specify the action type such as **File Expiration**. When configuring file expiration, specify a folder to which expired files will be moved.

- **Notification tab:** You can generate notifications to be sent in the form of an e-mail message, and entry in the event log, or the execution of a command or script. Options for these notifications are similar to those mentioned earlier in this section.

- **Report tab:** You can generate log files or reports in several formats. You can also configure report delivery by e-mail to an administrator in the format `account@domain`.

- **Condition tab:** Enables you to set conditions on the execution of the file-management task, such as the number of days since the file was created, last modified, or last accessed. You can also specify property conditions or a wild-card pattern matching the filename.

- **Schedule tab:** Enables you to use the Task Scheduler to specify a time and interval at which the file-management task will be executed. Options are similar to those discussed earlier for generating reports using FSRM.

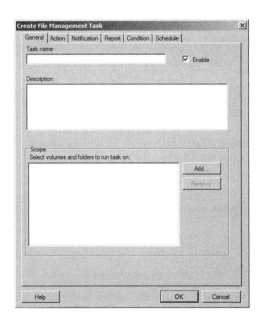

**Figure 12-11**  The Create File Management Task dialog box enables you to specify the properties and conditions for running a file-management task.

When you create a file-management task and click **OK**, summary information about the task is displayed in the details pane of FSRM. If you need to change the properties of the file-management task, simply right-click it and choose **Edit File Management Task Properties**. The Edit File Management Task dialog box that appears contains the same tabs and options as mentioned for the Create File Management Task.

**NOTE**   For more information on using FSRM to perform file-management tasks, refer to "Working with File Management Tasks" at http://technet.microsoft.com/en-us/library/dd758756(WS.10).aspx.

## Configuring Disk and Volume Quotas

First introduced in Windows 2000 and improved with each successive server version is the concept of disk quotas. This feature allows an administrator to set a limit on the amount of disk space used by an individual user. Added with Windows Server 2008 is the use of FSRM to enable quotas on shared folders within disk volumes, together with additional mechanisms for notifying users who are approaching or exceeding their quota limits.

You can send a warning to users when they reach a certain level of disk usage, and you can write an event to the event log if a user attempts to exceed his quota. When you enable disk quotas, Windows Server 2008 also collects disk usage statistics for all users enabled on the volume, thus allowing the administrator to keep track of disk usage. Thereby, the administrator can manage disks more efficiently and prevent users from "hogging" disk space.

You can enable disk and volume quotas from Windows Explorer or from the FSRM console. Enabling quotas from Windows Explorer permits you to set different quotas for different users; the quotas apply to all folders within the specified volume. Enabling quotas from FSRM, on the other hand, permits you to set quotas that apply to given folders (such as shares) on the server; however, you cannot specify different quota levels for different users when using FSRM.

### Using Windows Explorer to Enable Disk Quotas

Windows Explorer enables you to enable quotas on a per-volume, per-user basis. Use the following procedure to enable disk quotas from Windows Explorer:

1. In Windows Explorer, right-click the volume on which you want to enable disk quotas, and then select **Properties**.

2. In the Properties dialog box, click the **Quota** tab to display disk quota information.

3. On the Quota Properties dialog box, select the **Enable quota management** check box. Then, specify values for the quota parameters described in Table 12-3 and shown in Figure 12-12.

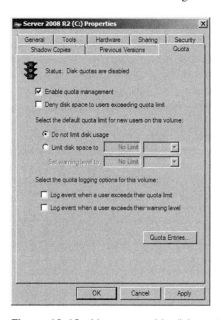

**Figure 12-12**    You can enable disk quotas for individual users on given disks.

4. To configure quota entries for specific users, click the **Quota Entries** button. From the Quota Entries dialog box, you can view the status of all quotas configured on the volume including the user name, amount of space used, quota limit, warning level, and percent used.

5. After making any changes and closing the Quota Entries dialog box, click **OK** or **Apply**. A Disk Quota message box (see Figure 12-13) warns you that the disk will be rescanned and that this may take several minutes.

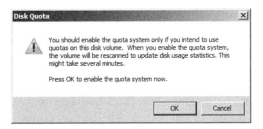

**Figure 12-13**  You are warned that the disk volume will be rescanned to update disk usage statistics.

6. Click **OK** to close this message box and start the scan.

Table 12-3 describes the options that are available on the Quota tab of the disk's Properties dialog box.

**Table 12-3**  Disk Quota Configuration Options

| Option | Description |
| --- | --- |
| Enable quota management | Enables quota management and enables the other options so that you can configure them. |
| Deny disk space to users exceeding quota limit | When users exceed their quota, they receive an `Out of disk space` message and they cannot write further data. |
| Do not limit disk usage | Select this option when you do not want to limit the amount of disk space used. |
| Limit disk space to | Configures the disk space limit per user. |
| Set warning level to | Configures the amount of disk space that a user can write before receiving a warning. |
| Log event when a user exceeds their quota limit | Writes an event to the Windows system log on the computer running disk quotas whenever a user exceeds her quota limit. |
| Log event when a user exceeds their warning level | Writes an event to the Windows system log on the computer running disk quotas any time a user exceeds his quota warning level, not his actual quota. |

When the disk quota system is active, a user checking the properties of the volume where it is enabled sees only the amount of space permitted on the quota; the available space is the permitted space minus the space already used. If a user tries to copy a file that is larger than the allowed space, he receives a message that the file cannot be copied. In addition, an event is written to the event log if you have selected the appropriate check box described in Table 12-3. You can view usage statistics by clicking the **Quota Entries** button.

**NOTE**   You can enable quotas only on volumes formatted with the NTFS file system. Only administrators can enable quotas, but they can permit users to view quota settings.

**TIP**   Set appropriate quotas on all volumes that a user can access. Provide warnings to the users, and log events when they exceed their quota limit and/or warning level.

### Using FSRM to Enable Quotas

FSRM provides a more comprehensive set of options for enabling quotas. You can enable quotas on shared folders as well as volumes, and you can define templates that can be used for setting common quota definitions across multiple servers and shares. FSRM enables you to create the following types of quotas:

- **Hard quota:** Denies additional disk space to a user exceeding her quota limit and generates notifications when data saved reaches configured thresholds. Equivalent to selecting the **Deny disk space to users exceeding quota limit** option, previously shown in Figure 12-12.

- **Soft quota:** Only generates the configured notifications when data saved reaches configured thresholds. Equivalent to clearing the preceding option.

FSRM can generate notification actions that are similar to those already discussed for file classification, including e-mail notifications, logged events, execution of commands or scripts, or generation of storage reports. Use the following procedure to create a quota:

1. Expand the Quota Management node in FSRM to reveal the Quotas and Quota Templates subnodes.

2. Right-click **Quotas** and choose **Create Quota**. The Create Quota dialog box appears (see Figure 12-14).

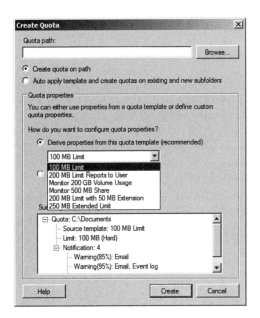

**Figure 12-14**  FSRM provides several default options for creating a shared folder-based quota.

3. Type or browse to the desired volume or folder.

4. If you have a quota template configured, select the **Auto apply template and create quotas on existing and new subfolders** option. Otherwise, leave the default of **Create quota on path** selected.

5. Select an option for configuring quota properties from the drop-down list shown in Figure 12-14 or select the **Define custom quota properties** radio button for specifying additional options.

6. When finished, click **Create** to create and enable the quota.

### Using FSRM to Create Quota Templates

FSRM in Windows Server 2008 R2 adds the capability of defining *quota templates*. By doing so, you can apply standard storage limits and notification thresholds to many volumes and folders on servers throughout your organization. In addition, you can automatically update all quotas based on your template simply by editing the template. This enables you to create a standard user quota template that limits each user's storage on the user's personal folder; you can easily modify all users' limits by editing this template.

FSRM provides several default quota templates that you can use or modify to suit your needs. You can also create a new quota template by performing the following procedure:

1. Select the **Quota Templates** subnode in the console tree of FSRM. The details pane displays the default quota templates.

2. Right-click **Quota Templates** and choose **Create Quota Template**. The Create Quota Template dialog box shown in Figure 12-15 appears.

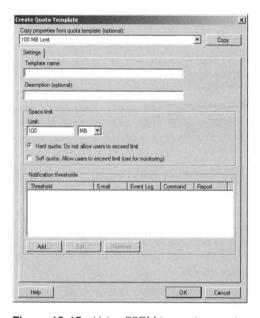

**Figure 12-15**   Using FSRM to create a custom quota template.

3. If you want to copy the properties of a default quota template, select it from the drop-down list provided and click **Copy**.

4. Type a name and optional description for the template in the text boxes provided.

5. Specify a space limit (in KB, MB, GB, or TB) and choose whether to enable a hard or soft quota.

6. Click **Add** to configure notification thresholds. The Add Threshold dialog box enables you to send e-mail messages to users and administrator, write events to the event log, execute commands or scripts, or generate reports. Options available are similar to those available with other FSRM actions. Click **OK** when finished.

7.  When finished, click **OK** to close the Create Quota Template dialog box and add your custom template to the list in the details pane of FSRM.

**NOTE**   For more information on using FSRM to configure quotas, refer to "Working with Quotas" at http://technet.microsoft.com/en-us/library/dd758768(WS.10).aspx.

**TIP**   Be aware that you can set quotas by user only by configuring them from Windows Explorer; conversely, you can set quotas by shared folder only by configuring them from FSRM. An exam question might test your knowledge of this fact.

### Some Guidelines for Using Quotas

The following are a few guidelines for using quotas on Windows Server 2008 file servers:

- If you need to specify different quotas for different users, use Windows Explorer to configure quotas. Conversely, if you need to specify quotas that apply to shared folders, use FSRM to configure quotas.

- When installing applications, use the Administrator account rather than your own user account. That way, the space used by the applications will not be charged against your quota if you have one.

- If you want to use disk quotas only to monitor disk space usage, specify a soft quota by clearing the **Deny disk space to users exceeding quota limit** check box in Windows Explorer or by selecting the **Soft quota** option in FSRM. That way, users are not prevented from saving important data.

- Be aware that use of hard quotas might cause applications to fail. Using FSRM to configure hard quotas provides additional reports and warnings that alert you to situations where quota limits are being approached and enable you to take action as needed.

- Monitor space used and increase the limits for those users who need larger amounts of space. When using FSRM, set up additional folders with less restrictive limits applied to users with access permissions for these folders.

- Set quotas on all shared volumes, including public folders and network servers, to ensure appropriate use of space by users.

- If a user no longer stores files on a certain volume, delete her disk quota entries. You can do this only after her files have been moved or deleted, or after someone has taken ownership of them.

**NOTE**   Be aware that NTFS file compression actually has no particular effect on the amount of quota space available to such a user. Disk quotas are calculated based on the amount of space occupied by uncompressed folders and files, regardless of whether files are compressed or not compressed.

## Storage Manager for SANs

First introduced with Windows Server 2003 R2, *Storage Manager for SANs* is an optional feature in all editions of Windows Server 2008 that enables you to create and manage logical unit numbers (LUN) on Fibre Channel and Internet SCSI (iSCSI) disk drive subsystems that support the Virtual Disk Service (VDS) in your *storage-area network* (SAN). A SAN is a discrete network that is dedicated to file storage using devices such as disk arrays or tape libraries that provides dedicated storage to servers in such a fashion that these devices appear to be locally attached to the servers that reference them. A LUN can comprise a disk, a portion of a disk, an entire disk array, or a section of a disk array in the subsystem; it serves as a logical identifier through which you can assign access control privileges, thereby simplifying the management of storage resources within the SAN. You can read from or write to a LUN in the same manner as you can from a physical or logical disk volume that you would manage from the Disk Management snap-in.

Storage Manager for SANs enables you to create the same types of LUNs as are possible with disk volumes, as follows:

- **Simple:** Uses a single physical drive or volume.

- **Spanned:** Spans more than one physical drive. Data is written to the first drive until it is full, then to the second drive, and so on.

- **Striped:** Also known as RAID-0, uses multiple physical drives and writes data in blocks across all the drives, thereby improving I/O performance. However, no fault tolerance is provided; if any drive fails, the entire LUN and its data are lost.

- **Mirrored:** Also known as RAID-1, provides fault tolerance by writing data simultaneously to two different physical drives.

- **Striped with parity:** Also known as RAID-5, uses three or more physical drives to write data in blocks across all the drives, including a parity stripe that provides fault tolerance. Provides better read performance than a simple LUN but write performance is reduced because of the parity calculation.

Storage Manager for SANs will be of special interest to administrators responsible for managing storage allocation on disk drive storage subsystems in a SAN and those who manage iSCSI storage subsystems and require a utility that enables them to create, configure, and manage iSCSI targets. Several of the tasks that you can perform using Storage Manager for SANs include the following:

- View details of supported storage subsystems. Storage Manager for SANs will automatically discover any Fibre Channel and iSCSI storage subsystems on the network. You can use information about available capacity and supported LUN types to plan the allocation of storage.

- Create LUNs on Fibre Channel and iSCSI disk drive storage subsystems, thereby enabling you to manage the allocation of storage within the SAN. You can create a new LUN and assign it to a server; display all LUNs on the storage subsystems, including information such as type, size, and online status; and assign a LUN to a cluster of servers making the storage highly available.

- Manage the connection between the storage subsystems in your SAN and the Windows Server 2008 computers that connect to the SAN. This includes specifying which host bus adapter ports or iSCSI initiator adaptors on servers in your SAN are granted access to LUNs you have created within the storage subsystems.

- Create and manage volumes on LUNs and assign LUNs to servers or clusters in the SAN. You can also configure security settings for iSCSI storage subsystems and run logon sessions with targets on the subsystems.

- Monitor the status of disk drives and LUNs in your storage subsystems.

Storage Manager for SANs is included as a server feature in Windows Server 2008 R2. You can install it by using the Add Features Wizard in Server Manager, similar to other server features discussed in other chapters. After the wizard informs you that installation has completed, you can access the Storage Manager for SANs snap-in from the Administrative Tools folder.

As shown in Figure 12-16, the Storage Manager for SANs snap-in provides the following three nodes in the console tree:

- **LUN Management:** Lists all the available LUNs and enables you to perform the following administrative tasks with LUNs:

    - **Create a LUN:** Right-click **LUN Management** and choose **Create LUN**. Then, follow the steps in the Provision Storage Wizard that appears.

    - **Extend a LUN:** Select **LUN Management** to display the available LUNs in the details pane. Right-click the required LUN and choose **Extend LUN**, and then type the required size for the LUN in the dialog box that appears.

    - **Delete a LUN:** In the details pane, right-click the required LUN and choose **Delete LUN**, and then confirm your action. Note that this action permanently deletes all data on all volumes on the LUN.

    - **Assign a LUN:** In the details pane, right-click the required LUN and choose **Assign LUN**. Then, follow the steps in the Assign LUN Wizard that appears.

    - **Unassign a LUN:** In the details pane, right-click the required LUN and choose **Unassign LUN**. This temporarily makes the LUN invisible without deleting any data contained within the LUN. You can re-assign the LUN at a later time to re-enable access to its data.

- **Subsystems:** Lists all the storage subsystems currently discovered in your SAN and allows you to rename a subsystem. For more information, refer to "Virtual Disk Service Technical Reference" at http://technet.microsoft.com/en-us/library/cc776012(WS.10).aspx.

- **Drives:** Select this node to display a list of all the drives in the subsystems contained within the SAN. You can make a light on the drive on which you are working blink in order to identify it. To do so, right-click the required drive and choose **Blink Drive Light**, and then click **Start** in the dialog box that appears. Click **Stop** to stop the blinking.

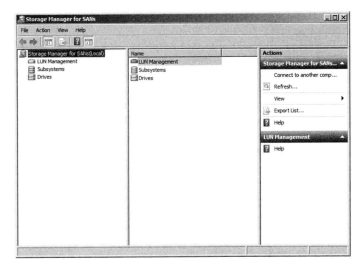

**Figure 12-16**   Storage Manager for SANs enables you to manage LUNs, subsystems, and drives.

**NOTE**   For more information on Storage Manager for SANs, refer to "Overview of Storage Manager for SANs" at http://technet.microsoft.com/en-us/library/cc753860. aspx. This reference provides links to other web pages providing details on procedures you can perform from this tool.

## Exam Preparation Tasks

## Review All the Key Topics

Review the most important topics in this chapter, noted with the key topics icon in the outer margin of the page. Table 12-4 lists a reference of these key topics and the page numbers on which each is found.

**Table 12-4**  Key Topics for Chapter 12

| Key Topic Element | Description | Page Number |
| --- | --- | --- |
| List | Introduces the tasks you can perform from the FSRM snap-in. | 500 |
| List | Describes the two types of file screening available with FSRM. | 501 |
| Figure 12-3 | Shows options available for configuring file screening. | 504 |
| Table 12-2 | Introduces the types of file storage reports you can create with FSRM. | 507 |
| List | Shows you how to configure FSRM to generate reports on a scheduled basis. | 509 |
| Figure 12-8 | Displays the property types you can use for file classification. | 512 |
| List | Shows you how to enable disk quotas from Windows Explorer. | 517 |
| Table 12-3 | Describes the available disk quota configuration options. | 518 |
| List | Shows you how to use FSRM to enable disk quotas. | 519 |
| Paragraph | Describes the purpose and use of Storage Manager for SANs. | 523 |

## Complete the Tables and Lists from Memory

Print a copy of Appendix B, "Memory Tables," (found on the CD), or at least the section for this chapter, and complete the tables and lists from memory. Appendix C, "Memory Tables Answer Key," also on the CD, includes the completed tables and lists to check your work.

## Definition of Key Terms

Define the following key terms from this chapter, and check your answers in the Glossary.

active file screen, disk quota, file classification, file screening, File Server Resource Manager (FSRM), logical unit number (LUN), passive file screening, quota template, storage-area network (SAN), Storage Manager for SANs, storage reports

This chapter covers the following subjects:

- **Printing Terminology in Windows Server 2008 R2:** This section introduces key terminology and concepts you must be aware of to administer printers. It also reviews the actions that occur when a user submits a print job.

- **Installing, Sharing, and Publishing Printers:** This section shows you how to install the Print and Document Services server role and then covers the installation, sharing, and publication of printers.

- **Managing and Troubleshooting Printers:** Print servers and printers come with a large array of properties you must be aware of to effectively manage a corporate printing environment. This section introduces you to the management of these properties, as well as the topic of granting permissions to printers and print servers and troubleshooting common printer problems.

# CHAPTER 13

# Configuring and Monitoring Print Services

Resources on a Windows Server 2008 network go beyond the subject of files and folders that have been the subject of Chapter 9, "Configuring File Servers," and subsequent chapters. An important component of any business network is the capability to print documents in a timely and accurate manner, and Windows Server 2008 R2 provides the Print and Document Services server role to assist administrators in setting up print servers and keeping printing capabilities operating properly. Typically, a print server is a computer to which you connect a print device and share so that many people across your network, and even across the Internet, can print to the printer.

In any case, clients that print to the printer can be running a variety of platforms and not just Windows systems. Windows Server 2008 supports hundreds of print devices from a large number of printer manufacturers. This chapter introduces you to the management of printers, which is an important topic—both in real life and on the 70-642 exam.

## "Do I Know This Already?" Quiz

The "Do I Know This Already?" quiz allows you to assess whether you should read this entire chapter or simply jump to the "Exam Preparation Tasks" section for review. If you are in doubt, read the entire chapter. Table 13-1 outlines the major headings in this chapter and the corresponding "Do I Know This Already?" quiz questions. You can find the answers in Appendix A, "Answers to the 'Do I Know This Already?' Quizzes."

**Table 13-1**  "Do I Know This Already?" Foundation Topics Section-to-Question Mapping

| Foundations Topics Section | Questions Covered in This Section |
|---|---|
| Printing Terminology in Windows Server 2008 R2 | 1–2 |
| Installing, Sharing, and Publishing Printers | 3–5 |
| Managing and Troubleshooting Printers | 6–12 |

1. In Microsoft terminology, which of the following is the best definition of a printer?

   a. The program that converts graphic commands into instructions that the print device is able to understand.

   b. The physical (hardware) device that produces the printed output.

   c. The computer that handles the printing process on the network.

   d. The software (logical) interface between the operating system and the physical print device.

2. Your print server is configured so that print jobs are copied to a reserved area within the system root folder of the computer before being sent to the print device. What is this action called?

   a. Preprinting

   b. Spooling

   c. Creation of an enhanced metafile (EMF)

   d. Routing

3. You purchased a new print device for your company's network. The print device is equipped with its own network adapter so that it can be directly connected to the network. You attached the print device to the network and are at the print server and want to install it. What program should you use? (Each correct answer represents a complete solution. Choose two answers).

   a. Print Management snap-in

   b. Add Roles Wizard in Server Manager

   c. Windows Explorer

   d. Device Manager

   e. Control Panel Devices and Printers

4. You installed and shared a new printer on your Windows Server 2008 R2 computer, which is configured with the Print and Document Service server role. Users printing documents from Windows 7 computers receive their documents properly, but users printing from Windows XP computers receive documents full of illegible characters. What should you do?

   a. From the Sharing tab of the Properties dialog box for the printer, select the **Render print jobs on client computers** option.

   b. From the Sharing tab of the Properties dialog box for the printer, click **Additional Drivers**. Then, select drivers for Windows XP from the Additional Drivers dialog box and click **OK**.

   **c.** From the Security tab of the Properties dialog box for the printer, add a group that contains the users of Windows XP computers and grant them the **Manage Documents** permission.

   **d.** Install a new printer from the Print Management snap-in. Configure this printer to point to the same print device and provide a unique share name that references users of Windows XP computers.

**5.** You are responsible for printers connected to Windows Server 2008 R2 print servers in you company's AD DS domain. These servers are configured as member servers in the domain. You installed a printer that should be accessible to computers in the Graphics department, but not to computers in other departments. All resources in this department are located in the Graphics organizational unit (OU). What should you do?

   **a.** From the Sharing tab of the printer's Properties dialog box, select the **List in the directory** option.

   **b.** Right-click this printer in the details pane of the Print Management snap-in and choose **List in Directory**.

   **c.** Right-click this printer in the details pane of the Print Management snap-in and choose **Deploy with Group Policy**. Choose a GPO that is linked to the Graphics OU and select the option labeled **The users that this GPO applies to (per user)**.

   **d.** Right-click this printer in the details pane of the Print Management snap-in and choose **Deploy with Group Policy**. Choose a GPO that is linked to the Graphics OU and select the option labeled **The computers that this GPO applies to (per machine)**.

**6.** You are responsible for the print servers and printers on your company's network. You configured a shared printer (HP40001) on Server1. Server2 also has an identical shared printer (HP40002). HP40001 on Server1 experiences a catastrophic paper jam. Many jobs are waiting to be printed in Server1's print queue. How can you ensure that these print jobs are printed without the need to ask the users to resubmit their print jobs to Server2?

   **a.** From the **Ports** tab of the HP40001 Properties dialog box, select **Enable printer pooling**. Include HP40002 and HP40001 in the pool.

   **b.** Rename the shared printer HP40001 to HP40002.

   **c.** In the Printers folder on the Server1, add a network printer called HP40003, pointing to HP40002 on Server2. Rename printer HP40001 to HP4000X. Then, rename HP40003 to HP40001.

   **d.** Select the **Ports** tab of the HP40001 Properties dialog box, click **Add Port**, choose **Local Port**, click **New Port**, and assign the UNC name \\ **Server2\HP40002** to the new port.

**7.** The boss is fed up with waiting for her documents to print and wants to be sure the account statement prints immediately when it is needed. What is the simplest thing to do so that this will happen properly?

    **a.** Ask her secretary to come in at 7 a.m. and print the account statement.

    **b.** When she needs to print the account statement, have her go to the printer properties and click **Cancel All Documents**, before printing the document.

    **c.** Configure a printer that points to the same print device and has the priority set at 99. Configure this printer's permissions so that only the boss has the Print permission and direct her to print the account statement on this printer.

    **d.** Configure her user account to have the **Prioritize Documents** permission.

**8.** You are responsible for managing the print servers and printers in your company's domain. A user calls and informs you that he has sent a large print job to the printer and has realized that he must make several changes to the document. So, he wants to delete the print job. What permission do you need to grant the user so that he can delete this job?

    **a.** Allow the user the **Manage this printer** permission.

    **b.** Allow the user the **Manage documents** permission.

    **c.** Allow the user the **Special permissions** permission, click **Advanced**, and then allow him the **Delete** permission.

    **d.** You don't need to do anything; he can delete his print jobs without additional permissions.

**9.** You are responsible for maintaining the printers on your company's AD DS network, which includes one domain with three print servers and 12 printers. You purchased a powerful new computer and installed Windows Server 2008 R2 and the Print and Document Management server role. You want to consolidate all the existing printers on the new server. What should you do to accomplish this task with the least amount of administrative effort?

    **a.** At each existing print server, select the **Export printers to a file** option. Complete the steps in the Printer Migration Wizard that starts to save printer export information to a file. Then, at the new server, select the **Import printers from a file** option. Then, use the Printer Migration Wizard to import the previously exported printer information.

    **b.** Use Windows Server Backup at each existing print server to back up the contents of the print server. Then, at the new server, use Windows Server Backup to restore the information that was backed up from each existing print server.

    **c.** Connect to the `%systemroot%\system32\spool\printers` folder on each existing print server and copy the contents of this folder to the same folder on the new print server. Repeat this task at each of the remaining print servers.

    **d.** At the new print server, run the Printer Installation Wizard to install each of the printers in turn, selecting the **Search the network for printers** option to ensure that you selected and installed the printers.

**10.** You are a tech-support specialist at your company. A Windows Server 2008 R2 computer is configured as a print server. This server supports several different types of printers, including color ink-jet and laser models. After updating the driver for the color ink-jet printers, users report that their print jobs printed at either the color ink-jet or laser printers contain unintelligible characters. Checking the website for the color ink-jet printer manufacturer, you notice that they have withdrawn the latest driver and will be issuing one within a few days. What action should you take to enable users to print from the laser printer with the least amount of delay?

    **a.** Install new printers for the laser print device at another server running Windows Server 2008 R2.

    **b.** Open Device Manager on the print server and access the Driver tab of the laser printer's Properties dialog box. Then, click the **Roll Back Driver** button.

    **c.** From the Print Management snap-in at the print server, right-click the driver and choose **Set Driver Isolation > None**.

    **d.** From the Print Management snap-in at the print server, right-click the driver and choose **Set Driver Isolation > Isolated**.

**11.** You are responsible for several printers installed on a Windows Server 2008 R2 print server on your network, which is configured as a workgroup. You want to allow a secretary named Evelyn to have the ability to view and manage print queues, but do not want her to have any other administrative capabilities on the network. What should you do?

   **a.** Access the **Security** tab of the Print Server Properties dialog box and add Evelyn to list of user or group names. Then, select the **View Server, Print, Manage Documents,** and **Manage Printer** permissions under the Allow column.

   **b.** Access the **Security** tab of the Print Server Properties dialog box and add Evelyn to list of user or group names. Then, select the **View Server** and **Manage Server** permissions under the Allow column.

   **c.** Open the Computer Management snap-in and select the Groups sub-node under the Local Users and Groups node. Then, add Evelyn's user account to the Print Operators group.

   **d.** Open the Computer Management snap-in and select the Groups sub-node under the Local Users and Groups node. Then, add Evelyn's user account to the Power Users group.

**12.** You are responsible for the printers installed on your Windows Server 2008 R2 print server named Server3. This server is a member server in your company's AD DS domain. A user attempting to print to a printer named Printer2 discovers that he is unable to print. Checking with several other users, you discover that nobody has been able to print since yesterday afternoon. Attempting to print from your Windows 7 desktop computer, you discover that you are unable to print and receive the following message: `Printer2 on Server3 is unable to connect`. But, you are able to ping Server3 from your desktop computer. What should you do to re-enable printing?

   **a.** From the Sharing tab of the Printer2 Properties dialog box, select the option labeled **Render print jobs on client computers**.

   **b.** Restart the Print Spooler service on Server3.

   **c.** In the details pane of the Print Management snap-in on Server3, right-click **Printer2** and choose **List in Directory**.

   **d.** Install a new printer on Server3, and configure this printer to print to the same print device. Then, instruct the users to resubmit their print jobs to this printer.

# Printing Terminology in Windows Server 2008 R2

We are all used to thinking of a printer as the machine that spews out printed pages. But, Microsoft has its own terminology (which it has used ever since the days of Windows NT and 9x), which you need to be aware of. Table 13-2 describes the official Microsoft definitions.

**Table 13-2**  Printing Terminology Used by Windows Computers

| Term | Description |
|------|-------------|
| **Printer** | The software (logical) interface between the operating system and the print device. In other words, a printer is part of the software and a print device is hardware. What this means is that a printer is the way that Windows sees where it is sending print jobs. This is true for all Windows versions, client or server. |
| **Print device** | The physical (hardware) device that produces the printed output. This device can be connected directly to your computer using a parallel (LPT) port, a USB connection, or a wireless connection (such as infrared [IR]); or it can be attached to the network by means of its own network interface card (NIC). |
| **Print server** | The computer that controls the entire printing process on a Windows network. The print server handles printing requests from all its clients. It can be running either a server operating system such as Windows Server 2003 or 2008, or a client such as Windows XP, Vista, or 7; however, print servers on client operating systems are limited to 10 concurrent connections. |
| **Print driver** | The program that converts graphics commands into instructions a given type of print device can understand. |
| **Printer ports** | The software interface (such as LPT1) between the computer and the print device. |
| **Print queue** | A waiting area where print jobs are stored and sequenced as they await the print device. Jobs are sequenced according to the order in which they are received as well as priority settings that are discussed later in this chapter. |
| **Print spooling** | The act of writing the contents of a print job to disk before sending it on to the print device. This can improve performance by eliminating the print device as a bottleneck that ties up the operating system or an application until the entire print job is output by the print device. In Windows 7 and Windows Server 2008, the default folder for spooling is located at `%systemroot%\system32\spool\printers`. You can change this location by altering the print server properties (Advanced tab) or the appropriate key in the Registry. |

**TIP**   Remember that Microsoft considers a "printer" to be the software interface between the print server and the physical print device, and a "print device" to be the actual hardware device that produces the printed output. This convention is used on Microsoft exams.

## Printing Process

When a user selects **File > Print** from an application, a series of steps must be completed for the printed document to appear. These steps have remained much the same over all recent versions of Windows:

1. When the user selects **File > Print**, a new print job is created, which includes all the data, and eventually, the printer commands that the system requires to output a document.

2. The client computer queries the print server for a version of the print driver for the default or a selected printer. If necessary, the most recent version of the driver is downloaded to the client computer.

3. The graphics device interface (GDI) and the printer driver may convert the print job into a rendered Windows enhanced metafile (EMF). (The GDI is the component that provides network applications with a system for presenting graphical information.) The GDI actually does double duty by producing WYSIWYG (what you see is what you get) screen output and printed output.

4. It is possible for Windows to convert the application's output (the print job) into either a metafile or a RAW format. (The RAW format is ready to print and requires no further rendering.) The driver then returns the converted print job to the GDI, which delivers it to the spooler.

5. The client side of the spooler (`Winspool.drv`) makes a remote procedure call (RPC) to the server side of the spooler (`Spoolsv.dll`). If a network-connected server is managing the print device, the spooler hands off the print job to the spooler on the print server. Then, that spooler copies the print job to a temporary storage area on that computer's hard disk. This step does not take place for locally managed print jobs. In that case, the job is spooled to disk locally.

6. The print server receives the job and passes it to the print router, `Spoolss.dll`. (You should not confuse a router in this context with the device that directs network packets from one subnetwork to another.)

7. The router checks the kind of data it has received and passes it on to the appropriate print processor component of the local print provider, or the remote print server if the job is destined for a network printer.

8. The local print provider may request that the print processor perform additional conversions as needed on the file, typically from EMF to RAW. (Print devices can only handle RAW information.) The print processor then returns the print job to the local print provider.

9. If a separator page is being used, the separator page processor on the local print provider adds a separator page to the print job and then passes the print job on to the appropriate print monitor. All recent versions of Windows support three types of print monitors: language, local port, and remote.

   - A language monitor provides the communications language used by the client and printer. In the case of bidirectional printers, this monitor allows you to monitor printer status and send notifications, such as `paper tray empty`.

   - The local port monitor (`Localspl.dll`) controls parallel, serial, and USB I/O ports where a printer may be attached, and sends print jobs to local devices on any of these ports.

   - The remote port monitor enables printing to remote printers. An example is the LPR port monitor, which can be used as an alternative to the standard port monitor for UNIX print servers.

10. The print monitor communicates directly with the print device and sends the ready-to-print print job to the print device.

11. The print device receives the data in the form it requires and translates it to a bitmap, producing printed output.

Although it may seem complicated, this sequence is designed to make printing more efficient and faster in a networked environment. In particular, the burden of spooling is distributed between client and server computers.

## Installing, Sharing, and Publishing Printers

By itself, Windows Server 2008 R2 is a very capable print server that provides a large range of capabilities for working with printers and documents, much like the capabilities that were included with previous Windows Server versions. The original version of Windows Server 2008 added the Print Services server role, which provided enhanced capabilities for sharing printers on the network and centralizing printer and print management tasks into its own Microsoft Management Console

(MMC) snap-in. In Windows Server 2008 R2 this role is replaced by the Print and Document Services role, which adds scanning management to the list of capabilities.

> **NOTE**   For additional introductory information on the Print and Document Services server role, refer to "Print and Document Services" at http://technet.microsoft.com/en-us/library/cc731636(WS.10).aspx.

### Installing the Print and Document Services Role

Use the following procedure to install the Print and Document Services server role on a Windows Server 2008 R2 computer:

1. Open Server Manager and expand the Roles node.

2. Click **Add Roles** to start the Add Roles Wizard.

3. From the Select Server Roles page, select **Print and Document Services** (as shown in Figure 13-1) and click **Next**.

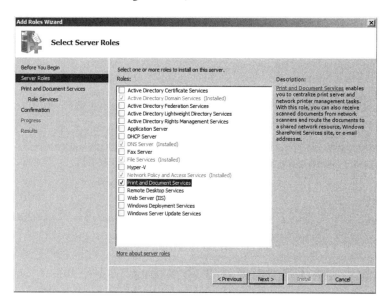

**Figure 13-1**   Selecting the Print and Document Services role.

4. The Introduction to Print and Document Services page provides links to information on this service. To learn more, click the links provided. When you're ready to proceed, click **Next**.

5. The Select Role Services page shown in Figure 13-2 enables you to select additional role services. The Print Server role is included by default. Make any desired selections and click **Next**.

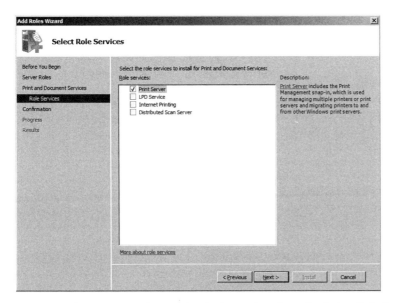

**Figure 13-2**   You can select optional role services from the Select Role Services page.

6. On the Confirm Installation Selections page, click **Install**.

7. The Installation Progress page tracks the progress of installing the Print and Document services server role. When informed that the installation is complete, click **Close**.

When finished, the Print Management snap-in is accessible from the Administrative Tools folder. This snap-in enables you to perform a large range of printer management tasks on printers installed on computers running any version of Windows from Windows 2000 or later. This chapter covers a large range of tasks you can perform from this snap-in.

## Installing Printers

You can install a printer on your Windows Server 2008 R2 computer from Control Panel even without installing the Print and Document Services server role. If you installed this role, you can also install a printer from the Print Management snap-in. This section looks at both methods of installing a printer.

### Using Control Panel to Install a Printer

Use the following procedure to install a printer from Control Panel:

1. Click **Start** > **Control Panel** > **Hardware**.

2. Under Devices and Printers, select **Add a printer**. The Add Printer Wizard starts and provides two options, as shown in Figure 13-3.

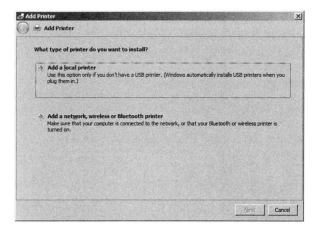

**Figure 13-3** Windows Server 2008 enables you to choose between installing a local or network printer.

3. Select the appropriate option and click **Next**.

4. If you select the **Add a network, wireless, or Bluetooth printer** option, Windows searches for network printers. Select the desired printer and click **Next**. If you select the **Add a local printer** option, the Add Printer page asks you to choose a printer port. Select the port to which the printer is attached and click **Next**.

5. You receive the Install the printer driver page. Select the make and model of the print device for which you're installing the printer (as shown in Figure 13-4) and click **Next**. To install a driver from an installation CD, click **Have Disk** and follow the instructions provided.

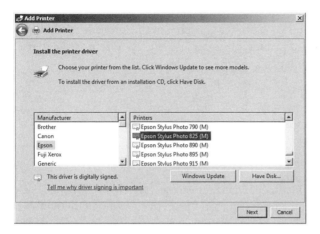

**Figure 13-4**    Selecting the make and model for which you're installing a printer.

6. The Type a Printer Name page provides a default name for the printer. Accept this or type a different name, and then click **Next**.

7. The Printer Sharing page shown in Figure 13-5 enables you to share the printer. Accept the share name or type a different name if necessary. Optionally, type location and comment information in the text boxes provided. (This information helps users when selecting a network printer.) When finished, click **Next**.

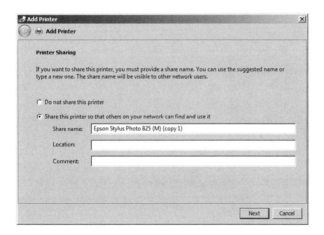

**Figure 13-5**    You are provided with options for sharing your printer.

8. You are informed that you successfully installed your printer. Click **Print a test page** to print a test page if desired to confirm printer installation. When done, click **Finish**.

> **NOTE**  If you are searching for a network printer at Step 4 of this procedure and the wizard is unable to locate the desired printer, click the link labeled **The printer that I want isn't listed**. The wizard displays a page that enables you to locate the printer in the directory, browse the network for a shared printer, or locate a printer based on IP address or hostname.

### Using the Print Management Console to Install a Printer

After you install the Print and Document Management server role as described earlier in this chapter, you can install a printer directly from this console. Use the following procedure:

1. Click **Start** > **Administrative Tools** > **Print Management** to open the Print Management console.

2. Expand the Print Server node to locate your print server.

3. Right-click your print server and choose **Add Printer**. The Network Printer Installation Wizard starts and displays options, as shown in Figure 13-6.

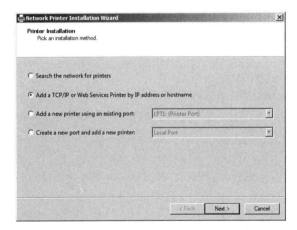

**Figure 13-6**  The Network Printer Installation Wizard facilitates installation of printers on the network.

4. Select the appropriate option and click **Next**.

5. If you select the **Add a TCP/IP or Web Services Printer by IP address or hostname** option, specify the host name or IP address as well as the port name on the Printer Address page, and then click **Next**. If you select the **Search the network for printers** option, the Network Printer Search page appears and displays the printers it finds. Select the desired printer and click **Next**.

6. On the Printer Driver page, select the make and model of the print device for which you're installing the printer, and then click **Next**.

7. The Type a printer name page provides a default name for the printer. Accept this or type a different name, and then click **Next**.

8. The Printer Sharing page provides options similar to those previously shown in Figure 13-5 that are provided when installing from Control Panel. Specify the required options and click **Next**.

9. If you receive a page asking for printer-specific configuration options, select the required options and then click **Next**. Options provided depend on the make and model of the print device associated with the printer you're installing.

10. You are informed that you successfully installed your printer. Click **Finish**.

When you finish installing the printer (whether from the Print Management snap-in or from Control Panel), the printer is displayed in the details pane of the Print Management snap-in when you select the **Printers** subnode under the node for your print server. From here, you can configure a series of management properties, as described in the sections to follow.

### Sharing Printers

As indicated in the previous section, you can share a printer at the time you install it. You can configure printer sharing at any time. Use the following procedure:

1. In the console tree of the Print Management snap-in, expand your print server to reveal the Printers node. All printers configured for your server will appear in the details pane.

2. Right-click your desired printer and choose **Manage Sharing**. This opens the printer's Properties dialog box to the Sharing tab.

3. Select the **Share this printer** check box. As shown in Figure 13-7, a default share name is provided automatically; accept this or type a different share name, as desired.

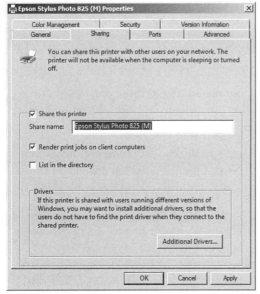

**Figure 13-7**   You can share your printer from the Sharing tab of the printer's Properties dialog box.

4. If users connecting to this printer are running different versions of Windows (including 32-bit as opposed to 64-bit Windows versions), click **Additional Drivers** to install drivers required by these users. From the Additional Drivers dialog box that appears, select the required drivers and click **OK**.

5. If client computers have the processing power for handling the print rendering process, select the check box labeled **Render print jobs on client computers**. To have the print server handle this processing load, clear this check box.

6. Click **OK**.

If you haven't installed the Print and Document Services server role, you can perform the same task from the Devices and Printers applet in Control Panel. Right-click your printer and choose **Printer Properties**. This brings up the same Properties dialog box; select the **Sharing** tab, as shown previously in Figure 13-7, and follow the same procedure as outlined here.

### Publishing Printers in Active Directory

If your print server is part of an Active Directory Domain Services (AD DS) domain, you can publish the printer to facilitate the task of users locating printers installed on the server. In the Print Management snap-in, right-click your printer and choose **List in Directory**, as shown in Figure 13-8. You can also publish your printer when configuring sharing (or from Control Panel if you have not installed the Print and Document Services server role), by selecting the **List in the Directory** check box, which was previously shown in Figure 13-7.

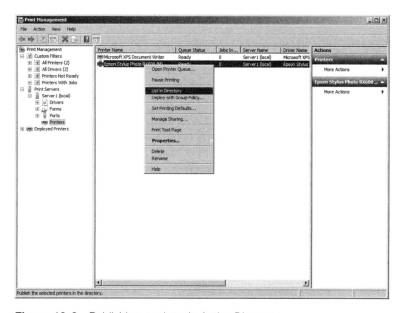

**Figure 13-8** Publishing a printer in Active Directory.

If you want to remove your printer from AD DS, right-click it and choose **Remove from Directory** or clear the **List in the Directory** check box.

You can also use the pubprn.vbs script to publish a printer in AD DS from the command line. The syntax is as follows:

```
Cscript Pubprn.vbs {<ServerName> | <UNCPrinterPath>}
"LDAP://CN=<Container>,DC=<Container>"
```

In this command, <ServerName> specifies the name of the server hosting the printer to be published. If omitted, the local server is assumed. <UNCPrinterPath> represents the UNC path to the shared printer being published. "LDAP://CN=<Container>,DC=<Container>" specifies the path to the AD DS container where the printer is to be published.

For example, to publish a printer named HPLaserJ located at Server1 to the Printers container in the que.com domain, use the following command at Server1:

```
Cscript Pubprn.vbs \\Server1\HPLaserJ LDAP://
CN=Printers,DC=Que,DC=com"
```

### Using Group Policy to Deploy Printer Connections

Group Policy enables you to deploy printers in an AD DS domain environment, automatically making printer connections available to users and computers in the domain or organizational unit (OU). Use the following procedure to add printer connections to a Group Policy object (GPO):

1. In the details pane of the Print Management snap-in, right-click the desired printer and choose **Deploy with Group Policy**. (This option is visible in Figure 13-8, which was previously shown.)

2. The Deploy with Group Policy dialog box shown in Figure 13-9 opens. Click **Browse** and locate an appropriate GPO. If necessary, you can also create a new GPO for storing the printer connections.

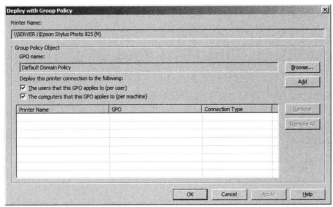

**Figure 13-9**   Using Group Policy to deploy printer connections.

3. Select either or both of the following options for deploying printer connections to users or computers, as required:

   - Select **The users that this GPO applies to (per user)** to deploy to groups of users, enabling these users to access the printer from any computer to which they log on.

   - Select **The computers that this GPO applies to (per machine)** to deploy to groups of computers, enabling all users of the computers to access your printer.

4. Click **Add**.

5. Repeat Steps 2 to 4 to deploy the printer connection settings to another GPO, if required.

6. Click **OK**.

# Managing and Troubleshooting Printers

Several factors must be considered in administering printers. Like any other shared resource, they can be assigned permissions and their use can be audited. Also, special printing configurations, such as printer pools, can be set up. Multiple printers can be configured for one print device to handle different types of jobs. Furthermore, lots of things can go wrong with print jobs. Complaints from users that they cannot print or are denied access can make up a significant portion of a network administrator or support specialist's job.

**NOTE** For detailed information on printer management including sample procedures, refer to "Print Management Step-by-Step Guide" at http://technet.microsoft.com/en-us/library/cc753109(WS.10).aspx.

## Using the Printer Properties Dialog box

Each printer has a Properties dialog box associated with it that enables you to perform a large quantity of management tasks. You already saw how to share a printer or publish it in AD DS. This section discusses several additional tasks that you can perform from this dialog box. Right-click the printer in the details pane of the Print Management snap-in and choose **Properties**, or right-click the printer in the Control Panel Devices and Printers applet and choose **Printer Properties** to bring up this dialog box. In addition to the tabs discussed here, some printers show additional tabs; for example, color printers possess a Color Management tab that enables you to adjust color profile settings. Some printers possess a Version Information tab, which merely displays version information and contains no configurable settings.

### General Tab

Use the General tab to rename the printer or modify the Location and Comment fields you supplied when installing the printer. You can also print a test page or modify printer preferences from this tab; click **Preferences** to open a dialog box that enables you to adjust settings, such as print quality, paper source, type, and size, maintenance factors such as print head cleaning, and so on. Appearance of, and options included in, this dialog box vary according to print device make and model.

### Ports Tab and Printer Pooling

As shown in Figure 13-10, the Ports tab enables you to select various available ports to which a document will be printed. Documents will print to the first available selected port. Click **Add Port** to bring up a dialog box that displays available port types and enables you to add new ports. From here, you can add a new TCP/IP port for accessing a network printer; a wizard is provided to guide you through the required steps. Options for configuring port options and deleting unneeded ports are also available.

**Figure 13-10**   The Ports tab of the printer's Properties dialog box enables you to configure printer ports and printer pooling.

The Ports tab also enables you to configure *printer pooling*. A printer pool is a group of print devices that are connected to a single printer through multiple ports on the print server. These print devices should be the same make and model so that they use the same printer driver. This method is useful because it allows pooling of similar print devices. In high volume print situations, if one print device is busy, print jobs directed to a printer can be spooled to another available print device that is part of the printer pool and printing jobs are completed more quickly. To configure printer pooling, specify a different port for each print device in the printer pool. Then, select the check box labeled **Enable printer pooling** and click **OK**.

To client computers, the printer pool appears as though it were a single printer. When users submit print jobs to the printer pool, the jobs are printed on any available print device. You should position the physical print devices in close proximity to each other so that the user does not have to search for print jobs. Enabling separator pages is a best practice that you should follow so that the users can locate their print jobs rapidly and conveniently.

This tab also enables you to redirect a printer should a problem occur with its print device and you need to take it offline for maintenance. Redirecting a printer on the print server redirects all documents sent to that printer. However, you cannot redirect individual documents. To do so, click **Add Port**, and on the Printer Ports dialog box, select **Local Port**, and then click **New Port**. In the Port Name dialog box that appears, enter the UNC or URL path to the other printer, and then click **OK**.

> **TIP** Configuration changes to the available ports on any print server affect all printers set up on that server. Also note that it is a good idea to locate all the print devices that make up a printer pool in the same general area of your operation. People won't need to roam the halls of your organization in search of printed out jobs.

### Advanced Tab

The Advanced tab enables you to control the availability of the printer and configure drivers and spool settings. Available settings on this tab are shown in Figure 13-11 and described in Table 13-3.

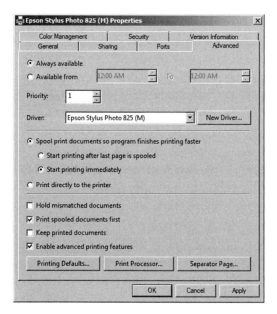

**Figure 13-11** The Advanced tab of the printer's Properties dialog box enables you to control availability, priority, and spooler settings.

**Table 13-3**   Configurable Advanced Printer Properties

| Setting | Description |
|---|---|
| **Always available** and **available from** | Enables you to specify the hours of the day when the printer is available. For example, you can configure a printer that accepts large jobs to print only between 6 p.m. and 8 a.m. so that shorter jobs can be printed rapidly. Jobs submitted outside the available hours are kept in the print queue until the available time. |
| **Priority** | Enables you to assign a numerical priority to the printer. This priority ranges from 1 to 99, with higher numbers receiving higher priority. The default priority is 1. For example, you can assign a printer for managers with a priority of 99 so that their print jobs are completed before those of other employees. |
| **Spool print documents so program finishes printing faster** | Enables spooling of print documents. Select from the following: <br><br> ■ **Start printing after last page is spooled:** Prevents documents from printing until completely spooled. Prevents delays when the print device prints pages faster than the rate at which they are provided. <br><br> ■ **Start printing immediately:** The default option causes documents to be printed as rapidly as possible. |
| **Print directly to the printer** | Sends documents to the print device without first writing them to the print server's hard disk drive. Recommended only for non-shared printers. |
| **Hold mismatched documents** | The spooler holds documents that do not match the available form until this form is loaded. Other documents that match the form can print. |
| **Print spooled documents first** | Documents are printed in the order that they finish spooling, rather than in the order that they start spooling. Use this option if you selected the **Start printing immediately** option. |
| **Keep printed documents** | Retains printed jobs in the print spooler. Enables a user to resubmit a document from the print queue rather than from an application. |
| **Enable advanced printing features** | Turns on metafile spooling and presents additional options like page order and pages per sheet. This is selected by default and should be turned off only if printer compatibility problems arise. |
| **Printing Defaults** command button | Selects the default orientation and order of pages being printed. Users can modify this from most applications if desired. Additional print device-specific settings may be present. |
| **Print Processor** command button | Specifies the available print processor, which processes a document into the appropriate print job. Available print processors are described in "Print Processor" at http://technet.microsoft.com/en-us/library/cc976744.aspx. |

| Setting | Description |
|---|---|
| **Separator Page** command button | Enables you to specify a separator page file, which is printed at the start of a print job to identify the print job and the user who submitted it. This is useful for identifying printed output when many users access a single print device. |

**TIP**   Unreadable output indicates incorrect printer drivers. If the printer produces a series of unintelligible characters rather than the expected output, the problem lies in the printer driver. Check with the manufacturer of the print device and ensure that you have installed the correct printer drivers.

**TIP**   You can configure different printers associated with the same print device so that managers' print jobs are printed before those of other users or so that long print jobs wait until after hours to prevent tying up a print device for an extended period of time. To do this, simply assign a priority of 99 to the managers' printer and 1 to the printer used by all other users. Also, assign permissions so that only the managers can print to their printer.

## Security Tab and Printer Permissions

Just as you can assign permissions to files and folders as you learned in Chapter 9, you can assign permissions to printers. Printers have access control lists (ACL) that you can modify in the same manner. Use the following steps to configure a printer's permissions from the Security tab of its Properties dialog box:

1. Select the **Security** tab of the printer's Properties dialog box, as shown in Figure 13-12.

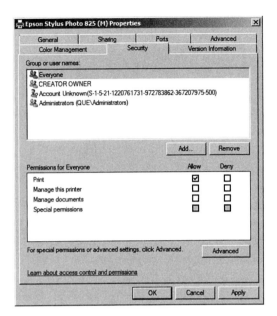

**Figure 13-12**   The Security tab of the printer's Properties dialog box enables you to configure printer permissions.

2. If you need to add users or groups to the ACL, click **Add** to open the Select Users, Computers, or Groups dialog box.

3. In this dialog box, click **Advanced**, and then click **Find now** to locate the required users or groups. You may also use the fields in the Common Queries area of the dialog box to narrow the search for the appropriate object.

4. Select one or more users or groups in the list, and then click **OK**. This returns you to the Security tab of the printer's Properties dialog box.

5. Select the permissions you want to allow or deny from the available list. Table 13-4 describes the available permissions.

6. If you need to assign special permissions or check the effective permissions granted to a specific user, click **Advanced**. The options available are similar to those discussed in Chapter 9 for files and folders.

7. When you finish, click **OK** or **Apply** to apply your settings.

**Table 13-4**   Windows Server 2008 Printer Permissions

| Permission | Description |
|---|---|
| Print | Enables users to connect to the printer to print documents and control settings for their own documents only. Users can pause, delete, and restart their own jobs only. |
| Manage this printer | Enables users to assign forms to paper trays and set a separator page. Users can also pause, resume, and purge the printer, change printer properties and permissions, and even delete the printer itself. Also enables users to perform the tasks associated with the Manage Documents permission. |
| Manage documents | Enables users to pause, resume, restart, and delete all documents. Users can also set the notification level for completed print jobs and set priority and scheduling properties for documents to be printed. |
| Special permissions | Similar to NTFS security permissions discussed in Chapter 9, the three default printer permissions are made up of granular permissions. Click Advanced to bring up the Advanced Security Settings dialog box, from which you can configure these permissions, if required. |

**NOTE**   The act of managing print jobs includes the two actions of resuming and restarting print jobs. Resuming a print job means to restart the job from the point at which it was paused, for example to add more paper to the printer. Restarting a print job means to restart it from the beginning, for example when the print job is being printed on the wrong type of paper. You can perform either of these tasks by right-clicking the print job in the print queue and selecting the appropriate option.

**TIP**   Print permissions behave in much the same fashion as file and folder permissions. As with file and folder permissions, printer permissions are cumulative, with the user receiving the sum of all permissions granted to any groups to which he belongs. If you explicitly deny a permission to a user or group by selecting a check box in the **Deny** column, this denial overrides any other allowed permissions the user might have, in exactly the same manner as discussed in Chapter 9 for file and folder permissions.

### Migrating Print Queues and Printer Settings

The Print Management snap-in enables you to export print queues, printer settings, printer ports, and language monitors, and then import these settings to another print server. Doing so enables you to consolidate multiple print servers or replace an older server.

Use the following procedure to perform a print migration:

1. In the console tree of the Print Management snap-in, expand the Print servers node, right-click the print server whose queues you want to export, and select **Export printers to a file**. The Printer Migration Wizard starts.

2. On the Review the list of items to be exported page, verify the objects listed that will be exported and click **Next**.

3. On the Select the file location page, type the path to the required file or click **Browse** to locate an appropriate file. The file you specified will be saved with a `.printerExport` extension.

4. The Exporting page tracks the progress of the export, and then displays an `Export complete` message. This page also informs you of any errors that might have occurred. You can obtain information on any errors from Event Viewer by clicking the **Open Event Viewer** command button provided on this page. This button opens Event Viewer to a Printer Migration Events subnode that displays events related to the migration process. For more information, refer to Chapter 20, "Configuring Event Logs." When done, click **Finish**.

Use the following steps to import the print queue to the new server:

1. In the console tree of the Print Management snap-in, expand the Print servers node, right-click the print server whose queues you want to import, and select **Import printers from a file**. The Printer Migration Wizard starts.

2. On the Select the file location page, type or browse to the location of the `.printerExport` file to be imported.

3. On the Review the list of items to be imported page, review the list of objects that will be imported, and then click **Next**.

4. On the Select import options page, select the following import options:

   - **Import mode:** Select **Keep existing printers** to maintain the settings on any existing printers that are installed on this print server, or select **Overwrite existing printers** to restore printer information from the backup file and overwrite the settings for existing printers on this print server.

- **List in the directory:** Select **List printers that previously existed** to maintain the current listing of printers in AD DS; select **List all printers** to add newly imported printers to the listing in AD DS; or select **Don't list any printers** to clear the listing of printers in AD DS.

- Select the **Convert LPR Ports to Standard Port Monitors** check box to convert Line Printer Remote (LPR) printer ports to the faster Standard Port Monitor when performing the import operation.

5. Click **Next**.

6. The Importing page tracks the progress of the import operation and displays an `Import Complete` operation when finished. This page also informs you of any errors that might have occurred. You can obtain information on any errors from Event Viewer by clicking **Open Event Viewer**, as previously described for the export action. When done, click **Finish**.

**NOTE** You can also migrate printer queues and settings from the command line by using the `Printbrm.exe` command. For more information on exporting and importing print queues and settings, refer to "Migrate Print Servers" at http://technet. microsoft.com/en-us/library/cc722360.aspx.

### Isolating Printer Drivers

Windows Server 2008 R2 introduces the capability to configure printer driver components to run in a process that is isolated from other processes including the spooler process. Doing so improves the reliability of the Windows print service by preventing a faulty printer driver from stopping all print operations on the print server. In previous Windows Server versions, including the original version of Windows Server 2008, printer drivers ran in the same process as the spooler; if a driver component were to fail, all print operations from the server would be halted.

Driver isolation is specified by an INF file that installs the printer driver. If this file indicates that the driver being installed supports driver isolation, the installer automatically configures the driver to run in an isolated process. This is specified by a `DriverIsolation` keyword in the INF file. If this variable is set to 2, the driver supports driver isolation; if it is omitted or set to 0, the driver does not support driver isolation.

To configure driver isolation, select the **Drivers** subnode under the print server in the Print Management snap-in. Right-click the driver and choose **Set Driver Isolation**

**> Isolated**, as shown in Figure 13-13. To disable driver isolation, choose **None** or **Shared**.

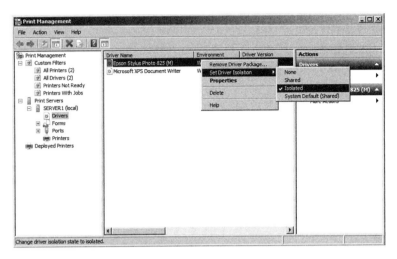

**Figure 13-13**   Configuring printer driver isolation.

**NOTE**   For more information on printer driver isolation, refer to "Printer Driver Isolation" at http://msdn.microsoft.com/en-us/library/ff560836(VS.85). aspx.

**TIP**   Sometimes, you might have a server on which you've installed different types of printers, such as laser, color laser, or color inkjet. Enabling printer driver isolation enables you to ensure that should a driver problem be encountered with one printer type, users can continue to use other printers of a different type on the same server.

### Configuring Location-Aware Printer Settings

Windows Server 2008 R2 introduces a location-aware default printer settings. Users with mobile computers running Windows 7 Professional, Enterprise, or Ultimate can configure a different default printer according to the network to which they are connected. For example, a user can specify a default printer when in the office, and a different default printer set for home. The laptop automatically selects the correct default printer according to the current location of the user.

Use the following procedure on a Windows 7 computer to configure location-aware printing:

1. Click **Start > Devices and Printers**. The Control Panel Devices and Printers applet opens.

2. Select a printer from those displayed under Printers and Faxes, and then click the **Manage Default Printers** option on the menu bar.

3. From the Manage Default Printers dialog box that appears, select the **Change my default printer when I change networks** radio button.

4. Select a printer for each network to which you connect, click **Add**, and then click **OK** when finished.

### Delegating Print Management

New to Windows Server 2008 R2 and Windows 7 is the ability to delegate print-management tasks directly to users who are not members of a group with built-in print-management capabilities, such as the Administrators, Server Operators, or Print Operators groups. This capability enables you to balance administrative work-loads across users without the need to grant excessive administrative capabilities; it also enables you to configure default printer security settings on print servers so that new printers inherit these settings automatically as you install them.

The Security tab of the print server's Properties dialog box introduces the following new permissions, which enable you to delegate print management tasks:

- **View Server:** Enables users to view the print server, including the printers that are managed by the server. By default, the Everyone group is granted this permission.

- **Manage Server:** Enables users to create and delete print queues with already installed drivers, add or delete ports, and add or delete forms. By default, administrators and the Interactive group are granted this permission. A user who has been granted this permission is referred to as a "delegated print administrator."

You need to be a member of the Administrators group or running with administrative privileges to create a delegated print administrator. Use the following procedure:

1. In the console tree of the Print Management snap-in, right-click the print server and choose **Properties**.

2. Select the **Security** tab to display the default permissions, as shown in Figure 13-14.

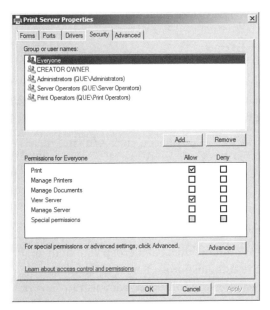

**Figure 13-14**    The Security tab of the print server's Properties dialog box enables you to delegate administrative control of printers attached to the server.

3. Click **Add** to add the user or group to which you want to delegate users, type the required user or group name, and then click **OK**. The user or group is added to the list in the Security tab.

4. Select this user or group and then select the check box under the **Allow** column for **Manage Server**. (This also selects the **View Server** permission.)

5. Also, select the **Print**, **Manage Documents**, and **Manage Printers** permissions in the Allow column.

6. To delegate just the ability to add printers, follow Step 3 to add the user or group, and then select the **Manage Server** and **Print** permissions only. (This also selects the **View Server** permission.)

7. To delegate just the ability to manage existing print queues, follow Step 3, and then select the **View Server**, **Print**, **Manage Documents**, and **Manage Printer** permissions.

8. When finished, click **OK** to apply the permissions and close the Security tab of the Print Server Properties dialog box.

**NOTE**   For more information on delegating administrative control of printers, refer to "Assigning Delegated Print Administrator and Printer Permission Settings in Windows Server 2008 R2" at http://technet.microsoft.com/en-us/library/ee524015(WS.10).aspx. Included in this reference are tables that describe the tasks that users granted the various permissions in the print server's Security tab are entitled to perform.

## Troubleshooting Printer Problems

Lots of things can go wrong in a print job's journey from an application to a print device, with stops in between at the operating system and its print drivers. By having reviewed the printing process described at the beginning of this chapter, you can often locate the source of printing problems.

### Some Common Problems

When a user complains that he cannot print, the first thing to do is check the physical aspects of the print device, such as the cable, power, and paper. If you need to check more advanced print device-related problems, refer to *CompTIA A+ Cert Guide, 220-701 and 220-702* (by Mark Edward Soper, Scott Mueller, and David L. Prowse) for more suggestions.

`Access Denied` errors usually indicate that printer permissions are not configured correctly or that they are not configured to the user's liking.

If the printed document comes out garbled, someone has installed an incorrect print driver. You should ensure that the correct driver for the problematic client is installed. (Click **Additional Drivers** on the Sharing tab of the printer's Properties dialog box to add a driver.) Occasionally, this problem can result from a resource conflict with the parallel port or a damaged printer cable. Check the printer cable for damage; also check for conflicts using Device Manager.

Occasionally, print jobs get stuck in the spooler. You might notice that no print jobs are coming out and the hard drive on the print server appears to be thrashing. If this should happen, you need to stop and restart the spooler service. Use the following procedure:

1. In the console tree of Server Manager, expand the **Configuration** node and select **Services**. This displays the list of services in the details pane.

2. Right-click **Print Spooler** and choose **Stop**.

**3.** Right-click it again and choose **Start**. This clears the jammed print job from the queue and allows other print jobs to print.

You can modify spool settings on a per-printer basis, making the printing process more efficient. The Advanced tab of the printer's Properties dialog box contains several settings previously shown in Figure 13-11 and described in Table 13-3 that you can modify to optimize the spool process if necessary.

### Printer Port Problems

Improperly configured printer ports can cause printing failures. Errors can occur if a user configures a computer to print directly to the printer or to use bidirectional printing when the print device does not support these functions.

TCP/IP printing, like the protocol itself, is subject to connectivity problems that require a good grounding in the TCP/IP protocol, as provided in Chapter 1, "Configuring IPv4 and IPv6 Addressing." If TCP/IP port problems occur, try configuring the standard TCP/IP port monitor for your printer. You may need to reconfigure the standard port monitor port from the printer's Properties dialog box. On the Ports tab of this dialog box (previously shown in Figure 13-10), click **Configure Port**. You may need to check with the manufacturer of the print device to see if it supports Simple Network Management Protocol (SNMP). Printers use SNMP to return print status. On print devices that support SNMP, printer status is returned to the user, including errors that occur during printing. If a print device does not support SNMP, you will either receive a generic printing error message or no error message when a printing error occurs.

You may need to add an additional TCP/IP port using the procedure described earlier in this chapter. You may also need to verify the port name and the printer name or IP address in the Ports tab of the printer's Properties dialog box. To do so, click **Configure Port**, and make the required modifications in the Configure Standard TCP/IP Port Monitor dialog box that appears. Then, click **OK** and click **Close** to close the printer's Properties dialog box.

### Enabling Notifications

The Print Management snap-in enables you to set up filters that can respond to printers encountering problem conditions such as paper jams or running out of paper. Such a filter can perform an action such as sending an e-mail to an administrator, running a script, or so on.

Use the following procedure to set up a filter for notification purposes:

1. In the console tree of the Print Management snap-in, right-click **Custom Filters** and choose **Add New Printer Filter**. This starts the New Printer Filter Wizard.

2. On the Printer Filter Name and Description page, type a name and optional description, and then click **Next**.

3. On the Define a filter page shown in Figure 13-15, specify values for the filter criteria, as follows:

   ■ **Field:** Specify a characteristic for the print server, queue, or status. By specifying **Queue Status**, you can evaluate a printer's current status.

   ■ **Condition:** Specify a Boolean characteristic, such as "is exactly," "begins with," "contains," or several others. Available conditions depend on the Field value.

   ■ **Value:** The value to be matched for the criteria to be met.

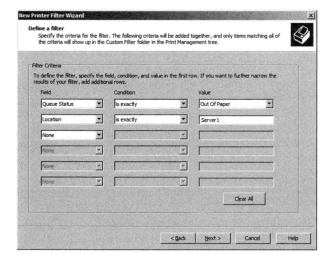

**Figure 13-15**   Defining a filter that alerts you to an out of paper condition on any printer attached to a server named Server1.

4. When finished specifying the appropriate criteria, click **Next** to display the Set Notifications (Optional) page.

5. On this page, select **Send e-mail notification** and type one or more e-mail addresses of individuals to be notified in the format `account@domain`. Also type the e-mail address of the sender, the name or IP address of the SMTP server that will relay the message, and message text to be included in the e-mail. If you want to run a script, select **Run script** and type the path to the required script or click **Browse** to locate the script. Use the Additional arguments field to include any required script parameters.

6. When done, click **Finish**.

## Exam Preparation Tasks

## Review All the Key Topics

Review the most important topics in this chapter, noted with the key topics icon in the outer margin of the page. Table 13-5 lists a reference of these key topics and the page numbers on which each is found.

**Table 13-5**  Key Topics for Chapter 13

| Key Topic Element | Description | Page Number |
| --- | --- | --- |
| Table 13-2 | Describes important terms that you might otherwise confuse with regard to printing. | 537 |
| List | Shows you how to install the Print and Document Services server role. | 540 |
| List | Shows you how to install a printer from Control Panel. | 542 |
| List | Shows you how to install a printer from the Print Management snap-in. | 544 |
| Figure 13-7 | Sharing a printer. | 546 |
| Figure 13-9 | Deploying a printer connection using Group Policy. | 548 |
| Table 13-3 | Describes configurable advanced printer properties. | 552 |
| Table 13-4 | Describes printer permissions. | 555 |
| Paragraph | Describes printer driver isolation. | 557 |
| List | Shows you how to delegate print management tasks. | 559 |

## Complete the Tables and Lists from Memory

Print a copy of Appendix B, "Memory Tables," (found on the CD), or at least the section for this chapter, and complete the tables and lists from memory. Appendix C, "Memory Tables Answer Key," also on the CD, includes the completed tables and lists to check your work.

## Definition of Key Terms

Define the following key terms from this chapter, and check your answers in the Glossary.

local printer, location-aware printing, network printer, print device, print driver, print driver isolation, print pooling, print queue, print server, print spooler, printer, printer pool, printer priority

This chapter covers the following subjects:

- **Remote Access Protocols:** This section sets the stage for the rest of this chapter by introducing the protocols you must be familiar with, both for creating remote access connections and for authenticating users accessing your network.

- **Configuring Dial-Up Connections:** Although dial-up hasn't been frequently used in recent years, users can still dial in to your network from a modem and phone line without accessing the Internet. This section shows you how to configure your remote access server to enable dial-up connections.

- **Network Address Translation:** When using IPv4, a Windows Server 2008 R2 computer can translate the limited number of public IP addresses to private addresses used only on an internal network. This section shows you how to configure your server for NAT, including its use as a DHCP allocator to provide IPv4 addressing information to incoming clients.

- **Virtual Private Networking:** An external client computer connecting to your network can access a dedicated tunnel across the Internet to complete the connection in a secure fashion. This section shows you how to create, authenticate, and secure a VPN connection.

- **Connection Manager:** This tool enables you to create profiles that can be downloaded to client computers to facilitate the process of creating dial-up or VPN connections in a secure, reproducible manner.

# CHAPTER 14

# Configuring Remote Access

You have already learned how to configure networking in the office environment, including technologies such as IPv4 and IPv6, DNS, DHCP, and file server configuration. But, the corporate LAN is only one part of the overall networking picture. Modern business extends far beyond the confines of the typical office—employees take work home, even spending entire days telecommuting with the consequent need to connect to office resources. Road warriors must connect to the network from hotels or client locations. And much more. These employees need reliable access to information stored on the corporate LAN, as well as the ability to collaborate with colleagues, regardless of where they are connecting. In this chapter and the next few chapters, you learn about remote access protocols and technologies offered by Windows Server 2008 R2.

## "Do I Know This Already?" Quiz

The "Do I Know This Already?" quiz allows you to assess whether you should read this entire chapter or simply jump to the "Exam Preparation Tasks" section for review. If you are in doubt, read the entire chapter. Table 14-1 outlines the major headings in this chapter and the corresponding "Do I Know This Already?" quiz questions. You can find the answers in Appendix A, "Answers to the 'Do I Know This Already?' Quizzes."

**Table 14-1** "Do I Know This Already?" Foundation Topics Section-to-Question Mapping

| Foundations Topics Section | Questions Covered in This Section |
| --- | --- |
| Remote Access Protocols | 1–3 |
| Configuring Dial-Up Connections | 4–6 |
| Network Address Translation | 7–8 |
| Virtual Private Networking | 9–12 |
| Connection Manager | 13–14 |

1. You are administering a network with a Windows Server 2008 RRAS server that users will be accessing from remote locations. You need to configure the server so that users connecting from locations without Internet access can dial-up directly to the server. Which protocol should you use?

   a. PPP

   b. SLIP

   c. PPTP

   d. L2TP

   e. IKEv2

2. Which of the following remote access protocols does not provide data encryption on its own?

   a. PPTP

   b. L2TP

   c. SSTP

   d. IKEv2

3. Which of the following remote access authentication protocols should you avoid because it sends credentials in unencrypted form?

   a. PAP

   b. CHAP

   c. EAP

   d. MS-CHAPv2

4. Which of the following should you do to begin configuring a Windows Server 2008 computer as a RRAS server?

   a. From Server Manager, use the Add Roles Wizard to install the Routing and Remote Access server role.

   b. From Server Manager, use the Add Features Wizard to install the Routing and Remote Access server feature.

   c. From Control Panel, use the Windows Components Wizard to install Routing and Remote Access.

   d. From Server Manager, use the Add Roles Wizard to install the Network Policy and Access Services server role and select Routing and Remote Access as a role feature.

**5.** You configured RRAS on your Windows Server 2008 R2 computer to accept dial-up clients. You want to ensure that RRAS can support as many as 20 clients that use PPTP to make their connections. How should you proceed?

   **a.** In the RRAS snap-in, right-click the server and choose **Properties**. From the PPTP tab of the server's Properties dialog box, click **Edit** and select the **Ports** tab on the dialog box that appears.

   **b.** In the RRAS snap-in, expand the entries under the server to reveal the Ports node. Right-click this node and choose **Properties**. Then, select **WAN Miniport (PPTP)** and click **Configure**.

   **c.** In the RRAS snap-in, right-click the server and choose **Properties**. From the Ports tab, select **WAN Miniport (PPTP)** and click **Configure**.

   **d.** In the RRAS snap-in, expand the entries under the server to reveal the **IPv4** node. Right-click this node and choose **Properties**. From the PPTP tab of the Properties dialog box that appears, click **Edit** and select the **Ports** tab on the dialog box that appears.

**6.** You added a new modem to your RRAS server to support an increased number of dial-up clients. However, the new modem does not appear in the Ports Properties dialog box. What should you do next to enable this modem?

   **a.** In the Ports Properties dialog box, click **Add** and select the modem from the list that appears. Then, click **Configure** to set the modem up to receive incoming calls.

   **b.** In the RRAS snap-in, right-click the server and choose **Properties**. From the Ports tab, click **Add** and select the modem from the list that appears. Then, click **Configure** to set the modem up to receive incoming calls.

   **c.** Access the Add Hardware Wizard in Control Panel to add the modem. Then, you should be able to configure it from the Ports Properties dialog box.

   **d.** In the RRAS snap-in, right-click your server and choose **Disable Routing and Remote Access**. Then, right-click the server and choose **Configure and Enable Routing and Remote Access**. In the Routing and Remote Access Setup Wizard, select the Remote Access option and when you reach the Ports page, ensure that the modem is present; if it is not present, click **Add** to add the modem.

7.  You are investigating the possibility of using NAT to enable Internet access on the client computers of your small company's network. Which are you able to do by configuring your Windows Server 2008 R2 computer as a NAT router? (Choose all that apply.)

    a.  Enable all client computers to access the Internet by means of a single IPv4 address configured on the Internet-facing adapter of your NAT router.

    b.  Enable all client computers to access the Internet by means of a single IPv6 address configured on the Internet-facing adapter of your NAT router.

    c.  Provide IP address configuration information to all client computers on your internal network.

    d.  Enable client computers to forward DNS name resolution requests to an Internet-based DNS server.

    e.  Enable routing of internal network traffic among more than one subnet.

8.  You configured your RRAS server to accept dial-up connections from external clients. Now, you want to enable the same server to provide NAT services to internal client computers. What should you do?

    a.  In the RRAS snap-in, right-click the server and choose **Configure and Enable Routing and Remote Access**. In the Routing and Remote Access Setup Wizard, select the **Network Address Translation** option.

    b.  In the RRAS snap-in, right-click the server and choose **Properties**. Select the NAT tab and click **Configure**, and then configure the required properties.

    c.  In the RRAS snap-in, expand the entry for your server to reveal the NAT node. Right-click this node and choose **Properties**, and then configure the required properties.

    d.  You cannot enable both dial-up access and NAT services on the same RRAS server. You must use a different server if you want to enable both these functions.

9.  Which of the following authentication types are supported for VPN connections in Windows Server 2008 R2? (Choose all that apply.)

    a.  Computer-level authentication using L2TP/IPSec

    b.  User-level authentication using PPP

    c.  Computer-level authentication using IKEv2

    d.  Data origin authentication and data integrity

**10.** You created a VPN connection but now need to enable the use of multiple transmission lines for increased speed of connections. You right-click the VPN connection and choose **Properties**. Which tab contains the option that you must configure?

- **a.** General
- **b.** Options
- **c.** Security
- **d.** Networking
- **e.** Sharing

**11.** You are responsible for configuring encryption levels on your Windows Server 2008 R2 computer, which runs RRAS for VPN connections to your network. All traveling workers have been issued Windows 7 laptop computers, and you want to ensure that computers running older versions of Windows are unable to access the network by means of the VPN connection. What should you do?

- **a.** Access the **Security** tab of the RRAS server's Properties dialog box and select the **Require encryption (disconnect if server declines)** option.
- **b.** Access the **Security** tab of the RRAS server's Properties dialog box and select the **Maximum strength encryption (disconnect if server declines)** option.
- **c.** Access the **Security** tab of the VPN Connection Properties dialog box and select the **Require encryption (disconnect if server declines)** option.
- **d.** Access the **Security** tab of the VPN Connection Properties dialog box and select the **Maximum strength encryption (disconnect if server declines)** option.

**12.** You are responsible for configuring your VPN server for connections by remote users. Users have reported that occasionally, downloads of important data while on the road have been interrupted and they have needed to resume these downloads from the beginning. Which feature should you enable?

- **a.** Connection Manager
- **b.** VPN Reconnect
- **c.** VPN Connection Security
- **d.** Advanced Security Auditing

**13.** You use the Connection Manager Administration Kit to create a profile that will provide settings for users on Windows 7 computers making VPN connections to your internal network. A user on a Windows XP laptop downloads and installs the profile. Later, when he attempts to connect to your network from home, he receives an error message and is unable to connect. Which of the following is the most likely reason he was unable to make this connection?

   **a.** You created a profile for a VPN connection. However, this user is attempting to make a dial-up connection and the profile is designed only for VPN connections.

   **b.** You specified the **Always use the same VPN server** option while running the CMAK Wizard, but the server whose name you specified is offline.

   **c.** You created a profile that enables Windows 7 computers to make the VPN connection. However, this user is using a Windows XP computer and the profile that he can use depends on the operating system in use.

   **d.** The user is using a computer running Widows XP Home Edition. He needs to upgrade his computer to Windows XP Professional.

**14.** You use the Connection Manager Administration Kit to create a profile that will provide settings for users on Windows 7 computers making VPN connections to your internal network. A user on a Windows 7 Professional laptop computer downloads and installs the profile. Later, she attempts to connect from a hotel location where she must type her username and password supplied by the hotel to access the Internet before she can complete the connection. She accesses the logon dialog box to connect to your network and types her domain username and password; however, she is unable to connect. She clicks Properties to bring up the connection's Properties dialog box, but the Internet Logon tab is missing. Which of the following is the most likely reason for this problem?

   **a.** While running the CMAK Wizard, you selected the **Use the same user name and password for VPN and dial-up connections** check box.

   **b.** While running the CMAK Wizard, you did not select the **Allow the user to choose a VPN server before connecting** check box.

   **c.** You should have created a profile for a dial-up connection instead.

   **d.** The user needs to upgrade her computer to Windows 7 Ultimate.

## Foundation Topics

# Remote Access Protocols

The remote access technology of Windows Server 2008 allows clients to dial into a Windows network over phone lines from remote points; for example, a salesperson calling in an order from a client location or hotel room. Windows Server 2008 includes the Routing and Remote Access (RRAS) server feature, to which you were introduced in Chapter 3, "Configuring Routing." In that chapter, you learned about the routing component; this chapter introduces the *Remote Access Service (RAS)* component, which facilitates this type of connection. Using RAS, remote access clients can dial-in from remote locations and access resources as if they were physically attached to the network.

You can achieve remote access connectivity by using either of two mechanisms described in Table 14-2.

**Table 14-2**   Remote Access Connection Mechanisms in Windows Server 2008

| Mechanism | Description |
|---|---|
| Dial-up remote access | A remote access client dials into the server through the telephone network or a dedicated digital line such as an Integrated Service Digital Network (ISDN) line to create a temporary network connection at a RAS server port. |
| Virtual private network | Uses an IP internetwork such as the Internet or a corporate intranet to create a virtual connection with a RAS server acting as the VPN server. |

Connectivity is the single most valuable capability in a computer. By connecting to other computers, a computer is able to access other information, applications, and peripheral equipment. Businesses have long since discovered that their employees will work longer hours and greatly increase their productivity when they are able to connect to the company's network from remote sites. For this reason, they provide RAS servers with either dial-up modems or VPN servers and Internet connections. Computers used by employees at remote locations link up with the Internet or corporate networks using dial-up or broadband networking connections. After a user's computer connects with a dial-up connection, she can open files and folders, use applications, print to printers, and pretty much use the network just as if she were connected to the network through its network adapter.

Standard protocols are used to make dial-up network connections:

- **Point-to-Point Protocol (PPP):** A dial-up protocol that can support multiple networking protocols, such as TCP/IP and Internetwork Packet Exchange/ Sequenced Packet Exchange (IPX/SPX), and can be used with compression and encryption. Note that support for the older Serial Line Interface Protocol (SLIP) has been removed from Windows Server 2008.

- **Point-to-Point Tunneling Protocol (PPTP):** A protocol used to transmit private network data across a public network in a secure fashion. PPTP supports multiple networking protocols and creates a secure VPN connection.

- **Layer 2 Tunneling Protocol (L2TP):** A protocol used to transmit private network data across a public network. L2TP supports multiple networking protocols. Used with IP Security (IPSec), it creates a secure VPN connection.

- **Internet Key Exchange version 2 (IKEv2):** A tunneling protocol that uses IPSec Tunnel Mode over UDP port 500. This combination of protocols also supports strong authentication and encryption methods.

> **NOTE** For more information on remote access protocols, refer to "VPN Tunneling Protocols" at http://technet.microsoft.com/en-us/library/dd469817(WS.10).aspx. Also, refer to "Overview of RRAS" at http://technet.microsoft.com/en-us/library/ dd469714(WS.10).aspx. This reference contains links to additional documents related to remote access servers.

## Remote Access Authentication Protocols

Authentication is the first perimeter of defense that a network administrator can define in a remote access system. The process of authenticating a user is meant to verify and validate a user's identification. If the user provides invalid input, the authentication process should deny the user access to the network. An ill-defined authentication system, or lack of one altogether, can open the door to mischief and disruption because the two most common methods for remote access are publicly available: the Internet and the public services telephone network. Table 14-3 discusses the authentication protocols supported by Windows Server 2008 dial-up network connections.

**Table 14-3**   Authentication Protocols for Remote Access

| Acronym | Name | Usage | Security |
|---|---|---|---|
| CHAP | Challenge Handshake Authentication Protocol | Client requests access. Server sends a challenge to client. Client responds using MD5 hash value. Values must match for authentication. | One-way authentication. Server authenticates client. |
| MS-CHAPv2 | Microsoft Challenge Handshake Authentication Protocol version 2 | Requires both the client and the server to be Microsoft Windows based. Does not work with LAN Manager. Client requests access, server challenges, client responds with an MD5 hash value and piggybacks a challenge to server. If a match is found, server responds with a success packet granting access to client, which includes an MD5 hash response to the client's challenge. Client logs on if the server's response matches what client expects. Note that the older MS-CHAP authentication protocol is no longer supported in Windows Server 2008. | Mutual (two-way) authentication |
| EAP | Extensible Authentication Protocol | Developed for PPP and can be used with IEEE 802.1X. Is capable of heading other authentication protocols, so improves interoperability between RAS systems, RADIUS servers, and RAS clients. Used with MD5-Challenge, smart cards, and certificate authentication in Windows Server 2008. | Provides additional authentication types based on plug-in modules, enables enhanced interoperability and efficiency of authentication process. |
| PEAP-TLS | Protected Extensible Authentication Protocol with Transport Layer Security | A highly secure password-based authentication protocol combination that utilizes certificate-based authentication. | Requires a computer certificate on the VPN server. |
| PAP | Password Authentication Protocol | Client submits a clear-text user identification and password to server. Server compares to information in its user database. If a match, client is authenticated. | Clear-text, one-way authentication. Least secure method. |

**Table 14-3** Authentication Protocols for Remote Access (*continued*)

| Acronym | Name | Usage | Security |
|---------|------|-------|----------|
| Smart cards | Certificates | User must have knowledge of PIN and possession of smart card. Client swipes card, which submits smart card certificate, and inputs PIN. Results are reviewed by server, which responds with its own certificate. If both client and server match, access is granted. Otherwise, error that credentials cannot be verified. | Certificate-based, two-way authentication. |

**NOTE** When using certificate authentication, the client computer must have a way of validating the server's certificate. To absolutely ensure that this validation will work, you can import the server's certificate into the client's Trusted Publishers list. If there is no way for a client to validate the server's certificate, an error displays stating that the server is not a trusted resource.

## New Features of RRAS in Windows Server 2008

Windows Server 2008 adds support for the following new RAS features:

- **Secure Socket Tunneling Protocol (SSTP):** A tunneling protocol that uses Secure Hypertext Transfer Protocol (HTTPS) over TCP port 443 to transmit traffic across firewalls and proxy servers that might block PPTP and L2TP traffic. SSTP uses Secure Sockets Layer (SSL) for transport-level security that includes enhanced key negotiation, encryption, and integrity checking.

- **VPN enforcement for Network Access Protection (NAP):** This is a client health policy creation, enforcement, and remediation technology that enables you to enforce security requirements such as security updates, required software such as antivirus, and other computer configuration settings. NAP is discussed in Chapter 16, "Configuring Network Access Protection (NAP)."

- **Support for IPv6:** Added is support for IPv6 remote access protocols such as version 6 of PPP (PPPv6), L2TP over IPv6, and DHCPv6 Relay Agent.

- **Cryptographic support:** Windows Server 2008 includes support for improved encryption algorithms for PPTP and L2TP connections, supporting new security requirements as mandated by U.S. and international government agencies.

- **VPN Reconnect:** Added in Windows Server 2008 R2, this allows a VPN connection to remain active even when a client's IP address changes. This functionality is useful in a case where a mobile network client changes wireless hotspots or changes from a wired to a wireless connection. VPN Reconnect is discussed in detail later in this chapter.

**NOTE** For more information on new RRAS technologies in Windows Server 2008, refer to "What's New in RRAS" at http://technet.microsoft.com/en-us/library/dd469840(WS.10).aspx.

## Configuring Dial-Up Connections

Dial-up networking connections are used for any type of connection—between two different computers, between a computer and a private network, between a computer and the Internet, and from a computer through the Internet to a private network using a tunneling protocol. You can share a dial-up connection using Internet Connection Sharing (ICS). All these functions and features offer different ways of connecting computers across large geographical distances.

When a computer connects to a remote access server, it performs functions nearly identical to logging on locally while connected to the network. The major difference is the method of data transport at the physical level, because the data is likely to travel across a rather slow telephone line for dial-up and Internet connections. Another difference between a local network user and a remote access user is the way that the user's identification is authenticated. If using Remote Authentication Dial-In User Service (RADIUS), the RADIUS server takes on the task of authenticating users and passing along their data to the directory service(s) in which the users' accounts are listed. We discuss RADIUS in Chapter 15, "Configuring Network Policy Server (NPS)."

### Configuring a RAS Server for Dial-Up

In Chapter 3, you learned how to install RRAS as a component of the Network Policy and Access Services Windows Server 2008 server role. If you selected the **Remote Access Service** option from the Select Role Services page of the Add Roles Wizard previously shown in Figure 3-5, you are ready to configure your server as a RAS server. Otherwise, access Server Manager and select the **Add Role Services** option under Network Policy and Access Services to access the Select Role Services page.

After you ensure that the RAS Server role feature has been installed, you can configure your server by accessing the Routing and Remote Access snap-in from the Administrative Tools menu. If you haven't configured your server as a router, you can
use the Routing and Remote Access Server Setup Wizard to configure your server
for dial-up. Use the following procedure:

1. In the console tree of the RRAS snap-in, right-click your server and choose
   **Configure and Enable Routing and Remote Access**. This starts the Routing and Remote Access Server Setup Wizard with a Welcome page.

2. Click **Next** to display the Configuration page. Select the default of **Remote
   access (dial-up or VPN)** (as shown in Figure 14-1), and then click **Next**. Alternately, if you want to configure your RRAS server for more than one of the
   functions provided by this wizard, select the **Custom Configuration** option
   and then select the required options from the Custom Configuration page of
   the wizard.

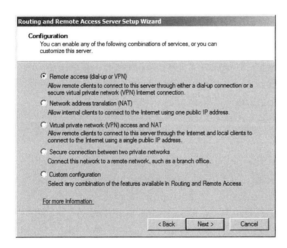

**Figure 14-1**   The Routing and Remote Access Server Setup Wizard enables you to configure
various functions available to your RRAS server.

3. From the Remote Access page of the wizard, select **Dial-up** and then click
   **Next**.

4. On the IP Address Assignment page, select **Automatically** if your network is
   configured with a DHCP server. Otherwise, select **From a specified range of
   addresses**. Then, click **Next**.

5. If you selected the **From a specified range of addresses** option, you receive
   the Address Range Assignment page. On this page, click **Add** to add a range of

IP addresses that the RRAS server will allocate to clients. Repeat if needed to add additional address ranges. When finished, click **Next**.

6. You receive the Managing Multiple Remote Access Servers page shown in Figure 14-2. For the present chapter, select **No, use Routing and Remote Access to authenticate connection** requests (as shown in Figure 14-2), and then click **Next**. The option to use RADIUS is discussed in Chapter 17.

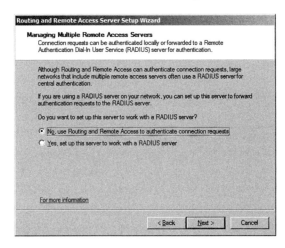

**Figure 14-2**   You can choose whether or not to use a RADIUS server to authenticate clients.

7. Review the options summarized on the Completing the Routing and Remote Access Server Setup Wizard page. If necessary, click **Back** to make any needed corrections. When done, click **Finish**.

8. If you receive a message box asking you to configure the properties of the DHCP relay agent with the IP address of your DHCP server, click **OK**. Refer to Chapter 2, "Configuring Dynamic Host Configuration Protocol (DHCP)," for information on configuring the DHCP relay agent.

### Configuring Dial-Up RAS Server Properties

After you enable your RRAS server, as described in the previous section, you can configure additional properties of the server from its Properties dialog box. Right-click your server and choose **Properties** to display the dialog box shown in Figure 14-3.

**Figure 14-3**   The RRAS server's Properties dialog box enables you to configure several properties related to dial-up remote access.

You can then configure the following properties for your RAS server:

- **General tab:** To enable dial-up clients to connect to your server, select **IPv4 Remote access server** and/or **IPv6 Remote access server** according to the IP protocol to be used by remote access clients.

- **Security tab:** Enables the selection of authentication and accounting providers and methods. Options available are discussed later in this chapter.

- **IPv4 tab:** If you are allowing IPv4 dial-up connections, access this tab and select the **Enable IPv4 Forwarding** check box. You can then select the method to be used by the server for IPv4 address assignment. Leave the default of **Dynamic Host Configuration Protocol (DHCP)** selected if you have a DHCP server that can assign IP addresses. To have the RAS server assign IPv4 addresses, select the **Static address pool** option and then click **Add** to add IPv4 address ranges to be assigned to remote access clients.

- **IPv6 tab:** If you are allowing IPv6 dial-up connections, access this tab and select the **Enable IPv6 Forwarding** and **Enable Default Route Advertisement** check boxes. Then, type the IPv6 network prefix to be used for assigning IPv6 addresses in the text box provided.

- **PPP tab:** From this tab, you can enable or disable the following settings pertaining to PPP connections to your server:

  - **Multilink connections:** Enable this option to allow multilink, which enables remote access clients to use multiple phone lines to increase their connection bandwidth.

  - **Dynamic bandwidth control using BAP or BACP:** When enabled, the server uses Bandwidth Allocation Protocol (BAP) or Bandwidth Allocation Control Protocol (BACP) to control the use of multiple phone lines for remote client connection.

  - **Link control protocol (LCP) extension:** When enabled, LCP sends Time-Remaining and Identification packets and requests callback during LCP negotiations. Clear this check box to prevent these actions if required.

  - **Software compression:** When selected, enables the server to use Microsoft Point-to-Point Compression Protocol (MPPC) to compress data sent on the connection.

- **Logging tab:** Enables you to select the level of logging (the server logs errors and warnings by default). You can choose to log errors only, log all events, or not to log any events. You can also log additional RRAS information for debugging purposes if desired.

### Enabling Modems used by the Dial-Up RAS Server

The Ports subnode within the RRAS snap-in enables you to configure modems for external users connecting to your RRAS server. Right-click this node and choose **Properties** to display the dialog box shown in Figure 14-4, which lists the ports available for users connecting to your server. To configure a modem shown in this list, select it and click **Configure** to display the dialog box shown in Figure 14-5. (Note that the check boxes that are enabled depend on the device you've selected from the Ports Properties dialog box.)

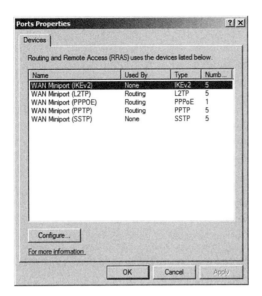

**Figure 14-4**   The Ports Properties dialog box displays all available RAS ports on your server.

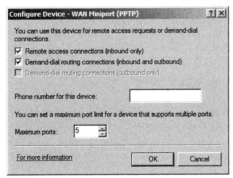

**Figure 14-5**   The Configure Device dialog box enables you to configure your modem to accept incoming connections.

- **Remote access connections (inbound only):** Enables your server to accept incoming calls on dial-up lines from remote users.

- **Demand-dial routing connections (inbound and outbound):** Enables demand-dial routing, as discussed previously in Chapter 3.

- **Demand-dial routing connections (outbound only):** Select this option to allow only outbound demand-dial connections.

- **Phone number for this device:** Specify the phone number that is used as the Called Station ID in BAP-enabled remote access connections. When a BAP-enabled device requests an additional connection, the RAS server returns a message containing this phone number, which needs to be dialed to complete the new connection. For PPTP or L2TP ports, you can type the IP address assigned to the interface of the VPN server on which VPN connections are received. VPN connections are discussed later in this chapter.

- **Maximum ports:** Specify the maximum number of ports for this device. This option is available only for devices that support a variable number of ports.

**TIP**   If your modem does not appear in the list on the Ports Properties dialog box, use the Control Panel Add Hardware Wizard to add the modem. When experimenting with modem settings for the purposes of the exam, you can add a dummy modem by choosing the option to manually select the hardware, and then selecting the **Standard 56000 Bps Modem** option from this wizard.

### Configuring Windows Server 2008 as a RAS Client

Although you would not normally want to do so, you can enable a Windows Server 2008 computer to dial-up to another RAS server located on your corporate network. To do so, open the Network and Sharing Center and select **Connect to a network**. You receive the Set Up a Connection or Network dialog box. Select either **Connect to a workplace** or **Set up a dial-up connection** (as shown in Figure 14-6) as required, and then follow the steps provided by the wizard. Options that you will encounter are similar to those in Windows 7. For more information, refer to *MCTS 70-680 Cert Guide, Windows 7, Configuring* (by Don Poulton, Pearson 2011).

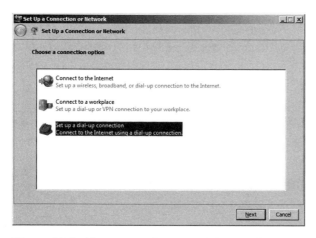

**Figure 14-6**   You can configure your Windows Server 2008 computer as a RAS client to connect to another server.

## Network Address Translation

*Network Address Translation (NAT)* is designed to address the problem of the limited number of IPv4 addresses still available by enabling the use of a single IPv4 external address with a series of client computers located on an internal network and configured with private IPv4 addresses. Refer to Chapter 1, "Configuring IPv4 and IPv6 Addressing," for information on how private IPv4 addressing works; Table 1-8 in that chapter describes the private IPv4 network addresses used by NAT.

RRAS includes a full-function NAT server capability that you would typically enable on a server that is located at the interface between your corporate network and the Internet. This server uses two network adapters, one connected to the Internet and the other to the local network. In doing so, it functions as the default gateway for all the client computers, enabling client computers on the local network to access the Internet without the need for public IP addresses. The NAT server changes the source IP address on each outbound packet to its public address and assigns a unique source port number, so that it can keep track of which client computer originated the network traffic and can properly route incoming traffic to the proper client.

> **NOTE**  The use of IPv6 eliminates the need for NAT; however, because IPv4 addresses are still in common usage, Windows Server 2008 R2 continues to support NAT and Microsoft expects you to know how to configure a server for NAT for the 70-642 exam.

The Windows Server 2008 computer that is configured for NAT is frequently referred to as a *NAT-enabled router*. This server provides the following capabilities:

- **Translation:** The NAT server translates IP addresses and TCP or UDP port numbers of packets that pass between the private internal network and the Internet.

- **Addressing:** The NAT server can act as a simplified DHCP server to provide IP address configuration information to client computers on the private network. This includes the allocation of an IP address, subnet mask, default gateway, and the IP address of a DNS server.

- **Name resolution:** The NAT server acts as a DNS forwarder for client computers on the private network by forwarding name resolution requests to the Internet-based DNS server for which it is configured.

**CAUTION** Because NAT provides addressing and name resolution services for client computers on the private network, you cannot configure the NAT server as a DHCP server or DHCP relay agent if NAT addressing is enabled; you also cannot configure this server as a DNS server if NAT-based name resolution is enabled.

As with other servers configured for routing, a NAT server must be multihomed—it is equipped with two network adapters, one connected to the Internet and provided with an IP address by the company's Internet service provider (ISP) and the other connected to the internal network. Furthermore, a NAT server cannot function as a dial-up RAS server, though it is possible for the NAT server to function as a VPN server, as discussed later in this chapter.

Use the following steps to configure your RRAS server for NAT:

1. In the RRAS snap-in, right-click your server and choose **Configure and Enable Routing and Remote Access**. (If you have been experimenting with other RRAS components on your server, you must first right-click the server and choose **Disable Routing and Remote Access**, click **Yes** to confirm your intentions, and then wait while the services are stopped and disabled.)

2. In the Routing and Remote Access Setup Wizard, click **Next** to display the page previously shown in Figure 14-1, and select the **Network address translation (NAT)** option.

3. Click **Next** to display the NAT Internet Connection page shown in Figure 14-7.

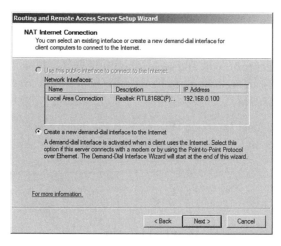

**Figure 14-7** The NAT Internet Connection page enables you to select an interface on which you want to enable NAT.

4. Select the required connection, click **Next**, and then click **Finish**.

5. If you selected the **Create a new demand-dial interface to the Internet** option in Step 4, the Demand-Dial Interface Wizard starts with a Welcome page. Click **Next**.

6. Type a name for the interface you're creating on the Interface Name page, and then click **Next**.

7. The Connection Type page shown in Figure 14-8 provides choices for the type of demand-dial interface. Available options depend on the hardware attached to your server. Make an appropriate choice and click **Next**.

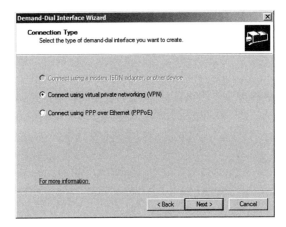

**Figure 14-8**   The Connection Type page presents options for the type of demand-dial interface to be created.

8. The remaining pages of the wizard depend on the connection type you choose. You will be asked to select protocols and security options that will be used for the connection and dial-out credentials to be used for connecting to the remote router, among other items.

9. After you complete the Demand-Dial Interface Wizard, you will receive a completion page for the Routing and Remote Access Server Setup Wizard. Click **Finish**.

### Enabling the NAT Server for DHCP

As already discussed, the NAT server can act as a simplified DHCP server to allocate IP addresses to client computers on the network. Use the following procedure:

1. In the RRAS snap-in, expand your server to reveal the IPv4 node, and expand this node to reveal the NAT subnode.

2. Right-click this node and choose **Properties**.

3. Select the **Address Assignment** tab and then select the check box labeled **Automatically assign IP addresses by using the DHCP allocator**, as shown in Figure 14-9.

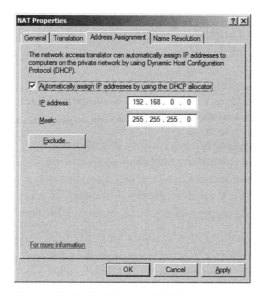

**Figure 14-9**   Enabling the DHCP allocator function on the NAT server.

4. Type the address and subnet mask of the network in the text boxes provided.

5. To exclude IP addresses from being assigned by the NAT server, click the **Exclude** command button, and then type the range of addresses to be excluded in the Exclude Reserved Addresses dialog box. Then click **OK**.

6. Click **OK** twice to exit the Properties dialog box.

**NOTE**   For more information on configuring the NAT server, refer to "Enable and Configure NAT" at http://technet.microsoft.com/en-us/library/dd469812(WS.10).aspx.

### Enabling Addresses, Services, and Ports on the NAT Server

When you have configured your Windows Server 2008 computer for NAT as already described, the server passes all standard ports and protocols. However, you can choose ports and services to be allowed across the NAT interface by configuring the properties of the interface. Proceed as follows:

1. In the RRAS snap-in, expand your server to reveal the IPv4 node and then expand this node to reveal the NAT subnode.

2. Select the NAT subnode to reveal the interfaces configured for NAT in the details pane.

3. Right-click the required interface and choose **Properties**.

4. From the interface's Properties dialog box, configure the following properties as required:

   - **NAT tab:** Enables you to specify whether the selected interface is a private interface connected to the internal network or the public interface that is connected to the Internet. For interfaces that are connected to the Internet, select **Enable NAT on this interface** to specify that the server performs TCP and UDP port translation in addition to IP address translation.

   - **Address Pool tab:** For the public interface that is connected to the Internet, enables you to list the configured ranges of public IP addresses assigned by your ISP. Click Add to specify the starting and ending addresses and the subnet mask to be used for NAT. You can also click **Reservations** to reserve public addresses from this list to be used by specific private network computers.

   - **Services and Ports tab:** Enables you to create, modify, and activate mappings between public IP addresses and ports, and services running on hosts on the private network at specified IP addresses and ports. For example, you can specify the services on the private network to which the Internet users can be directed. To add an additional service, click **Add** to display the Add Service dialog box shown in Figure 14-10 and specify the service description, ports, and private address in the fields provided. When finished, click **OK** to close the Add Service dialog box. Using this dialog box enables you to set up a web server that should be accessible only through the NAT device on a nonstandard port number by specifying the port number on this tab.

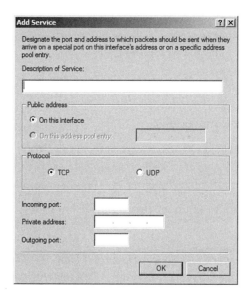

**Figure 14-10**   Enabling access by external users to an internal web server running on a non-standard port.

   **5.** Click **OK** to close the connection's Properties dialog box.

### Configuring Internet Connection Sharing

Windows Server 2008 also provides for a simplified version of NAT called *Internet Connection Sharing (ICS)*, which enables a small office or home network to use one computer on the network as the router to the Internet. Available on computers running Windows Vista and 7 as well as computers running both versions of Windows Server 2008, ICS includes the following components:

■ **Auto-dial:** For Internet connections that are not always on, the ICS computer can automatically establish the Internet connection when a client computer on the network attempts to access Internet resources.

■ **DHCP allocator:** Similar to full-fledged NAT, the ICS server can assign IP addresses to client computers. However, the available IP addresses are limited to the 192.168.0.0/24 network; the subnet mask of 255.255.255.0 and default gateway of 192.168.0.1 are also automatically assigned.

■ **DNS proxy:** The ICS server forwards DNS requests to the DNS server and forwards the DNS replies back to the clients.

As with NAT, the ICS server must be equipped with at least two network adapter cards. Use the following procedure to configure your Windows Server 2008 computer as an ICS server:

1. Click **Start**, right-click **Network**, and choose **Properties**. This displays the Network and Sharing Center.

2. Under Tasks, click **Manage Network Connections**.

3. Right-click the network interface connected to the network and choose **Properties**.

4. On the Sharing tab of the connection's Properties dialog box, select the check box labeled **Allow other network users to connect through this computer's Internet connection**.

You can also view ICS settings from the Network and Sharing Center. Click **Change adapter settings** to view the available adapters, then right-click the connection to the Internet and choose **Properties**. Select the **Sharing** tab to view the ICS settings. Note that this tab does not appear unless the server has at least two network adapters.

**NOTE**   For more information on ICS in Windows Server 2008 R2, refer to "Appendix F: Internet Connection Sharing, Network Bridge, and HomeGroup in Windows 7 and Windows Server 2008 R2" at http://technet.microsoft.com/en-us/library/ee126153(WS.10).aspx. For more information on the differences between ICS and NAT, refer to "How NAT differs from ICS" at http://technet.microsoft.com/en-us/library/dd469854(WS.10).aspx.

## Virtual Private Networking

A *virtual private network* (VPN) is exactly what its name infers—it's a virtual method of creating a private network across the inherently insecure Internet. In a nutshell, a VPN is a secure tunnel across the Internet. An administrator sets up a VPN server that sits basically between the private network and the Internet. When a remote computer connects to the Internet, whether via dial-up or other means, the remote computer can connect to the VPN server by using TCP/IP. Then the PPTP or L2TP protocols encapsulate the data inside the TCP/IP packets that are sent to the VPN server. After the data is received at the VPN server, it strips off the encapsulating headers and footers and then transmits the packets to the appropriate network servers and resources.

### How VPNs Function

A VPN provides a dedicated connection between one network and another. This can include the case of a remote user connecting across the Internet from home, hotel, or client site to the corporate network; it can also include connections between head office and branch offices within the company, where it is also called a site-to-site VPN. In any of these cases, the VPN connection provides for encapsulation, authentication, and data encryption.

### VPN Encapsulation

VPN networking emulates a point-to-point link by encapsulating each data packet with a header that provides routing information, which enables it to traverse the Internet or other public network to its destination. In other words, a tunnel across the public network is created that serves as a point-to-point connection from the remote user's computer and the VPN server on the corporate network. Logically, this acts as a wide-area network (WAN) connection between the two endpoints.

The four tunneling protocols introduced earlier in this chapter, although similar and all supported by Windows Server 2008 R2 and Windows 7 computers, act somewhat differently. PPTP incorporates security for encryption and authentication in the protocol by using Microsoft Point-to-Point Encryption (MPPE). SSTP encrypts data by encapsulating PPP traffic over the Secure Sockets Layer (SSL) channel of the HTTPS protocol. IKEv2 encapsulates datagrams by using IPSec Encapsulating Security Payload (ESP) or Authentication Header (AH) headers. L2TP does not provide encryption on its own. Instead, you must use IPSec to secure the data.

### Authentication

VPN networking with Windows Server 2008 R2 supports three types of authentication:

- **User-level authentication using PPP:** The client is authenticated by the VPN server by using a PPP user-level authentication method, which includes verification that the client has the appropriate authorization. If mutual authentication is in use, the VPN client also verifies the identity of the server, thereby providing protection against rogue VPN servers that an intruder might set up.

- **Computer-level authentication using IKEv2:** The VPN server and client use the IKEv2 protocol to establish an IPSec security association that exchanges either computer certificates or a preshared key, thereby establishing mutual authentication from each endpoint of the connection. Use of computer certificates is the strongest authentication method. Computer-level authentication is employed when connections are established using L2TP over IPSec or IKEv2.

- **Data origin authentication and data integrity:** Connections using L2TP over IPSec or IKEv2 can verify that the data sent across the connection has not been modified in transit. This is achieved by employing a cryptographic checksum based on an encryption key known only to the sender and receiver.

## Data Encryption

As the data is passed through the tunnel, it is encrypted by the sender and decrypted by the receiver. These processes depend on use of a common encryption key by both sender and receiver. An intruder attempting to intercept packets within the tunnel will discover that the data is unreadable. Use a larger encryption key for best security; however, the longer the key, the greater the computational power and time required to transmit the messages.

**NOTE** For more information on how a VPN functions, refer to "Virtual Private Networking" at http://technet.microsoft.com/en-ca/library/dd469653(WS.10).aspx. Detailed information on how VPNs function, including examples of VPN connections and encapsulated packet structures, is available from "Virtual Private Networking with Windows Server 2003: Overview" at http://technet.microsoft.com/en-ca/library/bb727041.aspx. Information in this reference is generally applicable to Windows Server 2008 VPNs.

### Configuring a RRAS Server for VPN

As with other RAS server configurations, your server must be equipped with two or more network interface cards (NIC). In addition, you should configure the Internet or perimeter network interface with a static IP address and default gateway, rather than as a DHCP client. Use a public IP address as assigned by the ISP with the appropriate subnet, plus the default gateway of an ISP router if the server is directly connected to the Internet, or the default gateway of the firewall connecting the VPN server to a perimeter network if available. It is also possible to use a NAT device between the Internet and the VPN server; in this case, configure the outbound network interface with a private IP address appropriate to the NAT device configuration. Once you're sure that your configuration meets these requirements, use the following procedure:

1. In the RRAS snap-in, right-click your server and choose **Configure and Enable Routing and Remote Access**. (If you have been experimenting with other RRAS components on your server, you must first right-click the server and choose **Disable Routing and Remote Access**, click **Yes** to confirm your intentions, and then wait while the services are stopped and disabled.)

2. In the Routing and Remote Access Setup Wizard, click **Next** to display the page previously shown in Figure 14-1, and select the **Virtual private network (VPN) access and NAT** option. Then, click **Next**.

3. On the VPN Connection page, select the network interface connected to the public network from which VPN clients will access the server, and then click **Next**.

4. On the IP Address Assignment page, select **Automatic** if a DHCP server is available for providing IP address assignment to VPN clients. To have the VPN server act as a DHCP allocator, select the **From a specified range of addresses** option, and then from the Address Range Assignment page, specify the starting and ending IP addresses of the ranges to be used for address assignment. When finished, click **Next**.

5. On the Managing Multiple Remote Access Servers page, select the appropriate option for using a RADIUS server for authenticating the VPN clients. If a RADIUS server is not in use, the VPN server uses the Active Directory Domain Services (AD DS) database if the server is joined to the domain; otherwise, it uses its local account database. Then, click **Next**.

6. You receive the completion page. Click **Finish**.

The procedure is slightly different if you are experimenting with a computer that has only one network interface. In this case, proceed as follows:

1. From the page previously shown in Figure 14-1, select the **Custom configuration** option. Then, click **Next**.

2. If you receive the Custom Configuration page, select **VPN access**, and then click **Next**.

3. On the completion page, click **Finish**.

4. You receive a Start the service message box. Click **Start service**.

**NOTE**   For more information on configuring the RRAS server for VPN, refer to "Enable RRAS as a VPN Server" at http://technet.microsoft.com/en-us/library/dd458983.aspx and "Enable RRAS as a VPN Server and a NAT Router" at http://technet.microsoft.com/en-us/library/dd458971.aspx. The latter reference contains a procedure that you can follow to set up a VPN server and NAT router on the same machine.

### Creating and Authenticating VPN Connections

To establish the VPN client connection on a Windows Server 2008 R2 or Windows 7 computer, use the following procedure. To follow along with this exercise and to test it, you should have a client computer and a VPN server that can both connect to the Internet. These two computers should not be connected in any other way than through the Internet:

1. Click **Start,** right-click **Network,** and choose **Properties**. The Network and Sharing Center opens.

2. Click **Set up a new connection or network**.

3. The Set Up a Connection or Network page previously shown in Figure 14-6 provides several connection options. Click **Connect to a workplace,** and then click **Next**.

4. You are given the option for selecting a dial-up or a VPN connection. Click **Use my Internet connection (VPN)**.

5. On the Type the Internet address to connect to page (see Figure 14-11), type the name of the organization and the Internet address (FQDN, IPv4 address, or IPv6 address). Select the other options displayed on this page as required and click **Next**.

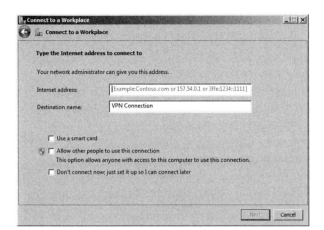

**Figure 14-11**  Type the Internet address and destination name of the network you want to access.

6. On the Type your user name and password page, type the username and password you will use to access the network. If this is a domain-based network, type the domain name. To remember the password for future access, select the **Remember this password** check box. Then, click **Connect**.

7. Windows displays a creation page as it creates the connection. When completed, it informs you that the connection is ready. Click **Connect Now** to connect.

8. To connect later to your connection, right-click it in the Network Connections dialog box and choose **Connect**. Type the required information in the Connect VPN Connection dialog box and then click **Connect**.

After you set up a VPN connection, you can modify its properties if required. Right-click the connection in the Network Connections folder and choose **Properties**. The connection's Properties dialog box consists of the tabs described in Table 14-4, each with different types of configurations:

**Table 14-4**  Options Provided by the VPN Connection Properties Dialog Box

| Tab | Options Available |
|-----|-------------------|
| General | Enables you to specify the host name or IP address of the destination, and the need to connect to a public network such as the Internet before attempting to set up the VPN connection. |

**Table 14-4**   Options Provided by the VPN Connection Properties Dialog Box (*continued*)

| Tab | Options Available |
| --- | --- |
| Options | Provides the presentation features, such as prompting for a name, password, certificate, and phone number, as well as the Windows domain, and redialing options if the line is busy or the connection dropped. The PPP Settings button enables you to use link control protocol (LCP) extensions and software compression, or to negotiate multi-link (use of multiple dial-up lines for increased transmission speed) for single-link connections. |
| Security | Enables you to select the type of VPN (automatic, PPTP, L2TP/IPSec, SSTP, or IKEv2), the security protocols to use, including EAP (for smart cards, certificates already on this computer, or trusted root certification authorities), PAP, CHAP, MS-CHAPv2, and so on. You can also configure encryption to be optional, required, or required at maximum strength. |
| Networking | Enables you to specify the use of TCP/IPv4 and TCP/IPv6, as well as File and Printer Sharing for Microsoft Networks, and the Client for Microsoft Networks. Click **Install** to install additional features, including network clients, services, and protocols. To install these features, you should have an installation disc. |
| Sharing | Lets you configure ICS in order to share the connection with other computers on your local network. You can also select an option to establish dial-up connections when other computers attempt to access the Internet. Click **Settings** to select the services on the network that Internet users can access. |

## Configuring VPN Connection Security

As already mentioned, any of PPTP, L2TP, SSTP, or IKEv2 enable you to set up a tunneled connection from a remote location across the Internet to servers in your office network and access shared resources as though you were located on the network itself. Recall that PPTP, SSTP, and IKEv2 include built-in security for encryption and authentication, whereas L2TP does not. You must use IPSec to secure data being sent across an L2TP connection.

An issue that you should be aware of concerns the encryption levels used by client and server computers when establishing a VPN connection. If these encryption levels fail to match, you might receive an error code 741 accompanied by the message stating that `The local computer does not support the required encryption type` or an error code 742 with the message `The remote server does not support the required encryption type`. This problem occurs if the server is using an encryption level different from that of your client computer. Servers running Windows 2000 Server or Windows Server 2003 use Rivest Cipher 4 (RC4) encryption at a level of either 40-bits or 56-bits. By default, Windows Server 2008, as well as Windows Vista and Windows 7 use 128-bit encryption. Use the following procedure to modify the encryption level:

1. From the Network and Sharing Center, click **Change adapter settings** to access the Network Connections dialog box.

2. Right-click the desired VPN connection and select **Properties**.

3. On the Security tab of the VPN Connection Properties dialog box shown in Figure 14-12, select **Maximum strength encryption (disconnect if server declines)**, and then click **OK**.

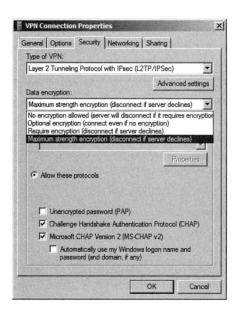

**Figure 14-12**   The Security tab of the connection's Properties dialog box enables you to specify the level of encryption used in a VPN connection.

**NOTE**   For more information on configuring VPN connection encryption, refer to "Configuring data encryption for a connection" at http://technet.microsoft.com/en-us/library/gg252641(WS.10).aspx.

**TIP**   Another issue you might encounter when securing a VPN connection that is configured to use PPTP is that of users receiving error 721 along with a message stating `The remote computer is not responding`. To ensure VPN connectivity, you need to ensure that TCP port 1723 is open on the firewall and that the firewall permits Generic Routing Encapsulation (GRE) protocol traffic. For more information, refer to "You receive an `'Error 721'` error message when you try to establish a VPN connection through your Windows Server-based remote access server" at http://support.microsoft.com/kb/888201.

### Enabling VPN Reconnect

New to Windows Server 2008 R2 and Windows 7 is the VPN Reconnect feature, which uses IKEv2 technology to automatically re-establish a VPN connection when a user has temporarily lost her Internet connection. This avoids the need to manually re-connect to the VPN and possibly having to re-start a download. VPN Reconnect can re-establish a connection as long as 8 hours after the connection was lost. A user could be connected to an airport Wi-Fi connection when his flight is called for boarding; when he lands at his destination, he can re-connect and finish his download.

Use the following procedure to set up VPN Reconnect:

1. Access the **Security** tab of the connection's Properties dialog box, as previously shown in Figure 14-12.

2. In the Type of VPN drop-down list, select **IKEv2** and click **Advanced settings**.

3. In the Advanced Properties dialog box shown in Figure 14-13, ensure that **Mobility** is selected, and then select a value (30 minutes by default) in the Network outage time dialog box.

4. Click **OK**, and then click **OK** again to close the connection's Properties dialog box.

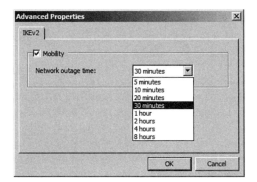

**Figure 14-13**   You can choose a reconnection time of up to 8 hours from the Advanced Properties dialog box.

**NOTE**   For further information and a sample detailed procedure, refer to "Remote Access Step-by-Step Guide: Deploying Remote Access with VPN Reconnect" at http://technet.microsoft.com/en-us/library/dd637783(WS.10). aspx.

### Configuring Advanced Security Auditing

Group Policy in Windows Server 2008 R2 provides a new set of advanced audit policy configuration settings that you can use to provide a high level of control over audit policies. As with other Group Policy settings, you can configure them in any Group Policy object (GPO) linked to an AD DS site, domain, or organizational unit (OU). Found in the Computer Configuration\Policies\Windows Settings\Security Settings\Advanced Audit Policy Configuration\System Audit Policies node of the Group Policy Management Editor, the advanced audit policies provide a total of 53 policy settings within ten categories, as shown in Figure 14-14. These policy settings are available for all editions of Windows Server 2008 R2, as well as Windows 7 Professional, Enterprise, and Ultimate.

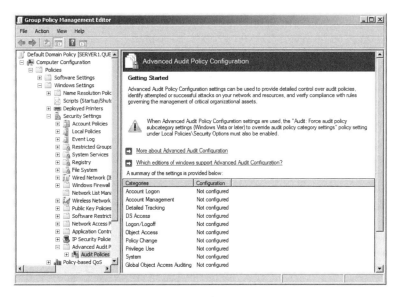

**Figure 14-14** Advanced Audit Policy Configuration provides a comprehensive set of audit policies classified into ten categories.

Previous versions of Windows supported basic audit policy settings. Although you
can still use these settings in Windows Server 2008 R2, they do not provide this
granular level of audit policy configuration. For example, the basic audit policy setting for account logon provides a single audit setting, whereas advanced audit policy
provides four settings. Enabling the basic setting is equivalent to enabling all of the
advanced settings. This provides greater control over auditing setting and enables
you to control the size and detail provided by the security logs to a much greater
extent.

To configure any of these settings, double-click the desired category in Figure 14-
14 to display the available settings. Double-click the desired setting to display its
**Properties** dialog box, select the **Configure the following audit events** check box,
and then select **Success** and/or **Failure** as required. Audited events will be displayed
in the Event Viewer Security log. For more information on each policy setting, click
its **Explain** tab.

**NOTE**    For more information on advanced audit policy settings as a whole, refer to
"Advanced Security Audit Policy Settings" at http://technet.microsoft.com/en-us/
library/dd772712(WS.10).aspx.

## Using Remote Access Policies

You can use remote access policies as well as user account dial-in properties for managing access to VPN connections. Using a remote access policy provides the following benefits:

- **Detailed administration:** You can use a separate group to grant dial-up or VPN access privileges. You can also delegate responsibility for managing access to this group to another administrator.

- **Using groups for access control:** This provides simplified administration of managing access permissions, compared to granting access on a per-user basis. You can utilize the same group for granting permissions to VPN, dial-up, and file share access.

- **Precise control of connections:** You can create policies that control different access technologies such as dial-up, VPN, or wireless access. You can also create different policies for users such as contractors who might need a different extent of access than regular employees. You can also configure callback settings and limit the locations from which callback is permitted.

Prior to Windows Server 2008, you could manage remote access policies by using the Remote Access Policies subnode of the RRAS snap-in. In both the original and R2 versions of Windows Server 2008, Network Policy Server (NPS) manages remote access policies. In the RRAS snap-in, right-click **Remote Access Logging & Policies** and choose **Launch NPS**. The topic of remote access policies is discussed in Chapter 15.

## Configuring VPN Packet Filters

By default, the Routing and Remote Access Server Setup Wizard creates filters that block all incoming traffic except incoming VPN connections. If the VPN server is running other services that depend on Internet access such as e-mail or web servers, you must manually create packet filters that allow traffic to and from these services. You can configure packet filters for each interface and configure them to either pass all traffic except those prohibited by filters or block all traffic except packets allowed by filters.

Use the following procedure to configure VPN packet filters:

1. In the console tree of the RRAS snap-in, expand either IPv4 or IPv6 according to the protocol for which you want to configure packet filters.

2. Select the **General** subnode to display the available interfaces in the details pane.

**3.** Right-click the desired interface and choose **Properties** to display the Properties dialog box shown in Figure 14-15.

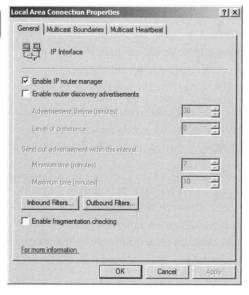

**Figure 14-15** The Properties dialog box for a VPN connection enables you to configure inbound and outbound packet filters among other properties.

**4.** Click the **Inbound Filters** or **Outbound Filters** command button according to the direction for which you want to configure packet filters.

**5.** In the Inbound Filters or Outbound Filters dialog box that appears, click **New** to create a new packet filter. This displays the Add IP Filter dialog box shown in Figure 14-16.

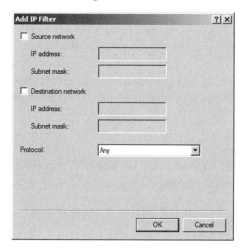

**Figure 14-16** The Add IP Filter dialog box enables you to specify the network parameters to be accepted or dropped by the VPN server.

6. Select **Source network** and/or **Destination network** as required, and type the IP address and subnet mask of the network for which you're configuring a packet filter. If you're configuring IPv6 packet filters, type the IPv6 address and prefix length. From the Protocol drop-down list, select a protocol to be filtered or leave this at the default setting of **Any**. If you select the **TCP** or **UDP** option, you can also specify source and destination port numbers (or leave these blank to allow the filter to work with all ports). When done, click **OK**.

7. You are returned to the Inbound Filters dialog box. As shown in Figure 14-17, the filter you specify appears in the Filters list. Select the desired filter action of receiving or dropping all packets except those that meet the specified criteria.

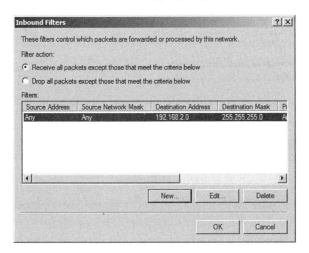

**Figure 14-17**   The Inbound (or Outbound) Filters dialog box enables you to add, edit, or delete packet filters.

8. To add additional packet filters, click **New** and repeat the process. If you need to modify any filter parameters, select it and click **Edit**. To remove a filter, select it and click **Delete**. When finished, click **OK** to return to the connection's Properties dialog box.

## Connection Manager

First introduced with Windows Server 2003, *Connection Manager* is a client network connection tool that provides support for local and remote connections to your network by means of different types of access points.

You can implement Connection Manager by using the Connection Manager Administration Kit (CMAK). This utility is designed for network administrators, information officers, and others that are responsible for developing, implementing, and supporting connection software for users remotely connecting to your network. This includes support for dial-up and VPN connections including the use of tunneling protocols to create tunnels through a public network. You can use Connection Manager to create a VPN connection through a dial-up session, digital subscriber line (DSL), or other connection type.

Connection Manager supports a large range of features that simplify and enhance the setup and use of connections by remote users connecting to your network from a dial-up modem or VPN connection. These features include the following:

- **Routing table updates:** Enables you to configure client routing tables for management of network traffic and security.

- **Automatic proxy server configuration:** Enables you to specify proxy server settings that ensure appropriate access to internal and external resources when a user is connected to the network.

- **Branding:** Enables you to customize the graphics, icons, messages, help file, and phone book support to assist remote users in accessing the network.

- **Custom actions and monitored applications:** Enables you to incorporate customized functionality including programs that can be set to run at various stages of the connection process, such as at logon or logoff.

- **Multiple user support for each service profile:** Enables you to provide support for users who share computers. You can maintain credentials for each user who shares the computer, so that they do not have to re-enter credentials each time they connect.

- **Simplified distribution:** When you complete running the CMAK Wizard as described later in this section, an executable file is created that you can distribute to all users who require the connection. This file includes all information necessary for setting up the connection with all parameters that you specified.

- **Custom phone books:** Enables you to specify the phone books that will be provided to the users. You can download the phone book and provide automatic updates as required at logon.

- **Custom help files:** Enables you to specify a customized help file that is displayed to users in place of the default file provided with Windows.

- **Support for VPN servers and protocols:** Enables users to choose a VPN server that will be used when connecting. You can also specify VPN protocols including PPTP, L2TP, SSTP, and IKEv2, as discussed earlier in this chapter.

**NOTE**   For more information on Connection Manager, refer to "Connection Manager" at http://technet.microsoft.com/en-us/library/cc771173.aspx, "Connection Manager Features" at http://technet.microsoft.com/en-us/library/dd672630(WS.10).aspx, and "Connection Manager Administration Kit Operations Guide" at http://technet.microsoft.com/en-us/library/dd672646(WS.10).aspx.

### Installing the Connection Manager Administration Kit

CMAK provides a wizard that guides you through the process of setting up connection profiles according to your business requirements. You can install the CMAK wizard on computers running Windows 7 or either version of Windows Server 2008; however, you must use a computer that is running the same processor architecture (32- or 64-bit) as the computers to which the CMAK profile is to be installed.

On a Windows Server 2008 computer, CMAK is installed as a server feature. Proceed as follows:

1. Open Server Manager and select the **Features** node to view the features installed on your computer.

2. In the details pane, click **Add Features** to start the Add Features Wizard.

3. On the Select Features page of the Add Features Wizard, select **Connection Manager Administration Kit** and click **Next**.

4. Click **Install** to proceed.

5. When you receive a message that installation succeeded, click **Close**.

### Using Connection Manager Administration Kit to Create a Profile

After completing this procedure, CMAK is available from the Administrative Tools folder. Use the following procedure to run the CMAK Wizard and create a connection profile:

1. Click **Start > Administrative Tools > Connection Manager Administration Kit**. The CMAK Wizard starts with a Welcome page.

2. Click **Next** to display the Select the Target Operating System page, as shown in Figure 14-18.

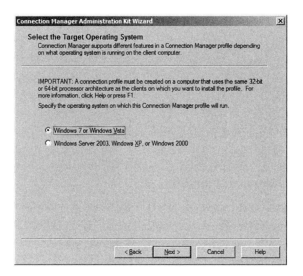

**Figure 14-18**   You must specify the correct operating system for which the Connection Manager profile will be used.

3. Select the correct target operating system and click **Next**.

4. The Create or Modify a Connection Manager profile page enables you to create a new profile or edit an existing one. Select the appropriate option and click **Next**.

5. On the Specify the Service Name and the File Name page, type the name of the profile to be created and the filename that identifies the Connection Manager profile, and then click **Next**.

6. On the Specify a Realm Name page, if the service requires one, select the **Add a realm name to the user name** option and type the realm name. Otherwise, leave the default of **Do not add a realm name to the user name** selected, and then click **Next**.

7. On the Merge Information from Other Profiles page, select any existing profiles to be added to the profile being created and click **Add** to merge them. When finished, click **Next**.

8. On the Add Support for VPN Connections page shown in Figure 14-19, select the **Phone book from this profile** option to add support for a VPN connection. Then select the appropriate options for VPN server name, username, and password. In addition, select the **Use the same user name and password for VPN and dial-up connections** check box if the user should use his domain credentials for logging on to the VPN or dial-up connection. When finished, click **Next**.

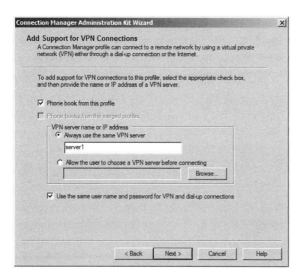

**Figure 14-19**    The CMAK Wizard enables you to add support for a VPN connection.

9. The Create or Modify a VPN Entry page enables you to create a new VPN entry or modify an existing one. A default VPN entry is supplied; click **New** to add another entry or **Edit** to modify this entry. When finished, click **Next**.

10. The Add a Custom Phone Book page enables you to add a custom phone book containing access numbers that users can dial to access a remote dial-up network. Type or browse to the required phone book file. If you need to specify text that users will see when accessing these phone numbers, type the desired text in the text box provided. When finished, click **Next**.

11. On the Specify an Automatic Phone Book Update Server page, type the phone book name and the URL for the connection point services server from which phone book updates will be downloaded, and then click **Next**.

12. The Configure Dial-Up Networking Entries page enables you to configure dial-up networking entries that contain additional configuration information for one or more phone numbers in the phone book such as IP settings to be used and scripts to be run. A default entry is provided. Click **Edit** to modify this entry or **New** to create a new entry. When finished, click **Next**.

13. The Specify Routing Table Updates page enables you to update the routing table if required. Routing tables were discussed in Chapter 3. If you need to make any changes, select the **Define a routing table update** radio button and provide the information required. Otherwise, leave the default of **Do not change the routing tables** selected, and then click **Next**.

14. The Configure Proxy Settings for Internet Explorer page enables you to configure proxy settings used by client computers. Select one of the options shown in Figure 14-20, browse to an appropriate proxy settings file if necessary, and then click **Next**.

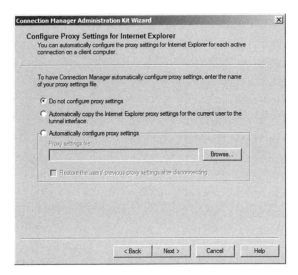

**Figure 14-20**   The CMAK Wizard enables you to specify Internet Explorer proxy settings if needed.

15. The Add Custom Actions page enables you to specify custom actions that perform additional configuration tasks on client computers. Specify any actions as desired, and then click **Next**.

16. The Display a Custom Logon Bitmap page enables you to change the default graphic that is displayed when a user runs the Connection Manager profile to create a connection. Select the default graphic or specify the path to a custom file if desired, and then click **Next**.

17. Also, specify a custom graphic for the phone book dialog box if desired or leave the **Default graphic** option selected, and then click **Next**.

18. The Display Custom Icons page enables you to select a custom icon for the profile that the user will see in the Network Center and the Network Connections folder. If desired, specify a custom icon. When finished, click **Next**.

19. The Include a Custom Help File page enables you to add a custom help file that is displayed when the user clicks **Help** in the Connection Manager window. To add a help file, select the **Custom Help file** option and specify the appropriate file. Otherwise leave the **Default Help file** option selected, and then click **Next**.

20. The Display Custom Support Information page enables you to display custom support information in the user's Connection Manager logon window. If you want to provide this information, type the desired text in the text box provided, and then click **Next**.

21. The Display a Custom License Agreement page enables you to display a custom agreement that the user must accept (or the installation will fail). To do so, type or browse to the text file containing your license agreement, and then click **Next**.

22. The Install Additional Files with the Connection Manager profile page enables you to specify additional files that will be installed on the client computer. Click **Add** to add any desired files. When finished, click **Next**.

23. You receive the Build the Connection Manager Profile and Its Installation Program page shown in Figure 14-21. You can make additional advanced customizations if desired by selecting the **Advanced customization** check box. Note the warning provided and click **Next** to create the Connection Manager profile.

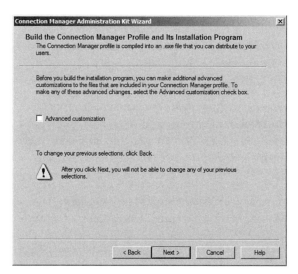

**Figure 14-21**   You are warned that you will be unable to change previous selections after you create your profile.

24. The wizard creates the Connection Manager profile and informs you that this profile is ready to distribute to clients. Note the path to the file and then click **Finish** to close the wizard.

After completing the wizard, copy the file created to suitable removable media for distribution to the users on a client computer for which the profile was created, or e-mail it to the required users.

---

**NOTE**   For more information on using the CMAK Wizard to create a customized connection protocol as well as advanced customization techniques, refer to "Connection Manager Administration Kit and the Customization Process" at http://technet. microsoft.com/en-us/library/dd672683(WS.10).aspx.

---

### Using the Connection Manager Client Interface

The user receiving the executable file as described in the previous section simply needs to run this executable; after doing so, he sees a logon dialog box that enables him to access the dial-up or VPN connection specified when running the wizard. This dialog box contains features and functions according to the options you've specified while running the CMAK Wizard. From this dialog box, users can specify their username and password for completing the connection; if you've specified a help file while running the CMAK Wizard, users can press **F1** to access help information. In addition, a user can click **Properties** from this dialog box to display a Properties dialog box that enables the following:

- **General tab:** Enables users to specify the way they connect to your service. If you've specified a VPN connection in the profile you've created, users can choose this connection, or alternatively use a dial-up modem and specify the required parameters. If you haven't specified a VPN connection, users can specify dial-up parameters only.

- **Internet logon tab:** Enables users to type a username and password for connecting to an ISP before establishing the VPN tunnel. Users receive this tab only if you've specified support for VPN connections and haven't selected the **Use the same user name and password for VPN and dial-up connections** check box as described in step 8 of the previous procedure and previously shown in Figure 14-19.

- **VPN tab:** Enables users to choose a VPN server for the connection. Users receive this tab only if you've specified support for VPN connections; selected the **Allow the user to choose a VPN server before connecting** radio button previously shown in Figure 14-19; and included a VPN server list file with the CMAK profile.

- **Options tab:** Enables users to change the connection defaults for establishing and maintaining active connections. Users can modify the number of redial attempts and the amount of idle time before the connection is terminated. Users can also choose to enable logging for the connection, and to view or clear the log.

- **Sharing tab:** Enables users to enable Internet Connection Sharing or Windows Firewall. These options are available only when the connection profile is used on a computer running either Windows Server 2003 or Windows XP.

**NOTE**   For more information on the Connection Manager user interface, refer to "Connection Manager User Interface" at http://technet.microsoft.com/en-us/library/dd672636(WS.10).aspx.

**TIP**   Users of all server and client-based Windows operating systems from Windows 2000 and later can use a profile established using CMAK to make dial-up and VPN connections to your network.

## Exam Preparation Tasks

## Review All the Key Topics

Review the most important topics in this chapter, noted with the key topics icon in the outer margin of the page. Table 14-5 lists a reference of these key topics and the page numbers on which each is found.

**Table 14-5** Key Topics for Chapter 14

| Key Topic Element | Description | Page Number |
|---|---|---|
| Table 14-2 | Introduces the two types of remote access connections supported by Windows Server 2008. | 573 |
| List | Introduces the four protocols used in creating dial-up remote access connections. | 574 |
| Table 14-3 | Introduces authentication protocols used by Windows Server 2008 RRAS. | 575 |
| List | Shows you how to configure your server for dial-up remote access. | 578 |
| Figure 14-3 | The RRAS server's Properties dialog box enables you to configure a large range of server properties. | 580 |
| List | Describes the properties you can configure from the RAS server's Properties dialog box. | 580 |
| Figure 14-5 | Configuring your modem to accept dial-up connections. | 582 |
| Paragraph | Describes the function of NAT for translating Internet IP addresses to private local addresses. | 584 |
| List | Shows you how to configure your RRAS server for NAT. | 585 |
| List | Shows you how to enable your NAT server for DHCP functionality. | 587 |
| Figure 14-11 | Shows you how to create a VPN connection to the network. | 595 |
| Table 14-4 | Describes available properties for VPN network connections. | 595 |
| Figure 14-12 | You can choose from several levels of encryption when configuring a VPN connection. | 597 |
| Figure 14-15 | Configuring VPN connection packet filters. | 602 |
| List | Shows you how to install the Connection Manager Administration Kit. | 605 |
| List | You can use the CMAK Wizard to configure a large range of properties for a dial-up or VPN remote access connection. | 605 |

## Complete the Tables and Lists from Memory

Print a copy of Appendix B, "Memory Tables," (found on the CD), or at least the section for this chapter, and complete the tables and lists from memory. Appendix C, "Memory Tables Answer Key," also on the CD, includes the completed tables and lists to check your work.

## Definition of Key Terms

Define the following key terms from this chapter, and check your answers in the Glossary.

Challenge Handshake Authentication Protocol (CHAP), Connection Manager Administration Kit (CMAK), dial-up networking, Extensible Authentication Protocol (EAP), Internet Key Exchange version 2 (IKEv2), Layer 2 Tunneling Protocol (L2TP), Microsoft Challenge Handshake Authentication Protocol version 2 (MS-CHAPv2), Network Access Protection (NAP), Network Address Translation (NAT), Point-to-Point Protocol (PPP), Point-to-Point Tunneling Protocol (PPTP), Protected Extensible Authentication Protocol (PEAP)-Transport Layer Security (PEAP-TLS), remote access policy, Remote Access Service (RAS), Routing and Remote Access service (RRAS), Secure Socket Tunneling Protocol (SSTP), virtual private network (VPN), VPN Reconnect

This chapter covers the following subjects:

- **Wireless Networking Protocols and Standards:** In this section, you learn about the wireless networking protocols and standards used by Windows Server 2008. You also learn how to configure wired and wireless remote access policies for clients connecting to your network.

- **RADIUS in Windows Server 2008 R2:** This section shows you how to configure RADIUS servers, clients, and proxies on a Windows Server 2008 R2 computer. You learn about connection request policies, RADIUS accounting, and templates that you can use to ease the configuration burden with these servers.

# CHAPTER 15

# Configuring Network Policy Server (NPS)

Chapter 14, "Configuring Remote Access," introduced you to the technologies and methodologies of connecting remotely to your network by means of dial-up and virtual private network (VPN) connection types. With either type of remote connection, you have the option of centralizing authentication of Remote Access Service (RAS) users by means of a specialized technology known as Remote Authentication Dial-In User Service (RADIUS). Formerly known in Windows Server 2003 as Internet Authentication Service (IAS), Windows Server 2008 provides for Network Policy Server (NPS), which is Microsoft's implementation of the RADIUS technology. This chapter introduces you to the use and configuration of NPS as a RAS network authentication service.

Nowadays, wireless networking is gaining popularity on many fronts, ranging from home networks to hotel, airport, coffee shop to complete office implementations of wireless local-area networks (WLAN). The Institute of Electrical and Electronics Engineers (IEEE) has introduced a series of wireless networking standards known collectively as 802.1X, several of which you must be aware of, both for the real world and for the 70-642 exam. We look at wireless networking standards and policies in this chapter before going on to discuss the NPS server.

## "Do I Know This Already?" Quiz

The "Do I Know This Already?" quiz allows you to assess whether you should read this entire chapter or simply jump to the "Exam Preparation Tasks" section for review. If you are in doubt, read the entire chapter. Table 15-1 outlines the major headings in this chapter and the corresponding "Do I Know This Already?" quiz questions. You can find the answers in Appendix A, "Answers to the 'Do I Know This Already?' Quizzes."

**Table 15-1**   "Do I Know This Already?" Foundation Topics Section-to-Question Mapping

| Foundations Topics Section | Questions Covered in This Section |
| --- | --- |
| Wireless Networking Protocols and Standards | 1–5 |
| RADIUS in Windows Server 2008 R2 | 6–10 |

1. You want to select a wireless networking standard that will enable you to transmit data at a rate of up to 150 Mbps while offering high resistance to interference from other electronic devices. Which of the following should you choose?

   a. 802.11a

   b. 802.11b

   c. 802.11g

   d. 802.11n

2. Which of the following authentication methodologies provides support for Extensible Authentication Protocol (EAP) for integration with an authenticating server such as a RADIUS server?

   a. Open authentication

   b. Shared key authentication

   c. 802.1X authentication standard

   d. IPSec

3. You are configuring security for your company's wireless network. You want to enable a security protocol that uses Advanced Encryption Service (AES) encryption by default; users should be required to type a security key or passphrase to access the network. What protocol should you choose?

   a. WPA-Personal

   b. WPA2-Personal

   c. WPA-Enterprise

   d. WPA2-Enterprise

4. You are configuring wireless access policies for client computers on your company's network. Client computers run a mix of Windows XP, Windows Vista, and Windows 7, so you are configuring two separate policies. Which of the following can you configure for Windows Vista/7 but *not* for Windows XP? (Choose all that apply.)

a. Choice of ad hoc or infrastructure wireless network types

b. Choice of PEAP-MS-CHAP v2, PEAP-TLS, or EAP-TLS authentication types

c. The ability to configure wireless network permissions

d. The option for caching user information for subsequent connections to the network

e. The ability to specify WPA2 authentication

5. You are configuring a wired access group policy in a GPO linked to your company's AD DS domain. You enable the policy labeled **Don't allow shared user credentials for network authentication** so that client computers must re-authenticate at each new connection to the network. Later, you find that a user on a Windows Vista Business computer is able to connect repeatedly without re-authentication. Which of these is the most likely reason for this occurrence?

a. This option is valid for Windows 7 client computers only.

b. You should have cleared the option labeled **Use Windows Wired Auto Config service for clients**.

c. You have selected 128-bit TKIP as an encryption option.

d. Another policy in a GPO linked to an OU is overriding your policy configuration.

6. Which of the following provides RADIUS services in Windows Server 2008?

a. Internet Authentication Service (IAS)

b. Network Access Protection (NAP)

c. Network Policy Server (NPS)

d. Wi-Fi Protected Access (WPA)

7. Which of the following can you configure as RADIUS clients? (Choose all that apply.)

a. A local client computer running Windows XP Professional

b. A wireless access point

c. A RAS server running Windows Server 2008 R2

d. A laptop running Windows 7 Ultimate making a VPN connection to your network

e. An 802.1X-capable switch

8. Which of the following best describes the function of a RADIUS proxy?

   a. A server that forwards RADIUS messages between RADIUS clients and servers that perform user authentication, authorization, and accounting

   b. A server that forwards RADIUS messages directly to a domain controller for authenticating remote users

   c. A wireless access point that passes remote user credentials to a RADIUS server

   d. A server that forwards RADIUS messages between IP subnets to access a domain controller for authenticating remote users

9. You are creating a new connection request policy for the RADIUS servers on your network. Which of the following types of network access servers can you specify for sending connection requests to the RADIUS server? (Choose all that apply.)

   a. Remote Desktop Gateway

   b. Remote Access Server

   c. DHCP server

   d. DNS server

   e. Health Registration Authority

10. You are responsible for configuring settings that will be applied to eight Windows Server 2008 R2 computers that will be used as RADIUS servers on your network. What should you do to configure settings such as shared secrets, RADIUS clients, IP filters, and remediation server groups with the least amount of administrative effort?

   a. Configure all these settings on one server, then use Windows Server Backup to back up these settings and restore them to each of the other servers.

   b. Create an OU and place all the RADIUS servers in this OU. Then configure all these settings in a GPO linked to this OU.

   c. Create a template and specify these settings in the template. Then apply the template to each RADIUS server in turn.

   d. You cannot do any of these actions. Simply configure each server in turn for RADIUS and then apply these settings to each server.

## Foundation Topics

# Wireless Networking Protocols and Standards

The recent advances in wireless networking technology have enabled individuals to connect to networks from virtually any place a wireless access point is available. Many offices are taking advantages of the ease of setup of WLANs, which allow for mobility and portability of computers and other devices located within the office. And public access points in locations such as restaurants and airports permit users to send and receive data from many places that would have been unthought-of not too many years ago. Along with this convenience comes an increased chance of unauthorized access to the networks and the data they contain.

Windows Server 2008 improves upon the wireless support included with Windows XP and Windows Server 2003 so that wireless networking is as well integrated with the operating system as normal networking. Consequently, wireless network reliability, stability, and security are considerably enhanced over that of Windows Server 2003. The following are some of the more important security improvements in Windows Server 2008 wireless networking:

- Windows Server 2008 minimizes the amount of private information—such as the service set identifier (SSID)—that is broadcast before connecting to a wireless network.

- When users connect to an unencrypted public network (such as an airport or restaurant Wi-Fi hotspot), Windows warns users of the risks so that they can limit their activities accordingly.

- Windows Server 2008 supports a complete range of wireless security protocols, from Wired Equivalent Privacy (WEP) to Wi-Fi Protected Access (WPA and WPA2), Protected Extensible Authentication Protocol (PEAP), and its combination with Microsoft Challenge Handshake Authentication Protocol version 2 (MS-CHAP v2) and Extensible Authentication Protocol Transport Layer Security (EAP-TLS).

- You can use Group Policy settings to configure Single Sign On (SSO) profiles that facilitate wireless domain logon. 802.1X authentication precedes the domain logon and users are prompted for wireless credentials only if absolutely necessary. The wireless connection is therefore in place before the domain logon proceeds.

**NOTE** Two types of wireless networks are possible. In nearly all cases involving servers, you will be concerned with an infrastructure network, which is a WLAN based on a fixed wireless access point to which all computers connect for network access. An ad-hoc network is also possible; this is a direct connection between two computers (usually two laptops or sometimes a laptop and a desktop) without going through a wireless access point. Keep these two definitions in mind.

### Wireless Networking Standards

Table 15-2 describes four wireless networking standards available to Windows Server 2008.

**Table 15-2**   Characteristics of Wireless Networking Standards

| Protocol | Transmission speed | Frequency used | Comments |
|---|---|---|---|
| 802.11a | 54 Mbps | 5 GHz | While reducing interference from other appliances, this technology has a shorter signal range and is not compatible with network adapters, routers, and WAPs using the 802.11b standard. However, some devices are equipped to support either 802.11a or 802.11b. |
| 802.11b | 11 Mbps | 2.4 GHz | The 2.4 GHz frequency is the same as that which is used by many appliances, such as cordless phones and microwave ovens; this can cause interference. This technology also is limited in that it supports fewer simultaneous users than the other standards. |
| 802.11g | 54 Mbps | 2.4 GHz | You can have 802.11b and 802.11g devices operating together on the same network. This standard was created specifically for backwards compatibility with the 802.11b standard. The signal range is better than that of 802.11a but this technology suffers from the same interference problems as 802.11a. |
| 802.11n | Up to 150–600 Mbps, depending on the number of data streams | 2.4 or 5 GHz | This technology is compatible with devices using the older standards at the same frequency. It also has the best signal range and is most resistant to interference, though it can have the same problems as 802.11b if using the 2.4 GHz frequency. |

### Planning the Authentication Methods for a Wireless Network

Any wireless device that is located within range of your access point can theoretically connect to your network. Such a connection can even come from outside the building; hence the popular term "war driving," in which a person in a car scouts around for any available wireless access point that he might use to initiate some type of attack. Consequently, you need to ensure that secure authentication policies are in effect that only permit authorized users to connect to your WLAN.

Authentication on a wireless network is not user authentication but device authentication. This first stage of authentication proves that the device is authorized to connect to the network; then, the user can be authenticated in the same way that she would when accessing a wired LAN. The following three means of wireless authentication are currently used:

- **Open authentication:** Allows access according to anyone providing the correct service set identifier (SSID) or WEP key for the access point. This method provides only minimum protection and should be used with an additional protection mechanism.

- **Shared key authentication:** Similar to a challenge-response authentication process, in this method, the client sends a request for access to the access point, which returns a challenge. The client returns an encrypted response. This method is vulnerable to an intruder intercepting the challenge and response signals. It is also known as *shared secret authentication*, because the client computer only needs this shared secret to authenticate.

- **802.1X authentication standard:** Uses Extensible Authentication Protocol (EAP) to integrate with the authenticating server such as a RADIUS server. EAP provides an open-ended conversation between a wireless client computer and the RADIUS server. In its basic form, this method provides a secure authentication of the client; however, it is vulnerable to a man-in-the-middle attack, in which an attacker intercepts the authentication data and gains unauthorized access. You can provide the highest level of security by using a version of EAP that provides mutual authentication, such as EAP-MS-CHAP v2, EAP-TLS, or EAP-MD5.

Windows Server 2008 uses the 802.1X standard for authenticating access to wired Ethernet networks and wireless 802.11 networks. It provides support for EAP used in conjunction with several different authentication protocols for wireless computers:

- **EAP-TLS:** Uses certificate-based mutual authentication, negotiation of the encryption method, and encrypted key determination between the client and the authenticating server.

■ **EAP-MS-CHAP v2:** Provides mutual authentication based on password-based user and computer authentication. Both server and client must prove knowledge of the user's password for successful authentication.

■ **Protected EAP (PEAP):** Provides several additional benefits within TLS, including an encrypted authentication channel, dynamic keying material from TLS, fast reconnect using cached session keys, and server authentication that protects against the setup of unauthorized access points. You can use PEAP along with EAP-TLS, EAP-MS-CHAP v2, and non-Microsoft EAP authentication methods; however, PEAP is not supported for use with EAP-MD5. As well as providing encrypted authentication, PEAP creates a session key that is used to derive data encryption keys that protect data being sent between the client and the access point during the session.

## Planning the Encryption Methods for a Wireless Network

When a user is authenticated to the network, she has access to all data on the network that would normally be available from a regular wired connection. At the same time, an attacker could intercept the transmissions and gain possession of the data. Consequently, encryption of data traveling across the wireless network is of paramount importance.

### Wired Equivalent Privacy

WEP is the most basic form of encryption that can be used on 802.11-based wireless networks to provide privacy of data sent between a wireless client and its access point. It uses a symmetric cryptography system known as RC4 with a standard 40-bit key, or in some cases, a 104-bit key to protect data against unauthorized access. You can configure the key that WEP uses in Windows 7 and Windows Server 2008, as well as older Windows computers dating back to Windows XP and Windows Server 2003. While utilities exist that can crack WEP encryption, you can still provide a moderate level of security by using WEP, particularly if you change the encryption keys frequently.

### 802.1X

802.1X provides port-based network access control for a stronger level of authentication and encryption of data compared to WEP. We already have discussed how 802.1X provides authentication services to clients (supplicants) requesting network access.

802.1X works along with EAP-MS-CHAP v2, EAP-TLS, or EAP-MD5 as already discussed to provide data encryption after a client has been authenticated to the wireless network.

### Use of IPSec with Wireless Networks

We have discussed the use of IPSec in detail in Chapter 4, "Configuring Windows Firewall with Advanced Security." IPSec by itself does not control access to the WLAN, but you can use it on the wired portion of the network to provide a complete security solution for data transmitted across the network. However, you can use IPSec in conjunction with 802.1X to provide security for data being sent to client computers that are roaming between access points on the same network. You should segment the wireless network by placing a firewall between the WLAN and the remainder of the network.

**TIP**   You can use IPSec to provide strong security between a RADIUS server and a domain controller, if these services are not provided on the same machine. You can also use IPSec to secure traffic to a partner organization's RADIUS servers where this capability is needed.

### The IEEE 802.3 Wired Standard

IEEE also includes, among its other networking standards, the *802.3* standard for Carrier Sense Multiple Access with Collision Detection (CSMA/CD) Access Method and Physical Layer Specifications. Included are a series of standards for Ethernet connections as described in "IEEE Get Program" at http://standards. ieee.org/about/get/802/802.3.html. In Windows Server 2008 R2, you can configure group policies for authentication and network connectivity settings within the properties of the Wired Network (IEEE 802.3) Policies Group Policy extension or from within the NPS Microsoft Management Console (MMC) snap-in. These policies specify the settings that enable domain member clients to access IEEE 802.3 Ethernet networks by using 802.1X authentication. Both of these configurations are discussed later in this chapter.

### Planning and Configuring Wireless Access Policies

We have seen how authentication and encryption form the cornerstones of securing your wireless network. Group Policy in Windows Server 2008 R2 enables you to create access policies that control the use of your wireless network. Available are separate policy configuration options for Windows Vista/7 and Windows XP clients. You can also create a remote access policy using a RADIUS server such as the Microsoft NPS server. In planning an access policy, you need to consider factors such as the following:

- **Users, groups, and computers allowed to access the WLAN:** You can control who has access to the WLAN and from where. You can also specify user account dial-in properties and whether unauthenticated access is permitted.

- **Domains and organizational units (OUs):** You can create policies in different Group Policy objects (GPO) and link them to sites, domains, and OUs as required.

- **Where and when users can access the WLAN:** You can define which resources users can wirelessly access and the time of day when access is permitted.

- **Authentication methods:** We already described the authentication methods you can use on your WLAN.

- **Software settings:** WLAN security requires the configuration of NPS-based network policy and Group Policy. We discuss these briefly in this section.

- **The type of network security to be used:** Do you need to use WEP, IPSec, or 802.1X encryption? Will you use NPS as a central authentication point? Using an NPS server allows you to configure a common wireless access policy for all users regardless of the access point to which they connect.

You should create a wireless access policy that matches your company's security policies while granting users the level of access needed to perform their duties. Create the minimum number of policies needed to achieve a goal that allows for flexible and simple management of network access. Remote access policies can contain criteria similar to those specified in the list directly above.

### Creating a Wireless Access Policy for Windows Vista/7 Clients

Perform the following steps to create a wireless access policy for Windows Vista/7 clients:

1. Open the Group Policy Management Editor focused on a GPO linked to the appropriate Active Directory Domain Services (AD DS) container (site, domain, or OU).

2. Expand the Computer Configuration\Policies\Windows Settings\Security Settings node to locate the Wireless Network (IEEE 802.11 Policies) subnode.

3. Right-click this subnode and choose **Create a New Wireless Network Policy for Windows Vista and Later Releases**.

4. You receive the New Wireless Network Policy Properties dialog box shown in Figure 15-1. Click **Add** and then select **Infrastructure** (you would not normally select the **Ad hoc** option with a server.)

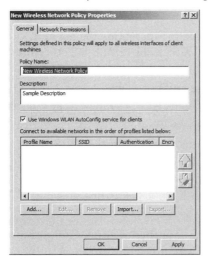

**Figure 15-1**   The New Wireless Network Policy Properties dialog box enables you to configure wireless access policies for Windows Vista and 7 clients.

5. You receive the New Profile properties dialog box shown in Figure 15-2. Type the name for your wireless network in the Profile Name dialog box and then type the SSID in the Network Name(s) (SSID) text box and click **Add** to add this SSID. Also, select the three self-explanatory options in the lower half of this dialog box as required.

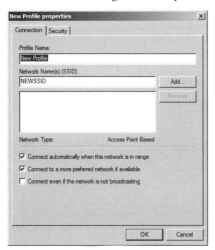

**Figure 15-2**   The New Profile properties dialog box enables you to configure the properties of the wireless network.

6. Select the **Security** tab. Then, configure the following settings, as shown in
   Figure 15-3:

   ■ **Authentication:** Select from the available authentication types, as de-
     scribed in Table 15-3.

   ■ **Encryption:** Select the method to be used for encryption of data sent
     across the wireless network. You can choose from 128-bit WEP, 128-bit
     Temporal Key Integrity Protocol (TKIP), or 128-bit Advanced Encryp-
     tion Standard (AES) according to the security type chosen (see Table 15-
     3). It is recommended that you should select **AES** if supported by your
     wireless access points and client network adapters.

   ■ **Select a network authentication method:** Available for the WPA-
     Enterprise, WPA2-Enterprise, or Open with 802.1X authentication
     types, you can choose either **Microsoft Protected EAP (PEAP)** or
     **Microsoft: Smart Card or other certificate**. Click **Properties** to
     specify properties of either authentication methods.

   ■ **Authentication mode:** Choose either **User authentication**, **Computer
     authentication**, **User or Computer authentication**, or **Guest authen-
     tication**, as required.

   ■ **Max. Authentication Failures:** You can choose a limit between 1 (default)
     and 100.

   ■ **Advanced button:** Enables you to specify additional settings related to
     advanced IEEE 802.1X settings, enabling single sign-on for the network,
     and fast roaming settings.

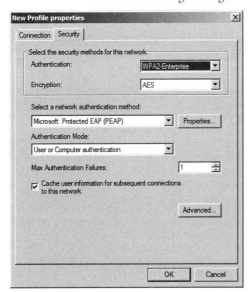

**Figure 15-3**   The Security tab enables you to specify authentication and encryption settings for
your wireless network.

**Table 15-3** Available Client Wireless Authentication Options

| Option | Description | Available Encryption Types |
|---|---|---|
| Open | Open system authentication with WEP or no encryption. | WEP |
| Shared | Open system authentication using WEP. | WEP |
| WPA-Personal | Wi-Fi Protected Access (WPA) using a preshared passphrase or key. | TKIP (default) or AES |
| WPA2-Personal | Version 2 of WPA using a preshared passphrase or key. | TKIP or AES (default) |
| WPA-Enterprise | WPA using IEEE 802.1X authentication. | TKIP (default) or AES |
| WPA2-Enterprise | Version 2 of WPA using IEEE 802.1X authentication. Note that this is the recommended option that you should select if supported by your wireless access points and client network adapters. | TKIP or AES (default) |
| Open with 802.1X | IEEE 802.1X authentication using WEP (also known as dynamic WEP). | WEP |

7. When finished specifying authentication and encryption settings, click **OK**.

8. You are returned to the New Wireless Network Policy Properties dialog box. To specify permissions for the wireless network, select the **Network Permissions** tab to display the options shown in Figure 15-4.

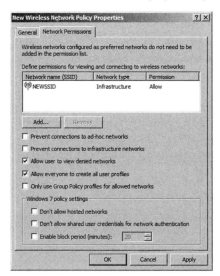

**Figure 15-4** The Network Permissions tab enables you to allow or deny network access and provides several options for setting permissions.

9. Specify the required permissions (click **Add** to add a network by its SSID) and select the permissions as displayed in the figure (defaults are as shown).

10. When finished, click **OK**. Your policy is displayed in the details pane of the Group Policy Object Editor.

> **TIP**   WPA2-Enterprise security provides the highest level of wireless networking authentication security. It requires authentication in two phases: first, an open system authentication; second, authentication using EAP. It is suitable for domain-based authentication and on networks using a RADIUS authentication server. In environments without the RADIUS server, use WPA2-Personal security.

> **NOTE**   For more information on configuring wireless group policies for Windows Vista/7 clients, refer to "Configure 802.1X Wireless Access Clients running Windows 7 and Windows Vista" at http://technet.microsoft.com/en-us/library/cc730674.aspx. Select the appropriate link for the authentication method in use.

### Creating a Wireless Access Policy for Windows XP Clients

Configuring a wireless access policy for Windows XP is slightly different. Use the following procedure:

1. Right-click the **Computer Configuration\Policies\Windows Settings\ Security Settings\Wireless Network (IEEE 802.11 Policies)** subnode and choose **Create a New Wireless Network Policy for Windows XP**.

2. In the General tab of the Windows XP Wireless Network (IEEE 802.11) Policies Properties dialog box (see Figure 15-5), type a name and description for the policy and select either **Any available network (access point preferred)** or **Access point (infrastructure) networks only** according to the requirements of your network. Also, ensure that the **Use Windows WLAN Auto-Config service for clients** option is selected.

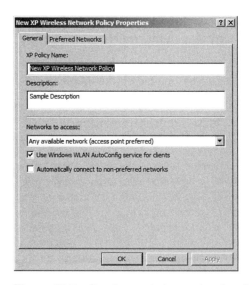

**Figure 15-5**   Creating a wireless network policy for Windows XP clients.

3. On the **Preferred Networks** tab, click **Add** and then select **Infrastructure**. (You would not normally select the **Ad hoc** option with a server.)

4. You see the New Preferred Settings Properties dialog box shown in Figure 15-6. On the Network Properties tab, specify the options required for your network; choices are similar to those provided for Windows Vista/7, including the authentication options previously described in Table 15-3.

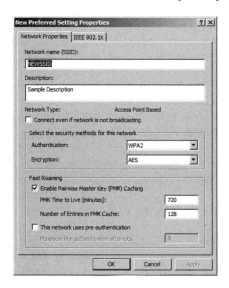

**Figure 15-6**   Configuring network authentication and encryption properties for Windows XP clients.

5. Select the **IEEE 802.1X** tab and then select either **Protected EAP (PEAP)** or **Smart Card or other Certificate**, according to the needs of your network.

6. Click **Settings** to configure additional properties for the authentication method you've chosen. Properties available here depend on the option selected in step 5. When finished, click **OK**.

7. Click **OK** to close the New XP Wireless Network Properties dialog box and save the settings you've configured. Your policy is displayed in the details pane of the Group Policy Object Editor.

> **NOTE** For more information on configuring access policies for Windows XP clients, refer to "Configure 802.1X Wireless Access Clients running Windows XP" at http://technet.microsoft.com/en-us/library/cc771557.aspx. Select the appropriate link for the authentication method in use. The web pages provide information on the settings available in Step 6 of this procedure.

### Configuring IEEE 802.3 Wired Access Policies

Group Policy in Windows Server 2008 R2 provides a Wired Network (IEEE 802.3) Policies subnode under the Computer Configuration\Policies\Windows Settings\ Security Settings node, which enables you to configure access policies for Windows XP with Service Pack 3, Windows Vista, and Windows 7 clients connecting to your server across the wired LAN. From this node, you can configure policies that support the following 802.1X authentication types:

- EAP-TLS or PEAP-TLS protocols for authenticating users with smart cards or other certificates

- PEAP-MS-CHAP v2 for authenticating users with secure passwords

Use the following procedure to configure an IEEE 802.3 wired access policy:

1. In a GPO linked to a suitable AD DS container object, right-click the **Computer Configuration\Policies\Windows Settings\Security Settings\ Wired Network (IEEE 802.3 Policies)** subnode and choose **Create a New Wired Network Policy for Windows Vista and Later Releases**.

2. In the General tab of the New Wired Network Policy Properties dialog box (see Figure 15-7), type a name and description for the policy and ensure that the **Use Windows Wired Auto Config service for clients** option is selected. Also, select the following settings for Windows 7 clients as needed:

- **Don't allow shared user credentials for network authentication:**
  Prevents users on Windows 7 computers from storing domain logon
  credentials. Clear this check box to enable users to store their domain
  credentials, which the computer can then use for network log on.

- **Enable block period (minutes):** Specifies the duration for which
  Windows 7 computers are prohibited from making auto connection attempts to the network. You can choose a range between 1 and 60 minutes.

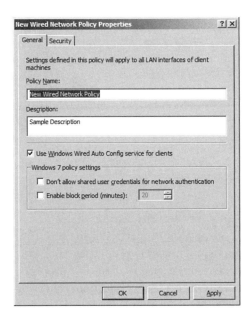

**Figure 15-7**   Creating a wired network policy for Windows Vista/7 client computers.

3. Select the **Security** tab. Ensure that the check box labeled **Enable use of
   IEEE 802.1X authentication for network access** is selected. Then, select
   the required authentication method from the choices of **Microsoft: Protected
   EAP (PEAP)** and **Microsoft: Smart Card or other certificate**. Also, select
   the authentication mode to be used; options are similar to those previously
   presented for wireless network connections in Figure 15-3, as well as other
   options shown in this figure for authentication failures and caching user
   information.

4. If you need to specify additional security settings, click the **Advanced** command button to display the Advanced security settings dialog box shown in
   Figure 15-8. Select the **Enforce advanced 802.1X settings** and **Enable
   Single Sign On for this network** options as required and then select any
   additional settings needed for access to your network.

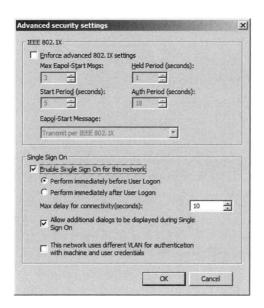

**Figure 15-8**    The Advanced security settings dialog box enables you to specify settings for advanced 802.1X and single sign on to the network.

5. When finished, click **OK** to close the Advanced security settings dialog box. This returns you to the Security tab of the policy's Properties dialog box. If you need to configure additional network authentication properties, click the **Properties** command button. This enables you to specify additional properties such as use of a smart card for authenticating a user connection, validating server certificates, and selecting trusted root certification authorities.

6. Click **OK** to close the New Wired Network Policy Properties dialog box. The wired network access policy you've configured is displayed in the details pane of the Group Policy Management Editor.

**NOTE**    For more information on configuring group policies for wired access clients, refer to "Configure 802.1X Wired Access Clients by using Group Policy Management" at http://technet.microsoft.com/en-us/library/cc731213.aspx. Select the appropriate link for the authentication method in use.

# RADIUS in Windows Server 2008 R2

As already introduced, RADIUS is a protocol first introduced in Windows 2000 that is used to provide secure authentication and accounting services for large-scale remote access networks. Use of this protocol allows a seamless authentication of remote clients regardless of the type of hardware they are using. It does this by providing a central point for multiple dial-up or VPN users to validate against, within a network of RRAS servers upon which this protocol runs. Users can dial in to different RRAS servers, depending on their current locations. For wireless connections, you can configure all wireless access points to send authentication requests to the RADIUS server. The RADIUS server provides the following benefits to your network:

- RADIUS provides a central authentication and authorization point for all dial-up, VPN, and wireless remote access connection requests.

- Use of a RADIUS server enables you to create a policy that can be applied at a single point on the network.

- RADIUS provides a central accounting point for logging remote access data to your network. You can store accounting information in a local log file or a Microsoft SQL Server database.

The RADIUS server is typically run on a RRAS server installed on a Windows Server 2008 computer; the RADIUS component is known as the *Network Policy Server (NPS)*. Any Windows 2000 or later computer accessing the network by means of a dial-up or VPN connection can be configured as a RADIUS client. A message called the shared secret is used that verifies secure communications between the client and host. In Windows Server 2008 R2, Microsoft has added new NPS templates, accounting improvements, and support for international, non-English character sets using UTF-8 encoding.

Situations in which you can use NPS as a RADIUS server include the following:

- You are using an AD DS domain or the local SAM user accounts database as your remote access client database. The NPS server uses this database to authenticate incoming clients; it communicates directly with a domain controller to complete all incoming authentication requests.

- You have set up multiple RRAS servers for dial-up connections, VPN connections, or demand-dial routers, and you want to centralize the configuration of network policies and accounting logging.

- You are outsourcing your dial-up, VPN, or wireless access to an external provider. The provider's servers can use NPS to authenticate and authorize all incoming connections.

■ You can centralize authentication, authorization, and accounting for various types of RRAS servers.

**NOTE** For additional introductory information on NPS in Windows Server 2008 R2, refer to "Network Policy Server Overview" at http://technet.microsoft.com/en-us/library/cc771347.aspx and "RADIUS Server" at http://technet.microsoft.com/en-us/library/cc755248.aspx.

### Installing NPS on a Windows Server 2008 RRAS Server

In Windows Server 2008, NPS is installed as a role service component of the Network Policy and Access Services server role. Use the following procedure to install NPS on a server already configured with this server role:

1. Open Server Manager, select the **Roles** node, and scroll the details pane to locate the **Network Policy and Access Services** role.

2. Click **Add role services**. The Add Role Services Wizard starts with a Select Role Services page.

3. On the Select Role Services page, select **Network Policy Server** as shown in Figure 15-9, and then click **Next**.

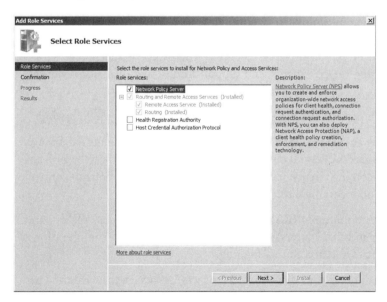

**Figure 15-9** NPS is installed as a role service in Network Policy and Access Services.

4. On the Confirm Installation Selections page, click **Install**. The NPS role service is installed.

5. When informed that the installation is complete, click **Close**.

After completing this procedure, you can administer NPS from its snap-in, which is installed in the Administrative Tools folder. If the Network Policy and Access Services server role is not installed on this server, use the Add Roles Wizard to select this role and then select the **Network Policy Server** role service as described in the previous procedure.

### Configuring the NPS Server for Wireless Access

Use the following procedure to configure the NPS server for wireless access:

1. Click **Start > Administrative Tools > Network Policy Server** to open the NPS snap-in.

2. The details pane displays the three options shown in Figure 15-10 for configuring your server. Select **RADIUS server for 802.1X Wireless or Wired Connections**.

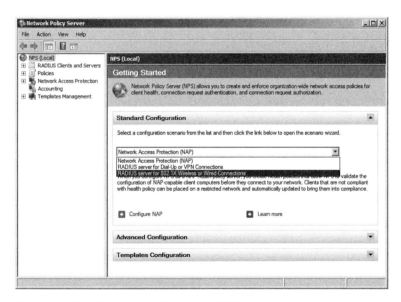

**Figure 15-10**   You can configure your NPS server for any of three standard configuration options.

3. Options on the details pane change to reflect the option selected. Click the link labeled **Configure 802.1X** to open a wizard that helps you configure this connection.

4. On the Select 802.1X Connections Type page, select **Secure Wireless Connections.** As shown in Figure 15-11, the wizard provides a default connection name. If desired, modify this name. Then, click **Next**.

**Figure 15-11**   You can configure either wireless or wired connections to your NPS server.

5. On the Specify 802.1X switches page, click **Add** to add your wireless access points as RADIUS clients.

6. On the New RADIUS Client dialog box shown in Figure 15-12, provide the name and address and shared secret information, and then click **OK**.

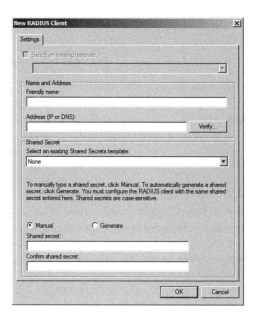

**Figure 15-12**   Specifying name, address, and shared secret information for a RADIUS client.

7.  The client is added to the list on the Specify 802.1X Switches page. Click **Add** to add another client if necessary. When done, click **Next**.

8.  On the Configure an Authentication Method page, select an authentication type from those shown in Figure 15-13. Click **Configure** to specify configuration options for the type chosen. Note that the EAP types provided require that a certificate be installed on the server. When finished, click **Next**.

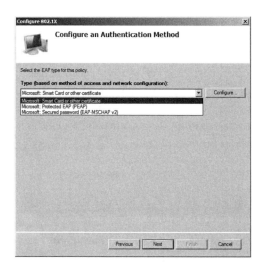

**Figure 15-13**   You can specify any of three authentication methods.

9. On the Specify User Groups page, click **Add** to specify domain security groups that will be allowed or denied access. When done, click **Next**.

10. The Configure Traffic Controls enables you to use virtual LANs (VLAN) and access control lists (ACL) to control network traffic. If you want to use traffic controls to limit the extent of network resources to which they can connect, click **Configure**. Otherwise, click **Next**.

11. Review the information presented on the completion page. If you want to change any settings, click **Previous**. When ready to proceed, click **Finish**.

To view the policy you've created, expand the **RADIUS Clients and Servers** node in the NPS snap-in and select the **RADIUS Clients** subnode. Summary information on the policy is provided in the details pane. If you need to modify the properties of the policy at a later time, right-click it and choose **Properties**. You can also disable the policy by right-clicking it and choosing **Disable**, or remove it by right-clicking it and choosing **Delete**.

### Configuring New RADIUS Clients

You can add Windows Server 2008 computers as RADIUS clients from the RADIUS Clients and Servers node of the NPS snap-in. Right-click this node and choose **New RADIUS Client**. This action displays the New RADIUS Client dialog box, which is similar to the dialog box previously shown in Figure 15-12, except that it also has an Advanced tab with several additional options. Using this dialog box, configure the following options for your RADIUS client:

- **Friendly name:** Provide a friendly name that facilitates identification of the proper client from the NPS snap-in.

- **Address (IP or DNS):** Provide the IPv4 or DNS address of the new RADIUS client.

- **Shared Secret:** Provide the same alphanumeric text string that is configured on the RADIUS server. This text string acts as a password between RADIUS servers, clients, and proxies. You can either type the shared secret in the two text boxes provided or click the **Generate** radio button to have NPS generate a shared secret for you.

- **Advanced tab:** Select this tab to specify the following options:

  - **Vendor:** In most cases, accept the default of RADIUS Standard. Or select the RADIUS client vendor from the drop-down list.

  - **Access-Request messages must contain the Message-Authenticator attribute:** This attribute is a message digest 5 (MD5) hash of the entire

RADIUS message. If this attribute is present, it is verified. If verification fails, the RADIUS message is discarded. If client settings require that this attribute be present (i.e., this check box is selected) and it is not present, the RADIUS message is discarded.

■ **RADIUS client is NAP-capable:** Select this option if the RADIUS client is compatible with Network Access Protection (NAP). NPS will send NAP attributes to the RADIUS client when accepting the access connection.

**CAUTION**   Be aware that client computers, such as laptops and others, making wireless or VPN connections to your network are not RADIUS clients. RADIUS clients are components such as wireless access points, 802.1X-capable switches, VPN servers, and dial-up servers. These components use the RADIUS protocol to communicate with NPS servers. For more information on RADIUS clients and their setup, refer to "Add a new RADIUS Client" at http://technet.microsoft.com/en-us/library/cc732929.aspx.

## Creating RADIUS Proxies and Proxy Groups

You can configure NPS as a *RADIUS proxy* to enable the forwarding of RADIUS messages between RADIUS clients and servers that perform user authentication, authorization, and accounting. In this case, the NPS server acts as a routing point through which RADIUS authentication and accounting messages are transmitted.

Use the following procedure to create a RADIUS proxy group:

1. In the NPS snap-in, expand the RADIUS Clients and Servers node, right-click **Remote RADIUS Server Groups**, and choose **New**.

2. In the New Remote RADIUS Server Group dialog box, type a name for the server group and then click **Add**.

3. In the Address tab of the Add RADIUS Server dialog box that appears, type the host name or IP address of the RADIUS server, as shown in Figure 15-14. From this tab, you can also specify a RADIUS template. Templates are discussed later in this chapter.

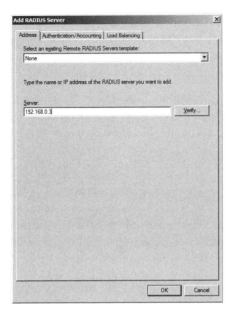

**Figure 15-14**   Adding a RADIUS server to a proxy group.

4. Select the **Authentication/Accounting** tab and type the shared secret you configured earlier in the Shared Secret and Confirm Shared Secret text boxes.

5. Select the **Load Balancing** tab. On this tab, adjust the values of Priority and Weight if necessary to balance requests among servers with different capacities (processing power, memory, and so on). If only one server is in use or if all servers have equal capacities, leave the settings at their defaults.

6. Click **OK**. The server is added to the list in the New Remote RADIUS Server Group dialog box.

7. Repeat Steps 2 to 6 to add additional RADIUS servers if required. When finished, click **OK** to close the New Remote RADIUS server Group dialog box. The group you've created appears in the details pane of the NPS snap-in.

**NOTE**   For more information on RADIUS proxies and proxy groups, refer to "RADIUS Proxy" at http://technet.microsoft.com/en-us/library/cc731320.aspx.

### Creating Connection Request Policies

A *connection request policy* is a set of conditions and settings that enable you to designate which RADIUS servers are entitled to perform the authentication and authorization of connection requests that the NPS server receives from RADIUS clients. You can specify which RADIUS servers are used for accounting.

Connection request policies enable you to use a NPS server as a RADIUS server or RADIUS proxy, according to factors such as the following:

- Time of day and day of the week

- Realm name in the connection request

- Type of connection in the request

- RADIUS client's IP address

Some of the ways that connection request policies can be utilized include the following:

- **NPS as a RADIUS server:** The local NPS server authenticates and authorizes all connection requests. This includes users from the NPS server's domain and trusted domains. This is the default connection request policy.

- **NPS as a RADIUS proxy:** The NPS server does not process connection requests locally; rather, it forwards requests to other RADIUS servers that are configured as members of remote RADIUS server groups. In this case, you need to delete the default connection request policy and create two new policies to forward requests to other domains.

- **NPS as both RADIUS server and RADIUS proxy:** The default connection request policy is retained and a new policy is created to forward requests to an NPS server in an untrusted domain. This proxy policy is placed first in the ordered policy list, so that if a connection request matches this proxy policy, it is forwarded to the server in the remote RADIUS group. If the connection request does not match the proxy policy but matches the default request connection policy, NPS processes the request locally.

- **NPS as RADIUS server with remote accounting servers:** In this case, local NPS does not perform accounting of connection requests. The default connection request policy is revised to forward accounting messages to another RADIUS server in a remote server group. The local NPS server still performs authentication and authorization of connection requests.

- **NPS with remote RADIUS to Windows user mapping:** The NPS server acts as both a RADIUS server and RADIUS proxy for each connection request by forwarding the authentication request to a remote RADIUS server while using a local Windows user account for authorization. This requires a local user account with the same name as the remote user account being authenticated by the remote RADIUS server.

Use the following procedure to configure new connection request policies:

1. In the NPS snap-in, expand the Policies node and select the **Connection Request Policies** folder. Three default connection request policies are displayed in the details pane, as shown in Figure 15-15.

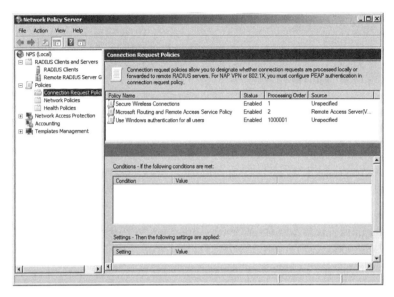

**Figure 15-15**    The NPS snap-in provides three default connection request policies.

2. Right-click **Connection Request Policies**, and choose **New**.

3. In the New Connection Request Policy Wizard, type a name for your policy and select from the options shown in Figure 15-16 for the type of network access server. Then, click **Next**.

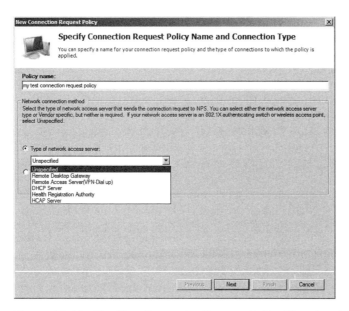

**Figure 15-16**  The New Connection Request Policy Wizard enables you to select several network access server types.

4.  On the Specify Conditions page, click **Add** to create a condition that determines whether the connection request policy is evaluated.

5.  On the Specify Conditions dialog box shown in Figure 15-17, select a condition to be added to the connection request policy and then click **Add**. Specify an appropriate value for the condition you selected and click **OK**.

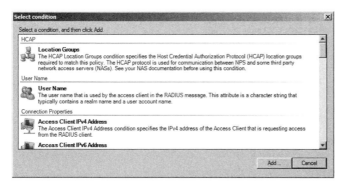

**Figure 15-17**  The Specify conditions dialog box contains a large series of conditions that you can use in creating your connection request policy.

6.  Repeat Step 5 if necessary to add additional conditions to your policy. When finished, click **Next**.

7. On the Specify Connection Request Forwarding page, leave the default of **Authenticate requests on this server** selected unless you are using a remote RADIUS server group for authentication. In this case, specify the required group, and then click **Next**.

8. On the Specify Authentication Methods page, if you want to use the default network authentication settings, leave the check box labeled **Override network policy authentication settings** cleared. If you need to specify a different authentication type, select this check box and select the appropriate authentication type from those presented. Then, click **Next**.

9. On the Configure Settings page, add any required additional attributes (realm name, standard RADIUS attributed, or vendor-specific attribute [a large number of vendor-specific attributes are available]). When finished, click **Next**.

10. The Completing Connection Request Policy Wizard page displays the conditions and settings you specified. Click **Previous** if you need to make any changes. When done, click **Finish**. You are returned to the NPS snap-in, where the policy you created is added to the list in the details pane.

The connection request policies are applied to a connection attempt in the order in which they appear in the details pane. You can modify the sequence of processing if needed; to do so, right-click a policy and choose **Move Up** or **Move Down**, as needed. You can disable a policy that should not be applied temporarily (right-click and choose **Disable**) or delete a policy that you're sure you'll never need again (right-click and choose **Delete**). If you need to change policy conditions, right-click the policy and choose **Properties**. The Properties dialog box that appears enables you to change any settings you've specified while running the New Connection Request Policy Wizard as described in the previous procedure.

**NOTE** For more information on connection request policies, including descriptions of all available policy settings, refer to "Connection Request Policies" at http://technet.microsoft.com/en-us/library/cc753603.aspx.

### Configuring RADIUS Accounting

NPS in Windows Server 2008 R2 enables you to track network usage for auditing and billing purposes. You can gather data in real time from a central location; you can also analyze NPS accounting information with non-Microsoft products to provide a series of reports on the usage of your remote access network.

NPS in Windows Server 2008 R2 supports the following logging types:

- **Event logging:** Enables you to audit and troubleshoot connection attempts. You can configure event logging in the NPS snap-in from the server's Properties dialog box.

- **Logging user authentication and accounting requests to a local file:** Enables you to perform connection analysis, billing, and security investigation actions.

- **Logging user authentication and connection requests to a Microsoft SQL Server database:** Enables you to log data from multiple NPS servers to a single location.

NPS provides the Accounting Configuration Wizard to facilitate the setup of logging to text files, SQL databases, or both destinations. Use the following steps to configure NPS accounting:

1. In the NPS snap-in, select the **Accounting** node to display accounting information in the details pane, as shown in Figure 15-18.

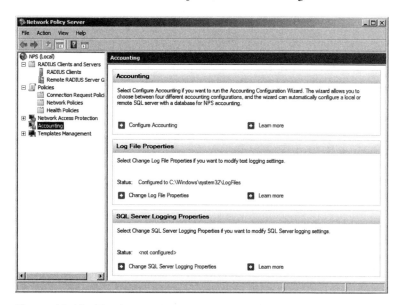

**Figure 15-18**   The Accounting node of the NPS snap-in enables you to perform actions related to accounting configuration.

2. Click **Configure Accounting**. The Accounting Configuration Wizard starts.

3. Click **Next** to display the Select Accounting Options page shown in Figure 15-19. Select one of these options and click **Next**.

**Figure 15-19** The Accounting Configuration Wizard provides four logging options.

4. On the Configure (selected option) Logging page, select the types of information to be logged: **Accounting requests, Authentication requests, Periodic accounting status**, and **Periodic authentication status**. These items are all selected by default. If you selected SQL server logging, click **Configure** to specify logging properties. If you selected local file logging, accept the default of C:\Windows\system32\LogFiles or type an alternate local file location. You can also click **Browse** to locate the desired file.

5. Review the information on the Summary page and then click **Next**. If you need to modify your settings, click **Previous** and make any needed corrections.

6. Click **Close**.

The details pane of the NPS snap-in also enables you to modify your log file settings. Click **Change Log File Properties** to modify settings for logging to a text file, or **Change SQL Server Logging Properties** to modify settings for logging to an SQL Server database. Available log file settings include a choice of format for the log file and a time interval at which a new log file is reached. A large range of properties for SQL Server logging are available.

**NOTE**   For more information on RADIUS accounting, refer to "RADIUS Accounting" at http://technet.microsoft.com/en-us/library/cc725566.aspx. Click the links at the bottom of this page for additional information on configuring text and SQL log file properties.

## Configuring NPS Templates

You can use *NPS templates* to create configuration components such as client lists, shared secrets, connection conditions, and so on, which you can use on a series of NPS servers. Doing so reduces the amount of time required to configure NPS servers in large environments, and assists in setting up parallel configuration options.

To configure NPS templates, access the Templates Management node in the console tree of the NPS snap-in. As shown in Figure 15-20, six NPS templates are provided.

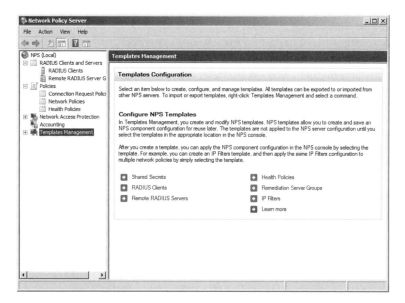

**Figure 15-20**   The Templates Management node of the NPS snap-in provides default templates that you can modify or create additional templates as needed.

To configure any of the NPS templates, expand the Templates Management node in the console tree of the NPS snap-in. Then, right-click the desired template and choose **New**. Provide a template name and then specify the following properties:

- **Shared Secrets:** Type and confirm the shared secret to be used. You can also automatically generate a shared secret by clicking the **Generate** radio button.

- **RADIUS Clients:** Type a friendly name and IP or DNS address of the RA-DIUS client. Also, either select a shared secrets template or manually type and confirm the required shared secret.

- **Remote RADIUS Servers:** Specify the name or IP address of the RADIUS server to be added. Then, click **Next** and specify shared secret and accounting information. Click **Next** another time and specify load balancing settings, as mentioned earlier. Then, click **Next** and click **Finish**.

- **IP Filters:** Specify IPv4 and IPv6 input and output filters, as required. For each filter, specify filters by source and destination IP address and subnet mask or IPv6 prefix length. Also, specify allowed protocols and source and destination port numbers. For each filter you create, choose a filter action from **Do not permit packets listed below** or **Permit only the packets listed below**.

- **Health Policies:** Enables you to create NAP health policy settings. Health policies are described in Chapter 16.

- **Remediation Server Groups:** Enables you to specify servers belonging to remediation groups that can be accessed by clients that do not conform to NAP health policy settings. See Chapter 16 for more information.

If you need to modify any template you create, select the template type in the console tree of the NPS snap-in to display the templates in the details pane. Right-click the required template and choose **Properties**, and then make any needed corrections in the dialog box that appears. From the right-click menu, you can also rename, delete, or duplicate the template, or view statistics on its usage.

**NOTE**   For more information on NPS templates, refer to "NPS Templates" at http://technet.microsoft.com/en-us/library/dd759185.aspx.

# Exam Preparation Tasks

## Review All the Key Topics

Review the most important topics in this chapter, noted with the key topics icon in the outer margin of the page. Table 15-4 lists a reference of these key topics and the page numbers on which each is found.

**Table 15-4**   Key Topics for Chapter 15

| Key Topic Element | Description | Page Number |
| --- | --- | --- |
| Table 15-2 | Describes wireless networking connection standards. | 620 |
| List | Describes wireless authentication methods. | 621 |
| List | Describes wireless authentication protocols. | 621 |
| List | Shows you how to create a group policy for Windows Vista/7 wireless access clients. | 624 |
| Table 15-3 | Describes available client wireless authentication options. | 627 |
| Figure 15-4 | You can specify a wide range of access permissions for Windows Vista/7 clients accessing the wireless network. | 627 |
| List | Shows you how to create a group policy for Windows XP wireless access clients. | 628 |
| Figure 15-7 | Creating a wired access policy for Windows Vista/7 clients. | 631 |
| Paragraph | Describes the use of RADIUS servers. | 633 |
| Figure 15-10 | You have three options for configuring access to your RADIUS server. | 635 |
| Figure 15-12 | Configuring RADIUS clients. | 637 |
| List | Describes several uses of connection request policies. | 641 |
| List | Shows you how to configure a connection request policy. | 642 |
| Figure 15-17 | Selecting conditions to be used in a connection request policy. | 643 |
| Figure 15-18 | Configuring RADIUS accounting. | 645 |
| Figure 15-20 | NPS provides six default templates. | 647 |

## Complete the Tables and Lists from Memory

Print a copy of Appendix B, "Memory Tables," (found on the CD), or at least the section for this chapter, and complete the tables and lists from memory. Appendix C, "Memory Tables Answer Key," also on the CD, includes the completed tables and lists to check your work.

## Definition of Key Terms

Define the following key terms from this chapter, and check your answers in the Glossary.

802.1X authentication, connection request policy, Extensible Authentication Protocol-Transport Layer Security (EAP-TLS), IEEE 802.11, IEEE 802.3, Network Policy Server (NPS), NPS template, Remote Authentication Dial-In User Service (RADIUS), RADIUS client, RADIUS proxy, service set identifier (SSID), Wi-Fi Protected Access (WPA and WPA2), wireless access policy, wired equivalent privacy (WEP)

This chapter covers the following subjects:

- **Concepts of NAP:** This section introduces the various types of NAP enforcement technologies and provides a brief outline of the components found on a typical NAP-enabled network.

- **NAP Enforcement:** This section provides information on the uses and requirements of each of the NAP enforcement types. It also shows you how to configure NAP to use these enforcement types.

- **System Health Validation:** This section discusses the criteria you can evaluate using system health validators and introduces the new multi-configuration system health validator in Windows Server 2008 R2.

# CHAPTER 16

# Configuring Network Access Protection (NAP)

You already learned how Windows Server 2008 protects your network by ensuring that only legitimate users can authenticate to your network and access its resources; in addition, you have learned about technologies such as IP Security (IPSec) that can be used to secure network transmissions against intrusion. But, a significant component of network security remains to be addressed—what about mobile computers used by individuals with legitimate user accounts that have downloaded inappropriate software on the Internet when attached to external networks? These computers might also have become infected with malware from compromised machines elsewhere on the external networks to which they were connected. Upon returning to your network, such computers can spread malware infections across your network despite being properly authenticated. *Network Access Protection (NAP)* is designed to address the problems these computers can present.

Chapter 15, "Configuring Network Policy Server (NPS)," introduced you to the Microsoft implementation of the Remote Authentication Dial-In User Service (RADIUS) server that you can use for providing a centralized authentication point for remote access users attempting to access your network. NAP is a component of NPS that examines client computers attempting to connect to the network for system health—in other words, the presence of adequate security features such as up-to-date antivirus and antispyware programs, Windows updates, and so on.

## "Do I Know This Already?" Quiz

The "Do I Know This Already?" quiz allows you to assess whether you should read this entire chapter or simply jump to the "Exam Preparation Tasks" section for review. If you are in doubt, read the entire chapter. Table 16-1 outlines the major headings in this chapter and the corresponding "Do I Know This Already?" quiz questions. You can find the answers in Appendix A, "Answers to the 'Do I Know This Already?' Quizzes."

**Table 16-1**  "Do I Know This Already?" Foundation Topics Section-to-Question Mapping

| Foundations Topics Section | Questions Covered in This Section |
| --- | --- |
| Concepts of NAP | 1–2 |
| NAP Enforcement | 3–7 |
| System Health Validation | 8–9 |

1. You are responsible for planning the implementation of NAP on your network. Which of the following types of servers would you typically include on the remediation network? (Choose all that apply.)

   a. Antivirus signature servers

   b. Windows Server Update Services (WSUS) servers

   c. NAP health policy servers

   d. NAP enforcement servers

   e. Domain controllers

   f. DHCP and DNS servers

   g. Troubleshooting servers

2. A laptop computer running Windows XP SP3 attempts to connect to your network by means of a VPN connection. What type of file does this computer send to the NAP enforcement server to determine whether it is in compliance?

   a. System Health Validator (SHV)

   b. Statement of Health (SoH)

   c. X.509 health certificate

   d. No file is sent. This computer is non-NAP capable and must be upgraded to either Windows Vista or Windows 7.

3. You are responsible for setting up NAP enforcement on your network. Your manager has requested you to enable DHCP enforcement. You installed the Network Policy and Access Services server role on a computer named Server1 and are planning to configure this server for NAP DHCP enforcement. DHCP is installed and running on another computer named Server2. Which of the following do you need to do to complete the enabling of DHCP-based NAP enforcement? (Each correct answer represents part of the solution. Choose two.)

   a. Install Certificate Services on the DHCP server.

   b. Install Certificate Services on the NAP server.

    **c.** Enable NAP on all DHCP scopes.

    **d.** Configure the DHCP server as a RADIUS client.

    **e.** Install Internet Information Services (IIS) on the NAP server.

**4.** Which of the following NAP enforcement types requires the use of a Health Registration Authority (HRA) server, together with servers running Certificate Services and Internet Information Services (IIS)? (Choose all that apply.)

    **a.** DHCP enforcement

    **b.** VPN enforcement

    **c.** IPSec enforcement

    **d.** 802.1X enforcement

    **e.** RDS enforcement

**5.** You are configuring Network Access Protection (NAP) for your company's AD DS domain. The company has many road warriors who connect to the network over the Internet using laptop computers. The company's security policy stipulates that external communications involving these users be secured at all times.

You must ensure that external users can access the network only from laptop computers that meet these requirements. What type of policy should you configure?

    **a.** 802.1X enforcement

    **b.** IPSec enforcement

    **c.** RDS enforcement

    **d.** VPN enforcement

**6.** You are planning to use IPSec enforcement as a NAP enforcement type on your Windows Server 2008 R2 network. Which of the following components are required on your network in order to use IPSec enforcement? (Choose all that apply.)

    **a.** DHCP scopes that are enabled for NAP.

    **b.** A public key infrastructure (PKI) with at least one CA.

    **c.** An AD DS domain with all clients joined to the domain.

    **d.** A health registration authority (HRA) server.

    **e.** Network access points must be configured as RADIUS clients.

7. Your network includes several wireless access points that client computers connect from. To ensure that all client computers accessing the network wirelessly are compliant with health policies, you configure NAP with 802.1X authentication. You also configure the access points to use 802.1X authentication. Which of the following must you do to ensure that all wireless clients are checked for health by NAP?

    a. On the Configure an Authentication Method page, select the EAP option **Secure Password (PEAP-MS-CHAP v2)** for authenticating wireless clients.

    b. Configure all wireless client computers as RADIUS clients.

    c. Configure all access points as RADIUS clients.

    d. Require that all client computers present an appropriate certificate.

8. You are configuring security settings in the Windows Security Health Validator (WSHV) to be used in conjunction with a NAP enforcement policy on your network. Client computers on the network run a mix of Windows XP Professional, Windows Vista Business, and Windows 7 Professional. Which of the following settings *cannot* be enforced on the Windows XP client computers?

    a. Windows Firewall or other firewall software is enabled.

    b. Antivirus software is installed, properly updated, and enabled.

    c. Antispyware software is installed, properly updated, and enabled.

    d. Windows Update Services is enabled and all current updates have been installed.

**9.** You just upgraded the servers on your network to Windows Server 2008 R2 and heard that you can set up a multi-configuration SHV. What do you need to do to create a policy that includes a multi-configuration SHV? (Each correct answer represents part of the solution. Choose two.)

    **a.** Right-click the **SHV** node in the console tree of the NPS snap-in and choose **New Multi-Configuration SHV**. Then, provide an appropriate name for the configuration and select the desired settings for each configuration in turn from the Windows Security Health Validator dialog box.

    **b.** Right-click the **Settings** subnode under the SHV node in the console tree of the NPS snap-in and choose **New**. Then, select the desired settings from the Windows Security Health Validator dialog box.

    **c.** Use the Configure NAP Wizard and select the 802.1X enforcement type. Then, on the Define NAP Health Policy page, specify the appropriate configuration of the multi-configuration SHV.

    **d.** Create a new health policy and select the appropriate setting from the multi-configuration SHV from the drop-down list in the Create New Health Policy dialog box.

**Foundation Topics**

## Concepts of NAP

Perhaps you have mobile computers that have been on the road bringing malware back to your network and creating havoc. Or these mobile computers, when making a virtual private network (VPN) connection might have been accessed by other computers externally that infect them with viruses, worms, spyware, and so on. NAP is designed to mitigate the problems these computers can create; it helps administrators ensure that the overall integrity and security of the network is maintained. NAP enables you to redirect noncompliant computers to a remediation segment on the network, where they can be brought into compliance with the security standards you have set.

First introduced with Windows Vista and the original version of Windows Server 2008, NAP can address health criteria, such as the following:

- Is the client's antivirus and antispyware software installed, enabled, and up-to-date?

- Is Windows Firewall enabled?

- Is automatic updating enabled?

- Are security updates installed according to a security severity rating in the Microsoft Security Response Center?

- Are all software updates installed and configured?

NAP uses *system health validators (SHV)* to assess these criteria. Windows Server 2008 R2 and Windows 7 enable you to use multiple SHV configurations. You can configure health policies in which you select one of these SHV configurations, such as one configuration for internal desktop computers and another one for portable computers that connect across the VPN.

On any NAP-capable computer (which includes client computers running Windows XP SP3, Vista, or 7, or servers running either the original or R2 versions of Windows Server 2008), you can check the status of the NAP security agent by accessing the Action Center from the System and Security category of Control Panel. Expand the Security section and scroll down to see the Network Access Protection listing, as shown in Figure 16-1. If the service is not running, you can start it from the Services snap-in, accessed from the Configuration node of Server Manager or by typing **services** in the Start menu Search field.

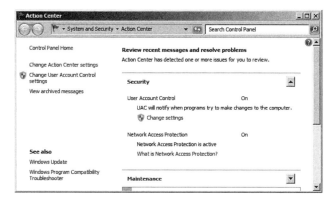

**Figure 16-1** Action Center informs you whether the Network Access Protection agent service is running.

Enforcement options against noncompliant clients in NAP include the following:

- **No enforcement:** Simply monitors the client's health state; can include auto-remediation.

- **IPSec:** Unhealthy client connection requests can be rejected; compliant clients receive an X.509 health certificate.

- **802.1X:** Can provide strong network restrictions and can be applied to both wired and wireless connections. Unhealthy clients reach a restricted VLAN.

- **Terminal Services Gateway:** Limits access to limited set of resources for purposes of remediation; only compliant clients can reach terminal services applications.

- **VPN:** Uses IP filters enforced by VPN server to route unhealthy clients to remediation servers.

- **DHCP:** Can check clients when they request IP address assignment, and restricts route to remediation servers.

- **DirectAccess:** Verifies client health before allowing an IPSec tunnel connection; rejects connections and requires new health certificates.

**NOTE** For more information on NAP in Windows Server 2008 R2 and Windows 7, refer to "NAP Client Configuration" at http://technet.microsoft.com/en-us/library/cc754803.aspx and "Network Access Protection" at http://technet.microsoft.com/en-us/network/bb545879.aspx.

### Components of a Typical NAP Deployment

A typical NAP implementation includes the following types of servers:

- **NAP health policy server:** This server receives and processes health credentials from NAP clients. It must be able to communicate with other NAP components, such as NAP enforcement servers and health requirement servers. This server can also provide domain user authentication for 802.1X and VPN-based connections; to do so, this server requires connection to Active Directory Domain Services (AD DS) domain controllers. You can have more than one health policy server to provide load balancing and failover, or to carry out health evaluation locally on multiple NAP enforcement servers. You can also use multiple health policy servers in conjunction with multiple domain controllers.

- **NAP enforcement server:** This server grants or denies access to NAP clients according to their health status. As shown in Figure 16-2, a NAP enforcement server checks a client's health status against standards you have configured on a NAP health policy server. According to the response received from the NAP health policy server, the NAP enforcement server can allow full network access to a compliant client; or in the case of a client that does not meet health standards, it can either deny access completely or allow restricted access, which means that the client can access only a portion of the network that contains resources that update the client as required so that it meets health standards.

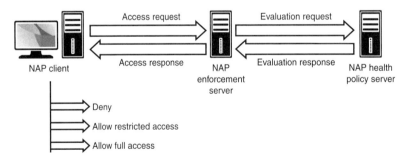

**Figure 16-2**    A simplified representation of how NAP works on your network.

- **NAP certification authority (CA) and Health Registration Authority (HRA) servers:** The *Health Registration Authority (HRA)* server plays a central role when IPSec enforcement is being used. The HRA works as a registration authority in an X.509 public key infrastructure (PKI). It validates client credentials and forwards them in a certificate request to the NAP CA on behalf of the client after the NAP health policy server determines that the client is fully compliant. The NAP CA server is required whenever you've deployed NAP using IPSec enforcement or with a no enforcement design. You can install the NAP CA on the same server as your HRA if desired.

- **NAP Remediation server:** This server provides updates and services to non-compliant client computers. You might need to include the following types of servers on your NAP remediation network:

  - **Antivirus signature servers:** Provide updates to signatures required for antivirus programs to be up to date.

  - **Windows Server Update Services (WSUS) servers:** Provide security updates or other software updates.

  - **Systems Center component servers:** Provide items such as software updates and distribution points. Client computers can download client policies, scan for software update compliance, and download required software updates.

  - **Domain controllers:** Provide domain services, such as authentication, Group Policy objects (GPO), and domain profile settings.

  - **DHCP and DNS servers:** Provide TCP/IP configuration settings and resolution of host names so that clients can access other required servers.

  - **Troubleshooting servers:** Provide instructions to users for bringing computers into compliance with health policies. You can provide URLs that enable users to connect to the appropriate locations; these URLs must be accessible on the remediation network.

  - **Other services:** You might want to provide Internet access for the purposes of reaching remediation services on the Internet, such as Windows Update or program vendor update locations.

- **NAP health requirement server:** Enables communication with the NAP health policy server to establish requirements for installed SHVs, which include settings that determine the compliance status of client computers attempting to connect to the network. The need for a NAP health requirement server depends on the design of an SHV. Types of health requirement servers include antivirus signature servers, domain controllers, and proprietary servers required by specific software applications.

Included within the NAP framework are the following network protection functionalities:

- **Health validation:** Determines whether client computers accessing the network meet all system health requirements.

- **Network restriction:** Restricts network access and communication for computers that do not meet system health requirements.

- **Remediation:** Enables noncompliant computers to receive the updates required to meet network compliance standards.

- **Ongoing compliance:** Ensures that the user's computer continues to meet health policy requirements as it accesses network resources.

When setting up the NAP health policy server, you configure one or more SHVs that include settings that determine the compliance status of client computers attempting to connect to the network. Each client computer sends a *statement of health (SoH)* to the NAP enforcement server, which evaluates the information in the SoH against the requirements defined in the health policy. Client computers that meet all SHV health requirements are allowed total access to the network. A client computer that does not meet the health requirements can be denied access or be restricted to a remediation network, as previously shown in Figure16-2. For purposes of testing the configuration of your SHVs, you can configure an option that enables a noncompliant computer to access the network without restriction; however, you should remove this option after you're sure that the SHV is working properly.

By default, Windows Server 2008 includes only the Windows Security Health Validator (WSHV) SHV. You can install additional SHVs on each NPS server in your NAP framework.

> **NOTE**   For details on the architecture of a typical NAP implementation, refer to "NAP Server-side Architecture" at http://msdn.microsoft.com/en-us/library/cc895519(v=VS.85).aspx.

### What's New with NAP in Windows Server 2008 R2

Windows Server 2008 R2 improves upon NAP by adding support for multiconfiguration SHV. This enables you to specify multiple SHV configurations; you can select one of these SHV configurations when setting up your health policy. You can have different network policies that specify different sets of health requirements according to situations such as internally connected computers and client computers that connect by means of a VPN. Note that all NAP health policy servers must be running Windows Server 2008 R2 to take advantage of multi-configuration SHVs. The original version of Windows Server 2008 required the use of a different NAP health policy server to specify a different set of configuration for the same SHV.

Included also are NAP client user interface improvements, available to Windows 7 client computers. In Windows 7, the response received from the NAP enforcement server is integrated into the Action Center.

# NAP Enforcement

NAP enforcement takes place whenever client computers attempt to access the network by any means including external dial-up or VPN connections or simple communication on the network with other resources such as servers, printers, and so on. NAP can be used to enforce different types of connections to your network, including the following:

- Communications with Dynamic Host Configuration Protocol (DHCP) servers

- VPN connections

- IPSec-protected communications

- Institute of Electrical and Electronics Engineers (IEEE) 802.1X-authenticated connections

- Remote Desktop Services (RDS) and other Terminal Services-brokered connections

NAP is included as a role service component of the Network Policy and Access Services server role. You must install the NPS server role as outlined in Chapter 15 before you can configure your server for NAP. After you do so, you can run the Configure NAP Wizard to configure your server for the enforcement type you want to set up. The following sections examine each enforcement type in detail.

## DHCP Enforcement

When using the DHCP enforcement method, the NAP health policy server evaluates client health according to the configured health policies and SHVs. NPS then instructs the DHCP server to provide compliant NAP client computers with full IP configuration parameters for access to the network. Noncompliant computers are provided restricted access using a subnet mask of 255.255.255.255 and no default gateway. When using this enforcement method, the DHCP server must have the NPS role service installed, running, and configured to forward connection requests to the health policy server for evaluation.

Use the following procedure to configure your NAP server for DHCP enforcement:

1. Click **Start** > **Administrative Tools** > **Network Policy Server** to open the NPS snap-in.

**2.** On the details pane of the NPS snap-in, ensure that **Network Access Protection (NAP)** is selected from the drop-down list under Standard Configuration, and then click **Configure NAP**.

**3.** The Configure NAP Wizard starts with the Select Network Connection Method For Use with NAP page, as shown in Figure 16-3.

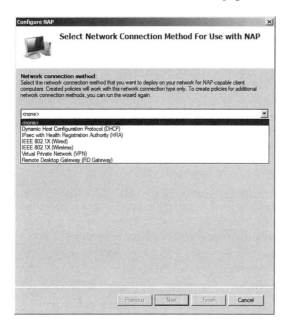

**Figure 16-3**   You must select a network connection method to proceed with installing NAP.

**4.** Select the **Dynamic Host Configuration Protocol (DHCP)** option and click **Next**.

**5.** On the Specify NAP Enforcement Servers Running DHCP Server page, click **Add** to add remote DHCP servers as RADIUS clients if necessary. If the local server is running DHCP, you can click **Next** without adding any clients.

**6.** On the Specify DHCP Scopes page, click **Add** to add any NAP-enabled scopes. If you want to apply the current NAP policy to all scopes on the specified DHCP server, leave this page blank. Then, click **Next**.

**7.** The Configure Machine Groups page enables you to grant or deny access to groups of computers. Click **Add** to display the Add Groups dialog box and specify a domain security group if necessary. Leave this page blank to apply the policy to all computers. Then, click **Next**.

8.  The Specify a NAP Remediation Server Group and URL page shown in
    Figure 16-4 enables you to select a remediation server group to enable non-
    compliant computers to install the required updates. Specify the group or click
    **New Group** to create a remediation server group. Also, type a URL in the
    text box provided to direct users at noncompliant computers to a help page if
    available. When finished, click **Next**.

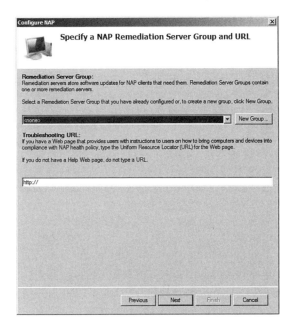

**Figure 16-4**    Specifying a NAP remediation server.

9.  On the Define NAP Health Policy page shown in Figure 16-5, specify at least
    one SHV to be enforced with the policy you're creating. Also, select one of the
    options given for NAP-ineligible client computers, and then click **Next**.

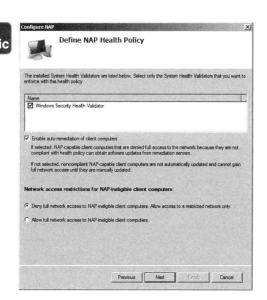

**Figure 16-5**   The Define NAP Health Policy page enables you to specify SHVs and options for ineligible computers.

10. The Completing NAP Enforcement Policy and RADIUS Client Configuration page shown in Figure 16-6 displays summary information about the policies that will be created, including connection request, network access, and health policies. If you need to make changes, click **Previous**. To create these policies, click **Finish**.

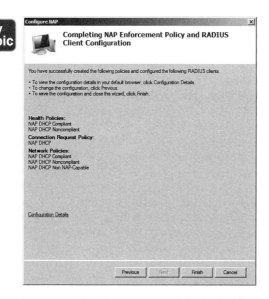

**Figure 16-6**   When you complete the Configure NAP Wizard, policies for connection request, network access, and health are created.

Regardless of the network enforcement method selected, the Configure NAP Wizard creates the following policies, each of which is named according to the name provided in Step 4 of the previous procedure and stored in its subnode of the Policies node of the Network Policy Server snap-in:

- A connection request policy

- Network policies for compliant and noncompliant clients

- Health policies for compliant and noncompliant clients

You can modify any of these policies at any time by right-clicking the required policy and choosing **Properties**.

### Enabling NAP on the DHCP Server's Scopes

After you enable DHCP enforcement as described here, you must also enable NAP on your DHCP scopes. Use the following procedure to enable NAP on all available scopes:

1. Click **Start > Administrative Tools > DHCP** to start the DHCP snap-in.

2. Expand the server in the console tree to reveal the **IPv4** node, right-click this node, and choose **Properties**.

3. Select the **Network Access Protection** tab.

4. As shown in Figure 16-7, click **Enable on all scopes**.

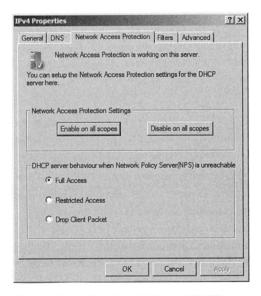

**Figure 16-7**   Enabling NAP on all DHCP scopes.

**5.** Choose from one of the following options for behavior when the NPS server is unavailable:

- **Full Access:** Provides full access for all clients whether compliant or not. Use this option only for testing and monitoring NAP. When you choose this option, NAP is considered to be running in *reporting mode*.

- **Restricted Access:** Limits access for noncompliant computers to servers in the remediation server group only.

- **Drop Client Packet:** Prevents assignment of DHCP-configured IP addresses. Noncompliant clients will receive an Automatic Private Internet Protocol Addressing (APIPA)-configured address on the 169.254.0.0/16 network.

**6.** Click **OK**.

If you want to enable NAP on a single scope, right-click the desired scope in the console tree of the DHCP snap-in and choose **Properties**. Then, perform Steps 3–6 of the preceding procedure.

> **NOTE**  For more information on DHCP enforcement, refer to "DHCP Enforcement Configuration" at http://technet.microsoft.com/en-us/library/dd125315(WS.10).aspx. For a detailed step-by-step procedure for configuring DHCP enforcement, refer to "Step-by-Step Guide: Demonstrate NAP DHCP Enforcement in a Test Lab" at www.microsoft.com/downloads/en/details.aspx?FamilyID=ac38e5bb-18ce-40cb-8e59-188f7a198897&displaylang=en.

### VPN Enforcement

When using VPN enforcement, the NAP health policy server evaluates client health according to the configured health policies and SHVs. NPS then instructs the VPN server to provide full access to compliant NAP client computers and restricted access to noncompliant computers. If Routing and Remote Access Service (RRAS) is installed on a separate server, you must configure the NAP VPN server as a RADIUS client, as discussed in Chapter 15. Use a connection request policy where the source is set to remote access server and the policy is configured to authenticate requests on this server. Select the **Override network policy authentication settings** option and configure Protected Extensible Authentication Protocol (PEAP) to enable health checks and allow secure password- or certificate-based authentication.

In addition, you need to have a CA server running Active Directory Certificate Services (AD CS) available to issue server certificates.

Use the following procedure to configure your NAP server for VPN enforcement:

1. Start the Configure NAP Wizard, as previously described and shown in Figure 16-3.

2. Select the **Virtual Private Network (VPN)** option and click **Next**.

3. On the Specify NAP Enforcement Servers Running VPN Server page, click **Add** to add remote VPN servers as necessary. If the NAP server is running RRAS as a VPN server, it is added automatically. When finished, click **Next**.

4. On the Configure User Groups and Machine Groups page, add groups that should be granted or denied access. Leave this page blank to apply the policy to all users and computers. When finished, click **Next**.

5. On the Configure an Authentication Method page shown in Figure 16-8, note that PEAP is the authentication method used. Select either or both of the EAP types, **Secure Password (PEAP-MS-CHAP v2)** and/or **Smart Card or other certificate (EAP-TLS)**, as required. Then, click **Next**.

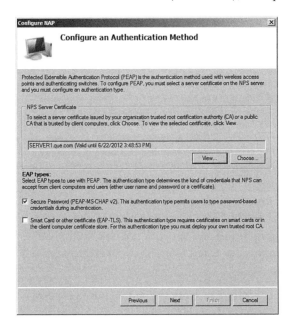

**Figure 16-8** The Configure an Authentication Method page enables you to view information about the NPS server certificate and to choose an EAP type to be used.

6. On the Specify a NAP Remediation Server Group and URL page, select a re-mediation server group from the drop-down list provided. If you need to cre-ate a remediation server group, click **New Group** and specify the group name and remediation servers to be included. When finished, click **Next**.

7. On the Define NAP Health Policy page, select the SHVs to be enforced with this health policy. By default, WSHV is included. (Creation of new SHVs is discussed later in this chapter.) Also, select an option for network access re-strictions for NAP-ineligible client computers, and then click **Next**.

8. The completion page displays summary information about the policies that will be created, including connection request, network access, and health poli-cies. This page is similar to that shown for DHCP enforcement in Figure 16-6. If you need to make changes, click **Previous**. To create these policies, click **Finish**.

> **NOTE** For more information on using the VPN enforcement configuration, refer to "VPN Enforcement Configuration" at http://technet.microsoft.com/en-us/library/dd125382(WS.10).aspx. For a detailed step-by-step procedure for configuring VPN enforcement, refer to "Step-by-Step Guide: Demonstrate NAP VPN Enforcement in a Test Lab" at www.microsoft.com/downloads/en/details.aspx?FamilyID=729bba00-55ad-4199-b441-378cc3d900a7&displaylang=en.

### IPSec Enforcement

When using IPSec enforcement, the NAP server works with the HRA server to de-termine compliance with configured health and network policies. The HRA server uses IIS to communicate with AD DS and authenticate connection requests. This server forwards authenticated clients to the NAP health policy server, where they are evaluated according to the configured health and network policies. Compliant clients receive a health certificate from the associated CA server and are granted full network access.

When IPSec enforcement is in use, the physical network is divided into the follow-ing three logical networks, of which any computer is a member of only one at any given time:

- **Secure network:** Includes computers that have received health certificates and use these certificates for authenticating incoming communication attempts.

This would include most server and client computers within an AD DS-based network.

- **Boundary network:** Includes computers that have received health certificates but do not use these certificates for authenticating incoming communication attempts. These include servers used for assessment and remediation of NAP clients, as well as HRA and remediation servers.

- **Restricted network:** Includes computers that do not have health certificates because they have not completed health checks, are noncompliant with policy, or non-NAP-capable computers, such as older Windows computers, Macintosh computers, or UNIX computers.

Setting up IPSec enforcement thus involves two separate procedures: installing and configuring the HRA server and using the Configure NAP Wizard to configure NAP for IPSec enforcement.

### Installing and Configuring an HRA Server

You must have an HRA server, which is configured with IIS, as well as a CA server. The CA server can be configured as either an enterprise or standalone CA, and can be placed on the same server as the HRA server. Use the following procedure to configure the HRA server:

1. Open Server Manager, select the **Roles** node, and scroll the details pane to locate the **Network Policy and Access Services** role.

2. Click **Add role services**. The Add Role Services Wizard starts with a Select Role Services page, as previously shown in Figure 15-9.

3. On the Select Role Services page, select **Health Registration Authority** and click **Next**.

4. You receive the message box shown in Figure 16-9, informing you that you need to install Internet Information Services (IIS) and Remote Server Administration Tools. Click **Add Required Role Services**, and then click **Next** to proceed.

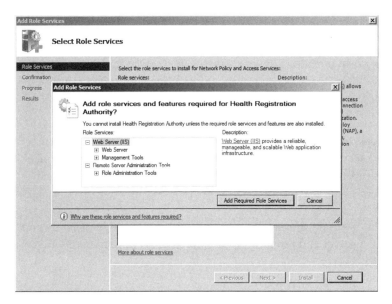

**Figure 16-9** You need to install additional role services and features to install the Health Registration Authority.

5. You are informed that the HRA requires at least one CA be associated with it, as shown in Figure 16-10. For learning purposes, it is sufficient to select the **Install a local CA** option to issue health certificates for this HRA server. Then, click **Next**.

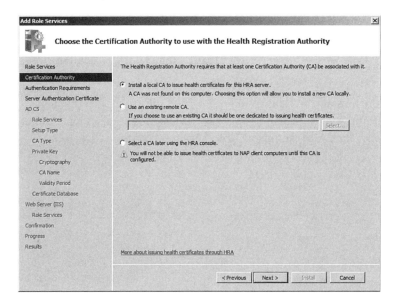

**Figure 16-10** You need to install a CA for the server to function as a HRA.

6. You receive the Choose Authentication Requirements for the Health Registration Authority page shown in Figure 16-11. Select the default option as shown
to require that users be authenticated, and then click **Next**.

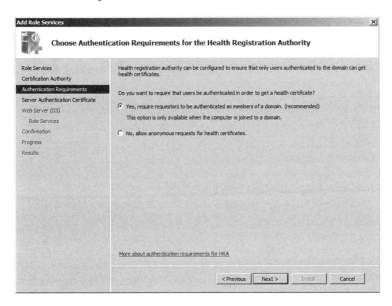

**Figure 16-11**    You should configure the HRA to require users to be authenticated in the domain.

7. On the Server Authentication Certificate page, select a certificate for using
Secure Sockets Layer (SSL) for encrypting network traffic. It is recommended
that you leave the default of **Choose an existing certificate for SSL encryption** selected. Then, click **Next**.

8. If you are installing IIS on this server, you receive the Introduction to Web
Server (IIS) page. Select links on this page to learn more about IIS if desired.
When finished, click **Next**.

9. On the Select Role Services page, it is sufficient to leave the IIS defaults selected. Click **Next**.

10. Review the information on the Confirm Installation Selections page. If you
need to modify any selections, click **Previous**. When finished, click **Install** to
proceed.

11. When informed that installation is completed, click **Close**.

## Configuring NAP for IPSec Enforcement

After you install the HRA server as described in the previous section, you need to configure NAP for IPSec enforcement. Use the following procedure:

1. Start the Configure NAP Wizard, as previously described and shown in Figure 16-3.

2. Select the **IPSec with Health Registration Authority (HRA)** option and click **Next**.

3. On the Specify NAP Enforcement Servers Running HRA page, click **Add** to add additional HRA servers as RADIUS clients if necessary. If you configured the local server with HRA as described previously, it is automatically added. Click **Next**.

4. On the Configure Machine Groups page, click **Add** to specify an AD DS security group containing client computers to be granted or denied access if necessary. Leave this page blank to apply the policy to all users. When finished, click **Next**.

5. On the Define NAP Health Policy page, specify at least one SHV to be enforced with the policy you're creating, and then click **Next**. This page is similar to the one previously shown in Figure 16-5, except that the options for NAP-ineligible client computers are not provided.

6. The completion page displays summary information about the policies that will be created, including connection request, network access, and health policies. This page is similar to that shown for DHCP enforcement in Figure 16-6. If you need to make changes, click **Previous**. To create these policies, click **Finish**.

## Configuring the HRA for Health Certificates

Before you can use IPSec enforcement, you also need to configure a CA that will issue health certificates to client computers. Use the following procedure:

1. Click **Start > Administrative Tools > Health Registration Authority** to open the Health Registration Authority snap-in.

2. Right-click the **Certification Authority** node in the console tree and choose **Add certification authority**.

3. In the Add Certification Authority dialog box that appears, type the name of the CA to be used by the HRA for requesting client certificates and then click **OK**. You can also click **Browse** to locate an appropriate CA.

If you're using an enterprise CA, you should specify this fact by right-clicking **Certification Authority** and choosing **Properties**. From the Properties dialog box that appears, select the radio button labeled **Use enterprise certification authorities**. From the same dialog box, you can modify the number of minutes between requests when a server is unavailable (5 minutes by default), and the time the certificates approved by the HRA will be valid (4 hours by default).

**TIP**    It is advisable to configure more than one CA by repeating the previous procedure. If a single CA goes offline, clients are unable to perform a NAP health check; if NAP enforcement is enabled, they are unable to access the full network.

### Using Group Policy to Specify IPSec Enforcement

You can specify IPSec enforcement in Group Policy by using the following procedure:

1.  Open the Group Policy Management Editor focused on an appropriate GPO.

2.  Navigate to the **Computer Configuration\Policies\Windows Settings\ Security Settings\Network Access Protection\NAP Client Configuration\Health Registration Settings\Trusted Server Groups** node.

3.  Right-click this node and choose **New**.

4.  Follow the steps presented by the New Trusted Server Group Wizard. This includes providing a name for the group you're creating and adding the URLs of the HRA servers to be trusted by the client.

5.  To enable IPSec enforcement, select the **Computer Configuration\Policies\Windows Settings\Security Settings\Network Access Protection\ NAP Client Configuration\Enforcement Clients** node. This displays several policies in the details pane, all of which are disabled by default.

6.  Right-click the **IPSec Relying Party** policy setting and choose **Enable**.

You can also use Group Policy to create IPSec connection security rules for servers that are to be accessed by compliant computers (but not by noncompliant computers). Refer to Chapter 4, "Configuring Windows Firewall with Advanced Security," for information on using either Group Policy or the Windows Firewall with Advanced Security snap-in to create connection security rules.

**TIP**   Ensure that you remember the following requirements for IPSec enforcement:

- IPSec enforcement requires that a PKI be deployed.

- A domain infrastructure is required and clients must be joined to the domain.

- Certificates are the only supported credential.

- The HRA server must be deployed and available on the network.

**NOTE**   For more information on configuring the IPSec enforcement option, refer to "IPSec Enforcement Configuration" at http://technet.microsoft.com/en-us/library/dd125312(WS.10).aspx. For a detailed step-by-step procedure for configuring IPSec enforcement, refer to "Step-by-Step Guide: Demonstrate NAP IPSec Enforcement in a Test Lab" at www.microsoft.com/download/en/details.aspx?displaylang=en&id=12609. For more information on the HRA server, refer to "Health Registration Authority" at http://technet.microsoft.com/en-us/library/cc732365.aspx. For more information on deploying a CA server, refer to "Active Directory Certificate Services Step-by-Step Guide" at http://technet.microsoft.com/en-us/library/cc772393(WS.10).aspx.

### 802.1X Enforcement

When using VPN enforcement, the NAP health policy server evaluates client health according to the configured health policies and SHVs. NPS then instructs the 802.1X authenticating switch or access point to provide full access to compliant NAP client computers and restrict access to noncompliant client computers. When setting up this enforcement method, you must configure the switch or access point as a RADIUS client. Set up a connection request policy to authenticate requests on this server, and configure PEAP to enable health checks and allow secure password- or certificate-based authentication. The 802.1X-capable device must be configured to forward authentication requests to a RADIUS server, which is also a NAP health policy server.

Use the following procedure to configure your NAP server for 802.1X enforcement:

1. Start the Configure NAP Wizard, as previously described and shown in Figure 16-3.

2. Select the **IEEE 802.1X (Wired)** or **IEEE 802.1X (Wireless)** option as appropriate, and then click **Next**.

3. On the Specify 802.1X Authenticating Switches or Access Points page, click **Add** to add network access serves such as authenticating switches or wireless access points as RADIUS clients, and then click **Next**.

4. On the Configure User Groups and Machine Groups page, add groups that should be granted or denied access. Leave this page blank to apply the policy to all users and computers. When finished, click **Next**.

5. On the Configure an Authentication Method page previously shown in Figure 16-8, select either or both of the EAP types, **Secure Password (PEAP-MS-CHAP v2)** and/or **Smart Card or other certificate (EAP-TLS)**, as required. Then, click **Next**.

6. On the Configure Traffic Controls page shown in Figure 16-12, click **Configure** to specify RADIUS attributes for computers being granted full or restricted network access, as required. The dialog box that appears enables you to specify RADIUS standard attributes and vendor-specific attributes. Then, click **Next**.

**Figure 16-12**  The Configure Traffic Controls page enables you to specify RADIUS attributes for computers being granted full or restricted network access.

7. Specify options for the SHVs to be enforced and network access restrictions for NAP-ineligible client computers, as previously shown in Figure 16-5, and then click **Next**.

8. The completion page displays summary information about the policies that will be created, including connection request, network access, and health policies. This page is similar to that shown for DHCP enforcement in Figure 16-6. If you need to make changes, click **Previous**. To create these policies, click **Finish**. The policies are created and added to the appropriate subnodes in the NPS snap-in.

---

**NOTE** For more information on configuring the 802.1X enforcement option, refer to "802.1X Enforcement Configuration" at http://technet.microsoft.com/en-us/library/dd125308(WS.10).aspx. For a detailed step-by-step procedure for configuring 802.1X enforcement, refer to "Step-by-Step Guide: Demonstrate 802.1X Enforcement in a Test Lab" at www.microsoft.com/download/en/details.aspx?displaylang=en&id=733.

---

### RDS Enforcement

When using RDS enforcement, the NAP health policy server evaluates client health according to the configured health policies and SHVs. NPS then instructs the RD Gateway server to either allow or deny access by the client according to the client health results. Note that the RD Gateway server is a machine running Windows Server 2008 that has the Remote Desktop Services server role installed, together with its RD Gateway role service.

Use the following procedure to configure your NAP server for RDS enforcement:

1. Start the Configure NAP Wizard, as previously described and shown in Figure 16-3.

2. Select the **Remote Desktop Gateway (RD Gateway)** option, and then click **Next**.

3. On the Specify NAP Enforcement Servers Running RD Gateway page, click **Add** to add remote servers running RD Gateway. If RD Gateway is running on the local computer, you do not need to do anything. Then, click **Next**.

4. On the Configure Client Device Redirection and Authentication Methods page shown in Figure 16-13, select the appropriate options according to your network configuration, and then click **Next**.

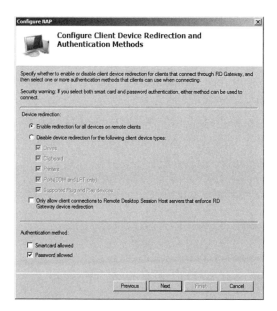

**Figure 16-13**  Specifying device redirection and authentication methods for RD Gateway connections.

5.  On the Configure the Idle Timeout and Session Timeout Actions page shown in Figure 16-14, select the **Enable idle timeout** and **Enable session timeout** options as appropriate to your network, and then click **Next**.

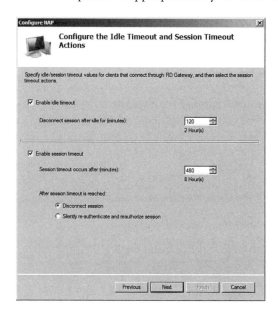

**Figure 16-14**  Specifying idle and session timeout values for RD Gateway connections.

6. On the Configure User Groups and Machine Groups page, add groups that should be granted access. Note that you must add at least one user group. When finished, click **Next**.

7. Specify options for the SHVs to be enforced and network access restrictions for NAP-ineligible client computers, and then click **Next**.

8. The completion page displays summary information about the policies that will be created, including connection request, network access, and health policies. This page is similar to that shown for DHCP enforcement in Figure 16-6. If you need to make changes, click **Previous**. To create these policies, click **Finish**. These policies are placed in the appropriate subnodes of the NPS snap-in.

**NOTE** For more information on configuring the RDS enforcement option with NAP, refer to "Configuring NAP Integration with RD Gateway Step-by-Step Guide" at http://technet.microsoft.com/en-us/library/gg618548(WS.10).aspx.

## System Health Validation

When using NAP in an AD DS environment, NAP client computers are evaluated according to settings in Group Policy. Use a Group Policy object (GPO) linked to an appropriate container, such as a site, domain, or organizational unit (OU). This enables you to configure NAP settings for client computers running Windows XP SP3, Windows Vista, Windows 7, or Windows Server 2008/R2.

As already mentioned, NAP uses SHVs to evaluate the health status of client computers. On the client side, a component called the system health agent (SHA) monitors client health. By default, Windows Server 2008/R2 and Windows Vista/7 include the Windows Security Health Validator (WSHV) and Windows Security Health Agent (WSHA). These components enforce the following security settings:

- Windows Firewall or other firewall software is enabled.

- Antivirus software is installed, properly updated, and enabled.

- Antispyware software is installed, properly updated, and enabled. Note that this check is not performed on Windows XP computers.

- Windows Update Services is enabled and all current updates have been installed.

**TIP**  When deploying a SHV that enforces NAP enforcement for VPNs, you should use a GPO linked to the appropriate AD DS container that enables Security Center on all affected client computers. Security Center is required for some NAP deployments that use the WSHV. You can do so by accessing the Computer Configuration\Policies\Administrative Templates\Windows Components\Security Center node and enabling the Turn on Security Center (Domain PCs only) policy. For more information, refer to "Windows Security Health Validator" at http://technet.microsoft.com/en-us/library/cc731260.aspx.

### Configuring the Windows Security Health Validator

You can modify the default WSHV settings by performing the following procedure:

1. Click **Start** > **Administrative Tools** > **Network Policy Server** to open the NPS snap-in.

2. In the console tree of the NPS snap-in, expand the **Network Access Protection** node to reveal the **System Health Validators** node, and then expand this node to reveal the **Windows Security Health Validator** subnode. As shown in Figure 16-15, Settings and Error Codes panels appear in the details pane.

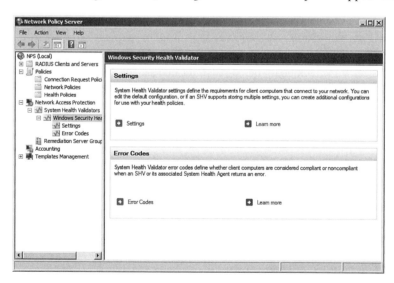

**Figure 16-15**  You can configure security settings and error codes for WSHV.

3. Click **Settings**.

**4.** The Windows Security Health Validator dialog box, as shown in Figure 16-16, appears. Select either **Windows7/Windows Vista** or **Windows XP** according to the operating system in use by clients that will be evaluated.

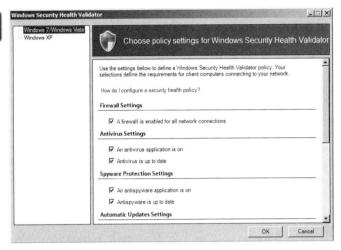

**Figure 16-16**   You can choose from a series of security settings that will be enforced by WSHV.

**5.** Select or clear the check boxes according to the items you want to have clients evaluated on. By default, all the items mentioned previously are selected, except for Security Updates Settings. To enable the use of security updates evaluation, select the check box labeled **Restrict access for clients that do not have all available security updates installed**. Then, select the following options as required:

- **Specify the minimum severity level required for updates:** Select the desired security level from the drop-down list. By default, this is `Important and above`. You can also choose **Critical only, Moderate and above, Low and above,** or **All**.

- **Specify the minimum number of hours allowed since the client has checked for new security updates:** Select the required number of hours (maximum 72 hours, default 22 hours).

- **Source of security updates:** By default, security updates are obtained from Microsoft Update. You can also select either or both of **Windows Update** and **Windows Server Update Services**.

**6.** Repeat for the other operating system if both types of operating system are in use on your network. When finished, click **OK**.

## Configuring Error Codes

You can also modify error code settings in WSHV. Error codes determine whether action will be taken against client computers that are noncompliant with regard to any of the security settings. Generally, you would leave all of these set to **Noncompliant**, but if problems arise because otherwise compliant machines are unable to contact external services because of connectivity problems, you might want to set one or more of these to **Compliant**. Use the following procedure to configure error codes:

1. In the console tree of the NPS snap-in, select the **Windows Security Health Validator** subnode to reveal the dialog box previously shown in Figure 16-15.

2. Click **Error Codes**.

3. You receive the Windows Security Health Validator dialog box, as shown in Figure 16-17. For any of the five error codes displayed, select the **Compliant** option from its drop-down list if you don't want to have clients sent to the remediation network should validation fail for the stated reason.

**Figure 16-17**   You can modify the error code resolution for each of five possible situations.

4. Click **OK**.

## Using Multi-Configuration SHV

Windows Server 2008 R2 and Windows 7 support the multi-configuration SHV feature, in which you can specify multiple configurations of a SHV. When configuring a health policy, you can select one specific configuration from the multi-configuration SHV. For example, you can set up a network policy that specifies that computers on the internal network must have antivirus enabled and another network policy that specifies that computers connecting by VPN must have antivirus enabled and signature files updated. Note that multi-configuration SHVs are only available for SHVs that support this feature, such as WSHV. A third-party SHV must be designed to support the multi-configuration feature.

To specify additional settings in a multi-configuration SHV, use the following procedure:

1. Right-click the **Settings** subnode under the SHV node in the console tree of the NPS snap-in and choose **New**.

2. Provide a friendly name for the new configuration, and then select the desired settings from the dialog box previously shown in Figure 16-16.

After performing this procedure you can later select the desired multi-configuration SHV option when creating a new health policy. (The procedure for doing so is explained later.)

### Configuring NAP Policies

You saw how NAP policies are created when you run the Configure NAP Wizard. You can create new policies at any time; the NPS snap-in provides several wizards to assist you in this process. The following procedure shows you how to create a new network policy:

1. In the console tree of the NPS snap-in, right-click **Network Policies** and choose **New**. This starts the New Network Policy Wizard.

2. On the Specify Network Policy Name and Connection Type page, type a name for your policy. Select the type of network access server to be used with this policy, and then click **Next**.

3. On the Specify Conditions page, click **Add** to add a condition that determines whether the network policy is evaluated for the connection request. This displays the dialog box shown in Figure 16-18 that enables you to select a condition from one of the following:

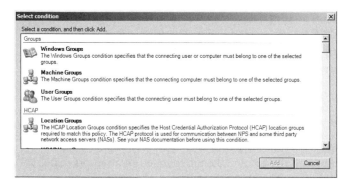

**Figure 16-18**  The Select Condition dialog box enables you to select a condition that determines whether the network policy is evaluated.

- **Groups:** Enables you to select a group to which the user and/or computer must belong.

- **HCAP:** Enables you to specify a Host Credential Authorization Protocol (HCAP) location or user group. This type of group is used to integrate with Cisco Network Access Control.

- **Day and time restrictions:** Enables you to specify the days and times when connection attempts are allowed or prohibited.

- **Network Access Protection:** Enables you to specify a range of conditions pertaining to NAP, such as identity type, health policies, NAP-capable computers, and operating system in use.

- **Connection Properties:** Enables you to specify properties that pertain to allowed or denied connections, such as an IP address range, authentication type, EAP types, service type and tunnel type.

- **RADIUS Client Properties:** Enables you to specify properties that pertain to the RADIUS client being accessed. Remember that this means components such as RRAS servers, wireless access points, and so on. Refer to Chapter 15 for more information.

- **Gateway:** Enables you to specify properties that pertain to a network access server (NAS) being contacted during the connection attempt. This includes properties such as the called station ID (phone number), IP address, and port type.

4. Repeat Step 3 to add additional conditions as required for your policy. Then, click **Next**.

5. On the Specify Access Permission page, choose either **Access granted** or **Access denied** to determine the action taken if connection attempts match policy conditions. Then, click **Next**.

6. On the Configure Authentication Methods page, specify the authentication methods required for the connection request to match the policy. Click **Add** if you need to specify an EAP type, as shown in Figure 16-19. Then, click **Next**.

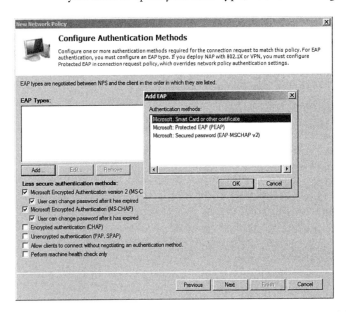

**Figure 16-19**   The Configure Authentication Methods page enables you to specify the authentication methods.

7. On the Configure Constraints page, specify additional constraints if required that must be met to match the connection request. You can specify an idle timeout, session timeout, called station ID, day and time restrictions, and NAS port type. When done, click **Next**.

8. On the Configure Settings page shown in Figure 16-20, select **NAP Enforcement** and specify one of the options shown for enforcement of the policy. You

should select the **Allow full network access** option when creating a policy for healthy computers or the **Allow limited access** option when creating a policy for noncompliant computers. Then, click **Next**.

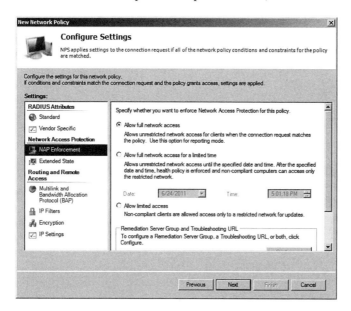

**Figure 16-20**   Specifying enforcement of the NAP policy.

9. On the Completing New Network Policy page, review the policy conditions and policy settings. If you need to make any changes, click **Previous**. Click **Finish** to create the policy and add it to the list in the details pane of the NPS snap-in.

If you want to create a connection request policy, right-click the **Connection Request Policies** subnode and choose **New**. The pages presented by the New Connection Request Policy Wizard are similar to those presented by the New Network Policy Wizard. You receive a Specify Connection Request Forwarding page that enables you to specify RADIUS authentication and accounting request settings. The Configure Settings page enables you to specify a realm name and RADIUS attributes.

If you want to create a new health policy, right-click **Health Policies** and choose **New**. This displays the Create New Health Policy dialog box shown in Figure 16-21. Provide a policy name and select an option for client SHV checks. (You have several options for various numbers of health checks passed or failed.) Specify the SHV used in the health policy; if you are using a multi-configuration SHV, select a setting from the drop-down list. Then, click **OK** to create the policy.

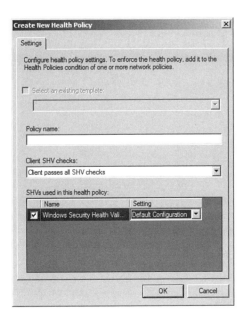

**Figure 16-21**    Creating a new health policy.

If you want to create a new health policy, use the following procedure:

1.  Right-click **Health Policies** and choose **New**.

2.  On the Create New Health Policy dialog box shown in Figure 16-21, provide a policy name and select an option for client SHV checks. (You have several options for various numbers of health checks passed or failed.)

3.  Specify the SHV used in the health policy; if you are using a multi-configuration SHV, select a setting from the drop-down list.

4.  Click **OK** to create the policy.

If you need to modify any policy you create, whether by using the Configure NAP Wizard or by means of the procedure in this section, right-click the desired policy in the details pane of the NPS snap-in and choose **Properties**. The Properties dialog box that appears enables you to modify any of the settings described in this section.

# Exam Preparation Tasks

## Review All the Key Topics

Review the most important topics in this chapter, noted with the key topics icon in the outer margin of the page. Table 16-2 lists a reference of these key topics and the page numbers on which each is found.

**Table 16-2** Key Topics for Chapter 16

| Key Topic Element | Description | Page Number |
|---|---|---|
| List | Introduces the types of health criteria that a NAP implementation can address. | 658 |
| List | Introduces the available types of NAP enforcement. | 659 |
| List | Describes the types of servers used in a NAP implementation. | 660 |
| Figure 16-5 | Defining health validators and the action to be applied to a NAP-ineligible client computer. | 666 |
| Figure 16-6 | Completing the Configure NAP Wizard creates a series of policies that will be applied to client computers requesting access to your network. | 666 |
| Figure 16-8 | Configuring an EAP authentication method to be used with VPN enforcement. | 669 |
| List | IPSec enforcement divides the network into three logical segments. | 670 |
| List | Shows you how to install an HRA server. | 671 |
| Figure 16-12 | Configuring RADIUS attributes for 802.1X authentication. | 677 |
| Figure 16-16 | Configuring security settings to be enforced by the Windows Security Health Validator. | 682 |
| List | Shows you how to create a new NAP network policy. | 684 |
| List | Describes the types of conditions you can specify in a NAP network policy. | 685 |

## Definitions of Key Terms

Define the following key terms from this chapter, and check your answers in the Glossary.

health policies, Health Registration Authority (HRA), Network Access Protection (NAP), remediation server, reporting mode, statement of health (SoH), system health agent (SHA), system health validator (SHV), Windows Security Health Validator (WSHV)

This chapter covers the following subjects:

- **Concepts of DirectAccess:** This section familiarizes you with how Direct Access works and the requirements that DirectAccess servers and client computers must meet.

- **Configuring the DirectAccess Server:** This section outlines the use of the DirectAccess Setup Wizard and the other configuration actions for running DirectAccess. It also introduces the concept of using DirectAccess on a perimeter network.

- **Group Policy and DirectAccess:** Group Policy enables you to configure policies that affect the functionality of DirectAccess clients. Group Policy also provides the Name Resolution Policy Table, which provides DNS name resolution and security options for DirectAccess clients.

# CHAPTER 17

# Configuring DirectAccess

Chapter 14, "Configuring Remote Access," introduced you to technologies involved in connecting remote clients to your network using dial-up and virtual private network (VPN) connections. Chapters 15, "Configuring Network Policy Server (NPS)," and 16, "Configuring Network Access Protection (NAP)," continued to explore the technologies provided by Microsoft that helps you ensure that only properly authenticated computers with the proper security configurations and updates receive access to your corporate network. Now, we turn our attention to another remote connectivity feature provided by Windows Server 2008 R2 that is especially valuable in creating secure, authenticated connections between external locations and corporate offices—the DirectAccess feature, which enables seamless access to the network from any location without the need for a VPN.

## "Do I Know This Already?" Quiz

The "Do I Know This Already?" quiz allows you to assess whether you should read this entire chapter or simply jump to the "Exam Preparation Tasks" section for review. If you are in doubt, read the entire chapter. Table 17-1 outlines the major headings in this chapter and the corresponding "Do I Know This Already?" quiz questions. You can find the answers in Appendix A, "Answers to the 'Do I Know This Already?' Quizzes."

**Table 17-1** "Do I Know This Already?" Foundation Topics Section-to-Question Mapping

| Foundations Topics Section | Questions Covered in This Section |
| --- | --- |
| Concepts of DirectAccess | 1–3 |
| Configuring the DirectAccess Server | 4–6 |
| Group Policy and DirectAccess | 7–8 |

1. You are planning an implementation of DirectAccess to facilitate network access by road warriors who connect to your company's network from various external locations such as client networks, hotels, and airports. You intend to set up a pilot implementation of DirectAccess using a server that is running the original version of Windows Server 2008. Which of the following actions do you need to take in order to run DirectAccess on this server? (Each correct answer represents part of the solution. Choose four.)

   a. Upgrade the server to Windows Server 2008 R2.

   b. Install the Web Server (IIS) server role on the server.

   c. Promote the server to a domain controller in your company's AD DS domain.

   d. Install Active Directory Certificate Services (AD CS) on the server.

   e. Install at least two network adapters on the server.

   f. Configure the network adapter that is connected to the Internet with one public IPv4 address.

   g. Configure the network adapter that is connected to the Internet with two consecutive public IPv4 addresses.

2. These road warriors who intend to access your company's network from various external locations are currently using laptops running a variety of Windows operating systems dating back to Windows XP. Which of the following do you need to do so that these users can connect to the network using DirectAccess? (Each correct answer represents part of the solution. Choose two.)

   a. Upgrade all laptops to Windows Vista Business, Enterprise, or Ultimate or Windows 7 Professional, Enterprise, or Ultimate.

   b. Upgrade all laptops to Windows Vista Enterprise or Ultimate or Windows 7 Enterprise or Ultimate.

   c. Upgrade all laptops to Windows 7 Professional, Enterprise, or Ultimate.

   d. Upgrade all laptops to Windows 7 Enterprise or Ultimate.

   e. Install DirectAccess client connection software on all laptops.

   f. Ensure that all client computers are joined to your company's AD DS domain.

3. Which of the following are required on DirectAccess client computers to ensure that they can be authenticated on the network? (Choose two.)

   a. The clients must be joined to the domain and belong to a special security group configured on the DirectAccess server.

   b. The clients must be configured with IPv6 globally routable addresses.

   c. The clients must have installed a certificate that specifies the Client Authentication and Server Authentication certificate purposes.

   d. The clients must be equipped with a smart card reader that includes a certificate that specifies the Client Authentication and Server Authentication certificate purposes.

4. Which of the following do you need to do to install DirectAccess on your server?

   a. Run the Add Roles Wizard to install the DirectAccess server role.

   b. Run the Add Roles Wizard to install the Network Policy and Access Services server role. On the Select Role Services page, select the DirectAccess role feature.

   c. Run the Add Roles Wizard to install the Web Server (IIS) server role. On the Select Role Services page, select the DirectAccess role feature.

   d. Run the Add Features Wizard to install the DirectAccess server feature.

5. You installed DirectAccess on your server and now you access the DirectAccess Management Console snap-in. After clicking **Setup**, you receive the DirectAccess Setup Wizard. Which of the following actions does this wizard direct you to perform? (Choose all that apply.)

   a. Specify the ports and protocols that are allowed to pass the perimeter and Internet-facing firewalls.

   b. Specify the name of the group containing the client computers that will be enabled for DirectAccess.

   c. Obtain and install a computer certificate on the server.

   d. Specify the certificates that client computers will access and the certificate used to secure remote client connectivity over HTTPS.

   e. Specify the URL that provides clients with location information plus the host name and IPv6 address for the domain controller.

   f. Specify the application servers that will accept secure connections from clients.

6. You are implementing DirectAccess along with Network Access Protection (NAP) on your company's network. Which of the following represents the best location for the various servers involved in this implementation?

   a. Place the DirectAccess server and all NAP servers such as the enforcement server, the health policy server, and Health Registration Authority (HRA) on the perimeter network between the internal network and the Internet. Place the remediation network servers within the internal network.

   b. Place the DirectAccess server on the perimeter network between the internal network and the Internet. Place all NAP servers as well as the remediation network servers within the internal network.

   c. Place the DirectAccess server and the NAP enforcement server on the perimeter network between the internal network and the Internet. Place the HRA server and the remediation network servers within the internal network.

   d. Place all servers, including the DirectAccess server and all NAP network servers within the internal network.

7. You are using Group Policy to create a Name Resolution Policy Table (NRPT) rule that will apply to external users using DirectAccess to reach the sales.que.com portion of your company's DNS namespace. Which of the following items can you specify within this rule? (Choose all that apply.)

   a. Names and IP addresses of DNS servers

   b. Use of Network Access Protection (NAP)

   c. Use of a Web proxy

   d. IPSec encryption type for communication between DNS client and DNS server

   e. Options for resolving only IPv6 queries or both IPv4 and IPv6 queries

**8.** You configured your network to use DirectAccess. A user named Jim, who has returned to the office after visiting several client locations, reports that he is unable to access servers on the network. Jim was able to reach these servers when he was at client locations. What should you do?

    **a.** Check the configuration of the DirectAccess server because the IP address specified for the DNS server in the DirectAccess snap-in must be incorrect.

    **b.** Specify a Name Resolution Policy Table (NRPT) exemption that exempts the DirectAccess location server from special handling by the NRPT rules.

    **c.** Specify a NRPT exemption that exempts the internal DNS servers from special handling by the NRPT rules.

    **d.** Specify an alternate IP configuration on Jim's computer that adds the IPv6 addresses of the internal DNS servers to the computer's TCP/IP properties.

**Foundation Topics**

## Concepts of DirectAccess

DirectAccess is a new feature of Windows Server 2008 R2 and Windows 7 that enables users to directly connect to corporate networks from any Internet connection. Once enabled, a user can access network resources as though he were actually at the office. DirectAccess uses IPv6 over IPSec to create a seamless, bidirectional, secured tunnel between the user's computer and the office network, without the need for a virtual private network (VPN) connection.

DirectAccess differs from a VPN implementation in that users are provided end-to-end authentication and end-to-end encryption. This means that they are connecting to an exact server with data encryption across the entire connection. Furthermore, IT professionals can service remote computers whenever the client computer has Internet connection.

The benefits of DirectAccess include the following:

- **Improved mobile workforce productivity:** Users have the same connectivity to network resources whether they are in or out of the office. Users can be connected through any Internet connection, such as a client's office, home, hotel, airport Wi-Fi connection, and so on.

- **Improved management of remote users:** You can apply Group Policy updates and software updates to remote computers whenever they are connected by means of DirectAccess.

- **Improved network security:** DirectAccess uses IPv6 over IPSec to enable encrypted communications and secured authentication of the computer to the corporate network even before the user has logged on. IPv6 also provides globally routable IP addresses for remote access clients. Encryption is provided using Data Encryption Standard (DES), which uses a 56-bit key, and Triple DES (3DES), which uses three 56-bit keys.

- **Access control capabilities:** You can choose to allow only specific applications or subnets of the corporate network or to allow unlimited network access by DirectAccess users.

- **Simplified network traffic:** Unnecessary traffic on the corporate network is reduced because DirectAccess separates its traffic from other Internet traffic. You can specify that DirectAccess clients send all traffic through the DirectAccess server.

Windows Server 2008 R2 includes the required server functionality to operate DirectAccess. Optionally, you can also include Microsoft Forefront Unified Access Gateway (UAG) 2010 Service Pack 1. This option provides enhanced security within and outside the corporate network, enabling DirectAccess for IPv4-only applications and resources on the network. Security is improved on the DirectAccess server and built-in wizards and tools simplify deployment and reduce configuration errors. In addition, UAG provides centralized management and policy control across all users, devices, and network resources.

A DirectAccess implementation includes the following key components:

- **DirectAccess server:** A Windows Server 2008 R2 computer that is a member of an Active Directory Domain Services (AD DS) domain and accepts connections from DirectAccess clients and facilitates client access to resources on the corporate intranet. You would typically install DirectAccess servers on your perimeter network between your Internet-facing firewall and your intranet.

- **DirectAccess client:** A domain member computer running Windows 7 Enterprise or Ultimate or Windows Server 2008 R2 that can utilize a DirectAccess server to automatically and transparently connect to the corporate network.

- **Network location server:** An intranet web server used by a DirectAccess client to determine whether it is located on the corporate intranet or the Internet. This server receives and processes requests for a Hypertext Transfer Protocol Secure (HTTPS)-based URL.

- **Certificate revocation list (CRL) distribution points:** Servers that provide access to the CRL published by the certification authority (CA) that issues certificates for DirectAccess. DirectAccess clients check the CRL to ensure the validity of the certificates used for the HTTPS connections to the network location server and DirectAccess server.

**NOTE** For more information on UAG, refer to "Forefront UAG DirectAccess deployment guide" at http://technet.microsoft.com/en-us/library/dd857320.aspx. For general information on DirectAccess, refer to "DirectAccess" at http://technet.microsoft.com/en-us/network/dd420463.aspx and links included in this document.

### DirectAccess Server Requirements

DirectAccess server computers must be running any edition of Windows Server 2008 R2. If your server is running the original version of Windows Server 2008, you must upgrade to the R2 version. DirectAccess requires an AD DS domain with one or more DirectAccess servers that meet the following requirements:

- The server must be configured as a member of an AD DS domain. This server needs to have the Web Server (Internet Information Services [IIS]) server role installed.

- The domain functional level must be Windows Server 2008 native or higher. If smart card authorization is in used, the domain functional level must be at least Windows Server 2008 R2.

- You need to install the DirectAccess Management Console server feature from the Server Manager Add Features Wizard to enable the server to act as a DirectAccess server.

- The server must be equipped with two network adapters: one connected directly to the network and one connected to the corporate intranet.

- The network adapter that is connected to the Internet must be configured with two consecutive IPv4 public addresses.

- The server requires digital certificates obtained from an Active Directory Certificate Services (AD CS) server that is configured as an Enterprise CA. DirectAccess clients use certificates from the same CA; doing so enables both client and server to trust each other's certificates.

By using two consecutive public IPv4 addresses on the perimeter network interface, the DirectAccess server acts as a Teredo server, and clients on the internal network can use this server to detect the type of Network Address Translation (NAT) device that they are behind. As defined in RFC 4380, a Teredo server is a machine that uses a globally routable IPv4 address to access the Internet, thereby helping to provide IPv6 connectivity to Teredo clients (which, in this case, are the DirectAccess clients).

**NOTE**   For more information on the types of NAT and the method that involves the use of two IPv4 addresses, refer to "Why Do I Need Two IP Addresses on the External Interface of the UAG DirectAccess Server?" at http://blogs.technet.com/b/tomshinder/archive/2011/01/19/why-do-i-need-two-ip-addresses-on-the-external-interface-of-the-uag-directaccess-server.aspx. For more information on Teredo, refer to "Teredo Overview" at http://technet.microsoft.com/en-us/network/cc917486.aspx.

**TIP** Without two public IPv4 addresses, DirectAccess will not work because these two addresses are required on the Teredo server to determine the type of NAT device behind which the DirectAccess client is located. Be aware of this requirement, both for the 70-642 exam and for setting up DirectAccess in the real world.

In addition, the domain must have at least one domain controller and DNS server that runs Windows Server 2008 SP2 or Windows Server 2008 R2. If UAG is not in use and connection to IPv4-only resources is required, you must have a Network Address Translation 64 (NAT64) device.

### Using IPv6 with DirectAccess

DirectAccess requires using IPv6 in order that DirectAccess clients can have globally routable addresses. This technology extends network infrastructure that already is configured with IPv6, so that clients can still use IPv4 to access the Internet if so desired. If the network infrastructure does not include IPv6, you can use the 6to4 and Teredo IPv6 technologies so that DirectAccess clients can connect to an intranet that includes IPv4 only. We introduced 6to4 and Teredo in Chapter 1, "Configuring IPv4 and IPv6 Addressing."

Table 17-2 summarizes these network connectivity options.

**Table 17-2** Options for Connecting DirectAccess Clients to the Network

| Type of IP Address Assigned to the Client | Preferred Method of Connection |
| --- | --- |
| Globally routable IPv6 address | Globally routable IPv6 address |
| Public IPv4 address | 6to4 |
| Private (NAT) IPv4 address | Teredo |
| If unable to connect using these methods | IP-HTTPS |

### Using Network Access Protection

You can use NAP with DirectAccess so that DirectAccess clients must submit a health certificate for initial authentication with the DirectAccess server. This health certificate proves that the client is free of malware and is up-to-date with regard to security updates and antimalware definitions. Clients obtain this certificate from a Health Registration Authority server prior to initial connection to the DirectAccess server.

### DirectAccess Client Requirements

DirectAccess client computers must be running Windows 7 Enterprise or Ultimate edition. In addition, Windows Server 2008 R2 computers can act as DirectAccess clients. The client computer does not require installation of any client connection software; their configuration is managed directly through membership in a AD DS domain with the appropriate Group Policy settings. A user at a DirectAccess client computer merely sees the remote network as an extension of the local network to which she is connected; no special DirectAccess connection interface is used or required.

All client computers must be joined to the AD DS domain and belong to a special security group that you configure when setting up the DirectAccess server. When connected to the internal network, a client receives its configuration via Group Policy. Each client computer also needs computer certificate installed that enables DirectAccess authentication. As already mentioned, a Windows Server 2008 R2 computer running AD CS provides this certificate.

### DirectAccess Connection Process

Connecting to corporate resources involves the following process:

1. The DirectAccess client computer connects to a network and determines whether it is connected to the corporate intranet. If it is already connected, it does not use DirectAccess; if it is external, it uses DirectAccess.

2. The client computer uses IPv6 and IPSec to connect to the DirectAccess server via an intranet website on the server that is configured when the server is set up. If the client is not on an IPv6 network, it uses 6to4 or Teredo to encapsulate the IPv6 traffic into the IPv4 connection.

3. If a firewall or proxy server prevents the client computer from using 6to4 or Teredo, the client computer tries to use IP over Secure Hypertext Transfer Protocol (IP-HTTPS) with Secure Sockets Layer (SSL) to encapsulate the IPv6 traffic.

4. The DirectAccess client and server authenticate each other using their computer certificates and the IPSec tunnel is set up. In addition, the DirectAccess server validates the client by means of group memberships configured in AD DS.

5. If NAP is in use, the DirectAccess client submits its health certificate to a NAP health policy server, which determines whether the client is in compliance with system health requirements.

6. The user logs on and the DirectAccess client establishes a second IPSec tunnel for access to the network resources.

7. The DirectAccess server forwards traffic between the client and the corporate network resources according to the user's access permissions.

Typically, this process happens automatically without intervention from the user apart from the logon process.

# Configuring the DirectAccess Server

DirectAccess is installed as a server feature in Windows Server 2008 R2. Before you install DirectAccess, you must have a Windows Server 2008 R2 computer that is equipped with two physical network adapters. The server must be joined to an AD DS domain.

### Installing and Configuring the DirectAccess Server Feature

You should perform the following preliminary steps before installing DirectAccess:

1. Obtain and install a computer certificate on the server. This certificate will be used for IPSec authentication.

2. Set up the server on the perimeter network with one network adapter connected to the Internet and one or more network adapters connected to the internal network. If no native IPv6 connectivity is available, both network adapters should be configured with public IPv4 addresses.

3. Ensure that the appropriate ports are open on the perimeter and Internet-facing firewalls. For the required ports, refer to "Requirements and Prerequisites" at http://technet.microsoft.com/en-gb/library/dd637780(WS.10).aspx.

4. Enable IPv6 on all clients and servers if not already enabled.

5. Create an AD DS security group and add the accounts for the client computers that will be using DirectAccess to this group.

6. Use the Add Roles Wizard in Server Manager to install the AD CS server role unless this role is installed on another available server. From the Certification Authority snap-in, configure a CRL distribution point on a shared folder accessible to the DirectAccess server and to client computers.

7. If the DirectAccess server is also the network location server, use the Add Roles Wizard to install the IIS server role on this server. For learning purposes,

it is sufficient to accept all the defaults presented by the wizard. Further, if you have followed along with the procedures of Chapter 16, these roles should already be installed on your computer.

8. Designate one of the server network adapters as the Internet-facing adapter. As already described, this interface requires two consecutive, public IPv4 addresses, both of which must be assigned to this interface.

9. Ensure that the Internet-facing interface is configured as either a **Public** or **Private** interface, depending on your network design. Configure the internal network interfaces as **Domain** interfaces. If additional interfaces are present, ensure that no more than two classification types are selected.

After you configure your server to meet these requirements, use the following procedure to install the DirectAccess server feature:

1. Open Server Manager and select the **Features** node.

2. Click **Add Features**, and on the Select Features page of the Add Features Wizard, select **DirectAccess Management Console**, as shown in Figure 17-1. Then, click **Next**.

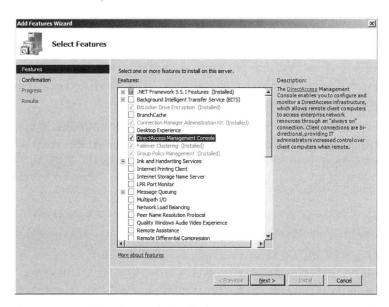

**Figure 17-1**    DirectAccess is installed as a server feature in Windows Server 2008 R2.

3. Click **Install**.

4. When informed that installation is complete, click **Close**.

This procedure adds the DirectAccess Management Console MMC snap-in to the Administrative Tools folder. Use the following procedure to set up DirectAccess for use:

1. Click **Start > Administrative Tools > DirectAccess Management**.

2. You receive the DAMgmt - [DirectAccess] snap-in, as shown in Figure 17-2. Select the **Setup** node from the console tree to display the DirectAccess Setup Wizard, which provides a four-step procedure in the details pane for setting up the DirectAccess server.

**Figure 17-2**   The DirectAccess Management Console snap-in enables you to manage Direct Access on your server.

3. In the details pane, click **Configure** for Step 1.

4. On the DirectAccess Client Setup page, click **Add**.

5. Type the name of the group containing the computers that will be configured as DirectAccess clients, click **OK**, and then click **Finish**.

6. Click **Configure** for Step 2.

7. On the Connectivity page that appears, select the network addresses for the interfaces connected to the Internet and the local network and click **Next**.

8. On the Certificate Components page, click **Browse** under **Select the certificate to which remote client certificates must chain** to locate the certificate that client computers will access when accessing your server. Select the appropriate certificate from the list that appears and then click **OK**.

9. Click **Browse** under **Select the certificate that will be used to secure remote client connectivity over HTTPS**. Select the appropriate certificate from the list that appears, click **OK**, and click **Finish**.

10. Click **Configure** for Step 3.

11. On the Location page, select **Network Location server is run on a highly available server (recommended)**. Type the URL to this server (this must begin with https:). Click **Validate** and then click **Next**.

12. On the DNS and Domain Controller page, note the entry for the host name and IPv6 address for the domain controller. The IPv6 address that appears consists of a 6to4 network prefix and an Intra-Site Automatic Tunnel Addressing Protocol (ISATAP)-based network identifier. Click **Next** and then click **Finish**.

13. Click **Configure** for Step 4.

14. On the DirectAccess Application Server Setup page, if additional end-to-end authentication and traffic protection is required, add the security groups that contain the servers requiring this authentication. Otherwise, accept the default of **Require no additional end-to-end authentication**. Click **Finish**.

15. Click **Save** and then click **Finish**.

16. You receive the DirectAccess Review dialog box. Review the settings displayed, click **Apply**, and then click **OK** in the DirectAccess Policy Configuration message box that appears.

---

**NOTE**   For more information on running the DirectAccess Setup Wizard, refer to "DirectAccess Setup Wizard Instructions" at http://technet.microsoft.com/en-us/library/dd637813(WS.10).aspx. For a detailed procedure that sets up both servers and client computers for DirectAccess, refer to "Test Lab Guide: Demonstrate DirectAccess" at www.microsoft.com/download/en/details.aspx?displaylang=en&id=24144. For information on manual configuration of a DirectAccess server from the command line, refer to "Appendix A—Manual DirectAccess Server Configuration" at http://technet.microsoft.com/en-us/library/ee649214(WS.10).aspx. You can use the commands described in this reference to configure DirectAccess on a Server Core machine or to create a script.

### DirectAccess and the Perimeter Network

The usual location of the DirectAccess server is on the perimeter network between the internal network and the Internet, such that the DirectAccess server essentially acts as a firewall between the internal and perimeter networks. See Figure 17-3.

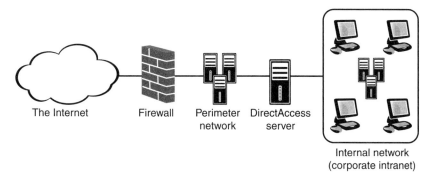

**Figure 17-3**    The DirectAccess server sits on the boundary between the perimeter network and the internal network.

When using NAP with DirectAccess, place all relevant NAP servers, such as the enforcement server, the health policy server, and Health Registration Authority (HRA), as well as the remediation network within the internal network. You can also implement a similar perimeter network design when using the Forefront UAG DirectAccess implementation.

**NOTE**    For more information on the placement of the DirectAccess server on the perimeter network, refer to "Where to Place the DirectAccess Server" at http://technet.microsoft.com/en-us/library/ee382264(WS.10).aspx and "Planning the placement of a Forefront UAG DirectAccess server" at http://technet.microsoft.com/en-us/library/ee809089.aspx.

**TIP**    Use a Hyper-V failover cluster to provide load balancing and hardware redundancy for the DirectAccess server. Microsoft suggests using two Hyper-V hosts with failover clustering supporting a single shared DirectAccess server in a virtual machine. Doing so protects against failure of one DirectAccess server and consequent loss of access to the internal network by external clients.

### Configuring Authentication

As already mentioned, DirectAccess authenticates the computer before the user logs on with the aid of the client computer and server certificates. This authentication provides access to DNS servers and domain controllers so that the user can log on with her username and password and be authenticated to AD DS.

You can also implement two-factor authentication using a smart card as well as the username/password combination. The user must insert her smart card and then log on and provide her password; however, she can access Internet resources from her client computer without the smart card. This increases security by preventing an unauthorized user who has obtained the legitimate user's password but not the smart card from accessing the network (or the smart card but not the password).

## Group Policy and DirectAccess

Windows Server 2008 R2 and Windows 7 provide Group Policy settings that enable you to specify settings for configuring the behavior of clients and name resolution in conjunction with the use of DirectAccess. We look at these policies in this section.

### Using Group Policy to Configure DirectAccess Clients

As already described, client computers that will be using DirectAccess must be joined to the AD DS domain. You can configure the required Group Policy settings in a Group Policy object (GPO) linked to the security group used for DirectAccess client computers. Figure 17-4 shows the available settings, which are found at the **Computer Configuration\Policies\Administrative Templates\Network\ TCPIP Settings\IPv6 Transition Technologies** node. These settings enable you to configure settings for client computers using the 6to4, Teredo, or IP-HTTPS connection technologies. Consult the Help text for each policy for information on what each policy does.

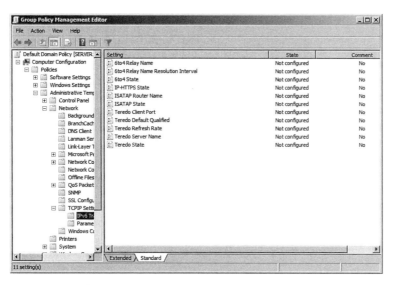

**Figure 17-4**  Group Policy provides these settings for configuring DirectAccess client computers.

You can use the Certificates snap-in to verify that each client computer has received an appropriate certificate. Add this snap-in to a blank Microsoft Management Console (MMC) and configure it for the local computer account. You should see a certificate in the Personal\Certificates node of this snap-in, and it should specify the Client Authentication and Server Authentication certificate purposes, as shown in Figure 17-5.

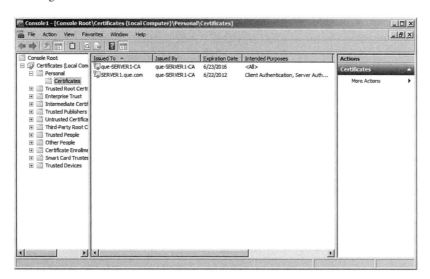

**Figure 17-5**  The Certificates snap-in should show that each client computer has received a certificate that specifies the Client Authentication and Server Authentication purposes.

### Name Resolution Policy Table

Chapter 8, "Configuring Client Computer Name Resolution," introduced you to the topic of using DNS and other name resolution technologies for resolving host names on the Internet and the internal network. Typically, client computers on a corporate network receive information on the location of DNS servers by means of DHCP or DHCPv6 configuration parameters, as was introduced in Chapter 2, "Configuring Dynamic Host Resolution Protocol (DHCP)." In Windows 7 and Windows Server 2008 R2, special handling of name queries can be applied for DNS names that match specific portions of the namespace. This is performed with the aid of a new Group Policy setting called the Name Resolution Policy Table (NRPT).

You can specify rules in the NRPT for either names or namespaces, as well as the settings for the required special handling. The DNS client service compares the name in a DNS query against each rule in the NRPT and performs special handling if the requested name matches a rule. Other queries are processed normally by interface-configured DNS servers as described in Chapter 8.

When DirectAccess is in use, clients send DNS name queries for intranet resources to the DNS servers specified in the NRPT. For secure intranet resources, the DNS client service can use DNS Security Extensions (DNSSEC) to verify the resolved name.

When you run the DirectAccess Setup Wizard as described earlier in the chapter, a default NRPT is automatically created. You can create additional NRPTs or modify an existing one if necessary, by using the following procedure:

1. Open the Group Policy Management Editor focused on an appropriate GPO.

2. Navigate to the **Computer Configuration\Policies\Windows Settings\ Name Resolution Policy** node. The details pane displays default settings for the NRPT, as shown in Figure 17-6.

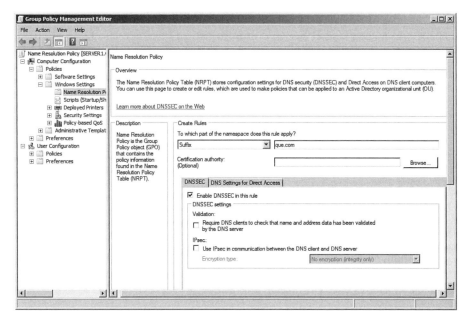

**Figure 17-6** Group Policy provides these settings for configuring a name resolution policy.

3. Under Create Rules, specify which part of the namespace that the rule should apply to. For example, to have the rule apply to all name requests in the que. com domain, select **Suffix** from the drop-down list and type que.com in the text box, as shown in Figure 17-6. The drop-down list also provides options for **FQDN, Subnet (IPv4), Subnet (IPv6), Prefix**, or **Any**.

> **NOTE** If you select the **Any** option, you should enable the **Computer Configuration\Policies\Administrative Templates\Network\Network Connections\ Route all traffic through the internal network** setting for DirectAccess tunneling. If a name matches multiple rules, the rule with the highest precedence applies; the order of precedence is FQDN, prefix, suffix, Any.

4. If you need to associate a certification authority with the rule you're creating, type the name or IP address in the text box provided or click **Browse** to locate the required CA.

5. To enable DNSSEC, select the check box labeled **Enable DNSSEC in this rule**. Then, to require validation of name resolution data, select the check box labeled **Require DNS clients to check that name and address data has been validated by the DNS server**.

6. To use IPSec for encrypted communications with the DNS server, select the check box labeled **Use IPSec in communication between the DNS client and DNS server**. Also, choose one of the following encryption options from the drop-down list:

- **No encryption (integrity only):** Does not encrypt communications, but ensures that information sent between the client and DNS server has not been altered in transit.

- **Low: 3DES, AES (128, 192, 256):** Uses 3DES or Advanced Encryption Standard (AES) with the indicated key lengths.

- **Medium AES (128, 192, 256):** Increases the AES key length as indicated.

- **High AES (192, 256):** Increases the key length further.

7. To configure settings for DirectAccess, select the **DNS Settings for Direct Access** tab and then select the check box labeled **Enable DNS settings for Direct Access in this rule**, as shown in Figure 17-7.

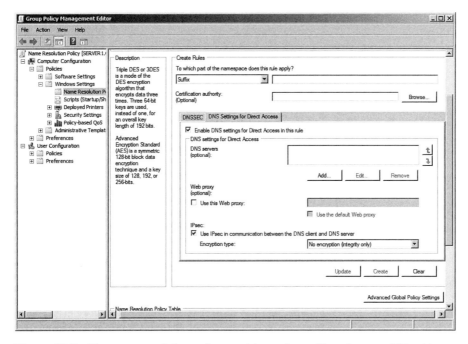

**Figure 17-7**   The name resolution policy provides policy settings for use of DirectAccess.

8.  To add DNS servers to the rule, click **Add** and type the name or IP address of each server in the text box provided. Also, select the options for using a web proxy and IPSec usage as shown. The options for IPSec encryption are the same as already described for DNSSEC.

9.  To add policy settings for network location dependency, query failure, and query resolution, click the **Advanced Global Policy Settings** command button and specify the settings needed for your policy, as shown in Figure 17-8. Click **OK** when finished.

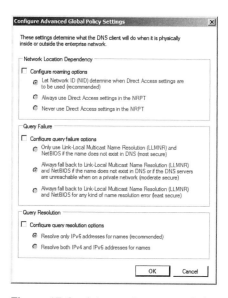

**Figure 17-8**   Advanced name resolution policy settings are available for network location dependency, query failure, and query resolution.

10.  When finished, click **Create** to create your policy. A summary of the settings you configured appears in the Name Resolution Policy Table section at the bottom of the details pane.

11.  Repeat Steps 3 to 10 to create additional name resolution policies as required.

12.  If you need to edit any rule later, select it and click **Edit Rule**, make the needed changes, and then click **Update**. To delete a rule, select it and click **Delete Rule**.

### Using NRPT Exemptions

In some cases, you might want to specify that individual names or namespaces within an overall DNS namespace be exempted from special handling by the NRPT rules. For example, suppose you want to enable DirectAccess for the que.com domain but not for policies.internal.que.com. This is needed when setting up an FQDN rule for the DirectAccess location server. For example, suppose you have set up a suffix rule for the intranet namespace that specifies the IPv6 addresses of intranet DNS servers, but the network location server is within the same DNS namespace. However, depending on your IPv6 configuration, the clients might be unable to access the intranet DNS servers at the specified IPv6 addresses, but are reachable from the interface-configured IPv4 addresses.

If you have not specified an exemption rule, the DirectAccess client on the intranet uses IPv6 in attempting to resolve the name of the network location server. Because the intranet DNS servers are not reachable, this client is unable to access the network location server and thinks that it is on the Internet rather than the intranet. Consequently, the client is unable to access intranet resources by name. Use an exemption rule for the network location server to mitigate this problem. The Direct Access Setup wizard automatically creates NRPT rules for the intranet namespace, including an exemption for the network location server.

**NOTE**   For more information on configuring the NRPT, refer to "The Name Resolution Policy Table" at http://technet.microsoft.com/en-us/magazine/ ff394369.aspx and "Design Your DNS Infrastructure for DirectAccess" at http:// technet.microsoft.com/en-us/library/ee382323(WS.10).aspx.

### Split-Brain DNS and the Name Resolution Policy Table

It is possible to use the same DNS domain name, for example, `que.com`, for both intranet and Internet resources. In this case, a user on a portable computer would see the intranet website when in the office and the Internet website when at an external location, such as at home or in a client location.

If you configured an NRPT with a rule for the corporate namespace that includes the IPv6 addresses of internal DNS servers, the user with a DirectAccess client machine at an Internet location will see the intranet version of the website when he types the URL for the company (such as www.que.com). If you want these users to see the public website when at an Internet location, you need to add the FQDN of the URL as an exemption rule to the NRPT. However, doing so prevents users on DirectAccess clients from accessing the intranet version of the URL.

If you want to retain the split-brain DNS configuration, you need to decide which resources with duplicate names should be accessible to DirectAccess clients and add the appropriate exemption rules for intranet resources that should be accessible to these clients. To make both versions available, use alternate names for the intranet resources that do not duplicate the names on the Internet resources.

But, in this instance, it is probably better to avoid using a split-brain DNS deployment. In other words, use a different Internet namespace from that used on the intranet; for example, internal.que.com on the intranet and que.com on the Internet. When doing so, DirectAccess clients can access both versions without the need for additional configuration of the NRPT.

## Exam Preparation Tasks

## Review All the Key Topics

Review the most important topics in this chapter, noted with the key topics icon in the outer margin of the page. Table 17-3 lists a reference of these key topics and the page numbers on which each is found.

**Table 17-3**   Key Topics for Chapter 17

| Key Topic Element | Description | Page Number |
|---|---|---|
| List | Summarizes DirectAccess server requirements. | 700 |
| Table 17-2 | Describes DirectAccess connection options. | 701 |
| List | Describes the DirectAccess connection process. | 702 |
| List | Using the DirectAccess Setup Wizard. | 705 |
| Figure 17-3 | Shows the typical location of a DirectAccess server on the perimeter network. | 707 |
| List | Shows you how to configure a Name Resolution Policy Table. | 710 |
| Paragraph | Describes the need for NRPT exemptions. | 714 |

## Complete the Tables and Lists from Memory

Print a copy of Appendix B, "Memory Tables," (found on the CD), or at least the section for this chapter, and complete the tables and lists from memory. Appendix C, "Memory Tables Answer Key," also on the CD, includes the completed tables and lists to check your work.

## Definitions of Key Terms

Define the following key terms from this chapter, and check your answers in the Glossary.

DirectAccess, Name Resolution Policy Table (NRPT), network location server

This chapter covers the following subjects:

- **Concepts of WSUS:** WSUS enables you to download updates to a central server on your network so that all computers on the network can obtain their updates from this server rather than having to access the Internet for these updates. This section introduces WSUS and explains how it works.

- **Installing and Configuring a WSUS Server:** WSUS provides a large range of settings that govern its use and application on the network. This section shows you how to install WSUS and work with it to ensure optimum delivery of updates to client computers while minimizing the chance of updates causing problems with these computers.

- **Configuring Client Computers for WSUS:** You must configure client computers to use WSUS for receiving updates rather than connecting to the Windows Update website. Group Policy provides a range of policies that help you configure consistent options across your network.

# CHAPTER 18

# Windows Server Update Services (WSUS) Server Settings

Windows Server Update Services (WSUS) is a server-based component that enables you to provide update services to computers on a corporate network without the need for individual computers to go online to the Microsoft Windows Update website to check for updates. It saves valuable bandwidth because only the WSUS server actually connects to the Windows Update website to receive updates, while all other computers on the network receive their updates from the WSUS server. On a multisite network, you can set up a hierarchy of WSUS servers in which only the top server in the hierarchy connects to the Windows Update website and other WSUS servers receive their updates from this server. Furthermore, WSUS provides network administrators with the ability to test updates for compatibility before enabling computers on the network to receive the updates, thereby reducing the chance of an update disrupting computer or application functionality across the network.

## "Do I Know This Already?" Quiz

The "Do I Know This Already?" quiz allows you to assess whether you should read this entire chapter or simply jump to the "Exam Preparation Tasks" section for review. If you are in doubt, read the entire chapter. Table 18-1 outlines the major headings in this chapter and the corresponding "Do I Know This Already?" quiz questions. You can find the answers in Appendix A, "Answers to the 'Do I Know This Already?' Quizzes."

**Table 18-1** "Do I Know This Already?" Foundation Topics Section-to-Question Mapping

| Foundations Topics Section | Questions Covered in This Section |
|---|---|
| Concepts of WSUS | 1–2 |
| Installing and Configuring a WSUS Server | 3–7 |
| Configuring Client Computers for WSUS | 8–10 |

1. You are planning a deployment of WSUS to your company's network, which includes a variety of client computers dating all the way back to Windows NT 4.0 Workstation. Which of the following operating systems can you configure to act as WSUS clients? (Choose all that apply.)

   a. Windows NT 4.0 Workstation with SP6a

   b. Windows 98

   c. Windows 2000 Professional with SP4

   d. Windows XP Professional with SP3

   e. Windows Vista Ultimate with SP2

2. Microsoft packaged a set of updates that is designed to fix problems with specific Windows components or software packages, such as Microsoft Office. What is this package known as?

   a. An update roll-up

   b. A critical security update

   c. An optional update

   d. A service pack

3. You are installing WSUS on a Windows Server 2008 R2 computer and want to ensure that communications between client computers and the WSUS server are secured by using HTTPS over TCP port 443. Which of the following must you install on the WSUS server that does not use secured communication to ensure proper communications?

   a. A database server running Microsoft SQL

   b. A web server running IIS

   c. A server running Network Access Protection (NAP)

   d. A Secure Sockets Layer (SSL) certificate

**4.** Your company's network consists of a head office and a branch office, which are connected by an ISDN line. You are deploying a WSUS server in the head office and would like to ensure that client computers in the branch office can also download updates across the ISDN link with the minimum bandwidth usage. What should you do?

    **a.** Install WSUS on a server at the branch office and select the **Synchronize from another Windows Server Update Services server** option at the head office server.

    **b.** Install WSUS on a server at the branch office and select the **Synchronize from another Windows Server Update Services server** option at the branch office server.

    **c.** Install WSUS on a server at the branch office and select the **Synchronize from Microsoft Update** option.

    **d.** Place all branch office client computers in a computer group named Branch Office Computers and configure a Group Policy object (GPO) linked to the branch office site that directs all client computers to the head office WSUS server to receive their updates.

**5.** You are deploying a WSUS server that will provide updates to all client computers in your organization, which has 10 servers and 100 client computers running various Windows versions from Windows XP onward. How should you configure your WSUS server to deploy updates to these client computers using the least amount of administrative effort?

    **a.** Create one or more computer groups containing the client computers in your organization. Then, use the Update Services snap-in to add individual client computers to the required groups.

    **b.** Create a global security group in AD DS and add the computer accounts of the client computers to this group. Then, use the Update Services snap-in to specify that this group will receive updates from the WSUS server.

    **c.** Create a global security group in AD DS and add the computer accounts of the client computers to this group. Then, use Group Policy to specify that this group will receive updates from the WSUS server.

    **d.** Create one or more computer groups containing the client computers in your organization. Then, use Group Policy to add client computers to these groups.

6. You deployed a WSUS server in your organization and want to ensure that client computers download approved updates within one week of your approving the updates. You already approved the updates you want the client computers to install. What should you do next?

   a. From the Approve Updates dialog box, right-click the approved updates, select **Deadline**, and then specify a deadline time or interval.

   b. In the console tree of the Update Services snap-in, right-click the **Updates** node and choose **Deadline**. Then, specify a deadline time or interval.

   c. After approving the updates, open a command prompt and type `gpupdate /force.`

   d. After approving the updates, open a command prompt and type `wuauclt. exe /detectnow.`

7. You want to view a report that informs you which updates have been installed on the client computers serviced by your WSUS server. You want to obtain the report in an easily readable format without needing to process the information in another application first. Which of the following formats can you obtain information in this fashion? (Each answer represents a complete solution. Choose two.)

   a. Microsoft Word document

   b. Microsoft Excel spreadsheet

   c. Microsoft Access database

   d. Adobe PDF document

8. You installed Windows Server Update Services on a server on your network, and you want to ensure that computers on the network do not attempt to access the Internet for downloading updates. What policy should you configure?

   a. Allow Automatic Updates immediate installation

   b. Turn on Software Notifications

   c. Specify intranet Microsoft update service location

   d. Enable client-side targeting

9. You configured a WSUS server to provide updates to all client computers on your company's network. The server is configured to use SSL certificates and you've configured a policy setting in a GPO that points client computers to the WSUS server. A user named John at a computer running Windows Vista Ultimate reports that his computer is not receiving updates from the WSUS server. No other users report problems with receiving updates. What should you do to ensure that John's computer receives all updates in a timely fashion from the WSUS server?

   a. At John's computer run the `wuauclt.exe /resetauthorization/ detectnow` command.

   b. At the WSUS server, run the `wuauclt.exe /resetauthorization/ detectnow` command.

   c. Configure John's computer to download updates directly from the Microsoft Update website.

   d. Upgrade John's computer to Windows 7 Ultimate.

10. You are responsible for administering a WSUS server. You configured a policy that specifies client computers will download and install updates every Thursday. A critical update has been issued and you've tested and approved this update. You want to deploy this update to clients on the network as soon as possible. What should you do?

    a. Run the `wsusutil.exe /detectnow` command.

    b. Run the `wuauclt.exe /detectnow` command.

    c. Run the `gpupdate /force` command.

    d. From the Approve Updates dialog box, right-click the approved updates, select **Deadline**, and then specify a short interval.

**Foundation Topics**

# Concepts of WSUS

Maintaining all the computers on your network can be a daunting job, especially on a large network with hundreds, or even thousands of computers to be kept updated. Microsoft provides updates for its operating systems and major applications, such as Exchange Server, SQL Server, and Microsoft Office on a monthly basis, generally the second Tuesday of each month. Although a few updates can introduce additional functionality to Windows or its applications, most updates offer fixes for software bugs or security issues, such as malware or exploits, that can open your network to compromise or denial of service. With only a few computers, it is simple enough to have each computer connect to the Windows Update website and download the required updates. But, imagine all the computers on a large network attempting to do this—the network bandwidth and configuration time required would rapidly become unmanageable. Microsoft recognized this years ago and created Software Update Services (SUS), which ran on a Windows 2000 or Windows Server 2003 computer and distributed updates to all other computers on the network.

Subsequently, Microsoft replaced SUS with Windows Update Services (WUS), which was almost immediately updated to WSUS and is now in version 3.0 with Service Pack (SP) 2. Using WSUS 3.0 SP2, you can deploy the latest Microsoft product updates to computers running Windows 2000 SP4, Windows XP SP2, Windows Server 2003, or more recent Windows server and client operating systems.

## Purposes of Windows Update and WSUS

Windows Update and WSUS enable you to maintain your computer in an up-to-date condition by automatically downloading and installing critical updates as Microsoft publishes them. By default, your computer automatically checks for updates at the Windows Update website; when configured for WSUS as described in this chapter, client computers contact the WSUS server for available updates. Updates are automatically installed on a daily basis and you are informed about optional updates that might be available. The following are several key features of Windows Update:

- Windows Update scans your computer and determines which updates are applicable to your computer. These updates include the latest security patches and usability enhancements that ensure your computer is kept as secure and functional as possible.

- Updates classified by Microsoft as High Priority and Recommended can be downloaded and installed automatically in the background without interfering with your work. At the same time, Windows Update can inform you about optional updates and Windows Ultimate Extras.

- Windows Update informs you if a restart is required to apply an update. You can postpone the restart so that it does not interfere with activities in progress. Should an update apply to a software program with files in use, Windows can save the files and close and restart the program.

In Windows Server 2008 R2 and Windows 7, Windows Update supports the distribution and installation of the following types of updates:

- **Critical security updates:** Updates that Microsoft has determined are critical for a computer's security. These are typically distributed on the second Tuesday of each month, which has become known as "Patch Tuesday." In general, they fix problems that intruders can exploit to perform actions, such as adding administrative accounts, installing rogue software, copying or deleting data on your computer, and so on.

- **Optional updates:** Potentially useful updates that are not security-related. These might include software and driver updates, language packs, and so on.

- **Update roll-ups:** Packaged sets of updates that fix problems with specific Windows components or software packages such as Microsoft Office.

- **Service packs:** Comprehensive operating system updates that package together all updates published since launch of the operating system or issuance of the previous service pack. In many cases, service packs also include new features or improvements to existing features.

## New Features of WSUS 3.0

WSUS 3.0 provides a series of new features that facilitate the use, deployment, and client support. The following are some of the more significant new features available with WSUS 3.0:

- **Ease of use:** WSUS provides a Microsoft Management Console (MMC) 3.0 snap-in that provides a series of home pages for each available task, filtering and sorting of updates, and custom views. You can also use the WSUS snap-in to remotely manage your server (or a hierarchy of WSUS servers) from a remote computer. Furthermore, several wizards are available performing tasks such as server setup and cleanup of older information.

- **Improved deployment options:** WSUS 3.0 enables you to receive updates automatically at specified intervals, even as frequently as once per hour (compared to once per day in WSUS 2.0). You can specify an auto-approval mode that uses pre-specified rules to automatically approve updates.

- **Improved support for server hierarchies:** WSUS 3.0 enables you to manage a hierarchy of WSUS servers in which a single server (often known as the *upstream* server) downloads updates and passes them on to other WSUS servers (known as *downstream servers*). You can also set up a cluster of servers set up for fault tolerance and load balancing purposes. Only the upstream server has to download updates from the Microsoft Update website; thereby only a single connection to this website is needed, minimizing network bandwidth required for downloading of updates.

- **Advanced extensibility features:** You can set up improved application programming interfaces (API) to extend the functionality and management of WSUS 3.0, including advanced management tools such as System Center Essentials and the capability of supporting third-party applications and updates. Microsoft provides a software development kit that helps you to create custom code for managing automatic updates and WSUS servers according to specific requirements on your network.

- **Automatic downloading and approval options for updates:** You can choose which updates are downloaded to a WSUS server according to criteria such as product or product family (such as Microsoft Office or Microsoft Windows 7), update classification (such as critical updates or drivers), or language. You can choose from approval actions for each update including automatic approval, removal of updates that support uninstall, or decline.

- **Choice of database options:** WSUS 3.0 uses a database the stores update information, event information about update actions at client computers, and WSUS server settings. You can store this database on an internal database that you can install when setting up your server or you can use a Microsoft SQL Server database running on a SQL server 2005 SP1 or later server.

- **Multiple reporting and troubleshooting options:** You can monitor the status of actions such as the level of update compliance and the need for specific updates on each client computer, update compliance for specific updates, synchronization or download activity for given time periods, and a summary of options that have been specified for the WSUS implementation. All reports can be printed or exported to Excel spreadsheets or .pdf files. Further, you can use the WSUS Management Pack to troubleshoot your WSUS infrastructure including network connectivity, permissions, SQL server connectivity, and WSUS-related services.

**NOTE**   For additional introductory information on WSUS, refer to links contained in the document "Microsoft Windows Server Update Services 3.0 Overview" at http://technet.microsoft.com/en-us/library/cc708429(WS.10).aspx.

## Installing and Configuring a WSUS Server

Before you install WSUS on your server, the server must meet the following requirements:

- The WSUS server must be able to communicate with the Windows Update website by using an HTTP connection. You might need to provide additional credentials if a proxy server is used on the network.

- If setting up a server hierarchy, the downstream WSUS servers must be able to communicate with the upstream server by means of an HTTP connection over TCP port 80. You can also use HTTPS over TCP port 443 if you have a Secure Sockets Layer (SSL) certificate available.

- The system volume and the volume on which you install WSUS must both be formatted with the NTFS file system. It is recommended that a minimum of 20 to 30 GB of free space be available on the volume on which WSUS stores update content; the more free space, the better.

- If an SQL server is not available on your network, WSUS installs Windows Internal Database. It is recommended that a minimum of 2 GB of free space be available on the volume where Windows Internal Database is installed.

**CAUTION**   If you have installed WSUS 3.0 SP2 on a server running the original version of Windows Server 2008, Microsoft cautions you that an upgrade to Windows Server 2008 R2 will fail. You must upgrade the Windows Internal Database before you can upgrade the server to Windows Server 2008 R2. Refer to "How to obtain the latest service pack for Windows Internal Database" at http://support.microsoft.com/kb/968854 for more information.

### Installing WSUS on a Windows Server 2008 R2 Computer

In the original version of Windows Server 2008, you had to download WSUS from the Microsoft website and then install it. In Windows Server 2008 R2, WSUS is directly available as a server role. Use the following procedure to install WSUS on a Windows Server 2008 R2 computer:

1. Open Server Manager and expand the Roles node.

2. Click **Add Roles** to start the Add Roles Wizard.

3. On the Select Server Roles page, select **Windows Server Update Services**.

4. If Internet Information Services (IIS) is not present on your computer, you receive the message box shown in Figure 18-1, which informs you that you must install this role. Click **Add Required Role Services**, and then click **Next**.

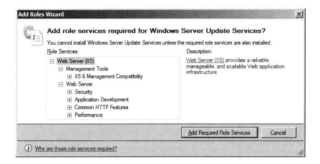

**Figure 18-1**    You need to install IIS with a specified set of role services in order to install WSUS.

**NOTE**    Even if you've installed IIS on your server for running DirectAccess, you may still receive this message box for purposes of installing additional IIS components required for the WSUS server.

5. You receive the Introduction to Web Server (IIS) page, which provides links to additional information on IIS. Click any of these links to obtain information as desired. When finished, click **Next**.

6. The Select Role Services page enables you to select additional IIS role services. Role services required for WSUS are selected by default. For learning purposes, you do not need to select any additional services. Click **Next**.

7. You receive the Introduction to Windows Server Update Services page. To obtain additional information, select any of the links provided. When finished, click **Next**.

8.  The Confirm Installation Selections page provides a summary of the role services that will be installed. To proceed, click **Install**.

9.  The Installation Progress page tracks the progress of installing WSUS. After IIS is installed, you receive the Welcome to the Windows Server Update Services 3.0 SP2 Setup Wizard page. Click **Next**.

**TIP**    The WSUS Setup Wizard appears in a separate window that might be hidden beneath the Add Roles Wizard. If the latter wizard appears to be "hung," press **Alt+Tab** until the WSUS Setup Wizard appears on screen.

10. On the License Agreement page, click **I accept the terms of the License agreement**, and then click **Next**.

11. The wizard displays the page shown in Figure 18-2 that informs you that the Microsoft Report Viewer 2008 Redistributable component is required and needs to be installed after you install WSUS. Click **Next**.

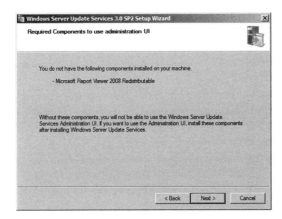

**Figure 18-2**    You are informed that you must install Microsoft Report Viewer 2008 Redistributable.

12. The Select Update Source page shown in Figure 18-3 provides options for storing updates. In most cases, you will want to accept the option of **Store updates locally**, which is selected by default. If necessary, click **Browse** to locate a different location for storing your updates. When finished, click **Next**.

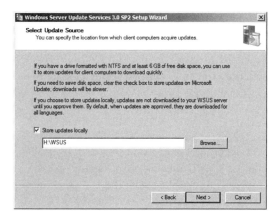

**Figure 18-3**   You are provided with options for storing updates.

13. The Database Options page shown in Figure 18-4 provides options for data storage. If you have an SQL server available, select one of the options provided for using a database server. Otherwise, accept the default option labeled **Install Windows Internal Database on this computer**. If necessary, click **Browse** to locate an alternate location for storing the database. When finished, click **Next**.

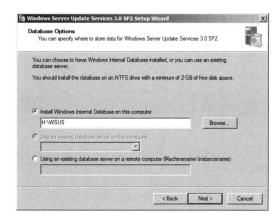

**Figure 18-4**   Select an appropriate option for storing the update database.

14. The Web Site Selection page provides two options for specifying the website to be used for WSUS Web services. In most cases, you will want to leave the default of **Use the existing IIS Default Web site** selected. Click **Next**.

15. The Ready to Install Windows Server Update Services 3.0 SP2 page displays options you have selected. Click **Next** to proceed.

16. The Installing page charts the progress of installing WSUS 3.0 SP2. This process takes several minutes. When informed that the installation is complete, click **Finish**, and then click **Close**.

After you install WSUS, the Update Services MMC snap-in is available from the Administrative Tools folder. You can also administer WSUS from a web browser by using the address `http://localhost/WSUSAdmin` on the local server. Substitute the server name for `localhost` when administering WSUS on a remote server.

### Installing Microsoft Report Viewer Redistributable 2008

As already mentioned, you need to install Microsoft Report Viewer Redistributable 2008 on your WSUS server. This is an executable file that you can download from the Microsoft Download Center. Use the following procedure:

1. In Internet Explorer or another suitable browser, navigate to www.microsoft. com/download/en/details.aspx?displaylang=en&id=6576 and click the **Download** button.

2. Click **Start download**, and then click **Run** to start the installation immediately or **Save** to save the downloaded file to your computer.

3. If you saved the installation file to your computer, double-click this file, and then click **Run** to start the installation.

4. The Microsoft Report Viewer Redistributable 2008 Setup Wizard appears. Click **Next**.

5. Review the license terms, select the check box labeled **I have read and accept the license terms**, and then click **Install**.

6. When informed that the installation is completed, click **Finish**.

> **NOTE**   For more information on installing the WSUS server, refer to "Install the WSUS 3.0 SP2 Server" at http://technet.microsoft.com/en-us/library/ dd939817(WS.10).aspx.

### Getting Started with WSUS

The first thing you need to do after installing WSUS is to obtain the latest updates from the Microsoft Update website. The Updates node of the Update Services snap-in makes it easy to perform this task, as described in the following procedure:

1. Click Start > Administrative Tools > Windows Server Update Services. The Update Services console opens.

2. In the console tree, select your server to display the view shown in Figure 18-5.

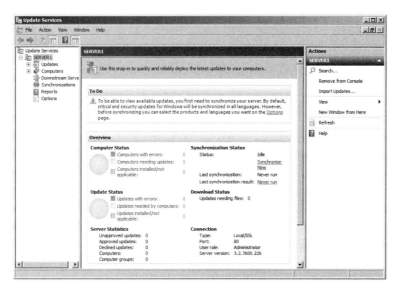

**Figure 18-5**   When first installed, the Update Services console informs you that a synchronization has never been run.

3. Click **Synchronize Now**.

4. The status display changes to Synchronizing and displays the percent of updates that have been downloaded to your server. Initially, this synchronization will take some time.

5. When synchronization is completed, the status changes to Idle and the last synchronization result displays Succeeded, as shown in Figure 18-6. As shown in this figure, you are also informed of several tasks that you should perform. These tasks are described more fully in the sections that follow.

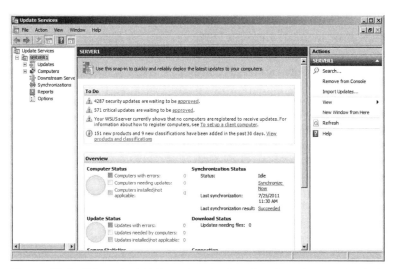

**Figure 18-6**   When the initial synchronization of updates is completed, the Update Services snap-in informs you of several tasks that you should perform.

## Configuring WSUS Options

The Update Services snap-in enables you to configure a large range of options that govern the behavior of the WSUS server. Click **Options** in the console tree of the snap-in to display the available configuration options in the details pane, as shown in Figure 18-7. Selecting an option displays a dialog box that enables you to configure the selected option. The following options are available from this node:

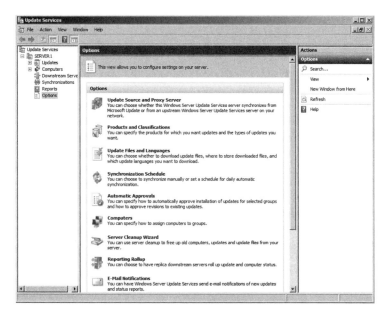

**Figure 18-7**   The WSUS console enables you to configure a comprehensive range of options.

- **Update Source and Proxy Server:** Enables you to configure your server to receive updates directly from Microsoft Update or act as a downstream server that receives its updates from another WSUS server. By default, the server synchronizes from Microsoft Update. If you want the server to function as a downstream server, click the **Update Source and Proxy Server** option, and then select the **Synchronize from another Windows Server Update Services server** option, as shown in Figure 18-8. In addition, you can specify options for use of SSL to securely synchronize updates or specify that the server is a replica of the upstream server. The Proxy Server tab enables you to configure the use of a proxy server when synchronizing, including user credentials required for connecting to the proxy server.

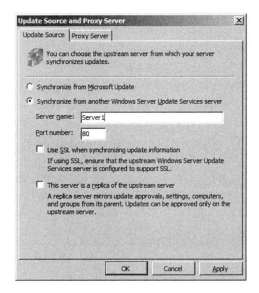

**Figure 18-8**   Configuring a WSUS server to act as a downstream server.

- **Products and Classifications:** Enables you to specify which products will receive updates from Microsoft Update or the upstream server. The Classification tab enables you to specify the classifications (critical updates, definition updates, security updates, service packs, update rollups, and so on) that will receive updates.

- **Update Files and Languages:** The Update Files tab provides options for storing update files locally (the default) or enabling computers to install from Microsoft Update. The Update Languages tab enables you to filter the updates according to language. Selecting the language or languages used on your network will dramatically reduce the number of updates downloaded and stored on your server.

**TIP**   If you want all WSUS client computers to download approved updates directly from the Microsoft Update servers, access the **Update Files** tab of the Update Files and Languages dialog box, select the option labeled **Do not store update files locally; computers install from Microsoft Update**, and then click **OK**. This is useful if you have a situation in which most of the client computers access the WSUS server over a slow WAN connection but have high-bandwidth Internet connections, or if there are only a small number of client computers. When you do so, client computes will report successful update installations to your WSUS server. For more information, refer to "Change WSUS update storage settings using the WSUS Administration Console" at http://technet.microsoft.com/en-us/library/hh334977(WS.10).aspx.

- **Synchronization Schedule:** Enables you to set a schedule for daily automatic synchronization, including the time for first synchronization and the number of times per day that synchronization occurs. The default is to perform manual synchronizations.

- **Automatic Approvals:** Enables you to specify rules for automatically approving updates when they are synchronized. You can create rules that specify which updates will be approved and the computer groups for which they are approved.

- **Computers:** Enables you to specify how computers are assigned to groups. You can choose between use of the Update Services console (the default) or using Group Policy or registry settings. Configuring this option enables you to choose between server-side and client-side targeting of updates, as discussed in more detail later in this section.

- **Server Cleanup Wizard:** Runs a wizard that removes out-of-date and unused update files, old revisions of updates, superseded updates, and computers that are no longer active. This wizard helps you reclaim disk space occupied by obsolete updates.

- **Reporting Rollup:** Enables you to choose whether downstream servers roll up computer and update status to this server.

- **E-Mail Notifications:** As shown in Figure 18-9, the General tab enables you to specify that WSUS sends e-mail notifications of new updates and status reports to e-mail addresses (for example, dpoulton@certguide.com) that you specify in this dialog box. You can also specify the frequency at which status reports are sent and the language used. The E-mail Server tab enables you to specify the e-mail server and the sender name and e-mail address to be used in the messages.

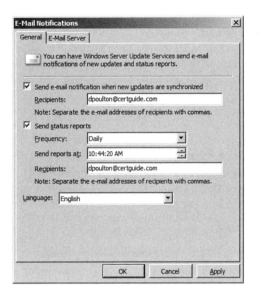

**Figure 18-9**   Specifying options for sending e-mail notifications and status reports.

- **Microsoft Update Improvement Program:** Select the check box provided to join the Microsoft Update Improvement Program, which enables your server to send information to Microsoft about the quality of updates, including the number of computers that successfully install or fail to install each update downloaded to the server. This option is not selected by default.

- **Personalization:** As shown in Figure 18-10, this option enables you to personalize the way information for the server is displayed. This includes information obtained from replica downstream servers in a WSUS hierarchy as well as the items that will be displayed in the To Do list for the server, as shown in the details pane when the server name is selected (refer to Figure 18-6 for a sample To Do list). When operating a hierarchy of WSUS servers, you can include information from replica downstream servers in the status reports by selecting the **Include computers and status from replica downstream servers** option (the default) or include information from the current server only by selecting the **Show computers and status from this server alone** option.

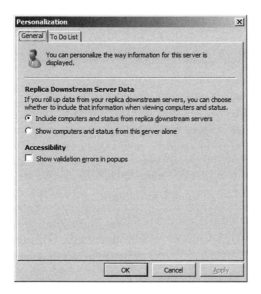

**Figure 18-10**   You can determine whether information from computers serviced by a down-stream server are included in the reports generated by an upstream server from the Personaliza-tion dialog box.

**TIP**   An exam question might ask you how you would ensure that the WSUS console only displays updates from the current server and not from downstream replica servers. To do so, select the **Show computers and status from this server alone** option, as shown in Figure 18-10.

- **WSUS Server Configuration Wizard:** Runs a wizard that helps you perform initial configuration of many of the actions normally run for server setup. Included are upstream and proxy servers, choice of languages, products, and classifications, and configuration of a sync schedule.

**NOTE**   For more information on these options and other aspects of configuring the WSUS server, refer to "Configure WSUS by Using the WSUS Administration Console" at http://technet.microsoft.com/en-us/library/hh334984(WS.10).aspx and the links contained within this reference.

### Testing Updates

All networks contain a diverse environment of computers running different operating systems with various combinations of applications installed on them. Although Microsoft tests updates thoroughly before releasing them to the public, this testing cannot cover the almost infinite combination of computers and applications present in the real world. Microsoft recommends that you create a test environment containing computers representative of those on your network; by doing so, you can install each update and assess its impact before you deploy it across the network.

Some of the results you can watch for when performing testing include the following:

- For updates that require a restart, the test computer should restart properly after the update is installed.

- Software updates should have an uninstall routine that can successfully remove the update. Alternately, the update should be removed properly by performing a system restore to a time previous to update installation.

- Business-critical applications and services should continue to function properly after installation of the update.

- Updates targeted to computers connected across slow or unreliable network connections should properly download and install to these computers.

### Using Computer Groups

WSUS enables you to create customized computer groups that enable you to target updates to specific computers on your network. WSUS provides the following two default computer groups, to which client computers are automatically added when they initially contact the WSUS server:

- **All Computers:** Contains every computer that has ever contacted the WSUS server for updates. You cannot remove computers from this group.

- **Unassigned Computers:** Contains computers that have not been assigned to another group that you've created. Initially, all computers that have contacted the WSUS server are included; as you create new computer groups and assign computers to them, these computers are removed from the Unassigned Computers group.

Typically, you should perform a staged deployment of updates that helps you to avoid problems with updates that are incompatible with computers or applications on your network. A typical deployment schedule involves the following stages:

- **Testing:** Set up a test lab that includes computers representative of the computers and applications in use on your network and add representative computers from your network to this group. Then, deploy the updates and run the various applications found on each computer. Initial testing of the updates can reveal many of the problems before any computers on your network are affected.

- **Pilot:** Assign tech-savvy users from various departments of the company to computers in a pilot group and ask them to report whether they encounter any problems running the various applications that they use in their day-to-day work.

- **Production:** Deploy updates to all remaining computers on the network (the All Computers group) once the users in the pilot group have worked for several days without reporting any problems.

To create a new computer group, right-click **All Computers** in the console tree of the Update Services snap-in and choose **Add Computer Group**. In the Add Computer Group dialog box that appears (see Figure 18-11), type a name for the group (for example, Pilot Test Computers) and click **Add**. The group is added as a subnode under the All Computers node.

**Figure 18-11**   Creating a new computer group.

After you set up computer groups, you can specify how computers are added to these groups and add them to the groups. Table 18-2 describes the two available options for configuring computer groups:

**Table 18-2**    Targeting of Client Computers

| Targeting Type | Description |
|---|---|
| Server-side targeting | Enables you to manually add computers to computer groups using the Update Services snap-in. This is best used only in small organizations. |
| Client-side targeting | Uses Group Policy to add computers to specified computer groups. New computers are automatically added to the appropriate group when they first contact the WSUS server. This is best used in large organizations configured with at least one Active Directory Domain Services (AD DS) domain. |

**NOTE**    For more information on planning and using computer groups in WSUS, refer to "Plan WSUS Computer Groups" at http://technet.microsoft.com/en-us/library/hh328559(WS.10).aspx.

### Configuring Server-Side Targeting

As already mentioned, computers that are not specifically assigned to a group are included in the Unassigned Computers group. To use server-side targeting to add computers to a different group, use the following procedure:

1. In the console tree of the Update Services snap-in, expand the **Computers** node to locate the **All Computers** and then the **Unassigned Computers** subnode.

2. Right-click the computer to be assigned to a group and choose **Change Membership**.

3. In the Set Computer Group Membership dialog box, select the group to which the computer should be assigned and then click **OK**.

**TIP**    You can change the group membership of multiple computers at the same time. Use the **Ctrl** key to select the computers to be configured (or use the **Shift** key to select a contiguous group of computers) before executing Step 2 of the preceding procedure.

## Configuring Client-Side Targeting

When client-side targeting is enabled, computers automatically assign themselves to the appropriate group the first time they contact the WSUS server. Use the following procedure to enable client-side targeting by means of Group Policy:

1. In the console tree of the Update Services snap-in, select the **Options** node, and then click **Computers** (as previously shown in Figure 18-7).

2. As shown in Figure 18-12, the Update Services console is used by default (server-side targeting). To specify client-side targeting, select the **Use Group Policy or registry settings on computers** option.

**Figure 18-12**   The Computers dialog box enables you to chose between server- or client-side targeting.

3. To specify the computer group to which client computers will be placed, open the Group Policy Management Editor focused on a Group Policy object (GPO) linked to the appropriate AD DS container in which the computer accounts are located. In a workgroup environment, open the Local Group Policy Editor at each client computer that needs to be configured.

4. Navigate to the **Computer Configuration\Policies\Administrative Templates\Windows Components\Windows Update** node.

5. Right-click the **Enable client-side targeting** policy and choose **Edit**.

6. As shown in Figure 18-13, select the **Enabled** option, type the name of the computer group to which the computers will be joined, and then click **OK**.

**Figure 18-13**    Specifying a computer group to which computers affected by this GPO will be added.

**NOTE**    You can also use the Registry Editor to configure client computers for client-side targeting. Registry values for WSUS are found in the HKEY_LOCAL_MACHINE\Software\Policies\Microsoft\Windows\WindowsUpdate key. For more information on configuring Registry settings, refer to "Configure Automatic Updates in a Non-Active Directory Environment" at http://technet.microsoft.com/en-us/library/cc708449(WS.10).aspx.

**TIP**    If computers are not being added to the correct WSUS target computer group, access the **Options** node, select **Computers**, and ensure that you've selected the **Use Group Policy or registry settings on computers** option.

### Approving Updates

Users will not receive updates from your WSUS server until you approve them. As already discussed, you can approve updates for deployment to any combination of the various computer groups you've configured. Use the following procedure to approve updates:

1. In the console tree of the Update Services snap-in, expand the **Updates** node. This displays the following four subnodes:

   - **All updates:** Displays all available updates. You would normally select this subnode for rapid approval of updates.

   - **Critical updates:** Displays all high-priority updates that are not security related. This can include items such as bug fixes.

   - **Security updates:** Displays all updates that are designed to fix security issues, such as denial of service, creation of rogue administrative accounts, installation of malicious software, and so on.

   - **WSUS updates:** Displays updates related to the WSUS server.

2. Ensure that the Approval drop-down list reads **Unapproved** and select **Any** from the Status drop-down list. If updates do not appear, click **Refresh** and wait for a few seconds.

3. Select the updates to be approved. To select multiple contiguous updates, click the first one and then shift-click the last one. To select multiple noncontiguous updates, hold the **Ctrl** key while you shift each one. To select all updates, press **Ctrl-A**.

4. Right-click the selected updates and choose **Approve**. You receive the Approve Updates dialog box shown in Figure 18-14.

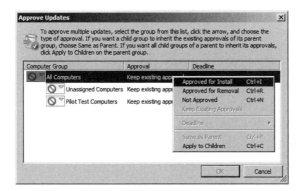

**Figure 18-14**   The Approve Updates dialog box provides several options for approving updates for distribution to client computers.

5. Select the computer group for which you want to approve the updates.

6. Right-click the selection and choose one of the options visible in Figure 18-14. To install the updates to the computers in the selected group, select the **Approved for Install** option. To specify a deadline by which the updates must be installed, right-click the selection again and choose **Deadline**, and then specify a deadline time or interval.

7. Repeat Steps 5 and 6 as necessary to approve the updates for additional computer groups as required. When finished, click **OK**.

8. If you receive a licensing dialog box, click **I Accept**.

9. The Approval Progress dialog box charts the progress of approving the selected updates. This process takes several minutes, especially if a large number of updates must be approved, such as when setting up a new WSUS server. Note any errors that are displayed. When the approval progress completes, click **Close**.

**TIP**   When working with a WSUS server hierarchy, you can ensure that downstream servers automatically approve updates you have approved on the upstream server. To do so, at the downstream server, ensure that you've selected the option labeled **This server is a replica of the upstream server**. This option is found on the Update Source and Proxy Server dialog box (refer to Figure 18-8).

### Declining Updates

If you encountered problematic updates during your test procedures, you can decline these updates so that they are not installed on client computers. Use the following procedure:

1. In the details pane of the Update Services snap-in, select the update or updates to be declined, according to the procedure in Steps 3 and 4 of the previous procedure.

2. Right-click the selection and choose **Decline**.

3. The Decline Update dialog box asks you if you are sure you want to decline these updates. Click **Yes** to proceed.

4. A message box charts the progress of declining updates. This dialog box disappears automatically when the process is complete.

## Viewing Reports

WSUS provides a series of reports that enables you to view the status of various updates and information on each computer that has contacted the WSUS server for updates. Use the following procedure:

1. In the console tree of the Update Services snap-in, select the **Reports** node to display the available reports, as shown in Figure 18-15.

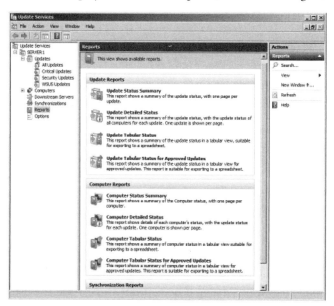

**Figure 18-15**   WSUS provides a series of reports that enable you to check the status of updates and client computers.

2. Select the desired report from the options displayed in the details pane. You receive the dialog box shown in Figure 18-16.

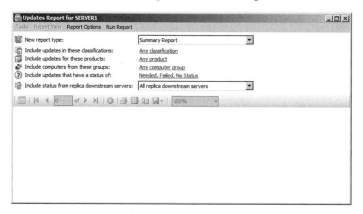

**Figure 18-16**   You receive several options that determine the content of the report that will be displayed.

**3.** Select the following options:

- **New report type:** The drop-down list displays the report type chosen from the Reports node, but you can choose one of the other report types, as previously shown in Figure 18-15.

- **Include updates in these classifications:** Enables you to choose update classifications such as critical updates, drivers, security updates, service packs, and so on.

- **Include updates for these products:** Enables you to choose Microsoft products such as server types, Office, and so on.

- **Include computers from these groups:** Enables you to choose the computer groups you've defined.

- **Include updates that have a status of:** Enables you to choose update statuses from **Installed/Not Applicable, Needed, Failed,** or **No Status.** Choose **Any** to display all statuses.

- **Include status from replica downstream servers:** Select **All replica downstream servers** or **Exclude replica downstream servers** as desired.

**4.** When finished selecting report options, click **Run Report** from the menu bar of the Updates Report dialog box. After a few seconds, information on the first update appears. To view information on other available updates, click the arrows provided in the menu bar of this dialog box. You can also expand the list in the left pane of this dialog box to display a list of the updates that have been reported on, and then select an update from this list to display information on the selected update. See Figure 18-17.

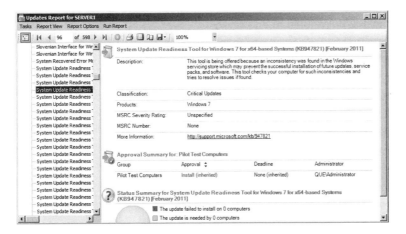

**Figure 18-17**   Viewing report information on a selected update.

5. Use the icons at the top of the dialog box to print or save the report as desired. You can export the report as an Adobe PDF file or an Excel spreadsheet.

You can also display information on synchronizations of updates that have occurred on this server. Select the **Synchronizations** node in the console tree. The information provided in the details pane shows you how many updates have been downloaded from Windows Update or from the upstream server in a multiple server WSUS hierarchy.

## Using WSUS on a Disconnected Network

If your network includes a segment that is not connected to the Internet, you can deploy a WSUS server that is connected to the Internet but is isolated from the disconnected network segment. After you download updates to the WSUS server, you can export the updates to removable media such as a USB memory stick or portable hard drive, and use this media to import the updates to a WSUS server located on the disconnected network.

The `wsusutil.exe` command-line utility is used for exporting and importing updates for disconnected networks. Use the following procedure:

1. Open an administrative command prompt at the server used for downloading updates from the Internet and navigate to the `C:\Program Files\Update Services\Tools` folder.

2. Type the following command:

   ```
   wsusutil.exe export packagename.cab logfile.log
   ```

   In this command, `Packagename.cab` is a unique filename that contains the export metadata, and `logfile.log` is a unique filename the contains the export log.

3. After this command has completed, copy the export files to the removable media.

4. Carry the removable media to the WSUS server on the disconnected network and transfer the files to this server.

5. Open an administrative command prompt at this server and navigate to the `C:\Program Files\Update Services\Tools` folder.

6. Type the following command:

   ```
   wsusutil.exe import packagename.cab logfile.log
   ```

**NOTE**   For more information on servicing a WSUS server located on a dis-connected network, refer to "Configure a Disconnected Network to Receive Updates" at http://technet.microsoft.com/en-us/library/dd939873(WS.10). aspx.

**NOTE**   The `wsusutil.exe` utility enables you to perform a large range of management actions from the command line. For more information including a description of the available subcommands and parameters, refer to "Manage WSUS 3.0 SP2 from the Command Line" at http://technet.microsoft.com/en-us/library/dd939838(WS.10).aspx. Also available is the `wuauclt.exe` utility, which provides some control over the functioning of the Windows Update Agent. For more information on this utility, refer to "Appendix H: The `wuauclt` Utility" at http://technet.microsoft.com/en-us/library/cc720477(WS.10).aspx.

## Configuring Client Computers for WSUS

On client computers running Windows Vista or Windows 7, Windows Update is used to maintain the computer in an up-to-date condition by automatically downloading and installing critical updates as Microsoft publishes them. By default, these computers automatically check for updates at the Windows Update website. On computers running Windows XP and Windows 2000, the Automatic Updates client performs much the same tasks. When a WSUS server is deployed on the network, this server takes over the task of providing approved updates to client computers from the Windows Update website, thereby dramatically reducing the amount of bandwidth used and enabling you to approve updates before clients download them, as discussed earlier in this chapter.

The most practical means of configuring client computers for WSUS in any corporate setting is to use Group Policy. Open the Group Policy Management Editor focused on the Default Domain Policy GPO or a GPO targeted at a specific site or OU in your organization as required, and navigate to the Computer **Configuration\Policies\Administrative Templates\Windows Components\Windows Update** node to obtain the policy settings shown in Figure 18-18.

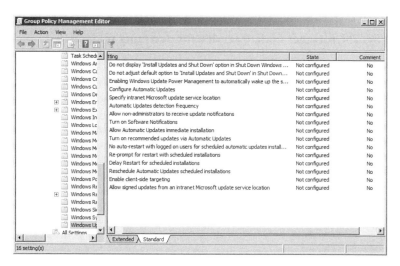

**Figure 18-18**   Group Policy provides a series of settings that govern the use of WSUS on your client computers.

Use the following procedure to specify that client computers affected by the GPO will use your WSUS server rather than Windows Update to obtain updates:

1. Right-click the **Specify intranet Microsoft update service location** policy and choose **Edit** to obtain the dialog box shown in Figure 18-19.

**Figure 18-19**   The Specify intranet Microsoft update service location policy is used to direct client computers to the WSUS server for updates.

2. Enable this policy and type the URL pointing to the WSUS server in the text box labeled **Set the intranet update service for detecting updates**.

3. You can also specify a server to which client computers upload statistical information on installed updates, by typing the URL to the desired statistical server (which might be the same as the WSUS server but is not necessarily so) in the text box labeled **Set the intranet statistics server**.

4. Click **OK**.

**TIP**   If you configured the WSUS website to use SSL, remember that the URL you enter must begin with `https:`.

It is also important to specify the behavior of the client computers in downloading and installing automatic updates. To do so, right-click the **Configure Automatic Updates** policy setting and choose **Edit** to receive the Configure Automatic Updates properties dialog box. Select **Enabled** and choose one of the following settings from the Configure automatic updating drop-down list shown in Figure 18-20.

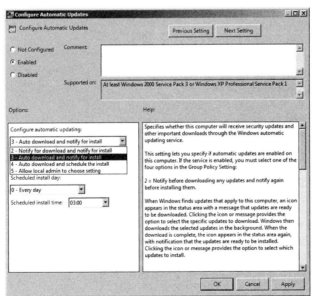

**Figure 18-20**   The Configure Automatic Updates dialog box offers four choices for configuring automatic updating of client computers.

- **2–Notify for downloading any updates and notify again before installing them:** WSUS notifies you when updates are available by displaying an icon in the notification area and a message stating that updates are available for download. The user can download the updates by clicking either the icon or the message. When the download is complete, the user is informed again with another icon and message; clicking one of them starts the installation.

- **3–Download the updates automatically and notify when they are ready to be installed:** WSUS downloads updates in the background without informing the user. After the updates have been downloaded, the user is informed with an icon in the notification area and a message stating that the updates are ready for installation. Clicking one of them starts the installation. This is the default option.

- **4–Automatically download updates and install them on the schedule specified below:** WSUS downloads updates automatically when the scheduled install day and time arrive. You can use the drop-down lists on the left side of the dialog box to specify the desired days and times, which, by default, are daily at 3:00 a.m.

- **5–Allow local administrators to select the configuration mode that Automatic Updates should notify and install updates:** Enables local administrators to select a configuration option of their choice from the Automatic Updates control panel, such as their own scheduled time for installations.

The following describes several of the other more important available policy settings shown in Figure 18-18:

- **Do not display "Install Updates and Shut Down" option in Shut Down Windows dialog box:** Prevents the appearance of this option in the Shut Down Windows dialog box, even if updates are available when the user shuts down his computer.

- **Do not adjust default option to "Install Updates and Shut Down" option in Shut Down Windows dialog box:** When enabled, changes the default shut down option from Install Updates and Shut Down to the last shut down option selected by the user.

- **Enabling Windows Update Power Management to automatically wake up the system to install scheduled updates:** Uses features of Windows Power Management to wake computers up from hibernation to install available updates.

- **Automatic Updates detection frequency:** Specifies the length of time in hours used to determine the waiting interval before checking for updates at an intranet update server. You need to enable the Specify Intranet Microsoft Update Service Location policy to have this policy work.

- **Allow non-administrators to receive update notifications:** Enables users who are not administrators to receive update notifications according to other Automatic Updates configuration settings.

- **Turn on Software Notifications:** Enables you to determine whether users see detailed notification messages that promote the value, installation, and usage of optional software from the Microsoft Update service.

- **Allow Automatic Updates immediate installation:** Enables Automatic Updates to immediately install updates that neither interrupt Windows services nor restart Windows.

- **Turn on recommended updates via Automatic Updates:** Enables Automatic Updates to include both important and recommended updates.

- **No auto-restart with logged on users for scheduled automatic updates installations:** Prevents Automatic Updates from restarting a client computer after updates have been installed. Otherwise, Automatic Updates notifies the logged-on user that the computer will automatically restart in five minutes to complete the installation.

- **Re-prompt for restart with scheduled installations:** Specifies the number of minutes from the previous prompt to wait before displaying a second prompt for restarting the computer.

- **Delay Restart for scheduled installations:** Specifies the number of minutes to wait before a scheduled restart takes place.

- **Reschedule Automatic Updates scheduled installations:** Specifies the length of time in minutes that Automatic Updates waits after system startup before proceeding with a scheduled installation that was missed because a client computer was not turned on and connected to the network at the time of a scheduled installation, as previously specified by option 4 from the Configure Automatic Updating drop-down list.

- **Enable client-side targeting:** Enables you to specify a target group name for client-side targeting of updates as described earlier in this chapter.

- **Allow signed updates from an intranet Microsoft update service location:** Enables you to manage whether Automatic Updates accepts updates signed by entities other than Microsoft when the update is found on an intranet Microsoft Update location.

For more information on these policies, consult the Help information provided on the right side of each policy's Properties dialog box.

Note that after you configure Group Policy settings, these may take some time to apply to client computers. As with other Group Policy settings, you can force an immediate refresh by opening a command prompt and typing `gpupdate /force`. To enable client computers to initiate detection by the WSUS server, open a command prompt at each client computer and type the command `wuauclt.exe /detectnow`. This option requests that the Automatic Updates client contact the WSUS server immediately.

If client computers are experiencing problems receiving updates from the WSUS server when SSL certificates are in use, run the command `wuauclt.exe /resetauthorization /detectnow` at each affected client. This forces the client to download a new certificate from the WSUS server and then download updates from the server.

**TIP**   If you do not want to use Group Policy to configure the use of WSUS on client computers, you can also edit the Registry of each client computer; however, this means it is more cumbersome and if done incorrectly could jeopardize the operation of the client computer. For more information, refer to "Configure Automatic Updates using Registry Editor" at http://technet.microsoft.com/en-us/library/dd939844(WS.10).aspx.

**NOTE**   For more information on configuring client computers, refer to "Update and Configure the Automatic Updates Client Computer" at http://technet.microsoft.com/en-us/library/dd939900(WS.10).aspx.

## Exam Preparation Tasks

## Review All the Key Topics

Review the most important topics in this chapter, noted with the key topics icon in the outer margin of the page. Table 18-3 lists a reference of these key topics and the page numbers on which each is found.

**Table 18-3**   Key Topics for Chapter 18

| Key Topic Element | Description | Page Number |
|---|---|---|
| List | Describes types of updates handled by Windows Update and by WSUS. | 725 |
| List | Shows you how to install a WSUS server. | 728 |
| Figure 18-6 | WSUS informs you of tasks you should perform after initial synchronization of updates. | 733 |
| Figure 18-7 | The WSUS console provides a large number of configurable options. | 733 |
| Paragraph | Describes the importance of testing updates before deploying them to client computers. | 738 |
| Table 18-2 | Describes server- and client-side targeting of updates. | 740 |
| Figure 18-12 | Shows you how to configure server-side or client-side targeting. | 741 |
| List | Shows you how to approve updates. | 743 |
| Figure 18-15 | WSUS provides several types of reports that provide information on update status. | 745 |
| Figure 18-16 | Shows options that determine the content of WSUS reports. | 745 |
| Figure 18-18 | Group Policy provides a series of policies for configuring use of WSUS on your network. | 749 |
| Figure 18-20 | Four options for configuring download and installation of updates are available. | 750 |

## Complete the Tables and Lists from Memory

Print a copy of Appendix B, "Memory Tables," (found on the CD), or at least the section for this chapter, and complete the tables and lists from memory. Appendix C, "Memory Tables Answer Key," also on the CD, includes the completed tables and lists to check your work.

## Definition of Key Terms

Define the following key terms from this chapter, and check your answers in the Glossary.

client-side targeting, computer groups, downstream server, Microsoft updates, server-side targeting, update classifications, update synchronization, upstream server, Windows Update, Windows Server Update Services

This chapter covers the following subjects:

- **Performance Monitor:** This section introduces the Performance Monitor tool included with every version of Windows and shows you how to create graphs and summaries of server performance in real time.

- **Data Collector Sets:** This section expands on the previous section by showing you how to log server performance data in a form that you can save so that you can perform trend analysis of server performance over longer periods of time and gain an insight into what types of upgrades you should be thinking about.

- **Analyzing Performance Data:** This section describes the most useful counters for monitoring your server's memory, processor, disk, and network performance.

- **Reliability Monitor:** This is a new tool in Windows Server 2008 that provides a system stability index, which is a measure of server reliability that you can track as a function of time. It provides a convenient means of tracking the frequency of occurrence of problems with your server's hardware and software.

# CHAPTER 19

# Configuring Performance Monitoring

When you purchase and install a new server on your network, the server usually offers a high level of performance and users on the network discover that they can rapidly access this server for files and applications contained on it. But as time passes, new applications are installed, and more data is stored on the server, performance tends to decrease and users notice that it takes longer to access their data. Windows Server 2008 R2 provides tools that help you monitor the performance of your server over time and assess the need for hardware upgrades to keep it humming along at a pace acceptable for users. In this chapter, you learn how to monitor and log server performance using tools that you need to be familiar with for the 70-642 exam and for the real world.

## "Do I Know This Already?" Quiz

The "Do I Know This Already?" quiz allows you to assess whether you should read this entire chapter or simply jump to the "Exam Preparation Tasks" section for review. If you are in doubt, read the entire chapter. Table 19-1 outlines the major headings in this chapter and the corresponding "Do I Know This Already?" quiz questions. You can find the answers in Appendix A, "Answers to the 'Do I Know This Already?' Quizzes."

**Table 19-1**  "Do I Know This Already?" Foundation Topics Section-to-Question Mapping

| Foundations Topics Section | Questions Covered in This Section |
| --- | --- |
| Performance Monitor | 1–4 |
| Data Collector Sets | 5–6 |
| Analyzing Performance Data | 7–8 |
| Reliability Monitor | 9–10 |

1. Which of the following tasks can you perform using Performance Monitor? (Choose all that apply.)

   a. Identify performance problems such as bottlenecks

   b. Monitor resource usage

   c. Establish trends of server performance with time

   d. Terminate misbehaving applications

   e. Monitor the effects of changes in server configuration

   f. Generate alerts when unusual conditions occur

2. You are learning how to use Performance Monitor for the first time, and note that this tool can monitor specific hardware or software components in your server. What term does Performance Monitor use to denote one of these components by?

   a. Object

   b. Counter

   c. Instance

   d. Component

3. You configured Performance Monitor to display 15 different counters and are uncertain as to which line on the chart is displaying information for the Processor\% Processor Time counter. Which of the following actions can you use to highlight the line generated by this counter? (Each answer represents a complete solution. Choose two answers.)

   a. Select this counter from the list at the bottom of the Performance Monitor display, and then press the **Backspace** key.

   b. Select this counter from the list at the bottom of the Performance Monitor display, and then press the **Insert** key.

   c. From the Add Counters dialog box, add a duplicate instance of the same counter.

   d. Access the **Graph** tab of the Performance Monitor Properties dialog box. Then, select a distinct color, width, and style for this counter.

   e. Access the **Data** tab of the Performance Monitor Properties dialog box. Then, select a distinct color, width, and style for this counter.

4. You need to provide a user named Sharon with the capability of running a data collector set you've configured, but you do not want her to be able to modify the data collector set. To which group should you add Sharon's user account in order to satisfy this requirement?

   a. Users

   b. Performance Monitor Users

   c. Performance Log Users

   d. Power Users

5. Ellen configured the Performance Monitor tool to track several network-related performance objects on her Windows Server 2008 R2 file server so that she can have a performance baseline against which she can compare future server performance. After viewing the graph for several minutes, she realizes she needs to save the data logged in the graph for future reference. What should she do to save all monitoring data, including the points that are no longer visible?

   a. She needs to right-click the graph and choose **Save Image As**. In the dialog box that appears, she needs to specify the name of a comma-delimited file to which Performance Monitor will save all data.

   b. She needs to choose the **File > Export** command. In the dialog box that appears, she needs to specify the name of a comma-delimited file to which Performance Monitor will save all data.

   c. She used the wrong Performance Monitor component. She needs to use the Data Collector Sets feature to configure logging so that she can save the performance data.

   d. She used the wrong tool. She needs to use Resource Monitor and select **File > Save As** so that she can save the performance data.

6. You want to run a script that cleans up unneeded files when disk space is getting low. What should you do?

   a. Use Performance Monitor to create a performance graph and add the LogicalDisk\% Free Space counter to this graph. Open the **Task** tab of the Properties dialog box for this graph and specify the path to a script that deletes unneeded files.

   b. Use Performance Monitor to create a data collector set that tracks the LogicalDisk\% Free Space counter. Then, configure a script that deletes unneeded files and specify the path to this script in the **Task** tab of the alert's Properties dialog box.

   c. Open Resource Monitor and expand the **Disk** section. Right-click the entry corresponding to the amount of free space in the desired disk and choose **Properties**. Then, configure a script that deletes unneeded files and specify the path to this script in the **Task** tab of the dialog box that appears.

   d. Use the Scheduled Tasks application to create a scheduled task that runs a script that deletes unneeded files and specify a low value of the LogicalDisk\% Free Space counter as a trigger for this task.

7. You think your computer might need more RAM, and you're wondering how much memory is committed to either physical RAM or running processes. What counter should you check in Performance Monitor?

   a. Memory\Pages/sec

   b. Memory\Available Bytes

   c. Memory\Committed Bytes

   d. Processor\% Processor Time

   e. System\Processor Queue Length

8. You suspect that your computer is running low on available memory when several applications are running at once, but you do not have the budget to add additional RAM at present. The computer is configured with two hard disks: disk 0 contains partitions C: and D:, while disk 1 contains partitions E: and F:. Operating systems files are on partition C:. Which of the following would most likely be the best solution to improve the performance of this computer?

   a. Increase the size of the paging file on the C: partition to twice the amount of RAM currently in the system.

   b. Select the **No paging file** option.

   c. Add a new paging file on the D: partition.

   d. Add a new paging file on the E: partition.

9. You are experimenting with Reliability Monitor and discovering what information you might be able to obtain using this tool. Which of the following types of information would be available from this tool? (Choose all that apply.)

   a. The date on which an application crashed

   b. The date on which processor utilization exceeded 90 percent

   c. The date on which updates were installed on the computer

   d. The date on which an application was uninstalled from the computer

10. You want to obtain summary statistics of processor, disk, network, and memory performance for your Windows Server 2008 R2 computer. You want to obtain this information quickly without spending a lot of time configuring options; at present, you do not want to save a lot of logging data. What application should you use?

   a. Reliability Monitor

   b. Resource Monitor

   c. Performance Monitor

   d. Event Viewer

   e. Data Collector Sets

## Foundation Topics

# Performance Monitor

The Windows Server 2008 R2 Performance Monitor snap-in replaces and updates the Performance Console tool used with Windows 2000 and Windows Server 2003. It is included as a component of the Diagnostics section of Server Monitor and also is accessible as a standalone MMC console from the Administrative Tools folder. As shown in Figure 19-1, it includes the following monitoring tools:

- **Performance Monitor:** Provides a real-time graph of server performance, either in the present time or as logged historical data.

- **Data Collector Sets:** Records server performance data into log files. Data collectors are separated into groups that you can use for monitoring performance under different conditions. We discuss Data Collector Sets later in this chapter.

- **Reports:** Produces performance report data. This feature was included as the Report function of the System Monitor console in previous Windows versions.

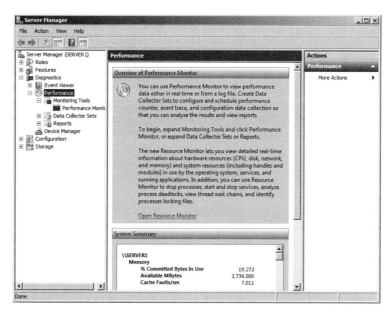

**Figure 19-1**   You can monitor and log your server's performance from the Performance Monitor snap-in, here shown as a component of the Server Manager console.

In the original version of Windows Server 2008, this tool is known as the Reliability and Performance Monitor console and includes a Resource Overview section that performs an overall reliability analysis of computer stability with time. This component has been replaced by the Resource Monitor tool mentioned later in this chapter.

**NOTE**   For additional information on Reliability and Performance Monitor and its various components, refer to "Performance and Reliability Monitoring Step-by-Step Guide for Windows Server 2008" at http://technet.microsoft.com/en-us/library/cc771692(WS.10).aspx and "Performance Monitor Getting Started Guide" at http://technet.microsoft.com/en-ca/library/dd744567(WS.10).aspx.

As shown in Figure 19-2, Performance Monitor provides a configurable real-time graph of computer performance and enables you to perform tasks such as the following:

- Identify performance problems such as bottlenecks

- Monitor resource usage

- Establish trends of server performance with time

- Monitor the effects of changes in server configuration

- Generate alerts when unusual conditions occur

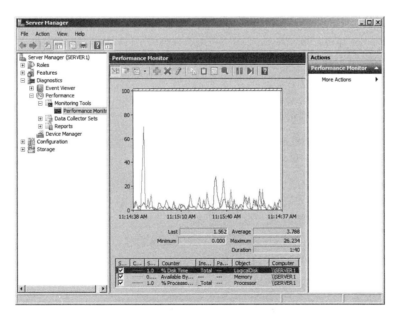

**Figure 19-2**   Performance Monitor displays a real-time graph of activity for selected objects and counters.

Before you learn more about the Performance Monitor tool, you need to be familiar with the terms defined in Table 19-2, which are used in a specific manner when referring to performance metrics.

**Table 19-2   Performance Monitor Terms**

| Term | Description |
| --- | --- |
| Object | A specific hardware or software component that Performance Monitor is capable of monitoring. It can be any component that possesses a series of measurable properties. Windows Server 2008 R2 comes with a defined set of objects; applications such as Internet Information Services (IIS) installed on Windows Server 2008 R2 may add more objects to the available set. |
| Counter | One of a series of statistical measurements associated with each object. |
| Instance | Refers to multiple occurrences of a given object. For example, if your computer has two hard disks, two instances of the PhysicalDisk object will be present. These instances are numbered sequentially, starting with 0 for the first occurrence. On a multiple processor server, the performance of each processor is recorded as an instance. An instance labeled "Total" is also present, yielding the sum of performance data for each counter. Note that not all objects have multiple instances. |

Information on objects and counters is displayed in the following format: *Object (_instance)\Counter*. For example, Processor (_0)\%Processor Time measures the %Processor time on the first processor. The instance does not appear if only a single instance is present.

### Using Performance Monitor to Collect Real-Time Data

Performance Monitor enables you to obtain a real-time graph of computer performance statistics. Use the following procedure:

1. Open Server Manager and select **Performance** from the console tree. Alternately, you can use one of the following procedures to open Performance Monitor in its own console:

   - Click **Start**, type `performance` in the Start Search text box, and then click **Performance Monitor**.

   - Click **Start > Administrative Tools > Performance Monitor**.

   - Click **Start**, type `msconfig` in the Start Menu Search Field. Select **Performance Monitor** from the Tools tab of System Configuration, and then click **Launch**.

2. If you receive a User Account Control (UAC) prompt, click **Yes** or supply administrative credentials.

3. In the Performance console, click **Performance Monitor**. Performance Monitor starts and displays the Processor\%Processor Time counter.

4. To add objects and counters, click the **+** icon on the toolbar.

5. In the Add Counters dialog box that appears (see Figure 19-3), select the server to be monitored from the Select Counters from Computer drop-down list. To monitor local computer performance, you can select **<Local Computer>**. Then, select the desired object and instance from the lists directly below the Select Counters list.

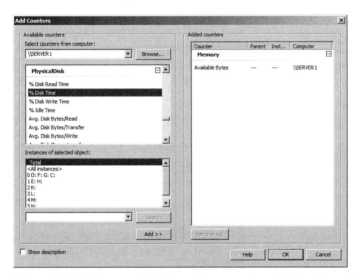

**Figure 19-3**   You can select from a large number of objects from the Performance Object drop-down list in the Add Counters dialog box.

6. Expand the desired object to display a list of available counters from which you can select one or more counters. To add counters to the graph, select the counter and click **Add**.

7. Repeat Steps 5 and 6 to add more counters. You learn about suitable counters in the following sections.

8. When you are finished, click **OK**.

**TIP**   You can highlight individual counters in Performance Monitor. To highlight an individual counter in the Performance Monitor display, select it from the list at the bottom of the details pane and click the highlight icon (looks like a highlighter pen) in the taskbar. You can also press the **Backspace** key to highlight the counter. The highlighted counter appears in a heavy line. You can use the up or down arrow keys to toggle through the list of counters and highlight each one in turn. This feature helps you to find the desired counter from a graph that includes a large number of counters.

### Customizing Performance Monitor

You can customize the appearance of the graph as well as the data source used for displaying performance data from the Performance Monitor Properties dialog box. In the console tree of Performance Monitor, right-click **Performance Monitor** and choose **Properties** to open the dialog box shown in Figure 19-4. This dialog box has the following five tabs:

- **General tab:** As shown in Figure 19-4, this tab enables you to specify the components that are displayed on the performance graph. You can choose the time interval and duration at which computer performance is sampled; to obtain performance data over a longer period of time, increase the values in the **Sample every** and **Duration** fields.

- **Source tab:** Enables you to display currently logged performance data or data that was previously logged into a data collector set. You can also display this tab by clicking the **View Log Data** icon (second icon from the left) in the toolbar displayed above the performance graph. If you are displaying logged data, you can choose a time range to be displayed on the graph. We discuss options on this tab later in this chapter.

- **Data tab:** Enables you to modify the color, width, and style of individual counters as displayed in the performance graph. This helps you identify specific counters from a complex graph that includes a large number of counters.

- **Graph tab:** Enables you to modify the overall type of graph that is displayed by Performance Monitor. By default, Performance Monitor displays a line graph, such as shown in the figures in this chapter. You can also choose a histogram view, which displays the value of each counter as a vertical bar, or a report view, which displays a numerical summary of each counter. In addition, you can choose to have the default line display scroll across the graph or to wrap, which causes the graph to slide along the viewing area in a manner similar to that presented by Task Manager. Additional options enable you to specify grids, scale numbers, and change the maximum and minimum values displayed.

- **Appearance tab:** Enables you to change the color of various graph components, text font, and border appearance.

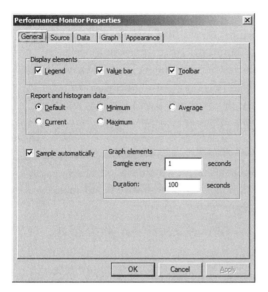

**Figure 19-4**   The Performance Monitor Properties dialog box enables you to customize various components of the performance graph.

### Permissions Required to Run Performance Monitor

Ordinary users who are members of the default Users group are entitled to run Performance Monitor to create real-time performance graphs and display data logged by a previously executed data collector set. Windows Server 2008 provides the following default groups that enable you to delegate permissions for performing additional tasks, such as creating and running data collector sets to nonadministrative users:

- **Performance Monitor Users:** Members of this group can modify the Performance Monitor display properties while viewing real-time data. They can also run data collector sets, but cannot create or modify data collector sets.

- **Performance Log Users:** Members of this group receive all the privileges of the Performance Monitor Users group. In addition, they are entitled to create and modify data collector sets after this group has been assigned the **Log on as a batch user** right. For more information on assigning this user right, refer to

"Enable Logging for Performance Log Users Group Members" at http://tech-net.microsoft.com/en-us/library/cc722184.aspx.

# Data Collector Sets

A Data Collector Set is a set of performance objects and counters that enables you to log computer performance over time while you are performing other tasks. Such logging is important because changes in computer performance often occur only after an extended period of time. Data Collector Sets are binary files that save performance statistics for later viewing and analysis in the Performance Monitor snap-in; you may also export them to spreadsheet or database programs for later analysis.

Previously known as Performance Logs and Alerts, this feature enables you to do the following:

- Establish a performance baseline for each server, which is a log of server performance that you can save for later comparison with future performance and tracking any changes that might have occurred over time.

- Identify potential bottlenecks in server performance so that you can take corrective action.

- Monitor the effectiveness of any changes you make to the server's configuration.

- Alert you to events of unusual server performance, such as a consistently high percentage of processor utilization or low available memory. These might indicate hardware or software problems, or the need to upgrade some system component. You can also trigger other actions such as running a program when an alert event occurs. These alerts are displayed in the Application log in Event Viewer.

## System-Defined Data Collector Sets

Windows Server 2008 and Windows Server 2008 R2 create a series of Data Collector Sets by default. Included are the following:

- **Active Directory Diagnostics:** Analyzes performance of Active Directory Domain Services (AD DS)-related counters on a domain controller.

- **System Diagnostics:** Enables you to create a report that contains details of local hardware resources, system response times, and local computer processes. System information and configuration data are also included. See Figure 19-5.

- **System Performance:** Enables you to create a report that provides details on local hardware resources, system response times, and local computer processes.

- **Wireless Diagnostics:** Enables you to create a report that provides data on wireless network-related performance and diagnostics traces on computers equipped with wireless network adapters.

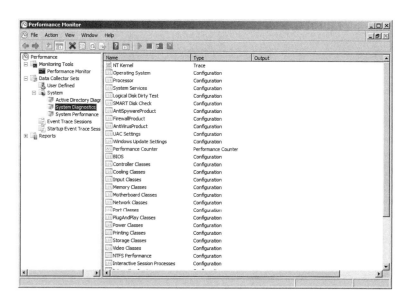

**Figure 19-5**  Performance Monitor includes a series of predefined system Data Collector Sets that you can use to log server performance data.

## Using System-Defined Data Collector Sets

To run any of these Data Collector Sets, right-click the desired set in the console tree of Performance Monitor and choose **Start**. By default, the Data Collector Set logs data for one minute and then displays information in the details pane of the Performance Monitor snap-in. This performance data is logged to `%systemdrive%\PerfLogs\System\Performance\<servername_date_number>`. Use the following procedure to view logged performance data:

1. In the console tree of the Performance Monitor snap-in previously shown in Figure 19-2, select and expand **Reports**, and then expand **System**.

2. Select and expand the type of Data Collector Set you logged. You see entries for each log you created for this Data Collector Set.

3. Select the desired computer and date combination. As shown in Figure 19-6, this displays summary performance information in the details pane of the Performance Monitor snap-in.

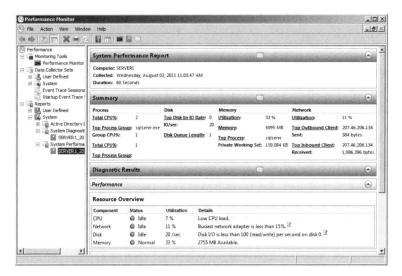

**Figure 19-6**   Performance Monitor displays summary information related to a system-defined Data Collector Set.

4. For more information on any of the displayed subsystems, click the triangle at the end of the desired subsystem's title bar. This expands the CPU, network, disk, and memory subsystems to display several sub-subsystems. Select a sub-subsystem to display information on the selected sub-subsystem.

**NOTE**   For more information on viewing reports, refer to "View Reports in Windows Performance Monitor" at http://technet.microsoft.com/en-us/library/cc766130.aspx.

**TIP**   You can generate a report using the System Diagnostics Data Collector Set rapidly from the command line by typing `perfmon /report`. Performance Monitor opens in a simplified window, runs this Data Collector Set for one minute, and then displays summary information similar to that shown in Figure 19-6.

## Viewing Logged Performance Data

Performance Monitor enables you to view a graph of the data logged by the Data Collector Set. Use the following steps to view this data:

1. In the console tree of the Performance Monitor snap-in, select the **Performance Monitor** node.

2. From the view previously shown in Figure 19-2, select the **View Log Data** icon (the second icon from the left in the toolbar immediately above the performance graph).

3. This displays the Source tab of the Performance Monitor Properties dialog box. Select the **Log Files** option and click **Add**.

4. Select the log file that contains the data you just logged in the Select Log File dialog box that appears, click **Open**, and then click **OK**.

5. Click the **+** icon in the toolbar to display the Add Counters dialog box previously shown in Figure 19-3 and select the desired objects and counters to be displayed as described earlier in this section, and then click **OK**. This displays the selected log in the performance graph.

> **TIP**  You can specify additional properties related to system Data Collector Sets by right-clicking the data collector set in the console tree of the Performance Manager snap-in and choosing **Data Manager**. The dialog box that appears enables you to specify properties, such as the minimum free disk space that must be available on the drive where log data is stored, the maximum number of subfolders allowed in the Data Collector Set data directory, and the maximum root path size of the Data Collector Set data directory. For example, you can use the Minimum free disk option to prevent the Data Collector Set from logging data if your server has less than a specified amount of available disk space. For more information, refer to "Performance Monitoring Getting Started Guide" referenced earlier in this chapter.

## User-Defined Data Collector Sets

Performance Monitor enables you to create your own user-defined Data Collector Set. Use the following procedure to create a Data Collector Set:

1. In the console tree of the Performance Monitor snap-in previously shown in Figure 19-2, select and expand **Data Collector Sets**.

2. Select **User Defined**.

3. To create a new Data Collector Set, right-click a blank area of the details pane and select **New > Data Collector Set**. The Create New Data Collector Set Wizard starts.

4. You receive the page shown in Figure 19-7. Provide a name for the new Data Collector Set. Select either **Create from a template (Recommended)** or **Create manually (Advanced)**, and then click **Next**. If you select the **Create manually (Advanced)** option, refer to the next procedure for the remainder of the steps you should perform.

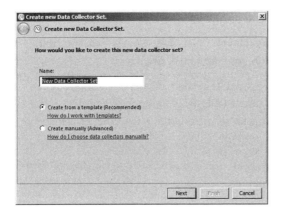

**Figure 19-7**   The How would you like to create this new data collector set? page of the Create New Data Collector Set Wizard enables you to name your Data Collector Set and choose whether to use a template.

5. If you select the **Create from a Template** option, you receive the dialog box shown in Figure 19-8, which enables you to use a template based on counters similar to those of the system Data Collector Sets already discussed, including Active Directory Diagnostics, System Diagnostics, and System Performance. You can also choose the **Basic** option, which enables you to use performance counters to create a basic Data Collector Set, which you can edit later if necessary.

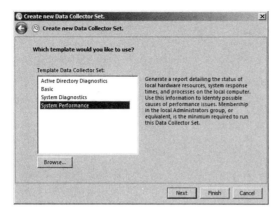

**Figure 19-8**    The Create New Data Collector Set Wizard enables you to use several different templates.

6. Select the desired template and click **Browse** to locate a template file (XML format) if one exists. Then, click **Next**.

7. You receive the Where would you like the data to be saved? page, as shown in Figure 19-9. Select a location to which you want the data to be saved (or accept the default location provided), and then click **Next**.

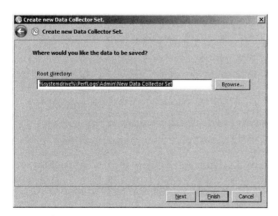

**Figure 19-9**    The Where would you like the data to be saved? page enables you to chose the folder to which you want to save the Data Collector Set.

8. The Create the data collector set? page shown in Figure 19-10 enables you to select the user under whom the Data Collector Set will be run. If you want to run it under a different user, click **Change** and supply the requested credentials. To start logging now, select **Start this data collector set now**. To configure additional properties, select **Open properties for this data collector**

**set**, and then modify settings on the Properties dialog box that appears. Then, click **Finish**.

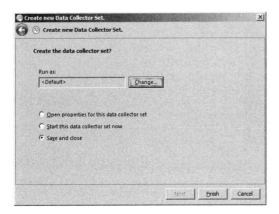

**Figure 19-10**   The Create the data collector set? page enables you to run the set as another user or open the properties of the Data Collector Set.

**TIP**   After you select the desired template, you can click **Finish** on any of the remaining pages of the wizard if you want to accept the remaining defaults.

### Creating a Custom Data Collector Set

To create a custom Data Collector Set, use the **Create manually (Advanced)** option in Step 4 of the previous procedure, and then use the following steps to complete the procedure:

1. After selecting the **Create manually (Advanced)** option and clicking **Next**, you receive the screen shown in Figure 19-11, which enables you to specify the following options:

   - **Performance counter:** Enables you to select performance objects and counters to be logged over time. Click **Next** to specify the performance counters to be logged and the desired sampling interval.

   - **Event trace data:** Enables you to create trace logs, which are similar to counter logs, but they log data only when a specific activity takes place, whereas counter logs track data continuously for a specified interval.

- **System configuration information:** Enables you to track changes in Registry keys. Click **Next** to specify the desired keys.

- **Performance Counter Alert:** Enables you to display an alert when a selected counter exceeds or drops beneath a specified value. Click **Next** to specify the counters you would like to alert and the limiting value (see Figure 19-12 for an example).

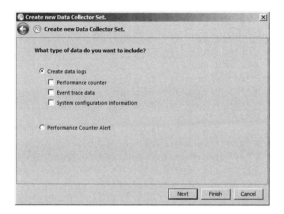

**Figure 19-11** You can create several types of logs or alerts from the Create manually option in the Create New Data Collector Set Wizard.

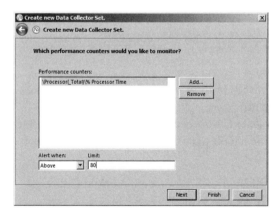

**Figure 19-12** Creating an alert that informs you when the Processor\% Processor Time value exceeds 80 percent.

2. After clicking **Next**, you receive the same dialog box shown previously in Figure 19-10. To configure additional properties such as actions to be taken in response to an alert condition, select the **Open properties for this data collector set** option.

3.  To specify a task that will run when the alert is triggered, select the **Task** tab of the **Properties** dialog box that appears. You receive the dialog box shown in Figure 19-13. Specify the information in the text boxes provided and then click **OK**.

**Figure 19-13**   The Task tab of the (Data Collector Set name) Properties dialog box enables you to specify a task that will run when the alert condition is triggered.

4.  To start the Data Collector Set now, click **Start this data collector set now**. Then, click **Finish**.

The Data Collector Set is created and placed in the User Defined section. If you select the **Start this data collector set now** option, logging begins immediately and continues until you right-click the Data Collector Set and choose **Stop**. To start the collector set later, right-click it in the details pane of the Performance Monitor snap-in and choose **Start**.

Use the same procedure to view data collected with a user-defined Data Collector Set as described earlier in this section for system Data Collector Sets.

### Using Performance Monitor to Create a Data Collector Set

Perhaps the simplest method to create a Data Collector Set is to use a set of counters you have already configured in Performance Monitor. The following steps show you how:

1. After creating a performance graph as described earlier in this section, right-click **Performance Monitor** in the console tree and select **New > Data Collector Set**. The Create New Data Collector Set Wizard starts, as previously described.

2. Provide a name for the Data Collector Set and click **Next**.

3. Accept the location to which the data is to be saved, or type or browse to the location of your choice, and then click **Next**.

4. In the Create the data collector set? page, select any required options, and then click **Finish**.

The Data Collector Set is created and placed in the User Defined section. If you select the option to start the Data Collector Set now, logging begins immediately and continues until you right-click the Data Collector Set and choose **Stop**.

**NOTE**  For more information on creating and working with Data Collector Sets, refer to "Creating Data Collector Sets" at http://technet.microsoft.com/en-us/library/cc749337.aspx and links contained within this reference.

## A Few Best Practices for Logging Server Performance

You should have a server performance-logging program in place so as to have a baseline record of how all servers are performing under normal load conditions, and to obtain trends over time in their performance as user patterns change. In this way, you can be prepared in the event that something unusual occurs.

Some suggestions for performance logging are as follows:

- Log server performance at 10- to 15-minute intervals for a week or two, and archive the logs that are created.

- While logging server performance, turn off services that are not essential to day-to-day server operation and logging.

- During periods of especially high server use, log server performance at 1 or 2 minute intervals.

- See Table 19-3 in the next section for suggestions regarding performance counters that you should log for given situations.

**Table 19-3**   Some Suggestions for Monitoring Server Performance

| Situation | Object | Counters |
|---|---|---|
| To check overall performance | Memory | Pages/Sec |
| | Network | % Network Utilization |
| | PhysicalDisk | % Disk Time |
| | Processor | % Processor Time |
| | Server | Bytes Total/Sec |
| To check if disks are the bottleneck | LogicalDisk and PhysicalDisk | % Disk Time, Disk Bytes/Sec, Avg. Disk Bytes/Transfer, Avg. Disk sec/Transfer, Avg. Disk Queue Length |
| | Memory | Pages/Sec |
| To check if the processor is the bottleneck | Processor | % Processor Time, Interrupts/Sec |
| | System | Processor Queue Length, % Total Processor Time |
| To check if RAM is the bottleneck | Memory | Pages/Sec, Available Bytes, Committed Bytes, Pool Nonpaged Bytes |
| Resource planning | LogicalDisk | % Free Space |
| | Memory | Pages/Sec, Available Bytes |
| | PhysicalDisk | % Disk Time, Average Disk Sec/Transfer |
| | Processor | % Processor time, Interrupts/Sec |
| | Server | Bytes Total/Sec |
| | System | File Read/Write Operations/Sec |

**NOTE**   For a comprehensive treatment of server monitoring scenarios as well as suggestions for tuning server hardware for optimum performance, refer to "Performance Tuning Guidelines for Windows Server 2008 R2" at http://msdn.microsoft.com/en-us/windows/hardware/gg463392.aspx.

**TIP**   Remember that you must use the Data Collector Sets feature of Performance Monitor if you want to retain a permanent record of performance data from any computer.

## Command-Line Utilities

You can perform several tasks associated with performance monitoring and optimization from the command line. The following are several available tools:

- **Perfmon /report:** Starts the System Diagnostics data collector set and displays a report of the results.

- **Perfmon /res:** Starts the Resource View.

- **Perfmon /rel:** Starts Reliability Monitor.

- **Perfmon /sys:** Starts Performance Monitor.

- **Logman:** Manages data collector logs. You can start, stop, and schedule the collection of performance and trace logging data.

- **Relog:** Creates new performance logs from data in existing logs by modifying the sampling rate and/or converting the file format.

- **Typeperf:** Writes performance data to the command prompt window or to a log file.

For information on running these tools, type the command name followed by **/?** at a command prompt.

## Monitoring Print Servers

Performance Monitor, as well as its Data Collector Sets feature, enables you to add counters for monitoring print servers. Included is the Print Queue performance object, which contains instances for each printer installed on your server. The following counters are available:

- **Add Network Printer Calls:** Shows the total number of calls from other print servers to add shared printers since the last restart.

- **Bytes Printed/sec:** Provides a rough indication of how busy the printer is by displaying the number of bytes printed from the print queue per second.

- **Enumerate Network Printer Calls:** Shows the number of calls to the server from browse clients since the last restart.

- **Job Errors:** Shows the total number of printer job errors due to network problems since the last restart.

- **Jobs:** Shows the current number of jobs in the print queue, thereby providing an estimate of usage.

- **Jobs Spooling:** Shows the current number of spooling jobs in the print queue.

- **Max Jobs Spooling:** Shows the maximum number of spooling jobs since the last restart.

- **Max References:** Shows the maximum number of open references to the printer.

- **Not Ready Errors:** Shows the total number of printer not ready errors since the last restart.

- **Out of Paper Errors:** Shows the total number of out of paper errors since the last restart.

- **References:** Shows the current number of references, such as a user or program connecting to the printer, to the print queue.

- **Total Jobs Printed:** Shows the total number of jobs in the queue printed since the last restart.

- **Total Pages Printed:** Shows the total number of pages in the queue printed since the last restart.

**NOTE**   The general performance counters discussed in previous sections are also useful when monitoring the performance of your print server. Also, use counters found in the spoolsv instance of the Process object. For more information on monitoring print servers, refer to "Performance Monitoring and Baseline Measurement" at http://technet.microsoft.com/en-us/library/cc782262(WS.10).aspx.

## Analyzing Performance Data

As discussed in the previous section, use of Data Collector Sets is the most convenient way to gather and store performance monitoring data from your servers. You can retain a series of Data Collector Sets collected at different times and under different server loads to track the performance of your servers over time as additional users and computers are added to the network, new applications are installed, updates are added, and other various changes to the server and network configurations take place. Such information enables you to spot potential bottlenecks and plan for additional hardware resources needed to keep up with increasing demand on your network over time.

The following sections present information on optimizing and troubleshooting key components of your server infrastructure, including memory, processor, disk, and network.

## Optimizing and Troubleshooting Memory Performance

The Memory object includes counters that monitor the computer's physical and virtual memory. Table 19-4 discusses the most important counters for this object.

**Table 19-4**   Important Counters for the Memory Object

| Counter | What It Measures | Interpretation and Remedial Tips |
|---|---|---|
| Pages/sec | The rate at which data is read to or written from the paging file | A value of 20 or more indicates a shortage of RAM and a possible memory bottleneck. To view the effect of paging file performance on the system, watch this counter together with LogicalDisk\% Disk Time. Add RAM to clear the problem. |
| Available Bytes | The amount of physical memory available | A value consistently below 4 MB indicates a shortage of available memory. This might be due to memory leaks in one or more applications. Check your programs for memory leaks. You may need to add more RAM. |
| Committed Bytes | The amount of virtual memory that has been committed to either physical RAM or running processes | Committed memory is in use and not available to other processes. If the amount of committed bytes exceeds the amount of RAM on the computer, you may need to add RAM. |
| Pool Nonpaged | The amount of RAM in the non-paged pool system memory (an area holding objects that cannot be written to disk) | If this value exhibits a steady increase in bytes without a corresponding increase in computer activity, check for an application with a memory leak. |
| Page Faults/sec | The number of data pages that must be read from or written to the page file per second | A high value indicates a lot of paging activity. Add RAM to alleviate this problem. |

In addition to these counters, the Paging File\% Usage counter is of use when troubleshooting memory problems. This counter measures the percentage of the paging file currently in use. If it approaches 100 percent, you should either increase the size of the paging file or add more RAM.

Lack of adequate memory may also have an impact on the performance of other subsystems in the computer. In particular, a large amount of paging, or reading/writing data from/to the paging file on the hard disk results in increased activity in both the processor and disk subsystems. You should monitor counters in these subsystems at the same time if you suspect memory-related performance problems. You learn more about monitoring counters later in the section, "Optimizing and Troubleshooting Processor Utilization."

The *paging file* (also called the page file) is an area on the hard disk that is used as an additional memory location for programs and data that cannot fit into RAM (in other words, virtual memory). By default, the paging file is located at `%systemdrive%\pagefile.sys` and has a default initial size of the amount of RAM in the computer plus 300 MB, and a default maximum size of 3 times the amount of RAM in the computer.

To improve performance on a computer equipped with more than one physical hard disk, you should locate the paging file on a different hard disk than that occupied by the operating system. You can also increase the size of the paging file or configure multiple paging files on different hard disks. Any of these configurations help to optimize performance by spreading out the activity of reading/writing data from/to the paging files. Note that you should retain a paging file on the system/boot drive to create a memory dump in case of a crash. This memory dump is useful for debugging purposes.

Use the following procedure to modify the configuration of the paging file:

1. Click **Start**, right-click **Computer** and choose **Properties**, and then select **Advanced system settings** from the Tasks list in the System applet.

2. On the Advanced tab of the System Properties dialog box, select **Settings** under **Performance**.

3. Select the **Advanced** tab of the Performance Options dialog box.

4. In the Virtual memory section of this tab, click **Change** to display the Virtual Memory dialog box, which displays the disk partitions available on the computer and the size of the paging file on each.

5. To add a paging file to a drive, first clear the **Automatically manage paging file size for all drives** dialog box. As shown in Figure 19-14, select the drive and choose **Custom size** to specify an initial and maximum size in MB or **System managed size** to obtain a default size. To remove a paging file, select the drive holding the file and click **No paging file**. Note that some programs may not work properly if you choose the **No paging file** option. Then, click **Set**.

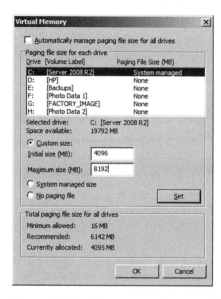

**Figure 19-14**    You can modify paging file properties from the Virtual Memory dialog box.

6. Click **OK** three times to apply your changes and to close the Performance Options and System Properties dialog boxes.

7. Click **Restart Now** to restart your computer if prompted.

## Optimizing and Troubleshooting Processor Utilization

The processor is the "heart" of the system because it executes all program instructions, whether internal to the operating system or in user-executed applications. The Processor object contains counters that monitor processor performance. Table 19-5 discusses the most important counters for this object.

**Table 19-5**   Important Counters for the Processor Object

| Counter | What It Measures | Interpretation and Remedial Tips |
| --- | --- | --- |
| % Processor Time | The percentage of time the processor is executing meaningful actions (excludes the Idle process) | If this value is consistently greater than 85%, the processor could be causing a bottleneck. You should check the memory counters discussed previously; if these are high, consider adding more RAM. Otherwise, you should consider adding a faster processor (or an additional one if supported by your motherboard). |
| Interrupts/sec | The rate of service requests from I/O devices that interrupt other processor activities | A significant increase in the number of interrupts, without a corresponding increase in system activity, may indicate some type of hardware failure. Brief spikes are acceptable. |

You should also look at the System\Processor Queue Length counter. If the value of this counter exceeds 2, a processor bottleneck may exist, with several programs contending for the processor's time.

As mentioned in Table 19-5, memory shortages may frequently manifest themselves in high processor activity. It is usually much cheaper and easier to add RAM to a computer than to add a faster or additional processor. Consequently, you may want to consider this step first when you are experiencing frequent high processor activity.

## Optimizing and Troubleshooting Disk Performance

Disk performance is measured by two processor objects: The PhysicalDisk counters measure the overall performance of a single physical hard disk rather than individual partitions. LogicalDisk counters measure the performance of a single partition or volume on a disk. These counters include the performance of spanned, striped, or RAID-5 volumes that cross physical disks.

PhysicalDisk counters are best suited for hardware troubleshooting. Table 19-6 describes the most important counters for this object.

**Table 19-6**   Important Counters for the PhysicalDisk Object

| Counter | What It Measures | Interpretation and Remedial Tips |
| --- | --- | --- |
| % Disk Time | The percentage of time that the disk was busy reading or writing to any partition | A value of over 50% suggests a disk bottleneck. Consider upgrading to a faster disk or controller. Also check the memory counters to see whether more RAM is needed. |
| Avg. Disk Queue Length | The average number of disk read and write requests waiting to be performed | If this value is greater than 2, follow the same suggestions as for % Disk Time. |
| Average Disk Sec/Transfer | The length of time a disk takes to fulfill requests. | A value greater than 0.3 may indicate that the disk controller is retrying the disk continually because of write failures. |

LogicalDisk counters are best suited for investigating the read/write performance of a single partition. Table 19-7 describes the most important counters for this object.

**Table 19-7**   Important Counters for the LogicalDisk Object

| Counter | What It Measures | Interpretation and Remedial Tips |
| --- | --- | --- |
| % Disk Time | The percentage of time that the disk is busy servicing disk requests | A value greater than 90% may indicate a performance problem except when using a RAID device. Compare to Processor\% Processor Time to determine whether disk requests are using too much processor time. |
| Average Disk Bytes/ Transfer | The amount of data transferred in each I/O operation | Low values (below about 20 KB) indicate that an application may be accessing a disk inefficiently. Watch this counter as you close applications to locate an offending application. |
| Current Disk Queue Length | The amount of data waiting to be transferred to the disk | A value greater than 2 indicates a possible disk bottleneck, with processes being delayed because of slow disk speed. Consider adding another faster disk. |
| Disk Transfers/ sec | The rate at which read or write operations are performed by the disk | A value greater than 50 may indicate a disk bottleneck. Consider adding another faster disk. |
| % Free Space | Percentage of unused disk space | A value less than about 15% indicates that insufficient disk space is available. Consider moving files, repartitioning the disk, or adding another disk. |

**TIP**   You should log disk activity to a different disk or computer. The act of recording performance logs places an extra "hit" on performance for the disk on which logs are recorded. To obtain accurate disk monitoring results, record this data to a different disk or computer.

### Optimizing and Troubleshooting Network Performance

The Network Interface object includes counters that monitor the server's network interface performance. Table 19-8 discusses the most important counters for this object.

**Table 19-8**   Important Counters for the Network Interface Object

| Counter | What It Measures | Interpretation and Remedial Tips |
| --- | --- | --- |
| Bytes Total/sec | The rate of successful transmissions across the network, both inbound and outbound | Indicates how the network adapter is performing. Values should be high, but preferably not more than 50% of available network bandwidth (see Current Bandwidth counter). |
| Bytes Sent/sec | The rate of successful outbound transmissions across the network | Similar to Bytes Total/sec. |
| Current Bandwidth | Measures each adapter's bandwidth or maximum transfer rate | If Bytes Total/sec approaches the maximum transfer rate, the probability of collisions on the network increases. If this occurs, you might want to consider adding a new network adapter with a higher bandwidth. |
| Packets Outbound Discarded | Measures the number of outbound packets dropped by the network interface | Increasing values might indicate that the network is so busy that network buffers cannot keep up with the outbound flow of packets. |
| Output Queue Length | Length of the output packet queue | This value should be 2 or lower. If it is higher, network saturation is occurring; you should install a faster network card or segment the network. |

You might also want to monitor counters in the Network Segment object. These provide statistics for the local network segment. Use of this object requires that the Network Monitor driver be installed on your server; refer to Chapter 21, "Collecting Network Data," for more information.

## Reliability Monitor

First introduced with Windows Vista and the original version of Windows Server 2008, Reliability Monitor utilizes the built-in Reliability Analysis Component (RAC) to provide a trend analysis of your computer's system stability over time. As shown in Figure 19-15, Reliability Monitor provides a graph of the *System Stability Index* against time. The System Stability Index correlates the trend of your computer's stability against events that might destabilize the computer. Events tracked include Windows updates; software installations and removals; device driver installations, updates, rollbacks, and removals, as well as driver failure to load or unload; application hangs and crashes; disk and memory failures; and Windows failures such as boot failures and system crashes. This graph enables you to track a reliability change directly to a given event. The System Stability Report at the bottom of the window provides information that helps you troubleshoot the root cause of reductions in system reliability and helps you to formulate a strategy for addressing the issues rapidly.

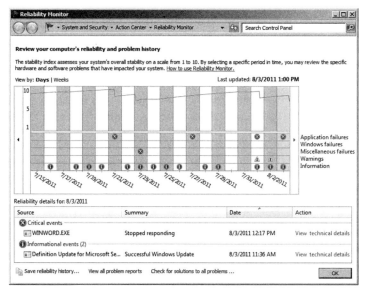

**Figure 19-15**    Reliability Monitor provides a trend analysis of your server's stability.

Use the following steps to run Reliability Monitor:

1. Ensure that you are logged on as an administrator or have administrator credentials available.

2. Click **Start > Control Panel > System and Security > Action Center.** Expand the Maintenance section, and then click **View reliability history**. You can also click **Start** and type reliability in the Start Search text box. Then, click **View reliability history** in the Programs list.

3. As shown in Figure 19-15, events that cause the performance index to drop are marked in one of the event rows. Click a date containing one of these marks and then expand the appropriate section to obtain more information for the following categories:

   ■ **Application failures:** Software programs that hang or crash. Information provided includes the name of the program, its version number, the type of failure, and the date.

   ■ **Windows failures:** Problems such as operating system crashes and boot failures. Information provided includes the type of failure, the operating system and service pack version, the Stop code or detected problem, and the failure date.

   ■ **Miscellaneous failures:** Other types of failures, such as improper shutdowns. Information includes the failure type, details, and date.

   ■ **Warnings:** Other problems, such as unsuccessful application reconfiguration or update installation. Information includes the type of reconfiguration attempted.

   ■ **Information:** Includes the successful installation of various updates and definition packs, as well as successful installation or uninstallation of software programs.

4. To view a comprehensive list of problems, click the **View all problem reports** link at the bottom of the dialog box. The list displayed includes the various types of failures noted here.

5. To export an XML-based reliability report, click **Save reliability history**, specify a path and file name, and then click **Save**.

6. To check for solutions to problems, click **Check for solutions to all problems**. Reliability Monitor displays a Checking for Solutions message box as it goes to the Internet and attempts to locate solutions to your problems. You may need to click **Send information** to send additional information to the Microsoft Error Reporting Service.

**NOTE**   To display data in the System Stability Chart, you must run your computer for at least 24 hours after first installation of Windows Server 2008 R2. For the first 28 days, Reliability Monitor uses a dotted line on the Stability Chart graph, indicating that the data is insufficient to establish a valid baseline for this index.

**TIP**   If Reliability Monitor does not display any data after you start it, you need to ensure that the RacTask task is enabled. By default, this task runs one time about an hour after you install Windows Server 2008. You need to use the Task Scheduler to configure a trigger that automatically starts this task. For more information and details on the required procedure, refer to "Reliability Monitor displays no information in Windows Server 2008 and in Window Server 2008 R2" at http://support.microsoft.com/kb/983386.

**NOTE**   For more information on Reliability Monitor, refer to "Performance and Reliability Monitoring Step-by-Step Guide for Windows Server 2008" at http://technet.microsoft.com/en-us/library/cc771692(WS.10).aspx and select the link labeled **Scenario 7: View system stability with Reliability Monitor**.

### Resource Monitor

Resource Monitor provides a summary of CPU, disk, network, and memory performance statistics including mini-graphs of recent performance of these four components. In the original version of Windows Server 2008, Resource Monitor was combined with Performance Monitor in a single MMC snap-in; Windows Server 2008 R2 (like Windows 7) separates these two applications into their own interfaces. To run Resource Monitor, open Task Manager and click **Resource Monitor** from the Performance tab. You can also open Resource Monitor by clicking **Start**, typing `resource` in the Start Menu Search Field, and then clicking **Resource Monitor** in the Programs list, or by clicking **Start**, typing msconfig in the Start Menu Search Field, selecting **Resource Monitor** from the Tools tab of System Configuration, and then clicking **Launch**.

Resource Monitor provides a summary of processor, disk, network, and memory performance statistics including mini-graphs of recent performance for these components, as shown in Figure 19-16. In the original version of Windows Server 2008, this tool was called Resource Overview and appeared as a default window when you first start Reliability and Performance Monitor.

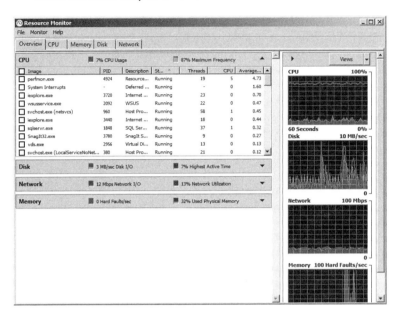

**Figure 19-16**   Resource Monitor provides a performance summary for important CPU, disk, network, and memory counters.

Click the downward-pointing arrow at the right side of each of these components on the Overview tab to display additional information. For each of the four components, the information provided on this tab includes the application whose resource usage is being monitored (known as the image) and the process identifier number (PID) of the application instance. By selecting the tab associated with each component, you can view additional details about the component selected. The following additional information is provided for each of the four components:

- **CPU tab:** A brief description of the monitored application, the number of threads per application, the CPU cycles currently used by each application instance, and the average CPU resulting from each instance as a percentage of total CPU usage.

- **Memory tab:** Current hard faults per second and memory usage information in KB for committed, working set, sharable, and private memory components.

- **Disk tab:** The file being read or written by each application instance, the current read and write speeds in bytes/minute, and the total disk input/output (I/O) in bytes/minute, the I/O priority level, and the response time in milliseconds.

- **Network tab:** The IP address of the network component with which the computer is exchanging data, the amount of data (bandwidth) in bytes per second (sent, received, and total) by each instance.

To filter the display of disk, network, and memory usage according to process, select the check box or boxes in the Image column of the CPU section, as previously shown in Figure 19-16. To change the size of the graphical displays on any tab, select **Large**, **Medium**, or **Small** from the Views drop-down list above the graphical displays.

**NOTE**   For more information on using Resource Monitor, refer to "Resource Availability Troubleshooting Getting Started Guide" at http://technet.microsoft.com/en-us/library/dd883276(WS.10).aspx.

**TIP**   Resource Monitor enables you to obtain information on the processor usage of various applications on the server. This is information that you cannot obtain by using Performance Monitor or its Data Collector Sets feature.

## Exam Preparation Tasks

# Review All the Key Topics

Review the most important topics in this chapter, noted with the key topics icon in the outer margin of the page. Table 19-9 lists a reference of these key topics and the page numbers on which each is found.

**Table 19-9**   Key Topics for Chapter 19

| Key Topic Element | Description | Page Number |
|---|---|---|
| Figure 19-2 | Performance Monitor displays a real-time graph of computer performance counters. | 763 |
| Table 19-2 | Describes terminology used with Performance Monitor. | 764 |
| List | Shows you how to configure Performance Monitor to display a series of counters. | 764 |
| Paragraph | Describes the purpose and use of data collector sets. | 768 |
| Figure 19-5 | Describes system data collector sets. | 769 |
| List | Shows you how to view logged performance data. | 771 |
| List | Shows you how to configure data collector sets for logging computer performance. | 771 |
| Figure 19-12 | Configuring data collector sets to display trace action alerts. | 775 |
| Table 19-4 | Describes the important counters for the Memory performance object. | 781 |
| List | Shows you how to configure the paging file. | 782 |
| Table 19-5 | Describes the important counters for the Processor performance object. | 784 |
| Figure 19-15 | Reliability Monitor provides a time-trend of your computer's stability against several types of failures. | 787 |

## Complete the Tables and Lists from Memory

Print a copy of Appendix B, "Memory Tables," (found on the CD), or at least the section for this chapter, and complete the tables and lists from memory. Appendix C, "Memory Tables Answer Key," also on the CD, includes the completed tables and lists to check your work.

## Definition of Key Terms

Define the following key terms from this chapter, and check your answers in the Glossary.

alert, data collector set, instance, paging file, performance counter, performance logs, Performance Monitor, performance object, Reliability Monitor, Resource Monitor. System Stability Index

This chapter covers the following subjects:

- **Event Viewer:** This section provides a background to the rest of the chapter by describing the various event logs generated by Windows Server 2008 and how to set up the properties of these logs for optimum viewing and analysis.

- **Customizing Event Logs:** This section shows you how to create custom views that contain only the information you need to have at your fingertips and make these customized logs available throughout your network.

- **Configuring Event Log Subscriptions:** By creating subscriptions, you can set up a single computer to collect event logs from many other computers on your network, thus simplifying the task of finding events of importance, regardless of the computer on which they occur.

- **Configuring Tasks from Events:** Event Viewer works together with Task Scheduler so that you can configure Windows to perform a task, such as running a program, sending an e-mail message, or displaying a message on your desktop to alert you of a problem condition on your network. This section shows you how to set up such tasks.

# CHAPTER 20

# Configuring Event Logs

Chapter 19, "Configuring Performance Monitoring," started the discussion of monitoring and maintaining the servers on your network at optimum capability. But, events are happening behind the scenes all the time, both on the servers and on the client computers that make up the heart of your network. Users must be able to access servers and locate their data and applications without delay. As problems occur anywhere on your network, your servers log messages into the built-in Windows event logs, and it is important that you monitor these logs continuously to detect emerging problems as they occur. At first glance, these logs might appear rather cryptic; however, Windows Server 2008 provides tools and utilities that assist you in the tasks of locating important event messages and collecting these messages together at one convenient location that simplifies your day-to-day server monitoring actions. This chapter familiarizes you with the actions that you need to know to separate the important facts from other routine, informational messages that would otherwise take up too much of your attention and time.

## "Do I Know This Already?" Quiz

The "Do I Know This Already?" quiz allows you to assess whether you should read this entire chapter or simply jump to the "Exam Preparation Tasks" section for review. If you are in doubt, read the entire chapter. Table 20-1 outlines the major headings in this chapter and the corresponding "Do I Know This Already?" quiz questions. You can find the answers in Appendix A, "Answers to the 'Do I Know This Already?' Quizzes."

**Table 20-1**  "Do I Know This Already?" Foundation Topics Section-to-Question Mapping

| Foundations Topics Section | Questions Covered in This Section |
| --- | --- |
| Event Viewer | 1–2 |
| Customizing Event Logs | 3–4 |
| Event Log Subscriptions | 5–7 |
| Configuring Tasks from Events | 8 |

1. Which of the following actions can you perform using Event Viewer in Windows Server 2008 R2? (Choose all that apply.)

   a. Create and save event log filters so that you can more rapidly locate event messages that inform you of a problem.

   b. Export a custom event view to another computer so that users at the latter computer can rapidly locate event messages.

   c. Generate alerts when a condition such as high processor utilization occurs on your computer.

   d. Schedule a task to run when a given event is logged.

   e. Collect events from multiple computers so that you can view all these events on a single computer.

2. You open Event Viewer and want to access logs that store events from single components, such as Distributed File Service (DFS) replication, Active Directory Domain Service (AD DS) events, and Domain Name System (DNS) events. In which Event Viewer log should you look for this information?

   a. Application

   b. Security

   c. System

   d. Applications and Services Logs

3. You want to reduce the number of events viewed in the System log of Event Viewer because you've found that you waste a lot of time going through thousands of minor events when trying to locate important events that can pinpoint problems. What should you do?

   a. Configure the log to overwrite events after 48 hours.

   b. Filter the log to display Error, Warning, and Information events.

   c. Filter the log to display only Critical, Warning, and Error events.

   d. Create an event log subscription.

**4.** You are responsible for maintaining the event logs on five file servers that run Windows Server 2008 R2. You have configured auditing on shared folders on each of these servers and want to configure a log on each server that will display only failed attempts to access these shares. You want to do this with the least amount of administrative effort. What should you do?

    **a.** At each server in turn, filter the Security log to display only failed attempts to access the shares.

    **b.** At one server, create a custom view focused on the Security log that displays only failed attempts to access the shares. Export this custom view as an XML file, and then import it to each of the other servers in turn.

    **c.** At each server in turn, filter the Applications and Services logs node to display only failed attempts to access the shares.

    **d.** At one server, create a custom view focused on the Applications and Services logs node that displays only failed attempts to access the shares. Export this custom view as an XML file, and then import it to each of the other servers in turn.

**5.** You are responsible for eight computers located in a small medical office that are configured as a workgroup. You want to collect event logs from all these computers onto a single computer so that you can spot problems more rapidly. What should you configure on this computer?

    **a.** A source-initiated event subscription

    **b.** A collector-initiated event subscription

    **c.** A filter that views logs by event source

    **d.** A filter that views logs by user and computer

**6.** You are configuring an event log subscription that will forward events from all the computers in one department of your company to a collector computer running Windows Server 2008 R2 so that you can monitor events occurring on all of these computers from your Windows Server 2008 R2 computer. Which of the following actions should you take? (Each answer represents part of the solution. Choose two.)

    **a.** Run the `wecutil qc` command at the Windows Server 2008 R2 computer.

    **b.** Run the `winrm quickconfig` command at the Windows Server 2008 R2 computer.

    **c.** Run the `wecutil qc` command at each client computer in the department.

    **d.** Run the `winrm quickconfig` command at each client computer in the department.

**7.** You are configuring an event log subscription and want to use HTTPS to provide for secure forwarding of event information to the collector computer. Which of the following actions should you undertake? (Choose all that apply.)

  **a.** Install a computer certificate at each source computer.

  **b.** Install a computer certificate at the collector computer.

  **c.** Create an exception in Windows Firewall for TCP port 443.

  **d.** From the Advanced Subscription Settings dialog box, select HTTPS and TCP port 443.

  **e.** Install Internet Information Services on the collector computer and configure the computer for HTTPS binding.

  **f.** Run the `winrm quickconfig -transport:https` command at each source computer.

  **g.** Run the `winrm quickconfig -transport:https` command at the collector computer.

**8.** A problematic service has been failing at random times on your Windows Server 2008 computer, and you want to have a message displayed on your desktop when this occurs. What should you do?

  **a.** In Event Viewer, right-click the error generated by the failing service and choose **Attach Task To This Event**. In the Create Basic Task Wizard, select the **Display a message** option and type the title and message to be displayed in the fields provided.

  **b.** Create a custom view in Event Viewer and specify the name and ID number of the error displayed by the failing service in the Query Filter dialog box.

  **c.** In Event Viewer, configure an event log subscription and specify the name and ID number of the error displayed by the failing service in the Query Filter dialog box.

  **d.** In Performance Monitor, configure an alert that is triggered by the failing service. Then, select the **Display a message** option and type the title and message to be displayed in the fields provided.

## Foundation Topics

# Event Viewer

Event Viewer, found as a component of Server Manager and as a separate MMC console in the Administrative Tools folder, enables you to view logs of events generated by Windows and its applications. Actions you can perform with Event Viewer include the following:

- View events stored in multiple event logs. This helps you locate events related to a particular problem that you might be encountering on your server.

- Create and save event log filters for later reuse as custom views that display a preconfigured set of events that you might want to analyze when troubleshooting a particular type of problem. You can use this custom view whenever you encounter such a problem; you can also export the view to other computers and share it with other people.

- View alerts generated by data collector sets you configured with Performance Monitor. We discussed Performance Monitor in Chapter 19.

- Schedule tasks to run when a given event is logged. Event Viewer integrates with Task Scheduler to run a specified task whenever the given event occurs.

- Create and manage event log subscriptions. This enables you to collect events from remote computers and store them at a single location.

You can open Event Viewer by using any of the following methods:

- In Server Manager, expand **Diagnostics** and then select **Event Viewer**. This opens Event Viewer as a snap-in within the Server Manager console, as shown in Figure 20-1.

- Click **Start** and type `msconfig` in the Start menu Search field. From the Tools tab of System Configuration, select **Event Viewer** and then click **Launch**.

- Click **Start > Administrative Tools> Event Viewer**.

- Click **Start** and type `event` in the Start menu Search field. Select **Event Viewer** from the Programs list. Any of these last three methods opens the Event Viewer snap-in within its own MMC console.

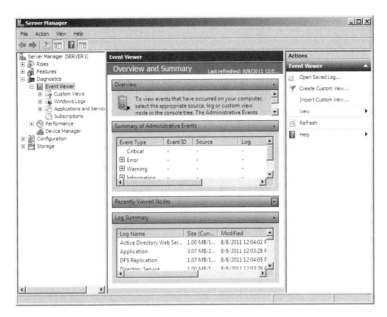

**Figure 20-1**   Here shown as a component of Server Manager, Event Viewer records events that have occurred on your server.

### Viewing Logs in Event Viewer

To view the actual event logs, expand the Event Viewer node in the console tree to reveal the Custom Views, Windows Logs, and Application Services Logs. The Custom Views node contains a Server Roles folder containing logs related to each server role installed on your server, as well as an Administrative Events and Printer Migration Events nodes.

Table 20-2 describes the event logs found in the Windows Logs node in Windows Server 2008.

**Table 20-2**   Windows Server 2008 Event Logs

| Event Log | Description |
| --- | --- |
| Application | Logs events related to applications running on the computer, including alerts generated by data collector sets. Any application written to Microsoft standards, including programs such as e-mail or antivirus applications, can record events in this log. |
| Security | Logs events related to security-related actions performed on the computer. To enable security event logging, you must configure auditing of the types of actions to be recorded. Remember that when you enable auditing of object access, you also need to configure NTFS auditing options on the files and folders you need to audit. |

| Event Log | Description |
|---|---|
| Setup | Logs events related to setup of applications. |
| System | Contains events related to actions taking place on the computer in general, including hardware-related events. Included are reasons for the failure of services to start and the cause of Stop (blue screen) errors. This log also records events related to network connectivity problems. |
| Forwarded Events | Contains events logged from remote computers. To enable this log, you must create an event subscription. |

Most logs in Event Viewer record three types of events—errors, warnings, and informational events—as shown in Figure 20-2. Error messages are represented by a red circle with a white exclamation mark in the center. Information messages are represented by a balloon with a blue "i" in the center, and warning messages are represented by a yellow triangle with a black exclamation mark in the center. Although not always true, an error is often preceded by one or more warning messages. A series of warning and error messages can describe the exact source of the problem, or at least point you in the right direction.

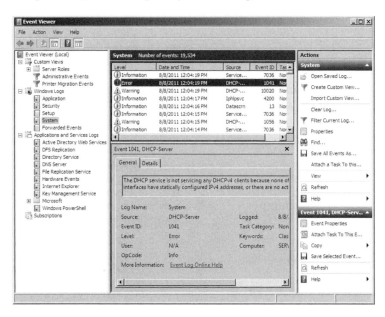

**Figure 20-2** Most Event Viewer logs record errors, warning events, and informational events.

To obtain additional information about an event, select it. The bottom of the central pane displays information related to the selected event. You can also right-click

an event and select **Event Properties** (or double-click the event) to display information about the event in its own dialog box (see Figure 20-3) that can be viewed without scrolling. From this dialog box, you can use the up and down arrows provided to
view the properties of other events. These arrows are useful in tracking the progress
of an incident that has recorded multiple events.

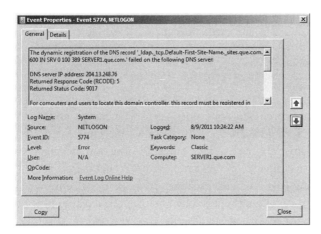

**Figure 20-3**    The Event Properties dialog box provides detailed information about the event.

**TIP**    You can view event logs generated by servers at your desktop computer running
Windows Vista or 7 by configuring an event log subscription for each server and using the Forwarded Events subnode mentioned in Table 20-2. Event log subscriptions
are discussed later in this chapter.

**NOTE**    For additional introductory information on Event Viewer and event logs, refer to "Event Logs" at http://technet.microsoft.com/en-us/library/cc722404.aspx and
"Threats and Countermeasures Guide: Event Log" at http://technet.microsoft.com/
en-us/library/hh125924(WS.10).aspx.

## Event Log Properties

Right-click any event log and choose **Properties** to bring up the log's Properties
dialog box, which provides general information about the event log, including its

current and maximum size. As shown in Figure 20-4, you can modify the maximum size (2 MB by default) and choose one of the following options for the action to be taken when the maximum log size is reached:

- **Overwrite events as needed (oldest events first):** The default option, this automatically overwrites the oldest events and is suitable in most situations.

- **Archive the log when full, do not overwrite events:** Automatically saves the event log as an .evtx file named with the current date when full. A new, empty log is started. This is the best option for use if you must ensure that no important events are lost.

- **Do not overwrite events (Clear logs manually):** When the log is full, no additional events are logged until you've cleared the log manually. If you select this option, you must commit to reviewing the log frequently enough so that the maximum size is not reached. To retain events and keep the log running, you must manually archive the log when it is nearing the full condition. Click the **Clear Log** command button to manually clear the logs.

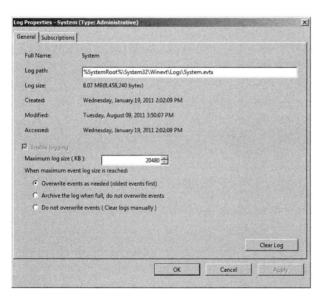

**Figure 20-4**  The Log Properties dialog box provides general information on the log and enables you to specify an option for the maximum log size.

To manually archive an event log, right-click the log in the console tree of Event Viewer and choose **Save All Events As**. Provide a log filename (file type .evtx), change the default path if necessary, and then click **Save**. You can view a saved log later by right-clicking the log and choosing **Open Saved Log**. Select the desired log and click **Open**.

### Applications and Services Logs

The Applications and Services Logs node contains events from single applications or services, as opposed to events with potential systemwide impact. The following four subtypes of logs are included:

- **Administrative:** Logs events that describe problems with well-defined solutions that an administrator can work with. For example, an event is logged when an application fails to connect to a printer. Included is a message that contains direct instructions providing steps to be done to rectify the problem.

- **Operational:** Logs events that can be used for analyzing and diagnosing a problem or occurrence. You can use these events to trigger utilities or tasks based on the problem or occurrence. For example, adding or removing a printer generates an operational event.

- **Analytic:** Contains events that aid in performance evaluations and trouble-shooting; such events might indicate problems that cannot be handled by user intervention. Because they are logged in high volume, you should only enable and log these types of events for limited time periods when diagnosing problems.

- **Debug:** Contains events that developers can use to troubleshoot issues with their programs.

**NOTE**   By default, the analytic and debug log types are hidden and disabled. To enable and use them, click **View > Show Analytic and Debug Logs** from the Event Viewer menu bar. This adds these logs to the console tree of Event Viewer. Then, right-click the log you want to enable and choose **Properties**. In the Properties dialog box that appears, select **Enable Logging** and then click **OK**.

Categories found under this node depend on the server roles and applications installed on the server, and typically include logs such as the following:

- **Active Directory Web Services:** Logs events related to the Active Directory Web Services (ADWS), which is a new Windows service in Windows Server 2008 R2 that provides a Web service interface to Active Directory Domain Services (AD DS) domains and Active Directory Lightweight Directory Services (AD LDS) instances. This log is created when you install AD DS or AD LDS on your server.

- **AppLocker:** Logs events related to the AppLocker feature, which is new to Windows Server 2008 R2 and provides enhanced capabilities for limiting what software can be installed and run on Windows 7/Server 2008 R2 computers.

- **DFS Replication:** Logs events related to the use of Distributed File System (DFS) replication. You are informed of the successful or failed status of replication, including the starting of the DFS Replication service. Refer to Chapter 10, "Configuring Distributed File System (DFS)," for more information.

- **Directory Service:** Found only on domain controllers, the Directory Service log records events related to actions taken on the AD DS database, such as online defragmentation. This log also records errors related to directory access problems.

- **DNS Server:** Found on DNS servers only, this log records events related to the operation of the DNS server service.

- **File Replication Service:** Similar to the DFS Replication log, but logs events related to the older file replication service used for AD DS replication and replication of the SYSVOL share prior to Windows Server 2008 R2.

- **Hardware Events:** Records events related to the server's hardware configuration.

- **Internet Explorer:** Records events related to the functioning of Internet Explorer.

- **Key Management Service:** Contains events related to Key Management Service (KMS), which is a lightweight service that assists you in activating multiple computers running Windows Vista/7/Server 2008 /R2.

- **Microsoft:** This folder expands to reveal a Windows subfolder containing sub-subfolders holding logs from a large range of services running on your computer. For example, the Windows Firewall With Advanced Security sub-subfolder holds event logs for ConnectionSecurity, ConnectionSecurityVerbose, Firewall, and FirewallVerbose.

## Customizing Event Logs

Windows Server 2008 enables you to customize your event logs so that you can more rapidly find events of particular interest. If you select a large number of auditable events, the Event Viewer logs can rapidly accumulate a large variety of events. Windows Server 2008 provides capabilities for customizing what appears in the Event Viewer window. For example, the System event log, by default, generates a large number of informational events with event ID 7036, which relate to Windows or particular services successfully starting or stopping, or other actions related to a computer's startup or shutdown. These events can easily be 75 percent of all events logged in the System log. Use the following steps to customize the information displayed:

1. Right-click the desired log and choose **Filter Current Log**. This displays the Filter Current Log dialog box, as shown in Figure 20-5.

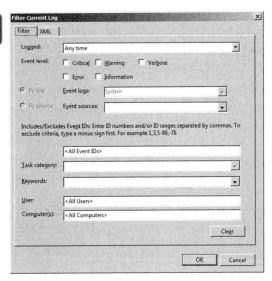

**Figure 20-5**   You can filter event logs according to several categories.

2. Configure the following properties as required:

   ▪ **Logged:** Select the time interval that you want to examine. You can choose from several default time ranges, including **Any time**, **Last hour**, **Last 12 hours**, **Last 24 hours**, **Last 7 days**, or **Last 30 days**. You can also select **Custom range** to display a dialog box that enables you to enter a custom date range or specify events logged on a specific date only.

   ▪ **Event level:** Choose the type(s) of events you want to view. Select **Verbose** to view extra details related to the viewed events.

   ▪ **By log:** Select the Windows logs or Applications and Services logs you want to include.

   ▪ **By source:** Select from an extensive range of Windows services, utilities, and components whose logs you want to include.

   ▪ **Event IDs:** Type the event IDs to be displayed by your custom view, separated by commas. You can include a range of IDs by using a hyphen; for example, to include IDs from 4624 to 4634, type `4624-4634`. To exclude an event ID, prefix it with a minus sign.

- **Task category:** Expand the drop-down list and select the categories you want to view.

- **Keywords:** Select the keywords that you want to include in the customized view.

- **User** and **Computer(s):** Select the usernames of the accounts to be displayed and the names of the computers to be displayed. Separate the names in each list by commas.

- **XML tab:** Enables you to specify an event filter as an XML query.

3. When finished, click **OK**. The details pane informs you that the log is filtered and provides a summary of the filter criteria used.

To edit filter criteria on a filtered event log, simply right-click it and choose **Filter Current Log** again. This re-opens the Filter Current Log dialog box, enabling you to make any desired changes. To remove the filter, right-click the log and choose **Clear Filter**.

### Creating and Using Custom Views

A custom view is essentially a filter that has been named and saved. You can reuse this filter on your computer or any other computer as desired. You can create a custom view based on any event log included in Event Viewer. Use the following steps:

1. Right-click the desired log in the console tree of Event Viewer and choose **Create Custom View**.

2. The Create Custom View dialog box appears and provides the same options as already shown in Figure 20-5 for filtering a log. Specify the desired options and click **OK**.

3. In the Save Filter to Custom View dialog box that appears (see Figure 20-6), select a node where the custom view is to be displayed and type a name and optional description for the custom view. If you want all users to be able to view the custom filter, select the **All Users** check box (as shown). Then, click **OK**.

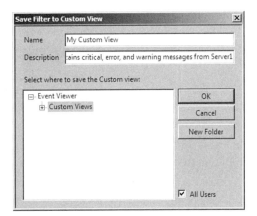

**Figure 20-6**    The Save Filter to Custom View dialog box enables you to save your custom view.

After you save the custom view, you can see this view by expanding the Custom Views node in the console tree to locate it by the name you provided.

**NOTE**    For more information on filtering event logs, refer to "Filter Displayed Events" at http://technet.microsoft.com/en-us/library/cc722058.aspx.

### Exporting and Importing Custom Views

Event Viewer also enables you to export custom views as XML files, so that you can import them to another computer using Event Viewer on that computer. Use the following steps:

1. Right-click the custom view in the console tree of Event Viewer and choose **Export Custom View**.

2. In the Save As dialog box that appears, accept the default path that is displayed or type a different path as required.

3. Specify a filename and click **Save**.

Use the following steps to import the custom view to another computer:

1. Right-click the node of Event Viewer under which you want the custom view to appear, and then choose **Import Custom View**.

2. In the Import Custom View dialog box that appears, navigate to the folder in which you stored the custom view, select the desired custom view, and click **Open**.

3. In the Import Custom View File dialog box, modify the name and add an optional description if desired. Select the location where the custom view is to be saved. To place the custom view in its own subfolder, click **New Folder** and type a name for the desired folder. If you want the view to be accessible to all users of the computer, select the **All Users** check box. Then, click **OK**.

**NOTE**   For more information on working with custom views, refer to "Create and Manage Custom Views" at http://technet.microsoft.com/en-us/library/cc766238. aspx.

## Configuring Event Log Subscriptions

Event Viewer includes a Subscriptions feature that enables you to collect event logs from a number of computers (termed *source computers* or *forwarding computers*) in a single, convenient location (termed the *collector computer*) that helps you keep track of events that occur on these computers. You can specify the events that will be collected and the local log in which they will be stored. After activating the subscription, you can view these event logs in the same manner as already discussed for local event logs.

The Event Subscriptions feature works by using Hypertext Transfer Protocol (HTTP) or Secure HTTP (HTTPS) to relay specified events from one or more source computers to a collector computer. It uses the Windows Remote Management (WinRM) and Windows Event Collector (Wecsvc) services to perform these actions and uses an XML file to store configuration information. To configure event log subscriptions, you must configure these services on both the source and collector computers.

You can configure Event Subscriptions to work in either of two ways:

- **Collector initiated:** The collector computer pulls the specified events from each of the source computers. This type is typically used where there are a limited number of easily identified source computers.

- **Source initiated:** Each source computer pushes the specified events to the collector computer. This type is typically used where there are a large number of source computers that are configured using Group Policy.

### Configuring the Source Computers to Forward Events

You need to run the `Winrm` and `Wecutil` commands at both the source and collector computers. To do so, log on to each source computer with an administrative user account (it is best to use a domain administrator account when configuring computers in an AD DS domain) and perform the following steps:

1. Add the computer account of the collector computer to the local Administrators group on each source computer.

2. Type the following command at an administrative command prompt:

   `Winrm quickconfig`

3. You receive messages stating `Create a WinRM listener on HTTP://* to accept WS-Man requests to any IP on this machine. Enable the WinRM firewall exception. Make these changes [y/n]?`. Type **y** and press **Enter** to make these changes.

4. Add a Windows Firewall exception for Remote Event Log Management at each source computer. We discussed configuring Windows Firewall in Chapter 4, "Configuring Windows Firewall with Advanced Security."

5. Add an account with administrative privileges to the Event Log Readers group at each source computer, and specify this account in the Configure Advanced Subscription Settings dialog box mentioned in the next section.

### Configuring the Collector Computer to Forward Receive Events

Also, log on to the collector computer with an administrative account and perform the following steps:

1. Open an administrative command prompt and type the following command:

   `Wecutil qc`

2. You receive the message `The service startup mode will be changed to Delay-Start. Would you like to proceed (Y- yes or N- no)?`. To proceed, type **y** and then press **Enter**.

3. Type `winrm set winrm/config/client @{TrustedHosts="<sources>"}`. In this command, `<sources>` is a list of the names of all workgroup source computers separated by commas.

Having run these commands, the computers are now ready to forward and collect events. Note that in a workgroup environment, you can only use collector-initiated subscriptions.

**TIP**   Remember that you must issue the `winrm quickconfig` command at each source computer, and the `wecutil qc` command at the collector computer (and not the other way around).

**NOTE**   For more information on the `winrm` and `wecutil` commands, refer to "Configure Computers to Forward and Collect Events" at http://technet.microsoft.com/en-us/library/cc748890.aspx.

### Configuring Event Log Subscriptions

After you complete the preceding procedures at all source and collector computers, you are ready to configure event log subscriptions at the collector computer by using the following procedure:

1. In the console tree of Event Viewer, right-click the type of log you want to configure a subscription for and choose **Properties**.

2. Select the **Subscriptions** tab of the Properties dialog box that appears.

3. If the Windows Event Collector Service is not running, Event Viewer displays the message box shown in Figure 20-7, asking you to start this service. Click **Yes** to proceed.

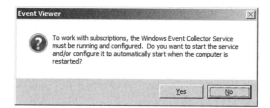

**Figure 20-7**   You are asked to start the Windows Event Collector Service before you can create an event log subscription.

4. Click **Create** to create your first event subscription. This displays the Subscription Properties dialog box, as shown in Figure 20-8.

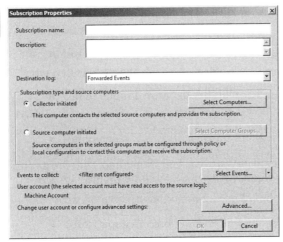

**Figure 20-8**   The Subscription Properties dialog box enables you to configure an event log subscription.

5. Under **Subscription name**, provide an informative name that you will use to locate your event log subscription later. If desired, type an optional description in the field provided.

6. By default, the **Destination log** field displays the log type, according to the Windows log you right-clicked in Step 1 of this procedure. To choose a different log type, select it from the drop-down list.

7. Under **Subscription type and source computers**, select **Collector initiated** and click the **Select Computers** button to specify the computers from which you want to collect event data. Or select **Source computer initiated** and click **Select Computer Groups** to specify groups of computers that have been configured through Group Policy to receive the subscription from the computer at which you are working. In either case, you can also select computers from an AD DS domain.

8. Under **Events to collect**, click **Select Events** to display the Query Filter dialog box, which provides the same options as shown previously in Figure 20-5 and enables you to select the event types that will be included in the subscription.

9. If necessary, click **Advanced** to display the Advanced Subscription Settings dialog box shown in Figure 20-9, which enables you to select the following options that specify the user account that has access to the source logs (appears only if you selected the **Collector initiated** option in Step 7) and optimize event delivery.

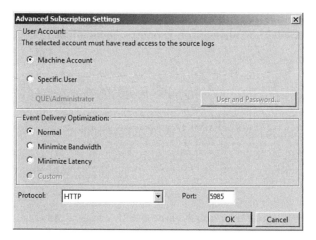

**Figure 20-9**  The Advanced Subscription Settings dialog box enables you to specify user account and event delivery settings.

- **Machine Account:** This is the default account that provides access to the required logs.

- **Specific User:** If necessary, you can specify a user other than the one indicated. To do so, click **Specific User**, click the **User and Password** button, and type the required user/password information.

- **Normal:** This is the default option, which provides reliable event delivery without conserving bandwidth. It is appropriate unless you need tighter control over bandwidth use or need forwarded events delivered as quickly as possible. It uses pull delivery mode, batches five items at a time, and specifies a batch timeout of 15 minutes.

- **Minimize Bandwidth:** This option controls the use of bandwidth by reducing the frequency of event delivery, using push delivery mode and setting a batch timeout of 6 hours.

- **Minimize Latency:** Ensures the most rapid delivery of events. Appropriate for collecting alerts or critical event, this option uses push delivery mode and sets a batch timeout of 30 seconds.

- **Protocol:** Normally set to HTTP, you can select **HTTPS** to provide for secure forwarding of event information using the encrypted HTTPS protocol. Use of HTTPS requires that you configure the server with a computer certificate and create an exception in Windows Firewall for TCP port 443 used by HTTPS. Also, at the collector computer, you need to run the following command:

```
Winrm quickconfig -transport:https
```

10. When finished, click **OK** to close the Advanced Subscription Settings dialog box and click **OK** again to close the Subscription Properties dialog box.

**TIP**   If you receive an `Access is denied` error message after configuring an event log subscription, verify the User Account settings. The specific user account that you configure should be a member of the computer's Event Log Readers group or the Administrators group. An exam question might test your knowledge of this fact.

**NOTE**   If you select a different user account from the Advanced Subscription Settings dialog box, the account you select must be a member of the local computer's Event Log Readers group or the Administrators group.

**TIP**   You can use the `Wecutil cs` command to create an event subscription from the command line. This is useful for scripting purposes or when working at a computer running the Server Core installation of Windows Server 2008 R2. For more information on the `Wecutil` command-line utility, refer to "`Wecutil`" at http://technet.microsoft.com/en-us/library/cc753183(WS.10).aspx.

**NOTE**   For more information on creating and managing event log subscriptions, refer to "Event Subscriptions" at http://technet.microsoft.com/en-us/library/cc749183.aspx and "Manage Subscriptions" at http://technet.microsoft.com/en-us/library/cc749140.aspx, plus the links contained therein.

## Configuring Tasks from Events

Event Viewer in Windows Server 2008 enables you to associate tasks with events. Event Viewer integrates with Task Scheduler to make this action possible. Use the following steps to create a task:

1. Right-click the desired event and choose **Attach Task To This Event**. This starts the Create Basic Task Wizard, as shown in Figure 20-10.

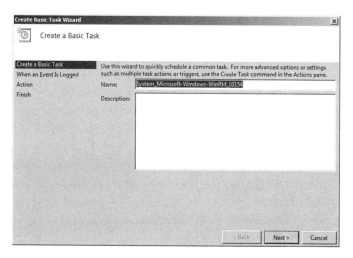

**Figure 20-10**  The Create Basic Task Wizard enables you to specify an action that will be taken each time a specific event takes place.

2. The wizard supplies a default name according to the selected event. If necessary, change this name and provide an optional description. Then, click **Next**.

3. The When a Specific Event Is Logged page displays information about the log, source, and event ID of the selected event. Review this information and click **Next**.

4. On the Action page, specify the action to be performed, and then click **Next**. You have the following options:

   ■ **Start a program:** Type the path to the executable file or click **Browse** to locate the desired program. Also specify arguments if needed.

   ■ **Send an e-mail:** Type the e-mail addresses, subject, and text to be sent. Click **Browse** to locate an attachment if you want to include one. Also, type the DNS name of the SMTP server that will relay the message.

   ■ **Display a message:** This action displays a message box on the desktop. Type the title and message to be displayed in the fields provided.

5. Review the information on the Summary page. If necessary, click **Back** to modify any components of the task. To specify additional properties, select the check box labeled **Open the Properties dialog for this task when I click Finish**. When done, click **Finish** to create the task.

You can also attach a task to an event log. Right-click the desired log in the console tree of Event Viewer and choose **Attach a Task To this Log**. Furthermore, you can attach a task to a custom view that you've created within the Custom Views node. Right-click the desired custom view and choose **Attach Task To This Custom View**. In either case, follow the steps in the Create Basic Task Wizard, which are similar to those in the preceding procedure.

**TIP**   Configuring an e-mail notification is a good way to ensure that you are kept up-to-date with regard to any events that happen on servers when you are not physically present at servers for which you are responsible.

## Exam Preparation Tasks

## Review All the Key Topics

Review the most important topics in this chapter, noted with the key topics icon in the outer margin of the page. Table 20-3 lists a reference of these key topics and the page numbers on which each is found.

**Table 20-3**   Key Topics for Chapter 20

| Key Topic Element | Description | Page Number |
|---|---|---|
| Table 20-2 | Describes available Windows logs in Windows Server 2008. | 800 |
| Figure 20-2 | Shows typical Windows event logs. | 801 |
| List | Describes the subtypes of logs in the Applications and Services Logs node of Event Viewer. | 804 |
| Figure 20-5 | Displays options available for filtering event logs. | 806 |
| List | Describes the two types of event log subscriptions. | 809 |
| Figure 20-8 | Displays options available for configuring event log subscriptions. | 812 |
| List | Shows you how to configure a task to be run when an event occurs. | 814 |

## Complete the Tables and Lists from Memory

Print a copy of Appendix B, "Memory Tables," (found on the CD), or at least the section for this chapter, and complete the tables and lists from memory. Appendix C, "Memory Tables Answer Key," also on the CD, includes the completed tables and lists to check your work.

## Definitions of Key Terms

Define the following key terms from this chapter, and check your answers in the Glossary.

collector computer, custom view, event log subscription, Event Viewer, filtering, source computer

This chapter covers the following subjects:

- **Simple Network Management Protocol (SNMP):** SNMP enables you to gather data such as network protocol information, hardware and software configuration data, usage, event, and error statistics, and so on. This section shows you how to use SNMP to gather data from network computers and devices such as bridges and routers.

- **Network Monitor:** Network Monitor is Microsoft's protocol analyzer tool that enables you to capture and analyze packets being transmitted across the network. This section shows you how to use Network Monitor to accomplish these actions.

- **Connection Security Rules Monitoring:** This section shows you how to obtain a quick summary of configured connection security rules information in Windows Firewall with Advanced Security.

# CHAPTER 21

# Collecting Network Data

The monitoring of servers and networks is vital in any organization to ensure that the network keeps humming along and users are able to access resources in a timely and proper fashion. In Chapter 19, "Configuring Performance Monitoring," you learned about monitoring and logging performance counters so that you could track changes in the performance of your servers over a period of time. Following up, Chapter 20, "Configuring Event Logs," showed you how to view and filter event logs, and customize these logs and forward them to a central point to facilitate the locating of troublesome occurrences. This chapter continues on the general theme of server monitoring by looking at methods used to collect and interpret network data. Problems or intrusions on the network often reveal themselves in the content of packets transmitted over the wire; in this chapter, you learn how to capture and interpret information contained in these packets as an aid in monitoring and troubleshooting events occurring on the network.

## "Do I Know This Already?" Quiz

The "Do I Know This Already?" quiz allows you to assess whether you should read this entire chapter or simply jump to the "Exam Preparation Tasks" section for review. If you are in doubt, read the entire chapter. Table 21-1 outlines the major headings in this chapter and the corresponding "Do I Know This Already?" quiz questions. You can find the answers in Appendix A, "Answers to the 'Do I Know This Already?' Quizzes."

**Table 21-1** "Do I Know This Already?" Foundation Topics Section-to-Question Mapping

| Foundations Topics Section | Questions Covered in This Section |
| --- | --- |
| Simple Network Management Protocol (SNMP) | 1–3 |
| Network Monitor | 4–9 |
| Connection Security Rules Monitoring | 10 |

1. Which of the following best describes the purpose of using SNMP on your network?

   a. For monitoring counters that provide information on how a server's network interface card is performing

   b. For providing a simple interface for mail delivery across the network

   c. For monitoring devices on your network in network management systems for situations that warrant administrative attention

   d. For viewing the content of packets being transmitted across the network to and from your server

2. Which of the following message types is the only one that an SNMP agent can send to the management system in an unsolicited fashion without first being requested by the management agent?

   a. Get-request

   b. Get-next-request

   c. Get-bulk-request

   d. Set-request

   e. Get-response

   f. Trap

3. You are configuring a computer to act as an SNMP agent. You want to enable this computer to process SNMP SET requests but not to create new entries in the SNMP tables, so you access the Security tab of the SNMP Service properties dialog box. Which of the following options should you specify?

   a. NOTIFY

   b. READ ONLY

   c. READ WRITE

   d. READ CREATE

4. You want to install Network Monitor on your Windows Server 2008 R2 computer so that you can capture and analyze network traffic that crosses the server's network adapter card. What method must you use to accomplish this task?

   a. In Server Manager, access the Add Roles Wizard and then select **Network Monitor** from the Select Server Roles page.

   b. In Server Manager, access the Add Roles Wizard and then select **Network Policy and Access Services** from the Select Server Roles page. Then, on the Select Role Services page, select **Network Monitor**.

   c. In Server Manager, access the Add Features Wizard and then select **Network Monitor** from the Select Server Features page.

   d. Download the Network Monitor installer file from Microsoft and then run this file on your server.

5. You are using Network Monitor to capture and analyze the traffic crossing the network adapter card on your server. Which of the following criteria can you use to filter the traffic to display only selected frames? (Choose all that apply.)

   a. Frames captured using a specified network adapter

   b. Frames using a specified protocol

   c. Frames originating from a specified IP address

   d. Frames originating from a computer running a specific operating system

6. A user at a client computer whose IPv4 address is 192.168.3.101 is having difficulty accessing network resources on your company's AD DS network, and you suspect that DNS name resolution is the problem. You want to run Network Monitor and capture DNS requests that are sent to and from this computer without capturing any other network packets. Which of the following filter expressions should you use to accomplish this task?

   a. **DNS && IPv4.address==192.168.3.101**

   b. **DNS || IPv4.address==192.168.3.101**

   c. **DNS && IPv4.sourceaddress==192.168.3.101**

   d. **DNS || IPv4.sourceaddress==192.168.3.101**

**7.** You have been running Network Monitor from a server named Server3, which also hosts several mission-critical applications. After several users reported slow access to applications on this server, you use Performance Monitor to check server performance, and discover that Network Monitor is consuming too much memory to allow the applications to run properly. You need to keep Network Monitor running on this machine but must ensure that the applications have enough memory to function properly. What should you do?

   **a.** Access the Capture tab of the Network Monitor Options dialog box and deselect the **Record Capture Filter** option.

   **b.** Access the Capture tab of the Network Monitor Options dialog box and deselect the **Enable Conversations** option.

   **c.** Access the Parser Profiles tab of the Network Monitor Options dialog box and select the **High Performance Capturing** profile.

   **d.** Access the Parser Profiles tab of the Network Monitor Options dialog box and select the **Faster Parsing** profile.

**8.** You are running Network Monitor 3.4 on a Windows Server 2008 R2 computer, which is a member server on your company's network, which includes over 20 different servers. After capturing some frames, you notice a bewildering array of IP addresses and you waste a lot of time deciphering these addresses to the corresponding server names. You want the server names to appear directly in the network captures. What should you do?

   **a.** Create a display filter and select **DHCP** from the filter list. Then, click **Apply** to apply the filter to your capture.

   **b.** Create a new capture filter that specifies **DHCP** and apply the filter to the capture.

   **c.** Right-click each IP address and select **Resolve to Name**.

   **d.** Access the Aliases dialog box and add the server name for each required IP address to the list on this table. Then, click **Apply**.

9. You have been using Network Monitor to obtain an overall view of the type of network packets being transmitted across the various segments of the network. A computer named Server7 appears to be sending and receiving a large number of packets and you want to obtain a quick view of the network traffic across Server7 without installing Network Monitor on it. You will later observe and interpret this capture from a different computer. What should you do?

   a. Open a command prompt on Server7 and run the `Nmcap /network * / capture /file caputrename.cap` command.

   b. From Network Monitor on another computer on your network, select the **Connect to another computer** option, and then specify **Server7**.

   c. Download Network Monitor OneClick from the Microsoft website and run this program on Server7.

   d. You cannot perform this task without downloading and installing Network Monitor on Server7.

10. Which of the following are properties of a connection security rule that you can display from the Connection Security Rules subnode of the Monitoring node in the Windows Firewall with Advanced Security snap-in? (Choose all that apply.)

    a. Addresses, ports, and protocols specified with the chosen rule.

    b. Information on any connections that have been blocked because of violating the chosen rule.

    c. Authentication methods being used with the chosen rule.

    d. Local and remote tunnel endpoints and interface types.

    e. Whether the rule applies authorization and exempts IPSec-protected connections.

## Foundation Topics

# Simple Network Management Protocol

*Simple Network Management Protocol* (SNMP) is a component of the TCP/IP protocol suite. Found within the Application layer of the Operation Systems Interconnection (OSI) model, SNMP was originally developed to monitor and troubleshoot routers and bridges on the Internet. Defined in RFC 1157, SNMP enables you to perform actions such as configuring devices remotely, monitoring network performance, or detecting network faults or inappropriate access to the network. It is essential that you understand SNMP to manage modern networks, and as such, Microsoft expects you to be familiar with SNMP for purposes of the 70-642 exam.

### How SNMP Functions

SNMP consists of the following two primary components:

- **SNMP management system:** A computer on which you have installed SNMP management software that sends information and update requests to devices configured as SNMP agents. The management system requests information from the agent such as the available hard disk space or the number of open files. If the management system has write access to the device, it can also modify the device's configuration.

- **SNMP agent:** A device such as a computer or network component on which SNMP software has been installed. The SNMP agent gathers information in response to requests from a SNMP management system. In general, agents only respond to messages from SNMP management systems; they do not originate messages except when configured to report a specific event such as an attempt at inappropriate access.

### Management Information Base

The Management Information Base (MIB) is a database that holds the information that a management system can request and the information returned by agents. Included within the MIB is a set of objects that represent various types of information about a network device, such as the number of active sessions or the operating system version. Objects within the MIB namespace are arranged in a hierarchical fashion such that each manageable object can be assigned a globally unique name. When the management system sends a request to an agent, it includes this globally unique name in the request. An example of a namespace is 1.3.6.1.4.311, which has been assigned to Microsoft. Under that branch, Microsoft is authorized to create additional MIBs. Organizations can assign names to objects under this branch that are unique to their network.

The Microsoft Windows SNMP service provides an internal infrastructure that allows third-party software and hardware developers to create their own MIBs for use with the Windows SNMP service. The following MIBs are supported by the SNMP service in Windows Server 2008:

- **Internet MIB II:** Internet MIB II is an extension of the previous standard, MIB I. Defined in RFC 1212, it defines 171 objects required for troubleshooting on fault and configuration analysis.

- **LAN Manager MIB II:** Contains approximately 90 objects required for networking, such as share, session, user, and log-on information. These objects are generally read-only because of the nonsecure nature of SNMP.

- **DHCP MIB:** Contains about 14 objects for monitoring DHCP server activity, including numbers of items such as actively leased addresses, failures, and DHCP discover requests.

- **WINS MIB:** Contains approximately 70 objects that monitor WINS server activity, including such items as the number of resolution requests that succeeded or failed and the date and time of the last replication.

- **IIS MIBs:** Define objects used by Internet Information Services (IIS) to monitor Hypertext Transfer Protocol (HTTP) and File Transfer Protocol (FTP) activity. They are automatically installed when you install IIS.

- **RADIUS Server MIBs:** Define objects used by the Remote Authentication Dial-In User Service (RADIUS) to monitor RADIUS server authentication and accounting activity. They are automatically installed when you install the Microsoft Internet Authentication Service (IAS).

## SNMP Messages

Messages exchanged by SNMP management systems and agents include the following:

- **Get-request:** Sent by the management system to request information about a single MIB object or an SNMP agent, such as the number of packets forwarded.

- **Get-next-request:** An extended request sent by an SNMP management system for browsing an entire tree of management objects. In response to this message, an agent returns the identity and value of the next object in the MIB.

This request type is useful for dynamic tables such as IPv4 or IPv6 routing tables.

- **Get-bulk-request:** Sent by the management system to request that the data sent by the agent be as large as possible within the constraints of maximum message size.

- **Set-request:** Sent by the management system to assign an updated value for an MIB object. This message type enables the management system to remotely configure SNMP agents.

- **Get-response:** Sent by the SNMP agent in response to a Get-request, Get-next-request, Get-bulk-request, or Set-request message.

- **Trap:** An unsolicited message sent by an SNMP agent to an SNMP management system when the agent detects a certain type of event, such as a system restart or an attempted intrusion.

> **CAUTION**   SNMP messages are sent unencrypted in a clear-text format. You need to use an encryption protocol, such as IP Security (IPSec), to protect SNMP messages. Refer to Chapter 4, "Configuring Windows Firewall with Advanced Security" for more information on IPSec.

### SNMP Communities

A *community* is a logical group of hosts that belong together and all run the SNMP service. Every community includes at least one management system and multiple agents. It serves to organize systems into groups for a logical management scheme.

A case-sensitive community name is used to identify communities. The default community name is `public` and all hosts initially belong to it. For proper security, you should supply a unique name. Agents can be members of multiple communities at the same time, in order to communicate with SNMP managers in different communities. Figure 21-1 shows a sample grouping containing two distinct communities, Alpha and Beta.

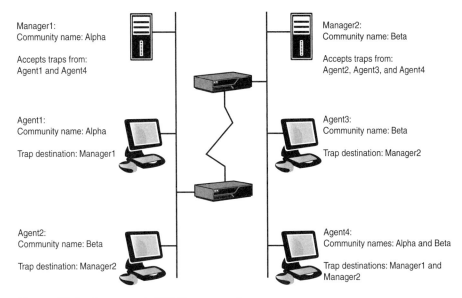

Manager1:
Community name: Alpha

Accepts traps from:
Agent1 and Agent4

Manager2:
Community name: Beta

Accepts traps from:
Agent2, Agent3, and Agent4

Agent1:
Community name: Alpha

Trap destination: Manager1

Agent3:
Community name: Beta

Trap destination: Manager2

Agent2:
Community name: Beta

Trap destination: Manager2

Agent4:
Community names: Alpha and Beta

Trap destinations: Manager1 and
Manager2

**Figure 21-1**   An example SNMP community.

Only managers and agents that belong to the same community can communicate. In
this example:

- Agent1 can send and receive messages to Manager1 because they are both
  members of the Alpha community.

- Agent2 and Agent3 can send and receive messages to Manager2 because they
  are both members of the Beta community.

- Agent4 can send and receive messages to both Manager1 and Manager2 because Agent4 is a member of both Alpha and Beta communities.

### How SNMP Functions

The following is a simple description of a typical SNMP request and response:

1. A SNMP management system sends a request to an SNMP agent, such as a
   Get-request or Get-next-request message. This message includes one or more
   data objects and a community name, and is sent to the agent's IPv4 address
   and the destination UDP port 161.

2. The SNMP agent receives the message. The agent verifies the community
   name; if invalid, the message is discarded. If the message is valid, it is passed to
   the appropriate MIB component, which returns the requested information to
   the agent.

3. The SNMP agent sends a Get-response message with the community name to the management system.

---

**NOTE**   For more introductory information on SNMP, refer to Appendix B of "TCP/IP Fundamentals for Microsoft Windows" at www.microsoft.com/download/en/confirmation.aspx?id=8781.

---

**TIP**   Remember that management systems and agents that must communicate with each other must belong to the same community. Also, remember that you can configure an agent to belong to multiple communities so that it can send messages to more than one management system.

---

### Installing and Configuring SNMP

In both the original and R2 versions of Windows Server 2008, SNMP is included as a server feature. Use the following procedure to install SNMP:

1. Open Server Manager to the Features node and click **Add Features**.

2. The Add Features Wizard opens with the Select Features page. Select **SNMP Services**, as shown in Figure 21-2, and click **Next**.

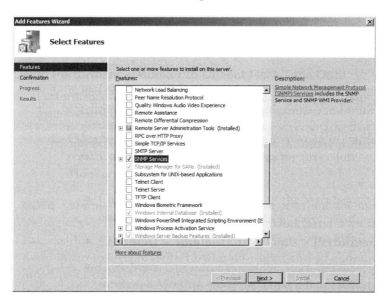

**Figure 21-2**   SNMP is installed as a server feature in Windows Server 2008 R2.

3. The Confirm Installation Services page informs you that the SNMP service and SNMP Windows Management Instrumentation (WMI) provider will be installed. Click **Install** to proceed.

4. The Installation Progress page tracks the installation of SNMP. When finished, the Installation Results page appears. Click **Close**.

5. If requested, click **Yes** to restart the server and complete the installation of the SNMP feature.

SNMP does not possess its own snap-in; rather, you configure SNMP from the Services snap-in. Use the following procedure:

1. Click **Start > Administrative Tools > Computer Management**, then expand **Services and Applications** and click **Services** to display the list of services in the details pane. You can also click **Start**, type `services` in the Start menu Search field, and click **Services**.

2. Right-click **SNMP Service** and choose **Properties** to display the SNMP Service Properties dialog box.

3. Configure the options described in Table 21-2 on the Agent, Traps, and Security tabs.

**Table 21-2**   Important Configurable SNMP Service Properties

| Tab | Configurable Properties |
|---|---|
| Agent | Enables you to specify the name of an individual responsible for maintaining the SNMP service, as well as the physical location of the computer. Also, select from the following services to be enabled on this computer, as shown in Figure 21-3:<br><br>• **Physical:** Specifies whether this computer manages physical devices, such as repeaters or hubs.<br><br>• **Applications:** Specifies whether this computer uses any applications that use TCP/IP to transmit data. You should always select this option, because by just using SNMP, you need to have TCP/IP set up.<br><br>• **Datalink and subnetwork:** Specifies whether the computer manages a bridge.<br><br>• **Internet:** Specifies whether this computer is an IP gateway (router).<br><br>• **End-to-end:** Specifies whether this computer is an IP host. This option should always be selected, because the computer is most likely an IP host. |

**Table 21-2**   Important Configurable SNMP Service Properties (*Countinued*)

| Tab | Configurable Properties |
| --- | --- |
| Traps | As shown in Figure 21-4, this tab enables you to specify the community name and trap destinations served by this computer. Type the required community name in the field provided and click **Add to list**. To add trap destinations, click **Add** and type the hostname or IP address in the SNMP Service Configuration dialog box that appears, and click **Add** again. Repeat these steps as needed to add additional communities and trap destinations. |
| Security | As shown in Figure 21-5, this tab enables you to restrict SNMP communications for the SNMP agent, permitting it to communicate with only a specific list of communities. To enable the agent to send trap messages, select the check box labeled **Send authentication trap** (as shown) and click **Add** under Accepted Community names. Note that a host communicating with this agent must belong to a community listed here for the SNMP service to accept requests. In the SNMP Service Configuration dialog box shown in Figure 21-6 that appears, add the required community name and choose from the following available rights for the community being added:<br><br>■ NONE: Prevents this host from processing any SNMP requests.<br><br>■ NOTIFY: Permits this host to send only SNMP traps to the community.<br><br>■ READ ONLY: Prevents this host from processing SNMP SET requests.<br><br>■ READ WRITE: Permits this host to process SNMP SET requests.<br><br>■ READ CREATE: Enables this host to create new entries in the SNMP tables.<br><br>To permit the computer to accept any queries originating from any host in any community, select the radio button labeled Accept SNMP packets from any host. To limit SNMP to respond to only a specified set of hosts, select Accept SNMP packets from these hosts and click Add to specify the name or IP address of a permitted host. Then repeat as necessary to add additional hosts. To modify any community name or host, including the specified community rights, select the appropriate Edit button and make the changes in the dialog box that appears. To remove a community name or host, select it and click the appropriate Delete button. |

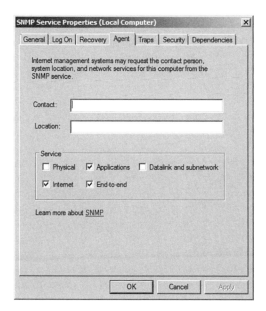

**Figure 21-3** Configuring SNMP Agent properties.

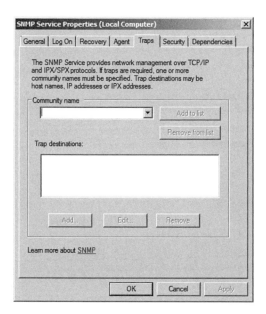

**Figure 21-4** Specifying properties for SNMP traps.

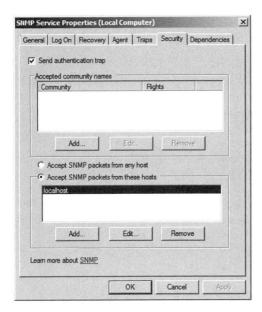

**Figure 21-5**   Specifying accepted community names and SNMP hosts.

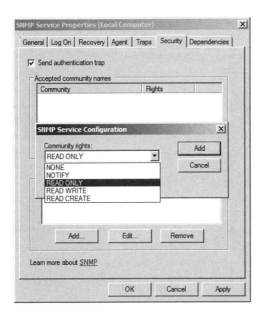

**Figure 21-6**   You can choose from five levels of community rights.

**NOTE**   For more information on configuring SNMP service properties, refer to "SNMP" at http://technet.microsoft.com/en-us/library/cc733024.aspx and select the appropriate tab from the list in the left-hand column of this page.

## Network Monitor

Troubleshooting problems on your network often involves the need to critically examine the frames (packets) being transmitted across the network in order to determine the cause. Doing so can involve the use of a *protocol analyzer*. Also known as a network analyzer or packet analyzer, a protocol analyzer is a hardware device or software program that enables you to capture, store, and analyze each packet that crosses your network. You can see a breakdown of each packet according to protocol in the order in which they were received. You can analyze packets at all levels of the OSI model to determine the cause of the problem. Refer to Chapter 1, "Configuring IPv4 and IPv6 Addressing," for information on the OSI model and its layers. Microsoft provides a very capable software-based protocol analyzer in *Network Monitor*.

### Concepts of Protocol Analyzers

The following steps describe the action of a protocol analyzer in simple fashion:

1. Capture a copy of every packet on the wire by operating in a promiscuous capture mode, which is a mode that captures all packets regardless of the address to which they are being sent.

2. Time stamp the packets.

3. Filter out the undesired packets.

4. Display a breakdown of the various layers of protocols in a bit by bit fashion.

You can save these packet traces and retrieve them later for analysis. After capturing a packet from the wire, the analyzer breaks down the headers and describes every bit of each header in detail.

Although the act of capturing and time stamping the packets is simple, beginners tend to capture every packet on a segment when attempting to troubleshoot a specific problem. The only problem is that such an action captures a very large volume of network traffic. Analyzing these packets can rapidly become a daunting task.

Network Monitor provides filters to help you quickly and easily isolate the problem, as you will see later in this chapter.

The problem at hand determines the type of packets you should be collecting. Ensure that you're familiar with the protocols so that you know what to look for. For example, if you are troubleshooting a DNS problem, you have a client that is unable to determine the IP address for a given network resource. You know the sequence of DNS name resolution; this fact should help you determine the packets that you should be looking for.

Network Monitor enables you to capture, view, and analyze frames (packets) as they are transmitted over a network to all network adapter cards on your computer. By analyzing these frames, you can troubleshoot network problems, for example when users cannot log on because they are unable to communicate with domain controllers, DNS servers, or other servers.

It can perform security-related actions, such as the following:

- Detection of intrusion attempts and successes.

- Detection of unauthorized users and tracing their activity on the network.

- Creation of a record of actions that can include unauthorized attempts at server or network access, by generating logs of captures that provide information on network actions including source and destination addresses, protocols, and data transferred.

You can filter Network Monitor to capture or display only frames that meet certain criteria, thereby shortening the long list of frames included in the Frame Summary pane and facilitating the location of a certain frame type. Some of the more common filter criteria are the following:

- Frames captured by a specified network adapter

- Frames using a specified protocol

- Frames with a specified property, such as those originating from a specified IP address

## Placement of Protocol Analyzers

For a protocol analyzer to capture every packet on the network, the network interface card and its driver must support promiscuous mode operations—in other words, it must capture error packets and packets addressed to other devices. Further, the analyzer must be able to capture broadcast and multicast traffic.

To provide a complete analysis of a network containing multiple LAN and/or WAN segments, you must figure out where to place your network analyzers. It is not necessary to place an analyzer on every network segment. On the other hand, it is advantageous to deploy multiple analyzers. The layout of your network and the type of devices connecting network segments affect your decision in placing your analyzers. The following are several considerations you should think of:

- A hub functions as a multiport repeater. Consequently, traffic sent or received by any one computer is visible to all computers connected to the hub. So you can connect your protocol analyzer to any port on the hub.

- A bridge isolates network traffic on each network segment that it spans. Consequently, you should place protocol analyzers on each side of the bridge.

- A switch is a multiport bridge that isolates traffic on multiple network segments. Consequently, you should use a hub to connect the switch port, the computer or host to be analyzed, and the protocol analyzer. This enables you to see all traffic being sent or received by the computer.

- A router isolates and directs traffic according to the network address. As a result, an analyzer placed on one side of the router sees only traffic on that side. Consequently, you should consider locating an analyzer on each side of the router or loading analyzer agents on the router.

- Testing of WAN links is similar in that you should deploy analyzers on both sides of the WAN links or connect analyzers or agents to the IP router. This might require assistance from your WAN link provider to properly make a physical connection to the WAN link.

### Installing and Running Microsoft Network Monitor

Network Monitor is not included with Windows Server 2008 R2 by default. You need to download the executable file and install it. You also need to download and install a parser file. This tool queries the captured network traffic and provides customized output formats. The parser can also query other monitoring data, such as log files, XML files, and CSV files, as well as data sources such as the event logs, the registry, the file system, and AD DS. Use the following steps:

1. Access www.microsoft.com/downloads/details.aspx?familyid=983b941d-06cb-4658-b7f6-3088333d062f&displaylang=en to download Network Monitor 3.4 (or the most recent version) as an executable (.exe) file. Also, access http://nmparsers.codeplex.com/releases/view/75878 to download the Log Parser 3.4.2748 file. Save these files to a convenient location on your computer.

2. Double-click the Network Monitor installer file and click **Run** on the Internet Explorer - Security Warning dialog box that appears.

3. You are informed that Microsoft Network Monitor Capture and Parser engine will be installed, followed by the Microsoft Network Monitor Parsers. Click **Yes** to continue.

4. The Microsoft Network Monitor 3.4 (Capture and Parser Engine) Setup Wizard starts with a Welcome page. Click **Next**.

5. Accept the end user license agreement and click **Next**.

6. You might be asked if you want to use Microsoft Update to keep your computer secure and up-to-date. Select an option as desired and click **Next**.

7. The Choose Setup Type page provides a choice of three setup types as shown in Figure 21-7. Choose the most appropriate setup type for your needs. (For learning purposes, it is adequate to select **Typical**.)

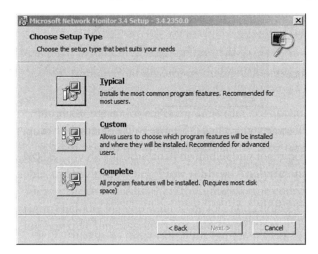

**Figure 21-7**   You receive a choice of three setup types when installing Network Monitor.

8. The Ready to Install page informs you that the wizard is ready to install Network Monitor. If desired, select the option to create a shortcut on the desktop. Click **Install**.

9. The Installing Network Monitor page tracks installation progress, and then the Completing the Setup Wizard page informs you when installation is complete. Click **Finish**. You might be asked to log off and log back on before performing a capture.

10. The Log Parser installation runs automatically. Accept the UAC prompt if you receive one.

11. When informed that the Log Parser 3.4.2748 has been installed, click **Finish**.

## Using Network Monitor to Capture Network Data

After installation completes, use the following steps to run Network Monitor and view captured data in real time:

1. Click **Start > All Programs > Microsoft Network Monitor 3.4** or double-click the desktop icon to start the program. Network Monitor starts and displays the interface shown in Figure 21-8 that includes a summary of new features as well as several how-to tips.

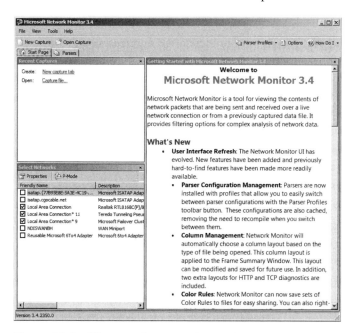

**Figure 21-8**   When you first start Network Monitor, you see a summary of new features.

2. To capture network traffic, click **New capture tab** in the Recent Captures section. A tab named Capture1 by default is added at the top of the window that displays a multipane arrangement within which captured data will be displayed.

3. Click **Start** from the toolbar or the Capture menu to capture network traffic across the network adapter card of your server.

4. As shown in Figure 21-9, each frame captured creates one line within the Frame Summary pane, including such details as source and destination computers (name or IP address), protocol name, and description. The time offset is the number of seconds elapsed since the capture was started.

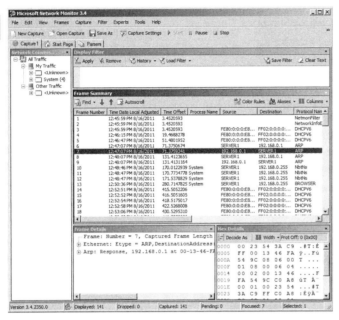

**Figure 21-9**   Network Monitor provides information on all frames that it captures.

5. To display information about a particular frame, select it. The Frame Details pane provides information on the selected frame, and the Hex Details pane provides a hexadecimal rendering of the bits contained within the frame.

6. To view additional information about the selected frame in the Frame Details panel, click any of the **+** icons visible at the beginning of lines.

7. You can also view this information in its own window by using Ctrl or Shift to select multiple frames from the Frame Summary panel, right-clicking, and choosing **View Selected Frame(s) in a New Window**. The Frame Display View dialog box that opens provides Frame Details and Hex Details panels similar to those in the main Network Monitor window.

8. To stop capturing frames, click **Stop** from the Capture menu.

9. To save your capture for later analysis, click **Save As** from the toolbar at the top of the Network Monitor window. Type a filename, change the path if desired, and click **Save**.

To display a previously saved capture, simply open Network Monitor to the Start Page previously shown in Figure 21-8. The Recent Capture section displays any capture files it finds in the default location; select the link to the desired file. To locate a capture file located elsewhere, select the **Capture file** link in the Recent Captures section. Navigate to the desired folder in the dialog box that appears, select the desired capture, and then click **Open**.

### Filtering Captured Network Data

When you run the preceding procedure to capture network data, Network Monitor captures everything that passes by your network adapter card. Locating a specific frame or frames that provide information on a specific problem would be like searching for a needle in a haystack were it not for the built-in filter capabilities of Network Monitor. Filtering enables you to view frames associated with a particular protocol, protocol element, or property, such as source and destination Ethernet (MAC) or IP addresses, port numbers, and so on. For example, you can choose to capture only network traffic originating from a given IP address.

Network Monitor 3.4 provides for a large number of standard built-in filters as shown in Figure 21-10. To filter your data using one of these filters, simply access the **Filter** menu, navigate to and select the desired filter, and click the **Apply** button on the toolbar in the Display Filter section. After you do this, the capture changes to display only those frames that conform to the selected filter.

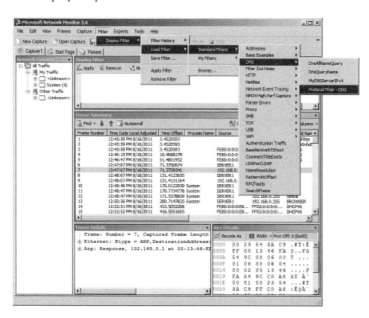

**Figure 21-10**   Network Monitor provides a comprehensive set of built-in filters, accessible from the Filter menu.

After you click the **Apply** button, the Display Filter section of the Network Monitor window displays the contents of the filter, as shown in Figure 21-11, and the Frame Summary section displays only those frames that match the selected filter.

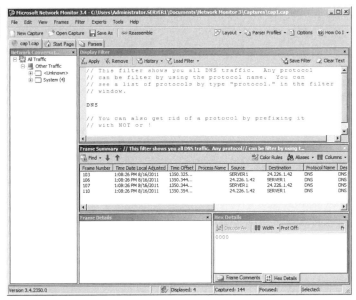

**Figure 21-11**    Filtering the network capture to display only DNS frames.

Network Monitor 3.4 uses a simple expression-based logical syntax to filter frames. You can create your own filter by typing the filter expression into the Display Filter window. Examples of filters include the following:

- **TCP:** Passes only frames using the TCP protocol

- **TCP OR UDP:** Passes frames using either the TCP or UDP protocol

- **Ethernet.Address==0x0012345678AB:** Passes only frames originating from or set to a computer with a network adapter of MAC address 00-12-34-56-78-AB

- **IPv4.sourceaddress==192.168.0.1:** Passes only frames originating from IPv4 address 192.168.0.1

- **IPv4.address==192.168.0.1:** Passes frames that either originate from or are sent to IPv4 address 192.168.0.1

To filter a capture so that it meets both of two criteria that you specified, separate the criteria using the AND or && operator. To filter a capture so that it meets either of two criteria, separate the criteria using the OR or || operator. For example, to filter a capture DNS traffic from a server at 192.168.0.11, you use the filter expression `DNS AND IPv4.sourceaddress==192.168.0.11`.

To facilitate the creation of customized filters, you can use the Intellisense coding feature first introduced with Visual Studio 2005. Intellisense provides features that facilitate the use of common language expressions (for example, context-appropriate code choices as you type code, such as properties, functions, and objects that help you to create a filter without searching for syntax options). To start Intellisense, type a period (.) in the Display Filter window. Doing so provides a list of available options. To obtain options for a given keyword, such as `protocol`, type the keyword followed by a period (for example, `protocol.`). This provides a list of available protocols, from which you can select the desired one. After typing a filter, you can click **Verify Filter** to test the validity of the filter you've created. After you create a filter that you're satisfied with, click **Save Filter** to save the filter for later use on any computer. At a later time, simply click **Load Filter**, browse to the filter location, select the filter, click **Open**, and then click **Apply** to load and apply the filter to a new capture.

**TIP**  If you're setting up a capture or display filter to pass only frames originating from or destined to a machine with a given MAC address, you must specify `Ethernet.Address` as the filter parameter and the 12-digit hexadecimal address must be prefixed with `0x`.

**NOTE**  For more information on the Intellisense coding feature, refer to "Using IntelliSense" at http://msdn.microsoft.com/en-us/library/hcw1s69b(VS.80).aspx and "Jscript IntelliSense Overview" at http://msdn.microsoft.com/en-us/library/bb385682.aspx.

### Using a Capture Filter

The previous section showed you how you can filter captured data to display only frames that meet criteria you have specified. You can also use a capture filter, which filters data during capture so that only those frames that meet your criteria are captured; other frames are passed through without capturing. Use the following procedure to create and use a capture filter:

1. From the Capture menu of Network Monitor, select **Filter**.

2. Select **Capture Filter** and then expand the list to locate the desired filter, in a manner similar to that described previously and shown in Figure 21-10 for

display filters. Alternately, you can type an expression or use Intellisense in the same fashion as with display filters.

3. Click **Start** to begin the capture using the capture filter. Proceed as described earlier in this section to run and save the capture.

4. To save the capture filter for later use, click **Save**, type a name for the filter, and click **Save** again.

### Configuring Network Monitor Options

Click **Tools > Options** to display the Options dialog box shown in Figure 21-12, which enables you to configure the following aspects of data capture in Network Monitor:

- **General tab:** Enables you to display several additional items in the Frame Details section. You can also specify or browse to a default alias file. Information about the alias file appears in the next section.

- **Capture tab:** Enables you to configure the following options pertaining to your capture session, as shown in Figure 21-12:

  - **Temporary capture file:** Specify the size and path to a file that stores captured data when you first create a new Capture tab in Network Monitor. This file is deleted when you close Network Monitor. (You are given an option to save the capture to a location of your choosing.)

  - **Stop capturing when free disk space is less than:** Specify the percent of free space or the number of megabytes remaining when you want the capture to automatically stop, in order to prevent running out of disk space.

  - **Capture only the first bytes of a frame:** Disabled by default, this limits the portion of a frame that is captured. You can use this option if you want to capture only the frame header as opposed to the entire frame.

  - **Record Capture Filter:** Saves the capture filter used as metadata information in the network capture. This data appears in the Frame Summary window.

  - **Record Active Network Adapters:** Records a list of network adapters on the capturing computer as metadata information in the network capture.

  - **Enable Conversations:** By selecting this option, you can group captured frames into conversations. When in use, frames are grouped and displayed in the Network Conversations pane in a tree structure (see the left side of Figure 21-12) according to the conversations to which they belong. Note that use of this option (which is selected by default) significantly increases memory usage and processor utilization; if the computer becomes unresponsive when performing a capture, deselect this option.

- **Show Processes in "Network Conversations' tree:** Only available if conversations are enabled, this option provides additional information about the processes in the Network Conversations pane.

- **Color Rules tab:** A color rule enables you to more easily distinguish the network traffic generated by a given protocol that appears in the Frame Summary window. Click **New** to create a color rule, from which you can specify a filter expression covered by the rule. You can then specify foreground and background colors, as well as text styles used in displaying frames that correspond to the filter expression.

- **Parser Profiles tab:** A *parser* is the component that converts the bits captured on the wire into a readable format. This tab enables you to select from several default parser profiles or add your own; currently, parsers are available for over 400 network protocols as well as applications such as Microsoft Office or SharePoint. Microsoft provides several different sets of parser profiles. It is suggested that for data collection, you should use the High Performance Capturing profile; for analyzing data, you can use the dedicated Office Communications Server or Windows profile.

- **Updates tab:** Enables you to specify that Network Monitor will automatically access the Microsoft Updates website once a month for updates. Note that you can manually check for updates at any time by clicking **Help > Check for Updates** on the menu bar.

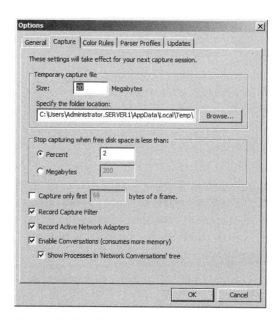

**Figure 21-12**  The Capture tab of the Options dialog box enables you to configure several properties of your capture sessions.

**NOTE** For more information on available parsers and links for downloading additional parsers, refer to "Using Network Monitor with the Microsoft Office and SharePoint Products Parsers" at http://msdn.microsoft.com/en-us/library/hh372964.aspx and "Network Monitor Open Source Parsers" at http://go.microsoft.com/fwlink/?LinkId=217711. Also, refer to "Information about Network Monitor 3" at http://support.microsoft.com/kb/933741 for information on several of the options available from the Options dialog box.

### Using Aliases

An alias is a friendly name that you can specify to replace IPv4, IPv6, and Ethernet addresses displayed in the Frame Summary panel with meaningful names such as hostnames of servers; for example, you can replace the IP address of the local computer with the alias `localhost`.

Use the following procedure to specify an alias:

1. Access a Capture tab in Network Monitor.

2. In the Frame Summary section, click the **Aliases** icon and then click **Manage Aliases**.

3. In the Aliases dialog box that appears (see Figure 21-13), click **New**.

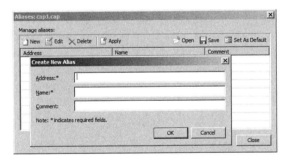

**Figure 21-13** Creating an alias in Network Monitor.

4. In the Create New Alias dialog box that appears, type the address to be replaced and the alias to be associated with it. You can also provide an optional comment. Click **OK**. Repeat Step 4 as needed to add additional aliases.

5. When finished, click **Close**. This information is added to the alias table.

6. Click the **Aliases** icon and then click the **Apply** button to apply the alias.

7. To save the alias for later usage, click the **Aliases** icon and then click **Manage Aliases**. Click the **Save** icon in the aliases toolbar, type a filename for the alias, and then click **Save**.

To load a saved alias, click the **Aliases** icon and then click **Manage Aliases**. Click the **Open** icon on the aliases toolbar, navigate to and select the aliases file to be used, and then click the **Apply** button in the toolbar.

### Performing a Capture from the Command Prompt

You can run Network Monitor from the command-line tool `nmcap.exe`, which is found in the `%systemdrive%\Program Files\Microsoft Network Monitor 3` folder by default. This is useful for scripting execution of Network Monitor, creating a scheduled task for running Network Monitor, or for use on a computer running the Server Core version of Windows Server 2008.

To perform a simple capture of all network traffic, use the following command:

```
nmcap /network * /capture /file capturename.cap
```

Where `capturename.cap` is the filename into which the captured data is stored. The capture runs automatically until you stop it by pressing **Ctrl+C**. To perform a filtered capture, type the filter capture in quotation marks after the /capture parameter. For example, use the following command to capture DHCP traffic:

```
nmcap /network * /capture "DHCP" /file capturename.cap
```

Another useful parameter of the `nmcap` utility is `/inputcapture`. Specify this parameter with the name of a previous Network Monitor capture to filter the specified capture and create a new capture containing only frames that meet the specifications of the filter. For example, to filter the `capture1.cap` file to create another capture that includes only DHCP-related traffic, use the following command:

```
nmcap /inputcapture capture1.cap /capture "DHCP" /file caputrename.cap
```

You can also quickly perform a network capture on a computer without Network Monitor installed by downloading and running Network Monitor OneClick. Access www.microsoft.com/download/en/details.aspx?displaylang=en&id=6537 and download and run the `OneClick_Autorun.exe` file. Open this file with administrative privileges. After accepting the license agreement, you receive the command-line window shown in Figure 21-14, from which you can specify a capture file location or accept the default provided. As instructed, press x to terminate the capture.

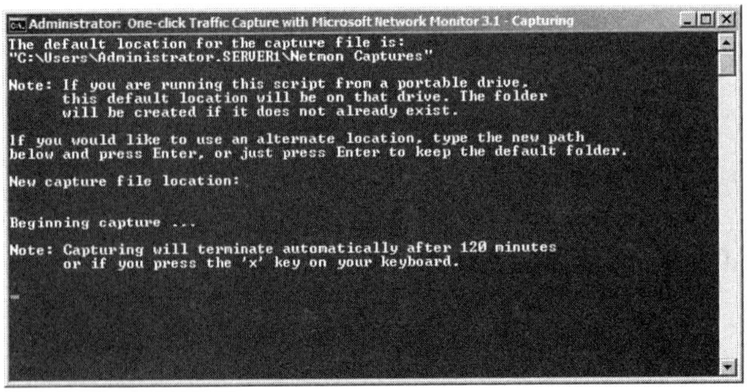

**Figure 21-14**   Using Network Monitor OneClick to perform a quick capture of network frames.

You can view and analyze a capture obtained from the command line or from Network Monitor OneClick by loading it into Network Monitor in the same fashion as used to load any other previously saved capture.

**NOTE**   For more information on `nmcap.exe`, refer to "NMCap: the easy way to Automate Capturing" at http://blogs.technet.com/b/netmon/archive/2006/10/24/ nmcap-the-easy-way-to-automate-capturing.aspx. For information on usage of this tool and its extensive list of options, open a command prompt and type **nmcap /?**. The Network Monitor Help files also includes a description of the available commands and options associated with this tool.

**TIP**   Keep in mind the difference between capture filters and display filters. A capture filter is applied during capture and captures only those packets that meet the conditions of the filter, thereby resulting in a smaller capture file. A display filter is applied after capture; the initial file is as large as an unfiltered capture, but only those packets that meet the filter criteria are displayed.

## Connection Security Rules Monitoring

In Chapter 4, you learned that Windows Firewall with Advanced Security provides connection security rules that use IPSec to manage authentication of two machines on the network and the encryption of network traffic sent between them using IPSec. These rules define which authentication, key exchange, data integrity, or encryption can be used when forming a security association that protects communication between the two computers. You also learned how to configure connection security rules using the Windows Firewall with Advanced Security snap-in.

The console tree of the Windows Firewall with Advanced Security snap-in contains a Monitoring node. Expand this node to reveal a Connection Security Rules subnode, as well as subnodes for Firewall and Security Associations. You need to configure at least one connection security node as described in Chapter 4 before you can configure monitoring from this subnode.

Select the **Connection Security Rules** subnode to display all configured rules in the details pane. Right-click the desired rule and choose **Properties** to display the dialog box shown in Figure 21-15. The tabs of this dialog box provide the following information, all of which is configured when running the New Connection Security Rule Wizard as described in Chapter 4 or later from the rule's Properties dialog box, accessed from the main Connection Security Rules node in the Windows Firewall with Advanced Security snap-in:

- **General:** Displays the IP addresses and ports (TCP or UDP) associated with each endpoint of the rule, as well as the protocol in use and the profile type (Domain, Private, and/or Public) associated with the rule. The rule displays Any if addresses, ports, or protocols have not been specified when configuring the rule.

- **Authentication:** Indicates the first and second authentication methods, such as Kerberos v5, NTLM v2, computer certificates, or other, used by the rule. The Details column provides information only when certificates or preshared keys are used for authentication.

- **Advanced:** Displays the local and remote tunnel endpoints (if the connection security rule is a tunnel rule) and the interface types. Also indicates whether or not authorization is applied and IPSec-protected connections are exempted from the rule.

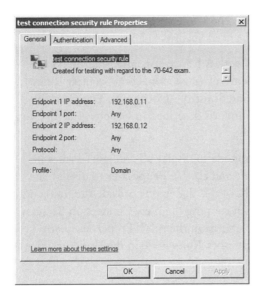

**Figure 21-15** Displaying connection security rules properties.

No configurable properties are present on any tabs of this dialog box.

**NOTE** For more information on monitoring connection security rules, refer to "Monitored Connection Security Rules Properties Page" at http://technet.microsoft. com/en-us/library/dd759099.aspx and select one of the three tabs present in this page.

### Configuring Authentication Properties

As already mentioned, the Authentication tab enables you to specify first and second authentication methods to be used in conjunction with connection security rules and IPSec-secured connections. Provided are the following two stages of authentication:

- **First authentication:** Enables computers to be authenticated to each other and is performed during the Main Mode phase of IPSec negotiations.

- **Second authentication:** Enables users at authenticated computers to be authenticated to each other and is performed by Authenticated IP in an Extended Mode of the Main Mode phase of IPSec negotiations.

Both the first and second authentications enable you to use multiple methods in the order that you specify. The first successful method is used. Available are the following:

- **Kerberos v5:** Enables you to authenticate peer computers belonging to the same AD DS domain or trusted domains. In second authentication, users logged onto these computers are authenticated.

- **Certificates:** Enables computer or user authentication by means of certificates generated by a trusted certification authority (CA). Useful when computers or users do not belong to the same domain or to trusted domains.

- **Health certificates:** You can use health certificates that are published by Network Access Protection (NAP) to ensure that only computers that are up-to-date with regard to security updates or antivirus protection. NAP was discussed in Chapter 16, "Configuring Network Access Protection (NAP)."

- **Preshared keys:** Uses a shared, secret key that was previously agreed upon by two users. Both parties must manually configure IPSec for use of this key. This method is not recommended except for testing purposes.

**CAUTION**   Microsoft recommends that you do not configure both the first and second authentications to be optional. Such a practice is equivalent to turning authentication off. You should require at least first authentication within a secure environment.

**NOTE**   For more information on configuring IPSec authentication methods, refer to "First Authentication" at http://technet.microsoft.com/en-us/library/cc772400(WS.10).aspx and "Second Authentication" at http://technet.microsoft.com/en-us/library/cc742501(WS.10).aspx.

## Exam Preparation Tasks

## Review All the Key Topics

Review the most important topics in this chapter, noted with the key topics icon in the outer margin of the page. Table 21-3 lists a reference of these key topics and the page numbers on which each is found.

**Table 21-3**   Key Topics for Chapter 21

| Key Topic Element | Description | Page Number |
|---|---|---|
| List | Describes the two major components of an SNMP implementation. | 824 |
| List | Describes types of messages exchanged by SNMP management systems. | 825 |
| Paragraph | Describes how SNMP communities function. | 826 |
| Table 21-2 | Describes important configurable SNMP service properties. | 829 |
| Paragraph | Describes the function of a protocol analyzer. | 833 |
| List | Describes components you should consider when planning the placement of a protocol analyzer. | 835 |
| List | Shows you how to install Network Monitor 3.4. | 835 |
| Figure 21-9 | Network Monitor displays information on all network traffic that passes across the server's adapter. | 838 |
| Figure 21-11 | When you filter Network Monitor, it displays only those frames that meet the requirements of the filter you've specified. | 840 |
| Paragraph | Shows you how to use Nmcap.exe to run Network Monitor from a command prompt. | 845 |
| Figure 21-14 | Network Monitor OneClick enables you to run Network Monitor quickly on a computer without the need to install the complete Network Monitor software. | 846 |

## Complete the Tables and Lists from Memory

Print a copy of Appendix B, "Memory Tables," (found on the CD), or at least the section for this chapter, and complete the tables and lists from memory. Appendix C, "Memory Tables Answer Key," also on the CD, includes the completed tables and lists to check your work.

## Definitions of Key Terms

Define the following key terms from this chapter, and check your answers in the Glossary.

Management Information Base (MIB), Network Monitor, `nmcap.exe`, protocol analyzer, Simple Network Management Protocol (SNMP), SNMP agent, SNMP community, SNMP management system, SNMP trap

# Practice Exam

1. Jack is the network administrator for The Knox Bakery Company, which operates an AD DS domain called `knoxbakery.com`. The domain includes a DNS server called NS01. Knox Bakery has prospered enough to buy out a competitor called Valley City Bakery. Valley City Bakery operations and offices will remain at their current location across town from Knox Bakery.

   Managers of the two companies decide that the Valley City Bakery network will become a subdomain called `vcb.knoxbakery.com`. This domain includes a DNS server called NS02.

   Jack needs to decide how clients at the headquarters domain, `knoxbakery.com`, will resolve names located in the `vcb.knoxbakery.com` domain. Which of the following actions can Jack perform to enable name resolution in this domain? (Each correct answer represents a complete solution. Choose two answers.)

   a. Add a pointer (PTR) resource record to NS01 that references `ns02.vcb.knoxbakery.com`.

   b. Add a start of authority (SOA) resource record to NS01 that references `ns02.vcb.knoxbakery.com`.

   c. Add a delegation to NS01 that delegates the zone `vcb.knoxbakery.com` to `ns02.vcb.knoxbakery.com`.

   d. Add a stub zone for `vcb.knoxbakery.com` to NS01.

   e. Add a _dns service locator (SRV) resource record to NS01 that references `ns02.vcb.knoxbakery.com`.

2. Sandy is the network administrator for a company that operates an AD DS network consisting of a single domain. The network uses a Windows Server 2008 R2 computer that is configured as a DHCP server to provide TCP/IP configuration information to client computers.

   Sandy has installed a new router that divides the network into two subnets. After installing and configuring this router, users on the new subnet report that they are unable to access computers located on the other subnet, despite the fact that clients on the original subnet can access each other without a problem.

Sandy goes to a Windows 7 Professional computer on the new subnet and issues the `ipconfig` command. The results of this command indicate that the computer is using an IP address of 169.254.0.43 with a subnet mask of 255.255.0.0. The default gateway is blank. What should Sandy do in order to configure network connectivity for the computers on the new subnet? (Each correct answer represents a complete solution to the problem. Choose two answers.)

   **a.** Configure a DHCP server to supply a default gateway to client computers.

   **b.** Manually specify a default gateway on each client computer in the newly created subnet.

   **c.** Configure the router to pass BOOTP broadcasts to the other subnet.

   **d.** Install a DNS server on the newly created subnet.

   **e.** Install a DHCP relay agent on the newly created subnet.

   **f.** Install a DNS Forwarder on the newly created subnet.

**3.** Greg has configured a collector-initiated event log subscription that is to collect events from servers named Server1 and Server2 onto a server named Server3. When checking the configuration of the subscription at Server3, Greg notices error messages stating `Access is denied` from the Server1 and Server2 computers. Which of the following should Greg configure so that the subscription collects event logs properly?

   **a.** Configure the settings in the Advanced Subscription Settings dialog box on Server3 to specify a specific user account that is a member of the local computer's Event Log Readers group or the Administrators group.

   **b.** Configure the settings in the Advanced Subscription Settings dialog box on Server3 to specify appropriate protocol and port settings.

   **c.** On the Server1 and Server2 computers, run the `wecutil qc` command.

   **d.** From the Subscription Properties dialog box, click **Select Events** and specify one or more event types to be included in the event subscription.

**4.** Sharon is the network administrator for a company that operates an AD DS domain in which all servers run either the original or R2 version of Windows Server 2008 and all client computers run either Windows Vista Enterprise or Windows 7 Enterprise. A server named EXCH1 runs the original version of Windows Server 2008 and Microsoft Exchange Server 2007.

As company business grows, the volume of e-mail is approaching the capacity of EXCH1, so the company purchases a new server, installs Windows Server 2008 R2 and Exchange Server 2010, and uses the name EXCH2 for this server.

Sharon's boss wants her to configure DNS so that incoming e-mail traffic is directed preferentially to EXCH2. How should she proceed?

    **a.** Create a new SRV resource record for EXCH2 and configure its priority to be 99 and its port number to be 25. Also, set the priority value for EXCH1's SRV resource record to 1.

    **b.** Create a new SRV resource record for EXCH2 and configure its priority to be 1 and its port number to be 25. Also, set the priority value for EXCH1's SRV resource record to 99.

    **c.** Create a new MX resource record for EXCH2 and configure its priority to be 99. Also, set the priority value for EXCH1's MX resource record to 1.

    **d.** Create a new MX resource record for EXCH2 and configure its priority to be 1. Also, set the priority value for EXCH1's MX resource record to 99.

**5.** Wayne is responsible for ensuring the security of remote access connections to his company's AD DS network. He deployed a VPN server running Windows Server 2008 R2 behind a firewall that is configured to allow only secured web-based communications using Secure Hypertext Transfer Protocol (HTTPS).

Employees connect to the network across the VPN using notebook computers running Windows 7. Wayne must ensure that these employees use the most secure means of connecting without the need to open additional ports on the firewall. What protocol should Wayne configure on the VPN server?

    **a.** PPTP

    **b.** L2TP over IPSec

    **c.** IKEv2

    **d.** SSTP

6. Shirley is the network administrator for a company that operates a network that is configured to use IPv6 exclusively. The network is configured with five different subnets.

Shirley deploys a new Windows Server 2008 R2 computer named Server25. She must ensure that this server can communicate with all client computers, regardless of the subnet they are located on. The address chosen must be one that is reserved for internal networks. Which of the following addresses should she select?

   a. **fc00::23d4:217a:1025**

   b. **2000::23d4:217a:1025**

   c. **fe80::23d4:217a:1025**

   d. **fec0::23d4:217a:1025**

7. Flora is the systems administrator for her company's AD DS network. A file server has suffered a catastrophic disk failure that required Flora to install several new hardware components including a new hard disk. She needs to perform a bare metal recovery of this server. What should she do first?

   a. Use the Windows Server 2008 R2 installation DVD-ROM to start the server, and then select **Repair your computer**.

   b. Use the Windows Server 2008 R2 installation DVD-ROM to start the server, and then select **Recovery Console**.

   c. Use the Windows Server 2008 R2 installation DVD-ROM to start the server, press **F8**, and then select **Safe Mode**.

   d. Merely select the disk containing the bare metal backup of the server.

8. Brenda is setting up Network Access Protection (NAP) to ensure that wireless clients connecting to her company's network from remote locations are up-to-date with system health policies. On using a laptop computer from home to test application of NAP policies, she discovers that her computer is not restricted to the remediation network, despite not having the latest service pack installed. Which of the following actions should Brenda perform? (Each correct answer represents part of the solution. Choose two answers.)

   a. Brenda should ensure that 802.1x enforcement is configured on the NAP server.

   b. Brenda should ensure that IPSec enforcement is configured on the NAP server.

   c. Brenda should ensure that all wireless access points are configured as RADIUS clients.

**d.** Brenda should ensure that all wireless access points are configured as RADIUS servers.

**e.** Brenda should ensure that a NAP certification authority (CA) is present on the network and accessible to the wireless access points.

9. David has used Windows Firewall with Advanced Security on a Windows Server 2008 R2 computer named Server3 to configure several custom outbound and inbound rules. He wants to copy these rules to another computer, named Server4, which also runs Windows Server 2008 R2. What should he do to accomplish this task with the least amount of administrative effort?

**a.** Use the `netsh advfirewall dump` command at Server3 to copy the Windows Firewall with Advanced Security rules. Then, use the `netsh advfirewall reset` command on Server4 to restore the rules on this computer.

**b.** Use the `wbadmin` utility on Server3 to back up the Windows Firewall with Advanced Security rules. Then, restore these rules at Server4.

**c.** In the Windows Firewall with Advanced Security snap-in on Server3, right-click **Inbound Rules** and choose **Export Policy**. After saving the export file, go to Server4, right-click **Inbound Rules**, and choose **Import Policy**. Click **Yes**, specify the name of the policy file to be imported, and then click **Open**. Then, repeat this procedure with the **Outbound Rules** node.

**d.** In the Windows Firewall with Advanced Security snap-in on Server3, right-click **Windows Firewall with Advanced Security** and choose **Export Policy**. After saving the export file, go to Server4, right-click **Windows Firewall with Advanced Security**, and choose **Import Policy**. Click **Yes**, specify the name of the policy file to be imported, and then click **Open**.

10. Hubert is responsible for maintaining remote access to his company's AD DS network. The network has a RADIUS server named Server11 that is configured as a Network Policy Server (NPS) machine. Because the company has added many new salespersons who will be connecting to the network from external client locations, Hubert has installed a new server named Server12 and configured this server with NPS.

Hubert wants to have authentication requests received by Server12 to be passed automatically to Server11 for processing. What should he do?

**a.** On Server11, add Server12 as a new RADIUS client.

**b.** On Server11, create a new remote RADIUS proxy group. Then, add Server12 on the Address tab of the Add RADIUS Server dialog box.

    **c.** On Server12, create a new remote RADIUS proxy group. Then, add Server11 on the Address tab of the Add RADIUS Server dialog box.

    **d.** On Server12, define a new connection request policy that passes all authentication requests automatically to Server11.

**11.** Michelle is responsible for ensuring the maintenance of DNS services for her company's AD DS network. The network is configured as a forest named `que.com` and consists of a root domain and three child domains. Each domain hosts two or three Windows Server 2008 R2 DNS servers, each of which hosts Active Directory–integrated zones for all four domains.

The company acquires a subsidiary named Certguide, which operates an AD DS forest named `certguide.com` that consists of a single domain.

Michelle needs to configure DNS in the `que.com` forest to enable name resolution for resources located in both forests. How should she proceed?

    **a.** She should create a new conditional forwarder and store it in Active Directory. She should replicate this forwarder to all DNS servers in the `que.com` forest.

    **b.** She should create a new application directory partition in the `que.com` forest and create application directory partition replicas on all DNS servers in the forest.

    **c.** She should configure a stub zone on the `certguide.com` DNS server that contains information about the authoritative name servers in the `que.com` DNS zones.

    **d.** She should configure a stub zone on the forest root `que.com` DNS server that contains information about the authoritative name servers in the `certguide.com` DNS zone.

    **e.** She should configure client computers in `que.com` to use the `certguide.com` DNS server as the alternate DNS server.

**12.** Eleanor has created a data collector set on her Windows Server 2008 R2 computer that will monitor several aspects of her server's performance. She wants the data collector set to stop logging if the server has less than 500 MB of available disk space on the volume she has specified for logging performance. What should she do?

    **a.** Right-click the data collector set in the console tree of the Performance Manager snap-in and choose **Data Manager**. On the Actions tab of the dialog box that appears, select **Size** and specify 500 MB as the size of the folder where log data is stored.

**b.** Right-click the data collector set in the console tree of the Performance Manager snap-in and choose **Data Manager**. On the Data Manager tab of the dialog box that appears, select **Minimum free disk** and specify 500 MB as the minimum amount of available space.

**c.** Right-click the **Data Collector Sets** node in the console tree of the Performance Manager snap-in and choose **Properties**. On the Actions tab of the dialog box that appears, select **Size** and specify 500 MB as the size of the folder where log data is stored.

**d.** Right-click the **Data Collector Sets** node in the console tree of the Performance Manager snap-in and choose **Properties**. On the Data Manager tab of the dialog box that appears, select **Minimum free disk** and specify 500 MB as the minimum amount of available space.

**13.** Karla is the network administrator for a company that operates an AD DS network consisting of a parent domain and two child domains. All DNS servers run Windows Server 2008 or Windows Server 2008 R2 and all DNS zones are configured as Active Directory–integrated zones hosted on domain controllers.

Karla notices that the zone data for one of the child domains contains several entries for unknown computers that are not domain members. What should she do to prevent this from occurring in the future?

**a.** Select the **Secure only** option on the General tab of the zone's Properties dialog box.

**b.** Change the zone replication scope to the **All DNS servers in this domain** option.

**c.** On the Zone Aging/Scavenging Properties dialog box, select the **Scavenge Stale Resource Records** option.

**d.** Right-click the server in the console tree of DNS Manager and choose **Scavenge Stale Resource Records**.

**14.** Gary administers the network for his company. His network contains eight Windows Server 2008 computers, a single UNIX server, and 90 Windows 7 Professional computers on a single subnet using the address 172.16.31.0/24. Client computers receive their IP configuration from a DHCP server. DNS resources records are updated dynamically. A user named Nancy complains that she cannot access the UNIX server, even though she can access the computers running Windows Server 2008 and other client computers. Other clients can reach Nancy without difficulty. Gary tries to ping the UNIX server by name from Nancy's Windows 7 Professional computer and receives the message `Unknown host unix1.que.com`. After several other troubleshooting attempts, he realizes that he is receiving the message because the UNIX server is not registered with the DNS server on the Windows Server 2008 network. He adds the UNIX server to the DNS server's database and tries again to ping the UNIX server from the Windows 7 Professional machine. However, he receives the same message.

Which of the following should Gary try next to correct this situation?

   **a.** Check to make sure that the subnet mask on the client machine is configured properly.

   **b.** At the Windows 7 Professional client, run the command `ipconfig /flushdns` to clear the DNS resolver cache.

   **c.** Configure a default gateway for the Windows 7 Professional client.

   **d.** At the Windows 7 Professional client, run the command `ipconfig /registerdns` to ensure that it is also registered in DNS.

   **e.** At the Windows 7 Professional client, run the commands `ipconfig /release` and `ipconfig /renew`.

**15.** Karen is the systems administrator for a company that runs a network with a single AD DS domain. She has been using Network Monitor to capture traffic at a file server for an entire work day. The resulting capture file, named `capture1.cap`, was almost 1 GB in size. She would like to create a smaller file named `dns1.cap` from this capture that contains only DNS-related traffic. What should Karen do?

   **a.** Use the `nmcap.exe /inputcapture capture1.cap /capture DNS /file dns1.cap` command.

   **b.** Use the `nmcap.exe /network * /capture "DNS" /file dns1` command.

   **c.** In Network Monitor, configure a capture filter using the DNS filter and then save the resulting file as `dns1.cap`.

   **d.** In Network Monitor, configure a display filter using the DNS filter and then save the resulting file as `dns1.cap`.

16. Joe is the network administrator for a company that operates an AD DS network containing a single domain named que.com. The network includes two Windows Server 2008 R2 computers named Server11 and Server12, which are configured as DHCP servers.

    Joe has configured a scope named Scope1 on Server11. He needs to ensure that DHCP clients receive IP addressing information from the IP address range in Scope1, even if Server11 is not available. He must also ensure that the DHCP servers do not assign duplicate IP addresses. What should he do?

    a. Create a scope named Scope2 on Server12, and configure this scope with the same IP address range as on Scope1.

    b. Create a superscope on Server11.

    c. Create a multicast scope on Server11

    d. Use the DHCP Split-Scope Configuration Wizard on Server11 to split the scope into two subscopes.

17. Susan has run the DirectAccess Setup Wizard to set up DirectAccess for enabling access to head office servers by users located at branch offices on her company's AD DS network. She wants to ensure that the DNS client service on client computers in the branch office make only secure intranet connections, and wants the DNS client services to securely verify all resolved names. Which of the following should she configure in Group Policy?

    a. DNS Security Extensions (DNSSEC)

    b. Split-brain DNS

    c. Name Resolution Policy Table (NRPT) exemptions

    d. Remote Desktop Services (RDS) enforcement

18. Spencer is the systems administrator for a company that operates an AD DS domain named que.com in which all servers run Windows Server 2008 R2 and all client computers run Windows 7 Ultimate. He has configured a Group Policy object (GPO) linked to the domain in which he has selected the **Require a smart card for EFS** option as shown in the exhibit so that users must insert their smart cards when accessing files and folders that have been encrypted using EFS.

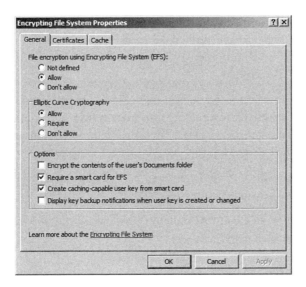

Spencer has discovered that users can still access encrypted files after they have removed their smart cards. He must ensure that users must keep their smart cards inserted at all times when accessing encrypted files. What should he do?

   **a.** Under Elliptic Curve Cryptography, select **Require**.

   **b.** Under Elliptic Curve Cryptography, select **Don't allow**.

   **c.** Clear the **Create caching-capable user key from smart card** option.

   **d.** Select the **Display key backup notifications when user key is created or changed** option.

**19.** Janet has configured an event log subscription that collects events from computers named Server1 and Server2, which run Windows Server 2008 R2 Enterprise Edition, so that she can read them on her desktop computer that runs Windows 7 Ultimate. She opens Event Viewer on her desktop computer. What should she do to locate these events on her desktop computer?

   **a.** Right-click **Event Viewer** and choose **Connect to Another Computer**. From the Select Computer dialog box, choose **Server1** to view events on this computer and then **Server2** to view events on that computer.

   **b.** From the Custom Views node in Event Viewer, select the **Server1** and **Server2** event logs in turn.

   **c.** From the Custom Views node in Event Viewer, select the **Forwarded Events** subnode.

   **d.** From the Windows Logs node in Event Viewer, select the **Forwarded Events** subnode.

20. Murray is the systems administrator for a manufacturing company that operates a Windows Server 2008 network consisting of a single domain. More specifically, he is responsible for ensuring that all users have an adequate amount of disk space available to store important files. When checking the contents of a file server named Server7, he notices a large number of files that have not been modified or accessed for several years.

Murray wants to obtain a list of all files that have not been accessed in the past two years. What should he do?

   a. In FSRM, create a passive file screen and specify the **Least Recently Accessed Files** option. Click **Edit Parameters** and specify an interval of 730 days.

   b. Use the Storage Reports feature in FSRM and select the **Least Recently Accessed Files** option. Click **Edit Parameters** and specify an interval of 730 days.

   c. Use FSRM to create a file quota template. Specify a limit of 730 days and apply this template to all users in the domain.

   d. From the Quota tab of the server's hard disk Properties dialog box, select **Enable quota management** and then select the **Least Recently Accessed Files** option. Specify a limit of 730 days.

21. Amanda is configuring IP addressing for a company that has a head office in midtown Manhattan and eleven branch offices in various locations throughout the New York metropolitan area. She has decided that each office will correspond to a single subnet on the company's wide-area network (WAN). The company itself can use a single Class C network for this purpose. Which of the following subnet masks would provide the most host addresses for each office?

   a. 255.255.255.192

   b. 255.255.255.224

   c. 255.255.255.240

   d. 255.255.255.248

22. Doug is a systems administrator for an environmental research organization that operates a large laboratory facility near Detroit. The laboratory's network consists of Windows Server 2008 and Windows 7 Professional computers. Research scientists are hosting a planning conference in a nearby hotel. Doug needs to configure dial-up connections between the hotel and the laboratory, using 12 temporary telephone lines installed into the conference room to facilitate connections to the laboratory by the scientists using laptop computers

that run either Windows XP Professional or Windows 7 Professional. Each of these temporary phone lines is configured with its own telephone number.

Doug has installed Routing and Remote Access (RRAS) on a Windows Server 2008 R2 computer in the laboratory. This server is equipped with 12 modems, each of which is connected to a new telephone line in the laboratory. These lines share a single telephone number. On testing the new connections, Doug notes that he is able to connect from the hotel to the laboratory. However, he is required to enter his user name and password.

The coordinators of the conference would like the scientists to be able to connect to the network without the need to enter their credentials during the dial-up process. These scientists log on to their portable computers by using cached domain credentials, and they have not been issued any advanced security devices such as digital certificates or smart cards. How should Doug configure the RRAS server so that they can connect without the need to re-enter their credentials during the dial-up process, while maintaining their access permissions on the network?

    **a.** Configure the RRAS server to use MS-CHAP v.2 for authentication. Also, configure the scientists' laptop computers to automatically use Windows logon names and passwords during dial-up authentication.

    **b.** Configure the RRAS server to use EAP-TLS for authentication. Also, configure the scientists' laptop computers to automatically use Windows logon names and passwords during dial-up authentication.

    **c.** Configure the RRAS server to use PAP for authentication. Also, configure the scientists' laptop computers to automatically use Windows logon names and passwords during dial-up authentication.

    **d.** Enable caller ID verification for each scientist.

**23.** Lisa is responsible for maintaining the DNS configuration of her company's AD DS domain. All servers run Windows Server 2008 R2 and client computers run either Windows Vista Business or Windows 7 Enterprise or Ultimate. DNS is configured as an Active Directory–integrated zone on two domain controllers and as a secondary zone on a single external DNS server located on the network's perimeter zone. The external DNS server hosts only the records for her company's web and mail servers.

Lisa deploys an additional secondary DNS server on the perimeter network to improve Internet-based name resolution. She uses Reliability and Performance Monitor to monitor the new DNS server and notices that the Transfer Start of Authority (SOA) Requests Sent value is high. She needs to minimize the bandwidth used by the perimeter network DNS servers across the firewall server for zone transfer requests. She must also ensure that only authorized servers can receive copies of this zone file.

Which of the following should Lisa configure on the external DNS server? (Each correct answer represents part of the solution. Choose two answers.)

    **a.** On the Notify list, select **Servers listed on the Name Servers tab**.

    **b.** On the Notify list, select **The following servers** and specify the IP addresses of the perimeter zone secondary DNS servers.

    **c.** Increase the value of the Refresh interval.

    **d.** Decrease the value of the Refresh interval.

    **e.** Increase the value of the Retry interval.

    **f.** Decrease the value of the Retry interval.

    **g.** Disable dynamic updates.

**24.** Chris is the systems administrator for an AD DS domain that includes nine servers running either the original or R2 version of Windows Server 2008 and 200 client computers that run either Windows Vista Business or Windows 7 Professional. The DNS domain does not connect to the Internet.

The DNS server is a Windows Server 2008 R2 member server called Server09. If Server09 is unable to resolve a DNS query, it should not be able to contact any other DNS server external to the network.

Chris has already removed all references to forwarders from the Forwarders tab of the server's Properties dialog box. What else should he do? (Each correct answer represents a complete solution to the problem. Choose two answers.)

    **a.** Delete the `cache.dns` file from the `%systemroot%\System32\Dns` folder.

    **b.** Configure Server09 as a caching-only DNS server.

    **c.** Delete all entries from the Root Hints tab and add any entries for other local DNS servers if necessary.

    **d.** Enable recursion for the DNS domain.

**25.** Carm is the systems administrator for a company whose network is configured as a single AD DS domain. Servers run a mix of the original and R2 versions of Windows Server 2008 and client computers run a mix of Windows XP Professional, Windows Vista Business, and Windows 7 Enterprise. Each department in the company is configured as a separate organizational unit (OU). Carm is configuring a Windows Server 2008 computer to act as a Windows Server

Update Services (WSUS) server. He wants users in the Developers department to receive updates separately from those in all other departments of the company. How should he configure the WSUS server? (Each correct answer represents part of the solution. Choose three answers.)

    **a.** Use the Update Services snap-in in WSUS to create two computer groups, one for computers in the Developers department and the other for all other company computers.

    **b.** Place the computer accounts of all computers in the Developers department into one security group in AD DS, and place the computer accounts of all other computers into a different security group.

    **c.** From the Options node of the Update Services snap-in, access the Computers dialog box and select the **Use Group Policy or registry setting on computers** option.

    **d.** From the Options node of the Update Services snap-in, access the Computers dialog box and select the **Use the Update Services console** option.

    **e.** In a Group Policy object (GPO) linked to the Developers OU, enable the **Enable client-side targeting** policy and specify the group containing the computers in the Developers department. In a separate GPO linked to the domain, enable the **Enable client-side targeting** policy and specify the group containing all other company computers.

    **f.** Use the Update Services snap-in to specify when the computers in the two groups will receive their updates.

**26.** Gerry is the network administrator for a company that operates an AD DS network consisting of a single domain and two sites corresponding to the downtown head office and a suburban branch office. The network is configured to use IPv4. He has installed a new computer running Windows Server 2008 R2 and equipped with two network adapter cards at the branch office.

Gerry needs to configure the branch office server as a router. Which of the following actions should he perform? (Each correct answer represents part of the solution. Choose two answers.)

    **a.** Install the Routing and Remote Access Services server role.

    **b.** Install the Network Policy and Access Services server role and the Routing and Remote Access Services role feature.

    **c.** From the Routing and Remote Access Server Setup Wizard, select the **Remote access (dial-up or VPN)** option.

   **d.** From the Routing and Remote Access Server Setup Wizard, select the **Secure connection between two private networks** option.

   **e.** From the Routing and Remote Access Server Setup Wizard, select the **Custom Configuration** option and then select the **LAN routing** option.

**27.** Rick is the systems administrator for his company, which operates an AD DS domain in which all servers run Windows Server 2008 R2 and all client computers run Windows 7 Enterprise. Rick has configured a Group Policy object (GPO) linked to the domain that specifies that client computers receive their updates from a Windows Server Update Services (WSUS) server on the network.

Company policy stipulates that all client computers must install all updates labeled by Microsoft as Critical or Important before being allowed to access network resources. Rick must configure Network Access Protection (NAP) to enforce this policy. What should he do?

   **a.** Configure NAP to disconnect all clients without proper security updates.

   **b.** Configure NAP to direct all clients without proper security updates to the remedial network.

   **c.** Configure NAP to direct all clients without proper security updates to the Microsoft Windows Update website.

   **d.** Configure NAP to enable Windows Firewall on all clients without proper security updates.

**28.** Kathleen is the systems administrator for a company that operates an AD DS network consisting of a single domain named que.com. The domain includes an Active Directory–integrated DNS zone, which is currently hosted on three Windows Server 2008 R2 domain controllers named Server01, Server02, and Server03.

Kathleen wants to configure a Windows Server 2008 R2 computer called Server11 as a secondary name server. After installing DNS, Kathleen runs the New Zone Wizard, specifies a secondary zone, and then specifies **Server01** as a master server from which Server11 should obtain updates.

A few weeks later, Server01 suffers a hardware failure and it will take several weeks before the required parts will be obtained. Kathleen accesses the DNS Manager snap-in on Server11, right-clicks the que.com zone, and chooses **Properties**. Kathleen must ensure that Server11 receives zone updates regularly while Server01 is unavailable. What should she do next?

**a.** Select the **General** tab and click **Edit** to add either Server02 or Server03 as a master server.

**b.** Select the **Name Servers** tab and click **Add** to add either Server02 or Server03 as a primary name server.

**c.** Select the **Start of Authority** tab and click **Browse** under the Primary Server option to add either Server02 or Server03 as a primary name server.

**d.** Select the **Zone Transfers** tab and select the **Allow Zone Transfers** option. Then, choose the **Only to the following servers** option and add either Server02 or Server03 as a primary name server.

29. Phil is in charge of maintaining the DNS servers in his company's AD DS domain. The domain contains two DNS servers: Server11 resolves internal name requests and Server12 resolves external name requests. Client computers are configured to send name resolution queries to Server11, which then forwards requests for external name resolution to Server12.

   Phil modifies the DNS configuration at Server12 to correct a problem with this server. Internal users report that they are unable to see the updated DNS record. What should Phil do to ensure that the updated DNS record is properly resolved by the clients?

   **a.** Run the `ipconfig /flushdns` command on Server11.

   **b.** Run the `ipconfig /flushdns` command on Server12.

   **c.** Instruct the users to run the `ipconfig /flushdns` command on their client computers.

   **d.** Run the `dnscmd /clearcache` command on Server11.

   **e.** Run the `dnscmd /clearcache` command on Server12.

30. Marisa is a network administrator for a company that operates a single-domain AD DS network named `examprep.com`. All servers on the network run either the original or R2 version of Windows Server 2008.

   After users report problems with data stored on a file server named Server9, Marisa monitors this server and discovers that intruders have compromised this computer. She must ensure that external communications to Server9 are blocked. What should she do?

   **a.** In Windows Firewall with Advanced Security, select the **Public Profile** tab and select the **Block all connections** option under Inbound connections.

**b.** In Windows Firewall with Advanced Security, select the **Private Profile** tab and select the **Block all connections** option under Inbound connections.

**c.** In Windows Firewall with Advanced Security, select the **Domain Profile** tab and select the **Block all connections** option under Inbound connections.

**d.** In Windows Firewall with Advanced Security, select the **Public Profile** tab and select the **Block** option under Inbound connections. Then, click **Customize** and specify the range of IP addresses that should be exempted from the rule.

**e.** In Windows Firewall with Advanced Security, select the **Private Profile** tab and select the **Block** option under Inbound connections. Then, click **Customize** and specify the range of IP addresses that should be exempted from the rule.

**f.** In Windows Firewall with Advanced Security, select the **Domain Profile** tab and select the **Block** option under Inbound connections. Then, click **Customize** and specify the range of IP addresses that should be exempted from the rule.

31. Brendan is responsible for administering a Windows Server 2008 computer called PrnSvr01 that is part of his company's AD DS domain and is performing the role of print server. He recently installed a high-speed laser print device on the network, created a logical printer named Phaser on PrnSvr01, and shared Phaser with the default settings.

Brendan wants Phaser to be available to all staff in the company. Management has asked him to limit use of the physical printer to members of the Traders domain local group between the hours of 8 a.m. and 4 p.m. They are to have shared use of the physical printer at other times of the day. What should Brendan do?

**a.** Create and share a new logical printer named Phaser2. Configure this printer to be available from 8 a.m. to 4 p.m. For Phaser2, remove the Everyone group from the print permissions list, and add the Traders group with the Print permission allowed. Instruct users in the Traders group to set Phaser2 as their default printer.

**b.** Create and share a new logical printer named Phaser2. Configure this printer to be available from 8 a.m. to 4 p.m. For Phaser2, deny the Everyone group the print permission, and add the Traders group with the Print permission allowed. Instruct users in the Traders group to set Phaser2 as their default printer.

**c.** Configure the Phaser logical printer to be available from 4 p.m. to 8 a.m. Create a new logical printer named Phaser2 and share it with the default settings. For Phaser2, deny the Everyone group the print permission, and add the Traders group with the Print permission allowed. Instruct users in the Traders group to set Phaser2 as their default printer.

**d.** Configure the Phaser logical printer to be available from 4 p.m. to 8 a.m. Create a new logical printer named Phaser2 and share it with the default settings. For Phaser2, remove the Everyone group from the print permissions list, and add the Traders group with the Print permission allowed. Instruct users in the Traders group to set Phaser2 as their default printer.

**32.** Jean is configuring SNMP to receive trap messages from client computers in the Accounting department of her company's network so that she can be informed rapidly when problem conditions occur on client computers. She has configured a server named Alpha as a management system with the community name alpha and added client computers in her department to this community as SNMP agents. Another administrator in the Marketing department named Carolyn has configured a server named Beta as a second management system with the community name beta and added client computers to this management system.

A user in the Accounting department at a Windows 7 Professional computer named Computer43 contacts Jean with a problem and on investigating, she discovers a condition that should have been reported by SNMP. Discussing the problem with Carolyn, Jean discovers that Carolyn has received a trap message from the Computer43 computer. Which of the following is the most likely cause for this error?

**a.** Computer43 belongs to both the alpha and beta communities, and SNMP permits only a single trap message to be sent.

**b.** Computer43 belongs to both the alpha and beta communities, but Carolyn has not configured the SNMP service on the Alpha server to receive trap messages.

**c.** Jean configured the Computer43 machine in error to belong to the beta community rather than the alpha community.

**d.** It is not possible to configure a computer to belong to more than one community; therefore, when Carolyn added this computer to the beta community, it was removed from the alpha community.

**33.** Francesca has configured a domain-based DFS namespace named \\que.com\dfs1 on two servers named Server01 and Server02, which are member servers in her company's AD DS domain, which is named que.com. Server01 is located in the company's head office and Server02 is located in a suburban branch office.

Francesca has configured Server01 as the namespace server for this namespace. She has configured a subfolder in the DFS namespace named Documents and specified folder targets of \\Server1\Documents and \\Server2\Documents.

Users in the suburban office report that they view different contents in the Documents folder than those in the head office. What should Francesca do to ensure that the content in the Documents folder is the same in both offices?

   **a.** Create an additional DFS namespace named \\que.com\documents and add the Documents folder to this namespace.

   **b.** Create a replication group that includes Server1 and Server2. From the Add Folder to Replicate dialog box, add the Documents folder.

   **c.** Configure Server02 as an additional namespace server.

   **d.** Move the namespace server for this namespace to Server02.

**34.** Mary is planning a wireless networking setup for her company's AD DS domain. She purchased new wireless access points that support the latest signal transmission technologies including frequencies of 2.4 or 5 GHz and a transmission speed of up to 600 Mbps. What wireless networking protocol should she implement?

   **a.** 802.11a

   **b.** 802.11b

   **c.** 802.11g

   **d.** 802.11n

**35.** Ben is responsible for ensuring that multiple backups of the Windows Server 2008 R2 file servers on his company's network are available at all times. He is scheduling backups to occur on a nightly basis. Which of the following can Ben use as possible backup locations to accomplish this task? (Each correct answer represents a complete solution to the problem. Choose three answers.)

   **a.** DVD-R drives

   **b.** Internal hard disks

   **c.** External hard disks

   **d.** Tape volumes

   **e.** Remote shared folders on other servers

**36.** Holly is the systems administrator for a manufacturing company. The company employs sales associates that need to connect to a virtual private networking (VPN) server running Windows Server 2008 R2 on the company's network. The VPN server is configured with a computer certificate obtained from the company's enterprise certification authority (CA) server.

Holly must ensure that connections to the VPN server are securely authenticated and that credentials sent by sales associates are encrypted. Which authentication protocol should she use?

   **a.** CHAP

   **b.** MS-CHAPv2

   **c.** PEAP-TLS

   **d.** PAP

**37.** Don is a network administrator for a company whose Windows Server 2008 network is divided into two subnets separated by a router. Some Windows 7 Professional computers are located on Subnet 1 as shown in the exhibit.

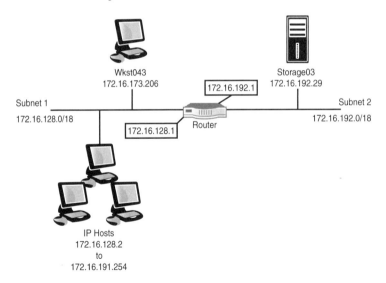

Manually configured IP addresses of the clients range from 172.16.128.2 to 172.16.191.254. The second router interface connects to the 172.16.192.0/18 network on which several Windows Server 2008 computers reside. A user with the IP address of 172.16.173.206 complains that she cannot connect to a file server called Storage03 on Subnet 2. Nor can she connect to some of the users on her own subnet. Don goes to her computer and discovers that he cannot ping either 172.16.128.1 or 172.16.192.1. He tries the `route print` command and obtains the results shown in the following table.

| Network Destination | Netmask | Gateway | Interface | Metric |
|---|---|---|---|---|
| 0.0.0.0 | 0.0.0.0 | 172.16.128.1 | 172.16.173.206 | 1 |
| 127.0.0.0 | 255.0.0.0 | 127.0.0.1 | 127.0.0.1 | 1 |
| 172.16.128.0 | 255.255.224.0 | 172.16.173.206 | 172.16.173.206 | 1 |
| 172.16.173.206 | 255.255.255.255 | 127.0.0.1 | 127.0.0.1 | 1 |
| 172.16.255.255 | 255.255.255.255 | 172.16.173.206 | 172.16.173.206 | 1 |
| 224.0.0.0 | 224.0.0.0 | 172.16.173.206 | 172.16.173.206 | 1 |
| 255.255.255.255 | 255.255.255.255 | 172.16.173.206 | 172.16.173.206 | 1 |

Why can this computer not reach the servers on Subnet 2?

   a. The router interface to the second subnet is configured with an incorrect IP address.

   b. This computer is configured with an incorrect default gateway address.

   c. This computer is configured with an incorrect IP address.

   d. This computer is configured with an incorrect subnet mask.

38. Harry is responsible for ensuring that all servers can be accessed using DNS on his company's AD DS network, which includes a single domain named `certguide.com`. The network includes a web server installed on a Windows Server 2008 machine named server8.certguide.com. Harry must ensure that users can reach the web server when they type **www.certguide.com** into their browser. What type of record should he add to the DNS zone to ensure that the web server is properly reached?

   a. Start of authority (SOA)

   b. Service location (SRV)

   c. Alias (CNAME)

   d. Host (A or AAAA)

   e. Well-known service (WKS)

39. Anna is planning a DirectAccess implementation for her company's AD DS domain, which includes a head office and three branch offices. She has set up a

Windows Server 2008 R2 computer on the perimeter network that is intended to function as a DirectAccess server and has also set up another server running Active Directory Certificate Services (AD CS) and configured certificate revocation list (CRL) distribution points that will be available to client computers.

Before installing DirectAccess, Anna needs to ensure that the server she has set up meets all requirements for functioning as a DirectAccess server. Which of the following must Anna do? (Each correct answer represents part of the solution. Choose all that apply.)

    **a.** The server must be a member server in the AD DS domain and have IIS installed.

    **b.** The server must be configured as a domain controller and have IIS installed.

    **c.** The domain functional level must be set to Windows Server 2008 or higher.

    **d.** The domain functional level must be set to Windows Server 2008 R2 or higher.

    **e.** The server must be equipped with two network adapters, one connected directly to the Internet and one connected to the corporate intranet.

    **f.** The server must have a network adapter connected to the Internet that is configured with two consecutive public IPv4 addresses.

    **g.** The server must have a network adapter connected to the Internet that is configured with two consecutive public IPv6 addresses.

    **h.** The server must be configured as a Network Access Protection (NAP) server and configured to require health certificates from client computers attempting to use DirectAccess.

    **i.** The server requires digital certificates obtained from an Active Directory Certificate Services (AD CS) server that is configured as an Enterprise CA.

**40.** Jane is administrator of Acme Construction, which operates an AD DS network consisting of a single domain. Acme is headquartered in Pittsburgh with branch offices in Columbus, Cleveland, and Harrisburg. Jane's company-wide domain name will be `acmeconstr.com`. Initially, Jane plans to install a DNS server at headquarters and another in each of the three branch offices. She plans to have the DNS server in Pittsburgh host her company's domain. Additionally, Jane intends to delegate responsibility for maintaining DNS systems and zone information to network administrators located at each of the branch offices.

Which of the following plans will achieve the desired results for Jane?

   **a.** The DNS server in Pittsburgh will host a standard primary zone for the `acmeconstr.com` domain. Each branch office will host a standard primary zone.

   **b.** The DNS server in Pittsburgh will host a standard primary zone for the `acmeconstr.com` domain. Branch offices will be configured as subdomains. Each branch office will host a standard secondary zone for its subdomain.

   **c.** The DNS server in Pittsburgh will host a standard primary zone for the `acmeconstr.com` domain. Branch offices will be configured as subdomains. Each branch office will host a standard primary zone for its subdomain.

   **d.** The DNS server in Pittsburgh will host a standard primary zone for the `acmeconstr.com` domain. Branch offices will be configured as subdomains. Each branch office will host a stub zone for its subdomain.

**41.** Tyson is the network administrator for a growing company whose IP network consists of three subnets all of which attach to a single Windows Server 2008 computer that functions as a router. The company has been assigned the 201.202.203.0/24 Class C network. The three subnets contain 82, 55, and 29 computers each, and it is anticipated that a fourth subnet holding up to 30 computers will eventually be added. Tyson needs to subnet the existing network by adding bits to the subnet mask, but there is no additional network address available to him. The router supports classless interdomain routing (CIDR) and variable length subnet masks (VLSM).

Which of the following subnet addresses should Tyson assign to the three existing networks while still leaving room for a future fourth subnet as specified in this scenario? (Each correct answer represents part of the solution. Choose three answers.)

   **a.** 201.202.203.0/26

   **b.** 201.202.203.0/25

   **c.** 201.202.203.192/27

   **d.** 201.202.203.128/26

   **e.** 201.202.203.192/25

   **f.** 201.202.203.192/26

**42.** Erin is the network administrator for a company that operates an AD DS domain. The domain includes a WSUS server that runs the original version of

Windows Server 2008 and is configured as a member server in the domain. In recent months, the company has been upgrading all servers on the network to Windows Server 2008 R2 with a view to upgrading the domain and functional forest levels to Windows Server 2008 R2 so that they can take advantage of the new features provided, such as the Active Directory Recycle Bin.

Erin starts the upgrade on the WSUS server, but receives an error that the upgrade cannot continue. What should she do to enable the upgrade to proceed successfully?

    **a.** She must run the `Adprep /forestprep` and `Adprep /domainprep` commands on the WSUS server.

    **b.** She must upgrade the Windows Internal Database first.

    **c.** She must remove WSUS from the server first. After the server has been upgraded, she can reinstall and reconfigure WSUS on the server.

    **d.** She cannot upgrade this server without performing a complete new installation of Windows Server 2008 R2.

**43.** Judy is the network administrator of her company's AD DS network, which operates a head office and a branch office. A mission-critical application that runs from both offices of the network requires NetBIOS name resolution.

Judy has configured two WINS servers to provide NetBIOS name resolution. A WINS server named Server8 is located in the head office and is configured with the IP address 192.168.0.18. Another WINS server is located in the branch office. This server is named Server9 and is configured with the IP address 192.168.1.19. All client computers in both offices are configured to access the WINS servers in the order of use 192.168.0.18, 192.168.1.19.

Judy reconfigures the WINS addresses on the branch office client computers in the following order of use: 192.168.1.19, 192.168.0.18. After doing so, users in the branch office report that they are no longer able to connect to the head office servers. What should Judy do to restore name resolution of head office computers to users at the branch office?

    **a.** From the Intervals tab of the WINS server properties dialog box at Server9, increase the Renew interval setting to 1 day.

    **b.** From the Intervals tab of the WINS server properties dialog box at Server9, reduce the Extinction timeout setting to 1 day.

    **c.** Configure Server8 and Server9 as WINS push/pull replication partners.

    **d.** Add static name-to-address mappings to the WINS database in Server9 that direct branch office client computers to the proper head office servers.

**44.** Keisha is a systems administrator for a company that operates an AD DS domain named `certguide.com`. The word-processing application in use on the network is configured so that all temporary files are created in the folder in which the document is located. A user named Wilson is working on some highly confidential information that must receive a high level of protection from unauthorized users. Keisha creates a folder on Wilson's Windows 7 Professional computer, and moves the confidential files into it. She needs to ensure that only Wilson has access to the confidential files and all temporary files created while he is working on them.

Which of the following should Keisha do? (Each correct answer represents part of the solution. Choose three.)

   **a.** Assign the Users group the Deny–Full Control permission for the folder.

   **b.** Assign Wilson's user account the Allow–Full Control permission for the folder.

   **c.** Encrypt the folder.

   **d.** Encrypt the files.

   **e.** Add Wilson's user account to the list of users that are allowed to open the folder.

   **f.** Designate Ben's user account as an EFS recovery agent.

**45.** Jennifer is responsible for maintaining the system health of client computers on her company's network. She has configured Network Access Protection (NAP) using the Windows Security Health Validator (WSHV) to enforce client computer health. A computer named Server5 on the remediation network is in need of new hardware components that will take a few days to obtain. In the meanwhile, Jennifer must enable client computers that would otherwise require Server5 access to access the company network on a temporary basis. What should she do?

   **a.** From the console tree of the Network Policy Server snap-in, expand **Network Access Protection\System Health Validators\Windows Security Health Validator\Error Codes**. Select the error code labeled **SHV unable to contact required services**, and then select the **Compliant** option.

   **b.** From the console tree of the Network Policy Server snap-in, expand **Network Access Protection\System Health Validators\Windows Security Health Validator\Error Codes**. Select the error code labeled **SHV unable to contact required services**, and then select the **Noncompliant** option.

c. From the console tree of the Network Policy Server snap-in, expand **Network Access Protection\System Health Validators\Windows Security Health Validator\Settings**. Clear the option labeled **Restrict access for clients that do not have all available security updates installed**.

d. From the console tree of the Network Policy Server snap-in, expand **Network Access Protection\System Health Validators\Remediation Server Groups**. Select the group to which Server5 belongs, and then remove this server from the group.

46. Adam is responsible for managing a DNS server named Server1 that runs Windows Server 2008 R2. Adam would like to receive e-mail notifications when the DNS service on Server1 logs errors or warnings. He must ensure that he does not receive e-mail notifications for informational events that occur at Server1. Which of the following tasks should he perform? (Each correct answer represents part of the solution. Choose two answers.)

a. Select the **DNS Server** log on Server1.

b. Use Event Viewer on Server1 to create a custom view from the Application log on Server1.

c. Use Event Viewer on Server1 to create a custom view from the DNS Server log on Server1.

d. Attach a task to the event log that sends an e-mail notification to his e-mail address.

e. On the Start of Authority tab of the DNS zone's Properties dialog box, add his e-mail address to the Responsible Person field.

f. Use the Data Collector Sets option in Performance Monitor to send alerts to his e-mail address.

47. Rob is the network administrator for a manufacturing company that operates an AD DS network consisting of a single domain in which all servers run Windows Server 2008 R2 and all client computers run Windows 7 Enterprise. Rob has created a connection security rule on a member server named Server3 that requires Kerberos authentication for inbound and outbound connections.

Rob must ensure that client computers can access Server3 and that all connections to this server are encrypted. What should he do?

a. Use Windows Firewall with Advanced Security to create an outbound rule and specify the **Allow the connection if it is secure** option. Then, click **Customize** and select the **Require the connections to be encrypted** option.

  b. Use Windows Firewall with Advanced Security to create an inbound rule and specify the **Allow the connection if it is secure** option. Then click **Customize** and select the **Require the connections to be encrypted** option.

  c. Use Windows Firewall with Advanced Security to create a connection security rule and specify the **Isolation** option. Then, specify **Require authentication for inbound and outbound connections** as well as the **Computer and user (Kerberos V5)** authentication method.

  d. Create a Group Policy object that enables the Client (Respond Only) IPSec policy on all client computers.

48. Several months after installing a new Windows Server 2008 R2 file server and configuring quotas for users in her company's AD DS domain, Kelly notices that the hard disk on which users' shared folders are located is over three quarters full. On checking through the contents of the shared folders, Kelly notices a large number of audio and video files.

   Kelly wants to prevent users from storing audio and video files on the shared folder. What should she do?

  a. Use File Server Resource Manager (FSRM) to create an active file screen that blocks audio and video files.

  b. Use File Server Resource Manager (FSRM) to create a passive file screen that blocks audio and video files.

  c. Modify the quota to reduce the amount of disk space available to each user.

  d. Modify the quota to disallow the saving of audio and video files.

49. Beth is in charge of administering the network printers for the branch of a large accounting firm. It's April and the tax return business has the network's heavy-duty laser printer running non-stop. An accountant informs her that his documents are "not coming out of the printer in a timely manner." Beth examines the printer queue on the Windows Server 2008 computer. The documents in the queue can neither be printed nor deleted. What should she try first to restore printer functionality?

  a. Pause the printer. From the Advanced tab of the printer's Properties dialog box, select the **Hold Mismatched Documents** option, and then start the printer again.

  b. Stop, then restart the Print Spooler service.

    **c.** Redirect the original printer's print queue to a newly installed instance of the same printer.

    **d.** Relocate the folder used by the Print Spooler service.

**50.** Robert is the network administrator for a company that runs an AD DS network with a single domain. One of the domain controllers has been running slowly during much of the day and Robert suspects that he might need to upgrade the processor. Robert has added additional RAM to the computer but he wants to be informed of potential processor bottlenecks.

Robert decides he wants to have the domain controller inform him when the processor utilization exceeds 85 percent. What should he do? (Each correct answer represents part of the solution. Choose two answers.)

    **a.** Configure Resource Monitor to generate an alert when the Processor\%Processor Time counter exceeds 85%.

    **b.** Configure Performance Monitor to generate an alert when the Processor\%Processor Time counter exceeds 85%.

    **c.** Configure a data collector set to generate an alert when the Processor\%Processor Time counter exceeds 85%.

    **d.** In Server Manager, ensure that the Alerter service is configured to start automatically and send a message to his computer. He will then receive a message box on his computer when an alert is created.

    **e.** View the Application log in Event Viewer to determine whether any alerts have been generated.

    **f.** View the System log in Event Viewer to determine whether any alerts have been generated.

**51.** Matt is responsible for ensuring that network infrastructure services operate smoothly on his company's AD DS network, which consists of a single domain. The network uses a DHCP server called Dogstar to lease IP addressing information to client computers found on the network. Budget constraints currently limit him to using a single Windows Server 2008 R2 member server computer for this purpose. The only other member server, called Server43, is currently used as a file server. Although it contains a large amount of disk space, it is unsuitable for use as a DHCP server. If his DHCP server should experience a hardware failure of some kind Matt could be in trouble. All his Windows XP and Windows 7 Professional computers are configured to implement dynamic DNS updates and DNS itself is configured to use Active Directory–integrated zones.

Matt wants to store a backup of his DHCP server's database in a location that will allow him to restore his DHCP server to full functionality as quickly as possible. How should Matt proceed?

- **a.** Manually back up the DHCP database to a shared folder on Server43.

- **b.** Manually back up the DHCP database to the `Windows\System32\dhcp\backup` folder on Dogstar, and then copy its contents to a shared folder on Server43.

- **c.** Stop the DHCP Server service on Dogstar, then manually back up the DHCP database to the `Windows\System32\dhcp\backup` folder on Dogstar, then copy contents to a shared folder on Server43.

- **d.** Use `wbadmin.exe` to back up the system state on Dogstar to a shared folder on Server43.

- **e.** Manually back up the DHCP database to the `Windows\System32\dhcp\backup` folder on Dogstar.

**52.** Carolyn administers a single AD DS domain called `que.com`. She has decided against configuring `que.com` as an Active Directory–integrated zone. Carolyn has designated her domain controllers as Scorpio01 and Scorpio02. Her DNS servers are called Taurus01, Taurus02, and Taurus03. Taurus01 is the master DNS server. Taurus02 and Taurus03 are secondary DNS servers.

Carolyn wants only Taurus01 and Taurus02 to be authoritative for the `que.com` zone, so she specifies these two servers on the Name Servers tab of the `que.com` Properties dialog box. She accesses the Zone Transfers tab and clicks **Notify** to open the Notify dialog box. How should she configure the options in this dialog box so that all DNS servers are notified of any DNS zone updates? (Each correct answer represents part of the solution. Choose two answers.)

- **a.** Select the **Automatically notify** check box.
- **b.** Clear the **Automatically notify** check box.
- **c.** Select the **Servers listed on the Name Servers tab** option.
- **d.** Select the option labeled **The following servers** and specify IP address information for Taurus01, Taurus02, and Taurus03.
- **e.** Select the option labeled **The following servers** and specify IP address information for Taurus01, Scorpio01, and Scorpio02.
- **f.** Select the option labeled **The following servers** and specify IP address information for Taurus02 and Taurus03.

**53.** Cindy is the systems administrator for a company whose AD DS network is configured with a single domain. All servers run Windows Server 2008 R2 and all client computers run Windows 7 Enterprise. The network includes three domain controllers that are all configured as DNS servers and host an Active Directory–integrated zone.

Recently, the network experienced a DNS cache poisoning attack that disrupted name resolution for several days. She wants to increase the size of the socket pool to 10,000 to provide increased protection against this type of attack in the future. What should she do?

   **a.** At each DNS server, open an administrative command prompt and type `dnscmd /Config /SocketPoolSize 10000`. Then, restart the DNS service.

   **b.** At one DNS server, open an administrative command prompt and type `dnscmd /Config /SocketPoolSize 10000`. Then, restart the DNS service.

   **c.** At each DNS server, access the **Advanced** tab of the server's Properties dialog box, select the **Socket Pool Size** option, and then type `10000` in the text box provided.

   **d.** At one DNS server, access the **Advanced** tab of the server's Properties dialog box, select the **Socket Pool Size** option, and then type `10000` in the text box provided.

**54.** John is the systems administrator for a company that operates a network consisting of a single AD DS domain in which all servers run Windows Server 2008 R2 and all client computers run Windows 7 Professional. A server named Server1 is configured with the Network Policy and Access Services, including the Routing and Remote Access Services (RRAS) role service. Server1 is equipped with two network adapter cards, one connected to the Internet and the second connected to the internal network. All connections to the internal network are configured with private IP addresses in the range 192.168.3.0/24.

A server named IIS2 that runs Internet Information Services hosts a secured website that allows connections over TCP port 3437 only. This server is connected to the internal network and does not have a direct Internet connection.

John must ensure that users can access the secure website on IIS2 from the Internet. How should he configure Server1 to permit this connection?

   **a.** Configure Server1 as a VPN server and add a packet filter that allows TCP port 3437.

   **b.** Configure Server1 for Routing Information Protocol (RIP) and add a route to the routing table that directs external web requests for IIS2 to this server.

    **c.** Enable NAT on Server1 and enable the Secure Web Server (HTTPS) service on the external interface.

    **d.** Enable NAT on Server1 and enable port 3437 on the NAT tab of the IPv4-NAT-Interface Properties dialog box.

**55.** Kristina is a consultant hired by an insurance agency to set up the WAN connectivity from the agency's downtown Phoenix office to its Scottsdale branch office. The two offices are connected by an ISDN line that is already set up and in working condition. The insurance company pays for the cost of this ISDN line according to the time the connection is active. Therefore, Kristina needs to optimize the connection for its connect time. She decides to set up an on-demand demand-dial connection. Only the remote office needs to initiate the link. In order to complete this task, Kristina needs to configure the static routes.

Which of the following does Kristina need to configure to complete the connection? (Each correct answer represents part of the solution. Choose two answers.)

    **a.** A static route using Routing and Remote Access Service on the head office server.

    **b.** A static route using Routing and Remote Access Service on the branch office server.

    **c.** The user account on the head office server.

    **d.** The user account on the branch office server.

**56.** Ruth administers a single domain AD DS network with four Windows Server 2008 domain controllers, three Windows Server 2008 member servers, 100 Windows Vista Business clients, and 100 Windows 7 Professional clients. There are frequent changes to client configuration on the network. DNS is configured on two of the domain controllers with one Active Directory–integrated zone, and DHCP is configured on one of the member servers. Ruth has configured the DHCP server to register both address (A) and pointer (PTR) resource records for all client computers. She has also configured the DNS zones to allow only secure dynamic update.

Last Thursday, the DHCP server crashed and Ruth replaced it with a standby DHCP server. On Friday, she upgraded 15 of the Windows Vista Business computers to Windows 7 Professional. A user working from a Windows 7 Professional computer that had earlier been upgraded tried to connect today to one of the newly upgraded client computers; however, it did not recognize the names of the upgraded client computers.

Which of the following should Ruth do in order to solve this problem with the least amount of administrative effort?

   **a.** Run the `ipconfig /registerdns` command.

   **b.** At the backup DHCP server, select the **Always dynamically update DNS A and PTR records** option from the DNS tab of the server's Properties dialog box.

   **c.** Run the `ipconfig /renew` command.

   **d.** Add both DHCP servers as members of the DnsUpdateProxy group.

**57.** Kathy is responsible for administering Windows Server Update Services (WSUS) on her network. As a result of recent corporate expansion, Kathy has acquired a new computer running Windows Server 2008 R2, on which she wants to install WSUS to relieve the load on the current WSUS server.

Kathy wants to have the new WSUS server receive its updates from the current WSUS server. How should she configure the new server?

   **a.** Configure the new server as a WSUS client.

   **b.** Configure the new server to communicate with a downstream server.

   **c.** Configure the new server to communicate with an upstream server.

   **d.** Configure the new server to communicate with a proxy server.

**58.** Carol is the network administrator for a company that operates an IPv6 network consisting of 20 subnets. She is deploying a new Windows Server 2008 R2 computer on the network and needs to ensure that this server can communicate with client computers on all subnets but cannot be accessed across the Internet by external computers. Which of the following IPv6 addresses should she configure this server with?

   **a.** fe80::6e00:f0aa:cbb8:0005/64

   **b.** 2000::6e00:f0aa:cbb8:0005/64

   **c.** fd00::6e00:f0aa:cbb8:0005/8

   **d.** ff00::6e00:f0aa:cbb8:0005/64

**59.** Kent is responsible for ensuring that wireless access to his company's AD DS network is properly authenticated and secured. Users will access his network using various laptop computers running Windows XP, Windows Vista, and Windows 7. The network includes a RADIUS server named Server08 that is configured as a Network Policy Server (NPS). Kent creates a GPO and accesses the New Wireless Network Policy Properties dialog box and selects the

**Infrastructure** option. He then creates a new profile and chooses the **WPA2-Enterprise** authentication and **AES** encryption methods.

On testing the policy from home the same evening, Kent is able to connect to the network properly using a laptop running Windows 7 Professional. However, a few days later, several users with Windows XP Professional laptops report that they are unable to connect. What should Kent do?

a. Kent needs to specify the **WPA-Enterprise** authentication method.

b. Kent needs to select the **TKIP** encryption method.

c. Kent needs to select the **Ad hoc** option from the New Wireless Network Policy Properties dialog box.

d. Kent needs to create a second wireless access policy, this one directed at Windows XP clients.

60. Rod has configured several computers on his company's network to act as an SNMP community. A computer named Server4 is configured as an IP router to connect two subnets on the network. Rod accesses the Agent tab of the SNMP Service Properties dialog box on Server4. Which of the following options should Rod select to ensure that this computer participates fully in the SNMP community? (Each answer represents part of the solution. Choose three answers.)

a. **Physical**

b. **Applications**

c. **Datalink and subnetwork**

d. **Internet**

e. **End-to-end**

61. Erica is the network administrator for a company that operates an AD DS domain named certguide.com. The network includes two web servers named www and www2, both of which run Windows Server 2008 R2. The company's website is hosted on the www server and the www2 server includes a copy of the current website.

A web developer named Trevor is working on updates to the corporate website by making changes on the www2 server. Erica needs to enable Trevor to connect to the www2 server from his Windows 7 desktop computer when he types the address **www.certguide.com** into his browser. All other users should continue to access the **www** server when they type the same address. What should Erica do to accomplish this task?

    **a.** At Trevor's desktop computer, add a record to the LMHOSTS file.

    **b.** At Trevor's desktop computer, add a record to the HOSTS file.

    **c.** At Trevor's desktop computer, access the Alternate Configuration tab of the TCP/IP Properties dialog box and add the IP address of the `www2` server as a preferred DNS server.

    **d.** At the DNS server, create an alias (CNAME) resource record.

**62.** Natalie is setting up DirectAccess to facilitate access by users at her company's branch office to servers located at the head office. She sets up a server running Windows Server 2008 R2 in the branch office that is equipped with two physical network adapters and joins the server to the company's AD DS domain. She also installs a computer certificate on the server that will be used for IPSec authentication. Next, she creates a global security group named Branch Office Users and adds the user accounts of the users in the branch office to this group. Finally, she installs the Active Directory Certificate Services (AD CS) and Internet Information Services (IIS) server roles and the DirectAccess server feature on this server. While running the DirectAccess Management console, Natalie adds the Branch Office Users group as DirectAccess clients, adds certificates to be used by client computers accessing the server as well as certificates to be used to secure remote client connectivity over HTTPS. She also specifies the URL to the network location server as well as the host name and IPv6 address for the domain controller.

Users report that they are unable to access head office servers using DirectAccess. Which of the following is the most likely reason that they were unable to do so?

    **a.** Natalie should have specified an IPv4 address for the domain controller.

    **b.** Natalie should have added the computer accounts of branch office computers to the global security group, not the user accounts.

    **c.** Natalie should have generated certificates for each user in the branch office and specified these certificates for securing remote connectivity over HTTPS.

    **d.** Natalie has configured DirectAccess properly. The link to the head office servers must be offline.

**63.** Ruby is the systems administrator for a company that operates an AD DS network with a single domain called `que.com`. All servers run either the original or R2 version of Windows Server 2008. One Monday, she notices that the hard disk on DHCP server named Server6 has failed. She installs a new hard disk and performs a bare metal restore from a recent backup.

Ruby must ensure that DHCP clients do not receive IP addresses that have already been leased to other DHCP clients. What should she do?

   **a.** Set the DHCP server option 47 value to 0.

   **b.** Set the DHCP server option 47 value to 1.

   **c.** Set the Conflict Detection value to 0.

   **d.** Set the Conflict Detection value to 1.

**64.** Brent is the network administrator for a company that operates an AD DS network consisting of a single domain and four sites representing the company's offices, which are located in San Francisco, Oakland, San Jose, and Stockton. Each site has at least one domain controller that runs DNS and hosts an Active Directory–integrated zone. Domain controllers in the company run a mix of Windows 2000 Server, Windows Server 2003, and Windows Server 2008.

Brent's company places a contract with a second company in San Jose to provide extensive educational materials for company employees. Brent configures a conditional forwarder on a San Jose DNS server to point to a private web server at the second company's network, but employees in the San Francisco, Oakland, and Stockton offices report that they are unable to access the private web server.

On contacting administrators in the San Francisco, Oakland, and Stockton offices, Brent discovers that the conditional forwarder setting does not appear in their DNS servers. What should Brent to?

   **a.** Use Active Directory Sites and Services to force intersite replication.

   **b.** Configure the conditional forwarder with the **All domain controllers in this domain** option.

   **c.** Configure the conditional forwarder with the **All DNS servers in this domain** option.

   **d.** Configure a new zone delegation for each of the San Francisco, Oakland, and Stockton sites.

**65.** Julian is the systems administrator for a teaching hospital with specific responsibility for securing access to documents and records located on three Windows Server 2008 file servers. One of these servers contains a folder named `Research`, which resides on an NTFS partition. Julian's boss has instructed him to provide the following levels of access to this folder (all access to the folder is from client computers across the network):

Doctors should have Change control for all content in the `Research` folder. Nurses need Read access to the folder.

Students need Read access to a file called `Lesson1.doc` found in the `Research` folder. They should not be able to access any other files in the folder in any other way.

How should Julian configure permissions for the Research folder?

a. Share: Doctors-Full Control, Nurses-Read, Students-Read. NTFS: Doctors-Modify, Nurses-Read, Students-Read.

b. Share: Doctors-Change, Nurses-Change, Students-Read. NTFS: Doctors-Full Control; Nurses-Full Control, Students-Read for Lesson1.doc only; List for the folder.

c. Share: Doctors-Full Control, Nurses-Full Control, Students-Read. NTFS: Doctors-Modify, Nurses-Read, Students-Read for Lesson1.doc only; List for the folder.

d. Share: Doctors-Full Control, Nurses-Full Control, Students-Full Control. NTFS: Doctors-Read, Nurses-Read, Students-Read for Lesson1.doc only.

66. Betsy is the systems administrator for a company that operates an AD DS domain. The network includes a Windows Server 2008 R2 computer that is configured as a Network Policy Server (NPS) server for authenticating external users making VPN connections to the network.

Betsy must limit VPN access to the network to standard working hours of 8 a.m. to 5 p.m. She must ensure that this access limitation applies before any other limits she might need to apply. What should she do?

a. Create a new connection request policy that specifies the **Remote Access Server (VPN-dial up)** type of network access server. Then, add a Day and Time Restriction condition granting access between the hours of 8 a.m. and 5 p.m. Specify a processing order of 1 for this condition.

b. Create a new connection request policy that specifies the **Remote Access Server (VPN-dial up)** type of network access server. Then, add a Day and Time Restriction condition granting access between the hours of 8 a.m. and 5 p.m. Specify a processing order of 99 for this condition.

c. Create a new connection request policy that specifies the **Remote Desktop Gateway** type of network access server. Then, add a Day and Time Restriction condition granting access between the hours of 8 a.m. and 5 p.m. Specify a processing order of 1 for this condition.

d. Create a new connection request policy that specifies the **Remote Desktop Gateway** type of network access server. Then, add a Day and Time Restriction condition granting access between the hours of 8 a.m. and 5 p.m. Specify a processing order of 99 for this condition.

**67.** Nolan is the network administrator for a company that operates an AD DS network with a single domain. The company has a head office and a branch office, each of which is configured as a separate site in AD DS. The head office contains a server named App1 that hosts several mission-critical applications. Nolan has configured App1 with an inbound rule in Windows Server with Advanced Security that is designed to permit all domain users to access App1.

The week after configuring the firewall rule, several users in the branch office report that they are unable to access App1. These users are able to access several file servers in the head office; in addition, users in the head office report no problems in accessing App1. What should Nolan modify in the firewall rule?

   **a.** Edge traversal settings

   **b.** Protocol and Port settings

   **c.** Scope settings

   **d.** Tunnel settings

**68.** Ashley is setting up a NAP enforcement strategy for her network. In addition to ensuring that client computers meet health requirements, she wants to make sure that all communication between remote access clients connecting to her network from external locations is encrypted. What should she do?

   **a.** Run the Configure NAP Wizard on the NPS server, select the **Virtual Private Network (VPN)** option, and then select the **Smart Card or other certificate (EAP-TLS)** option from the Configure an Authentication Method page. Then, complete the remaining pages of the wizard.

   **b.** Run the Configure NAP Wizard on the NPS server, select the **IPSec with Health Registration Authority (HRA)** option, and then select the **Smart Card or other certificate (EAP-TLS)** option from the Configure an Authentication Method page. Then, complete the remaining pages of the wizard.

   **c.** Use the Add Role Services Wizard to install the Health Registration Authority role service on an appropriate server. While running this wizard, select a certificate for using SSL for encrypting network traffic and leave the default of **Choose an existing certificate for SSL encryption** selected. Then, run the Configure NAP Wizard on the NPS server, select the **Virtual Private Network (VPN)** option, and complete the remaining pages of the wizard.

   **d.** Use the Add Role Services Wizard to install the Health Registration Authority role service on an appropriate server. While running this wizard, select a certificate for using SSL for encrypting network traffic and leave the default of **Choose an existing certificate for SSL encryption** selected. Then, run the Configure NAP Wizard on the NPS server, select the **IPSec with Health Registration Authority (HRA)** option, and complete the remaining pages of the wizard.

69. Kate is the network administrator for a company that has a network that consists of a single AD DS domain with three sites corresponding to the head office and two branch offices. DNS is configured with Active Directory–integrated zones hosted on all head office domain controllers and secondary zones on member servers in the branch offices. Each branch office also includes a file server, which users access by specifying its fully qualified domain name (FQDN).

Occasionally, outages on the WAN links can last as long as two days. Kate needs to ensure that users can access the file server by its FQDN even if the WAN links are down for two days. What should she do?

   a. On the Start of Authority tab of the zone's Properties dialog box, set the **Minimum (default) TTL** value to 3 days.

   b. On the Start of Authority tab of the zone's Properties dialog box, set the **TTL for this record** value to 3 days.

   c. On the Start of Authority tab of the zone's Properties dialog box, set the **Expires after** value to 3 days.

   d. On the General tab of the zone's Properties dialog box, click **Aging**. Then set the Refresh interval to 3 days.

70. Steve is responsible for ensuring that applications and data on a server named FS01 are available at all times. He has scheduled backups to occur on a nightly basis during the week. One Monday, he discovers that FS01 has stopped responding. Because FS01 needs new hardware components that will take a few days to receive, Steve installs a new server named FS02 to ensure that the applications and data from FS01 are available. What should he do?

   a. Use the `vssadmin start recovery` command to restore the applications and data.

   b. Use the `vssadmin start sysrecovery` command to restore the applications and data.

   c. Use the `ntbackup restore` command to restore the applications and data.

   d. Use the `wbadmin start recovery` command to restore the applications and data.

**e.** Use the `wbadmin start sysrecovery` command to restore the system state.

**71.** Julio is the network administrator for Salty Dogs, LLC. The company's Design Director, Elizabeth, uses a portable laptop computer that has been installed with Windows 7 Ultimate. Julio's company requires that all users use smart cards to access company resources. He has therefore provided Elizabeth with a portable smart card reader. Company policy also requires that all users connect with the highest level of security possible when using an Internet, VPN, or modem link.

Julio is now creating the modem connection for Elizabeth to dial into the network. Which authentication protocol should he select so that Elizabeth can use her smart card for access to the VPN?

**a.** Microsoft Challenge Handshake Authentication Protocol (MS-CHAP) version 2

**b.** Extensible Authentication Protocol (EAP)

**c.** Challenge Handshake Authentication Protocol (CHAP)

**d.** Password Authentication Protocol (PAP)

**72.** Ellen is the systems administrator for a company that operates an AD DS network consisting of a single domain. The company has been using a Windows 2000 Server computer running WINS for single-name resolution of computer names on the network.

As part of a move to decommission all older servers and convert the network to using Windows Server 2008 R2 servers exclusively, Ellen needs to configure DNS to provide forestwide single name resolution. What should she do?

**a.** Create a primary zone named GlobalNames. Add host (A) resource records for all computers that require single name resolution. Then create corresponding secondary zones on all other DNS servers on the network.

**b.** Create an Active Directory–integrated zone named GlobalNames. Add host (A) resource records for all computers that require single name resolution.

**c.** Create SRV resource records for all computers that require single name resolution.

**d.** Create CNAME resource records for all computers that require single name resolution.

**73.** Gertrude is the network administrator for a company that operates an AD DS domain with two sites representing the company's Boston head office and a branch office located in Providence. The two offices are connected with a 128-kbps ISDN link. Each office has a Windows Server 2008 Routing and Remote Access (RRAS) computer that is configured as a router and uses RIP v.2.

The company has obtained a dedicated T1 link to provide an upgraded connection between the Boston and Providence offices, and Gertrude's manager has asked her to configure the two RRAS servers to use the T1 link as the primary connection but retain the ISDN connection as a backup link. How should Gertrude proceed to accomplish this objective?

    **a.** Configure the RRAS servers with a higher metric for the ISDN link.

    **b.** Configure the RRAS servers with a higher metric for the T1 link.

    **c.** Upgrade the RIP v.1 protocol to OSPF.

    **d.** Configure an IP Security policy in a GPO that specifies the T1 link as a primary connection.

**74.** Lynda is responsible for managing print services for users in her company's AD DS domain. The domain includes several Windows Server 2008 computers that are configured as print servers, each of which includes one or more shared printers.

Lynda needs to ensure that user can locate all shared printers on any of these servers. What should she do at each server? (Each correct answer represents a complete solution to the problem. Choose three answers.)

    **a.** Open a Windows PowerShell session and execute the `Set-ADOjbect` cmdlet.

    **b.** Open a Windows PowerShell session and execute the `Set-ADPrinter` cmdlet.

    **c.** From a command prompt, run the `pubprn.vbs` script.

    **d.** Right-click each printer in the Print Management console and choose **List in Directory**.

    **e.** Right-click the print server in the Print Management console and choose **Properties**. From the Ports tab of the print server's Properties dialog box, select **List in the Directory**.

    **f.** Right-click each printer in the Print Management console and choose **Properties**. From the Sharing tab of the printer's Properties dialog box, select **List in the Directory**.

g. From the Printer Sharing page of the Add Printer Wizard, select **Share this printer so that others on your network can find and use it**. Then, provide a share name that points to the print server on which the print device is installed.

**75.** Tony is the network administrator for a company that operates a network consisting of two subnets separated by a router, as shown in the exhibit.

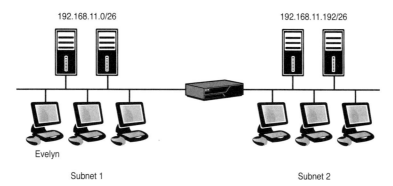

The subnets are configured with IPv4 addresses according to the network ranges shown in the exhibit. The router interfaces are configured with the IP addresses 192.168.11.1 and 192.168.11.193, respectively, and all client computers are configured with static IP addresses.

A user named Evelyn reports that she is unable to access any computers on Subnet 2. She does not have any difficulty accessing computers and their shared resources on Subnet 1. Tony runs `ipconfig` on Evelyn's computer and notices that it is configured with the IP address 192.168.11.101, the subnet mask of 255.255.255.0, and the default gateway 192.168.11.1. How should he modify the configuration of Evelyn's computer so that she is able to reach computers on Subnet B?

a. Change the subnet mask on Evelyn's computer to 255.255.255.192.

b. Change the subnet mask on Evelyn's computer to 255.255.0.0.

c. Change the default gateway on Evelyn's computer to 192.168.11.193.

d. Access the Advanced TCP/IP Settings dialog box on Evelyn's computer and configure an additional IP address on the 192.168.11.192/26 network.

**76.** Stan administers Distributed File System (DFS) within his company's AD DS domain. He has created a large domain-based namespace called \\que.com\ documents. The namespace contains a large number of subfolders with folder targets that enable access to its contents from any of the six offices operated by the company. He has configured shared folder and NTFS permissions for each subfolder that enable members of different security groups in the domain access according to their job requirements.

Lately, help desk technicians have received numerous calls from users receiving Access denied messages when attempting to reach subfolders in the \\que.com\documents namespace for which they have not been granted access. Stan verified that these users do not require access to these subfolders.

What can Stan do to reduce the instance of Access denied messages?

   **a.** Enable access-based enumeration on the DFS namespace.

   **b.** Subdivide the DFS namespace into several namespaces according to the requirements of specific groups of users.

   **c.** Disable referrals.

   **d.** Create replication groups and add the security groups configured with access permissions to these groups.

**77.** Mike is the systems administrator for his company's network, which is configured as an AD DS domain in which all servers run Windows Server 2008 R2 and all client computers run Windows 7 Enterprise. Mike has configured Network Monitor 3.4 on a server named Server1. After capturing data for several days, Mike is confused by the various IP addresses and names indicated on the capture file.

Mike wants to have the host names of the various servers on the network displayed on this capture file. What should he do to accomplish this task? (Each answer represents part of the solution. Choose two answers.)

   **a.** Create aliases that specify the host names and IP addresses on the company network.

   **b.** Create a display filter that specifies the host names and IP addresses on the company network.

   **c.** Use the nmcap.exe command with the /inputcapture and /capture parameters to specify the host names of the required servers.

   **d.** Apply the filter to the capture.

   **e.** Apply the aliases to the capture.

  **f.** Mike cannot display the host names on the current capture file. He must use a capture filter on a new capture tab before starting the capture.

  **g.** Mike cannot display the host names on the current capture file. He must apply the aliases to a new capture tab before starting the capture.

**78.** Teresa administers the network for Exam Prep Inc., which operates a website with the DNS name www.examprep.com. A single web server has been hosting the site since Teresa first began working for Exam Prep.

As a result of an increased amount of traffic to the website, Teresa's boss has asked her to add two additional server computers running Windows Server 2008 R2 and IIS to handle the increased traffic. Teresa configures each of the three web server computers to use the name www.examprep.com. As per the rules of TCP/IP she configures each server to use a different IP address. Teresa would like to ensure that the web servers be accessed equally, so she accesses the Advanced tab of the DNS server's Properties dialog box as shown in the exhibit.

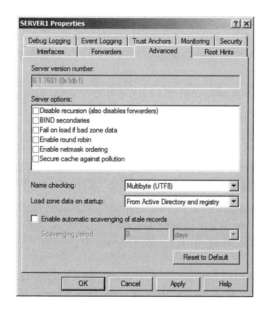

Which item should Teresa select to distribute user access equally among the web servers?

  **a.  Disable recursion (also disables forwarders)**

  **b.  BIND secondaries**

  **c.  Fail on load if bad zone data**

    **d. Enable round robin**

    **e. Enable netmask ordering**

    **f. Secure cache against pollution**

**79.** Evan is responsible for managing disk space usage on a Windows Server 2008 R2 computer named FileSrv1. The server contains two hard disks: disk C contains the operating system and application files and disk D includes a large shared folder that contains subfolders for each user in the company.

Users in different departments of the company store data on their subfolders. Space requirements for these users depends on their specific job functions, and Evan has created several global security groups to which he has added user accounts according to job function.

Evan wants to create disk quotas according to these groups. What should he do?

    **a.** In FSRM, create a quota template for each group he has configured. Then, apply these templates to the shared folder in the D: volume.

    **b.** In FSRM, right click **Quotas** and choose **Create Quota**. From the Create Quota dialog box, specify a disk quota for each global group he has configured.

    **c.** In FSRM, right click **Quotas** and choose **Create Quota**. From the Create Quota dialog box, specify a disk quota for each individual user that needs to store data in the folder.

    **d.** From the Quota tab of the disk D: Properties dialog box, select **Enable quota management** and click **Quota Entries**. Then, specify a disk quota for each global group he has configured.

    **e.** From the Quota tab of the disk D: Properties dialog box, select **Enable quota management** and click **Quota Entries**. Then, specify a disk quota for each individual user that needs to store data in the folder.

**80.** Evelyn is the network administrator for her company, which operates an AD DS domain in which all servers run Windows Server 2008 R2 and all client computers run Windows 7 Enterprise. Evelyn has set up a Windows Server Update Services (WSUS) server to distribute updates from the Microsoft Windows Update website, and must ensure that all computers access this server for their updates, rather than going across the Internet to the Windows Update website.

Evelyn sets up a Group Policy object (GPO) linked to the domain. Which of the following policies should she enable to accomplish this objective?

    **a.** Configure Automatic Updates

    **b.** Turn on Software Notifications

    **c.** Enable client-side targeting

    **d.** Specify intranet Microsoft update service location

**81.** Bruce is the network administrator for his company, which operates a Windows Server 2008 network consisting of a single AD DS domain named `cert-guide.com`. All computers on the domain run either Windows Server 2008 R2 or Windows 7 Professional. The Windows 7 Professional client computers are configured to obtain their IP information from one of three DHCP servers operating on the network. Bruce has configured all DHCP options at the scope level. He has also configured client reservations and client-level options for several Windows 7 Professional clients that require fixed IP addresses.

Bruce has just added a new DNS server to the network and wants to ensure that all clients access this server as the primary DNS server for servicing name resolution requests. At the scope level on each DHCP server, he has configured the 006 DNS Servers DHCP option with the IP address of the new DNS server. He has also requested that all users use the `ipconfig /renew` command to receive new IP lease information, and then use `ipconfig /all` to verify that they have received the IP address of the new DNS server as the primary DNS server. Every user except those that receive fixed IP leases reports that they have received the IP address of the new DNS server; however, the users that receive fixed IP leases have not been updated to the IP address of the new DNS server.

Which of the following actions should Bruce take in order to update the computers with fixed IP addresses to receive the IP address of the new DNS server?

    **a.** For the clients receiving IP address reservations, configure the 006 DNS Servers DHCP option at the vendor class level.

    **b.** For the clients receiving IP address reservations, configure the 006 DNS Servers DHCP option at the server level.

    **c.** For the clients receiving IP address reservations, configure the 006 DNS Servers DHCP option at the client level.

    **d.** Ask the users with fixed IP addresses to use the `ipconfig /flushdns` command.

    **e.** Ask the users with fixed IP addresses to shut down and restart their computers.

898   MCTS 70-642 Cert Guide: Windows Server® 2008 Network Infrastructure, Configuring

**82.** Ryan is a systems administrator for a company that operates an AD DS forest containing an empty forest root domain and two child domains named `east.que.com` and `west.que.com`. All servers on the network run Windows Server 2008 R2 and all client computers run Windows 7 Enterprise.

Users in the `west.que.com` domain report that it takes a long time to access resources in the `east.que.com` domain. What action should Ryan perform to improve the response times? (Each correct answer represents part of the solution. Choose two answers.)

   **a.** Create a GPO that enables the **Primary DNS Suffix Devolution Level** policy and specify a minimum number of two labels to be retained.

   **b.** Create a GPO that enables the **DNS Suffix Search List** policy and specify the `east.que.com` and `west.que.com` DNS suffixes.

   **c.** Create a GPO that enables Link-Local Multicast Name Resolution.

   **d.** Link the GPO to the `west.que.com` domain.

   **e.** Link the GPO to the `east.que.com` domain.

   **f.** Link the GPO to the `que.com` domain.

**83.** Yvonne is the network administrator for a company that has a head office and three branch offices. Each branch office has a server running Windows Server 2008 R2. Yvonne wants to collect event logs from the branch office servers to a server named Server1 at the head office so she can be informed of problems in the branch offices in an expedient manner. What should Yvonne do?

   **a.** At the head office server, run the `winrm quickconfig` command. Then, run the `winrm set winrm/config/client @{TrustedHosts="Server1"}` command at each branch office server, in which she specifies the name of the head office server in the `<sources>` parameter. Also, run the `wecutil qc` command at each branch office server.

   **b.** At the head office server, run the `winrm quickconfig` command. Then, run the `winrm set winrm/config/client @{TrustedHosts="Server1"}` command at the same server, in which she specifies the names of the branch office computers in the `<sources>` parameter. Also, run the `wecutil qc` command at each branch office server.

   **c.** At the head office server, run the `wecutil qc` command. Then, run the `winrm set winrm/config/client @{TrustedHosts="Server1"}` command at the same server, in which she specifies the names of the branch office computers in the `<sources>` parameter. Also, run the `winrm quickconfig` command at each branch office server.

    **d.** At the head office server, run the `wecutil qc` command. Then, run the `winrm set winrm/config/client @{TrustedHosts="Server1"}` command at each branch office server, in which she specifies the name of the head office server in the `<sources>` parameter. Also, run the `winrm quickconfig` command at each branch office server.

**84.** Ursula is responsible for administering a single AD DS domain for a small university. At present, the only DNS server is a domain controller called Deecee01. Deecee01's zone is a primary zone and is not stored in Active Directory. Because students' client computers need to only access the university's server computers, A records for these servers have been added to the zone.

Enrollment is up and a building expansion program promises to expand IT services. Ursula wants to streamline DNS administration by configuration dynamic updates. Dr. Hilliard, who sits on the IT planning committee, has expressed "profound concern" that dynamic updates will open the door to hacker/students using rogue PCs to register and insinuate their records into the zone. This activity could mark the revival of a peer-to-peer file-sharing problem that has been brought under control.

How can Ursula assure Dr. Hilliard that dynamic updates are performed safely on the university network? (Each correct answer represents part of the solution. Choose two answers.)

    **a.** Convert the standard primary zone to an Active Directory–integrated zone.

    **b.** In the General tab of the zone Properties dialog box, select **Secure only** at the Dynamic Updates list.

    **c.** In the General tab of the zone Properties dialog box, select **Nonsecure and secure** at the Dynamic Updates list.

    **d.** In the Zone Transfers tab of the zone Properties dialog box, select **Only to the servers listed on the Name Servers tab**.

    **e.** Configure the DNS server to not support incremental zone transfers.

**85.** Tom is planning the use of Network Access Protection (NAP) on his company's AD DS network. The network contains a Windows Server 2008 R2 computer named Server1 that is configured as an enterprise root certification authority. Another server named Server2 is configured with Routing and Remote Access Service (RRAS), and will be used as an access point for remote clients making a VPN connection to the network. Tom is configuring a server named Server3 as a Network Policy server and System Health Validation server.

What does Tom need to do to ensure that the system health policy is applied to all client computers that attempt to make a VPN connection?

   **a.** Configure Server2 as a RADIUS client.

   **b.** Configure Server3 as a RADIUS client.

   **c.** Configure all domain controllers on the network to be RADIUS clients.

   **d.** Select the **RDS Enforcement** option.

**86.** Kelly is responsible for ensuring that communications between the various sites on her company's AD DS network are properly authenticated and secured. The network includes five sites representing the head office and four branch offices, each of which is connected to the head office with a T1 WAN link.

The manager wants Kelly to use IPSec to secure communications across the WAN links. She must ensure that the method used provides data confidentially, authentication, integrity, and anti-replay for the payload contained within each packet. How should she set up IPSec?

   **a.** She should use IPSec transport mode with Authentication Header (AH).

   **b.** She should use IPSec tunnel mode with AH.

   **c.** She should use IPSec transport mode with Encapsulating Security Protocol (ESP).

   **d.** She should use IPSec tunnel mode with ESP.

**87.** Shirley is responsible for maintaining the servers on her company's AD DS network. Users are reporting slow access to a file server named Server8 when they attempt to access shared documents located on this server. Shirley opens Performance Monitor on Server8 to collect real-time performance data and notices that the processor runs at 100 percent of capacity most of the time. She would like to obtain additional information to ascertain why the processor is overtaxed. What should she do?

   **a.** Use Performance Monitor to attach performance counters to each process running on Server8 and monitor these for processor usage.

   **b.** Create a custom view from the Application log in Event Viewer that provides information on errors generated by each process running on Server8.

   **c.** Use Resource Monitor to obtain information on the processor usage of each application running on Server8.

   **d.** Use Reliability Monitor to obtain information on the processor usage of each application running on Server8.

**88.** Connie is the systems administrator for a company that operates an AD DS network with a single domain. All servers run Windows Server 2008 R2. In recent months, Connie has removed a number of Windows XP Professional computers from the network and replaced them with new Windows 7 Professional machines, so that now all client computers run Windows 7 Professional or Ultimate.

A server named Server4 is configured as a DNS server and includes a primary zone that holds name resolution data for the network. Connie notices that the primary zone contains entries for old Windows XP computers that have been removed from the network. What should she do to remove these stale resource records from the zone file immediately?

 **a.** In the console tree of DNS Manager, right-click **Server4** and choose **Properties**. On the Advanced tab of the server's Properties dialog box, select the **Enable automatic scavenging of stale records** option and specify a short time frame as the scavenging period.

 **b.** In the console tree of DNS Manager, right-click **Server4** and choose **Set Aging/Scavenging for All Zones**. Then, select the **Scavenge stale resource records** check box.

 **c.** In the console tree of DNS Manager, right-click the primary forward lookup zone and choose **Properties**. In the General tab of the Properties dialog box, click **Aging**, and then select the **Scavenge stale resource records** check box.

 **d.** In the console tree of DNS Manager, right-click **Server4** and choose **Scavenge Stale Resource Records**. Then, click **Yes** in the message box that appears.

**89.** Grant is responsible for managing remote access connections to his company's network. He would like to create a profile that facilitates remote connections to the company's VPN server. The profile should include items such as a custom phone book containing access numbers and supported protocols for the VPN connection, a URL that points to the connection point services server, Internet Explorer proxy settings, and custom files that will be installed on each client's computer. Grant should also be able to distribute this profile by e-mail to all clients that require connection to the network. What should Grant do?

 **a.** Create a Group Policy object (GPO) that contains the required settings. Back this GPO up and distribute a backup copy to each required client, who can then restore the GPO with the Local Group Policy Editor.

 **b.** Run the Routing and Remote Access Setup Wizard, select the **Virtual private network (VPN) access and NAT** option, and then configure options presented by this wizard to complete a profile that he can distribute to the required clients.

   **c.** Run the Routing and Remote Access Setup Wizard, select the **Custom configuration** option, and then configure options presented by this wizard to complete a profile that he can distribute to the required clients.

   **d.** Use Connection Manager to create a custom profile that he can distribute to the required clients.

**90.** Roberta is the network administrator for a company that operates an Active Directory Domain Services (AD DS) domain that includes a head office and two regional offices. The head office has domain controllers and member servers running Windows Server 2008 R2 and client computers running a mix of Windows Vista and Windows 7. Each regional office has two Windows Server 2003 R2 servers and 80 client computers running a mix of Windows Vista and Windows 7. These offices are organized into a network that includes two subnets in each office.

Roberta wants to set up BranchCache so that computers in the regional offices can easily access data on head office servers. Which of the following steps must she take? (Each answer represents part of the solution. Choose four answers.)

   **a.** Install BranchCache in Distributed Cache mode.

   **b.** Install BranchCache in Hosted Cache mode.

   **c.** Upgrade branch office servers to Windows Server 2008 R2.

   **d.** Upgrade Windows Vista head office client computers to Windows 7.

   **e.** Upgrade Windows Vista branch office client computers to Windows 7.

   **f.** Create a Group Policy object (GPO) that includes a predefined firewall rule that specifies **BranchCache–Content Retrieval (Uses HTTP)** and select the **Allow the Connection** option.

   **g.** Create a Group Policy object (GPO) that includes a custom firewall rule that allows all local ports and select the **Allow the Connection If It Is Secure** option.

**91.** Bob is the network administrator for a company that operates an AD DS network named `certguide.com`. The network includes a head office and one branch office. The head office is configured with the network address 192.168.2.0/24 and the branch office has a network address of 192.168.3.0/26. Bob has recently deployed a Windows Server 2008 R2 computer with Routing and Remote Access Services (RRAS) to act as a router to join the head office with one of the branch offices. This server is configured with the IP address

192.168.2.1 on the head office interface and 192.168.3.1 on the branch office interface.

A user at a client computer in the second branch office reports that she is unable to access the head office with her computer's current configuration. What action should Bob take on her computer's routing table to provide it with a persistent route to the head office servers?

    **a.** Bob should execute the route `-p` add `192.168.3.0` `mask` `255.255.255.0` `192.168.2.1` command.

    **b.** Bob should execute the route `-p` add `192.168.2.0` `mask` `255.255.255.0` `192.168.3.1` command.

    **c.** Bob should execute the route `-p` add `192.168.3.0` `mask` `255.255.255.192` `192.168.2.1` command.

    **d.** Bob should execute the route `-p` add `192.168.2.0` `mask` `255.255.255.192` `192.168.3.1` command.

**92.** Arlene is configuring a Windows Server 2008 R2 computer to act as an SNMP management system. She wants to configure the SNMP service properties to accept SNMP packets from only a predetermined set of hosts. So, she right-clicks the **SNMP** service in the Services node of the Computer Management snap-in and chooses **Properties** to display the SNMP Service properties dialog box, as shown in the exhibit.

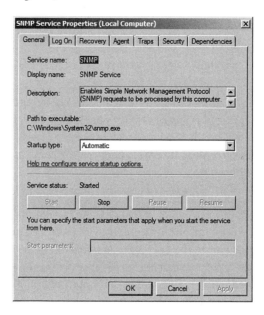

Which tab of this dialog box should she select to accomplish this task?

**a.** General

**b.** Log On

**c.** Recovery

**d.** Agent

**e.** Traps

**f.** Security

**g.** Dependencies

**93.** Marilyn is responsible for maintaining DNS on her company's AD DS network, which consists of a single domain in which all servers run Windows Server 2008 R2. The company operates an office in downtown Denver and a suburban office in Littleton.

After upgrading a member server in the company's suburban office to a domain controller, users at that office report that logon to the domain is slow. Upon investigating the problem, Marilyn notices that the service (SRV) resource records for the new domain controller are not registered in the DNS zone for the suburban office. What should she do to re-register these SRV resource records as fast as possible?

**a.** Restart the DNS Server service.

**b.** Restart the DNS Client service.

**c.** Restart the Netlogon service.

**d.** Reboot the domain controller.

**94.** Edward is responsible for managing computers on a network segment used by developers in building customized point-of-service applications. Because of intrusions that have occurred several times in recent months, he has disconnected this network segment from the Internet and from the remaining corporate network, and has configured it as a workgroup.

Edward must ensure that all computers on this segment are kept updated with respect to the latest Microsoft updates, and to this end he has configured a Windows Server 2008 R2 computer on the segment with WSUS. Another server running WSUS is present on the corporate network. Which of the following means should he use to ensure that the WSUS server on the isolated segment receives all required updates with the least amount of administrative effort? (Each correct answer represents a complete solution to the problem. Choose two answers.)

a. At the WSUS server on the corporate network, type the command `wsusutil.exe export packagename.cab logfile.cab`. Copy the `logfile.cab` file to removable media, take this media to the WSUS server on the isolated segment, and then type the command `wsusutil.exe import packagename.cab logfile.cab`.

b. At the WSUS server on the corporate network, type the command `wuauclt.exe export packagename.cab logfile.cab`. Copy the `logfile.cab` file to removable media, take this media to the WSUS server on the isolated segment, and then type the command `wuauclt.exe import packagename.cab logfile.cab`.

c. At the WSUS server on the corporate network, use `wbadmin.exe` to back up the folder containing the Windows Internal Database. Copy this backup to removable media, take this media to the WSUS server on the isolated segment, and then use `wbadmin.exe` to restore the folder to this server.

d. At the WSUS server on the corporate network, use `ntbackup.exe` to back up the folder containing the Windows Internal Database. Copy this backup to removable media, take this media to the WSUS server on the isolated segment, and then use `ntbackup.exe` to restore the folder to this server.

e. At the WSUS server on the corporate network, use the Update Source and Proxy Server dialog box to specify synchronization of this server with the server on the isolated network. Select the option labeled **This server is a replica of the upstream server**.

f. At the WSUS server on the isolated network, use the Update Source and Proxy Server dialog box to specify synchronization of this server with the server on the corporate network. Select the option labeled **This server is a replica of the upstream server**.

**95.** Charles is responsible for managing disk usage on three file servers that are member servers in his company's AD DS domain. He has created a file quota template and uses this template to apply quotas to several shared folders accessed by 150 users. After upgrading the hard disks on each of the file servers, Charles would like to increase the amount of disk space available to all 150 users. What should he do to accomplish this task with the least amount of administrative effort?

a. Create and apply a new quota template.

b. Add additional shared folders and create an additional quota template that applies quotas to these folders.

    **c.** Modify the file screen settings for each user.

    **d.** Simply modify the quota template.

**96.** Andrea is responsible for monitoring and maintaining the servers on her company's AD DS network. Servers run a mix of the original and R2 versions of Windows Server 2008. After installing and running a new DHCP server that runs Windows Server 2008 R2 for one month, Andrea checks Reliability Monitor and discovers that no data is available for the System Stability Index. What should Andrea do to ensure that the server collects Reliability Monitor information?

    **a.** Configure the Task Scheduler service with a trigger that automatically starts the RacTask task.

    **b.** In Event Viewer, scroll the System log to locate an error event related to Reliability Monitor, right-click the event, and choose **Attach Task To This Event**. On the Action page of the Create Basic Task Wizard, specify the path to the Reliability Monitor executable file.

    **c.** In Performance Monitor, expand **Data Collector Sets > System > System Diagnostics**, right-click this node, and choose **Start**. After one minute, expand the **Reports > System Performance** node and select the data collector set corresponding to the current date and time.

    **d.** Open the Services snap-in, right-click the **Performance Logs & Alerts** service, and choose **Properties**. On the dialog box that appears, set the startup type for this service to **Automatic**.

**97.** Jocelyn is the systems administrator for a company that has converted its network to using IPv6 exclusively. She has configured a server named Server04 as a DHCP server for leasing IPv6 addresses to client computers. Jocelyn must ensure that all TCP/IP settings, including IPv6 addresses, are allocated to DHCP clients on subnets that are configured for use of IPv6. DHCP clients on subnets that are not configured for use of IPv6 should not receive any configuration information. How should she configure the DHCP server to meet this requirement?

    **a.** She should set the Managed Address Configuration (M) flag to 0 and the Other Stateful Configuration (O) flag to 1.

    **b.** She should set the M flag to 1 and the O flag to 0.

    **c.** She should set both the M flag and the O flag to 1.

    **d.** She should set both the M flag and the O flag to 0.

**98.** Tyrone is the network administrator for a company named All Roads Engineering Consultants, which operates an AD DS network configured as a single domain. The Designing department has recently acquired a high-speed laser printer to handle printing requirements of the various staff.

Tyrone created three domain local groups on the print server for purposes of managing the printer: Designers have Print permission, Supervisors have Manage Documents permission, and Managers have Manage Printer permission.

Tyrone needs to give a staff member in the Designing department named Yolanda the ability to pause, resume, and cancel documents printed by all staff, but not control the permissions assigned to other staff members on the printer.

To which group should Tyrone add Yolanda's user account?

    **a.** Supervisors.

    **b.** Designers.

    **c.** Managers.

    **d.** Tyrone does not need to add Yolanda to any of these groups; she can perform these tasks by default.

**99.** Ralph is responsible for managing VPN connections to his company's AD DS network. Employees connecting from client locations use Secure Sockets Tunneling Protocol (SSTP) to make the connection to a VPN server running Windows Server 2008. A user named Linda reports that when she attempts to complete the connection from a laptop running Windows XP Professional, she receives an error code 741 accompanied by the message stating that The local computer does not support the required encryption type. What should Ralph do to enable Linda to make a successful connection to the VPN server?

    **a.** On Linda's computer, access the **Security** tab of the VPN Connection Properties dialog box, select **No encryption allowed (server will disconnect if it requires encryption)**, and then click **OK**.

    **b.** On Linda's computer, access the **Security** tab of the VPN Connection Properties dialog box, select **Require encryption (disconnect if server declines)**, and then click **OK**.

    **c.** On Linda's computer, access the **Security** tab of the VPN Connection Properties dialog box, select **Maximum strength encryption (disconnect if server declines)**, and then click **OK**.

    **d.** On Linda's computer, reconfigure her VPN connection to use the Point to Point Tunneling Protocol (PPTP) instead.

**100.** Mick is responsible for ensuring that a server named Terminal1, which runs Remote Desktop Protocol (RDP), can be accessed by users in his domain. How should he configure Windows Firewall on Terminal1?

    **a.** Configure an inbound rule that passes traffic on UDP port 500.

    **b.** Configure an inbound rule that passes traffic on TCP port 1723.

    **c.** Configure an inbound rule that passes traffic on TCP port 1812.

    **d.** Configure an inbound rule that passes traffic on TCP port 3389.

**101.** Julie is responsible for maintaining VPN access to her company's network, which is configured as an AD DS forest with an empty forest root domain and two child domains named east.que.com and west.que.com. The network includes a standalone Network Policy Server (NPS) server named Alpha and a VPN server named Beta. Julie has configured Beta as a RADIUS client to Alpha.

Julie needs to ensure that users from both east.que.com and west.que.com domains can make VPN connections through Beta by using their own domain user accounts. How should she proceed?

    **a.** Create connection request policies on Alpha.

    **b.** Create connection request policies on Beta.

    **c.** Add all domain client computers to a global group in each domain. Then, add the global groups as RADIUS clients to the Alpha server.

    **d.** From the Accounting node of the NPS snap-in on Alpha, add an option that logs user authentication and accounting requests for both domains.

**102.** Diana is the network administrator for a small company that operates a single domain AD DS network. Currently, all servers run Windows Server 2003 and all client computers run Windows XP Professional. The network has been using IPv4 exclusively and has not experienced any communication problems.

The company has purchased a new file server running Windows Server 2008 R2 and Diana is responsible for deploying this server on the network. Her boss has asked her to disable the use of IPv6 on this server. What should she do?

    **a.** Access the Local Area Connection Properties dialog box, select **Internet Protocol Version 6 (TCP/IPv6)** and click **Uninstall**. Then, click **Yes** to confirm her intention to uninstall this protocol.

    **b.** Access the Local Area Connection Properties dialog box and deselect the check box labeled **Internet Protocol Version 6 (TCP/IPv6)**.

    **c.** From a command prompt, type `netsh interface IPv6 delete`.

    **d.** In Windows Firewall with Advanced Security, create an incoming rule that blocks all IPv6 communications.

**103.** Eric is network administrator for Acme Construction Ltd. The company's network consists of a single AD DS domain called `acmeconstr.com`. Servers in the domain run either Windows Server 2003 or Windows Server 2008, and client computers run either Windows XP Professional or Windows 7 Professional. Two Windows Server 2008 computers named NS01 and NS02 host DNS zones for the `acmeconstr.com` domain; NS01 hosts a standard primary zone and NS02 hosts a standard secondary DNS zone. Queries that cannot be resolved by these servers are forwarded to Acme Construction's ISP.

Because Acme Construction has put a number of jobs out for tender in the past few months its DNS servers are receiving an exceptionally high number of requests and are becoming bogged down as a result. Eric creates a new zone called `bids.acmeconstr.com` to handle the traffic. He decides to configure a new Windows Server 2008 R2 DNS server called NS03 and dedicate it exclusively to servicing DNS requests for the `bids.acmeconstr.com` zone, where all future bids will be directed. To do this, he needs to delegate control of the `bids.acmeconstr.com` zone to the NS03 server. How should Eric proceed?

- **a.** Manually create an A record for the NS03 server computer.
- **b.** Use the New Delegation Wizard in the DNS console to delegate control of the new zone.
- **c.** Manually create an A record and an NS record for the NS03 server computer.
- **d.** Add the appropriate IP address for NS03 to the Forwarders tab on the NS01 and NS02 server computers.

**104.** Maggie is responsible for monitoring and maintaining the servers on her company's AD DS network. The network includes four servers that run the Server Core version of Windows Server 2008 R2. These servers are named SRV1, SRV2, SRV3, and SRV4. Maggie has used the `winrm` and `wecutil` commands to enable event log subscriptions on these servers. Now, she wants to configure SRV1 with an event log subscription that collects events from the other three servers. Which action should Maggie perform?

- **a.** At SRV1, execute the `Wevtutil cs subscription.xml` command to create an event log subscription named `subscription.xml`.
- **b.** At SRV1, execute the `Wecutil cs subscription.xml` command to create an event log subscription named `subscription.xml`.
- **c.** At SRV1, create a custom view named `subscription.xml` and export this view to each of the other servers.

  **d.** At SRV2, SRV3, and SRV4, attach tasks to the event types to be collected, and configure the task to write information to an event log file named `subscription.xml` on SRV1.

**105.** Melanie is responsible for ensuring that DNS services are operating properly in her company's AD DS domain. She has installed a new Windows Server 2008 R2 computer on the network and configured it as a secondary DNS name server on the network. To ensure that the server is functioning properly, she selects the simple and recursive query test types, and then runs these tests. The test columns display a `Pass` result for the simple test and a `Fail` result for the recursive test.

What should Melanie do first to troubleshoot this failure?

  **a.** Determine whether the root hints are correct.

  **b.** Restart the DNS server service.

  **c.** Access the **Debug Logging** tab and specify logging of incoming and outgoing packets with the Queries/Transfers option.

  **d.** Determine whether the server contains the `1.0.0.127.in-addr.arpa` zone.

**106.** Laura is a member of the Faculty and Department Heads groups at a local community college, and has been granted the right to log on locally at a Windows Server 2008 R2 file server that is maintained by the Humanities Department. The server contains a shared folder named `Policies` that is protected by shared folder and NTFS permissions (allowed unless otherwise specified) that are configured as follows:

| Type of Permission | Group | Permission |
|---|---|---|
| Shared folder | Faculty | Deny read |
| | Department Heads | Read |
| NTFS | Faculty | Modify |
| | Department Heads | Full control |

What is Laura's permission to the Policies folder when she logs on to the file server, and what is her permission to the Policies folder when she logs on to her Windows 7 Professional desktop computer?

  **a.** Read at both the server and desktop

  **b.** Read at the server and no access from the desktop

  **c.** Full control at the server and no access from the desktop

**d.** Full control at both the server and desktop

**e.** No access from either the server or desktop

**107.** Debbie is a network administrator for PQR Company, which operates an Active Directory Domain Services (AD DS) domain named pqr.com. She set up a Windows Server 2008 R2 computer as a DirectAccess server to facilitate employee connections to the network from client locations. On this server, she created a security group named DA.

Debbie must now configure employee client computers for DirectAccess connections. Which of the following must she do? (Each answer represents part of the solution. Choose four answers.)

**a.** Install a computer certificate on each client computer that enables DirectAccess authentication.

**b.** Enroll each employee with a user certificate that enables DirectAccess authentication.

**c.** Add the user account of each employee to the DA security group.

**d.** Add the computer account of each client computer to the DA security group.

**e.** Configure a Group Policy object (GPO) linked to the domain that specifies IPv6 transition technologies for connection to the DirectAccess server.

**f.** Configure a GPO linked to the domain that specifies Secure Sockets Layer (SSL) configuration settings for connection to the DirectAccess server.

**g.** Configure a GPO linked to the domain that specifies a name resolution policy including WINS security and DirectAccess settings.

**h.** Configure a GPO linked to the domain that specifies a name resolution policy including configuration settings for DNS security and DNS settings for DirectAccess.

**108.** Brenda is the network administer for a company that operates an AD DS forest that contains two domains, que.com and certguide.com. She is responsible for a DNS server named Server21, which hosts Active Directory–integrated zones for both que.com and certguide.com.

Users at computers in the certguide.com domain report that they are unable to access computers in the que.com domain by using single-label names. However, users in the que.com domain do not experience any difficulty in using single-label names to access computers in the certguide.com domain.

What should Brenda do to enable users in the `certguide.com` domain to use single-label names to access computers in the `que.com domain`, with the least amount of administrative effort?

    **a.** Enable the **DNS Suffix Search List** Group Policy setting in a GPO linked to the `certguide.com` domain and then add `que.com` as a DNS suffix in the property settings for this policy.

    **b.** Enable the **Allow DNS Suffix Appending to Unqualified Multi-Label Name Queries** Group Policy setting in a GPO linked to the `certguide.com` domain and then add `que.com` as an additional suffix in the property settings for this policy.

    **c.** Add `que.com` as an additional primary DNS suffix at the DNS Suffix and NetBIOS Computer Name dialog box on the affected client computers.

    **d.** Add `que.com` to the DNS suffix search order on the affected client computers.

**109.** Stephanie is the systems administrator for an AD DS domain that includes nine computers running Windows Server 2008 R2 and 225 client computers running Windows 7 Professional. Most servers are configured to use static IP addresses. Two member servers named Server3 and Server4 are configured as DHCP servers. A single DNS server, running on a domain controller named Server1, provides name resolution services. This server does not employ dynamic updating for its resource records.

The network includes a file server named Server9. Stephanie wants Server9 to receive the same IP address every time that it makes a request for one. She configures a reservation for Server9 on Server3 as shown in the exhibit so that the name "Server9" can be resolved to the IP address 192.168.1.114 without using broadcasts. She also creates a DNS host (A) record for Server9 on the DNS server.

Several days later, some users report that they can no longer access shared resources on Server9. On executing the `ipconfig /all` command on Server9,
Stephanie discovers that it is using an IP address of 192.168.1.51. What should
she do to correct this problem?

   a. At the command prompt on Server9 type **`ipconfig /release`**, then type
      **`ipconfig /renew`**.

   b. Configure a reservation for Server9 on Server4 that matches the one for
      Server3 as shown in the exhibit.

   c. Configure a reservation for Server9 on Server3 that uses the IP address
      192.168.1.51.

   d. Ensure that the MAC address displayed by the `ipconfig /all` com-
      mand matches the MAC address displayed in the exhibit.

110. Jim is responsible for maintaining security on his company's network, which
      includes a Windows Server 2008 R2 computer that runs WSUS to deliver up-
      dates to all client computers on the network. Company policy stipulates that
      all communication with the WSUS server be secured. What should Jim do to
      ensure that this policy is met?

   a. Configure the WSUS server to use BitLocker Drive Encryption.

   b. Configure the WSUS server to use MS-CHAPv2.

   c. Configure the WSUS server with NTFS permissions that limit access to
      administrative users.

   d. Install a Secure Sockets Layer (SSL) certificate and configure the WSUS
      server to use HTTPS over TCP port 443.

**111.** Wendy is responsible for managing a Windows Server 2008 R2 computer that is configured as a VPN server to enable remote access clients to connect to her company's network using the Point-to-Point Tunneling Protocol (PPTP). Users attempting to connect to the network receive a message stating `Error 721: The remote computer is not responding`.

Wendy checks the firewall settings on the VPN server. Which of the following ports should she open on the firewall so that remote users are able to access this server?

   **a.** 47

   **b.** 443

   **c.** 1723

   **d.** 3389

**112.** Betty is the network administrator for a company named North American Focus, which operates an AD DS network consisting of a single domain named `nafocus.com`. The Windows Server 2008 R2 domain controllers are configured as DNS servers and use an Active Directory–integrated zone. Included is a domain controller named Comstock. The `nafocus.com` domain connects to the Internet through an RRAS server called Oshtemo. Oshtemo uses Network Address Translation (NAT) to appear on the Internet as an external IP address. Two Windows 7 Professional client computers called Decatur and Wayland reside on the North American Focus network. These computers are configured with IP addresses as shown in the exhibit.

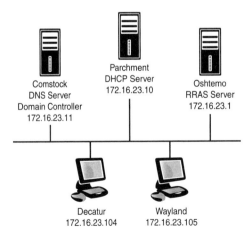

A subsidiary of Betty's company is called Exam Prep Inc., and operates a DNS domain named `examprep.com`. A Windows Server 2008 computer called Parchment provides TCP/IP configuration information via DHCP to computers running client operating systems and to computers acting as member servers.

A user on the Decatur computer needs to access a remote website to exchange confidential financial information. Decatur is the only computer in the `nafocus.com` domain that should be permitted to do this. What should Betty do to enable the Decatur computer to make the connection to the external website? (Each correct answer represents part of the solution. Choose two answers.)

- **a.** Configure NAT services on Comstock.
- **b.** Configure DNS services on Oshtemo.
- **c.** Configure an inbound packet filter on Oshtemo.
- **d.** Configure an outbound packet filter on Oshtemo.
- **e.** Configure an inbound packet filter on Decatur.
- **f.** Configure RRAS services on Comstock.

**113.** Brett is a desktop support specialist who is responsible for ensuring that up-to-date versions of users' files are available at all times. Users store their files on several shared folders on a Windows Server 2008 R2 computer. Several users have reported that files have become corrupted and he has had to perform restores from backup that have taken much of his time, not to mention users' time while waiting for the files to become available. What should Brett do to ensure that users can rapidly recover files to an older state?

- **a.** Enable the VSS service on each disk volume containing user data.
- **b.** Enable the VSS service on each shared folder that contains user data.
- **c.** Configure Windows Server Backup to perform incremental backups on each disk volume on an hourly basis.
- **d.** Configure Windows Server Backup to perform incremental backups on each shared folder that contains user data on an hourly basis.

**114.** Shelley is the network administrator for her company, which operates an AD DS network consisting of a single domain. She is setting up Network Access Protection (NAP) to enforce system health of VPN connections to the network. She must ensure that all client computers are monitored and protected properly. What should she do? (Each correct answer represents part of the solution. Choose two answers.)

    **a.** Create a Group Policy object (GPO) linked to the Domain Controllers organizational unit (OU).

    **b.** Create a GPO linked to the domain.

    **c.** Enable the Require trusted path for credential entry policy.

    **d.** Disable the Do not allow Digital Locker to run policy.

    **e.** Enable the Turn on Security Center policy.

**115.** Kim is responsible for ensuring the security of DNS-related network traffic in her company's AD DS domain, which includes three sites representing the head office and two branch offices. DNS is configured on two domain controllers at the head office and a member server in each of the branch offices. In the branch offices, DNS is configured as a secondary zone, receiving updates from one of the head office servers, where an Active Directory–integrated zone exists.

What should Kim do to ensure that replication traffic between the head office and branch office DNS servers is encrypted?

    **a.** Use Encrypting File System (EFS) to encrypt the drives containing the zone.dns file on each DNS server.

    **b.** Configure digital signing for all zone transfers.

    **c.** Use Group Policy to configure an IPSec connection security rule.

    **d.** Configure a trust anchor for the zone.DNS file on each server.

**116.** Krista wants to obtain a summary performance report of the CPU, network, disk, and memory subsystems of a server that runs Windows Server 2008 R2. Which of the following actions would provide her with a report that summarizes one minute's worth of performance of these subsystems?

    **a.** In Resource Monitor, allow the utility to collect data for one minute and then select **Monitor > Stop Monitoring**. Then, select the **CPU**, **Memory**, **Disk**, and **Network** tabs in turn and view data displayed by this tool.

    **b.** Click **Start**, type `msinfo32.exe`, and then press **Enter**. Then, select the various nodes under System Summary in turn to display performance reports on these subsystems.

    **c.** In Performance Monitor, expand the **Data Collector Sets > Event Trace Sessions** node, right-click this node, and choose **Start**. After one minute, expand the **Reports > Event Trace Sessions** node and select the data collector set corresponding to the current date and time. This displays a performance report in the details pane of Performance Monitor.

    **d.** In Performance Monitor, expand the **Data Collector Sets > System > System Performance** node, right-click this node, and choose **Start**. After one minute, expand the **Reports > System Performance** node and select the data collector set corresponding to the current date and time. This displays a performance report in the details pane of Performance Monitor.

**117.** Neil administers a network that is configured as a single AD DS domain for his firm. He is assigned the task of maintaining his company's DNS and DHCP servers. He decides that DHCP clients running Windows XP Professional or Windows 7 Professional should be configured to automatically select their primary DNS server.

Neil configures a Windows Server 2008 computer named Server4 as a DNS server. In the DHCP server's scope options for a subnet containing 25 client computers, he configures Server4's IP address in the 006 DNS Servers option. He also ensures that a DHCP reservation exists for Server4. Next, he restarts all the client computers on the subnet. He makes his way to a client computer and is disappointed to discover that it is still configured to use as its DNS server a computer that was taken offline just before Neil began making changes to the network. How can Neil correct this problem?

    **a.** Execute the `ipconfig/release` and `ipconfig /renew` commands on each computer.

    **b.** Configure both the 006 and the 015 options for the DNS server in the DHCP scope.

    **c.** Use `ipconfig /setclassid` at each client computer to set DHCP class ID information.

    **d.** Manually edit the TCP/IP properties on each client computer.

    **e.** Isolate the subnet to eliminate the possibility that clients are receiving scope information from a remote subnet.

**118.** Veronica is a network administrator for a company named Trilatera Corporation. The company is headquartered in Harrisburg, PA, with branch offices located in Peoria, IL, South Bend, IN, and Battle Creek, MI. The company's AD DS domain is named `trilatera.com` and has four sites corresponding to these offices.

Veronica configured a domain-based DFS namespace called `\\trilatera.com\documents`, which hosts shared folders on 20 different servers located in the various offices and is updated frequently. She must configure this namespace to reduce the load placed on the PDC emulator, so she right-clicks the namespace in the DFS Management snap-in and chooses **Properties**. Which option should she configure?

   **a.** From the Referrals tab, select **Random order**.

   **b.** From the Referrals tab, select **Lowest cost**.

   **c.** From the Referrals tab, select **Exclude targets outside of the client's site**.

   **d.** From the Advanced tab, select **Optimize for consistency**.

   **e.** From the Advanced tab, select **Optimize for scalability**.

**119.** Jason is the systems administrator for a company that operates a network consisting of a single AD DS domain and two sites, one representing the head office in Chicago and the other representing the branch office in Milwaukee. The network contains two print servers running Windows Server 2008 R2: Server01 is located in Chicago and Server11 in Milwaukee. Each server manages all printers in its office.

Jason wants to know when a printer in Milwaukee becomes unavailable. He adds Server11 to the Print Management console at Server01. What should he do in order to receive notification when a printer in Milwaukee is unavailable?

   **a.** At the top of the Event Viewer console, right-click **Event Viewer** and choose **Connect to Another Computer**. Select **Server11**. Then, right-click an event from the printers on Server11 and choose **Attach Task To This Event**. Then, from the Create Basic Task Wizard, select the **Send an e-mail** option.

   **b.** In Event Viewer, configure an event log subscription that collects error and warning events from Server11 and sends them to Server01. Right-click an event from the printers on Server11 and choose **Attach Task To This Event**. Then, from the Create Basic Task Wizard, select the **Send an e-mail** option.

**c.** From the New Printer Filter Wizard, define a filter that specifies **Printers Not Ready** and alerts him to problems on any printer attached to Server11 and select the **Send e-mail notification** option.

**d.** In the console tree of the Print Management snap-in, right-click **Server11** and choose **Properties**. From the Advanced tab of the Server Properties dialog box, select **Show informational notifications for network printers.**

**120.** Jill is the systems administrator for a company that operates an AD DS network consisting of a single domain. All servers run Windows Server 2008 R2 and all client computers run either the Professional or Ultimate edition of Windows 7. The network includes a server named Server6 that runs a legacy application that requires parameters such as Service, Protocol, Weight, and Port Number to be specified in DNS so that the application can run properly.

Which type of resource record should Jill configure?

**a.** Start of authority (SOA)

**b.** Service location (SRV)

**c.** Alias (CNAME)

**d.** Host (A or AAAA)

**e.** Well-known service (WKS)

# Answers to Practice Exam

1. C, D. Jack can add a delegation resource record for `ns02.vcb.knoxbakery.com` on NS01 or he can create a stub zone for `ns02.vcb.knoxbakery.com`. Delegation occurs when a name server (NS) resource record in a parent zone lists the DNS server that is authoritative for a child zone. When a DNS server delegates a domain to a child zone on a different DNS server the parent is made aware of new authoritative DNS servers for the child zone only when the resource records for these new DNS servers are added to the parent zone hosted on the DNS server. This addition must be accomplished by adding a delegation record manually. Alternately Jack can add a stub zone for `vcb.knoxbakery.com` to NS01. Stub zones can be created on a DNS server in the parent domain so that DNS is kept up-to-date regarding changes to the authoritative server list for the child domains. DNS uses the PTR resource records to resolve IP addresses to their corresponding FQDN; these records are found in the server's reverse-lookup zone. Because the scenario does not indicate any problem with resolving IP addresses to FQDNs, there is no reason to believe that adding a PTR record would aid clients at headquarters in name resolution for the child domain; consequently, answer A is incorrect. A SOA record lets clients or servers know which DNS server is authoritative for a particular domain. Only one SOA record exists in any zone; it is the first record in each zone file. So Jack does not need to add a SOA record, and answer B is incorrect. A SRV record enables Jack to find the server providing a specific service. AD DS uses SRV records to locate domain controllers. Jack does not need to add a SRV record, so answer E is incorrect. For more information, refer to "Stub Zones" and "Subdomains and Zone Delegation" in Chapter 6.

2. C, E. Sandy should enable a DHCP relay agent on the new subnet on which the new computers are located. She could also configure the router to pass BOOTP broadcasts to the other network, assuming that the router in use is so configurable. If a DHCP server is unreachable from a new computer joining the network, client computers use Automatic Private IP Addressing (APIPA) to obtain an IP address from the 169.254.0.0/16 network, which is a reserved network used for this purpose. Configuring

a DHCP server to supply a default gateway or manually specifying a default gateway will not solve the problem, so answers A and B are incorrect. Configuring a DNS server on this subnet provides host name-to-IP address resolution but does not provide IP addresses for new clients, so answer D is incorrect. A DNS forwarder is used to pass a DNS request that it is unable to resolve to one of the designated forwarders. But, the problem here is related to DHCP and not DNS, so answer F is incorrect. For more information, refer to "Configuring DHCP Relay Agents" in Chapter 2.

3. A. This error can occur if the specified user account is not a member of the local computer's Event Log Readers group or the Administrators group. So, Greg should ensure that the proper user account has been specified; he can find this option in the Advanced Subscription Settings dialog box, which he can access by clicking **Advanced** in the Subscription Properties dialog box. This error is not symptomatic of improper protocol and port settings, so answer B is incorrect. He does not need to run the `wecutil qc` command on the source computers, so answer C is incorrect. This error also does not indicate a problem in the events that have been specified for collection, so answer D is incorrect. For more information, refer to "Configuring Event Log Subscriptions" in Chapter 20.

4. D. The priority value contained in the mail exchanger (MX) resource record determines which mail server is contacted first when more than one mail server is present. The lower the number, the higher the priority. The priority needs to be set on the MX record, not on the SRV record; further the SRV records are automatically created when the servers are first added to the network. It is necessary to create the MX resource records manually for each new mail server when it is added to the network. Consequently, answers A and B are incorrect. If the priority for EXCH1 is set to 1 and that for EXCH2 is set to 99, then e-mail would be directed preferentially to EXCH1, so answer C is incorrect. For more information, refer to "New Mail Exchanger (MX) Records" in Chapter 7.

5. D. Wayne should configure the VPN server to use Secure Socket Tunneling Protocol (SSTP). This tunneling protocol uses HTTPS over TCP port 443 to transmit traffic across firewalls and proxy servers that might block PPTP and L2TP traffic. Neither PPTP nor L2TP use HTTPS to secure VPN access; further, these protocols require additional ports to be opened on the firewall. Therefore, answers A and B are incorrect. IKEv2 is a tunneling protocol that uses IPSec Tunnel Mode over UDP port 500; because it requires this port to be open on the firewall, answer C is incorrect. For more information, refer to "New Features of RRAS in Windows Server 2008" and "Configuring VPN Connection Security" in Chapter 14.

6. A. Of the address choices provided, Shirley should use **fc00::23d4:217a:1025**. An IPv6 address that begins with the fc00 prefix is a unique local IPv6 unicast address, which provides an address that is private to an organization but unique across all the organization's sites. Thus, it is reachable by all client computers on any subnet. An IPv6 address beginning with 2000 is a global unicast address, which is equivalent to a public IPv4 address. Because this address is not reserved for internal networks, answer B is incorrect. An address beginning with fe80 is a link-local unicast address, which is a nonroutable address used for communication within the same subnet. If she were to use this address, communication would be limited to those client computers on the same subnet as Server25, so answer C is incorrect. An address beginning with fec0 is a site local unicast address and is used for communication between nodes located in the same site. Again, communication would be limited to those client computers on the same subnet, so answer D is incorrect. For more information, refer to "IPv6 Prefixes" in Chapter 1.

7. A. Flora needs to use the Windows Server 2008 R2 installation DVD-ROM to start the server, and then select **Repair your computer**. After selecting this option, she will receive the System Recovery Options dialog box, from which she can select **System Image Recovery** and then select the backup that she wants to restore from. Recovery Console was used in older Windows Server versions for performing certain recovery actions; it is no longer used in Windows Server 2008, so answer B is incorrect. She cannot use Safe Mode in these circumstances so answer C is incorrect. She needs to use the Windows Server 2008 R2 DVD-ROM to start the bare metal recovery process, so answer D is incorrect. For more information, refer to "Performing a Full Server or Bare Metal Recovery of a Windows Server 2008 R2 Computer" in Chapter 11.

8. A, C. Brenda should ensure that 802.1x enforcement is configured on the NAP server. She should also ensure that all wireless access points are configured as RADIUS clients. Other enforcement types such as IPSec are used to verify client health when making wired connections to the network, so answer B is incorrect. The 802.1X-capable devices (wireless access points) must be configured to forward authentication requests to a RADIUS server, which is also a NAP health policy server. Consequently, they must be configured as RADIUS clients and not as RADIUS servers, so answer D is incorrect. The CA is required when the network is configured for VPN enforcement; it is optional when using 802.1X enforcement. Therefore answer E is incorrect. For more information, refer to "802.1X Enforcement" in Chapter 16.

9. D. David can export Windows Firewall with Advanced Security rules for use on another computer by using the Export Policy command, which is available by right-clicking **Windows Firewall with Advanced Security** and choosing **Export Policy**. He can then import the rules to another computer by using

the Import Policy command in a similar fashion. The `netsh advfirewall dump` command does not produce the required output, so answer A is incorrect. (Note, however, that David could use the `netsh advfirewall export` and `netsh advfirewall import` commands to export the rules from Server3 and import them to Server4; these perform the same tasks as the right-click commands mentioned here). It might be possible to back up the rules using `wbadmin`, but this would be more complex and difficult to perform than using the Export Policy and Import Policy commands, so answer B is incorrect. The right-click menus available for the Inbound Rules and Outbound Rules nodes in the Windows Firewall with Advanced Security snap-in do not contain **Export Policy** and **Import Policy** options, so answer C is incorrect. For more information, refer to "Importing and Exporting Policies" in Chapter 4.

10. B. By accessing the New Remote RADIUS Server Group dialog box, Hubert can make Server12 a proxy to Server11, which means that Server12 passes all authentication requests to Server11 for processing. He can access this dialog box by expanding the RADIUS Clients and Servers node in the NPS snap-in, right-clicking **Remote RADIUS Server Groups**, and choosing **New**. A RADIUS client is a network component such as a wireless access point or a VPN server, not another RADIUS server, so answer A is incorrect. Hubert must make Server12 a proxy to Server11, not the other way around, so answer C is incorrect. A connection request policy does not operate in the manner suggested by answer D, so this answer is incorrect. For more information, refer to "Creating RADIUS Proxies and Proxy Groups" in Chapter 15.

11. A. Michelle should create a new conditional forwarder and store it in Active Directory. She should replicate this forwarder to all DNS servers in the `que. com` forest. The conditional forwarder forwards all queries that it receives for names ending with a specific domain name (in this case, `certguide.com`) to the `certguide.com` DNS servers. By default, DNS stores zone data for Active Directory–integrated zones in two application directory partitions, which are automatically created and replicated among DNS servers in the forest. She does not need to create an additional application directory partition, so answer B is incorrect. Configuring a stub zone on the `certguide.com` DNS server might help to enable users in the certguide.com domain to access resources in the `que.com` forest, which is the opposite direction to that desired here, so answer C is incorrect. Configuring a stub zone on the forest root `que.com` DNS server that contains information about the authoritative name servers in the `certguide.com` DNS zone might help to provide users in the `que.com` root domain access to resources in `certguide.com`, but users in child domains would not have access. So answer D is incorrect. Configuring the `certguide.com` DNS server as the alternate DNS server would only send

DNS queries to this server if the local DNS server was unavailable; the local server would be unable to resolve queries directed to the `certguide.com` domain, so answer E is incorrect. For more information, refer to "Conditional Forwarders" in Chapter 5.

12. B. By right-clicking the data collector set in the console tree of the Performance Manager snap-in and choosing **Data Manager**, Eleanor can select the **Minimum free disk** setting and specify the minimum amount of free disk space that must be available for the data collector set to continue logging (in this case, 500 MB). The Size option on the Actions tab enables Eleanor to specify the maximum size of the log file, not the minimum amount of available free disk space, so answer A is incorrect. The Properties dialog box that she received when right-clicking the **Data Collector Sets** node in the console tree of the Performance Manager snap-in and choosing **Properties** does not have a Data Manager tab, so answers C and D are incorrect. For more information, refer to "System-Defined Data Collector Sets" in Chapter 19.

13. A. Karla should select the **Secure only** option on the General tab of the zone's Properties dialog box. This option prevents computers that are not domain members from registering resource records in DNS. The problem observed here is not caused by an improper zone replication scope, so answer B is incorrect. Scavenging removes resource records from computers that have been disconnected from the network, such as remote access computers that have improperly disconnected and have left invalid (stale) resource records behind. Scavenging would remove the improper resource records but would not prevent them from being added by non-domain computers in the future. Therefore answers C and D are incorrect. For more information, refer to "Dynamic DNS, Non-Dynamic DNS, and Secure Dynamic DNS" in Chapter 6.

14. B. Gary should run the command `ipconfig /flushdns` at the Windows 7 Professional client, in order to clear its DNS resolver cache. By running this command, Gary can flush and reset the contents of the DNS client resolver cache. It gives him the opportunity to discard negative cache entries from the cache, as well as, any other dynamically added entries, as needed during troubleshooting of DNS problems.

In this scenario, the clients are all receiving their TCP/IP configuration from the DHCP server. This would include the subnet mask, so an incorrect subnet mask would not be a likely issue; consequently, answer A is incorrect. As there is only one subnet, it is not necessary to configure a default gateway, so answer C is incorrect. The `ipconfig /registerdns` command is used to force a DNS client to renew its registration with the DNS server. This is necessary if a client's name records are missing from the server. This is not the situation here, as other clients can reach the problematic client; therefore, answer D is incorrect. Although Nancy's computer receives its IP address information from a DHCP server, IP communication appears to be functional. Using the `ipconfig /release` and `ipconfig /renew` commands is unlikely to solve the problem, because the location of DNS services has not changed, so answer E is incorrect. For more information, refer to "Using the `ipconfig` Command to Update and Register DNS Records" in Chapter 8.

15. A. Karen should use the **nmcap.exe /inputcapture capture1.cap /capture DNS /file dns1.cap** command. This command filters the `capture1.cap` file and produces a smaller file named `dns1.cap`, deleting all other frames from the initial file and creating a much smaller file. The **nmcap. exe /network \* /capture "DNS" /file dns1** command creates a capture filter, which Karen would use to create a new capture, not filter an existing capture, so answer B is incorrect. This is also true for creating a capture filter in the GUI version of Network Monitor, so answer C is incorrect. Creating a display filter enables Karen to display only DNS-related frames but does not enable her to create a smaller file; the resulting file would still be as large as the initial file, so answer D is incorrect. For more information, refer to "Performing a Capture from the Command Prompt" in Chapter 21.

16. D. Windows Server 2008 R2 provides the DHCP Split-Scope Configuration Wizard, which enables Joe to split the scope he has configured on Server11 into two separate scopes or subscopes. Doing so provides increased fault toler- ance and redundancy over using just a single DHCP server. If Joe were to cre- ate a scope named `Scope2` on Server12, and configure this scope with the same IP address range as on `Scope1`, both DHCP servers would be assigning IP ad- dresses from the same range, resulting in duplicate IP address assignment, so answer A is incorrect. A superscope combines two or more scopes into a single logical scope and enables a DHCP server to hand out IP addresses from either scope. This does not solve the problem here, so answer B is incorrect. A multi- cast scope is used to service multicast-enabled applications that send messages to more than one destination computer on the network. This is not relevant to the problem here, so answer C is incorrect. For more information, refer to "Split Scopes" in Chapter 2.

17. A. For secure intranet resources, Susan can specify the use of DNSSEC to verify resolved DNS names on the local intranet. Split-brain DNS enables her to use the same DNS domain name for both intranet and Internet resources according to a client's location. She would use NRPT exemptions to specify that individual names or namespaces within an overall DNS namespace be exempted from special handling by the NRPT rules. Neither of these provides secure name verification, so answers B and C are incorrect. RDS enforcement

is used in evaluating client health within a Network Access Protection environment; it is not used with DirectAccess, so answer D is incorrect. For more information, refer to "Name Resolution Policy Table" in Chapter 17.

18. C. When selected, the **Create caching-capable user key from smart card** option generates a session key that is valid for an entire session of working with EFS-encrypted files when a user first inserts her smart card. Consequently, the user can remove her smart card after starting an EFS session. Clearing this option requires that the smart card remain inserted for the duration of the session. Elliptic Curve Cryptography enables EFS to be compliant with Suite B encryption requirements as defined by the U.S. National Security Agency. Its use is not relevant to this scenario, so answers A and B are incorrect. The **Display key backup notifications when user key is created or changed** option prompts uses to back up EFS keys when created or changed; this option is also not relevant here, so answer D is incorrect. For more information, refer to "EFS Group Policies" in Chapter 9.

19. D. Janet needs to select the **Forwarded Events** subnode, which is found in the Windows Logs node. She could view event logs on the servers by connecting to them in Event Viewer, but this negates the advantage of having created event log subscriptions; therefore, answer A is incorrect. The Custom Views node in Event Viewer does not contain a Forwarded Events subnode, nor does it contain event logs for other computers; therefore, answers B and C are incorrect. For more information, refer to "Viewing Logs in Event Viewer" in Chapter 20.

20. B. Murray should use the Storage Reports feature in FSRM and select the **Least Recently Accessed Files** option. By clicking **Edit Parameters**, he can specify the number of days since a file was accessed—in this case, 730 days (2 years). A file screen prevents storage of files of specified types but does not monitor the age of stored files, so answer A is incorrect. A file quota template limits the amount of disk space available on shared folders to users, whether configured from FSRM or from the Quota tab of the disk's Properties dialog box. It does not limit the age of stored files, so answers C and D are incorrect. For more information, refer to "Managing Storage Reports" in Chapter 12.

21. C. The purpose of subnetting is always to make more networks available by altering the subnet mask applied to a network ID. This is done by borrowing bits from the host ID and assigning them to the network ID. Once this is done, there are more networks available with fewer hosts on each network. Of the choices available, the subnet mask 255.255.255.240 borrows the fewest number of bits, while still providing for 14 networks. Hence, it provides the

most hosts. Valid subnet masks for a Class C address that can create appropriate combinations of subnets and hosts include the following:

| Subnet Mask | Networks | Hosts |
| --- | --- | --- |
| 255.255.255.192 | 2 | 62 |
| 255.255.255.224 | 6 | 30 |
| 255.255.255.240 | 14 | 14 |
| 255.255.255.248 | 30 | 6 |
| 255.255.255.252 | 62 | 2 |

Subnet masks ending in 192 or 224 do not provide enough networks to fit
this scenario, so answers A and B are incorrect. A subnet mask ending in 248
provides enough networks, but does not provide the maximum possible hosts
within a single network, so answer D is incorrect. For more information, refer
to "Subnetting and Supernetting in IPv4" in Chapter 1.

22. A. Doug should configure the RRAS server to use MS-CHAP v.2 for authentication. He should also configure the scientists' laptop computers to automatically use Windows logon names and passwords during dial-up authentication.
MS-CHAP v.2 provides the strongest level of security that is commensurate
with the needs of this situation. It provides mutual authentication and bases
the cryptographic key on the user's password and an arbitrary challenge string,
which changes every time the user connects.

Doug could use EAP-TLS for authentication if the scientists were using digital certificates or smart cards for authentication. However, it cannot be used
within the constraints of this scenario, so answer B is incorrect. PAP provides
for clear-text password transmission and should only be used when other authentication protocols are impractical because it does not provide any security.
Therefore answer C is incorrect. RRAS in Windows Server 2008 does not
have an authentication option for using the originating telephone number of
the call to authenticate a user, so answer D is incorrect. For more information,
refer to "Remote Access Authentication Protocols" in Chapter 14.

23. B, C. Lisa should access the Zone Transfers tab of the same dialog box, click
**Notify,** and then ensure that **The following servers** is selected and that
the IP addresses of the perimeter zone secondary DNS servers are specified.
Specifying this option on the Notify list will ensure that only the authorized
secondary DNS servers receive notifications of zone updates. Lisa should also
access the Start of Authority (SOA) tab of the zone's Properties dialog box
and increase the value of the Refresh interval. An increase in the value of this
interval reduces the bandwidth required for the zone transfer SOA requests

sent by both perimeter network DNS servers. Specifying **Servers listed on the Name Servers tab** would cause additional zone transfers that involve the primary DNS servers in the internal network, so answer A is incorrect. Decreasing the value of the Refresh interval would increase the amount of zone transfer traffic across the firewall server, so answer D is incorrect. The Retry interval specifies how much time will elapse before the secondary server tries again to contact the master server, in the event that the master server does not respond to the initial refresh attempt. Its value is immaterial to the problem specified in this scenario, so answers E and F are incorrect. Dynamic updates are used by the master DNS servers to maintain the Active Directory–integrated zone and are not utilized by the secondary servers on the perimeter zone. She should not modify this setting, so answer G is incorrect. For more information, refer to "Configuring DNS Notify" in Chapter 6 and "Configuring SOA Resource Record Properties" in Chapter 7.

**24.** A, C. Chris should delete the `cache.dns` file from the `%systemroot%\System32\Dns` folder. He could also delete all entries from the Root Hints tab and add any entries for other local DNS servers if necessary. He can alter either the cache.dns file or the Root Hints tab to change how far up an inverted DNS tree any particular DNS server will query before it concludes that a given name cannot be resolved. It is a common and recommended practice to clear the names found in the `cache.dns` file or delete that file when a network using DNS should not connect to the Internet and the root DNS servers that are found there. This speeds resolution for the internal network and provides a measure of security. The cache maintained by a DNS server configured as a caching-only server contains only the names of hosts that the caching-only server has successfully resolved and, as such, is not relevant to the purpose of isolated name resolution within the internal domain, so answer B is incorrect. If Chris were to enable recursion for his domain, Server09 would attempt to resolve a DNS query after a forwarder failed to do so. Since the domain contains no forwarders, he should leave recursion disabled; therefore, answer D is incorrect. For more information, refer to "Root Hints Tab" in Chapter 5.

**25.** A, C, E. A situation like this one calls for Carm to set up a system of client-side targeting of updates. This causes new computers to be automatically added to the appropriate group when they first contact the WSUS server. Carm should use the Update Services snap-in to create these groups, and not security groups in AD DS, so answer B is incorrect. If Carm were to select the **Use the Update Services console** option from the Options node, he would be setting up server-side targeting. Because this option is not desired here, answer D is incorrect. Use of the Update Services snap-in as described in option F is also part of server-side targeting, so answer F is incorrect. For more information, refer to "Using Computer Groups" and "Configuring Client Computers for WSUS" in Chapter 18.

**26.** B, E. Gerry needs to install the Network Policy and Access Services server role and the Routing and Remote Access Services role feature. Then he needs to right-click the server in the RRAS snap-in and choose **Configure and Enable Routing and Remote Access**. This starts the Routing and Remote Access Server Setup Wizard, in which he must select the **Custom Configuration** option and then select the **LAN routing** option. Routing and Remote Access Services is not a server role; it is a role feature that is a component of the Network Policy and Access Services server role, so answer A is incorrect. Gerry would select the **Remote access (dial-up or VPN)** option only if he is setting up the server as a dial-in or VPN server, so answer C is incorrect. He would select the **Secure connection between two private networks** option in order to configure the server to send data securely across the Internet to another server, not to send data across the WAN link as required here, so answer D is incorrect. For more information, refer to "Configuring RRAS as a Router" in Chapter 3.

**27.** B. Rick should configure NAP to direct all clients without proper security updates to the remedial network. The purpose of the remedial network is to provide services that update noncompliant clients so that they can access the corporate network; the remedial network will include the WSUS server so that clients are properly updated. The setting Rick must configure is found in the System Health Validator (SHV) in use, under Settings. He must select the option labeled **Restrict access for clients that do not have all available security updates installed**, and then specify the **Important or above** option from the drop-down list displayed. Disconnecting noncompliant clients prevents them from being updated and eventually accessing the corporate network, so answer A is incorrect. Directing noncompliant clients to the Windows Update website exposes them to possible vulnerabilities; further, this circumvents any testing and approval of updates Rick might have done and creates unnecessary connections to the Internet. Furthermore, this does not allow these clients to become compliant, so answer C is incorrect. Windows Firewall should always be enabled regardless of compliance status, so answer D is incorrect. For more information, refer to "Concepts of NAP" in Chapter 16.

**28.** A. Kathleen should select the **General** tab. For a secondary name server, this tab enables her to specify one or more master servers, which are primary or Active Directory–integrated servers from which the secondary name server will receive zone updates. The Name Servers tab enables her to view the list of name servers in her domain; on a secondary name server, it is not possible to add servers here, so answer B is incorrect. The Start of Authority (SOA) tab enables her to configure the SOA record for the DNS zone. No configurable options are available on this tab for a secondary name server, so answer C is incorrect. The Zone Transfers tab allows her to configure how zone information is transferred from one DNS server to another in a traditional (non-Active Directory–integrated) domain. She cannot specify a primary server here, so answer D is incorrect. For more information, refer to "Configuring DNS Zone Properties" in Chapter 6.

**29.** D. Phil should run the `dnscmd /clearcache` command on Server11. This server caches all DNS name resolution information it has received from the external DNS server (Server12) so that it can immediately reply to additional queries for the same FQDN. The `dnscmd /clearcache` command clears resource records from the DNS cache memory on the server on which it is executed. Running the `ipconfig /flushdns` command clears the cache generated at the server from its own name resolution activities, not the cache generated by the DNS servers, so answers A and B are incorrect. Running this command at each client computer clears incorrect name resolutions from their cache, but they would still pick up the incorrect name resolution from Server11 if its cache has not been cleared, so answer C is incorrect. Phil must run this command on Server11 and not Server12, so answer E is incorrect. For more information, refer to "Using the `Dnscmd` Command to Update the DNS Server Cache" in Chapter 8 and "Using the Command-Line for DNS Server Administration" in Chapter 5.

**30.** C. By selecting the **Block all connections** option under Inbound connections, Marisa can ensure that unauthorized external connections will always be disabled. By doing this under the Domain Profile tab, firewall settings are configured for use when connected to an AD DS domain, as is the case in this situation. Public profile settings are used when connected to an insecure public network such as a Wi-Fi access point at a hotel or airport. Private profile settings are used when connected to a small private non-domain network. Neither of these are the case here, so answers A and B are incorrect. The Customize option enables Marisa to specify the network adapter on the server that will be covered by the firewall rule. It does not enable her to specify a range of IP addresses, so answers D, E, and F are all incorrect. For more information, refer to "Configuring Multiple Firewall Profiles" in Chapter 4.

**31.** D. By configuring the Phaser printer to be available only between 4 p.m. to 8 a.m., everyone will be able to use this print device during these hours. Meanwhile, members of the Traders group will have use of the print device between 8 a.m. and 4 p.m., by printing to it through Phaser2. It would be possible to configure Phaser2 to be available from 8 a.m. to 4 p.m.; however, if Brendan had kept Phaser available for all hours as these options suggest, the Traders group would not have exclusive use of the print device during these hours, so answer A is incorrect. Brendan must not specifically deny the Everyone group the print permission, as members of the Traders group are also members of this group and a specific denial overrides all allowed permissions; therefore no one would be able to use the physical print device between 8:00 a.m. and 4:00 p.m. and answers B and C are incorrect. For more information, refer to "Security Tab and Printer Permissions" in Chapter 13.

**32.** C. In this case, it is most likely that Computer43 was configured in error to belong to the `beta` community rather than the `alpha` community. Jean needs to ensure that the proper community name and trap destination are specified on the Traps tab of the SNMP Service Properties dialog box, which she can access from the Services snap-in by right-clicking **SNMP Service** and choosing **Properties**. A SNMP agent computer can send traps to only the management system in its own community so Jean did not receive the trap message at her server. It is possible for a SNMP agent computer to belong to more than one community. In such a case, SNMP permits trap messages to be sent to each management system; in addition, the SNMP service automatically receives trap messages. Therefore, answers A and B are incorrect. Because a computer can belong to more than one community, answer D is incorrect. For more information, see "How SNMP Functions" in Chapter 21.

**33.** B. To use DFS replication, it is necessary to create replication groups and add replicated folders (which means the `Documents` folder, in this case). She should not add an additional DFS namespace, so answer A is incorrect. Configuring an additional server as a namespace server for the same DFS namespace root or moving the namespace server to a different server does not solve this problem, so answers C and D are incorrect. For more information, refer to "Setting Up DFS Replication" in Chapter 10.

**34.** D. Mary should implement the 802.11n protocol. This provides for use of the wireless access points with the latest technologies as of 2011. The other protocols mentioned have various limitations including lower transmission speeds (11-54 Mbps), so answers A, B, and C are incorrect. For more information, refer to "Wireless Networking Protocols and Standards" in Chapter 15.

**35.** B, C, E. Ben can store scheduled backups on any of internal hard disks, external hard disks, or remote shared folders. It is not possible to perform scheduled backups to DVD-R drives because manual attention is needed to insert additional discs as required, so answer A is incorrect. Windows Server 2008 no longer supports tape volumes as backup media, so answer D is incorrect. For more information, refer to "Scheduling a Backup" in Chapter 11.

**36.** C. Holly should configure the VPN server to use PEAP-TLS (Protected Extensible Authentication Protocol with Transport Layer Security). This highly secure password-based authentication protocol combination uses certificate-based authentication. CHAP and MS-CHAPv2 are versions of the Challenge Handshake Authentication Protocol in which an MD5 hash value is sent for authentication. These protocols do not use certificates, so answers A and B are incorrect. PAP is the Password Authentication Protocol, which sends credentials in clear text. This is the least secure authentication method available, so answer D is incorrect. For more information, refer to "Remote Access Authentication Protocols" in Chapter 14.

**37.** D. The computer that cannot connect to the servers is configured with a subnet mask of 255.255.224.0, as shown on the third line of the output produced by the `route print` command. However, the /18 suffix on the class B network address of 172.16.128.0/18 indicates that two bits of the third octet are used to subnet the network, or a subnet mask of 255.255.192.0. This is consistent with the fact that the IP addresses of the clients range from 172.16.128.2 to 172.16.191.254, as stated in the problem. Therefore, the subnet mask is incorrect and no connection beyond the router is possible.

The subnet mask of 255.255.192.0 divides the 172.16.0.0 network into four subnets, as follows: 172.16.0.0, 172.16.64.0, 172.16.128.0, and 172.16.192.0. The subnet mask of 255.255.224.0 would divide the 172.16.0.0 network into eight subnets, and place the addresses of the problematic computer and its default gateway onto separate subnets of 172.16.160.0/19 and 172.16.128.0/19, respectively. Hence, the computer cannot reach its default gateway of 172.16.128.1 and cannot communicate across the router. If the router interface on the second subnet were configured with an incorrect IP address, then none of the client computers would be able to reach the servers; since the other client computers were able to access the servers, this interface is correct and answer A is incorrect. The entry under `Gateway` on the first line indicates that the default gateway is correctly specified, so answer B is incorrect. The IP address configured on the problematic computer is within the range specified; the fact that the user cannot connect to some of the computers on the local network indicates that the subnet mask is incorrect, and answer C is incorrect. As configured, she cannot connect to any computer whose IP address lies in the range of 172.16.128.1 to 172.16.159.254, and can connect only to computers whose IP addresses are within the range of 172.16.160.1 to 172.16.191.254, thus explaining why she cannot connect to some of the computers on the local network. For more information, refer to "IPv4 Addressing" in Chapter 1 and "Routing Table" in Chapter 3.

**38.** C. The CNAME record provides an alias (canonical names), which is an additional name (in this case, www) that points to a single host (`server8.certguide.com`). Machines will respond to either the original name or the alias. The SOA resource record is always the first record in any zone file and identifies the primary name server (which would not be Server8). The SRV record enables him to add additional parameters such as Service, Protocol, Weight, and Port Number. The A or AAAA record defines the name-to-IP address mapping. The WKS record describes the well-known TCP/IP services supported by a particular protocol on a specific IP address. None of these other resource record types enable Harry to provide an alias for Server8, so answers A, B, D, and E are incorrect. For more information, refer to "Creating New Resource Records" in Chapter 7.

**39.** A, C, E, F, I. A DirectAccess server must meet all these requirements. Note that the server must be a member server and does not need to be a domain controller, so answer B is incorrect. Although the server must be running Windows Server 2008 R2, the domain functional level can be at either Windows Server 2008 or Windows Server 2008 R2, so answer D is incorrect. The server must be configured with two consecutive public IPv4 (not IPv6) addresses, so answer G is incorrect. NAP is not required, so answer H is incorrect. For more information, refer to "DirectAccess Server Requirements" in Chapter 17.

**40.** C. Jane should configure the branch offices as subdomains. Additionally, each branch office should host a standard primary zone for its subdomain. Because the scenario states that the administrators in the branch offices are to be responsible for their specific DNS information, and that their DNS servers be configured to host standard primary zones, the branch offices must be configured as subdomains, because primary zones require their own domain. This is the only option that allows administrators to control the information stored in their respective DNS zones. If each branch office were to host a standard primary zone, it would not be possible for administrators in each branch office to administer that office's DNS configuration, so answer A is incorrect. Secondary zones are read-only and must receive their information from a primary standard zone; consequently, local administrators cannot control their zone data and answer B is incorrect. A stub zone contains read-only copies of the SOA record plus NS and A records for authoritative names servers only. It does not allow local administrative control, so answer D is incorrect. For more information, refer to "DNS Zone Types" in Chapter 6.

**41.** B, C, D. Variable length subnet masks (VLSM) allow an administrator to partition a network address range into subnets of different sizes. This scenario provides for three subnets that contain 82, 55, and 29 computers and requires that a fourth subnet be available that will hold up to 30 computers. The network prefix attached to each network address specifies the number of bits used by the subnet mask in masking off the subnet ID from the host ID. The maximum number of hosts available on any subnet is given by the formula $2^n -2$, where n is the number of zero bits remaining in the subnet mask, in other words, 32 minus the number of masked bits. The network 201.202.203.0/25 consequently has 7 zero bits and permits $2^7-2 = 126$ hosts, satisfying the requirement of the first subnet of 82 hosts. The network 201.202.203.128/26 has 6 zero bits and likewise permits 62 hosts, satisfying the requirement of the second subnet of 55 hosts. The network 201.202.203.192/27 permits 30 hosts, satisfying the requirement of the third subnet containing 29 hosts, and leaves room for another subnet of up to 30 hosts, namely 201.202.203.224/27.

The 201.202.203.0/26 network permits only up to 62 hosts, which is insufficient for the first subnet. Although it would accommodate the second subnet, no other listed option is available for the first subnet; therefore, answer A is incorrect. The option of 201.202.203.192/25 is invalid as a /25 subnet can begin only from a 0 or 128 as the last octet of the network address, answer E is incorrect. The 201.202.203.192/26 subnet would permit 62 hosts but leaves no room for a future fourth subnet among the given choices, so answer F is incorrect. For more information, refer to "Subnetting and Supernetting in IPv4" in Chapter 1.

**42.** B. Erin must upgrade the Windows Internal Database first. Without doing this, Microsoft cautions you that an upgrade to Windows Server 2008 R2 will fail. The `Adprep /forestprep` and `Adprep /domainprep` commands are never run on a member server, so answer A is incorrect. It is not necessary to remove and reinstall WSUS, so answer C is incorrect. Because she can upgrade the server after upgrading the Windows Internal Database, answer D is incorrect. For more information, refer to "Installing and Configuring a WSUS Server" in Chapter 18.

**43.** C. Judy should configure Server8 and Server9 as WINS push/pull replication partners. She can do this from the Replication Partners subnode in the console tree of the WINS snap-in. The Renew interval setting specifies the interval (Time to Live [TTL]) before a WINS client must refresh its NetBIOS name. The Extinction interval specifies the amount of time before a record marked as released is marked as extinct. Neither of these settings is pertinent to the situation described here, so answers A and B are incorrect. Adding static name-to-address mappings to the WINS database in Server9 that direct branch office client computers to the proper head office servers would accomplish the task but would take more effort and be prone to error. Furthermore, if IP address assignments change, these mappings would become invalid. Therefore, answer D is incorrect. For more information, refer to "WINS Servers" in Chapter 8.

**44.** B, C, E. Keisha should assign Wilson's user account the Allow–Full Control permission for the folder, encrypt the folder, and then add Wilson's user account to the list of users that are allowed to open the folder. She should not assign the Users group the Deny–Full Control permission for the folder; doing so would prevent Wilson from accessing the folder because all users are automatically members of this group and an explicit denial overrides all allowed permissions, so answer A is incorrect. If she were to encrypt the files rather than the folder, new files including the temporary files would not be encrypted, so answer D is incorrect. It is not necessary to designate Wilson's user account as an EFS recovery agent in this scenario, so answer F is incorrect. For more information, refer to "NTFS File and Folder Permissions" and "Encrypting File System" in Chapter 9.

**45.** A. NAP uses SHVs including the WSHV to evaluate the health status of client computers. Jennifer can modify error code settings; these settings determine whether action will be taken against client computers that are noncompliant with regard to any of the security settings. Generally, they are set to **Non-compliant**, but if problems arise because otherwise compliant machines are unable to contact external services because of problems such as the hardware components mentioned here, she should use the **Compliant** setting. The Noncompliant setting is the default setting and would render clients unable to contact Server5 as noncompliant, so answer B is incorrect. The **Restrict access for clients that do not have all available security updates installed** option determines the minimum security level of updates downloaded from Windows Update or from a WSUS server. It does not stop network access because of an unavailable server, so answer C is incorrect. Removing Server5 from the remediation server group might not prevent clients from being considered noncompliant, so answer D is incorrect. For more information, refer to "Configuring Error Codes" in Chapter 16.

**46.** C, D. Adam should create a custom view from the DNS Server log that collects only the error or warning events. He should then attach a task to the event log that sends an e-mail notification to his e-mail address. If he simply selects the **DNS Server** log, he would receive far more e-mail notifications than needed, so answer A is incorrect. The Application log does not contain DNS-related messages, so answer B is incorrect. Adding his e-mail address to the Responsible Person field on the Start of Authority tab would send a message if zone transfers are not working properly. However errors or warnings logged by the DNS service would not send messages, so answer E is incorrect. The Data Collector Sets option in Performance Monitor sends alerts for performance issues and not for DNS errors, so answer F is incorrect. For more information, refer to "Creating and Using Custom Views" and "Configuring Tasks from Events" in Chapter 20.

**47.** B. Rob can ensure that client computers can use encrypted communications to access Server3 by configuring an inbound rule in Windows Firewall with Advanced Security and specifying the **Allow the connection if it is secure** option. Because he needs to secure access by client computers into Server3, he needs an inbound rule and not an outbound rule, so answer A is incorrect. Using a connection security rule that specifies the **Computer and user (Kerberos V5)** authentication method would require authentication of all connections but would not require encryption, so answer C is incorrect. Windows

Server 2008 R2 no longer supports the IPSec policies found in the original version of Windows Server 2008 or Windows Server 2003, so answer D is incorrect. For more information, refer to "Configuring New Firewall Rules" in Chapter 4.

**48.** A. Kelly should use FSRM to create an active file screen that blocks audio and video files. A passive file screen would send messages to users who save these file types, but would not prevent the users from saving them, so answer B is incorrect. Reducing the amount of disk space available to each user might prevent them from saving important business data; further, it would not stop them from saving audio or video files, so answer C is incorrect. It is not possible to modify the quota to disallow the saving of audio or video files, so answer D is incorrect. For more information, refer to "Managing File Screening" in Chapter 12.

**49.** B. The quickest and least complicated solution to the problem is to stop, then restart the Print Spooler service. This risks little and assumes nothing, except that the Spooler service has stopped. Users might need to resubmit their documents after the service is restarted. Holding mismatched documents preserves documents in the print queue when a document's settings conflict with the printer's settings. Documents held for this reason do not prevent other documents from printing, so answer A is incorrect. Another printer, newly installed, presumably on the same physical print device, won't necessarily behave any differently, especially in the face of hardware problems, such as paper jams; therefore, answer C is incorrect. It is possible that the print server might not have sufficient disk space to store spooled print jobs. If restarting the print spooler service does not enable documents to be printed, Beth should check the amount of disk space available; if insufficient, she can relocate the folder used to hold spooled print jobs to a more spacious area if necessary. Nonetheless, stopping and restarting the Spool Service is the first solution that she should try, so answer D is incorrect. For more information, refer to "Troubleshooting Printer Problems" in Chapter 13.

**50.** C, E. Robert needs to create a manually configured data collector set and access the Performance Counter Alert option. When he does this, he can view alerts in the Application log in Event Viewer. Note that he can connect to the domain controller from his desktop computer to view these alerts (right-click **Event Viewer**, choose **Connect to another computer**, and then type the name of the required server). Resource Monitor and Performance Monitor both enable Robert to view performance data in real time; however, neither one is able to create alerts, so answers A and B are incorrect. Robert cannot configure the Alerter service to display alerts to his desktop, so answer D is incorrect.

964 MCTS 70-642 Cert Guide: Windows Server® 2008 Network Infrastructure, Configuring

He needs to look in the Application log and not the System log to find alerts, so answer F is incorrect. For more information, refer to "Data Collector Sets" in Chapter 19.

51. B. Matt should manually back up the DHCP database to the `Windows\System32\dhcp\backup` folder on Dogstar, then copy the backup folder's contents to a shared folder on Server43. Matt needs to use a manual backup, because this type of backup is useable by any other Windows Server 2008 computer running the DHCP Server service. In the event of a hardware disaster on Dogstar a manual DHCP backup stored on Dogstar would in all likelihood be unavailable; therefore Matt should copy or move the backup to another computer with adequate disk space, such as Server43. Consequently, answer A is incorrect. Matt is not required to stop the DHCP server service to run a manual backup, so answer C is incorrect. A manual DHCP backup operation cannot be backed up to a remote path. The system state backup does not include the DHCP database, so answer D is incorrect. The path must exist on the local computer, so answer E is incorrect. For more information, refer to "Managing and Troubleshooting a DHCP Server" in Chapter 2.

52. A, F. Carolyn should select the **Automatically notify** check box. She should also select **The following servers** and specify IP address information for Taurus02 and Taurus03. This enables these two servers to be kept up-to-date regarding the status of the DNS zone. Clearing the **Automatically notify** check box eliminates the other options found in the dialog box from further consideration, so answer B is incorrect. Specifying the **Servers listed on the Name Servers tab** option would not enable Taurus03 to be notified of updates, so answer C is incorrect. Taurus01 is the master DNS server, and as such, should not be specified in the Notify list, so answer D is incorrect. In this scenario, the domain controllers Scorpio01 and Scorpio02 are not running DNS, so answer E is incorrect. For more information, see "Configuring DNS Notify" in Chapter 6.

53. A. Cindy needs to type `dnscmd /Config /SocketPoolSize 10000` and then restart the DNS service. She needs to type this command at each DNS server for it to be effective across the network, so answer B is incorrect. The **Advanced** tab of the server's Properties dialog box does not have a **Socket Pool Size** option, so answers C and D are incorrect. For more information, refer to "DNS Socket Pooling" in Chapter 5.

54. D. Network Address Translation (NAT) provides translation of IP addresses and TCP or UDP port numbers of packets passing between the internal network and the Internet. By enabling NAT on Server1, John can ensure that external requests to the secure website on IIS2 are passed to this server. A VPN server can be configured to allow packets on a specific port to pass, but it

cannot translate IP addresses to direct external requests to a given machine on the internal network, so answer A is incorrect. It is not possible to configure a routing table as described in answer B, so this answer is incorrect. Enabling the Secure Web Server (HTTPS) service on the external interface would permit packets for TCP port 443 to pass, but IIS2 requires a nonstandard port number to be enabled, so answer C is incorrect. For more information, refer to "Network Address Translation" in Chapter 14.

55. B, C. Kristina needs to configure a static route using RRAS on the branch office server and the user account on the head office server. When a connection needs to be initiated from one end only, a one-way demand-dial connection should be used. This enables the limiting of the traffic and reducing the connect time, which is important if the company must pay for it by the length of time it is used. In order to configure the one-way connection, Kristina must configure a demand-dial interface with a static route from the station that initiates the call (in this case, the branch office), and configure a user account on the computer that receives the call (in this case, the head office). This user account must be specified in the Demand Dial Interface Wizard while configuring the outbound connection at the branch office. Kristina would need to configure the user account at the branch office and the static route at the head office only if a two-way demand-dial connection were required (in other words, connection to be initiated from either end); therefore, answers A and D are incorrect. For more information, refer to "Establishing a Demand-Dial Interface" in Chapter 3.

56. D. Ruth needs to add both DHCP servers as members of the DnsUpdateProxy group. When secure dynamic update has been enabled, the DHCP server can be configured to automatically register downlevel clients' A and PTR resource records in DNS. However, the updated resource records are owned by the original DHCP server, and only this server can modify them. A replacement DHCP server is unable to modify these records by default. The DnsUpdateProxy group is a special security group that handles the ownership of the DNS resource records. When the DHCP servers are added to this group, they do not take ownership of the resource records and updates can occur properly. The **ipconfig /registerdns** command manually refreshes the computer names that are registered in DNS. Its use would correct the problem given here; but it needs to be run on every client computer and therefore requires much more administrative effort; consequently, answer A is incorrect. In this scenario, the **Always dynamically update DNS A and PTR records** option should already be selected; because of the ownership issue here, this option by itself does not solve the problem, so answer B is incorrect. The **ipconfig /renew** command renews the client's TCP/IP lease in DHCP but does

not update the information in DNS, so answer C is incorrect. For more information, refer to "Using the DnsUpdateProxy Group" in Chapter 7.

57. C. Kathy should configure the new server to communicate with an upstream server. In a WSUS server hierarchy, the upstream server connects to the Windows Update website, downloads all updates as they become available, and passes these updates to the downstream servers. Kathy can configure this behavior by selecting the **Synchronize from another Windows Server Update Services server** option, available on the Update Source and Proxy Server dialog box, which Kathy can access by selecting it from the Options list in the Update Services snap-in. If Kathy were to configure the server as a WSUS client, it would receive updates in a fashion similar to other client computers on the network, but would be unable to distribute them to other computers. Therefore answer A is incorrect. Configuring the server to communicate with a downstream server is backwards to this scenario, so answer B is incorrect. Kathy would configure communication with a proxy server only if such a connection is required for enabling connection to the Internet. This is not needed here because the new server only needs to communicate with the old one, so answer D is incorrect. For more information, refer to "Configuring WSUS Options" in Chapter 18.

58. C. The fd00::6e00:f0aa:cbb8:0005/8 address is a unique local unicast address that is not routed to the Internet but is available to all internal network segments. The fe80::6e00:f0aa:cbb8:0005/64 address is a link-local unicast address, which is equivalent to an APIPA IPv4 address and only allows communication with similarly configured hosts on the same subnet; consequently, answer A is incorrect. The 2000::6e00:f0aa:cbb8:0005/64 address is a global unicast address, which is a globally routable Internet address and is reachable by external computers, so answer B is incorrect. The ff00::6e00:f0aa:cbb8:0005/64 address is a multicast address which provides multiple interfaces to which packets can be delivered to all network interfaces identified by this address. This is not desired here, so answer D is incorrect. For more information, refer to "Types of IPv6 Addresses" in Chapter 1.

59. D. Windows Server 2008 R2 provides two different wireless access policies, one directed at Windows Vista/7 clients and the other directed at Windows XP clients. In this scenario, Kent has configured only the policy for Windows Vista/7 clients. The WPA2-Enterprise authentication method and AES encryption methods are indeed suitable for Windows XP clients, so answers A and B are incorrect. Kent should not select the **Ad hoc** option; this is used only for connections directly between two portable computers without use of a wireless access point, which is not normally the case for wireless access to a domain network. Therefore answer C is incorrect. For more information, refer to "Planning and Configuring Wireless Access Policies" in Chapter 15.

**60.** B, D, E. The Applications option specifies whether this computer uses any applications that use TCP/IP to transmit data. You should always select this option, as by just using SNMP you need to have TCP/IP set up. The End-to-end option specifies whether this computer is an IP host. This option should always be selected, as the computer is most likely an IP host. So, Rod must ensure that both these options are always selected on any computer that is configured for SNMP. Finally, the Internet option specifies whether this computer is an IP gateway (router); consequently, Rod must ensure that this option is also selected. The Physical option specifies whether this computer manages physical devices, such as repeaters or hubs; and the Datalink and subnetwork option specifies whether the computer manages a bridge. Consequently, Rod does not need to select these options, and answers A and C are incorrect. For more information, refer to "Installing and Configuring SNMP" in Chapter 21.

**61.** B. Erica should add a record to the HOSTS file at Trevor's desktop computer. This file contains static host name-to-IP address mappings, and entries in the file override any information that the client computer might obtain from a DNS server. The LMHOSTS file contains NetBIOS name mappings; however, NetBIOS is not used in contacting web servers, so answer A is incorrect. The Alternate Configuration tab enables Trevor to provide a different IP address configuration when connected to a different network. It is not used in this type of situation, so answer C is incorrect. A CNAME resource record would direct all computers to the alternate server, which is not desired here; therefore, answer D is incorrect. For more information, refer to "HOSTS Files" in Chapter 8.

**62.** B. When preparing to set up a DirectAccess installation, Natalie must specify a group containing the computer accounts of branch office computers, not a group containing user accounts of branch office users. The DNS and Domain Controller page of the setup wizard must show an IPv6 address that consists of a 6-to-4 network prefix and an Intra-Site Automatic Tunnel Addressing Protocol (ISATAP)-based network identifier, not an IPv4 address; therefore, answer A is incorrect. DirectAccess requires the use of computer certificates, not user certificates, so answer C is incorrect. Because she has not specified a group containing computer accounts, answer D is incorrect. For more information, refer to "Installing and Configuring the DirectAccess Server Feature" in Chapter 17.

**63.** D. Ruby should set the Conflict Detection value to 1. When this parameter is set to a nonzero value, the DHCP server uses the `ping` utility to test an IP address before leasing it to a client; the value represents the number of times the server performs this test. The value can range from 0 to 6; higher values perform a more thorough test at the expense of server resources. The DHCP option 47 refers to the NetBIOS scope ID. Hosts can communicate only with other hosts configured with the same scope ID. This value is irrelevant to the situation here, so answers A and B are incorrect. If the Conflict Detection value is set to 0 (which is the default), the DHCP server does not check for IP address conflicts. This would allow DHCP clients to receive IP addresses that have already been leased to other clients, so answer C is incorrect. For more information, refer to "Managing and Troubleshooting a DHCP Server" in Chapter 2.

**64.** B. Brent should configure the conditional forwarder with the **All domain controllers in this domain** option. This option enables replication to all do-main controllers including those running Windows 2000. The problem in this scenario is not with a directory replication failure, so answer A is incorrect. The **All DNS servers in this domain** option replicates to Windows Server 2003 and Windows Server 2008 domain controllers only. Because Windows 2000 domain controllers are present on the network, conditional forwarding on this zone will not be established on these servers, so answer C is incorrect. Zone delegation is not an issue in this scenario, so answer D is incorrect. For more information, refer to "Replication Scope" in Chapter 6.

**65.** C. Remember that when NTFS and shared folder permission combine the most restrictive permission applies. For Doctors to have Change control to the `Research` folder, the combination of Full Control shared folder permis-sion and Modify NTFS permission works. The combination of Change shared folder and Full Control NTFS permission would also work. How-ever, granting the Doctors group only Read NTFS permission for this folder would prevent them from modifying content, so answer D is incorrect for this reason. Students must receive a specific Read NTFS permission for only the `Lesson1.doc` file; it is not possible to configure this type of permission at the shared folder level. Providing an overall access level of Read for the Students group enables them to read other documents, so answer A is incorrect. The combination of Change shared folder permission and Full Control NTFS permission would enable Nurses to make changes, which is not desired here; consequently, answer B is incorrect. For more information, refer to "Effective Permissions" in Chapter 9.

**66.** A. Betsy should create a new connection request policy that specifies the **Re-mote Access Server (VPN-dial up)** type of network access server. By speci-fying a processing order of 1, she ensures that this condition is applied before any others, including the default connection request policies created when she accesses the New Connection Request Policy Wizard. If she were to specify a processing order of 99, other policy conditions might be processed first, so an-swer B is incorrect. A Remote Desktop Gateway network access server is used for accessing applications on a Remote Desktop Gateway (formerly Terminal

Services) server, and not for VPN connections. Therefore, answers C and D are incorrect. For more information, refer to "Creating Connection Request Policies" in Chapter 15.

**67.** C. Nolan should modify the rule scope settings. The Scope tab of the rule's Properties dialog box enables him to limit the scope of connections from the internal network, and also block connections from undesired network segments, internal or external. Doing so, Nolan can limit access to a specific server to users or computers that have the need to access resources on this server. Edge traversal settings would enable him to receive or block unsolicited Internet traffic through a NAT device; since NAT is not in use here, answer A is incorrect. If the protocol or port settings were incorrect, users in the head office would be unable to access App1, so answer B is incorrect. Tunnel settings enable him to secure communications between two computers by means of IPSec tunnel mode. Security of connections is not the concern here, so answer D is incorrect. For more information, refer to "Configuring Rule Properties" in Chapter 4.

**68.** D. To enforce the encryption of communications on a NAP-protected network, Ashley must choose the IPSec enforcement method. This method enables her to select a certificate for using SSL encryption. Ashley must configure the HRA server to obtain this certificate from a CA, for which she can use Active Directory Certificate Services (AD CS) installed on the same computer as the HRA server. She cannot specify encryption of communications on a NAP-protected network by specifying VPN enforcement (or any enforcement type other than IPSec), so answers A and C are incorrect. Specifying EAP-TLS does not provide for encrypted communications, so answer B is incorrect. For more information, refer to "IPSec Enforcement" in Chapter 16.

**69.** C. Kate should set the **Expires after** value to 3 days. This value determines the length of time that a secondary server will resolve queries using the current information when it has been unable to contact the master server for an update. By default, this value is one day, which means that in the event of a longer WAN outage, users will be unable to contact the file server after one day. The **Minimum (default) TTL** value specifies the time interval used by other servers before cached information becomes expired and is discarded. It does not determine the validity period of zone data on the secondary DNS server, so answer A is incorrect. The **TTL for this record** value specifies the TTL for this specific resource record (in other words, the SOA resource record). But, other records including the file server's A record can still expire, so answer B is incorrect. The Refresh interval determines the earliest time when a stale resource record can be scavenged. This is not related to the problem at hand, so answer D is incorrect. For more information, refer to "Configuring SOA Resource Record Properties" in Chapter 7.

**70.** D. Using the `wbadmin start recovery` command enables Steve to restore the applications and data originally on FS01 to the new FS02 server. The `vssadmin` command enables Steve to administer Volume Shadow Copies and not to recover applications and data, so answers A and B are incorrect. The `ntbackup` command was used in older Windows versions to perform backups and restores. It has been replaced in Windows Server 2008 by the `wbadmin` command; consequently, answer C is incorrect. The `wbadmin start sysrecovery` command would recover system state. This would not include restoring the data required by this situation, so answer E is incorrect. For more information, refer to "Using the `Wbadmin` Command to Recover Your Server" in Chapter 11.

**71.** B. Julio should use the EAP authentication protocol. This is the only authentication protocol that works with smart cards. None of PAP, CHAP, or MS-CHAPv2 work with smart cards, so answers A, C, and D are incorrect. For more information, refer to "Remote Access Authentication Protocols" in Chapter 14.

**72.** B. Ellen should create an Active Directory–integrated zone named Global-Names. Add host (A) resource records for all computers that require single name resolution. This action is suitable in a situation such as this one where WINS is being retired. This zone must be Active Directory–integrated; a primary zone will not suffice, so answer A is incorrect. SRV resource records enable Ellen to specify parameters such as Service, Protocol, Weight, and Port Number for a service running on the network. CNAME resource records enable Ellen to define aliases for servers on the network. Neither of these record types enables single-name resolution, so answers C and D are incorrect. For more information, refer to "GlobalNames Zones" in Chapter 6.

**73.** A. Gertrude should configure the RRAS servers with a higher metric for the ISDN link. The metric is a parameter used by RIP to determine the optimum route when more than one route exists for a connection between two locations. The router will select the route with the lowest metric to make the connection when more than one route with different metric values exists. It will fall back on the other route only if the optimum one is unavailable. Consequently, by assigning the higher metric to the ISDN link, Gertrude assures that the T1 link will be used when it is available and the ISDN link will only be used as a backup. If Gertrude specifies a higher metric for the T1 link, the ISDN link will be used preferentially. This is not desired, so answer B is incorrect. Windows Server 2008 no longer supports the OSPF protocol, so answer C is incorrect. IP Security policies specify the level of security required for IPSec communications and do not include preferred routing; consequently, answer D is incorrect. For more information, refer to "Configuring Static Routing" in Chapter 3.

**74.** C, D, F. Lynda can right-click each printer in the Print Management console and choose **List in Directory**. She can also select this option from the Sharing tab of the printer's Properties dialog box. She can also publish printers by executing the `pubprn.vbs` script. Either of these actions publishes the printer in AD DS and enables users to search the directory for the available printers. The `Set-ADObject` cmdlet enables her to modify the properties of an object in AD DS. It does not enable her to publish a shared printer, so answer A is incorrect. The `Set-ADPrinter` cmdlet does not exist, so answer B is incorrect. The Ports tab of the print server's Properties dialog box does not have a **List in the Directory** option, so answer E is incorrect. The **Share this printer so that others on your network can find and use it** option enables Lynda to share the printer but does not publish it to AD DS, so answer G is incorrect. For more information, refer to "Publishing Printers in Active Directory" in Chapter 13.

**75.** A. Tony should change the subnet mask on Evelyn's computer to 255.255.255.192. This subnet mask reserves the first 2 bits of the fourth octet as part of the network ID and the last 6 bits of this octet as part of the host ID. The subnet mask of 255.255.255.0 currently on her computer makes the computer think that IP addresses on Subnet 2 are actually on Subnet 1. Consequently, attempts to access Subnet 2 computers do not cross the router and these computers cannot be found. If Tony were to change the subnet mask to 255.255.0.0, Evelyn's computer would still be unable to access Subnet 2 computers and would also be unable to access some Subnet 1 computers, so answer B is incorrect. The default gateway is correctly specified and changing it would not enable connection, so answer C is incorrect. It does not help to give Evelyn's computer a second IP address on the Subnet 2 network; moreover, this option is not available when IP addresses are statically assigned. Therefore, answer D is incorrect. For more information, see "Static IPv4 Addressing" in Chapter 1.

**76.** A. Stan should enable access-based enumeration on the DFS namespace. Doing so hides subfolders for which a user does not have access permissions from the user; consequently, each user sees only a folder tree containing documents for which he has access. Subdividing the DFS namespace would reduce the number of subfolders viewed by a given user, but would not remove the view of all subfolders to which he is not granted access, so answer B is incorrect. A referral is an ordered list of targets that a user receives when she accesses a namespace root or folder from a namespace server or domain controller. Disabling referrals might cause users to be unable to access portions of namespace for which they have access permissions granted. Stan would disable referrals to specific namespace servers only for taking servers offline for maintenance purposes, so answer C is incorrect. Replication groups are groups of servers configured for replicating DFS namespaces. They do not host security groups containing user accounts, so answer D is incorrect. For more information, refer to "Enabling Access-Based Enumeration of a DFS Namespace" in Chapter 10.

77. A, E. By using an alias file, Mike can specify that the IP addresses on the existing capture file be replaced by the corresponding host names as indicated in the alias file. After creating the alias file, Mike must click **Apply** on the toolbar of the Aliases dialog box to apply the aliases he has specified to the file. He would use a filter to capture and display only those frames with a specified characteristic; he cannot use a filter in the fashion described here, so answers B and D are incorrect. The nmcap.exe command is not used in this fashion, so answer C is incorrect. Because he can display the host names on the current capture file by using an alias as described here, answers F and G are incorrect. For more information, refer to "Using Aliases" in Chapter 21.

78. D. Teresa should select **Enable round robin**. Round robin rotates the order of matching resource records in the response list for the web server addresses returned to DNS clients. This ensures that web servers will be accessed equally by users. It's the most common approach for performing DNS load balancing. It is selected by default on a Windows Server 2008 computer. Selecting **BIND secondaries** prevents a DNS server from performing fast zone transfers to the secondary DNS servers. This is required for older UNIX servers, running versions of BIND earlier than version 4.9.4, which cannot handle fast zone transfers. Selecting **Fail on load if bad zone data** causes a DNS server to reject zone transfers if errors are discovered in the transfer. The **Enable netmask ordering** option causes the DNS server to reorder the A or AAAA resource records based on local subnet priority if the request is for a multihomed computer. Selecting **Secure cache against pollution** enables a server to clean up responses to prevent adding unrelated resource records to the cache that have come from another server during a recursive request. None of these options are required by this scenario, so answers A, B, C, E, and F are all incorrect. Note that, on the exam, a question similar to this might be presented as a "hot spot" where you must click on the exhibit at the place that you must configure. For more information, refer to "Configuring Round Robin" in Chapter 7.

79. E. To specify different quotas on a per-user basis, it is necessary to use the Properties dialog box for the disk in use. By clicking **Quota Entries**, he can specify disk quotas for each user. Note that he cannot specify groups in this context, so answer D is incorrect. It is not possible to create quotas on a per-user basis in FSRM, either by using quota templates or by configuring them from the Create Quota dialog box, so answers A, B, and C are all incorrect. For more information, refer to "Configuring Disk and Volume Quotas" in Chapter 12.

80. D. By enabling the **Specify intranet Microsoft update service location** policy, Evelyn can specify the name of the WSUS server from which client computers will receive their updates. The **Configure Automatic Updates** policy governs how the computer will receive and install updates. The **Turn on Software Notifications** policy enables her to determine whether users see detailed notification messages that promote the value, installation, and usage of optional software from the Microsoft Update service. Neither of these two policies will prevent clients from accessing the Microsoft Windows Update website across the Internet, so answers A and B are incorrect. The **Enable client-side targeting** policy enables Evelyn to specify a target group name to be used for receiving updates from an intranet server, such as a WSUS server; however, this policy by itself does not ensure that all computers access the WSUS server to receive their updates, so answer C is incorrect. For more information, refer to "Configuring Client Computers for WSUS" in Chapter 18.

81. A. Bruce needs to configure the 006 DNS servers DHCP option at the vendor class level for the clients receiving IP address reservations. In Windows Server 2008 DHCP, options can be set at any of four levels: server, scope, option class, and client. Option classes include vendor classes and user classes. It is likely that client-level options have been set for these clients when configuring their IP lease reservations, and these options would override those that are set at the scope level. By defining a vendor class option for client computers that receive IP address reservations, he can specify the 006 DNS Servers option for all clients at once. If he were to specify this option at the server level, it would apply to all computers on the network, not just those receiving IP address reservations, so answer B is incorrect. He could configure this option at the client level (in fact, this was required in Windows Server 2003 and older DNS servers); however, he would need to do this individually for each required client. Because this would take more effort, answer C is incorrect. Use of the `ipconfig /flushdns` command flushes the DNS client information that has been cached at the user in their DNS cache file; it does not provide for updating the client with the new DNS server information; consequently, answer D is incorrect. Merely shutting down and restarting the client computers that have reserved IP address will renew their IP lease information but not modify the DNS server information if it has not been first configured at the vendor class level, so answer E is incorrect. For more information, refer to "Configuring DHCP Options" in Chapter 2.

82. B, D. Ryan should create a GPO that enables the **DNS Suffix Search List** policy and specify the `east.que.com` and `west.que.com` DNS suffixes. He should then link this GPO to the `west.que.com` domain. The **Primary DNS Suffix Devolution Level** setting enables Ryan to specify the minimum

number of labels that must be retained in a query string when primary DNS suffix devolution takes place. This setting is not relevant to this scenario, so answer A is incorrect. Link-Local Multicast Name Resolution provides name resolution for computers running IPv6 without the need for contacting any infrastructure server. This is also not relevant, so answer C is incorrect. The name resolution problem is occurring in the `west.que.com` domain and not the `east.que.com` domain, so this is where the GPO should be linked. Consequently, answers E and F are incorrect. For more information, refer to "Configuring DNS Suffix Search Order Lists" and "Using Group Policy to Configure DNS Client Settings" in Chapter 8.

**83.** C. To prepare the head office (collector) server for using an event log subscription, Yvonne must run the `wecutil qc` command. At the same server, she must run the `winrm set winrm/config/client @{TrustedHosts="Server1"}` command. At the branch office (source) servers, Yvonne must run the `winrm quickconfig` command. She should not run the `winrm quickconfig` command at the head office server, so answers A and B are incorrect. Furthermore, she runs the `winrm set winrm/config/client @{TrustedHosts="Server1"}` command at the head office server and not the branch office servers, so answers A and D are incorrect. For more information, refer to "Configuring the Collector Computer to Forward Receive Events" in Chapter 20.

**84.** A, B. Ursula should convert the standard primary zone to an Active Directory–integrated zone. Only Active Directory–integrated zones can be configured for secure dynamic update. When secure dynamic updating is enabled, the authoritative name server accepts updates only from clients and servers that are authorized to make dynamic updates to the DNS zone database. This protects zones and resource records from unauthorized attempts at modification. By allowing only secure dynamic update, she can control which computers register with DNS. Allowing both nonsecure and secure dynamic updates would open up possibilities for nonsecure updates modifying the zone, so answer C is incorrect. Selecting the **Only to the servers listed on the Name Servers tab** option limits the scope of zone transfers but does not ensure the security of dynamic updates, so answer D is incorrect. Incremental zone transfers permit replication of only the portions of the zone database when changes have occurred. Permitting zone transfers reduces the amount of bandwidth that the zone transfer process consumes, but does not compromise the security of the zone database in any particular way. Removing support for incremental zone transfers won't tighten security. Therefore, answer E is incorrect. For more information, refer to "Dynamic DNS, Non-Dynamic DNS, and Secure Dynamic DNS" in Chapter 6.

**85.** A. Tom should configure Server2 as a RADIUS client. This is needed to ensure that the VPN server can communicate with the RADIUS server for authentication. In this scenario, Server3 acts as the RADIUS server and not as the RADIUS client, so answer B is incorrect. The RADIUS server communicates with the domain controllers to authenticate VPN clients and not the other way around, so answer C is incorrect. The **RDS Enforcement** option is used for communicating with Remote Desktop (RD) Gateway servers and not VPN servers, so answer D is incorrect. For more information, refer to "NAP Enforcement" in Chapter16.

86. D. Kelly should use IPSec tunnel mode with ESP. Tunnel mode enables her to secure communications between two networks by creating a tunneled path across the WAN through which secured data passes. She would use transport mode to secure transmissions within a single network, such as server-to-server or client-to-server. This is not needed in this scenario, so answers A and C are incorrect. AH provides data authentication, integrity, and anti-replay for the entire packet (including both the IP header and the data contained within the packet). However, AH does not provide data confidentiality, so answers A and B are incorrect. For more information, refer to "IPSec Modes" in Chapter 4.

87. C. Resource Monitor enables Shirley to obtain information on the processor usage of each application on the server. She cannot attach performance counters to each individual process in Performance Monitor, so answer A is incorrect. A custom view in Event Viewer enables Shirley to view events related to certain happenings on the server, but does not provide performance information, so answer B is incorrect. Reliability Monitor provides information on errors generated by applications but does not provide processor usage data, so answer D is incorrect. For more information, refer to "Resource Monitor" in Chapter 19.

88. D. Connie should right-click **Server4** and choose **Scavenge StaleResource Records**. Then, click **Yes** in the message box that appears. This action performs an immediate scavenging of all stale resource records. If she selects the **Enable automatic scavenging of stale records** option and specifies a short time frame as the scavenging period, scavenging takes place only after the time interval she has specified, not immediately, so answer A is incorrect. If she selects the **Scavenge stale resource records** option either for the server (which affects all DNS zones) or from any zone, scavenging takes place, but only after the no-refresh and refresh intervals have expired, not immediately; therefore, answers B and C are incorrect. For more information, refer to "Zone Scavenging" in Chapter 6.

89. D. Connection Manager provides the Connection Manager Administration Kit (CMAK) Wizard, which enables Grant to create custom profiles that include all the items mentioned here as well as several others. Group Policy does not contain policy settings for all these items, so answer A is incorrect. Grant

cannot specify all these items by running the Routing and Remote Access Setup Wizard, with either the **Virtual private network (VPN) access and NAT** or the **Custom configuration** option, so answers B and C are incorrect. For more information, refer to "Connection Manager" in Chapter 14.

90. B, C, E, F. This scenario requires that Roberta install BranchCache in Hosted Cache mode, which uses a server running Windows Server 2008 R2 in each branch office that hosts files cached from head office servers. She cannot use Distributed Cache mode because this mode works only with a single subnet with no more than 50 client computers, so answer A is incorrect. She must upgrade the branch office servers because BranchCache does not work on a Windows Server 2003 R2 machine. She must also upgrade branch office (but not head office) client computers to Windows 7 because BranchCache does not work on a Vista machine; therefore, answer D is incorrect. She must also create a GPO including a predefined firewall rule that enables BranchCache messages to pass, and the indicated predefined firewall rule works for this scenario, so she does not need to create any custom firewall rules. Therefore answer G is incorrect. For more information, refer to "Configuring BranchCache" in Chapter 9.

91. B. The `route -p add` command enables Bob to add a persistent route to any computer's routing table, ensuring that it will make this connection at any future time. Its parameters are the destination IP address, its subnet mask or netmask (identified with the `mask` keyword), and the gateway, which is the default gateway or router interface on the client computer's network. So in this case, the destination network IP address is 192.168.2.0 (the network address of the head office network), the netmask is 255.255.255.0 (which corresponds to the head office network's /24 CIDR notation), and the gateway is 192.168.3.1, which is the router interface in the branch office. The `route -p add 192.168.3.0 mask 255.255.255.192 192.168.2.1` command would create a persistent route for a computer in the head office connecting to the branch office, which is backwards to the given situation, so answer A is incorrect. The netmask must refer to the head office network, not the branch office network; in this case, the /26 CIDR notation in the branch office corresponds to a subnet mask of 255.255.255.192. Answers C and D are incorrect because they refer to the branch office subnet mask and not the head office subnet mask. For more information, refer to "Using Subnetting to Divide a Network" in Chapter 1 and "Using the Route Command to Create a Static Route" in Chapter 3.

92. F. Arlene must select the **Security** tab. This tab enables her to restrict SNMP communications for the SNMP agent, permitting it to communicate with only a specific list of communities. It also enables her to specify the hosts from which SNMP packets will be accepted as required by this question. None of

the other tabs in this dialog box enable her to perform this task, so answers A, B, C, D, E, and G are incorrect. Note that, on the exam, a question similar to this might be presented as a "hot spot" where you must click on the exhibit at the place that you must configure. For more information, refer to "Installing and Configuring SNMP" in Chapter 21.

**93.** C. Marilyn should restart the Netlogon service at the suburban office domain controller. Doing so re-registers the domain controller's SRV resource records. She can perform this action from the Services branch of Server Manager or by typing `net stop netlogon` followed by `net start netlogon`. Neither the DNS Server service nor the DNS Client service is responsible for re-registering the SRV resource records, so answers A and B are incorrect. She could re-register these records by rebooting the domain controller, but this would take more time, so answer D is incorrect. For more information, refer to "Additional New Resource Records" in Chapter7.

**94.** A, C. Edward can use the `wsusutil.exe` command-line utility with the `export` subcommand to export WSUS update metadata to a package file on removable media, and then use this utility with the import subcommand to import the metadata to the server on the isolated network. Edward can also back up the database from the server on the corporate network and restore this database to the server on the isolated network; it is possible to perform an incremental backup when doing so, to limit the amount of data that must be transferred. The `wuauclt.exe` command provides control over the functioning of the Windows Update Agent. It does not provide import/export capability, so answer B is incorrect. The `ntbackup.exe` utility was used in Windows Server 2003 but is no longer used in either the original or R2 version of Windows Server 2008, so answer D is incorrect. Configuring the two WSUS servers as an upstream/downstream combination is not possible because the isolated network is not connected in any way to the corporate network, so answers E and F are incorrect. For more information, refer to "Using WSUS on a Disconnected Network" in Chapter 18.

**95.** D. Charles just needs to modify the quota template to accomplish this action. It is not necessary to create and apply a new quota template or to add additional shared folders, so answers A and B are incorrect. File screens are concerned with the types of files that users are permitted to store in their shared folders, not with the amount of disk space available to each user, so answer C is incorrect. For more information, refer to "Using FSRM to Create Quota Templates" in Chapter 12.

**96.** A. Andrea must ensure that the RacTask task is enabled, which she can do by using Task Scheduler to configure a trigger that automatically starts this task. This task needs to be running so that System Stability Index data is collected.

Attaching a task to an error event does not ensure that the task is running, so answer B is incorrect. This scenario does not call for use of a system defined data collector set or for automatic startup of the Performance Logs & Alerts service, so answers C and D are incorrect. For more information, refer to "Reliability Monitor" in Chapter 19.

**97.** C. Jocelyn should set both the M flag and the O flag to 1. The M flag determines when DHCPv6 is used to obtain IPv6 stateful addresses, enabling clients to receive non-link-local addresses and other IPv6 configuration parameters. If the M flag is set to 0, stateless IPv6 addresses (which correspond to IPv4 APIPA addresses) are assigned to clients. This is not desired, so answers A and D are incorrect. The O flag determines how additional IPv6 configuration parameters such as the addresses of DNS servers are obtained. When set to 1, DHCPv6 is used to obtain these types of information. If set to 0, other methods such as manual configuration are used to specify these parameters, so answer B is incorrect. For more information, refer to "How DHCPv6 Works" in Chapter 2.

**98.** A. In order to perform the stated tasks on documents produced by all staff members at this printer, Yolanda needs the Manage Documents permission. This permission also allows her to modify document priorities and scheduling, as well as set notifications for users. It does not allow her to control the permissions of other staff or take ownership of print jobs; these tasks require the Manage Printer permission. The Print permission granted to the Designers group does not enable Yolanda to perform the required tasks, so answer B is incorrect. The Manage Printer permission would enable Tyrone to control the permissions assigned to other task members. Because this is not desired, answer C is incorrect. The default permission is Print, which does not enable her to perform these tasks, so answer D is incorrect. For more information, refer to "Security Tab and Printer Permissions" in Chapter 13.

**99.** C. Linda can use any of PPTP, L2TP, SSTP, or IKEv2 to set up a tunneled connection from a remote location across the Internet to servers in the office network and access shared resources as though she were located on the network itself. If she is using a client computer running Windows 2000 or Windows XP to connect to a server running Windows Server 2008, her client computer uses Rivest Cipher 4 (RC4) encryption at a level of either 40-bits or 56-bits. However, the server to which she is connecting uses 128-bit encryption by default; the error observed indicates an encryption mismatch and she must select the **Maximum strength encryption (disconnect if server declines)** option to correct this problem. The other encryption options will not correct the encryption mismatch. Linda will obtain the same error regardless of the type of VPN connection protocol she is using. Therefore, answers A, B, and D are incorrect. For more information, refer to "Configuring VPN Connection Security" in Chapter 14.

**100.** D. Windows Firewall enables Mick to create inbound or outbound rules for a specific TCP or UDP port number to enable traffic on the specified port to pass the firewall. In this case, he should configure an inbound rule that passes traffic on TCP port 3389. This port is the standard port used by RDP connections. UDP port 500 is used by IPSec communications; TCP port 1723 is used by PPTP communications to a RRAS or VPN server, TCP port 1812 is used for connections to a RADIUS server such as Microsoft's Network Policy Server (NPS). None of these other port numbers enable RDP traffic, so answers A, B, and C are all incorrect. For the exam, you should know the most commonly used standard port numbers. For more information, refer to "Configuring Inbound Rules or Outbound Rules" in Chapter 4.

**101.** A. Julie should create connection request policies on Alpha. On the connection request policies, she should specify groups containing users in each domain and grant these groups access. The connection request policies are created on the RADIUS server and not the VPN server, so answer B is incorrect. RADIUS clients are components such as wireless access points or VPN servers. Domain client computers are not RADIUS clients, so answer C is incorrect. Options on the Accounting node track authentication and accounting requests. They do not enable users from different domains to connect to the RADIUS server, so answer D is incorrect. For more information, refer to "Creating Connection Request Policies" in Chapter 15.

**102.** B. Diana should access the Local Area Connection Properties dialog box and deselect the check box labeled **Internet Protocol Version 6 (TCP/IPv6)**. Doing so prevents the server from communicating by means of IPv6. In older Windows versions such as Windows Server 2003 and Windows XP, she could have uninstalled IPv6. This is no longer possible in either the original or R2 version of Windows Server 2008, so answer A is incorrect. The `type netsh interface IPv6 delete` command is used to delete an address, not to delete the IPv6 protocol, so answer C is incorrect. Although it might be possible to block IPv6 communications in Windows Firewall, this does not remove IPv6 from the server, so answer D is incorrect. For more information, refer to "Connecting to a TCP/IP Version 6 Network" in Chapter 1.

**103.** B. Eric should use the New Delegation Wizard in the DNS console to delegate control of the new zone to the NS03 server computer. The wizard automatically creates the A and NS resource records required by the NS03 server. Manually creating and configuring these records would require an excessive amount of administrative effort, so answers A and C are incorrect. Aside from the fact that delegation takes precedence over forwarding if Eric added the appropriate IP address for NS03 to the Forwarders tab on the NS01 and NS02 server computers, those computers would still need to handle queries for the new zone in some fashion. Therefore answer D is incorrect. For more information, refer to "Subdomains and Zone Delegation" in Chapter 6.

**104.** B. The `Wecutil cs` command enables Maggie to create event log subscriptions at computers running the Server Core version of Windows Server 2008. Using this command, she can configure all required actions for setting up the event log subscription including such items as the events to be collected and the user accounts to be used. The `wevtutil` command enables her to retrieve information about event logs and publishers, but not to create event log subscriptions. So, answer A is incorrect. Maggie does not need to create a custom view in this situation, so answer C is incorrect. She cannot perform this task by attaching tasks to events, so answer D is incorrect. For more information, refer to "Configuring Event Log Subscriptions" in Chapter 20.

**105.** A. As well as checking connectivity to the master DNS server, Melanie should check the presence and correctness of the root hints file (`cache.dns`). If this file is correct, she should then stop and restart the DNS server service. This is not the first step she should try, so answer B is incorrect. Collecting debug logging data might help if all other troubleshooting steps fail, but it is also not the first step, so answer C is incorrect. If the `1.0.0.127.in-addr.arpa` zone were missing, the simple test would fail. Because the simple test passed in this situation, this zone must be present and answer D is incorrect. For more information, refer to "Monitoring Tab" in Chapter 5.

**106.** C. When Laura logs on locally to the file server, she has the Full Control permission. When a user logs on locally to a server, the shared folder permissions do not apply; they only apply when the user logs on across the network. Therefore the denied access to the Faculty group through the shared folder permissions does not apply. Her permission from the server is the least restrictive of the permissions that she receives from her membership in the various groups. In this case she has the Read permission from the Faculty group and the Full Control permission from the Department Heads group. Thus her effective permission is Full Control. However, at the desktop, both the shared folder and NTFS permissions apply, and a specific denial always overrides other access; therefore, her effective permission from the desktop is no access. Because the least restrictive permission is applied from multiple group memberships, the Read permission does not apply in her case, and answers A and B are incorrect. Because the specific denial overrides granted access, answer D is incorrect. Because shared folder permissions do not apply when the folder is accessed from the file server, answer E is incorrect. For more information, refer to "Effective Permissions" in Chapter 9.

**107.** A, D, E, H. For DirectAccess connections to work, each client computer must have a computer certificate that enables DirectAccess authentication, and its computer account must be added to the special security group set up on the DirectAccess server, in this case the DA group. Debbie must also configure a GPO that specifies IPv6 transition technologies as well as DNS security (DNSSEC) and DNS settings for DirectAccess. User certificates are not required, nor should the user accounts be added to the DA group, so answers B and C are incorrect. DirectAccess does not use SSL configuration settings; nor does DirectAccess use WINS name resolution technologies, so answers F and G are incorrect. For more information, refer to "Configuring the DirectAccess Server" in Chapter 17.

**108.** A. Brenda should enable the **DNS Suffix Search List** Group Policy setting in a GPO linked to the `certguide.com` domain and then add `que.com` as a DNS suffix in the property settings for this policy. This policy setting enables her to add one or more DNS suffixes to be attached to a query for an unqualified computer name, and applies to all client computers affected by the GPO. The **Allow DNS Suffix Appending to Unqualified Multi-Label Name Queries** policy does not enable Brenda to add an additional DNS suffix to the search order list, so answer B is incorrect. The DNS Suffix and NetBIOS Computer Name dialog box enables her to change the primary DNS suffix of a client computer; she cannot add an additional primary DNS suffix using this dialog box, so answer C is incorrect. Brenda could add `que.com` to the DNS suffix search order on the affected client computers; however, this would take far more administrative effort than using Group Policy, so answer D is incorrect. For more information, refer to "Using Group Policy to Configure DNS Client Settings" in Chapter 8.

**109.** B. Stephanie should configure a reservation for Server9 on Server4 that matches the one for Server3 as shown in the exhibit. Typically, more than one DHCP server is employed on a network so that if one DHCP cannot perform its function for some reason the other DHCP server can then perform that function in a similar fashion. In the case of a reservation, in particular, there can be no discrepancies. What appears to have happened is that Server9 had requested IP configuration information while Server3 was offline. The DHCP server Server4 was not configured with a reservation for Server9 so it simply allocated an address from its scope (192.168.1.51) to fulfill the request from Server9. It is true that typing `ipconfig /release`, then typing `ipconfig /renew` might actually fix the problem described in the question; however, this is true only if Server3 happens to receive and service the request before Server4. In that case, it will configure Server9 with the reserved IP address 192.168.1.114. That cannot be guaranteed, however, because DHCP servers do not share configuration information or attempt to reconcile differences in their con-

·figurations when they are used to configure clients on the same network. Thus, answer A is incorrect. If Stephanie were to configure a reservation for Server9 on Server3 that uses the IP address 192.168.1.51, she would also have to change the A host record on the DNS server. Because this takes more effort and is prone to error (also she would have to exclude this IP address from the scope on both DHCP servers), answer C is incorrect. Because Server9 has successfully received the reserved IP address in the past, it is unlikely that an incorrect MAC address is the source of the problem, so answer D is incorrect. For more information, refer to "Client Reservations and Options" in Chapter 2.

**110.** D. Jim can use SSL to secure communications between the WSUS server and client computers by installing an SSL certificate on the server and configuring it to use HTTPS over TCP port 443. Use of BitLocker Drive Encryption on the WSUS server encrypts the contents of the server's hard disk, but does not encrypt communications, so answer A is incorrect. He would use MS-CHAPv2 to secure authentication, not to encrypt communications, so answer B is incorrect. Using NTFS permissions to limit access would prevent nonadministrative users from receiving updates; further, updates to administrative users would not be encrypted, so answer C is incorrect. For more information, refer to "Installing and Configuring a WSUS Server" in Chapter 18.

**111.** C. Wendy must ensure that TCP port 1723 is open on the firewall protecting the VPN server. This problem can occur if the network firewall does not permit Generic Routing Encapsulation (GRE) protocol traffic. GRE uses IP protocol 47; to pass GRE traffic, TCP port 1723 must be open. GRE does not use port 47, so answer A is incorrect. TCP port 443 is used for secured Hypertext Transfer Protocol (HTTPS) traffic; port 3389 is used by Remote Desktop Protocol (RDP; formerly known as Terminal Services). These ports are not needed in this scenario, so answers B and D are incorrect. For more information, refer to "Remote Access Protocols" in Chapter 14.

**112.** C, D. Betty needs to create both inbound and outbound packet filters on the Oshtemo computer. Betty can configure an outbound packet filter that will only allow outbound communication from the Decatur computer to the external website. She can also configure an inbound packet filter on the Oshtemo computer that will intercept packets that originate from the external website and ensure that those packets are directed exclusively to the Decatur computer. Although domain controllers such as Comstock provide security for their domains, Betty can implement additional security options on RRAS servers that provide routing and NAT services to the network. Packet filtering is one of the more common examples of those services. NAT services are not required on Comstock to implement packet filtering that will have an effect on the network as a whole; therefore, answer A is incorrect. The RRAS server, Oshtemo, does not need to perform name resolution on behalf of any computers on either the Internet or the internal network. It need not become a DNS server, so answer B is incorrect. Once packets arrive at the Decatur computer there would be no particular need to filter them, so a packet filter is not required on Decatur, and answer E is incorrect. Further, Oshtemo provides RRAS services for the entire network; it is not necessary to configure Comstock as a RRAS server, and answer F is incorrect. For more information, refer to "Specifying Packet Filtering" in Chapter 3.

**113.** A. Volume Shadow Service (VSS) enables Brett to create shadow copies of files stored on the file server on a per-volume basis. Users can access previous versions of such files by selecting the **Previous Versions** tab of the file's Properties dialog box, thereby enabling them to recover rapidly from problems such as incorrect modification or file corruption, as required in this scenario. VSS is enabled on a per-volume basis, not a per-shared folder basis, so answer B is incorrect. Brett could use Windows Server Backup to create incremental backups, but this would take more effort and users would still need to contact him when problems occur, so answers C and D are incorrect. For more information, refer to "Volume Shadow Copies" in Chapter 11.

**114.** B, E. Shelley should create a GPO linked to the domain, and in this GPO, she should enable the Turn on Security Center policy. Found at the Computer Configuration\Administrative Templates\Windows Components\Security Center node, this policy enables the monitoring of essential security settings and notifies the user when the computer might be at risk. This policy must be linked to the domain so that it affects all users, so answer A is incorrect. The Require trusted path for credential entry policy requires users to enter Microsoft Windows credentials using a trusted path, to prevent malicious software such as a Trojan horse from stealing a user's credentials. It does not enforce system health requirements, so answer C is incorrect. Digital Locker is a download manager associated with Windows Marketplace and has nothing to do with network security, so answer D is incorrect. For more information, refer to "VPN Enforcement" in Chapter 16.

**115.** C. Kim should use Group Policy to configure an IPSec connection security rule, specifying the rule properties in a GPO linked to the domain. EFS encrypts the zone data while stored on each server, but does not protect zone data during replication, so answer A is incorrect. Digital signing of zone transfers verifies that zone transfers are being received from a trusted source, but does not enable encryption of data in transit, so answer B is incorrect. A trust anchor is a preconfigured public key associated with a specific zone in DNS. It provides additional security against certain types of intrusions such as spoofing, man-in-the-middle, and cache-poisoning attacks. However, it does not encrypt replication traffic, so answer D is incorrect. For more information, refer to "Secure Zone Transfers" in Chapter 6.

**116.** D. Windows Server 2008 provides system-defined data collector sets that enable Krista to obtain a rapid readout of summary performance information for these subsystems. More specifically, the System Performance data collector set enables her to create a report that provides details on local hardware resources, system response times, and local computer processes. Resource Monitor provides much of the same information, but not in as convenient a format, so answer A is incorrect. The `msinfo32.exe` tool provides configuration information but not performance information, so answer B is incorrect. Event trace sessions enables her to create trace logs that track data only when a specific activity takes place. They do not provide the data desired in this situation, so answer C is incorrect. For more information, refer to "System-Defined Data Collector Sets" in Chapter 19.

**117.** D. Neil should manually edit the TCP/IP properties on each client computer. More specifically, he needs to select the **Obtain DNS server address automatically** option on the General tab of the Internet Protocol version 4 (TCP/IPv4) Properties dialog box. The most likely reason that clients remain configured to use a DNS server other than the one specified in the scope for their subnet is that they have been previously configured manually with DNS information. Scope information will not override information that has been manually configured for a client computer, even when that computer has been configured as a DHCP client and has been restarted properly. The `ipconfig/release` and `ipconfig /renew` commands are designed to reset any TCP/IP configurations that have been applied to DHCP client computers, but these commands won't reset manual configurations, so answer A is incorrect. Typically, the options 006 for DNS Servers and 015 for Domain Name need to be specified in a scope designed to configure DNS options for such clients. If Neil needed to enable certain computers on the subnet to use a different DNS server than what all other computers use, he might consider configuring an advanced user class option. He can apply those types of options using the command `ipconfig /setclassid` at each client computer to set DHCP class ID information for those computers. Nothing in the question suggests that this requirement exists in this instance, so answers B and C are incorrect. Isolating the subnet does not make sense because the problem would not be solved when he eventually reconnects the subnet to the rest of the network, so answer E is incorrect. For more information, refer to "Configuring IPv4 Address Options" and "Using TCP/IP Utilities to Troubleshoot TCP/IP" in Chapter 1.

**118.** E. Veronica should access the Advanced tab and select the **Optimize for scalability** option. By selecting this option, scalability is improved and load on the PDC emulator is reduced when there are more than 16 namespace servers in the domain. The option selected from the Referrals tab determines how the targets in the various sites are presented to the client; however, the option chosen here does not affect the load placed on the PDC emulator, so answers A, B, and C are incorrect. The **Optimize for consistency** option is the default presented on the Advanced tab causes the PDC emulator to be polled hourly, causing increased load on this machine; therefore, answer D is incorrect. For more information, refer to "Configuring Polling of Domain Controllers" in Chapter 10.

**119.** C. From the New Printer Filter Wizard, Jason needs to define a filter that sends him an e-mail message whenever a printer on Server11 is unavailable. An unavailable printer can generate any of several different event log messages. Therefore, Jason would need to locate all such messages and create a task to send e-mail; consequently, answers A and B are incorrect. The **Show informational notifications for network** option would provide Jason with information about jobs that have printed successfully on a network printer. It would not provide a notification about a printer that is unavailable, so answer D is incorrect. For more information, refer to "Enabling Notifications" in Chapter 13.

**120.** B. Jill can configure the SRV resource record to specify these parameters for Server6. The SOA resource record is always the first record in any zone file and identifies the primary name server (which would not be Server6). The CNAME record provides additional names that point to a given server. The A or AAAA record defines the name-to-IP address mapping. The WKS record describes the well-known TCP/IP services supported by a particular protocol on a specific IP address. None of these other resource record types enable Jill to specify the required parameters, so answers A, C, D, and E are incorrect. For more information, refer to "Creating New Resource Records" in Chapter 7.

# Answers to the "Do I Know This Already?" Quizzes

## Chapter 1

1.  **C.** The session layer of the OSI model is responsible for performing these actions. The network layer translates logical network names and addresses into physical addresses. The transport layer provides flow control and error handling and aids in solving problems related to the transmission and reception of segments of data over a network. The presentation layer translates data into a format that can be understood by the different applications and the computers they run on.

2.  **D.** The TCP protocol operates at the transport layer of the TCP/IP reference model layer stack, while the IP protocol operates at the Internet layer. The application layer holds application-related protocols, such as HTTP, FTP, SNMP, and SMTP. The network interface layer provides an interface for the layer above it to the network media and holds only media-related protocols, such as Ethernet and Frame Relay. The presentation layer does not exist in the TCP/IP reference model, only in the seven-layer OSI model.

3.  **C.** The default gateway is the IP address of the router that connects your computer's subnet to other subnets on your company's network, as well as the Internet. Although important for your computer's TCP/IP configuration, the other items given here do not address this objective.

4.  **B.** Any IP address in the range 128.0.0.0 to 191.255.255.255 belongs to Class B. Class A addresses are in the range 1.0.0.0 to 126.255.255.255; Class C addresses are in the range 192.0.0.0 to 223.255.255.255; Class D addresses are in the range 224.0.0.0 to 239.255.255.255; Class E addresses are in the range 240.0.0.0 to 254.255.255.255.

5.  **A, C.** To configure your computer to use DHCP, you should ensure that the **Obtain an IP address automatically** and **Obtain DNS server address automatically** options are selected. You would specify the other two options if you were configuring your computer to use static IP addressing.

6. **A**. If your computer is using an IPv4 address on the 169.254.0.0/16 network, it is configured to use APIPA. An address on this network is assigned when the computer is configured to receive an IP address automatically, but is unable to reach a DHCP server. An alternate IP configuration is a separate static IP address that you can configure on a computer that is using DHCP; it would not be using this address. Private IPv4 addressing is in use if the IP address is on any of the 10.0.0.0/8, 172.16.0.0/16, or 192.168.0.0/24 networks.

7. **A**. A global unicast address is a globally routable Internet address that is equivalent to a public IPv4 address. A link-local unicast address is used for communication between neighboring nodes on the same link; a site-local unicast address is used for communication between nodes located in the same site; a multicast address provides multiple interfaces to which packets are delivered; and an anycast address is utilized only as destination addresses assigned to routers. None of these address types are suitable for direct Internet contact. Note that site-local addresses have been deprecated.

8. **C**. A link-local IPv6 address has an address prefix of fe80::/64. This address is equivalent to an APIPA-configured IPv4 address. The other address types have different network prefixes.

9. **A**. An ISATAP address uses the locally administrative interface identifier ::0:5efe:*w.x.y.z*, where *w.x.y.z* is any private unicast IPv4 address, or ::200:5efe:*w.x.y.z*, where *w.x.y.z* is a public IPv4 unicast address. Teredo uses a 2001::/32 prefix, and 6to4 uses a 2002::/16 prefix. An IPv4-mapped address would contain an ffff prefix.

10. **D**. A 6to4 relay forward 6to4 addressed traffic between 6to4 routers and 6to4 host/routers on the IPv4 Internet and hosts on the IPv6 Internet. Such computers use ICS to enable IPv6 forwarding on both the 6to4 tunneling and private interfaces. The other 6to4 components mentioned do not utilize ICS in forwarding network traffic.

11. **B**. You should use the `ipconfig /renew` command. This command forces the computer to try again to connect to the DHCP server and obtain an IP address lease. In this case, the computer was unable to access the DHCP server and configured itself with an APIPA address. The `/release` parameter releases the current IP address configuration but does not contact the DHCP server. The `/flushdns` parameter flushes the contents of the DNS cache. You would use this parameter when the computer has connected to an incorrect network because of incorrect information in the DNS resource records. The `/displaydns` parameter displays the contents of the DNS cache. This is also useful if the computer connects to an incorrect network.

12. **D, C, A, E, B.** You should perform the indicated actions in the following sequence: Run `ipconfig /all` to validate the IP address, subnet mask, default gateway, and DNS server, and whether you are receiving a DHCP leased address. Ping 127.0.0.1 or ::1 to validate that TCP/IP is functioning. Ping the computer's own IP address to eliminate a duplicate IP address as the problem. Ping the default gateway, which tells you whether data can travel on the current network segment. Ping a host that is on another subnet, which shows whether the router will be able to route your data. Microsoft exams might ask you to select actions you must perform and place them in the required sequence.

13. **A.** If two computers on the network are configured with the same IP address, the first one will connect properly, but the second one that attempts to connect will fail to do so and this problem will result. If your computer is configured for static IP addressing, it will never use APIPA. If the subnet mask is incorrect, your computer would not connect to machines on another subnet at any time. If your computer is configured with static IP addressing, the alternate IP address option will be unavailable.

14. **B, D, E.** When verifying IPv6 network connectivity, you may need to specify a zone ID for the sending interface with the `ping` command. You can obtain this zone ID by running either the `netsh interface ipv6 show interface` command or the `ipconfig /all` command (but not the `ipconfig /displaydns` command). Before using `ping` to check IPv6 network connectivity, clear the neighbor cache on your computer by running the `netsh interface ipv6 delete neighbors` command. You may optionally run the `netsh interface ipv6 show neighbors` command to view the neighbor cache; however, you are not required to run this command. After you perform these steps, you can run the `ping` command, suffixing it with the `%<ID>` parameter to include the zone ID.

# Chapter 2

1. **F, A, B, D.** When an IPv4 client is requesting an address from the DHCP server, it first sends a DHCPDISCOVER message to locate a server. The server sends a DHCPOFFER message to offer an IP address lease. The client sends a DHCPREQUEST message to indicate it is requesting this lease, and finally, the server sends a DHCPACK message to acknowledge acceptance of the lease. DHCPINFORM is used by workgroup DHCP servers for locating other DHCP servers on the network. There is no such message as DHC-PADVERTISE; however, DHCPv6 servers use an Advertise message to offer a lease to a client computer. Note that on the exam, you must sequence your answers in the proper order or the answer will be considered incorrect.

2. **A**. A client will first attempt to renew its lease with the DHCP server that provided its lease and configuration information after 50 percent of the lease time has elapsed. If a client still does not have a renewed lease after 87.5 percent of the active lease period has gone by, it will attempt to communicate with any DHCP server on the network to secure IP addressing and configuration information. No specific action occurs after either 80 or 95 percent of the lease time.

3. **B**. An IPv6 client can use the process of stateless address configuration to automatically configure itself without the use of DHCPv6 using a link-local address and router discovery. This process uses Router Solicitation and Router Advertisement messages which are exchanged with neighboring routers. Stateful address configuration used DHCPv6 to obtain non-link-local addresses and other IPv6 configuration parameters. Managed address configuration is not a configuration procedure; it is a flag that determines when DHCPv6 is used to obtain IPv6 stateful addresses. Automatic Private IP addressing is used to auto-assign IPv4 addresses in the absence of a DHCP server; it is not used with IPv6.

4. **E, C, D, G**. The messages sent are Solicit, Advertise, Request, and Reply. These correspond to the DHCPDISCOVER, DHCPOFFER, DHCPREQUEST, and DHCPACK messages sent when requesting an IPv4 address lease. The Confirm message is sent by a client to all servers to determine the validity of a client's configuration. The other options mentioned do not exist with DHCPv6.

5. **B, D**. To install DHCP on a server, you must be logged on as an administrator and the server must be configured with a static IP address. It does not matter whether the server is configured with IPv4, IPv6, or both; it also does not matter whether the server is a domain controller or not.

6. **D**. Pre-Windows 2000 computers, such as Windows NT or 9x, use WINS as a primary naming solution and may be unable to locate resources on the network if they are unable to locate a WINS server. You would want a DHCP relay agent if the DHCP server needs to service clients on other network segments. Remote users logging onto the network use DNS rather than WINS to locate network resources. Windows XP and Windows Server 2003 computers are able to locate local resources with the aid of a DNS server; consequently, they do not need a WINS server for this purpose.

7. **B**. You would use the `Dism /online /enable-feature /featurename:DHCPServerCore` command to install DHCP on a Windows Server 2008 R2 Server Core computer. The `Start /w ocsetup DHCPServerCore` command would install DHCP on a Server Core computer running the original version of Windows Server 2008 but not the R2 version.

The `servermanagercmd -install` command installs certain roles and role features with Server Core, but not DHCP. It is not possible for security reasons to install a server role from a remote computer.

8. **B**. DHCP options are always applied in the sequence server, scope, class, client. This is important to know because options applied at a later stage of this sequence always overwrite options applied earlier in the sequence. For example, server options are overwritten by any conflicting option applied at any of the other levels and client options always overwrite other options.

9. **A**. You should specify a user class option that sets the lease interval to 12 hours for all laptop computers. This type of class is used to differentiate clients according to their type, such as desktop, laptop, or server computer. A vendor class option might be applicable if all laptops are obtained from one vendor but this is not normally the case. Specifying client options for each laptop would take more work than specifying a user class option, and would be open to error. It might be possible to use a separate scope, but this would also take more effort and be error-prone.

10. **A, C**. To ensure that these servers retain their IP addresses but receive other IP configuration information from the DHCP server, you need to create an exclusion range within the scope plus reservations for each of the servers. The exclusion range prevents the server from assigning these IP addresses to other computers and the reservation ensures that these computers always receive their proper IP address. If you create two scopes as described in option B, the file servers would not receive other IP configuration information from the DHCP server. This is also true if you assign these servers static IP addresses. Superscopes are not relevant to this scenario.

11. **D**. You need to authorize the DHCP server in Active Directory. This requirement is necessary to prevent rogue DHCP servers from coming online and assigning improper IP addresses to clients, which would disrupt network communications. Reactivating the scope in this situation does not help. There is no such option in DHCP that would prevent the use of APIPA. A DHCP server on an AD DS domain does not need to be a domain controller.

12. **B**. The DHCP relay agent is a server configured with RRAS that listens for DHCP broadcast messages from client computers on its own subnet and forwards these messages to the DHCP server. The relay agent must be configured on the subnet away from the DHCP server and not on the subnet (A in this case) where the DHCP server is located. There is no scope option that specifies the IP address of a remote DHCP server. There is also no option within a client's TCP/IP Properties dialog box from which you can specify the IP address of a DHCP server.

13. **A**. The message stating `The specified DHCP client is not a reserved client` indicates that you have attempted to reserve an IP address that is outside the range of the DHCP server's scope. To correct the problem, modify the scope so that the desired IP address is within the scope or select a different IP address. There is no such scope option to specify a reserved IP address. If a duplicate IP address were configured on another computer, you would still be able to create a reservation but connectivity problems would occur afterward. You could specify a static IP address at the server in question, but then this server would not receive other IP options from the DHCP server.

# Chapter 3

1. **B**. A metric is a measuring standard, such as a hop count, that is employed by routing algorithms in calculating the best path to the destination. A hop is an individual step from one router to another as the message proceeds to its destination. A protocol is a standard created by some authority, such as the IANA that describes some workings of networks and the Internet (for example, any component protocol that makes up the TCP/IP protocol suite). A proxy is any entity that performs a task on behalf of something else, such as the DHCP relay agent.

2. **C**. RIP v2 provides all these capabilities, including support for CIDR and variable length subnet masks for RRAS routers in Windows Server 2008. OSPF was supported in Windows Server 2003 RRAS, but the support was removed in Windows Server 2008. RIP v1 is supported in Windows Server 2008 RRAS but does not provide all the support capabilities of RIP v2. BOOTP provides support for client computers without an operating system during PXE boot and enables such computers to locate DHCP and WDS servers to install Windows 7 or Windows Server 2008 R2.

3. **B**. The `route print` command displays the complete routing table, including dynamic routes added by RIP. There is no such command as `route display`. The **Show IP Routing Table** option displays the static routing table from the RRAS snap-in. However, it does not include dynamic routes added by RIP. This option is not available when you right-click the **General** node in the RRAS snap-in.

4. **A, E**. To configure your server as a router, you must first install RRAS and then configure RRAS for LAN routing. RRAS is installed as a component of the Network Policy and Access Service server role, so you must select this server role using the Add Roles Wizard; you select RRAS after selecting this server role and not directly as a server role. RRAS is not a feature, so it is not installed from the Add Features Wizard. The Remote Access (dial-up or VPN)

option does not provide the capabilities of installing a router, only a remote access server (although you could add routing later to a RAS server from its Properties dialog box).

5.  **A, B, C, E.** The New Routing Protocol dialog box enables you to install any of DHCP relay agent, IGMP Router and Proxy, NAT (Network Address Translation), or RIP version 2 for Internet Protocol. RIP version 1 for Internet Protocol is outdated. Although limited communications with RIP v1 routers is possible with Windows Server 2008 R2 routers, you cannot configure your server with this protocol. OSPF was supported in Windows Server 2003 RRAS, but the support was removed in Windows Server 2008.

6.  **D.** The **Security** tab of the RIP Properties dialog box enables you to specify the addresses of routers from which announcements will be ignored. Neither the **Neighbors** tab of the RIP Properties dialog box nor the **Security** tab of the RRAS server properties dialog box provides this option. The `route` command does not have a `-i` parameter.

7.  **A.** The `route -p add 192.168.3.0 MASK 255.255.255.0 192.168.2.1 metric 2` command correctly adds the desired route to your server's routing table. The `-p` parameter makes the route persistent; otherwise, the route is removed when the server is rebooted; the `-f` parameter clears the routing table of all gateway entries and is not used here. The order of the parameters in the `route -p add 192.168.2.1 MASK 255.255.255.0 192.168.3.0 metric 2` command is incorrect. (The destination must be specified first and the gateway address last.)

8.  **C.** If the network mask is specified as 255.255.255.255, only an exact match of the destination network number can use the route. If the mask is 0.0.0.0, any destination can use the route. If it is 255.255.255.0, any destination matching the first three octets can use the route. The mask is never going to be equal to the network number.

9.  **B.** The Options tab of the demand-dial interface's Properties dialog box enables you to specify the maximum number of redial attempts and the redial interval. The Security tab enables you to specify encryption, authentication, and authentication protocols, but not redial properties. The Networking tab enables you to specify networking protocols and their properties but not redial properties; further, this tab does not have an **Advanced** button.

10. **D.** In this case, you need to configure the RRAS server's inbound interface for IGMP proxy mode. This action connects a single-router intranet to a multicast-capable intranet or the Internet. Configuring a single-router intranet to a multicast-capable intranet or the Internet would enable the server to forward multicast traffic in a single-router intranet. The other configurations mentioned would not provide any particular benefit.

# Chapter 4

1. **B**. By selecting the **Block all incoming connections, including those in the list of allowed programs** option, you stop all attempts by outsiders to reach your server. This enables you to perform whatever detective and remedial measures you need to perform before putting the server back online. You need to do this within the Home or Work (Private) Network Location settings because your computer is connected to the work network. Public network location settings are used with mobile computers connecting from an insecure location, such as a public Wi-Fi hotspot; although present on the server interface, this option should never be used on a server. You would use the **Turn off Windows Firewall** option only when troubleshooting a connectivity problem and not when troubleshooting improper access to your computer.

2. **B, C, E**. You can configure Windows Firewall to specify programs that are allowed to communicate, or you can configure Windows Firewall to block all incoming connections, from the Windows Firewall Control Panel applet. You can also specify firewall settings for home, work, and public networks from this location. However, you must use the Windows Firewall with Advanced Security snap-in to configure ports and logging. (The Windows Firewall applet in the original version of Windows Server 2008 allowed specifying allowed ports, but this function was removed from this location in Windows Server 2008 R2.)

3. **C**. Windows Firewall with Advanced Security does not include any connection security rules by default. You can use the New Rules Wizard to set up connection security rules as well as additional rules for the other rule types.

4. **C, D, E**. Windows Firewall with Advanced Security enables you to configure settings for the domain, private, and public profiles. There are no user or computer profiles in this tool.

5. **A**. To enable privacy, you must ensure that accepted communications are encrypted. To do so, you need to select the **Allow the connection if it is secure** option from the Action page of the wizard. Then, select the **Require the connections to be encrypted** option on the Customize Allow if Secure Settings dialog box that appears. If you select the **Allow the connection if it is authenticated and integrity-protected** option, it does not ensure that all accepted communications will be encrypted. If you select the **Allow the connection** option from the Action page, you do not receive the Customize Allow if Secure Settings dialog box and, therefore, do not have a chance to select the **Require the connections to be encrypted** option. The **Authentication exemption** option enables specified computers to be exempted from authentication and does not meet the requirements of this scenario; furthermore, it

is found in the New Connection Security Rule Wizard and not in the New Incoming Rule Wizard.

6. **A**. When you select the **Allow the connection if it is secure** option in the New Rule Wizard, you are provided with a Users page that enables you to select the users or groups that are permitted access using the firewall rule you're creating. To grant access to the Research group, you must select the check box labeled **Only allow connections from these users**, click **Add**, and then add the Research group. If you select the **Skip this rule for connections from these users** option, you would designate the Research group as being blocked from access, which is not the desired result. You could complete the wizard after selecting the **Allow the connection if it is secure** option and then access the rule's Properties dialog box; however, this would take more administrative effort; further, you would have to change the rule action to **Allow the connection if it is secure** in order to make changes at the Users tab.

7. **D**. It is not possible to change a rule from Inbound to Outbound from any setting that is available in the rule's Properties dialog box. It is also not possible to drag a rule from one node to another in Windows Firewall with Advanced Security. You must create a new outbound rule to perform this action.

8. **C**. ESP provides data confidentially, authentication, integrity, and anti-replay for the payload contained within each packet. On the other hand, AH does not provide confidentiality so does not meet the requirements indicated here. Tunnel mode enables you to secure transmissions between two networks. This mode creates a tunneled path between subnets or across the Internet, through which secured data passes. Transport mode only secures transmissions within a single network, and so is not suited to this situation.

9. **B**. This scenario requires the use of Triple Data Encryption Standard (3DES). This provides a higher level of security than DES. AES provides even better security, but is not supported on computers running Windows XP or Windows Server 2003. ESP (which is required in this scenario) is not an encryption algorithm, but an IPSec protocol.

10. **A**. You should use Kerberos authentication. This is the default protocol used for AD DS authentication, and it can be used across all domains in a multiple domain forest. Although certificates provide a high level of authentication and are useful for authenticating computers from outside the forest, its use is not necessary in this situation. Preshared keys are used only if it is not possible to use other methods of authentication; this is a less secure method. IKE is Internet Key Exchange, which is a key exchange protocol that is part of the IPSec protocol suite. It is used for accomplishing the safe exchange of secret keys but not for authentication of users.

**11. D.** An IPSec exemption enables you to choose whether or not to exempt ICMP from IPSec requirements. Choosing the **Yes** option enables ICMP packets such as `ping` or `tracert` to pass without being examined by IPSec rules, thereby enabling the desktop support technician to use these tools. The Client (Respond Only) setting is no longer available to Windows 7 or Windows Server 2008 R2 computers; anyway, it would not enable ICMP packets to pass. An authorization exemption is used to designate computers that do not require authentication. IPSec tunnel authorization is used in conjunction with tunnel mode IPSec, which is not used here; it would not permit ICMP packets to pass anyway.

**12. B.** You should configure a server isolation policy. This policy, which can be configured in a domain-based GPO, enables you to isolate specific domain member servers to accept only authenticated and secured communication from other computers within the domain. Domain isolation is similar, but isolates all domain computers from non-domain computers; you use server isolation here because you want to isolate the indicated server and not other domain servers. IPSec tunnel authorization is used in conjunction with tunnel mode IPSec, which is not needed in this scenario. IPSec exemptions are used to enable ICMP packets such as `ping` or `tracert` to pass without being examined by IPSec rules. This is not needed here.

# Chapter 5

**1. A, B, C, D.** The DNS namespace includes root domains, top-level domains, second-level domains, and host names. You can even have additional subdomains at levels beneath the second level. However, NetBIOS names are not a component of the DNS namespace.

**2. C, D, F.** These three computer names qualify as FQDNs, which generally consist of a host name, second-level domain name, and top-level domain name separated by periods. SERVER1 is a NetBIOS name, not a FQDN. http://www is an incomplete name; further, a FQDN does not start with http:. webserver.anydomain. is an incomplete name.

**3. C.** In an iterative query, the name is resolved in the sequence root domain, top-level domain, second-level domain, and then host name. If the ISP's DNS server can resolve the query, this is a recursive query and not an iterative query. Beginners might think that a query is resolved from the front of the name to the back (parallel to a filename plus extension), but this sequence as described in option B is backwards. A client does not communicate directly with a root server, as option D suggests.

4. **A, D, E**. You can install DNS on a Windows Server 2008 R2 computer by using the Add Roles Wizard or the `Start /w ocsetup` command. In addition, if you promote your server to domain controller using the `dcpromo` command, the Active Directory Installation Wizard automatically installs DNS if another DNS server is not available on the network. Because DNS is a server role and not a feature, you cannot use the Add Features Wizard. The Control Panel Add or Remove Programs applet was used to install DNS on servers running Windows 2000 Server or Windows Server 2003, but it is no longer used for this purpose. DNS Manager is used to configure DNS after installation; it is installed when you install DNS.

5. **B**. When installing a DNS server, you should ensure that it has a static IP address. If it is configured to use DHCP to obtain an IP address automatically, then its IP address could change and client computers would be unable to locate the DNS server. The server does not need to be configured as a domain controller or an application server; further, it can function properly with only a single network adapter.

6. **D**. The error with ID 408 means that you have configured the Interfaces tab of the DNS server's properties to respond only to a specified IP address, but the IP address you've entered is incorrect. Unlike DHCP requests, a DNS request can cross any router on the network. If the DNS server's network adapter had failed, clients would be unable to resolve the intranet server's host name unless an alternate name resolution service such as a HOSTS file were present; however, you would not receive a 408 error. It is not necessary to specify the IP address of the intranet server on the Forwarders tab; in fact, the IP addresses specified here should be DNS servers and not web servers.

7. **A**. By specifying the DNS server of the partner company as a conditional forwarder, requests for resources in this company are automatically forwarded to this DNS server. If you specified the IP address and FQDN of the partner company DNS server on the Forwarders tab of your DNS server, the partner company DNS server could receive requests from your company's users for Internet resources. Specifying your DNS server's IP address and FQDN on the partner company's DNS server would forward requests in the opposite direction. Specifying the partner DNS server on the Root Hints tab would cause requests for Internet resources to go to the partner DNS server.

8. **B**. You should check the root hints on the DNS server. These specify the IP addresses of the Internet root servers that contain information for all the top-level Internet domains. If they are incorrect or missing, users will be unable to access external websites. A conditional forwarder is a DNS server that handles name resolution for specific domains. If the conditional forwarder were incorrect, errors would occur for the domain name specified in the New Conditional Forwarder dialog box only and not for other domains. Trust anchors

are used with signed zones on a DNS server that validates DNS zone data and provide security against certain types of intrusions; they would not stop the access to external websites as described here. Round robin randomizes access to multiple DNS servers that resolve names on the same zone. None of these provide Internet name resolution.

9. **D**. Debug logging records information on packets sent to and from the DNS server and stores this information in a text file named dns.log. DNS monitoring enables you to run test queries that check your server's configuration, but does not create this log file. Event logging determines what type of events are recorded in the Event Viewer log. DNS Notify enables a master server to notify secondary servers of changes to its zone but does not perform logging.

10. **B**. Cache locking is a security feature that enables you to control the overwriting of information stored in the DNS cache. If an intruder successfully overwrites information in the cache, he might be able to redirect network traffic to a malicious site. Root hints direct a query to servers that are authoritative for the DNS root zone. Conditional forwarders direct requests for specified DNS domains to a specified DNS server. Trust anchors are used with signed zones on a DNS server that validates DNS zone data and provide security against certain types of intrusions. If any of these were at fault, clients would be able to receive the proper website after clearing their cache; or they would be unable to reach any website.

# Chapter 6

1. **D**. A stub zone contains source information about authoritative name servers for its zone only. This zone information is obtained from another server that hosts a primary or secondary copy of the same zone data. Primary zones, secondary zone, and Active Directory–integrated zones all contain complete zone information. There is no such thing as a forwarding zone; only forwarding servers that forward name resolution requests to other DNS servers.

2. **B**. A secondary zone is a backup copy of DNS zone data hosted on a DNS server that is a secondary source for this zone information. A primary zone is a master copy of DNS zone data and is not used here. A stub zone contains source information about authoritative name servers for its zone only; it does not contain a complete set of zone information. You cannot configure an Active Directory–integrated zone on a server that is not a domain controller. There is no such thing as a forwarding zone; there are only forwarding servers that forward name resolution requests to other DNS servers.

3. **C**. A GlobalNames zone is a special type of Active Directory–integrated zone that enables you to resolve static, global records with single-label names without the need for a WINS server. A primary zone is a master copy of DNS

zone data and is not used here. A secondary zone is a backup copy of DNS zone data hosted on a DNS server that is a secondary source for this zone information. A stub zone contains source information about authoritative name servers for its zone only; it does not contain a complete set of zone information.

4. **D**. Benefits of secondary name servers include load balancing, fault tolerance, and improved name resolution across a slow link. However, not being involved with zone transfers is not a benefit of a secondary name server because these servers are indeed involved with zone transfers; this is a benefit of a caching-only server.

5. **A**. The reverse lookup zone contains the octets of the network portion of the IP address in reverse sequence and uses a special domain name ending in `in-addr.arpa`. Thus the correct address is `8.168.192.in-addr.arpa`. You do not use the host portion of the IP address, so `0.8.168.192.in-addr.arpa` is incorrect. The octets must be specified in reverse sequence, so the other two choices are both incorrect.

6. **C**. The General tab of a zone's Properties dialog box includes an option for changing the type of the zone. By clicking **Change**, you can choose from the primary, secondary, and stub zone types, and you can also choose to store the zone in Active Directory if your server is configured as a domain controller. The server's Properties dialog box does not have an option to select a primary name server option. (There is no General tab on this dialog box; furthermore, the same DNS server can be configured as primary for one zone and secondary for a different zone.) The Name Servers tab does not have an option for specifying the current server as a primary server. Because you can change the zone type from its Properties dialog box, you do not have to delete and re-create the zone.

7. **A**. The **Scavenge Stale Resource Records** option, available in the server's right-click menu in DNS Manager, enables you to immediately scavenge all stale resource records. The other options presented here enable scavenging, but not on an immediate basis.

8. **D**. This scenario calls for the creation of a new delegated subdomain, which enables the administrator in the Engineering department to manage his own DNS name space within the overall company's namespace. Creation of a new primary or secondary set of forward or reverse lookup zones, or creation of a non-delegated subdomain will not accomplish this objective.

9. **C**. You should select the **To all domain controllers in this domain** option. Of the possible DNS replication scopes available, this is the only one that will replicate properly to a DNS server running Windows 2000.

**10. A.** To enable the use of IPSec for securing zone transfers, you need to create a connection security rule in a domain-focused GPO. You need to specify the IP address ranges between which secure zone transfers are to be permitted, and you must require authentication using Kerberos V5 for inbound and outbound connections. Creating inbound and outbound rules does not work for securing zone transfers. Limiting zone transfers to servers on the Name Servers tab or to servers with specified IP addresses does not impose IPSec-based security. There is no **Enable zone transfers using IPSec** option in the Properties dialog box for the DNS server.

**11. A, B, D. E.** Performing any of these tasks might provide you with information as to why the user was unable to ping the file server by name. The `ipconfig /release` and `ipconfig /renew` commands renew the user computer's TCP/IP configuration but do not provide any troubleshooting information.

**12. B.** The `nslookup 10.0.5.25` command will provide you with the host name of the computer with this IP address. If the host name returned is incorrect, you can suspect some type of cache poisoning. The `ping 10.0.5.25` command tests conductivity to this machine but does not provide the host name. The `ipconfig /all` command provides comprehensive TCP/IP information for the computer from which it is issued but no information on other computers. The `ipconfig 10.0.5.25` command is invalid.

## Chapter 7

**1. B.** An AAAA resource record is used for mapping the host name to an IPv6 address. An A resource record is used with IPv4 addresses only. A NS resource record lists the DNS servers that are authoritative in the domain. A PTR resource contains IP address-to-name mappings (reverse lookup, the reverse of what is needed in this question).

**2. C.** A CNAME resource record provides aliases (canonical names), which are additional names that point to the same host. This facilitates the action required in this scenario. You would not use duplicated A address records here. A NS resource record specifies the DNS servers that are authoritative in the domain. An SRV resource record locates servers that provide a defined service on the network. A MX resource record identifies preferred mail servers on the network.

**3. E.** An SRV (service location) resource record is used to locate servers that provide a defined service, such as LDAP service as used by domain controllers. An A record maps host names to IPv4 addresses. A NS resource record specifies the DNS servers that are authoritative in the domain. A CNAME resource record provides aliases, which are additional names that point to the same host.

A PTR resource contains IP address-to-name mappings. None of these latter resource records point to services on the network.

4. **C.** The TTL value specifies the length of time that a DNS server retains cached information for a zone. Increasing this value enables information to be retained for a longer time, thereby reducing the amount of DNS traffic but with the potential of errors should the IP address configuration of a requested host change within this interval. Reducing the TTL value would have the opposite effect and would increase the amount of DNS traffic. The refresh interval is used with secondary DNS servers and is not relevant here.

5. **D.** Reducing the refresh interval enables a secondary server to be more up-to-date, but at the expense of increased network traffic. The retry interval specifies how much time elapses before the secondary server tries again to contact the master server in the event that the master server does not respond on the first attempt. Its value is not relevant to this situation. Increasing the refresh interval would have the opposite effect to what is needed here.

6. **A.** The Edit Name Server Record dialog box enables you to add the second IP address to the record used for DNS2. It is not possible to have two NS resource records for the same server. Deleting the existing resource record for DNS2 and adding a new record with two IP addresses is also not possible. The Name Server (NS) option is not available from the right-click menu in DNS Manager or from the Resource Record Type dialog box.

7. **B.** This problem occurs because Server05 is the owner of the client computers A and PTR records and only this server can update these records when secure dynamic update is configured. By adding all DHCP servers to the DnsUpdateProxy group, the servers are permitted to automatically update a client's A and PTR records whenever it updates the client's TCP/IP configuration. You need to add the DHCP servers and not the DNS servers to this group. You would use the `ipconfig /registerdns` command only in the case of a client that is configured with a static IP address. Selecting the option to allow both nonsecure and secure dynamic updates presents a potential security problem because rogue servers could produce improper updates. At any rate, it would not help in this case because Server05 would still own the records for these users' machines.

8. **D.** You should ensure that the **Enable netmask ordering** option is selected. This option is found on the Advanced tab of the DNS server's Properties dialog box. Adjusting the Priority value in the SRV resource record properties modifies the priority of accessing servers that provide a defined service. The NS record properties does not have a Priority value. The **Enable round robin** option provides load balancing among multiple DNS servers.

## Chapter 8

1. **C**. The DNS tab of the Advanced TCP/IP settings dialog box enables you to specify more than two DNS server addresses. It also allows you to sequence these server addresses in the order of most likely usage. The Internet Protocol (TCP/IP) Properties dialog box (either version 4 or 6) allows you to specify only two DNS server addresses. Another way you could solve this problem is to add the first two DNS server addresses from this dialog box and then click **Advanced** to add the third DNS server address from the DNS tab, as already described. The Alternate Configuration tab enables you to specify an alternate set of TCP/IP addressing parameters for use at a different location, such as when using a portable computer; it does not allow the specification of additional DNS server addresses.

2. **A**. When devolution is performed, a client computer that has appended a multiple-domain DNS suffix such as `certguide.com` to an unqualified host name such as `server1` attempts to resolve the FQDN `server1.certguide.com`; if this query fails, the client attempts to resolve the FQDN `server1.com`. It does not use the opposite sequence; while some type of iterative query might take place, this is not part of devolution. Searching multiply sequenced domain suffixes is also not part of devolution.

3. **D**. The **Use this connection's DNS suffix in DNS registration** option enables the use of DNS dynamic update to register the IP addresses and the connection-specific domain name of this connection, in addition to the primary name of the computer. The **Append parent suffixes of the primary DNS suffix** option enables the client to search the parent suffixes of the primary DNS suffix up to the second-level domain, when resolving unqualified host names. The **Append these DNS suffixes (in order)** option enables you to specify a list of DNS suffixes to be used for resolution of an unqualified name. The **Register this connection's addresses in DNS** option must be selected, not cleared, to select the **Use this connection's DNS suffix in DNS registration** option.

4. **B**. The DNS Suffix and NetBIOS Computer Name dialog box enables you to type a primary DNS suffix that is used by a standalone client computer. This dialog box is reached from the Computer Name/Domain Changes dialog box, which in turn is accessed from the Computer Name tab of the System Properties dialog box. You cannot specify a primary DNS suffix using the Workgroup field. Also, you cannot specify this setting from any of the fields in the DNS tab of the Advanced TCP/IP Settings dialog box.

5. **A**. You should ask Beth to open a command prompt on her computer and type `ipconfig /flushdns`. This command flushes incorrect information, including negative responses from failed DNS queries, from her computer's DNS

client cache. The `ipconfig /registerdns` command forces a registration of all client host records in DNS, but does not correct the name resolution problem. Logging off and logging back on can be used to reset access permissions (which you learn about later in this book) but does not clear the DNS cache (though rebooting her computer would clear the cache). Because Beth's computer still has incorrect information in the DNS client cache, you do not need to check the web server or network connections unless problems continue to occur.

6. **D**. If changes have been made to resource records at one DNS server, other DNS servers that reference these resource records do not automatically update their information. By typing the `dnscmd /clearcache` command at these servers, you can clear the cache of obsolete information and force the server to retrieve the current information. The `ipconfig /flushdns` command clears the client cache at whatever computer it has been typed, but this computer will still obtain incorrect information if the server cache has not been cleared. The `ipconfig /renew` command renews TCP/IP configuration information from a DHCP server; it does not clear incorrectly cached data.

7. **C**. If the computer first tries a broadcast to resolve a NetBIOS name query and, if unsuccessful, then tries to locate a NetBIOS name server, the computer is using m-node (mixed). If it were using b-node (broadcast), it would only try the broadcast method and not the NetBIOS name server. If it were using p-node (point-to-point), it would try the NetBIOS name server but not a broadcast. If it were using h-node (hybrid), it would try both methods but in the opposite sequence to that specified here.

8. **A**. When using a computer configured for IPv4 without a DHCP server, you should select the **Enable NetBIOS over TCP/IP** option to ensure that NetBIOS names can be resolved. You would not want to disable NetBIOS in this situation. Disabling the **Turn off Multicast Name Resolution** policy enables the use of LLMNR; however, this allows name resolution only on IPv6 networks. The `ipconfig /registerdns` command forces a registration of all client host records in DNS, but does not enable the use of NetBIOS.

9. **C**. The HOSTS file is a static file containing host name to IP address mappings that is found in the `%systemroot%\system32\drivers\etc` folder. It can be used to resolve host names in the absence of a DNS server. Entries in this file are automatically loaded into the DNS resolver cache when the DNS Client service starts. There is no specific file named Cache, though DNS uses a `Cache.dns` file for caching recent name resolution queries. WINS is a server-based dynamic NetBIOS name resolution feature and not a static name resolution file. The LMHOSTS file is a static database file of NetBIOS name-to-IPv4 address mappings that has been used since the days of early Windows computers and can still be used nowadays for the same purpose.

**10. B.** When you ping a remote host and receive a response that includes the IPv6 address of the remote host but no domain name suffix, your computer is using Link Local Multicast Name Resolution (LLMNR) to resolve this name. If it were using NetBIOS or WINS, you would see an IPv4 address, not an IPv6 address. If it were using a connection specific DNS suffix, you would see a domain name suffix appended to the host name in the response.

# Chapter 9

**1. A, C, E.** You can specify any of Read, Change, or Full Control shared folder permissions. The Modify and Read & Execute permissions are NTFS security permissions; they are not shared folder permissions.

**2. B.** You would use the `net share` command to create a shared folder from the Server Core version of Windows Server 2008 R2. There is no such command as `share`. The `net user` command enables you to create or modify user accounts but not share folders. The `netsh` command provides a variety of subcommands useful for networking configuration but not folder sharing.

**3. E.** Assign the Read & Execute permission to enable users to view files and run programs in the folder. The Full Control permission and Modify permission would enable users to edit or delete files in the folder. The Read permission does not enable them to run programs. The Change permission is a shared folder permission only.

**4. D.** Although NTFS permissions are cumulative such that a user receives the least restrictive permission, an explicit denial of permission overrides all allowed permissions. Therefore, in this scenario, Alice does not have access to the Documents folder.

**5. B, C, D, F.** The Read NTFS permission consists of the List folder/read data attributes, Read attributes, Read extended attributes, and Read special access permissions. The Traverse folder/execute file permission is included in the Read & Execute or higher basic NTFS permission; the Delete permission is included in the Modify or higher basic NTFS permission; and the Take ownership permission is included in the Full Control basic NTFS permission only.

**6. A.** Because all NTFS permissions are inherited, permissions granted to the Documents folder are by default inherited by the Specifications folder. So that members of the Interns group do not receive the permission to modify contents of this folder, you must remove the inherited permission by selecting the **Remove** option. If you select the **Add** option, members of the Interns group receive the inherited permissions and members of the Interns group can modify this folder. If you deny the Full Control permission to members of the Interns group, they will be unable to access the contents of this folder. If you don't do anything, members of the Interns group can modify the contents of the folder by way of the inherited permission.

7. **C**. If a shared folder has both shared folder and NTFS permissions assigned to it and a user accesses this folder across the network, the most restrictive permission is the effective permission. Therefore, in this scenario, Peter has Read permission on the Documents folder.

8. **A**. When a user accesses a shared folder on the same computer on which it is located, the shared folder permission does not apply and the user receives only the NTFS permission that has been assigned to the folder. Therefore, in this scenario, Fred has Full Control permission on the Documents folder.

9. **B, C**. To encrypt a file or folder, the file or folder must be located on a volume that is formatted with the NTFS file system. So, you need to convert the volume to the NTFS file system or move the folder to another volume that is formatted with the NTFS file system. If you were to format the D:\ volume with the NTFS file system, you would destroy the Confidential folder. The folder cannot be decompressed because this is also a function of the NTFS file system.

10. **B**. You should use Group Policy on a domain-based GPO to run the Add Recovery Agent Wizard and designate George's user account as a recovery agent. This enables him to decrypt and recover files at any domain member computer. You could accomplish the same by using Local Group Policy at each user's computer, but this would take far more time. The backed-up encryption certificate and keys would not enable George to decrypt users' files. Membership in the Domain Admins group is not sufficient privilege to enable George to recover other users' encrypted files.

11. **A, D**. You need to use Group Policy to enable the **Require additional authentication at startup**, enable this policy and select the **Allow BitLocker without a compatible TPM** option. You also need to use the Add Features Wizard in Server Manager to install BitLocker. After you perform these two tasks, the option to encrypt any operating system or fixed data drive with BitLocker will become available. You need to perform these actions before you can configure the use of a startup key. You don't need to upgrade your server to Windows Server 2008 Enterprise Edition or install the File Server role to use BitLocker.

12. **C, E**. You need to supply the password that was created when you first enabled BitLocker. You can do this either by pressing **Enter**, type the recovery password, and pressing **Enter** again, or by inserting a USB key on which the password is stored. You cannot start the computer using any of the options supplied by the System Recovery tool. Windows XP does not support Bit-

Locker; even if it did, it would not be possible to decrypt the partition in the manner suggested here.

13. **C**. The **All files and programs that users open from the shared folder are automatically available offline** option makes every file in the share available for caching by a remote user. When a user opens a file from the share, the file is downloaded to the client's cache and replaces any older versions of the file. The **Only the files and programs that users specify will be available offline** option requires that users specifically indicate which files are to be available. The **Enable BranchCache** option enables a branch office computer to serve files to other branch office client computers. The **Optimize for performance** option improves performance, but only on computers running Windows XP or older versions of Windows.

14. **B**. Because the branch office has a server available to all users, it is best to use BranchCache in the Hosted Cache mode. It would be possible to use the Distributed Cache mode, but when client computers containing cached content were offline, additional bandwidth would be used to access content on the head office server. Copying the contents of the shared folder on your file server to a shared folder on the branch office server would be possible but would not keep this share up-to-date and would not likely minimize bandwidth needs. The Offline Files option would enable users in the branch office to cache copies of required files on their computers but would also not likely minimize bandwidth needs.

15. **B, D, E**. Administrative shares are created by default when you first install Windows Server 2008. These shares are suffixed with the $ symbol and are visible from the Share and Storage Management snap-in; they can be accessed by entering the UNC path to the share in the Run command. Because they are hidden, you cannot see them in an Explorer window, nor can you access them from the Network and Sharing Center.

# Chapter 10

1. **A, B**. The Add Role Services Wizard enables you to create a DFS namespace that is either standalone or integrated with Active Directory at the same time that you're installing the DFS role service. The wizard enables you to install the software for DFS Replication, but it does not enable you to create a DFS replication group or specify a replication topology; you need to perform these tasks later.

2. **D**. A folder target is a UNC path of a shared folder or another namespace that is associated with a folder in a namespace. Folder targets are used to direct clients to specific server locations, generally the location nearest to their computers. The starting point of the namespace and is specified by users

when connecting to any object within the namespace is actually the definition of a DFS root. The others are types of folders that can be contained in a namespace hierarchy but are not specifically folder targets.

3. **C**. You should select the **Exclude targets outside of the client's site** option. This option prevents targets in other sites from being listed; if no same-site targets exist, the client is unable to access that portion of the DFS namespace. The **Random order** and **Lowest cost** options would list targets in other sites and clients might need to cross the WAN when these options are selected. The **Clients fail back to preferred targets** option is available only for individual folders in a namespace and not for the entire namespace.

4. **B**. Access-based enumeration displays only those files and folders that a user has permission to access. When you have enabled access-based enumeration, which you can do from the Advanced tab of the namespace's Properties dialog box, users will not see folders to which they do not have access, and will therefore receive fewer `Access denied` messages. The other options do not reduce the frequency of users receiving these messages; further, configuring additional namespaces would increase administrative overhead considerably.

5. **A, C, D**. You should upgrade all servers in the replication group to Windows Server 2003 R2 or higher. You should also convert any FAT32 partitions on replication member servers to the NTFS file system, and ensure that your antivirus software is compatible with DFS replication. These are all among the requirements for DFS replication. Furthermore, ensure that all servers are located in the same AD DS forest. You do not need to upgrade servers to Windows Server 2008 R2. Also, you do not need to create folder targets that point to all replication member servers; this is a component of DFS Namespaces, not DFS Replication.

6. **B**. The `Dfsrdiag.exe` command enables you to force members to poll domain controllers immediately for configuration changes, thereby helping to make the new configuration available for use as soon as possible. The `Dfsdiag.exe` command is used to diagnose issues with DFS Namespaces, not DFS Replication. `Dfsutil.exe` enables you to perform many actions with regard to configuring DFS from a command prompt including configuring access-based enumeration. `Dfsradmin.exe` enables you to add replicated folders to a replication group. None of these latter three commands enables you to expedite the availability of the new DFS configuration.

7. **D**. By right-clicking the **Publications** folder and choosing **Make read-only**, you can ensure that users accessing this replicated folder from branch-office member servers cannot make changes at these locations. If you were to right-click the replication group and choose **Make read-only**, nobody (even the managers and journalists) could make changes to this folder. If you were to

allow the Managers and Journalists group the Modify NTFS permission and allow the Read shared folder permission to the Everyone group, the managers and journalists would be able to make changes only at the server that actually hosts the Publications folder and not at the other two head office servers. If you were to allow the Managers and Journalists group the Modify NTFS permission and the Full Control shared folder permission, the managers and journalists would be able to modify this folder from the branch offices as well as the head office.

8. **C**. A health report provides information on replication statistics, error and warning events, backlogged files, and other information for each member of the replication group in the form of an HTML file. You can create this report by right-clicking the desired replication group in the console tree of the DFS Management snap-in and choose **Create Diagnostic Report**. This starts a wizard that provides three options, of which you must choose **Health Report**. The Propagation test option creates test files for propagating to other replication members and the Propagation report option creates a report that tracks the replication progress of these files. You cannot select **Create Health Report** directly from the right-click menu of the replication group.

# Chapter 11

1. **D**. In both the original and R2 versions of Windows Server 2008, Windows Server Backup is not installed by default when you install the operating system. You need to install Windows Server Backup as a server feature from the Features node in Server Manager. Windows Server Backup is not an option found in the console tree of either the Computer Management or Server Manager snap-ins. The `ntbackup` utility was used for performing backups in Windows Server 2003 and older server versions; it has been replaced by Windows Server Backup in Windows Server 2008.

2. **A**. You should select the **Bare metal recovery** option. The backup performed using this procedure is essentially a complete backup that enables you to recover your server from the Windows Recovery Environment should a catastrophic failure of some kind occur. System State provides a backup of all critical items including the Registry, System and boot files, and several other items depending on the roles installed on your server. It is a portion of the bare metal backup, but is not a complete backup that enables recovery from the Windows Recovery Environment. The system and boot volumes would also not provide a complete backup for recovery from the Windows Recovery Environment. The `vssadmin` tool enables you to configure shadow copies from the command line, but not to configure regular backups. VSS full backup is an option for enabling volume shadow copies, not for full server backup.

3. **A**. When you select the **Back up to a hard disk that is dedicated for backups (recommended)** option, the disk you've selected is formatted and dedicated to only store backups. This caused the partition containing the images to be erased. You would have received a warning message to this effect, which should have caused you to choose a different disk or backup option. The **Back up to a volume** option does not cause items on a different partition of the drive to be erased; if the selected partition is not large enough, an error message is generated and the backup does not take place. This procedure does not create multiple backups; each backup performed erases the previous one.

4. **C**. You use the `wbadmin` tool to configure backups from the command line in Windows Server 2008. This tool includes the capability of scripting backups. The `ntbackup` tool was used in Windows Server 2003 and older versions for this purpose, but its use is no longer supported. The `ntdsutil` tool is used for performing a variety of actions on AD DS domain controllers including authoritative restore operations, but it is not used for backups. The `vssadmin` tool enables you to configure shadow copies from the command line, but it doesn't allow you to configure regular backups.

5. **B**. You should open the Windows Server Backup tool, select **Recover Catalog**, and specify the path to the folder containing the current backups. This action restores the catalog and enables future backups to take place as scheduled. Replacing the backup disk with a new disk or changing the location of the stored backups does not restore the catalog and does not enable future backups to take place. It is not necessary to recover system state in this situation.

6. **D**. You should enable shadow copies on all drives containing user files. Users can then access the Previous Versions tab of a file's Properties dialog box whenever they need to restore a damaged file. Most client computers already come with backup software but this does not enable backup of data stored on remote server shares. Adding user accounts to the Backup Operators group enables users to back up their own files but would create extra administrative overhead with all users attempting to perform various backup and restore procedures. Duplicated files would likely also become corrupted at the same time and would not solve this problem.

7. **B**. Although all these procedures would enable recovery of the deleted file, downloading and installing client software from Microsoft on his computer is by far the simplest method to solve this problem. By default, only computers running Windows Vista, Windows Server 2008, and later have native support for volume shadow copies.

8. **A, B, E**. Windows Server Backup enables you to restore individual files and folders or the entire volume that does not include the operating system. You can also make an additional copy of restored files and folders in another loca-

tion; this enables you to ensure that files and folders are being properly backed up. You cannot restore operating systems to either the same or another server using this method.

**9. A.** The `wbadmin start systemstaterecovery -version:MM/DD/YYYY-HH:MM -backuptarget:target_drive: -machine:backup_server_name -quiet` command enables you to restore the system state on a Windows Server 2008 R2 Server Core computer. The `wbadmin start sysrecovery` command performs a bare metal recovery, and must be started from the Command Prompt option of the System Recovery Options dialog box. The `ntbackup` program is no longer used with Windows Server 2008; it was used with Windows Server 2003 and older server operating systems.

**10. C.** You should start the server from the Windows Server 2008 R2 DVD-ROM, select **Repair your computer**, select **System Image Recovery**, and then select **Use the latest available system image (recommended)**. This procedure enables a bare metal recovery of the server. It is not possible to start in Safe Mode because you have installed a new hard disk without an operating system. Safe Mode is not an option that is available from the System Recovery Options dialog box. It is not necessary to first install a new copy of the operating system because the bare metal recovery procedure recovers the operating system and data files.

# Chapter 12

**1. B, C, D, E.** FSRM enables you to create quotas that limit the amount of disk space users can store within a folder or volume; create file screens that restrict the file types users can save; define rules that set classification properties on files; and create scheduled tasks that can be used for applying actions to subsets of files. However, you cannot configure shared folder and NTFS permissions on files and folders using FSRM.

**2. C.** You should use FSRM to create a file group and give the group an appropriate name. Specify `*.mp*` as a set of files to include and `*.mpp` as a set of files to exclude. Then, create a file screen, specifying the **Active screening** type and the name of the file group that you created. If you specify `*.mpp` as a set of files to include and `*.mp*` as a set of files to exclude, this is backwards and will allow the storage of audio files as well as Microsoft Project files. If you specify the Passive screening type, users will still be able to save audio files; this option provides for monitoring but not blocking the specified file type.

3. **B, D**. To accomplish this objective, you can create a file screen that specifies the **Passive screening** option and select the **Image Files** file group as a group to block. You can also select the **Storage Reports** tab of the File Server Resource Manager Options dialog box and specify the **Files by File Group** option as a group to be reported on. If you select the **Active screening** option, users will be prevented from storing their image files, which is not the objective stated here. The File Screen Audit tab enables you to select an option for storing file screening activity in an auditing database; however, it does not include any options for specifying the type of files to be reported on.

4. **A**. The Action tab of the Create File Management Task dialog box enables you to configure a File Expiration task including the folder to which expired files will be moved, and the Condition tab enables you to specify the number of days after which the file will be considered as expired. The Properties dialog box for the shared folder does not provide these options. The **Least Recently Accessed Files** option enables you to create a report but does not enable you to move the files to another location. You might be able to accomplish this task by creating a file screen and specifying an appropriate file group and command, but you would need to write a script to accomplish this task, which would be more complicated than using the Create File Management Task dialog box.

5. **B**. FSRM enables you to configure a quota that applies to a specific shared folder rather than the entire volume. You cannot use FSRM to configure different quotas that apply to individual users; this action is only possible from Windows Explorer. You can deny additional space to users or write events to the event log from either FSRM or Windows Explorer; the denial of additional disk space configured from FSRM is termed a hard quota.

6. **C**. FSRM enables you to create a custom quota template that enables you to specify a soft quota and then apply this quota to all shared folders on all servers. You want to create a soft quota and not a hard quota because the latter would deny disk space if users exceed their limit, which is not the objective in this scenario. Windows Explorer does not enable you to create quota templates. You can create quotas from Windows Explorer that apply to individual disk volumes but not to shared folders; further, this takes more administrative effort.

7. **D**. The **Unassign LUN** option enables you to temporarily make the LUN invisible without deleting any data. The **Delete LUN** option would delete all data on all volumes on the LUN, which is not the objective here. There is no **Rename LUN** option. The Subsystems node lists all the storage subsystems currently discovered in your SAN and allows you to rename a subsystem; it does not allow you to work with individual LUNs.

# Chapter 13

1. **D**. It is important to remember that, in Microsoft terminology, the printer is the software (logical) interface between the operating system and the physical print device. Microsoft refers to the physical (hardware) device that produces the printed output as the print device. The program that converts graphics commands into instructions is called the print driver, and the computer that controls the printing process on the network is referred to as the print server.

2. **B**. The act of copying a print job to a reserved area within the system root folder of the computer before being sent to the print device is known as spooling. Doing so can improve performance by eliminating the print device as a bottleneck that ties up the operating system or an application until the entire print job is output by the print device. There is no such an action as preprinting. An EMF is the rendering of the print job by the graphics device interface (GDI) and the print driver before spooling takes place. The print router (not to be confused with a network router) is a program that routes a print job to the appropriate print processor component of the local provider or to a remote print server for processing on a network printer.

3. **A, E**. You can use either the Print Management snap-in or Control Panel Devices and Printers to install a printer on the network. None of the other tools mentioned here enable you to install a printer, either on the local computer or across the network.

4. **B**. When print jobs come out with unintelligible drivers, this means that the print driver is incorrect. Computers running different versions of Windows such as Windows XP or 7 might user different drivers. The Additional Drivers dialog box enables you to install a driver that enables Windows XP users to print their documents properly. The **Render print jobs on client computers** option transfers the processing load of rendering print jobs to the client computers (rather than the print server); however, this does not fix the problem encountered here. Granting users the Manage Documents permission or adding a new printer also will not solve this problem.

5. **D**. By using Group Policy to deploy the printer and choosing the option labeled **The computers that this GPO applies to (per machine)**, you can ensure that the printer is available to all computers in the Graphics OU. If you use the **List in the directory** option from either source, the printer will be available everywhere in the domain. If you select the option **The users that this GPO applies to (per user)**, users in the Graphics OU will be able to access the printer from computers in other departments of the company and users in other OUs will not be able to access it when printing from a computer in the Graphics OU.

6. **D**. The Ports tab of the printer's Properties dialog box enables you to redirect a printer should a problem occur with its print device and you need to take it offline for maintenance. By specifying the UNC path to the other printer as described in the option, all print jobs are automatically redirected to the other printer. You would use printer pooling to enable multiple print devices with a single printer but not to redirect print jobs. Renaming shared printers will not cause existing print jobs to be redirected.

7. **C**. By configuring a second printer with a priority of 99 and granting only the boss permission to print documents to this printer, she can ensure that her documents are printed promptly. Consequently, it is not necessary to ask her secretary to come in at 7 a.m. to print the documents. She could print her documents more promptly by clicking **Cancel All Documents**, before printing the document, provided she is granted the Manage Documents permission; however, this would make her unpopular with all other users who would need to resubmit their print jobs. There is no such permission as Prioritize Documents.

8. **D**. Because a user can with the Print permission delete his print jobs by himself without the need for additional permissions, you don't need to grant him any additional permissions.

9. **A**. The Printer Migration Wizard enables you to migrate all printer settings for each printer from one server to another. This includes print queues, printer settings, printer ports, and language monitors, and enables you to consolidate multiple print servers as being done in this scenario. You might be able to accomplish this task using Windows Server Backup but this is less convenient and takes more administrative effort. Simply moving the spooler file from each old print server to the new server will not accomplish the objective of this task. You could reinstall each printer at the new print server but this would take far more effort and, in itself, would not copy over any customized printer-specific settings that you might have configured in the past.

10. **D**. Printer driver isolation enables you to configure printer driver components to run in an isolated process that improves the reliability of the Windows print service by preventing a faulty printer driver from stopping all print operations on the print server. You can enable driver isolation by choosing the **Set Driver Isolation > Isolated** option. It would be possible to restore the laser printers by installing them to a different print server, but that would take more administrative effort. Because the print drivers run in the same process as the spooler, rolling back the drivers in Device Manager would not restore the laser printers. The **None** option disables driver isolation and does not solve this problem.

11. **A**. You should access the **Security** tab of the Print Server Properties dialog box and add Evelyn to list of user or group names. Then, select the **View Server**, **Print, Manage Documents**, and **Manage Printer** permissions under the Allow column. By granting Evelyn these permissions, you delegate her the ability to manage print queues without granting her excess administrative capabilities. Granting her the Manager Server permission would provide her with excess administrative capabilities. The Print Operators group exists only in a domain environment; you would need to create a similar group in a workgroup environment. The Power Users group exists only to provide backward compatibility with earlier Windows operating systems; its use would not provide Evelyn with the required capabilities.

12. **B**. You should restart the Print Spooler service on Server3. This clears a stalled print spooler; however, the user that submitted the job must resubmit his job. The **Render print jobs on client computers** option transfers the processing load of rendering print jobs to the client computers (rather than the print server); however, this does not fix the problem encountered here. Publishing the printer in AD DS will not solve this problem. It is not necessary to install a new printer to solve this problem.

## Chapter 14

1. **A**. PPP is a dial-up protocol that is supported by Windows Server 2008 and enables you to set up dial-up connections for users as described here. Remember that SLIP is an older protocol that is no longer supported in either edition of Windows Server 2008. PPTP, L2TP, and IKEv2 are VPN networking protocols that do not support dial-up connections.

2. **B**. All of PPTP, SSTP, and IKEv2 provide data encryption on their own. L2TP does not; you must use IPSec with L2TP to provide encryption of data sent across a remote access connection.

3. **A**. Password Authentication Protocol (PAP) sends its credentials in clear-text (unencrypted) form, so is the least secure method of authenticating a remote access connection. All the other protocols mentioned provide some kind of credential security.

4. **D**. To install RRAS, you need to access Server Manager and use the Add Roles Wizard to install the Network Policy and Access Services server role and select Routing and Remote Access as a role feature. RRAS is a role feature and not a server role or feature unto itself. You would use Control Panel to install RRAS on a Windows Server 2003 computer, but this functionality has been moved to Server Manager in Windows Server 2008.

5. **B**. The Ports Properties dialog box, accessed by right-clicking the Ports node and choosing **Properties**, enables you to configure properties of ports on your RRAS server. By clicking **Configure**, you access the Configure Device dialog box, which enables you to specify the maximum number of ports for any device that supports multiple ports. The RRAS server's Properties dialog box, accessed by right-clicking the server and choosing **Properties**, does not have either a PPTP or a Ports tab. The IPv4 node enables you to configure NAT; its Properties dialog box does not have a PPTP tab.

6. **C**. You need to use the Add Hardware Wizard to add the modem before you can configure it to accept dial-up clients. The Ports tab does not have an Add button for adding a modem. The RRAS server's Properties dialog box does not have a Ports tab that would enable you to perform this action. It is not necessary to disable and re-enable the RRAS server; further, the Routing and Remote Access Server Setup Wizard does not contain a Ports page.

7. **A, C, D**. By using NAT, you enable all client computers to access the Internet by means of a single IPv4 address. The NAT server can act as a DHCP server and provide IP addressing information as well as the address of an external DNS server for your client computers. However, NAT does not work with IPv6; neither does it enable routing among different internal subnets.

8. **D**. You cannot enable both dial-up access and NAT services on the same RRAS server. You must use a different server if you want to enable both these functions. To enable NAT services, you must first disable RRAS and then re-enable it, which removes the dial-up access functionality.

9. **B, C, D**. VPN in Windows Server 2008 R2 supports user-level authentication using PPP, computer-level authentication using IKEv2, and data origin authentication and data integrity. L2TP/IPSec provides data encryption but not authentication.

10. **B**. The Options tab provides presentation features for the VPN connection. By clicking the **PPP Settings** button, you can negotiate multi-link connections, which is the use of multiple lines for increased transmission speed. None of the other tabs enable you to configure these options.

11. **D**. You should access the **Security** tab of the VPN Connection Properties dialog box and select the **Maximum strength encryption (disconnect if server declines)** option. This provides for 128-bit encryption, which is supported by Windows Server 2008, Windows Vista, and Windows 7, but not by older operating systems such as Windows XP. Selecting the **Require encryption (disconnect if server declines)** option would allow Windows XP computers to connect using 40-bit or 56-bit encryption. These options are found in the Security tab of the VPN Connection Properties dialog box and not in the Security tab of the RRAS server's Properties dialog box.

12. **B**. The VPN Reconnect feature uses IKEv2 technology to automatically reestablish a VPN connection when a user has temporarily lost her Internet connection. Using VPN Reconnect, a user at a Windows 7 or Windows Server 2008 R2 computer can resume an interrupted download at a later time without needing to start over. Connection Manager provides the ability to set up consistent parameters for dial-up and VPN connections. VPN Connection Security enables you to specify the encryption level used by VPN connections. Advanced Security Auditing enables you to set up detailed audit policies. None of these items enable the re-establishment of an interrupted VPN connection.

13. **C**. The profiles created by the CMAK Wizard are specific to operating system architecture, and a profile created for Windows 7 computers will not work with a Windows XP computer. Profiles will work for either dial-up or VPN connections. The user could receive an error if the specified VPN server is offline, but this is not the fundamental reason why the error occurred in this scenario. Also, it does not matter which edition of Windows XP was on the user's computer; a profile for Windows XP rather than Windows 7 is required for him to connect successfully.

14. **A**. Users receive the Internet logon tab only if you've specified support for VPN connections and haven't selected the **Use the same user name and password for VPN and dial-up connections** check box, while running the CMAK wizard. The option for choosing a VPN server would determine whether the VPN tab appears, and not the Internet Logon tab. The user would use a dial-up connection only if she were connecting over a phone line and not the Internet. The edition of Windows 7 on her computer is not relevant to this situation.

## Chapter 15

1. **D**. 802.11n is a newer wireless networking standard that is compatible with devices using older standards but enables a transmission speed of up to 150-600 Mbps. It has the best signal range and is most resistant to interference. No other wireless standard offers this much transmission speed.

2. **C**. The 802.1X standard, as developed by the Institute of Electrical and Electronics Engineers (IEEE), uses EAP to integrate with the authenticating server such as a RADIUS server, thereby providing an open-ended conversation between the client and server. Open authentication provides only minimum authentication security when used on its own. Shared key authentication acts like a challenge-response process by using a shared secret to authenticate. Neither of these uses EAP. IPSec provides encryption services but not authentication.

3. **B**. By default, the WPA2-Personal protocol uses AES encryption and requires a security key or passphrase. WPA-Personal and WPA-Enterprise both use

TKIP encryption by default. Both WPA-Enterprise and WPA2-Enterprise do not require the user to type a security key or passphrase.

4. **C, D**. The wireless network policy for Windows Vista/7 clients provides the ability to configure wireless network permissions and the option for caching user information for subsequent connections to the network; neither of these are provided in the wireless network policy for Windows XP. Both network policies provide for the other options mentioned in this question.

5. **A**. The **Don't allow shared user credentials for network authentication** option is valid for Windows 7 computers only, and is ignored for Windows Vista computers. The **Use Windows Wired Auto Config service for clients** option must be selected, not cleared, for you to specify the **Don't allow shared user credentials for network authentication** option. 128-bit TKIP is used with wireless connections only, not with wired connections. Because the stated option is valid for Windows 7 computers only, this is not a case of the setting being overridden by another GPO linked to an OU.

6. **C**. In Windows Server 2008, NPS provides RADIUS services. IAS was the RADIUS server in Windows Server 2003, but it has been replaced by NPS in both the original and R2 versions of Windows Server 2008. NAP provides system health validation. WPA is a wireless client authentication option, not a provider of RADIUS services.

7. **B, C, E**. RADIUS clients include components such as wireless access points, 802.1X-capable switches, RAS servers running any version of Windows Server, VPN servers, and dial-up servers. Client computers in any capacity and running any Windows operating system are not considered to be RADIUS clients.

8. **A**. A RADIUS proxy forwards RADIUS messages between RADIUS clients and servers that perform user authentication, authorization, and accounting. Servers that forward RADIUS messages to domain controllers and wireless access points are RADIUS clients, not proxies. A server that forwards messages between IP subnets is acting as a router, not a RADIUS proxy.

9. **A, B, C, E**. When specifying the type of network access server that sends a connection request to a NPS server, you can choose Remote Desktop Gateway, Remote Access Server (VPN-Dial up), DHCP server, or Health Registration Authority. You can also choose an Unspecified option or Host Credential Authorization Protocol (HCAP) server. However, you cannot choose a DNS server.

10. **C**. You should create an NPS template, specify these settings in the template, and then apply the template to each RADIUS server in turn. Using a template reduces the amount of time required to configure NPS servers in a large environment. You do not need to use Windows Server Backup. Also, you cannot

configure these settings in a GPO and apply them in that fashion. Because you can use a NPS template to specify these settings, you do not need to configure them individually on each server.

# Chapter 16

1. **A, B, E, F, G**. A typical NAP remediation network can include antivirus signature servers, WSUS servers, domain controllers, DHCP and DNS servers, and troubleshooting servers. It might also include Systems Center component servers and other servers for Internet access to Windows Update or program vendor update locations. However, NAP health policy and enforcement servers are not part of a remediation network.

2. **B**. Each client computer attempting to connect sends a SoH to the NAP enforcement server, which evaluates its information against the requirements defined in the health policy. The SHV includes settings that the client must meet. It is a list of criteria supplied by the NAP server, not a file sent by the client to the server. The X.509 health certificate is given to compliant client computers when the 802.1X enforcement option is in use. A computer running Windows XP SP3 can be a NAP client, so the computer does not need to be upgraded.

3. **C, D**. Because DHCP and NPS are running on two different servers, you need to configure the DHCP server as a RADIUS client. You also need to enable NAP on all DHCP scopes used by NAP clients. (This will generally be all scopes on the DHCP server, although it is possible to selectively enable NAP on individual scopes.) You do not need Certificate Services on either the DHCP or NAP server; this role is needed only for 802.1X enforcement. IIS is not needed on the NAP server; this is also used with 802.1X enforcement. (It might also be used to host a web page within the remediation network to provide instructions for users at noncompliant computers.)

4. **C only**. Be aware that the IPSec enforcement method is the only one of the five enforcement types that requires that the network include HRA, Certificate Services, and IIS servers. The NAP server works with the HRA server to determine compliance with configured health and network policies. The HRA server uses IIS to communicate with AD DS and authenticate connection requests. These servers are not needed with the other enforcement types, though an IIS server might be present on the remediation network to serve web pages that direct users at noncompliant computers to the proper remediation locations.

5. **B**. You should configure NAP to use IPSec enforcement. This enforcement method uses a Health Registration Authority (HRA) server with IIS to communicate with AD DS and authenticate connection requests. In addition, the

network must have a CA server (which can be the same server as the HRA). The CA generates a certificate for using Secure Sockets Layer (SSL) for encrypting network traffic, thereby meeting the requirements of this scenario. You cannot specify encryption of communications on a NAP-protected network by specifying any of the other enforcement types mentioned.

6. **B, C, D**. When using IPSec enforcement, you must have a PKI with at least one CA. You must be running an AD DS domain with all clients joined to the domain, and a HRA server must be present on the network. You only need to enable DHCP scopes for NAP when using DHCP enforcement. You only need to configure network access points as RADIUS clients when using 802.1X enforcement.

7. **C**. You need to configure all access points as RADIUS clients to ensure that client computers connecting through these access points are evaluated by NAP. Using PEAP-MS-CHAP v2 authentication or requiring certificated does not enforce NAP health checks. Remember that the access points and not the client computers are configured as RADIUS clients.

8. **C**. On Windows XP computers, WSHV does not check that antispyware software is installed, properly updated, and enabled. It is possible to perform all the other types of checks on Windows XP computers.

9. **B, D**. To create and use a multi-configuration SHV, you need to right- click the **Settings** subnode under the SHV node in the console tree of the NPS snap-in and choose **New**. Then, select the desired settings from the Windows Security Health Validator dialog box. Then, you need to create a new health policy and select the appropriate setting from the multi-configuration SHV from the drop-down list in the Create New Health Policy dialog box. To use a different configuration from the multi-configuration SHV, you would simply repeat these steps, selecting the required setting in the drop-down list. The right-click menu for the SHV node in the NPS snap-in does not include a **New Multi-Configuration SHV** option. Use of multi-configuration SHVs is not specific to the 802.1X enforcement type; further, you cannot specify multi-configuration SHV options from the Define NAP Health Policy page of the Configure NAP Wizard.

# Chapter 17

1. **A, B, E, G**. You must upgrade the server to Windows Server 2008 R2, install the Web Server (IIS) server role on the server, install at least two network adapters on the server, and configure the network adapter that is connected to the Internet with two consecutive IPv4 addresses. DirectAccess is a new feature in Windows Server 2008 R2 and is not supported by the original version of Windows Server 2008. The use of two consecutive public IPv4 addresses

on the perimeter network interface enables the DirectAccess server to act as a Teredo server, enabling clients on the internal network to use this server to detect the type of network address translation (NAT) device that they are behind. If the network adapter has just a single IPv4 address, DirectAccess will not work because these two addresses are required on the Teredo server to determine the type of NAT device behind which the DirectAccess client is located. Although the DirectAccess server must be a member of an AD DS domain, it does not need to be a domain controller. Also, while AD CS is required, this role can be installed on a different server.

2. **D, F**. You need to upgrade all laptops to Windows 7 Enterprise or Ultimate. DirectAccess is not supported on Windows 7 Professional; it is also not supported on any edition of Windows Vista. All laptops must be joined to the AD DS domain. There is no such thing as DirectAccess connection software.

3. **A, C**. Clients must be joined to the domain and belong to the security group configured on the DirectAccess server; they must have a certificate that specifies the Client Authentication and Server Authentication certificate purposes. They do not require a smart card reader. It is preferable to have an IPv6 globally routable IP address, but clients with IPv4 addresses can use 6to4, Teredo, or HTTPS to access the network.

4. **D**. DirectAccess is installed as a server feature from Server Manager. DirectAccess is not a server role; further, it is not a role feature in either the Network Policy and Access Services or Web Server (IIS) server role.

5. **B, D, E, F**. The DirectAccess Setup Wizard consists of four steps that accomplish these actions. Before you run the wizard, ensure that the appropriate ports are open on the server and obtain and install a computer certificate for the server, because these actions are not included in the wizard.

6. **B**. Microsoft recommends that you place the DirectAccess server on the perimeter network between the internal network and the Internet. Place all NAP servers and the remediation network servers within the internal network. In this way, the DirectAccess server essentially acts as a firewall between the internal and perimeter networks.

7. **A, C, D, E**. When setting up a NRPT, you can specify DNS servers, web proxies, IPSec encryption, and query resolution options. Note that you must access the Configure Advanced Global Policy Settings dialog box to specify query resolution options. You cannot configure the use of NAP from a NRPT.

8. **C**. You should specify a NRPT exemption that exempts the internal DNS servers from special handling by the NRPT rules. If the IP address specified for the DNS server in the DirectAccess snap-in were incorrect, Jim would have been unable to connect while on the road. The exemption needs to be

specified for the internal DNS servers and not for the DirectAccess location server. It is not necessary to add an alternate IP configuration to Jim's computer.

# Chapter 18

1. **C, D, E**. You can configure computers dating back to Windows 2000 Professional with SP4 as WSUS clients. However, you cannot configure Windows NT 4.0 or Windows 9x computers as WSUS clients.

2. **A**. An update roll-up is a packaged set of updates that fix problems with specific Windows components or software packages such as Microsoft Office. A critical security update is a single update that Microsoft issues to fix a problem that is critical for a computer's security. An optional update is a potentially useful non-security-related update. A service pack is a comprehensive operating system update that often adds new features or improvements to existing features.

3. **D**. When using HTTPS for secured communication, the WSUS server must have an SSL certificate installed. If an SQL server is not available, the installation wizard will install the Windows Internal Database on your server; this is true whether or not HTTPS is being used. IIS is required whether or not HTTPS is being used. NAP checks client computers for system health; the presence or absence of a NAP server on the network is immaterial to this scenario.

4. **B**. You should install WSUS on a server at the branch office and select the **Synchronize from another Windows Server Update Services server** option at the branch office server. This option is found in the Update Source and Proxy Server dialog box, which you can access from the Options node of the Update Services snap-in. You must configure this option at the branch office WSUS server, not the head office server. The **Synchronize from Microsoft Update** option would direct all client computers to obtain updates from the Microsoft Update website and would increase the amount of traffic on the ISDN link. A GPO that directs branch office computers to the head office WSUS server would also increase the amount of traffic on the ISDN link.

5. **D**. You should create one or more computer groups containing the client computers in your organization. Then, use Group Policy to add client computers to these groups. This enables client-side targeting, which is the most efficient way to set up WSUS in a domain environment. Using the Update Services snap-in to add individual client computers to the required groups would enable server-side targeting, which is a manual method that takes more effort, particularly when new computers are added or existing ones moved.

You cannot use an AD DS global security group to target computers for WSUS, either with the Update Services snap-in or by using Group Policy.

6. **A**. You can specify a deadline by which updates are to be downloaded by right-clicking the computer group to which the updates have been approved in the Approve Updates dialog box and choosing **Deadline**. The dialog box that appears allows you to specify a deadline time or interval. This option is not available from the console tree of the Update Services snap-in. Neither the `gpupdate /force` nor the `wuauclt.exe /detectnow` command would set a deadline for installing updates.

7. **B, D**. The Reports node of the Update Services snap-in enables you to create reports in either the Microsoft Excel spreadsheet or Adobe PDF document format. You would need to perform additional actions to create either a Microsoft Word document or Microsoft Access database.

8. **C**. The **Specify intranet Microsoft update service location** policy enables you to specify a WSUS server on your network that client computers will access to receive software updates without accessing the Internet. With the other policies mentioned, client computers will still attempt to access the Internet for updates.

9. **A**. You need to run the `wuauclt.exe /resetauthorization /detectnow` command at John's computer (and not at the WSUS server). This command forces the client to download a new certificate from the WSUS server and then download updates from the server. It is not necessary to configure John's computer to download updates directly from the Microsoft Update website; doing this would defeat the entire reason for setting up a WSUS server in the first place. WSUS is entirely capable of updating computers back as far as Windows 2000, so it is not necessary to update John's computer to Windows 7.

10. **B**. You should run the `wuauclt.exe /detectnow` command. Running this command forces the Automatic Updates clients contact the WSUS server immediately. While the `wsusutil.exe` command has many subcommands and options, the `/detectnow` option is not one of them. The `gpupdate /force` command forces update of Group Policy but does not force clients to contact the WSUS server. Neither does setting a short interval from the Approve Update dialog box.

# Chapter 19

1. **A, B, C, E, F**. Performance Monitor can be used to perform all of these tasks except for terminating misbehaving applications, which you can do from Task Manager. Note that the action of generating alerts when unusual conditions

occur uses the data collector set capability, which is a component of Performance Monitor.

2. **A**. Performance Monitor uses the term *object* to denote a specific hardware or software component that it is capable of monitoring. A counter specifies one of a series of statistical measurements associated with each object. An instance refers to multiple occurrences of a given object, such as two discrete hard disks. The term component does not have a specific meaning associated with it in Performance Monitor.

3. **A, E**. By selecting the desired counter from the list at the bottom of the Performance Monitor display then pressing the **Backspace** key, you can highlight the counter in the Performance Monitor display. The **Insert** key does not perform this action. You can also use the up and down arrows to cycle the emphasis to other counters. The Data tab of the Performance Monitor Properties dialog box also enables you to emphasize a selected counter by modifying its color, width, and style. The Graph tab provides other customization capabilities, but does not enable you to highlight a given counter. You cannot add a duplicate instance of any counter; Performance Monitor displays a warning message if you attempt to do so.

4. **B**. You need to add Sharon's user account to the Performance Monitor Users group. All user accounts are automatically members of the Users group; this group can view data logged by a previously executed data collector set, but they cannot run a data collector set. The Performance Log Users group would entitle Sharon to create and modify a data collector set, which is not desired by this scenario. The Power Users group is provided only for backward compatibility with Windows XP and Windows Server 2003, and does not grant Sharon the right to execute a data collector set.

5. **C**. Ellen needs to use the Data Collector Sets tool to log data over a period of time in order to obtain a performance baseline for the domain controller. The Save Image As option saves an image of the currently visible data, but does not save data that is no longer visible. Performance Monitor does not have an Export option for saving performance data. Resource Monitor enables her to view a summary of performance data; the **File > Save As** option enables her to save configuration files but not monitoring data.

6. **B**. You should use Performance Monitor to create a data collector set that tracks the LogicalDisk\% Free Space counter. Then, configure a script that deletes unneeded files and specify the path to this script in the **Task** tab of the alert's Properties dialog box. The Properties dialog box associated with a performance graph in Performance Monitor does not have a Task tab. You cannot use either Resource Monitor or Task Scheduler to perform this action.

7. **C**. You should check the Memory\Committed Bytes counter. This counter measures the amount of virtual memory that has been committed to either physical RAM or running processes. Although useful for determining whether additional RAM is needed, the other counters mentioned here do not provide this specific information. Increasing the size of the paging file on the system partition or adding a paging file on another partition of the same disk helps to improve performance, but not as much as adding a paging file on another disk. Removing the paging file would have the opposite effect (performance would be worse and some programs might not run).

8. **D**. You should add a new paging file on the E: (or F:) partition. The paging file acts as an additional memory location for programs and data that cannot fit into RAM (in other words, virtual memory). You can achieve the best improvement in performance by locating the paging file on a different hard disk than that occupied by the operating system.

9. **A, C, D**. Reliability Monitor informs you of the date that various actions that might affect your computer's stability took place. Included are application failures (crashes), Windows failures, miscellaneous failures, warnings, and information events that include application uninstalls and update installations. Reliability Monitor cannot inform you when a performance counter exceeds a specified value; you need to use the Data Collector Sets feature of Performance Monitor to obtain this information.

10. **B**. Resource Monitor enables you to obtain this information. Performance Monitor and data collector sets require you to add counters to obtain the information. Event Viewer provides information on events that have occurred on the computer, but not time trends of computer performance.

## Chapter 20

1. **A, B, D, E**. Using Event Viewer, you can create and save event log filters, export a custom event view to another computer, schedule a task to run when a given event is logged, and collect events from multiple computers so that you can view all these events on a single computer. Event Viewer enables you to view alerts generated by data collector sets from Performance Monitor; however, it does not enable you to generate alerts from conditions such as high processor utilization.

2. **D**. You should look in the Applications and Services logs for this type of information. These logs are located in their own subnode and provide information for single applications, as opposed to the Application log, which logs events related to all applications on the computer. The Security log records information on audited events, and the System log records events related to actions occurring on the computer in general.

3. **C.** By filtering the log to display only Critical, Warning, and Error events, you can reduce the number of visible events and more easily locate events of interest. Information events make up the vast bulk of events recorded in the System log and do not represent problematic situations. Configuring the log to overwrite events after 48 hours would reduce the number of events appearing in the log, but might cause loss of events indicating significant problems unless you always look at the logs more frequently. Event log subscriptions collect data from several computers and are not relevant here.

4. **B.** You should create a custom view focused on the Security log at one server that displays only failed attempts to access the shares, and then export this custom view as an XML file, and then import it to each of the other servers in turn. Because the ability to export and import custom views exists in Windows Server 2008 Event Viewer, you do not need to configure a filter or custom view on each of the servers in turn; this would take more administrative effort. The Applications and Services logs node contains events from single applications or services such as AD DS or DNS; it does not track events related to successful or failed access to audited shares.

5. **B.** You should use a collector-initiated event subscription, which pulls events from the specified computers. A source-initiated event subscription is more appropriate where there are a large number of computers configured with Group Policy. A filter that views logs by event source displays logs according to Windows services, utilities, and components; this is not what is needed here. You could use a filter that views logs by user and computer, but this would be less convenient than creating an event log subscription, which is new to Windows Server 2008 R2.

6. **A, D.** You should run the `wecutil qc` command at the Windows Server 2008 R2 computer and the `winrm quickconfig` command at each client computer in the department. The `wecutil qc` command needs to be run at the collector computer (the computer that receives events from the other computers) and the `winrm quickconfig` command needs to be run at each source computer (the computers whose events are to be forwarded).

7. **B, C, D, G.** To use HTTPS to provide for secure forwarding of event information to the collector computer, you must install a computer certificate at the collector computer. You also need to create an exception in Windows Firewall for TCP port 443 used by HTTPS. In the Advanced Subscription Settings dialog box, you need to select HTTPS and TCP port 443. Finally, you need to run the `winrm quickconfig -transport:https` command at the collector computer. You do not need to install IIS on the collector computer.

8. **A.** Event Viewer enables you to attach a task to any event and one of the tasks you can specify is to display a message box to your desktop. You can customize this message box to provide text that alerts you to the failing service. Neither the Custom Views feature nor the event log subscription feature provides you with this capability. You can configure alerts from Performance Monitor using the Data Collector Service feature, but this monitors performance counters and not error conditions.

# Chapter 21

1. **C.** SNMP is used for monitoring devices on your network in network management systems for situations that warrant administrative attention. You would use Performance Monitor and network-related counters for monitoring counters that provide information on how a server's network interface card is performing. Providing a simple interface for mail is the purpose of Simple Mail Transfer Protocol (SMTP), not SNMP. Network Monitor, not SNMP, is used for viewing the content of network packets.

2. **F.** A trap is an unsolicited message sent by an SNMP agent to an SNMP management system when the agent detects a certain type of event such as a system restart or an attempted intrusion. All other message types are sent only as a response to a request sent by the management system.

3. **C.** To specify that the host is permitted to process SNMP SET requests, you should specify the READ WRITE option. Neither the NOTIFY nor the READ ONLY option would enable the host to process SNMP SET requests. The READ CREATE option would enable the host to create new entries in the SNMP tables.

4. **D.** To install Network Monitor, you must download the Network Monitor installer file from Microsoft and then run this file on your server. Network Monitor is not included in the default installation of Windows Server 2008 R2, either as a server rule, role service, or server feature.

5. **A, B, C.** Network Monitor enables you to filter captured traffic using any of these criteria and others. Captured frames do not include information on the operating system used by the originating computer.

6. **A.** You should use the filter **DNS && IPv4.address==192.168.3.101.** This is equivalent to **DNS AND IPv4.address==192.168.3.101** and requires that the capture include only DNS-based packets being sent either to or from the machine with IPv4 address 192.168.3.101. The || operator is equivalent to the OR operator and would capture any DNS-based packet as well as any packets being sent to and from the given IP address. If you use the **IPv4.sourceaddress**

keyword, only packets being sent from the given IP address would be captured, not the packets being received by this computer.

7. **B**. You should access the Capture tab of the Network Monitor Options dialog box and deselect the **Enable Conversations** option. This option consumes more memory and can cause other applications to run slowly or the server to become unresponsive. The Record Capture Filter option saves the capture filter used as metadata information. Parser profiles determine how the bits captured on the wire are converted to a readable format. The effect on memory usage by these options is much less than that of the Enable Conversations option.

8. **D**. You should access the Aliases dialog box and add the server name for each required IP address to the list on this table, and then click **Apply**. Doing so replaces each IP address with the name you've specified in the Aliases dialog box. You cannot obtain this information by using a display or capture filter and selecting **DHCP**; doing so would simply limit the frames displayed to those associated with the DHCP protocol. There is no **Convert to Name** option available.

9. **C**. You should download Network Monitor OneClick from the Microsoft website and run this program on Server7. This utility performs a capture that runs until you press X or until 120 minutes have elapsed, and then removes itself from the computer. The Nmcap command is not available until you install Network Monitor on the computer in concern. Unlike many other administrative programs, Network Monitor does not have a **Connect to another computer** option. Because you can install Network Monitor OneClick on Server7, you do not need to install the full version of Network Monitor.

10. **A, C, D, E**. The properties of a connection security rule that are visible under the Monitoring node in Windows Firewall with Advanced Security include all the items mentioned except for information on any connections that have been blocked because of violating the chosen rule.

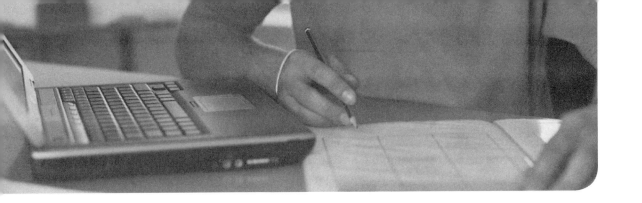

# Index

## Numerics

## A

# M

# N

# S

# X-Y-Z

DON POULTON

## Cert Guide
Learn, prepare, and practice for exam success

- Master every topic on Microsoft's newest MCTS 70-642 exam.
- Assess your knowledge and focus your learning.
- Get the practical workplace knowledge you need!

# MCTS
## 70-642
Windows Server 2008
Network Infrastructure,
Configuring

PEARSON

# Safari
### Books Online

# FREE
# Online Edition

Your purchase of **MCTS 70-642 Cert Guide** includes access to a free online edition for
45 days through the Safari Books Online subscription service. Nearly every Pearson IT
Certification book is available online through Safari Books Online, along with thousands of
books and videos from publishers such as Addison-Wesley Professional, Cisco Press, Exam
Cram, IBM Press, O'Reilly Media, Prentice Hall, Que, Sams, and VMware Press.

Safari Books Online is a digital library providing searchable, on-demand access to thousands
of technology, digital media, and professional development books and videos from leading
publishers. With one monthly or yearly subscription price, you get unlimited access to learning
tools and information on topics including mobile app and software development, tips and tricks
on using your favorite gadgets, networking, project management, graphic design, and much
more.

## Activate your FREE Online Edition at
## informit.com/safarifree

**STEP 1:**    Enter the coupon code: YOEGXBI.

**STEP 2:**    New Safari users, complete the brief registration form.
Safari subscribers, just log in.

If you have difficulty registering on Safari or accessing the online edition,
please e-mail customer-service@safaribooksonline.com